# ENGLISH
# FOOTBALL LEAGUE
# AND
# F.A. PREMIER LEAGUE
# TABLES
# 1888-2013

EDITOR
Michael Robinson

British Library Cataloguing in Publication Data

A catalogue record for this book is available from the British Library

ISBN: 978-1-86223-272-3


Copyright © 2013,   Soccer Books Limited, 72 St. Peters Avenue,
Cleethorpes, DN35 8HU     (01472) 696226


E-mail –   info@soccer-books.co.uk
Web site –   www.soccer-books.co.uk

**Manufactured in the UK by Ashford Colour Press Ltd.**

# THE FORMATION OF THE FOOTBALL LEAGUE

By 1888, there were around 1,000 clubs in England playing football according to the laws and rules of the Football Association. These clubs would arrange a set of fixtures that began in early September and ended in mid-April with the vast majority of games being played on Saturday afternoons. Most fixtures were kept but there was no guarantee that they would be. Sometimes, visiting teams would not turn up at all, or they might turn up with a reserve side because they had arranged another, more attractive game elsewhere, or they might arrive late, or with less than 11 players.

In the early, 'free and easy' days of football, this did not matter too much but after the legalisation of professionalism in 1885, things were very different. The leading clubs, most of whom were based in the North and the Midlands, as well as their normal running costs, also now had to pay their players. While supporters knew that games in the F.A. Cup and other major cup competitions would generally mean that both clubs would field their strongest teams, they could not be so sure about the ordinary 'friendly' games that filled most of the fixture calendar. It was by no means uncommon for supporters to turn up at the ground to find that one of the clubs 'could not raise a team' or 'had missed their (railway) connection'.

Unsurprisingly then, crowds for 'friendly' games were usually very much smaller than those for cup games, a worrying fact for clubs now facing a weekly wage bill. Furthermore, with the random nature of cup draws, even the best clubs could find themselves making an early exit from the most attractive competitions, a situation that could prove to be absolutely disastrous as the 'friendlies' that had been already arranged were liable to be cancelled if the opponents were still making progress in the cup competitions and the dates clashed.

This was the background that on 2nd March 1888 caused Mr. William McGregor, an Aston Villa official, to write to 5 leading clubs – Aston Villa, Blackburn Rovers, Bolton Wanderers, Preston North End and West Bromwich Albion. His letter read:

> "Every year it is becoming more and more difficult for football clubs of any standing to meet their friendly engagements and even arrange friendly matches. The consequence is that at the last moment, through cup-tie interference, clubs are compelled to take on teams who will not attract the public.
>
> I beg to tender the following suggestion as a means of getting over the difficulty – that ten or twelve of the most prominent clubs in England combine to arrange home and away fixtures each season, the said fixtures to be arranged at a friendly conference about the same time as the International Conference. This Combination might be known as the Association Football Union, and could be managed by a representative from each club.
>
> Of course, this is in no way to interfere with the National Association. Even the suggested matches might be played under Cup-tie rules. However, this is a detail. My object in writing at present is merely to draw your attention to the subject, and to suggest a friendly conference to discuss the matter more fully. I would take it as a favour if you would kindly think the matter over, and make whatever suggestion you may deem necessary."

The initial response was not encouraging. McGregor received only 2 replies, 1 of which was from Bolton Wanderers who suggested the inclusion of 8 more clubs: Accrington, Burnley, Halliwell (a Lancashire club), Notts County, Mitchell St. George's (from Birmingham), Old Carthusians (a prominent amateur club), Stoke and Wolverhampton Wanderers.

When the idea was more widely discussed, it was received with doubt, or even suspicion, in some quarters. In Sheffield for example, it was feared that the proposed organisation would be antagonistic to the F.A. and would be too costly for clubs. It was because of this that Sheffield Wednesday were excluded from the list of clubs invited to take part.

However, in Derby, Stoke, West Bromwich and Wolverhampton, the idea was warmly received and in Nottingham, where Forest were at the time still an amateur club, County readily agreed to join the nascent organisation. It should be noted that Mr. McGregor originally intended that there should be only one club from each town or city. With support growing, a meeting was organised at Anderton's Hotel, London on 22nd March. Those represented were: Aston Villa, Blackburn Rovers, Burnley, Notts County, Stoke, West Bromwich Albion and Wolverhampton Wanderers. Preston and Bolton each decided not to send a delegate while Derby County's delegate attended, but only as an observer.

The meeting decided "To form a League or Union of twelve of the most prominent clubs, the twelve selected being Accrington, Aston Villa, Blackburn Rovers, Bolton Wanderers, Burnley, Derby County, Everton, Notts County, Preston North End, Stoke, West Bromwich Albion and Wolverhampton Wanderers". Note that Accrington and Everton had been added to raise the number from 10 to 12. Note also that the only club south of Birmingham who had even been suggested were Old Carthusians but they, along with all clubs in the South-East, were strictly amateur and the playing standards of the top professional clubs were by 1888 so far ahead of the rest that it is highly unlikely that any amateurs could have competed effectively.

It was agreed that all league games would be played under the Cup rules of the F.A. and that clubs would play full strength teams in all matches. There were also rules regarding players' eligibility, admission prices (to be set at the discretion of the home club) and how gate money would be divided.

The 'average' that would determine the finishing order in the league was to be calculated from wins, draws and losses and not from goals scored but how that 'average' was to be calculated was not yet decided. It was, however, decided that the four clubs having the lowest 'average' would retire at the end of the season but be eligible for re-election.

Another meeting took place, at the Royal Hotel in Manchester on 17th April, attended by all 12 clubs and it was then that it was definitely decided to proceed with the idea. Thus, 17th April 1888 is the generally accepted date for the league's formation.

It was thought though that the proposed title of the 'Association Football Union' might be confused with the Rugby Football Union and so instead, it was decided to call it the Football League, a title about which Mr. McGregor had some misgivings as the word 'League' was often used by political and other organisations.

Three other clubs – Nottingham Forest, Sheffield Wednesday and Halliwell – also attended the meeting in the hope of gaining admittance but they were unsuccessful as it was felt that no more than 22 league fixtures could be fitted in.

McGregor also had the idea that there should be a subsidiary competition for the members' reserve teams and although that was not taken forward then, it eventually happened when the Central League was formed in 1911, followed by the London Combination a few years later.

There were a multitude of details to be agreed which were settled during the summer months but one, extremely important, area took a while longer. That was the means by which the order of clubs in the final table would be decided, what Mr. McGregor originally referred to as the 'average'.

While the principle of 2 points for a win and 1 for a draw was proposed at an early stage, there was a school of thought led by West Bromwich Albion that preferred that only wins would count, draws and defeats both being ignored. Eventually, the 2 points for a win and 1 for a draw system was adopted but only by 6 votes to 4 and not until 21st November 1888, when the season was already well under way.

There was one further point of particular interest in the League's first set of rules, that being the rule that there would be 'two classes of League clubs – First and Second – each to consist of twelve clubs'. The rules went on to state: 'There shall be first and second-class championships, and last four in each class to retire, but be eligible for re-election. The League shall have power to order any of the retiring clubs or the first four of the second class, to compete in order to decide the question of superiority'.

The second 'class' or 'division' eventually came into existence in 1892 but for 1888-89, there was just the 12-club 'first class', the world's first ever football league. The first games were played on Saturday 8th September 1888 and the results were as follows:

| | | | |
|---|---|---|---|
| Bolton Wanderers | 3 | Derby County | 6 |
| Everton | 2 | Accrington | 1 |
| Preston North End | 5 | Burnley | 2 |
| Stoke | 0 | West Bromwich Albion | 2 |
| Wolverhampton Wanderers | 1 | Aston Villa | 1 |

Blackburn Rovers' first ever league game was on 15th September, a 5-5 home draw with Accrington and Notts County's first game was on the same day, a 2-1 defeat at Everton.

## Record of the founder members

Altogether, 17 clubs were considered for, or hoped to be, included in the League. The table below shows the last survivors in the most important cup competitions in the 3 previous seasons, i.e. 1885-86, 1886-87 and 1887-88 and demonstrates clearly the dominance of the 12 actually selected.

The 12 selected clubs are in Bold Type, the 5 clubs who were considered or hoped to be considered but were ultimately not selected (Halliwell, Mitchell St. George's, Nottingham Forest, Old Carthusians and Sheffield Wednesday) are in Normal Type and those that were not even considered are in Italics.

| | 1885-86 | 1886-87 | 1887-88 |
|---|---|---|---|
| **F.A. Cup** | | | |
| Winners | **Blackburn Rovers** | **Aston Villa** | **West Bromwich Albion** |
| Finalists | **West Brom. Albion** | **West Brom. Albion** | **Preston North End** |
| Semi-Finalists | *Small Heath Alliance* | **Preston North End** | *Crewe Alexandra* |
| | *Swifts* | *Rangers (Glasgow)* | *Derby Junction* |
| **Birmingham Senior Cup** | | | |
| Winners | **West Brom. Albion** | *Long Eaton Rangers* | **Aston Villa** |
| Finalists | *Walsall Swifts* | **West Brom. Albion** | **West Bromwich Albion** |
| Semi-Finalists | **Wolverhampton W.** | *Burslem Port Vale* | **Stoke** |
| | *Burslem Port Vale* | *Small Heath Alliance* | **Wolverhampton Wands.** |
| **Lancashire Cup** | | | |
| Winners | **Bolton Wanderers** | **Preston North End** | **Accrington** |
| Finalists | **Blackburn Rovers** | **Bolton Wanderers** | **Preston North End** |
| Semi-Finalists | **Preston North End** | *Padiham* | *Witton* |
| | *Darwen* | *Witton* | *Darwen Old Wanderers* |
| **Staffordshire Senior Cup** | | | |
| Winners | **West Brom. Albion** | **West Brom. Albion** | **Wolverhampton Wands.** |
| Finalists | **Stoke** | *Walsall Swifts* | **West Bromwich Albion** |
| Semi-Finalists | *Burton Wanderers* | **Wolverhampton W.** | **Stoke** |
| | *Walsall Town* | *Burslem Port Vale* | *Walsall Town* |
| **Lord Mayor of Birmingham's Charity Cup** | | | |
| Winners | **Aston Villa** | **Wolverhampton W.** | **Aston Villa** |
| Finalists | *Wednesbury Old Ath.* | **Aston Villa** | Mitchell St. George's |

| | 1885-86 | 1886-87 | 1887-88 |
|---|---|---|---|
| **Liverpool Senior Cup** | | | |
| Winners | Everton | Everton | *Bootle* |
| **Sheffield Challenge Cup** | | | |
| Winners | *Mexborough* | Sheffield Wednesday | Sheffield Wednesday |
| **Wharncliffe Charity Cup** | | | |
| Winners | Sheffield Wednesday | *Staveley* | Sheffield Wednesday |
| **Nottinghamshire Senior Cup** | | | |
| Winners | Nottingham Forest | Nottingham Forest | *Notts Rangers* |

## How the league expanded

The table below shows the number of clubs in each division of the Football League.

| | F.L. | | | | Total |
|---|---|---|---|---|---|
| 1888-1891 | 12 | | | | 12 |
| 1891-1892 | 14 | | | | 14 |
| | **Div. 1** | **Div. 2** | | | |
| 1892-1893 | 16 | 12 | | | 28 |
| 1893-1894 | 16 | 15* | | | 31 |
| 1894-1898 | 16 | 16 | | | 32 |
| 1898-1905 | 18 | 18 | | | 36 |
| 1905-1915 | 20 | 20 | | | 40 |
| 1919-1920 | 22 | 22 | | | 44 |
| | **Div. 1** | **Div. 2** | **Div. 3(S)** | **Div. 3(N)** | |
| 1920-1921 | 22 | 22 | 22 | 0 | 66 |
| 1921-1923 | 22 | 22 | 22 | 20 | 86 |
| 1923-1950 | 22 | 22 | 22 | 22 | 88 |
| 1950-1958 | 22 | 22 | 24 | 24 | 92 |
| | **Div. 1** | **Div. 2** | **Div. 3** | **Div. 4** | |
| 1958-1987 | 22 | 22 | 24 | 24 | 92 |
| 1987-1988 | 21 | 23 | 24 | 24 | 92 |
| 1988-1991 | 20 | 24 | 24 | 24 | 92 |
| 1991-1992 | 22 | 24 | 24 | 23 | 93 |
| | **P.L.** | **Div. 1** | **Div. 2** | **Div. 3** | |
| 1992-1993 | 22 | 24 | 24 | 22† | 92 |
| 1993-1995 | 22 | 24 | 24 | 22 | 92 |
| 1995-2004 | 20 | 24 | 24 | 24 | 92 |
| | **P.L.** | **Champsh.** | **Lge. 1** | **Lge. 2** | |
| 2004-2012 | 20 | 24 | 24 | 24 | 92 |

* Excluding Bootle who resigned just before the start of the season.

† Excluding Maidstone United who resigned before playing a game.

## Changes to League membership

When the league was formed, the last 4 clubs in the table had to seek re-election. In 1889, at the end of the first season, all of the bottom 4 were re-elected. All subsequent changes are listed below. Years when there were no changes in membership are omitted.

1890    Sunderland were elected in place of Stoke. Sunderland had previously played only cup-ties and friendlies. Stoke joined the Football Alliance for the 1890-91 season.

1891    The League expanded from 12 to 14 members. The clubs elected to fill the 2 vacancies were Stoke (Football Alliance champions) and Darwen, who had finished 6th in the Football Alliance.

1892    The League expanded from 14 to 16 members. Darwen were not re-elected and so 3 new members were elected. They were: Nottingham Forest (Football Alliance champions), Newton Heath (runners-up in the Football Alliance) and Sheffield Wednesday (4th in the Football Alliance).

It was also decided to form a Second Division of 12 clubs with the original Football League becoming known as the First Division.

The 12 clubs elected to the new Second Division were: Darwen (following their failure to win re-election to the First Division) and 8 of the 9 remaining members of the Football Alliance. They were: Small Heath (who had finished 3rd), Burton Swifts (5th), Crewe Alexandra (6th), Ardwick (7th), Bootle (8th), Lincoln City (9th), Grimsby Town (10th) and Walsall Town Swifts (11th). The Football Alliance club who were not elected were Birmingham St. George, who had disbanded. The clubs elected to fill the final 3 places were Burslem Port Vale who had finished 3rd in the Midland League, Northwich Victoria (2nd in The Combination) and Sheffield United (3rd in the Northern League).

The League had invited 2 clubs to join from the Northern League but both declined. The 2 clubs invited were Newcastle East End who had finished 4th, and a proposed club to be formed by a merger of Middlesbrough Ironopolis (champions) and Middlesbrough (runners-up). The merger was abandoned and the 2 clubs continued separately.

1893    Division Two expanded from 12 to 16 clubs. The 4 clubs elected to the vacancies were: Liverpool (Lancashire League champions), Newcastle United (2nd in the Northern League), Rotherham Town (Midland League champions) and Woolwich Arsenal who had never played in a league. Later, when Accrington decided to join the Lancashire League rather than accept relegation to the Second Division, Middlesbrough Ironopolis (Northern League champions) accepted an invitation to take their place. Shortly before the start of the new season, Bootle resigned and disbanded, leaving 15 clubs in Division Two.

1894    Ardwick were declared bankrupt and, on 16th April 1894, they were wound up. A new club called Manchester City was formed to replace them and they were elected to take Ardwick's place in the League. Northwich Victoria chose not to seek re-election to the League and joined The Combination instead. Rotherham Town were not re-elected but, soon afterwards, Middlesbrough Ironopolis resigned and disbanded. Rotherham Town subsequently accepted an invitation to replace them. Bootle had resigned the previous August and so there were 3 vacancies. The clubs elected to fill these were Burton Wanderers (Midland League champions), Leicester Fosse (Midland League runners-up) and Bury (Lancashire League runners-up).

1895    Walsall Town Swifts were not re-elected and joined the Midland League, changing their name to Walsall. Loughborough Town (Midland League champions) were elected to replace them.

1896    The number of clubs required to seek re-election was reduced from 4 to 3. Rotherham Town did not seek re-election and disbanded soon afterwards. Burslem Port

Vale and Crewe Alexandra were not re-elected. Burslem Port Vale joined the Midland League and Crewe Alexandra joined The Combination. The 3 clubs elected to fill the vacancies were Gainsborough Trinity (Midland League runners-up), Walsall (3rd in the Midland League) and Blackpool (13th in the Lancashire League).

1897    Burton Wanderers were not re-elected and joined the Midland League. Luton Town (United League runners-up) were elected to replace them.

1898    Both divisions were expanded to 18 clubs. The 4 clubs elected to fill the vacancies created in the Second Division were Burslem Port Vale (5th in the Midland League), Barnsley (Midland League runners-up), Glossop North End (9th in the Midland League) and New Brighton Tower (Lancashire League champions).

1899    Glossop North End changed their name to Glossop. Darwen did not seek re-election and disbanded soon afterwards. However, they were quickly reformed and, after taking over a local junior club called Darwen Woodfold, joined the Lancashire League. Blackpool were not re-elected and joined the Lancashire League. The 2 clubs elected to fill the vacancies were Chesterfield (4th in the Midland League) and Middlesbrough (3rd in the Northern League, Division One).

1900    Luton Town did not seek re-election and joined the Southern League, Division One instead. Loughborough Town were not re-elected and applied to join the Midland League but disbanded before the start of the new season. The 2 clubs elected to fill the vacancies were Stockport County (Lancashire League champions) and Blackpool (3rd in the Lancashire League).

1901    Burton Swifts merged with Burton Wanderers of the Midland League and were re-elected under their merged name of Burton United. Walsall were not re-elected and moved to the Midland League. Bristol City (runners-up in the Southern League, Division One) were elected in their place. Shortly before the start of the new season, New Brighton Tower resigned and disbanded and Doncaster Rovers (Midland League runners-up) accepted an invitation to replace them.

1902    Newton Heath changed their name to Manchester United.

1903    Doncaster Rovers were not re-elected and joined the Midland League instead. Newly formed Bradford City, who had not played a single game, were elected in their place.

1904    Stockport County were not re-elected and joined the Lancashire Combination, Division One instead. Doncaster Rovers (11th in the Midland League) were elected in their place. Chesterfield changed their name to Chesterfield Town.

1905    Small Heath changed their name to Birmingham. Burton United and Doncaster Rovers were not re-elected. Leeds City (11th in the West Yorkshire League) and Chelsea (a newly formed club who had not played a single game) were elected in their places.

However, it was then decided to extend both divisions to 20 clubs, creating 4 more Second Division places. The clubs elected to take these were Burton United, who were thus re-elected, Hull City, who had previously played only friendlies, Clapton Orient (8th in the Southern League, Division Two and 7th in the London League, Premier Division) and Stockport County (Lancashire Combination, First Division champions). Doncaster Rovers then moved to the Midland League.

1907    Burton United were not re-elected and joined the Birmingham League. Fulham (Southern League First Division champions) were elected in their place. Subsequently, Burslem Port Vale resigned and disbanded, creating a further vacancy. Oldham Athletic (Lancashire Combination, First Division champions) accepted an invitation to fill it. A new club called Port Vale were quickly formed and joined the North Staffordshire Federation.

1908    Lincoln City were not re-elected and joined the Midland League. Bradford Park Avenue (13th in the Southern League, First Division) were elected in their place. Later, Stoke resigned and disbanded. They quickly reformed and asked to withdraw their resignation but were refused and Tottenham Hotspur (7th in the Southern League First Division) were elected in their place. Stoke joined the Birmingham League.

1909      The number of clubs required to seek re-election was reduced from 3 to 2. Chesterfield Town were not re-elected and moved to the Midland League. Lincoln City (Midland League champions) were elected in their place.

1910      Grimsby Town were not re-elected and moved to the Midland League. Huddersfield Town (5th in the Midland League) were elected in their place.

1911      Lincoln City were not re-elected and became a founder member of the Central League. Grimsby Town (Midland League champions) were elected in their place.

1912      Gainsborough Trinity were not re-elected and moved to the Midland League. Lincoln City (Central League champions) were elected in their place.

1913      Woolwich Arsenal changed their name to Arsenal.

1915      Glossop were not re-elected and joined the Lancashire Combination for 1915-16. In 1916, they closed down until 1919 when they rejoined the Lancashire Combination. Stoke (Southern League, Second Division champions) were elected in their place. However, it was later decided that the league should close down until the war ended.

1919      It was decided to extend both divisions to 22 clubs, creating 4 Second Division vacancies. The clubs elected into these vacancies (with their 1914-15 positions in brackets) were: Coventry City (5th in the Southern League, Division Two), Rotherham County (Midland League champions), South Shields (North-Eastern League champions) and West Ham United (4th in the Southern League, Division One). Leicester Fosse changed their name to Leicester City.

1919      On 19th October 1919, Leeds City refused to submit their books to a committee investigating illegal war-time payments to players. As a result, the club were expelled from the League and disbanded by order of the F.A.

Their record at the time of expulsion was: P8 W4 D2 L2 F17 A10 P10. Port Vale, who were playing in the Central League where they had finished 3rd in 1914-15, accepted an invitation to take over Leeds' fixtures and completed the season in their place.

1920      Grimsby Town and Lincoln City were not re-elected. The clubs elected in their places were Cardiff City (4th in the Southern League, First Division) and Leeds United, who were formed immediately after the demise of Leeds City and had gained entry to the Midland League for the rest of the 1919-20 season, finishing 12th.

It was then decided to form a Third Division which would consist of two sections, South and North. Only the champions of each section would be promoted to Division Two from where the bottom 2 would be relegated as replacements. The bottom 2 clubs in each of the Third Division sections would be required to seek re-election.

The Southern section was to start in 1920-21 by the absorption en masse of all clubs in the Southern League, Division One. These were, (their 1919-20 finishing positions in brackets):

Brentford (15th), Brighton & Hove Albion (16th), Bristol Rovers (17th), Crystal Palace (3rd), Exeter City (10th), Gillingham (22nd), Luton Town (20th), Merthyr Town (21st), Millwall (14th), Newport County (18th), Northampton Town (19th), Norwich City (12th), Plymouth Argyle (5th), Portsmouth (1st), Queens Park Rangers (6th), Reading (7th), Southampton (8th), Southend United (11th), Swansea Town (9th), Swindon Town (13th), Watford (2nd).

The other club who had been in the Southern League, First Division were Cardiff City, who had already been elected to Division Two and so one vacancy remained. Grimsby Town, who had not been re-elected to Division Two, accepted an invitation to fill it. Lincoln City, the other club not to have been re-elected, moved to the Midland League

The Northern section of the Third Division would start in 1921-22, as long as enough clubs of the desired strength could be found.

1921    It was agreed that Division Three (North) would be formed with 20 clubs, which would include the bottom club in Division Two (Stockport County) and Grimsby Town, who were transferred from Division Three (South). 14 of the remaining 18 vacancies were accepted on the recommendation of the Management Committee. Those 14, with their 1920-21 finishing position in brackets, consisted of 4 clubs from the Central League: Crewe Alexandra (2nd), Tranmere Rovers (7th), Rochdale (10th) and Nelson (17th); 4 clubs from the North-Eastern League: Darlington (champions), Hartlepools United (8th), Ashington (9th) and Durham City (11th); 2 clubs from the Lancashire Combination, Division One: Barrow (champions) and Accrington Stanley (6th); 2 clubs from the Midland League: Lincoln City (champions) and Chesterfield (3rd); and 2 clubs from the Birmingham League: Wrexham (3rd) and Walsall (5th).

The clubs elected to the remaining 4 places were Wigan Borough (11th in the Lancashire Combination, Division One), Halifax Town (11th in the Midland League), Stalybridge Celtic (13th in the Central League) and Southport (18th in the Central League).

Third Division (South) champions (Crystal Palace) had been promoted and Grimsby Town had been transferred to Division Three (North) so, with no club being relegated from Division Two, there were 2 vacancies in Division Three (South). The clubs elected to fill these vacancies were Aberdare Athletic (Welsh League champions and runners-up in the Southern League, Welsh Section) and Charlton Athletic (8th in the Southern League, English Section and 6th in the South-Eastern League).

1923    It was decided to expand Division Three (North) from 20 to 22 clubs while Stalybridge Celtic resigned and moved to the Cheshire League, creating a total of 3 vacancies. Two clubs were relegated from Division Two to Division Three (North) and none to Division Three (South) which thus had 1 vacancy. Bournemouth & Boscombe Athletic (runners-up in the Southern League, English Section) were elected to fill it. The 2 clubs elected to fill the vacancies in Division Three (North) were Doncaster Rovers (Midland League runners-up and New Brighton (4th in the Lancashire Combination).

1925    Stoke changed their name to Stoke City and Rotherham County merged with Rotherham Town (12th in the Midland League) to form Rotherham United.

1926    Aberdare Athletic merged with Aberaman Athletic (15th in the Welsh League) but continued in Division Three (South) as Aberdare Athletic. Coventry City transferred from Division Three (North) to Division Three (South).

1927    Walsall transferred from Division Three (North) to Division Three (South). Aberdare Athletic were not re-elected and moved to the Southern League, Western Section as Aberdare & Aberaman and to the Welsh League as Aberdare. Torquay United (champions of the Southern League, Western Section and runners-up in the Western League, Division One) were elected to Division Three (South) in their place.

1928    Durham City were not re-elected and moved to the North-Eastern League, Division One. Carlisle United (runners-up in the North-Eastern League, Division One) were elected to Division Three (North) in their place.

1929    Ashington were not re-elected and moved to the North-Eastern League, Division Two. York City (9th in the Midland League) were elected to Division Three (North) in their place.

1930    Merthyr Town were not re-elected and moved to the Southern League, Western Section and Welsh League, Division One. Thames Association (3rd in the Southern League, Eastern Section) were elected to Division Three (South) in their place. South Shields moved from South Shields to a new ground in Gateshead and changed their name to Gateshead.

1931      Walsall transferred from Division Three (South) to Division Three (North). Newport County were not re-elected and moved to the Southern League, Western Section and Welsh League, Division One. Mansfield Town (10th in the Midland League) were elected to Division Three (South) in their place. Nelson were not re-elected and moved to the Lancashire Combination. Chester (runners-up in the Cheshire League) were elected to Division Three (North) in their place.

1931      One 26th October 1931, Wigan Borough resigned and disbanded. Their record was P12 W3 D1 L8 F12 A33 P7. Merthyr Town offered to take over their fixtures but the offer was refused.

1932      Mansfield Town transferred from Division Three (South) to Division Three (North) where they replaced Wigan Borough. Thames Association resigned and disbanded. The clubs elected to fill the 2 vacancies in Division Three (South) were Newport County (6th in the Southern League, Western Section and runners-up in the Welsh League, Division One) and Aldershot (9th in the Southern League, Eastern Section and 7th in the London Combination, Division Two).

1936      Walsall transferred from Division Three (North) to Division Three (South).

1937      Mansfield Town transferred from Division Three (North) to Division Three (South).

1938      Port Vale transferred from Division Three (North) to Division Three (South). Gillingham were not re-elected and moved to the Southern League. Ipswich Town (3rd in the Southern League) were elected to Division Three (South) in their place.

1945      Birmingham changed their name to Birmingham City.

1946      Clapton Orient changed their name to Leyton Orient.

1947      Mansfield Town transferred from Division Three (South) to Division Three (North).

1950      It was decided to extend both sections of the Third Division from 22 to 24 clubs. The 2 clubs elected to the vacancies in the Southern Section were Colchester United (runners-up in the Southern League) and Gillingham (5th in the Southern League). The 2 clubs elected to the vacancies in the Northern Section were Scunthorpe & Lindsey United (3rd in the Midland League) and Shrewsbury Town (10th in the Midland League).

1951      Shrewsbury Town transferred from Division Three (North) to Division Three (South). New Brighton were not re-elected and moved to the Lancashire Combination, Division One. Workington (5th in the North-Eastern League) were elected to Division Three (North) in their place.

1952      Port Vale transferred from Division Three (South) to Division Three (North).

1958      Scunthorpe & Lindsey United changed their name to Scunthorpe United.

It was decided to restructure the two regional sections of the Third Division into two national divisions, Division Three and Division Four. The 1957-58 champions of each of the two regional sections were promoted to Division Two as usual, while the new Division Three was made up of the clubs finishing from 2nd to 12th in each of the two regional sections plus the 2 clubs relegated from Division Two. Division Four was made up of the clubs finishing 13th to 24th in each of the two regional sections. The bottom four clubs in Division Four would be required to seek re-election.

1960      Gateshead were not re-elected and moved to the Northern Counties League. Peterborough United (Midland League champions) were elected in their place.

1962      On 6th March 1962, Accrington Stanley resigned from the League. Their record at the time was P33 W5 D8 L20 F19 A60 P18. They joined the Lancashire Combination, Division Two in 1962-63. At the 1962 A.G.M., Oxford United (champions of the Southern League, Premier Division) were elected to replace them.

1967    Leyton Orient changed their name to Orient.

1968    Hartlepools United changed their name to Hartlepool.

1970    Swansea Town changed their name to Swansea City. Bradford Park Avenue were not re-elected and moved to the Northern Premier League. Cambridge United (champions of the Southern League, Premier Division) were elected in their place.

1971    Bournemouth & Boscombe Athletic changed their name to A.F.C. Bournemouth.

1972    Barrow were not re-elected and moved to the Northern Premier League. Hereford United (runners-up in the Southern League, Premier Division) were elected in their place.

1977    Hartlepool changed their name to Hartlepool United. Workington were not re-elected and moved to the Northern Premier League. Wimbledon (champions of the Southern League, Premier Division) were elected in their place.

1978    Southport were not re-elected and moved to the Northern Premier League. Wigan Athletic (runners-up in the Northern Premier League) were elected in their place.

1983    Chester changed their name to Chester City.

1987    Orient changed their name to Leyton Orient.

Re-election was scrapped and instead, automatic promotion and relegation was introduced between Division Four and the Football Conference, the champions of the latter replacing the bottom club in Division Four. The first club promoted under this system were Scarborough who replaced Lincoln City.

1988    Newport County were relegated to the Football Conference from where Lincoln City were promoted.

1989    Darlington were relegated to the Football Conference from where Maidstone United were promoted.

1990    Colchester United were relegated to the Football Conference from where Darlington were promoted.

1991    The League was expanded to 93 clubs. No club was relegated and Barnet were promoted from the Football Conference.

1992    On 25th March 1992, Aldershot resigned from the League and disbanded. Their record at the time was P36 W3 D8 L25 F21 A63 P17. A new club called Aldershot Town was quickly formed and joined the Isthmian League, Division Three in 1992-93.

1992    The clubs who were members of Division One all joined the new F.A. Premier League, an organisation outside of the control of the Football League. The rules for promotion and relegation between the new Premier League and Football League remained unchanged. The remaining Divisions of the Football League were all renamed, Division Two becoming Division One, Division Three becoming Division Two and Division Four becoming Division Three.

No clubs were relegated from the Football League but Colchester United were promoted from the Football Conference. Shortly before the start of the 1992-93 season, Maidstone United resigned and disbanded. A club called Maidstone Invicta was formed as a replacement in 1992 and joined the Kent County League, Division Four (West) in 1993-94.

1993    Halifax Town were relegated to the Football Conference from where Wycombe Wanderers were promoted.

1997    Hereford United were relegated to the Football Conference from where Macclesfield Town were promoted.

1998    Doncaster Rovers were relegated to the Football Conference from where Halifax Town were promoted.

1999    Scarborough were relegated to the Football Conference from where Cheltenham Town were promoted.

2000    Chester City were relegated to the Football Conference from where Kidderminster Harriers were promoted.

2001    Barnet were relegated to the Football Conference from where Rushden & Diamonds were promoted.

2002    Halifax Town were relegated to the Football Conference from where Boston United were promoted.

2003    The number of clubs to be promoted and relegated to the Football Conference increased from 1 to 2. Shrewsbury Town and Exeter City were relegated and Doncaster Rovers and Yeovil Town were promoted.

2004    Wimbledon moved to a new ground in Milton Keynes and changed their name to Milton Keynes Dons. Carlisle United and York City were relegated to the Football Conference from where Chester City and Shrewsbury Town were promoted. Division One of the Football League was renamed The Championship, Division Two was renamed League One and Division Three was renamed League Two.

2005    Kidderminster Harriers and Cambridge United were relegated to the Football Conference from where Carlisle United and Barnet were promoted.

2006    Oxford United and Rushden & Diamonds were relegated to the Football Conference from where Hereford United and Accrington Stanley were promoted.

2007    Boston United were relegated to the Football Conference (North) and Torquay United were relegated to the Football Conference from where Dagenham & Redbridge and Morecambe were promoted.

2008    Mansfield Town and Wrexham were relegated to the Football Conference from where Aldershot Town and Exeter City were promoted.

2009    Chester City and Luton Town were relegated to the Football Conference from where Burton Albion and Torquay United were promoted.

2010    Grimsby Town and Darlington were relegated to the Football Conference from where Stevenage Borough and Oxford United were promoted.

2011    Lincoln City and Stockport County were relegated to the Football Conference from where Crawley Town and A.F.C. Wimbledon were promoted.

2012    Macclesfield Town and Hereford United were relegated to the Football Conference from where Fleetwood Town and York City were promoted.

2013    Barnet and Aldershot Town were relegated to the Football Conference from where Mansfield Town and Newport County were promoted.

## Test Matches and Play-offs

It was anticipated when the League was first formed that there would be two 'classes' of clubs and that promotion and relegation between the two would be decided by 'Test Matches' (see under 'The Formation of the Football League', on page 3).

The Second Division was formed in 1892 and initially, there were 3 one-off games between the top Second Division clubs and the bottom First Division clubs. This, though, produced the occasional anomaly such as at the end of the very first season in which they were used when Second Division champions Small Heath lost their Test Match and so were not promoted whereas Sheffield United and Darwen, who had finished 2nd and 3rd, won their games and so leapfrogged Small Heath into the First Division.

In 1895-96, the system was refined into a mini-league for 2 places but Test Matches were scrapped altogether in 1898 after Stoke and Burnley drew their final mini-league game 0-0 when both clubs needed a point to ensure a top flight place.

The idea of extra games to decide promotion was revived in 1986 with the introduction of the play-offs. Initially, the club finishing just above the relegation zone competed for one place in the higher division with the 3 clubs who had finished just out of the promotion places in the division below. This was changed in 1988 to the present system whereby the 4 clubs finishing just below the automatic promotion places compete for one promotion place. The results of all Test Matches are listed below and results of the the play-offs are included alongside the tables for each season they have been held.

### 1892-93

| | |
|---|---|
| Darwen vs Notts County | 3-2 |
| *(played at Hyde Road, Ardwick)* | |
| Sheffield United vs Accrington | 1-0 |
| *(played at the Town Ground, Nottingham)* | |
| Small Heath vs Newton Heath | 1-1 |
| *(played at the Victoria Ground, Stoke)* | |

**Replay**

| | |
|---|---|
| Newton Heath vs Small Heath | 5-2 |
| *(played at the Olive Grove, Sheffield)* | |

Promoted:  Darwen, Sheffield United

Relegated:  Notts County, *Accrington

*Accrington resigned rather than accept relegation.

### 1893-94

| | |
|---|---|
| Liverpool vs Newton Heath | 2-0 |
| *(played at Ewood Park, Blackburn)* | |
| Preston North End vs Notts County | 4-0 |
| *(played at the Olive Grove, Sheffield)* | |
| Small Heath vs Darwen | 3-1 |
| *(played at the Victoria Ground, Stoke)* | |

Promoted:  Liverpool, Small Heath

Relegated:  Newton Heath, Darwen

## 1894-95

| | |
|---|---|
| Bury vs Liverpool | 1-0 |
| *(at Ewood Park, Blackburn)* | |
| Derby County vs Notts County | 2-1 |
| *(at Walnut Street, Leicester)* | |
| Stoke vs Newton Heath | 3-0 |
| *(at the Athletic Ground, Cobridge, Burslem)* | |

Promoted: Bury

Relegated: Liverpool

## 1895-96

The Test Match format changed into a mini-league in which each of the bottom two in Division One played home and away against each of the top two in Division Two. The top two in the table were promoted to, or remained in, Division One.

| | P | W | D | L | F | A | Pts |
|---|---|---|---|---|---|---|---|
| Liverpool | 4 | 2 | 1 | 1 | 6 | 2 | 5 |
| West Bromwich Albion | 4 | 2 | 1 | 1 | 9 | 4 | 5 |
| Small Heath | 4 | 1 | 1 | 2 | 8 | 7 | 3 |
| Manchester City | 4 | 1 | 1 | 2 | 5 | 15 | 3 |

Promoted: Liverpool

Relegated: Small Heath

## 1896-97

| | P | W | D | L | F | A | Pts |
|---|---|---|---|---|---|---|---|
| Notts County | 4 | 2 | 2 | 0 | 3 | 1 | 6 |
| Sunderland | 4 | 1 | 2 | 1 | 3 | 2 | 4 |
| Burnley | 4 | 1 | 1 | 2 | 3 | 4 | 3 |
| Newton Heath | 4 | 1 | 1 | 2 | 3 | 5 | 3 |

Promoted: Notts County

Relegated: Burnley

## 1897-98

| | P | W | D | L | F | A | Pts |
|---|---|---|---|---|---|---|---|
| Stoke | 4 | 2 | 1 | 1 | 4 | 2 | 5 |
| Burnley | 4 | 2 | 1 | 1 | 5 | 3 | 5 |
| Newcastle United | 4 | 2 | 0 | 2 | 9 | 6 | 4 |
| Blackburn Rovers | 4 | 1 | 0 | 3 | 5 | 12 | 2 |

Stoke and Burnley both needed 1 point from their last game to secure a place in Division One and they subsequently drew 0-0. Both divisions were later extended to 18 clubs with the above 4 teams all being placed in Division One.

Test matches were then replaced by automatic promotion and relegation for the following season.

## 1872 F.A. Cup

**Semi-finals**

Wanderers vs Queen's Park                    0-0
Royal Engineers vs Crystal Palace            3-0

**Final**

Kennington Oval, 16 March 1872

**Wanderers 1**  (Betts)
**Royal Engineers 0**

*Attendance 2,000*

## 1873 F.A. Cup

**Semi-finals**

Queen's Park vs Oxford University              †
(Wanderers received a bye)
† After playing Oxford, Queen's Park scratched from the final because they could not afford to travel to London.

**Final**

Lillie Bridge, 29th March 1873

**Wanderers 2**  (Kinnaird, Wollaston)
**Oxford University 0**

*Attendance 3,000*

## 1874 F.A. Cup

**Semi-finals**

Oxford University vs Clapham Rovers           1-0
Royal Engineers vs Swifts                     2-0

**Final**

Kennington Oval, 14th March 1874

**Oxford University 2**  (Mackarness, Patton)
**Royal Engineers 0**

*Attendance 2,500*

## 1875 F.A. Cup

**Semi-finals**

Royal Engineers vs Oxford University          1-0
Old Etonians vs Shropshire Wanderers          1-0

**Final**

Kennington Oval, 13th March 1875

**Royal Engineers 1**  (Scorer Not Known)
**Old Etonians 1 (aet.)**  (Bonsor)

*Attendance 3,000*

**Replay**

Kennington Oval, 16th March 1875

**Royal Engineers 2**  (Renny-Tailyour, Stafford)
**Old Etonians 0**

*Attendance 3,000*

## 1876 F.A. Cup

**Semi-finals**

Wanderers vs Swifts                           2-1
Oxford University vs Old Etonians             0-1

**Final**

Kennington Oval, 11th March 1876

**Wanderers 1**  (Edwards)
**Old Etonians 1**  (Bonsor)

*Attendance 3,500*

**Replay**

Kennington Oval, 18th March 1876

**Wanderers 3**  (Hughes 2, Wollaston)
**Old Etonians 0**

*Attendance 3,200*

## 1877 F.A. Cup

**Semi-finals**

Wanderers vs Cambridge University             1-0
(Oxford University received a bye)

**Final**

Kennington Oval, 24th March 1877

**Wanderers 2**  (Heron, Kenrick)
**Oxford University 1**  (Kinnaird (og))

*Attendance 3,000*

## 1878 F.A. Cup

**Semi-finals**

Royal Engineers vs Old Harrovians             2-1
(Wanderers received a bye)

**Final**

Kennington Oval, 23rd March 1878

**Wanderers 3**  (Kenrick 2, Kinnaird)
**Royal Engineers 1**  (Scorer Not Known)

*Attendance 4,500*

## 1879 F.A. Cup

**Semi-finals**

Old Etonians vs Nottingham Forest             2-1
(Clapham Rovers received a bye)

**Final**

Kennington Oval, 29th March 1879

**Old Etonians 1**  (Clerke)
**Clapham Rovers 0**

*Attendance 5,000*

## 1880 F.A. Cup

**Semi-finals**

Oxford University vs Nottingham Forest        1-0
(Clapham Rovers received a bye)

**Final**

Kennington Oval, 10th April 1880

**Clapham Rovers 1**  (Lloyd-Jones)
**Oxford University 0**

*Attendance 6,000*

## 1881 F.A. Cup

**Semi-finals**

Old Carthusians vs Clapham Rovers             4-1
(Old Etonians received a bye)

**Final**

Kennington Oval, 9th April 1881

**Old Carthusians 3**  (Page, Wynyard, Parry)
**Old Etonians 0**

*Attendance 4,500*

## 1882 F.A. Cup

**Semi-finals**

Old Etonians vs Great Marlow                  5-0
Blackburn Rovers vs The Wednesday         0-0, 5-1

**Final**

Kennington Oval, 25th March 1882

**Old Etonians 1**  (Anderson)
**Blackburn Rovers 0**

*Attendance 6,500*

## 1883 F.A. Cup

**Semi-finals**

| | |
|---|---|
| Blackburn Olympic vs Old Carthusians | 4-0 |
| Old Etonians vs Notts County | 2-1 |

**Final**

Kennington Oval, 31st March 1883

**Blackburn Olympic 2**  (Matthews, Costley)
**Old Etonians 1 (aet.)**  (Goodhart)

*Attendance 8,000*

## 1884 F.A. Cup

**Semi-finals**

| | |
|---|---|
| Blackburn Rovers vs Notts County | 1-0 |
| Queen's Park vs Blackburn Olympic | 4-1 |

**Final**

Kennington Oval, 29th March 1884

**Blackburn Rovers 2**  (Brown, Forrest)
**Queen's Park 1**  (Christie)

*Attendance 4,000*

## 1885 F.A. Cup

**Semi-finals**

| | |
|---|---|
| Blackburn Rovers vs Old Carthusians | 5-0 |
| Queen's Park vs Nottingham Forest | 1-1, 3-0 |

**Final**

Kennington Oval, 4th April 1885

**Blackburn Rovers 2**  (Forrest, Brown)
**Queen's Park 0**

*Attendance 12,500*

## 1886 F.A. Cup

**Semi-finals**

| | |
|---|---|
| Blackburn Rovers vs Swifts | 2-1 |
| West Bromwich vs Small Heath Alliance | 4-0 |

**Final**

Kennington Oval, 3rd April 1886

**Blackburn Rovers 0**
**West Bromwich Albion 0**

*Attendance 15,000*

**Replay**

Racecourse Ground, Derby, 10th April 1886

**Blackburn Rovers 2**  (Brown, Sowerbutts)
**West Bromwich Albion 0**

*Attendance 12,000*

## 1887 F.A. Cup

**Semi-finals**

| | |
|---|---|
| Aston Villa vs Glasgow Rangers | 3-1 |
| West Bromwich Albion vs Preston North End | 3-1 |

**Final**

Kennington Oval, 2nd April 1887

**Aston Villa 2**  (Hunter, Hodgetts)
**West Bromwich Albion 0**

*Attendance 15,500*

## 1888 F.A. Cup

**Semi-finals**

| | |
|---|---|
| West Bromwich Albion vs Derby Junction | 3-0 |
| Preston North End vs Crewe Alexandra | 4-0 |

**Final**

Kennington Oval 24th March 1888

**West Bromwich Albion 2**  (Woodhall, Bayliss)
**Preston North End 1**  (Dewhurst)

*Attendance 19,000*

## FOOTBALL LEAGUE 1888-89

| | | | | | | | |
|---|---|---|---|---|---|---|---|
| **PRESTON NORTH END** | 22 | 18 | 4 | 0 | 74 | 15 | 40 |
| Aston Villa | 22 | 12 | 5 | 5 | 61 | 43 | 29 |
| Wolverhampton Wanderers | 22 | 12 | 4 | 6 | 50 | 37 | 28 |
| Blackburn Rovers | 22 | 10 | 6 | 6 | 66 | 45 | 26 |
| Bolton Wanderers | 22 | 10 | 2 | 10 | 63 | 59 | 22 |
| West Bromwich Albion | 22 | 10 | 2 | 10 | 40 | 46 | 22 |
| Accrington | 22 | 6 | 8 | 8 | 48 | 48 | 20 |
| Everton | 22 | 9 | 2 | 11 | 35 | 46 | 20 |
| Burnley | 22 | 7 | 3 | 12 | 42 | 62 | 17 |
| Derby County | 22 | 7 | 2 | 13 | 41 | 61 | 16 |
| Notts County | 22 | 5 | 2 | 15 | 40 | 73 | 12 |
| Stoke | 22 | 4 | 4 | 14 | 26 | 51 | 12 |

## 1889 F.A. Cup

**Semi-finals**

| | |
|---|---|
| Preston North End vs West Bromwich Albion | 1-0 |
| Wolverhampton Wands. vs Blackburn Rovers | 1-1, 3-1 |

**Final**

Kennington Oval, 30th March 1889

**Preston North End 3**  (Dewhurst, J. Ross, Thompson)
**Wolverhampton Wanderers 0**

*Attendance 22,000*

## FOOTBALL LEAGUE 1889-90

| | | | | | | | |
|---|---|---|---|---|---|---|---|
| **PRESTON NORTH END** | 22 | 15 | 3 | 4 | 71 | 30 | 33 |
| Everton | 22 | 14 | 3 | 5 | 65 | 40 | 31 |
| Blackburn Rovers | 22 | 12 | 3 | 7 | 78 | 41 | 27 |
| Wolverhampton Wanderers | 22 | 10 | 5 | 7 | 51 | 38 | 25 |
| West Bromwich Albion | 22 | 11 | 3 | 8 | 47 | 50 | 25 |
| Accrington | 22 | 9 | 6 | 7 | 53 | 56 | 24 |
| Derby County | 22 | 9 | 3 | 10 | 43 | 55 | 21 |
| Aston Villa | 22 | 7 | 5 | 10 | 43 | 51 | 19 |
| Bolton Wanderers | 22 | 9 | 1 | 12 | 54 | 65 | 19 |
| Notts County | 22 | 6 | 5 | 11 | 43 | 51 | 17 |
| Burnley | 22 | 4 | 5 | 13 | 36 | 65 | 13 |
| *Stoke* | 22 | 3 | 4 | 15 | 27 | 69 | 10 |

## 1890 F.A. Cup

**Semi-finals**

| | |
|---|---|
| Blackburn Rovers vs Wolverhampton Wanderers | 1-0 |
| Bolton Wanderers vs The Wednesday | 1-2 |

**Final**

Kennington Oval, 29th March 1890

**Blackburn Rovers 6**  (Townley 3, Lofthouse, John
Southworth, Walton)
**The Wednesday 1**  (Bennett)

*Attendance 20,000*

## FOOTBALL LEAGUE 1890-91

| | | | | | | | |
|---|---|---|---|---|---|---|---|
| **EVERTON** | 22 | 14 | 1 | 7 | 63 | 29 | 29 |
| Preston North End | 22 | 12 | 3 | 7 | 44 | 23 | 27 |
| Notts County | 22 | 11 | 4 | 7 | 52 | 35 | 26 |
| Wolverhampton Wanderers | 22 | 12 | 2 | 8 | 39 | 50 | 26 |
| Bolton Wanderers | 22 | 12 | 1 | 9 | 47 | 34 | 25 |
| Blackburn Rovers | 22 | 11 | 2 | 9 | 52 | 43 | 24 |
| Sunderland | 22 | 10 | 5 | 7 | 51 | 31 | 23 |
| Burnley | 22 | 9 | 3 | 10 | 52 | 63 | 21 |
| Aston Villa | 22 | 7 | 4 | 11 | 45 | 58 | 18 |
| Accrington | 22 | 6 | 4 | 12 | 28 | 50 | 16 |
| Derby County | 22 | 7 | 1 | 14 | 47 | 81 | 15 |
| West Bromwich Albion | 22 | 5 | 2 | 15 | 34 | 57 | 12 |

Sunderland had two points deducted

## 1891 F.A. Cup

**Semi-finals**

| | |
|---|---|
| Blackburn Rovers vs West Bromwich Albion | 3-2 |
| Sunderland vs Notts County | 3-3, 0-2 |

**Final**

Kennington Oval, 21st March 1891

**Blackburn Rovers 3**  (Southworth, Dewar, Townley)
**Notts County 1**  (Oswald)

*Attendance 23,000*

## FOOTBALL LEAGUE 1891-92

| | | | | | | | |
|---|---|---|---|---|---|---|---|
| **SUNDERLAND** | 26 | 21 | 0 | 5 | 93 | 36 | 42 |
| Preston North End | 26 | 18 | 1 | 7 | 61 | 31 | 37 |
| Bolton Wanderers | 26 | 17 | 2 | 7 | 51 | 37 | 36 |
| Aston Villa | 26 | 15 | 0 | 11 | 89 | 56 | 30 |
| Everton | 26 | 12 | 4 | 10 | 49 | 49 | 28 |
| Wolverhampton Wanderers | 26 | 11 | 4 | 11 | 59 | 46 | 26 |
| Burnley | 26 | 11 | 4 | 11 | 49 | 45 | 26 |
| Notts County | 26 | 11 | 4 | 11 | 55 | 51 | 26 |
| Blackburn Rovers | 26 | 10 | 6 | 10 | 58 | 65 | 26 |
| Derby County | 26 | 10 | 4 | 12 | 46 | 52 | 24 |
| Accrington | 26 | 8 | 4 | 14 | 40 | 78 | 20 |
| West Bromwich Albion | 26 | 6 | 6 | 14 | 51 | 58 | 18 |
| Stoke | 26 | 5 | 4 | 17 | 38 | 61 | 14 |
| *Darwen* | *26* | *4* | *3* | *19* | *38* | *112* | *11* |

## 1892 F.A. Cup

**Semi-finals**

| | |
|---|---|
| West Brom. Albion vs Nottingham Forest | 1-1, 1-1, 6-2 |
| Aston Villa vs Sunderland | 4-1 |

**Final**

Kennington Oval, 12th March 1892

**West Bromwich Albion 3**   (Nicholls, Geddes, Reynolds)

**Aston Villa 0**

*Attendance 25,000*

## DIVISION ONE 1892-93

| | | | | | | | |
|---|---|---|---|---|---|---|---|
| **SUNDERLAND** | 30 | 22 | 4 | 4 | 100 | 36 | 48 |
| Preston North End | 30 | 17 | 3 | 10 | 57 | 39 | 37 |
| Everton | 30 | 16 | 4 | 10 | 74 | 51 | 36 |
| Aston Villa | 30 | 16 | 3 | 11 | 73 | 62 | 35 |
| Bolton Wanderers | 30 | 13 | 6 | 11 | 56 | 55 | 32 |
| Burnley | 30 | 13 | 4 | 13 | 51 | 44 | 30 |
| Stoke | 30 | 12 | 5 | 13 | 58 | 48 | 29 |
| West Bromwich Albion | 30 | 12 | 5 | 13 | 58 | 69 | 29 |
| Blackburn Rovers | 30 | 8 | 13 | 9 | 47 | 56 | 29 |
| Nottingham Forest | 30 | 10 | 8 | 12 | 48 | 52 | 28 |
| Wolverhampton Wanderers | 30 | 12 | 4 | 14 | 47 | 68 | 28 |
| The Wednesday | 30 | 12 | 3 | 15 | 55 | 65 | 27 |
| Derby County | 30 | 9 | 9 | 12 | 52 | 64 | 27 |
| *Notts County* | *30* | *10* | *4* | *16* | *53* | *61* | *24* |
| *Accrington* | *30* | *6* | *11* | *13* | *57* | *81* | *23* |
| Newton Heath | 30 | 6 | 6 | 18 | 50 | 85 | 18 |

## DIVISION TWO 1892-93

| | | | | | | | |
|---|---|---|---|---|---|---|---|
| Small Heath | 22 | 17 | 2 | 3 | 90 | 35 | 36 |
| **Sheffield United** | 22 | 16 | 3 | 3 | 62 | 19 | 35 |
| Darwen | 22 | 14 | 2 | 6 | 60 | 36 | 30 |
| Grimsby Town | 22 | 11 | 1 | 10 | 42 | 41 | 23 |
| Ardwick | 22 | 9 | 3 | 10 | 45 | 40 | 21 |
| Burton Swifts | 22 | 9 | 2 | 11 | 47 | 47 | 20 |
| Northwich Victoria | 22 | 9 | 2 | 11 | 42 | 58 | 20 |
| *Bootle* | *22* | *8* | *3* | *11* | *49* | *63* | *19* |
| Lincoln City | 22 | 7 | 3 | 12 | 45 | 51 | 17 |
| Crewe Alexandra | 22 | 6 | 3 | 13 | 42 | 69 | 15 |
| Burslem Port Vale | 22 | 6 | 3 | 13 | 30 | 57 | 15 |
| Walsall Town Swifts | 22 | 5 | 3 | 14 | 37 | 75 | 13 |

## 1893 F.A. Cup

**Semi-finals**

| | |
|---|---|
| Wolverhampton Wanderers vs Blackburn Rovers | 2-1 |
| Everton vs Preston North End | 2-2, 0-0, 2-1 |

**Final**

Fallowfield, Manchester, 25th March 1893

**Wolverhampton Wanderers 1**   (Allen)

**Everton 0**

*Attendance 45,000*

## DIVISION ONE 1893-94

| | | | | | | | |
|---|---|---|---|---|---|---|---|
| **ASTON VILLA** | 30 | 19 | 6 | 5 | 84 | 42 | 44 |
| Sunderland | 30 | 17 | 4 | 9 | 72 | 44 | 38 |
| Derby County | 30 | 16 | 4 | 10 | 73 | 62 | 36 |
| Blackburn Rovers | 30 | 16 | 2 | 12 | 69 | 53 | 34 |
| Burnley | 30 | 15 | 4 | 11 | 61 | 51 | 34 |
| Everton | 30 | 15 | 3 | 12 | 90 | 57 | 33 |
| Nottingham Forest | 30 | 14 | 4 | 12 | 57 | 48 | 32 |
| West Bromwich Albion | 30 | 14 | 4 | 12 | 66 | 59 | 32 |
| Wolverhampton Wanderers | 30 | 14 | 3 | 13 | 52 | 63 | 31 |
| Sheffield United | 30 | 13 | 5 | 12 | 47 | 61 | 31 |
| Stoke | 30 | 13 | 3 | 14 | 65 | 79 | 29 |
| The Wednesday | 30 | 9 | 8 | 13 | 48 | 57 | 26 |
| Bolton Wanderers | 30 | 10 | 4 | 16 | 38 | 52 | 24 |
| Preston North End | 30 | 10 | 3 | 17 | 44 | 56 | 23 |
| *Darwen* | *30* | *7* | *5* | *18* | *37* | *83* | *19* |
| *Newton Heath* | *30* | *6* | *2* | *22* | *36* | *72* | *14* |

## DIVISION TWO 1893-94

| | | | | | | | |
|---|---|---|---|---|---|---|---|
| Liverpool | 28 | 22 | 6 | 0 | 77 | 18 | 50 |
| Small Heath | 28 | 21 | 0 | 7 | 103 | 44 | 42 |
| Notts County | 28 | 18 | 3 | 7 | 70 | 31 | 39 |
| Newcastle United | 28 | 15 | 6 | 7 | 66 | 39 | 36 |
| Grimsby Town | 28 | 15 | 2 | 11 | 71 | 58 | 32 |
| Burton Swifts | 28 | 14 | 3 | 11 | 79 | 61 | 31 |
| Burslem Port Vale | 28 | 13 | 4 | 11 | 66 | 64 | 30 |
| Lincoln City | 28 | 11 | 6 | 11 | 59 | 58 | 28 |
| Woolwich Arsenal | 28 | 12 | 4 | 12 | 52 | 55 | 28 |
| Walsall Town Swifts | 28 | 10 | 3 | 15 | 51 | 61 | 23 |
| *Middlesbrough Ironopolis* | *28* | *8* | *4* | *16* | *37* | *72* | *20* |
| Crewe Alexandra | 28 | 6 | 7 | 15 | 42 | 73 | 19 |
| Ardwick | 28 | 8 | 2 | 18 | 47 | 71 | 18 |
| Rotherham Town | 28 | 6 | 3 | 19 | 44 | 91 | 15 |
| *Northwich Victoria* | *28* | *3* | *3* | *22* | *30* | *98* | *9* |

## 1894 F.A. Cup

**Semi-finals**

| | |
|---|---|
| Notts County vs Blackburn Rovers | 1-0 |
| Bolton Wanderers vs The Wednesday | 2-1 |

**Final**

Goodison Park, 31st March 1894

**Notts County 4**   (Logan 3, Watson)

**Bolton Wanderers 1**   (Cassidy)

*Attendance 37,000*

## DIVISION ONE 1894-95

| | | | | | | | |
|---|---|---|---|---|---|---|---|
| **SUNDERLAND** | 30 | 21 | 5 | 4 | 80 | 37 | 47 |
| Everton | 30 | 18 | 6 | 6 | 82 | 50 | 42 |
| Aston Villa | 30 | 17 | 5 | 8 | 82 | 43 | 39 |
| Preston North End | 30 | 15 | 5 | 10 | 62 | 46 | 35 |
| Blackburn Rovers | 30 | 11 | 10 | 9 | 59 | 49 | 32 |
| Sheffield United | 30 | 14 | 4 | 12 | 57 | 55 | 32 |
| Nottingham Forest | 30 | 13 | 5 | 12 | 50 | 56 | 31 |
| The Wednesday | 30 | 12 | 4 | 14 | 50 | 55 | 28 |
| Burnley | 30 | 11 | 4 | 15 | 44 | 56 | 26 |
| Bolton Wanderers | 30 | 9 | 7 | 14 | 61 | 62 | 25 |
| Wolverhampton Wanderers | 30 | 9 | 7 | 14 | 43 | 63 | 25 |
| Small Heath | 30 | 9 | 7 | 14 | 50 | 74 | 25 |
| West Bromwich Albion | 30 | 10 | 4 | 16 | 51 | 66 | 24 |
| Stoke | 30 | 9 | 6 | 15 | 50 | 67 | 24 |
| Derby County | 30 | 7 | 9 | 14 | 45 | 68 | 23 |
| *Liverpool* | *30* | *7* | *8* | *15* | *51* | *70* | *22* |

## DIVISION TWO 1894-95

| Bury | 30 | 23 | 2 | 5 | 78 | 33 | 48 |
|---|---|---|---|---|---|---|---|
| Notts County | 30 | 17 | 5 | 8 | 75 | 45 | 39 |
| Newton Heath | 30 | 15 | 8 | 7 | 78 | 44 | 38 |
| Leicester Fosse | 30 | 15 | 8 | 7 | 72 | 53 | 38 |
| Grimsby Town | 30 | 18 | 1 | 11 | 79 | 52 | 37 |
| Darwen | 30 | 16 | 4 | 10 | 74 | 43 | 36 |
| Burton Wanderers | 30 | 14 | 7 | 9 | 67 | 39 | 35 |
| Woolwich Arsenal | 30 | 14 | 6 | 10 | 75 | 58 | 34 |
| Manchester City | 30 | 14 | 3 | 13 | 82 | 72 | 31 |
| Newcastle United | 30 | 12 | 3 | 15 | 72 | 84 | 27 |
| Burton Swifts | 30 | 11 | 3 | 16 | 52 | 74 | 25 |
| Rotherham Town | 30 | 11 | 2 | 17 | 55 | 62 | 24 |
| Lincoln City | 30 | 10 | 0 | 20 | 52 | 92 | 20 |
| *Walsall Town Swifts* | *30* | *10* | *0* | *20* | *47* | *92* | *20* |
| Burslem Port Vale | 30 | 7 | 4 | 19 | 39 | 77 | 18 |
| Crewe Alexandra | 30 | 3 | 4 | 23 | 26 | 103 | 10 |

## 1895 F.A. Cup

### Semi-finals

| Aston Villa vs Sunderland | 2-1 |
|---|---|
| West Bromwich Albion vs The Wednesday | 2-0 |

### Final

Crystal Palace, 20th April 1895

**Aston Villa 1** (Chatt)
**West Bromwich Albion 0**

*Attendance 42,560*

## DIVISION ONE 1895-96

| ASTON VILLA | 30 | 20 | 5 | 5 | 78 | 45 | 45 |
|---|---|---|---|---|---|---|---|
| Derby County | 30 | 17 | 7 | 6 | 68 | 35 | 41 |
| Everton | 30 | 16 | 7 | 7 | 66 | 43 | 39 |
| Bolton Wanderers | 30 | 16 | 5 | 9 | 49 | 37 | 37 |
| Sunderland | 30 | 15 | 7 | 8 | 52 | 41 | 37 |
| Stoke | 30 | 15 | 0 | 15 | 56 | 47 | 30 |
| The Wednesday | 30 | 12 | 5 | 13 | 44 | 53 | 29 |
| Blackburn Rovers | 30 | 12 | 5 | 13 | 40 | 50 | 29 |
| Preston North End | 30 | 11 | 6 | 13 | 44 | 48 | 28 |
| Burnley | 30 | 10 | 7 | 13 | 48 | 44 | 27 |
| Bury | 30 | 12 | 3 | 15 | 50 | 54 | 27 |
| Sheffield United | 30 | 10 | 6 | 14 | 40 | 50 | 26 |
| Nottingham Forest | 30 | 11 | 3 | 16 | 42 | 57 | 25 |
| Wolverhampton Wanderers | 30 | 10 | 1 | 19 | 61 | 65 | 21 |
| *Small Heath* | *30* | *8* | *4* | *18* | *39* | *79* | *20* |
| West Bromwich Albion | 30 | 6 | 7 | 17 | 30 | 59 | 19 |

## DIVISION TWO 1895-96

| Liverpool | 30 | 22 | 2 | 6 | 106 | 32 | 46 |
|---|---|---|---|---|---|---|---|
| Manchester City | 30 | 21 | 4 | 5 | 63 | 38 | 46 |
| Grimsby Town | 30 | 20 | 2 | 8 | 82 | 38 | 42 |
| Burton Wanderers | 30 | 19 | 4 | 7 | 69 | 40 | 42 |
| Newcastle United | 30 | 16 | 2 | 12 | 73 | 50 | 34 |
| Newton Heath | 30 | 15 | 3 | 12 | 66 | 57 | 33 |
| Woolwich Arsenal | 30 | 14 | 4 | 12 | 59 | 42 | 32 |
| Leicester Fosse | 30 | 14 | 4 | 12 | 57 | 44 | 32 |
| Darwen | 30 | 12 | 6 | 12 | 72 | 67 | 30 |
| Notts County | 30 | 12 | 2 | 16 | 57 | 54 | 26 |
| Burton Swifts | 30 | 10 | 4 | 16 | 39 | 69 | 24 |
| Loughborough | 30 | 9 | 5 | 16 | 40 | 67 | 23 |
| Lincoln City | 30 | 9 | 4 | 17 | 53 | 75 | 22 |
| *Burslem Port Vale* | *30* | *7* | *4* | *19* | *43* | *78* | *18* |
| *Rotherham Town* | *30* | *7* | *3* | *20* | *34* | *97* | *17* |
| *Crewe Alexandra* | *30* | *5* | *3* | *22* | *30* | *95* | *13* |

## 1896 F.A. Cup

### Semi-finals

| The Wednesday vs Bolton Wanderers | 1-1, 3-1 |
|---|---|
| Wolverhampton Wanderers vs Derby County | 2-1 |

### Final

Crystal Palace, 18th April 1896

**The Wednesday 2** (Spiksley 2)
**Wolverhampton Wanderers 1** (Black)

*Attendance 48,836*

## DIVISION ONE 1896-97

| ASTON VILLA | 30 | 21 | 5 | 4 | 73 | 38 | 47 |
|---|---|---|---|---|---|---|---|
| Sheffield United | 30 | 13 | 10 | 7 | 42 | 29 | 36 |
| Derby County | 30 | 16 | 4 | 10 | 70 | 50 | 36 |
| Preston North End | 30 | 11 | 12 | 7 | 55 | 40 | 34 |
| Liverpool | 30 | 12 | 9 | 9 | 46 | 38 | 33 |
| The Wednesday | 30 | 10 | 11 | 9 | 42 | 37 | 31 |
| Everton | 30 | 14 | 3 | 13 | 62 | 57 | 31 |
| Bolton Wanderers | 30 | 12 | 6 | 12 | 40 | 43 | 30 |
| Bury | 30 | 10 | 10 | 10 | 39 | 44 | 30 |
| Wolverhampton Wanderers | 30 | 11 | 6 | 13 | 45 | 41 | 28 |
| Nottingham Forest | 30 | 9 | 8 | 13 | 44 | 49 | 26 |
| West Bromwich Albion | 30 | 10 | 6 | 14 | 33 | 56 | 26 |
| Stoke | 30 | 11 | 3 | 16 | 48 | 59 | 25 |
| Blackburn Rovers | 30 | 11 | 3 | 16 | 35 | 62 | 25 |
| Sunderland | 30 | 7 | 9 | 14 | 34 | 47 | 23 |
| *Burnley* | *30* | *6* | *7* | *17* | *43* | *61* | *19* |

## DIVISION TWO 1896-97

| Notts County | 30 | 19 | 4 | 7 | 92 | 43 | 42 |
|---|---|---|---|---|---|---|---|
| Newton Heath | 30 | 17 | 5 | 8 | 56 | 34 | 39 |
| Grimsby Town | 30 | 17 | 4 | 9 | 66 | 45 | 38 |
| Small Heath | 30 | 16 | 5 | 9 | 69 | 47 | 37 |
| Newcastle United | 30 | 17 | 1 | 12 | 56 | 52 | 35 |
| Manchester City | 30 | 12 | 8 | 10 | 58 | 50 | 32 |
| Gainsborough Trinity | 30 | 12 | 7 | 11 | 50 | 47 | 31 |
| Blackpool | 30 | 13 | 5 | 12 | 59 | 56 | 31 |
| Leicester Fosse | 30 | 13 | 4 | 13 | 59 | 56 | 30 |
| Woolwich Arsenal | 30 | 13 | 4 | 13 | 68 | 70 | 30 |
| Darwen | 30 | 14 | 0 | 16 | 67 | 61 | 28 |
| Walsall | 30 | 11 | 4 | 15 | 53 | 69 | 26 |
| Loughborough | 30 | 12 | 1 | 17 | 50 | 64 | 25 |
| Burton Swifts | 30 | 9 | 6 | 15 | 46 | 61 | 24 |
| *Burton Wanderers* | *30* | *9* | *2* | *19* | *31* | *67* | *20* |
| Lincoln City | 30 | 5 | 2 | 23 | 27 | 85 | 12 |

## 1897 F.A. Cup

### Semi-finals

| Aston Villa vs Liverpool | 3-0 |
|---|---|
| Everton vs Derby County | 3-2 |

### Final

Crystal Palace, 10th April 1897

**Aston Villa 3** (Campbell, Wheldon, Crabtree)
**Everton 2** (Bell, Boyle)

*Attendance 62,017*

## DIVISION ONE 1897-98

| SHEFFIELD UNITED | 30 | 17 | 8 | 5 | 56 | 31 | 42 |
|---|---|---|---|---|---|---|---|
| Sunderland | 30 | 16 | 5 | 9 | 43 | 30 | 37 |
| Wolverhampton Wanderers | 30 | 14 | 7 | 9 | 57 | 41 | 35 |
| Everton | 30 | 13 | 9 | 8 | 48 | 39 | 35 |
| The Wednesday | 30 | 15 | 3 | 12 | 51 | 42 | 33 |
| Aston Villa | 30 | 14 | 5 | 11 | 61 | 51 | 33 |
| West Bromwich Albion | 30 | 11 | 10 | 9 | 44 | 45 | 32 |
| Nottingham Forest | 30 | 11 | 9 | 10 | 47 | 49 | 31 |
| Liverpool | 30 | 11 | 6 | 13 | 48 | 45 | 28 |
| Derby County | 30 | 11 | 6 | 13 | 57 | 61 | 28 |
| Bolton Wanderers | 30 | 11 | 4 | 15 | 28 | 41 | 26 |
| Preston North End | 30 | 8 | 8 | 14 | 35 | 43 | 24 |
| Notts County | 30 | 8 | 8 | 14 | 36 | 46 | 24 |
| Bury | 30 | 8 | 8 | 14 | 39 | 51 | 24 |
| Blackburn Rovers | 30 | 7 | 10 | 13 | 39 | 54 | 24 |
| Stoke | 30 | 8 | 8 | 14 | 35 | 55 | 24 |

## DIVISION TWO 1897-98

| | | | | | | | |
|---|---|---|---|---|---|---|---|
| **Burnley** | 30 | 20 | 8 | 2 | 80 | 24 | 48 |
| **Newcastle United** | 30 | 21 | 3 | 6 | 64 | 32 | 45 |
| Manchester City | 30 | 15 | 9 | 6 | 66 | 36 | 39 |
| Newton Heath | 30 | 16 | 6 | 8 | 64 | 35 | 38 |
| Woolwich Arsenal | 30 | 16 | 5 | 9 | 69 | 49 | 37 |
| Small Heath | 30 | 16 | 4 | 10 | 58 | 50 | 36 |
| Leicester Fosse | 30 | 13 | 7 | 10 | 46 | 35 | 33 |
| Luton Town | 30 | 13 | 4 | 13 | 68 | 50 | 30 |
| Gainsborough Trinity | 30 | 12 | 6 | 12 | 50 | 54 | 30 |
| Walsall | 30 | 12 | 5 | 13 | 58 | 58 | 29 |
| Blackpool | 30 | 10 | 5 | 15 | 49 | 61 | 25 |
| Grimsby Town | 30 | 10 | 4 | 16 | 52 | 62 | 24 |
| Burton Swifts | 30 | 8 | 5 | 17 | 38 | 69 | 21 |
| Lincoln City | 30 | 6 | 5 | 19 | 43 | 82 | 17 |
| Darwen | 30 | 6 | 2 | 22 | 31 | 76 | 14 |
| Loughborough | 30 | 6 | 2 | 22 | 24 | 87 | 14 |

## 1898 F.A. Cup

**Semi-finals**

| | |
|---|---|
| Southampton vs Nottingham Forest | 1-1, 0-2 |
| Derby County vs Everton | 3-1 |

**Final**

Crystal Palace, 16th April 1898

**Nottingham Forest 3**   (Capes 2, McPherson)

**Derby County 1**   (Bloomer)

*Attendance 62,017*

## DIVISION ONE 1898-99

| | | | | | | | |
|---|---|---|---|---|---|---|---|
| **ASTON VILLA** | 34 | 19 | 7 | 8 | 76 | 40 | 45 |
| Liverpool | 34 | 19 | 5 | 10 | 49 | 33 | 43 |
| Burnley | 34 | 15 | 9 | 10 | 45 | 47 | 39 |
| Everton | 34 | 15 | 8 | 11 | 48 | 41 | 38 |
| Notts County | 34 | 12 | 13 | 9 | 47 | 51 | 37 |
| Blackburn Rovers | 34 | 14 | 8 | 12 | 60 | 52 | 36 |
| Sunderland | 34 | 15 | 6 | 13 | 41 | 41 | 36 |
| Wolverhampton Wanderers | 34 | 14 | 7 | 13 | 54 | 48 | 35 |
| Derby County | 34 | 12 | 11 | 11 | 62 | 57 | 35 |
| Bury | 34 | 14 | 7 | 13 | 48 | 49 | 35 |
| Nottingham Forest | 34 | 11 | 11 | 12 | 42 | 42 | 33 |
| Stoke | 34 | 13 | 7 | 14 | 47 | 52 | 33 |
| Newcastle United | 34 | 11 | 8 | 15 | 49 | 48 | 30 |
| West Bromwich Albion | 34 | 12 | 6 | 16 | 42 | 57 | 30 |
| Preston North End | 34 | 10 | 9 | 15 | 44 | 47 | 29 |
| Sheffield United | 34 | 9 | 11 | 14 | 45 | 51 | 29 |
| *Bolton Wanderers* | 34 | 9 | 7 | 18 | 37 | 51 | 25 |
| *The Wednesday* | 34 | 8 | 8 | 18 | 32 | 61 | 24 |

## DIVISION TWO 1898-99

| | | | | | | | |
|---|---|---|---|---|---|---|---|
| **Manchester City** | 34 | 23 | 6 | 5 | 92 | 35 | 52 |
| **Glossop North End** | 34 | 20 | 6 | 8 | 76 | 38 | 46 |
| Leicester Fosse | 34 | 18 | 9 | 7 | 64 | 42 | 45 |
| Newton Heath | 34 | 19 | 5 | 10 | 67 | 43 | 43 |
| New Brighton Tower | 34 | 18 | 7 | 9 | 71 | 52 | 43 |
| Walsall | 34 | 15 | 12 | 7 | 79 | 36 | 42 |
| Woolwich Arsenal | 34 | 18 | 5 | 11 | 72 | 41 | 41 |
| Small Heath | 34 | 17 | 7 | 10 | 85 | 50 | 41 |
| Burslem Port Vale | 34 | 17 | 5 | 12 | 56 | 34 | 39 |
| Grimsby Town | 34 | 15 | 5 | 14 | 71 | 60 | 35 |
| Barnsley | 34 | 12 | 7 | 15 | 52 | 56 | 31 |
| Lincoln City | 34 | 12 | 7 | 15 | 51 | 56 | 31 |
| Burton Swifts | 34 | 10 | 8 | 16 | 51 | 70 | 28 |
| Gainsborough Trinity | 34 | 10 | 5 | 19 | 56 | 72 | 25 |
| Luton Town | 34 | 10 | 3 | 21 | 51 | 95 | 23 |
| *Blackpool* | 34 | 8 | 4 | 22 | 49 | 90 | 20 |
| Loughborough | 34 | 6 | 6 | 22 | 38 | 92 | 18 |
| *Darwen* | 34 | 2 | 5 | 27 | 22 | 141 | 9 |

## 1899 F.A. Cup

**Semi-finals**

| | |
|---|---|
| Sheffield United vs Liverpool | 2-2, 4-4, 0-1*, 1-0 |
| Derby County vs Stoke | 3-1 |

* match abandoned

**Final**

Crystal Palace, 15th April 1899

**Sheffield United 4**   (Bennett, Priest, Beers, Almond)

**Derby County 1**   (Boag)

*Attendance 73,833*

## DIVISION ONE 1899-1900

| | | | | | | | |
|---|---|---|---|---|---|---|---|
| **ASTON VILLA** | 34 | 22 | 6 | 6 | 77 | 35 | 50 |
| Sheffield United | 34 | 18 | 12 | 4 | 63 | 33 | 48 |
| Sunderland | 34 | 19 | 3 | 12 | 50 | 35 | 41 |
| Wolverhampton Wanderers | 34 | 15 | 9 | 10 | 48 | 37 | 39 |
| Newcastle United | 34 | 13 | 10 | 11 | 53 | 43 | 36 |
| Derby County | 34 | 14 | 8 | 12 | 45 | 43 | 36 |
| Manchester City | 34 | 13 | 8 | 13 | 50 | 44 | 34 |
| Nottingham Forest | 34 | 13 | 8 | 13 | 56 | 55 | 34 |
| Stoke | 34 | 13 | 8 | 13 | 37 | 45 | 34 |
| Liverpool | 34 | 14 | 5 | 15 | 49 | 45 | 33 |
| Everton | 34 | 13 | 7 | 14 | 47 | 49 | 33 |
| Bury | 34 | 13 | 6 | 15 | 40 | 44 | 32 |
| West Bromwich Albion | 34 | 11 | 8 | 15 | 43 | 51 | 30 |
| Blackburn Rovers | 34 | 13 | 4 | 17 | 49 | 61 | 30 |
| Notts County | 34 | 9 | 11 | 14 | 46 | 60 | 29 |
| Preston North End | 34 | 12 | 4 | 18 | 38 | 48 | 28 |
| *Burnley* | 34 | 11 | 5 | 18 | 34 | 54 | 27 |
| *Glossop* | 34 | 4 | 10 | 20 | 31 | 74 | 18 |

## DIVISION TWO 1899-1900

| | | | | | | | |
|---|---|---|---|---|---|---|---|
| **The Wednesday** | 34 | 25 | 4 | 5 | 84 | 22 | 54 |
| **Bolton Wanderers** | 34 | 22 | 8 | 4 | 79 | 25 | 52 |
| Small Heath | 34 | 20 | 6 | 8 | 78 | 38 | 46 |
| Newton Heath | 34 | 20 | 4 | 10 | 63 | 27 | 44 |
| Leicester Fosse | 34 | 17 | 9 | 8 | 53 | 36 | 43 |
| Grimsby Town | 34 | 17 | 6 | 11 | 67 | 46 | 40 |
| Chesterfield | 34 | 16 | 6 | 12 | 65 | 60 | 38 |
| Woolwich Arsenal | 34 | 16 | 4 | 14 | 61 | 43 | 36 |
| Lincoln City | 34 | 14 | 8 | 12 | 46 | 43 | 36 |
| New Brighton Tower | 34 | 13 | 9 | 12 | 66 | 58 | 35 |
| Burslem Port Vale | 34 | 14 | 6 | 14 | 39 | 49 | 34 |
| Walsall | 34 | 12 | 8 | 14 | 50 | 55 | 32 |
| Gainsborough Trinity | 34 | 9 | 7 | 18 | 47 | 75 | 25 |
| Middlesbrough | 34 | 8 | 8 | 18 | 39 | 69 | 24 |
| Burton Swifts | 34 | 9 | 6 | 19 | 43 | 84 | 24 |
| Barnsley | 34 | 8 | 7 | 19 | 46 | 79 | 23 |
| *Luton Town* | 34 | 5 | 8 | 21 | 40 | 75 | 18 |
| *Loughborough* | 34 | 1 | 6 | 27 | 18 | 100 | 8 |

## 1900 F.A. Cup

**Semi-finals**

| | |
|---|---|
| Nottingham Forest vs Bury | 1-1, 2-3 |
| Southampton vs Millwall Athletic | 0-0, 3-0 |

**Final**

Crystal Palace, 21st April 1900

**Bury 4**   (McLuckie 2, Wood, Plant)

**Southampton 0**

*Attendance 68,945*

## DIVISION ONE 1900-01

| | | | | | | | |
|---|---|---|---|---|---|---|---|
| **LIVERPOOL** | 34 | 19 | 7 | 8 | 59 | 35 | 45 |
| Sunderland | 34 | 15 | 13 | 6 | 57 | 26 | 43 |
| Notts County | 34 | 18 | 4 | 12 | 54 | 46 | 40 |
| Nottingham Forest | 34 | 16 | 7 | 11 | 53 | 36 | 39 |
| Bury | 34 | 16 | 7 | 11 | 53 | 37 | 39 |
| Newcastle United | 34 | 14 | 10 | 10 | 42 | 37 | 38 |
| Everton | 34 | 16 | 5 | 13 | 55 | 42 | 37 |
| The Wednesday | 34 | 13 | 10 | 11 | 52 | 42 | 36 |
| Blackburn Rovers | 34 | 12 | 9 | 13 | 39 | 47 | 33 |
| Bolton Wanderers | 34 | 13 | 7 | 14 | 39 | 55 | 33 |
| Manchester City | 34 | 13 | 6 | 15 | 48 | 58 | 32 |
| Derby County | 34 | 12 | 7 | 15 | 55 | 42 | 31 |
| Wolverhampton Wanderers | 34 | 9 | 13 | 12 | 39 | 55 | 31 |
| Sheffield United | 34 | 12 | 7 | 15 | 35 | 52 | 31 |
| Aston Villa | 34 | 10 | 10 | 14 | 45 | 51 | 30 |
| Stoke | 34 | 11 | 5 | 18 | 46 | 57 | 27 |
| *Preston North End* | *34* | *9* | *7* | *18* | *49* | *75* | *25* |
| *West Bromwich Albion* | *34* | *7* | *8* | *19* | *35* | *62* | *22* |

## DIVISION TWO 1900-01

| | | | | | | | |
|---|---|---|---|---|---|---|---|
| **Grimsby Town** | 34 | 20 | 9 | 5 | 60 | 33 | 49 |
| **Small Heath** | 34 | 19 | 10 | 5 | 57 | 24 | 48 |
| Burnley | 34 | 20 | 4 | 10 | 53 | 29 | 44 |
| *New Brighton Tower* | *34* | *17* | *8* | *9* | *57* | *38* | *42* |
| Glossop | 34 | 15 | 8 | 11 | 51 | 33 | 38 |
| Middlesbrough | 34 | 15 | 7 | 12 | 50 | 40 | 37 |
| Woolwich Arsenal | 34 | 15 | 6 | 13 | 39 | 35 | 36 |
| Lincoln City | 34 | 13 | 7 | 14 | 43 | 39 | 33 |
| Burslem Port Vale | 34 | 11 | 11 | 12 | 45 | 47 | 33 |
| Newton Heath | 34 | 14 | 4 | 16 | 42 | 38 | 32 |
| Leicester Fosse | 34 | 11 | 10 | 13 | 39 | 37 | 32 |
| Blackpool | 34 | 12 | 7 | 15 | 33 | 58 | 31 |
| Gainsborough Trinity | 34 | 10 | 10 | 14 | 45 | 60 | 30 |
| Chesterfield | 34 | 9 | 10 | 15 | 46 | 58 | 28 |
| Barnsley | 34 | 11 | 5 | 18 | 47 | 60 | 27 |
| *Walsall* | *34* | *7* | *13* | *14* | *40* | *56* | *27* |
| Stockport County | 34 | 11 | 3 | 20 | 38 | 68 | 25 |
| Burton Swifts | 34 | 8 | 4 | 22 | 34 | 66 | 20 |

## 1901 F.A. Cup

### Semi-finals

| | |
|---|---|
| Tottenham Hotspur vs West Bromwich Albion | 4-0 |
| Sheffield United vs Aston Villa | 2-2, 3-0 |

### Final

Crystal Palace, 20th April 1901

**Tottenham Hotspur 2**　(Brown 2)
**Sheffield United 2**　(Bennett, Priest)

*Attendance 114, 815*

### Replay

Burnden Park, Bolton, 27th April 1901

**Tottenham Hotspur 3**　(Cameron, Smith, Brown)
**Sheffield United 1**　(Priest)

*Attendance 20,740*

## DIVISION ONE 1901-02

| | | | | | | | |
|---|---|---|---|---|---|---|---|
| **SUNDERLAND** | 34 | 19 | 6 | 9 | 50 | 35 | 44 |
| Everton | 34 | 17 | 7 | 10 | 53 | 35 | 41 |
| Newcastle United | 34 | 14 | 9 | 11 | 48 | 34 | 37 |
| Blackburn Rovers | 34 | 15 | 6 | 13 | 52 | 48 | 36 |
| Nottingham Forest | 34 | 13 | 9 | 12 | 43 | 43 | 35 |
| Derby County | 34 | 13 | 9 | 12 | 39 | 41 | 35 |
| Bury | 34 | 13 | 8 | 13 | 44 | 38 | 34 |
| Aston Villa | 34 | 13 | 8 | 13 | 42 | 40 | 34 |
| The Wednesday | 34 | 13 | 8 | 13 | 48 | 52 | 34 |
| Sheffield United | 34 | 13 | 7 | 14 | 53 | 48 | 33 |
| Liverpool | 34 | 10 | 12 | 12 | 42 | 38 | 32 |
| Bolton Wanderers | 34 | 12 | 8 | 14 | 51 | 56 | 32 |
| Notts County | 34 | 14 | 4 | 16 | 51 | 57 | 32 |
| Wolverhampton Wanderers | 34 | 13 | 6 | 15 | 46 | 57 | 32 |
| Grimsby Town | 34 | 13 | 6 | 15 | 44 | 60 | 32 |
| Stoke | 34 | 11 | 9 | 14 | 45 | 55 | 31 |
| *Small Heath* | *34* | *11* | *8* | *15* | *47* | *45* | *30* |
| *Manchester City* | *34* | *11* | *6* | *17* | *42* | *58* | *28* |

## DIVISION TWO 1901-02

| | | | | | | | |
|---|---|---|---|---|---|---|---|
| **West Bromwich Albion** | 34 | 25 | 5 | 4 | 82 | 29 | 55 |
| **Middlesbrough** | 34 | 23 | 5 | 6 | 90 | 24 | 51 |
| Preston North End | 34 | 18 | 6 | 10 | 71 | 32 | 42 |
| Woolwich Arsenal | 34 | 18 | 6 | 10 | 50 | 26 | 42 |
| Lincoln City | 34 | 14 | 13 | 7 | 45 | 35 | 41 |
| Bristol City | 34 | 17 | 6 | 11 | 52 | 35 | 40 |
| Doncaster Rovers | 34 | 13 | 8 | 13 | 49 | 58 | 34 |
| Glossop | 34 | 10 | 12 | 12 | 36 | 40 | 32 |
| Burnley | 34 | 10 | 10 | 14 | 41 | 45 | 30 |
| Burton United | 34 | 11 | 8 | 15 | 46 | 54 | 30 |
| Barnsley | 34 | 12 | 6 | 16 | 51 | 63 | 30 |
| Burslem Port Vale | 34 | 10 | 9 | 15 | 43 | 59 | 29 |
| Blackpool | 34 | 11 | 7 | 16 | 40 | 56 | 29 |
| Leicester Fosse | 34 | 12 | 5 | 17 | 38 | 56 | 29 |
| Newton Heath | 34 | 11 | 6 | 17 | 38 | 53 | 28 |
| Chesterfield | 34 | 11 | 6 | 17 | 47 | 68 | 28 |
| Stockport County | 34 | 8 | 7 | 19 | 36 | 72 | 23 |
| Gainsborough Trinity | 34 | 4 | 11 | 19 | 30 | 80 | 19 |

## 1902 F.A. Cup

### Semi-finals

| | |
|---|---|
| Sheffield United vs Derby County | 1-1, 1-1, 1-0 |
| Southampton vs Nottingham Forest | 3-1 |

### Final

Crystal Palace, 19th April 1902

**Sheffield United 1**　(Common)
**Southampton 1**　(Wood)

*Attendance 76,914*

### Replay

Crystal Palace, 26th April 1902

**Sheffield United 2**　(Hedley, Barnes)
**Southampton 1**　(Brown)

*Attendance 33,068*

## DIVISION ONE 1902-03

| | | | | | | | |
|---|---|---|---|---|---|---|---|
| **THE WEDNESDAY** | 34 | 19 | 4 | 11 | 54 | 36 | 42 |
| Aston Villa | 34 | 19 | 3 | 12 | 61 | 40 | 41 |
| Sunderland | 34 | 16 | 9 | 9 | 51 | 36 | 41 |
| Sheffield United | 34 | 17 | 5 | 12 | 58 | 44 | 39 |
| Liverpool | 34 | 17 | 4 | 13 | 68 | 49 | 38 |
| Stoke | 34 | 15 | 7 | 12 | 46 | 38 | 37 |
| West Bromwich Albion | 34 | 16 | 4 | 14 | 54 | 53 | 36 |
| Bury | 34 | 16 | 3 | 15 | 54 | 43 | 35 |
| Derby County | 34 | 16 | 3 | 15 | 50 | 47 | 35 |
| Nottingham Forest | 34 | 14 | 7 | 13 | 49 | 47 | 35 |
| Wolverhampton Wanderers | 34 | 14 | 5 | 15 | 48 | 57 | 33 |
| Everton | 34 | 13 | 6 | 15 | 45 | 47 | 32 |
| Middlesbrough | 34 | 14 | 4 | 16 | 41 | 50 | 32 |
| Newcastle United | 34 | 14 | 4 | 16 | 41 | 51 | 32 |
| Notts County | 34 | 12 | 7 | 15 | 41 | 49 | 31 |
| Blackburn Rovers | 34 | 12 | 5 | 17 | 44 | 63 | 29 |
| *Grimsby Town* | *34* | *8* | *9* | *17* | *43* | *62* | *25* |
| *Bolton Wanderers* | *34* | *8* | *3* | *23* | *37* | *73* | *19* |

## DIVISION TWO 1902-03

| | | | | | | | |
|---|---|---|---|---|---|---|---|
| **Manchester City** | 34 | 25 | 4 | 5 | 95 | 29 | 54 |
| **Small Heath** | 34 | 24 | 3 | 7 | 74 | 36 | 51 |
| Woolwich Arsenal | 34 | 20 | 8 | 6 | 66 | 30 | 48 |
| Bristol City | 34 | 17 | 8 | 9 | 59 | 38 | 42 |
| Manchester United | 34 | 15 | 8 | 11 | 53 | 38 | 38 |
| Chesterfield | 34 | 14 | 9 | 11 | 67 | 40 | 37 |
| Preston North End | 34 | 13 | 10 | 11 | 56 | 40 | 36 |
| Barnsley | 34 | 13 | 8 | 13 | 55 | 51 | 34 |
| Burslem Port Vale | 34 | 13 | 8 | 13 | 57 | 62 | 34 |
| Lincoln City | 34 | 12 | 6 | 16 | 46 | 53 | 30 |
| Glossop | 34 | 11 | 7 | 16 | 43 | 58 | 29 |
| Gainsborough Trinity | 34 | 11 | 7 | 16 | 41 | 59 | 29 |
| Burton United | 34 | 11 | 7 | 16 | 39 | 59 | 29 |
| Blackpool | 34 | 9 | 10 | 15 | 44 | 59 | 28 |
| Leicester Fosse | 34 | 10 | 8 | 16 | 41 | 65 | 28 |
| *Doncaster Rovers* | *34* | *9* | *7* | *18* | *35* | *72* | *25* |
| Stockport County | 34 | 7 | 6 | 21 | 39 | 74 | 20 |
| Burnley | 34 | 6 | 8 | 20 | 30 | 77 | 20 |

## 1903 F.A. Cup

### Semi-finals

| | |
|---|---|
| Aston Villa vs Bury | 0-3 |
| Derby County vs Millwall Athletic | 3-0 |

### Final

Crystal Palace, 18th April 1903

**Bury 6**   (Leeming 2, Ross, Sagar, Plant, Wood)
**Derby County 0**

*Attendance 63,102*

## DIVISION ONE 1903-04

| | | | | | | | |
|---|---|---|---|---|---|---|---|
| THE WEDNESDAY | 34 | 20 | 7 | 7 | 48 | 28 | 47 |
| Manchester City | 34 | 19 | 6 | 9 | 71 | 45 | 44 |
| Everton | 34 | 19 | 5 | 10 | 59 | 32 | 43 |
| Newcastle United | 34 | 18 | 6 | 10 | 58 | 45 | 42 |
| Aston Villa | 34 | 17 | 7 | 10 | 70 | 48 | 41 |
| Sunderland | 34 | 17 | 5 | 12 | 63 | 49 | 39 |
| Sheffield United | 34 | 15 | 8 | 11 | 62 | 57 | 38 |
| Wolverhampton Wanderers | 34 | 14 | 8 | 12 | 44 | 66 | 36 |
| Nottingham Forest | 34 | 11 | 9 | 14 | 57 | 57 | 31 |
| Middlesbrough | 34 | 9 | 12 | 13 | 46 | 47 | 30 |
| Small Heath | 34 | 11 | 8 | 15 | 39 | 52 | 30 |
| Bury | 34 | 7 | 15 | 12 | 40 | 53 | 29 |
| Notts County | 34 | 12 | 5 | 17 | 37 | 61 | 29 |
| Derby County | 34 | 9 | 10 | 15 | 58 | 60 | 28 |
| Blackburn Rovers | 34 | 11 | 6 | 17 | 48 | 60 | 28 |
| Stoke | 34 | 10 | 7 | 17 | 54 | 57 | 27 |
| *Liverpool* | *34* | *9* | *8* | *17* | *49* | *62* | *26* |
| *West Bromwich Albion* | *34* | *7* | *10* | *17* | *36* | *60* | *24* |

## DIVISION TWO 1903-04

| | | | | | | | |
|---|---|---|---|---|---|---|---|
| Preston North End | 34 | 20 | 10 | 4 | 62 | 24 | 50 |
| Woolwich Arsenal | 34 | 21 | 7 | 6 | 91 | 22 | 49 |
| Manchester United | 34 | 20 | 8 | 6 | 65 | 33 | 48 |
| Bristol City | 34 | 18 | 6 | 10 | 73 | 41 | 42 |
| Burnley | 34 | 15 | 9 | 10 | 50 | 55 | 39 |
| Grimsby Town | 34 | 14 | 8 | 12 | 50 | 49 | 36 |
| Bolton Wanderers | 34 | 12 | 10 | 12 | 59 | 41 | 34 |
| Barnsley | 34 | 11 | 10 | 13 | 38 | 57 | 32 |
| Gainsborough Trinity | 34 | 14 | 3 | 17 | 53 | 60 | 31 |
| Bradford City | 34 | 12 | 7 | 15 | 45 | 59 | 31 |
| Chesterfield | 34 | 11 | 8 | 15 | 37 | 45 | 30 |
| Lincoln City | 34 | 11 | 8 | 15 | 41 | 58 | 30 |
| Burslem Port Vale | 34 | 10 | 9 | 15 | 54 | 52 | 29 |
| Burton United | 34 | 11 | 7 | 16 | 45 | 61 | 29 |
| Blackpool | 34 | 11 | 5 | 18 | 40 | 67 | 27 |
| *Stockport County* | *34* | *8* | *11* | *15* | *40* | *72* | *27* |
| Glossop | 34 | 10 | 6 | 18 | 57 | 64 | 26 |
| Leicester Fosse | 34 | 6 | 10 | 18 | 42 | 82 | 22 |

## 1904 F.A. Cup

### Semi-finals

| | |
|---|---|
| Manchester City vs The Wednesday | 3-0 |
| Bolton Wanderers vs Derby County | 1-0 |

### Final

Crystal Palace, 23rd April 1904

**Manchester City 1**   (Meredith)
**Bolton Wanderers 0**

*Attendance 61,374*

## DIVISION ONE 1904-05

| | | | | | | | |
|---|---|---|---|---|---|---|---|
| NEWCASTLE UNITED | 34 | 23 | 2 | 9 | 72 | 33 | 48 |
| Everton | 34 | 21 | 5 | 8 | 63 | 36 | 47 |
| Manchester City | 34 | 20 | 6 | 8 | 66 | 37 | 46 |
| Aston Villa | 34 | 19 | 4 | 11 | 63 | 43 | 42 |
| Sunderland | 34 | 16 | 8 | 10 | 60 | 44 | 40 |
| Sheffield United | 34 | 19 | 2 | 13 | 64 | 56 | 40 |
| Small Heath | 34 | 17 | 5 | 12 | 54 | 38 | 39 |
| Preston North End | 34 | 13 | 10 | 11 | 42 | 37 | 36 |
| The Wednesday | 34 | 14 | 5 | 15 | 61 | 57 | 33 |
| Woolwich Arsenal | 34 | 12 | 9 | 13 | 36 | 40 | 33 |
| Derby County | 34 | 12 | 8 | 14 | 37 | 48 | 32 |
| Stoke | 34 | 13 | 4 | 17 | 40 | 58 | 30 |
| Blackburn Rovers | 34 | 11 | 5 | 18 | 40 | 51 | 27 |
| Wolverhampton Wanderers | 34 | 11 | 4 | 19 | 47 | 73 | 26 |
| Middlesbrough | 34 | 9 | 8 | 17 | 36 | 56 | 26 |
| Nottingham Forest | 34 | 9 | 7 | 18 | 40 | 61 | 25 |
| Bury | 34 | 10 | 4 | 20 | 47 | 67 | 24 |
| Notts County | 34 | 5 | 8 | 21 | 36 | 69 | 18 |

## DIVISION TWO 1904-05

| | | | | | | | |
|---|---|---|---|---|---|---|---|
| Liverpool | 34 | 27 | 4 | 3 | 93 | 25 | 58 |
| **Bolton Wanderers** | **34** | **27** | **2** | **5** | **87** | **32** | **56** |
| Manchester United | 34 | 24 | 5 | 5 | 81 | 30 | 53 |
| Bristol City | 34 | 19 | 4 | 11 | 66 | 45 | 42 |
| Chesterfield Town | 34 | 14 | 11 | 9 | 44 | 35 | 39 |
| Gainsborough Trinity | 34 | 14 | 8 | 12 | 61 | 58 | 36 |
| Barnsley | 34 | 14 | 5 | 15 | 38 | 56 | 33 |
| Bradford City | 34 | 12 | 8 | 14 | 45 | 49 | 32 |
| Lincoln City | 34 | 12 | 7 | 15 | 42 | 40 | 31 |
| West Bromwich Albion | 34 | 13 | 4 | 17 | 56 | 48 | 30 |
| Burnley | 34 | 12 | 6 | 16 | 43 | 52 | 30 |
| Glossop | 34 | 10 | 10 | 14 | 37 | 46 | 30 |
| Grimsby Town | 34 | 11 | 8 | 15 | 33 | 46 | 30 |
| Leicester Fosse | 34 | 11 | 7 | 16 | 40 | 55 | 29 |
| Blackpool | 34 | 9 | 10 | 15 | 36 | 48 | 28 |
| Burslem Port Vale | 34 | 10 | 7 | 17 | 47 | 72 | 27 |
| Burton United | 34 | 8 | 4 | 22 | 30 | 84 | 20 |
| *Doncaster Rovers* | *34* | *3* | *2* | *29* | *23* | *81* | *8* |

## 1905 F.A. Cup

### Semi-finals

| | |
|---|---|
| Everton vs Aston Villa | 1-1, 1-2 |
| Newcastle United vs The Wednesday | 1-0 |

### Final

Crystal Palace, 15th April 1905

**Aston Villa 2**   ( Hampton 2)
**Newcastle United 0**

*Attendance 101,117*

## DIVISION ONE 1905-06

| | | | | | | | |
|---|---|---|---|---|---|---|---|
| LIVERPOOL | 38 | 23 | 5 | 10 | 79 | 46 | 51 |
| Preston North End | 38 | 17 | 13 | 8 | 54 | 39 | 47 |
| The Wednesday | 38 | 18 | 8 | 12 | 63 | 52 | 44 |
| Newcastle United | 38 | 18 | 7 | 13 | 74 | 48 | 43 |
| Manchester City | 38 | 19 | 5 | 14 | 73 | 54 | 43 |
| Bolton Wanderers | 38 | 17 | 7 | 14 | 81 | 67 | 41 |
| Birmingham | 38 | 17 | 7 | 14 | 65 | 59 | 41 |
| Aston Villa | 38 | 17 | 6 | 15 | 72 | 56 | 40 |
| Blackburn Rovers | 38 | 16 | 8 | 14 | 54 | 52 | 40 |
| Stoke | 38 | 16 | 7 | 15 | 54 | 55 | 39 |
| Everton | 38 | 15 | 7 | 16 | 70 | 66 | 37 |
| Woolwich Arsenal | 38 | 15 | 7 | 16 | 62 | 64 | 37 |
| Sheffield United | 38 | 15 | 6 | 17 | 57 | 62 | 36 |
| Sunderland | 38 | 15 | 5 | 18 | 61 | 70 | 35 |
| Derby County | 38 | 14 | 7 | 17 | 39 | 58 | 35 |
| Notts County | 38 | 11 | 12 | 15 | 55 | 71 | 34 |
| Bury | 38 | 11 | 10 | 17 | 57 | 74 | 32 |
| Middlesbrough | 38 | 10 | 11 | 17 | 56 | 71 | 31 |
| *Nottingham Forest* | *38* | *13* | *5* | *20* | *58* | *79* | *31* |
| *Wolverhampton Wanderers* | *38* | *8* | *7* | *23* | *58* | *99* | *23* |

## DIVISION TWO 1905-06

| | | | | | | | |
|---|---|---|---|---|---|---|---|
| Bristol City | 38 | 30 | 6 | 2 | 83 | 28 | 66 |
| Manchester United | 38 | 28 | 6 | 4 | 90 | 28 | 62 |
| Chelsea | 38 | 22 | 9 | 7 | 90 | 37 | 53 |
| West Bromwich Albion | 38 | 22 | 8 | 8 | 79 | 36 | 52 |
| Hull City | 38 | 19 | 6 | 13 | 67 | 54 | 44 |
| Leeds City | 38 | 17 | 9 | 12 | 59 | 47 | 43 |
| Leicester Fosse | 38 | 15 | 12 | 11 | 53 | 48 | 42 |
| Grimsby Town | 38 | 15 | 10 | 13 | 46 | 46 | 40 |
| Burnley | 38 | 15 | 8 | 15 | 42 | 53 | 38 |
| Stockport County | 38 | 13 | 9 | 16 | 44 | 56 | 35 |
| Bradford City | 38 | 13 | 8 | 17 | 46 | 60 | 34 |
| Barnsley | 38 | 12 | 9 | 17 | 60 | 62 | 33 |
| Lincoln City | 38 | 12 | 6 | 20 | 69 | 72 | 30 |
| Blackpool | 38 | 10 | 9 | 19 | 37 | 62 | 29 |
| Gainsborough Trinity | 38 | 12 | 4 | 22 | 44 | 57 | 28 |
| Glossop | 38 | 10 | 8 | 20 | 49 | 71 | 28 |
| Burslem Port Vale | 38 | 12 | 4 | 22 | 49 | 82 | 28 |
| Chesterfield Town | 38 | 10 | 8 | 20 | 40 | 72 | 28 |
| Burton United | 38 | 10 | 6 | 22 | 34 | 67 | 26 |
| Clapton Orient | 38 | 7 | 7 | 24 | 35 | 78 | 21 |

## 1906 F.A. Cup

**Semi-finals**

| | |
|---|---|
| Everton vs Liverpool | 2-0 |
| Woolwich Arsenal vs Newcastle United | 0-2 |

**Final**

Crystal Palace, 21st April 1906

**Everton 1** (Young)
**Newcastle United 0**

*Attendance 75,609*

## DIVISION ONE 1906-07

| | | | | | | | |
|---|---|---|---|---|---|---|---|
| NEWCASTLE UNITED | 38 | 22 | 7 | 9 | 74 | 46 | 51 |
| Bristol City | 38 | 20 | 8 | 10 | 66 | 47 | 48 |
| Everton | 38 | 20 | 5 | 13 | 70 | 46 | 45 |
| Sheffield United | 38 | 17 | 11 | 10 | 57 | 55 | 45 |
| Aston Villa | 38 | 19 | 6 | 13 | 78 | 52 | 44 |
| Bolton Wanderers | 38 | 18 | 8 | 12 | 59 | 47 | 44 |
| Woolwich Arsenal | 38 | 20 | 4 | 14 | 66 | 59 | 44 |
| Manchester United | 38 | 17 | 8 | 13 | 53 | 56 | 42 |
| Birmingham | 38 | 15 | 8 | 15 | 52 | 52 | 38 |
| Sunderland | 38 | 14 | 9 | 15 | 65 | 66 | 37 |
| Middlesbrough | 38 | 15 | 6 | 17 | 56 | 63 | 36 |
| Blackburn Rovers | 38 | 14 | 7 | 17 | 56 | 59 | 35 |
| The Wednesday | 38 | 12 | 11 | 15 | 49 | 60 | 35 |
| Preston North End | 38 | 14 | 7 | 17 | 44 | 57 | 35 |
| Liverpool | 38 | 13 | 7 | 18 | 64 | 65 | 33 |
| Bury | 38 | 13 | 6 | 19 | 58 | 68 | 32 |
| Manchester City | 38 | 10 | 12 | 16 | 53 | 77 | 32 |
| Notts County | 38 | 8 | 15 | 15 | 46 | 50 | 31 |
| *Derby County* | *38* | *9* | *9* | *20* | *41* | *59* | *27* |
| *Stoke* | *38* | *8* | *10* | *20* | *41* | *64* | *26* |

## DIVISION TWO 1906-07

| | | | | | | | |
|---|---|---|---|---|---|---|---|
| Nottingham Forest | 38 | 28 | 4 | 6 | 74 | 36 | 60 |
| Chelsea | 38 | 26 | 5 | 7 | 80 | 34 | 57 |
| Leicester Fosse | 38 | 20 | 8 | 10 | 62 | 39 | 48 |
| West Bromwich Albion | 38 | 21 | 5 | 12 | 83 | 45 | 47 |
| Bradford City | 38 | 21 | 5 | 12 | 70 | 53 | 47 |
| Wolverhampton Wanderers | 38 | 17 | 7 | 14 | 66 | 53 | 41 |
| Burnley | 38 | 17 | 6 | 15 | 62 | 47 | 40 |
| Barnsley | 38 | 15 | 8 | 15 | 73 | 55 | 38 |
| Hull City | 38 | 15 | 7 | 16 | 65 | 57 | 37 |
| Leeds City | 38 | 13 | 10 | 15 | 55 | 63 | 36 |
| Grimsby Town | 38 | 16 | 3 | 19 | 57 | 62 | 35 |
| Stockport County | 38 | 12 | 11 | 15 | 42 | 52 | 35 |
| Blackpool | 38 | 11 | 11 | 16 | 33 | 51 | 33 |
| Gainsborough Trinity | 38 | 14 | 5 | 19 | 45 | 72 | 33 |
| Glossop | 38 | 13 | 6 | 19 | 53 | 79 | 32 |
| *Burslem Port Vale* | *38* | *12* | *7* | *19* | *60* | *83* | *31* |
| Clapton Orient | 38 | 11 | 8 | 19 | 45 | 67 | 30 |
| Chesterfield Town | 38 | 11 | 7 | 20 | 50 | 66 | 29 |
| Lincoln City | 38 | 12 | 4 | 22 | 46 | 73 | 28 |
| *Burton United* | *38* | *8* | *7* | *23* | *34* | *68* | *23* |

## 1907 F.A. Cup

**Semi-finals**

| | |
|---|---|
| Woolwich Arsenal vs The Wednesday | 1-3 |
| West Bromwich Albion vs Everton | 1-2 |

**Final**

Crystal Palace, 20th April 1907

**The Wednesday 2** (Stewart, Simpson)
**Everton 1** (Sharp)

*Attendance 84,584*

## DIVISION ONE 1907-08

| | | | | | | | |
|---|---|---|---|---|---|---|---|
| MANCHESTER UNITED | 38 | 23 | 6 | 9 | 81 | 48 | 52 |
| Aston Villa | 38 | 17 | 9 | 12 | 77 | 59 | 43 |
| Manchester City | 38 | 16 | 11 | 11 | 62 | 54 | 43 |
| Newcastle United | 38 | 15 | 12 | 11 | 65 | 54 | 42 |
| The Wednesday | 38 | 19 | 4 | 15 | 73 | 64 | 42 |
| Middlesbrough | 38 | 17 | 7 | 14 | 54 | 45 | 41 |
| Bury | 38 | 14 | 11 | 13 | 58 | 61 | 39 |
| Liverpool | 38 | 16 | 6 | 16 | 68 | 61 | 38 |
| Nottingham Forest | 38 | 13 | 11 | 14 | 59 | 62 | 37 |
| Bristol City | 38 | 12 | 12 | 14 | 58 | 61 | 36 |
| Everton | 38 | 15 | 6 | 17 | 58 | 64 | 36 |
| Preston North End | 38 | 12 | 12 | 14 | 47 | 53 | 36 |
| Chelsea | 38 | 14 | 8 | 16 | 53 | 62 | 36 |
| Blackburn Rovers | 38 | 12 | 12 | 14 | 51 | 63 | 36 |
| Woolwich Arsenal | 38 | 12 | 12 | 14 | 51 | 63 | 36 |
| Sunderland | 38 | 16 | 3 | 19 | 78 | 75 | 35 |
| Sheffield United | 38 | 12 | 11 | 15 | 52 | 58 | 35 |
| Notts County | 38 | 13 | 8 | 17 | 39 | 51 | 34 |
| *Bolton Wanderers* | *38* | *14* | *5* | *19* | *52* | *58* | *33* |
| *Birmingham* | *38* | *9* | *12* | *17* | *40* | *60* | *30* |

## DIVISION TWO 1907-08

| | | | | | | | |
|---|---|---|---|---|---|---|---|
| Bradford City | 38 | 24 | 6 | 8 | 90 | 42 | 54 |
| Leicester Fosse | 38 | 21 | 10 | 7 | 72 | 47 | 52 |
| Oldham Athletic | 38 | 22 | 6 | 10 | 76 | 42 | 50 |
| Fulham | 38 | 22 | 5 | 11 | 82 | 49 | 49 |
| West Bromwich Albion | 38 | 19 | 9 | 10 | 61 | 39 | 47 |
| Derby County | 38 | 21 | 4 | 13 | 77 | 45 | 46 |
| Burnley | 38 | 20 | 6 | 12 | 67 | 50 | 46 |
| Hull City | 38 | 21 | 4 | 13 | 73 | 62 | 46 |
| Wolverhampton Wanderers | 38 | 15 | 7 | 16 | 50 | 45 | 37 |
| *Stoke* | *38* | *16* | *5* | *17* | *57* | *52* | *37* |
| Gainsborough Trinity | 38 | 14 | 7 | 17 | 47 | 71 | 35 |
| Leeds City | 38 | 12 | 8 | 18 | 53 | 65 | 32 |
| Stockport County | 38 | 12 | 8 | 18 | 48 | 67 | 32 |
| Clapton Orient | 38 | 11 | 10 | 17 | 40 | 65 | 32 |
| Blackpool | 38 | 11 | 9 | 18 | 51 | 58 | 31 |
| Barnsley | 38 | 12 | 6 | 20 | 54 | 68 | 30 |
| Glossop | 38 | 11 | 8 | 19 | 54 | 74 | 30 |
| Grimsby Town | 38 | 11 | 8 | 19 | 43 | 71 | 30 |
| Chesterfield Town | 38 | 6 | 11 | 21 | 46 | 92 | 23 |
| *Lincoln City* | *38* | *9* | *3* | *26* | *46* | *83* | *21* |

## 1908 F.A. Cup

**Semi-finals**

| | |
|---|---|
| Wolverhampton Wanderers vs Southampton | 2-0 |
| Newcastle United vs Fulham | 6-0 |

**Final**

Crystal Palace, 25th April 1908

**Wolverhampton Wanderers 3** (Hunt, Hedley, Harrison)
**Newcastle United 1** (Howie)

*Attendance 74,967*

## DIVISION ONE 1908-09

| | | | | | | | |
|---|---|---|---|---|---|---|---|
| **NEWCASTLE UNITED** | 38 | 24 | 5 | 9 | 65 | 41 | 53 |
| Everton | 38 | 18 | 10 | 10 | 82 | 57 | 46 |
| Sunderland | 38 | 21 | 2 | 15 | 78 | 63 | 44 |
| Blackburn Rovers | 38 | 14 | 13 | 11 | 61 | 50 | 41 |
| The Wednesday | 38 | 17 | 6 | 15 | 67 | 61 | 40 |
| Woolwich Arsenal | 38 | 14 | 10 | 14 | 52 | 49 | 38 |
| Aston Villa | 38 | 14 | 10 | 14 | 58 | 56 | 38 |
| Bristol City | 38 | 13 | 12 | 13 | 45 | 58 | 38 |
| Middlesbrough | 38 | 14 | 9 | 15 | 59 | 53 | 37 |
| Preston North End | 38 | 13 | 11 | 14 | 48 | 44 | 37 |
| Chelsea | 38 | 14 | 9 | 15 | 56 | 61 | 37 |
| Sheffield United | 38 | 14 | 9 | 15 | 51 | 59 | 37 |
| Manchester United | 38 | 15 | 7 | 16 | 58 | 68 | 37 |
| Nottingham Forest | 38 | 14 | 8 | 16 | 66 | 57 | 36 |
| Notts County | 38 | 14 | 8 | 16 | 51 | 48 | 36 |
| Liverpool | 38 | 15 | 6 | 17 | 57 | 65 | 36 |
| Bury | 38 | 14 | 8 | 16 | 63 | 77 | 36 |
| Bradford City | 38 | 12 | 10 | 16 | 47 | 47 | 34 |
| *Manchester City* | 38 | 15 | 4 | 19 | 67 | 69 | 34 |
| *Leicester Fosse* | 38 | 8 | 9 | 21 | 54 | 102 | 25 |

## DIVISION TWO 1908-09

| | | | | | | | |
|---|---|---|---|---|---|---|---|
| **Bolton Wanderers** | 38 | 24 | 4 | 10 | 59 | 28 | 52 |
| **Tottenham Hotspur** | 38 | 20 | 11 | 7 | 67 | 32 | 51 |
| West Bromwich Albion | 38 | 19 | 13 | 6 | 56 | 27 | 51 |
| Hull City | 38 | 19 | 6 | 13 | 63 | 39 | 44 |
| Derby County | 38 | 16 | 11 | 11 | 55 | 41 | 43 |
| Oldham Athletic | 38 | 17 | 6 | 15 | 55 | 43 | 40 |
| Wolverhampton Wanderers | 38 | 14 | 11 | 13 | 56 | 48 | 39 |
| Glossop | 38 | 15 | 8 | 15 | 57 | 53 | 38 |
| Gainsborough Trinity | 38 | 15 | 8 | 15 | 49 | 70 | 38 |
| Fulham | 38 | 13 | 11 | 14 | 58 | 48 | 37 |
| Birmingham | 38 | 14 | 9 | 15 | 58 | 61 | 37 |
| Leeds City | 38 | 14 | 7 | 17 | 43 | 53 | 35 |
| Grimsby Town | 38 | 14 | 7 | 17 | 41 | 54 | 35 |
| Burnley | 38 | 13 | 7 | 18 | 51 | 58 | 33 |
| Clapton Orient | 38 | 12 | 9 | 17 | 37 | 49 | 33 |
| Bradford Park Avenue | 38 | 13 | 6 | 19 | 51 | 59 | 32 |
| Barnsley | 38 | 11 | 10 | 17 | 48 | 57 | 32 |
| Stockport County | 38 | 14 | 3 | 21 | 39 | 71 | 31 |
| *Chesterfield Town* | 38 | 11 | 8 | 19 | 37 | 67 | 30 |
| Blackpool | 38 | 9 | 11 | 18 | 46 | 68 | 29 |

## 1909 F.A. Cup

**Semi-finals**

| | |
|---|---|
| Manchester United vs Newcastle United | 1-0 |
| Bristol City vs Derby County | 1-1, 2-1 |

**Final**

Crystal Palace, 24th March 1909

**Manchester United 1**  (A. Turnbull)
**Bristol City 0**

*Attendance 71,401*

## DIVISION ONE 1909-10

| | | | | | | | |
|---|---|---|---|---|---|---|---|
| **ASTON VILLA** | 38 | 23 | 7 | 8 | 84 | 42 | 53 |
| Liverpool | 38 | 21 | 6 | 11 | 78 | 57 | 48 |
| Blackburn Rovers | 38 | 18 | 9 | 11 | 73 | 55 | 45 |
| Newcastle United | 38 | 19 | 7 | 12 | 70 | 56 | 45 |
| Manchester United | 38 | 19 | 7 | 12 | 69 | 61 | 45 |
| Sheffield United | 38 | 16 | 10 | 12 | 62 | 41 | 42 |
| Bradford City | 38 | 17 | 8 | 13 | 64 | 47 | 42 |
| Sunderland | 38 | 18 | 5 | 15 | 66 | 51 | 41 |
| Notts County | 38 | 15 | 10 | 13 | 67 | 59 | 40 |
| Everton | 38 | 16 | 8 | 14 | 51 | 56 | 40 |
| The Wednesday | 38 | 15 | 9 | 14 | 60 | 63 | 39 |
| Preston North End | 38 | 15 | 5 | 18 | 52 | 58 | 35 |
| Bury | 38 | 12 | 9 | 17 | 62 | 66 | 33 |
| Nottingham Forest | 38 | 11 | 11 | 16 | 54 | 72 | 33 |
| Tottenham Hotspur | 38 | 11 | 10 | 17 | 53 | 69 | 32 |
| Bristol City | 38 | 12 | 8 | 18 | 45 | 60 | 32 |
| Middlesbrough | 38 | 11 | 9 | 18 | 56 | 73 | 31 |
| Woolwich Arsenal | 38 | 11 | 9 | 18 | 37 | 67 | 31 |
| *Chelsea* | 38 | 11 | 7 | 20 | 47 | 70 | 29 |
| *Bolton Wanderers* | 38 | 9 | 6 | 23 | 44 | 71 | 24 |

## DIVISION TWO 1909-10

| | | | | | | | |
|---|---|---|---|---|---|---|---|
| **Manchester City** | 38 | 23 | 8 | 7 | 81 | 40 | 54 |
| **Oldham Athletic** | 38 | 23 | 7 | 8 | 79 | 39 | 53 |
| Hull City | 38 | 23 | 7 | 8 | 80 | 46 | 53 |
| Derby County | 38 | 22 | 9 | 7 | 72 | 47 | 53 |
| Leicester Fosse | 38 | 20 | 4 | 14 | 79 | 58 | 44 |
| Glossop | 38 | 18 | 7 | 13 | 64 | 57 | 43 |
| Fulham | 38 | 14 | 13 | 11 | 51 | 43 | 41 |
| Wolverhampton Wanderers | 38 | 17 | 6 | 15 | 64 | 63 | 40 |
| Barnsley | 38 | 16 | 7 | 15 | 62 | 59 | 39 |
| Bradford Park Avenue | 38 | 17 | 4 | 17 | 64 | 59 | 38 |
| West Bromwich Albion | 38 | 16 | 5 | 17 | 58 | 56 | 37 |
| Blackpool | 38 | 14 | 8 | 16 | 50 | 52 | 36 |
| Stockport County | 38 | 13 | 8 | 17 | 50 | 47 | 34 |
| Burnley | 38 | 14 | 6 | 18 | 62 | 61 | 34 |
| Lincoln City | 38 | 10 | 11 | 17 | 42 | 69 | 31 |
| Clapton Orient | 38 | 12 | 6 | 20 | 37 | 60 | 30 |
| Leeds City | 38 | 10 | 7 | 21 | 46 | 80 | 27 |
| Gainsborough Trinity | 38 | 10 | 6 | 22 | 33 | 75 | 26 |
| *Grimsby Town* | 38 | 9 | 6 | 23 | 50 | 77 | 24 |
| Birmingham | 38 | 8 | 7 | 23 | 42 | 78 | 23 |

## 1910 F.A. Cup

**Semi-finals**

| | |
|---|---|
| Newcastle United vs Swindon Town | 2-0 |
| Barnsley vs Everton | 0-0, 3-0 |

**Final**

Crystal Palace, 23rd April 1910

**Newcastle United 1**  (Rutherford)
**Barnsley 1**  (Tufnell)

*Attendance 77,747*

**Replay**

Goodison Park, 28th April 1910

**Newcastle United 2**  (Shepherd 2 (1 pen))
**Barnsley 0**

*Attendance 69,000*

## DIVISION ONE 1910-11

| | | | | | | | |
|---|---|---|---|---|---|---|---|
| **MANCHESTER UNITED** | 38 | 22 | 8 | 8 | 72 | 40 | 52 |
| Aston Villa | 38 | 22 | 7 | 9 | 69 | 41 | 51 |
| Sunderland | 38 | 15 | 15 | 8 | 67 | 48 | 45 |
| Everton | 38 | 19 | 7 | 12 | 50 | 36 | 45 |
| Bradford City | 38 | 20 | 5 | 13 | 51 | 42 | 45 |
| The Wednesday | 38 | 17 | 8 | 13 | 47 | 48 | 42 |
| Oldham Athletic | 38 | 16 | 9 | 13 | 44 | 41 | 41 |
| Newcastle United | 38 | 15 | 10 | 13 | 61 | 43 | 40 |
| Sheffield United | 38 | 15 | 8 | 15 | 49 | 43 | 38 |
| Woolwich Arsenal | 38 | 13 | 12 | 13 | 41 | 49 | 38 |
| Notts County | 38 | 14 | 10 | 14 | 37 | 45 | 38 |
| Blackburn Rovers | 38 | 13 | 11 | 14 | 62 | 54 | 37 |
| Liverpool | 38 | 15 | 7 | 16 | 53 | 53 | 37 |
| Preston North End | 38 | 12 | 11 | 15 | 40 | 49 | 35 |
| Tottenham Hotspur | 38 | 13 | 6 | 19 | 52 | 63 | 32 |
| Middlesbrough | 38 | 11 | 10 | 17 | 49 | 63 | 32 |
| Manchester City | 38 | 9 | 13 | 16 | 43 | 58 | 31 |
| Bury | 38 | 9 | 11 | 18 | 43 | 71 | 29 |
| *Bristol City* | 38 | 11 | 5 | 22 | 43 | 66 | 27 |
| *Nottingham Forest* | 38 | 9 | 7 | 22 | 55 | 75 | 25 |

## DIVISION TWO 1910-11

| West Bromwich Albion | 38 | 22 | 9 | 7 | 67 | 41 | 53 |
|---|---|---|---|---|---|---|---|
| Bolton Wanderers | 38 | 21 | 9 | 8 | 69 | 40 | 51 |
| Chelsea | 38 | 20 | 9 | 9 | 71 | 35 | 49 |
| Clapton Orient | 38 | 19 | 7 | 12 | 44 | 35 | 45 |
| Hull City | 38 | 14 | 16 | 8 | 55 | 39 | 44 |
| Derby County | 38 | 17 | 8 | 13 | 73 | 52 | 42 |
| Blackpool | 38 | 16 | 10 | 12 | 49 | 38 | 42 |
| Burnley | 38 | 13 | 15 | 10 | 45 | 45 | 41 |
| Wolverhampton Wanderers | 38 | 15 | 8 | 15 | 51 | 52 | 38 |
| Fulham | 38 | 15 | 7 | 16 | 52 | 48 | 37 |
| Leeds City | 38 | 15 | 7 | 16 | 58 | 56 | 37 |
| Bradford Park Avenue | 38 | 14 | 9 | 15 | 53 | 55 | 37 |
| Huddersfield Town | 38 | 13 | 8 | 17 | 57 | 58 | 34 |
| Glossop | 38 | 13 | 8 | 17 | 48 | 62 | 34 |
| Leicester Fosse | 38 | 14 | 5 | 19 | 52 | 62 | 33 |
| Birmingham | 38 | 12 | 8 | 18 | 42 | 64 | 32 |
| Stockport County | 38 | 11 | 8 | 19 | 47 | 79 | 30 |
| Gainsborough Trinity | 38 | 9 | 11 | 18 | 37 | 55 | 29 |
| Barnsley | 38 | 7 | 14 | 17 | 52 | 62 | 28 |
| *Lincoln City* | *38* | *7* | *10* | *21* | *28* | *72* | *24* |

## DIVISION TWO 1911-12

| Derby County | 38 | 23 | 8 | 7 | 74 | 28 | 54 |
|---|---|---|---|---|---|---|---|
| Chelsea | 38 | 24 | 6 | 8 | 64 | 34 | 54 |
| Burnley | 38 | 22 | 8 | 8 | 77 | 41 | 52 |
| Clapton Orient | 38 | 21 | 3 | 14 | 61 | 44 | 45 |
| Wolverhampton Wanderers | 38 | 16 | 10 | 12 | 57 | 33 | 42 |
| Barnsley | 38 | 15 | 12 | 11 | 45 | 42 | 42 |
| Hull City | 38 | 17 | 8 | 13 | 54 | 51 | 42 |
| Fulham | 38 | 16 | 7 | 15 | 66 | 58 | 39 |
| Grimsby Town | 38 | 15 | 9 | 14 | 48 | 55 | 39 |
| Leicester Fosse | 38 | 15 | 7 | 16 | 49 | 66 | 37 |
| Bradford Park Avenue | 38 | 13 | 9 | 16 | 44 | 45 | 35 |
| Birmingham | 38 | 14 | 6 | 18 | 55 | 59 | 34 |
| Bristol City | 38 | 14 | 6 | 18 | 41 | 60 | 34 |
| Blackpool | 38 | 13 | 8 | 17 | 32 | 52 | 34 |
| Nottingham Forest | 38 | 13 | 7 | 18 | 46 | 48 | 33 |
| Stockport County | 38 | 11 | 11 | 16 | 47 | 54 | 33 |
| Huddersfield Town | 38 | 13 | 6 | 19 | 50 | 64 | 32 |
| Glossop | 38 | 8 | 12 | 18 | 42 | 56 | 28 |
| Leeds City | 38 | 10 | 8 | 20 | 50 | 78 | 28 |
| *Gainsborough Trinity* | *38* | *5* | *13* | *20* | *30* | *64* | *23* |

## 1911 F.A. Cup

### Semi-finals
| | |
|---|---|
| Bradford City vs Blackburn Rovers | 3-0 |
| Newcastle United vs Chelsea | 3-0 |

### Final
Crystal Palace, 22nd April 1911

**Bradford City 0**
**Newcastle United 0**

*Attendance 69,098*

### Replay
Old Trafford, 26th April 1911

**Bradford City 1** (Spiers)
**Newcastle United 0**

*Attendance 58,000*

## 1912 F.A. Cup

### Semi-finals
| | |
|---|---|
| Swindon Town vs Barnsley | 0-0, 0-1 |
| Blackburn Rovers vs West Bromwich Albion | 0-0, 0-1 |

### Final
Crystal Palace, 20th April 1912

**Barnsley 0**
**West Bromwich Albion 0**

*Attendance 54,556*

### Replay
Bramall Lane, 24th April 1912

**Barnsley 1** (Tufnell)
**West Bromwich Albion 0 (aet.)**

*Attendance 38,555*

## DIVISION ONE 1911-12

| BLACKBURN ROVERS | 38 | 20 | 9 | 9 | 60 | 43 | 49 |
|---|---|---|---|---|---|---|---|
| Everton | 38 | 20 | 6 | 12 | 46 | 42 | 46 |
| Newcastle United | 38 | 18 | 8 | 12 | 64 | 50 | 44 |
| Bolton Wanderers | 38 | 20 | 3 | 15 | 54 | 43 | 43 |
| The Wednesday | 38 | 16 | 9 | 13 | 69 | 49 | 41 |
| Aston Villa | 38 | 17 | 7 | 14 | 76 | 63 | 41 |
| Middlesbrough | 38 | 16 | 8 | 14 | 56 | 45 | 40 |
| Sunderland | 38 | 14 | 11 | 13 | 58 | 51 | 39 |
| West Bromwich Albion | 38 | 15 | 9 | 14 | 43 | 47 | 39 |
| Woolwich Arsenal | 38 | 15 | 8 | 15 | 55 | 59 | 38 |
| Bradford City | 38 | 15 | 8 | 15 | 46 | 50 | 38 |
| Tottenham Hotspur | 38 | 14 | 9 | 15 | 53 | 53 | 37 |
| Manchester United | 38 | 13 | 11 | 14 | 45 | 60 | 37 |
| Sheffield United | 38 | 13 | 10 | 15 | 63 | 56 | 36 |
| Manchester City | 38 | 13 | 9 | 16 | 56 | 58 | 35 |
| Notts County | 38 | 14 | 7 | 17 | 46 | 63 | 35 |
| Liverpool | 38 | 12 | 10 | 16 | 49 | 55 | 34 |
| Oldham Athletic | 38 | 12 | 10 | 16 | 46 | 54 | 34 |
| *Preston North End* | *38* | *13* | *7* | *18* | *40* | *57* | *33* |
| *Bury* | *38* | *6* | *9* | *23* | *32* | *59* | *21* |

## DIVISION ONE 1912-13

| SUNDERLAND | 38 | 25 | 4 | 9 | 86 | 43 | 54 |
|---|---|---|---|---|---|---|---|
| Aston Villa | 38 | 19 | 12 | 7 | 86 | 52 | 50 |
| The Wednesday | 38 | 21 | 7 | 10 | 75 | 55 | 49 |
| Manchester United | 38 | 19 | 8 | 11 | 69 | 43 | 46 |
| Blackburn Rovers | 38 | 16 | 13 | 9 | 79 | 43 | 45 |
| Manchester City | 38 | 18 | 8 | 12 | 53 | 37 | 44 |
| Derby County | 38 | 17 | 8 | 13 | 69 | 66 | 42 |
| Bolton Wanderers | 38 | 16 | 10 | 12 | 62 | 63 | 42 |
| Oldham Athletic | 38 | 14 | 14 | 10 | 50 | 55 | 42 |
| West Bromwich Albion | 38 | 13 | 12 | 13 | 57 | 50 | 38 |
| Everton | 38 | 15 | 7 | 16 | 48 | 54 | 37 |
| Liverpool | 38 | 16 | 5 | 17 | 61 | 71 | 37 |
| Bradford City | 38 | 12 | 11 | 15 | 50 | 60 | 35 |
| Newcastle United | 38 | 13 | 8 | 17 | 47 | 47 | 34 |
| Sheffield United | 38 | 14 | 6 | 18 | 56 | 70 | 34 |
| Middlesbrough | 38 | 11 | 10 | 17 | 55 | 69 | 32 |
| Tottenham Hotspur | 38 | 12 | 6 | 20 | 45 | 72 | 30 |
| Chelsea | 38 | 11 | 6 | 21 | 51 | 73 | 28 |
| *Notts County* | *38* | *7* | *9* | *22* | *28* | *56* | *23* |
| *Woolwich Arsenal* | *38* | *3* | *12* | *23* | *26* | *74* | *18* |

## DIVISION TWO 1912-13

| | | | | | | | |
|---|---|---|---|---|---|---|---|
| Preston North End | 38 | 19 | 15 | 4 | 56 | 33 | 53 |
| Burnley | 38 | 21 | 8 | 9 | 88 | 53 | 50 |
| Birmingham | 38 | 18 | 10 | 10 | 59 | 44 | 46 |
| Barnsley | 38 | 19 | 7 | 12 | 57 | 47 | 45 |
| Huddersfield Town | 38 | 17 | 9 | 12 | 66 | 40 | 43 |
| Leeds City | 38 | 15 | 10 | 13 | 70 | 64 | 40 |
| Grimsby Town | 38 | 15 | 10 | 13 | 51 | 50 | 40 |
| Lincoln City | 38 | 15 | 10 | 13 | 50 | 52 | 40 |
| Fulham | 38 | 17 | 5 | 16 | 65 | 55 | 39 |
| Wolverhampton Wanderers | 38 | 14 | 10 | 14 | 56 | 54 | 38 |
| Bury | 38 | 15 | 8 | 15 | 53 | 57 | 38 |
| Hull City | 38 | 15 | 6 | 17 | 60 | 56 | 36 |
| Bradford Park Avenue | 38 | 14 | 8 | 16 | 60 | 60 | 36 |
| Clapton Orient | 38 | 10 | 14 | 14 | 34 | 47 | 34 |
| Leicester Fosse | 38 | 13 | 7 | 18 | 50 | 65 | 33 |
| Bristol City | 38 | 9 | 15 | 14 | 46 | 72 | 33 |
| Nottingham Forest | 38 | 12 | 8 | 18 | 58 | 59 | 32 |
| Glossop | 38 | 12 | 8 | 18 | 49 | 68 | 32 |
| Stockport County | 38 | 8 | 10 | 20 | 56 | 78 | 26 |
| Blackpool | 38 | 9 | 8 | 21 | 39 | 69 | 26 |

## 1913 F.A. Cup

**Semi-finals**

| | |
|---|---|
| Aston Villa vs Oldham Athletic | 1-0 |
| Sunderland vs Burnley | 0-0, 3-2 |

**Final**

Crystal Palace, 19th April 1913

**Aston Villa 1** (Barber)

**Sunderland 0**

*Attendance 120,081*

## DIVISION ONE 1913-14

| | | | | | | | |
|---|---|---|---|---|---|---|---|
| BLACKBURN ROVERS | 38 | 20 | 11 | 7 | 78 | 42 | 51 |
| Aston Villa | 38 | 19 | 6 | 13 | 65 | 50 | 44 |
| Middlesbrough | 38 | 19 | 5 | 14 | 77 | 60 | 43 |
| Oldham Athletic | 38 | 17 | 9 | 12 | 55 | 45 | 43 |
| West Bromwich Albion | 38 | 15 | 13 | 10 | 46 | 42 | 43 |
| Bolton Wanderers | 38 | 16 | 10 | 12 | 65 | 52 | 42 |
| Sunderland | 38 | 17 | 6 | 15 | 63 | 52 | 40 |
| Chelsea | 38 | 16 | 7 | 15 | 46 | 55 | 39 |
| Bradford City | 38 | 12 | 14 | 12 | 40 | 40 | 38 |
| Sheffield United | 38 | 16 | 5 | 17 | 63 | 60 | 37 |
| Newcastle United | 38 | 13 | 11 | 14 | 39 | 48 | 37 |
| Burnley | 38 | 12 | 12 | 14 | 61 | 53 | 36 |
| Manchester City | 38 | 14 | 8 | 16 | 51 | 53 | 36 |
| Manchester United | 38 | 15 | 6 | 17 | 52 | 62 | 36 |
| Everton | 38 | 12 | 11 | 15 | 46 | 55 | 35 |
| Liverpool | 38 | 14 | 7 | 17 | 46 | 62 | 35 |
| Tottenham Hotspur | 38 | 12 | 10 | 16 | 50 | 62 | 34 |
| The Wednesday | 38 | 13 | 8 | 17 | 53 | 70 | 34 |
| *Preston North End* | 38 | 12 | 6 | 20 | 52 | 69 | 30 |
| *Derby County* | 38 | 8 | 11 | 19 | 55 | 71 | 27 |

## DIVISION TWO 1913-14

| | | | | | | | |
|---|---|---|---|---|---|---|---|
| Notts County | 38 | 23 | 7 | 8 | 77 | 36 | 53 |
| Bradford Park Avenue | 38 | 23 | 3 | 12 | 71 | 47 | 49 |
| The Arsenal | 38 | 20 | 9 | 9 | 54 | 38 | 49 |
| Leeds City | 38 | 20 | 7 | 11 | 76 | 46 | 47 |
| Barnsley | 38 | 19 | 7 | 12 | 51 | 45 | 45 |
| Clapton Orient | 38 | 16 | 11 | 11 | 47 | 35 | 43 |
| Hull City | 38 | 16 | 9 | 13 | 53 | 37 | 41 |
| Bristol City | 38 | 16 | 9 | 13 | 52 | 50 | 41 |
| Wolverhampton Wanderers | 38 | 18 | 5 | 15 | 51 | 52 | 41 |
| Bury | 38 | 15 | 10 | 13 | 39 | 40 | 40 |
| Fulham | 38 | 16 | 6 | 16 | 46 | 43 | 38 |
| Stockport County | 38 | 13 | 10 | 15 | 55 | 57 | 36 |
| Huddersfield Town | 38 | 13 | 8 | 17 | 47 | 53 | 34 |
| Birmingham | 38 | 12 | 10 | 16 | 48 | 60 | 34 |
| Grimsby Town | 38 | 13 | 8 | 17 | 42 | 58 | 34 |
| Blackpool | 38 | 9 | 14 | 15 | 33 | 44 | 32 |
| Glossop | 38 | 11 | 6 | 21 | 51 | 67 | 28 |
| Leicester Fosse | 38 | 11 | 4 | 23 | 45 | 61 | 26 |
| Lincoln City | 38 | 10 | 6 | 22 | 36 | 66 | 26 |
| Nottingham Forest | 38 | 7 | 9 | 22 | 37 | 76 | 23 |

## 1914 F.A. Cup

**Semi-finals**

| | |
|---|---|
| Sheffield United vs Burnley | 0-0, 0-1 |
| Aston Villa vs Liverpool | 0-2 |

**Final**

Crystal Palace, 25th April 1914

**Burnley 1** (Freeman)

**Liverpool 0**

*Attendance 72,778*

## DIVISION ONE 1914-15

| | | | | | | | |
|---|---|---|---|---|---|---|---|
| EVERTON | 38 | 19 | 8 | 11 | 76 | 47 | 46 |
| Oldham Athletic | 38 | 17 | 11 | 10 | 70 | 56 | 45 |
| Blackburn Rovers | 38 | 18 | 7 | 13 | 83 | 61 | 43 |
| Burnley | 38 | 18 | 7 | 13 | 61 | 47 | 43 |
| Manchester City | 38 | 15 | 13 | 10 | 49 | 39 | 43 |
| Sheffield United | 38 | 15 | 13 | 10 | 49 | 41 | 43 |
| The Wednesday | 38 | 15 | 13 | 10 | 61 | 54 | 43 |
| Sunderland | 38 | 18 | 5 | 15 | 81 | 72 | 41 |
| Bradford Park Avenue | 38 | 17 | 7 | 14 | 69 | 65 | 41 |
| West Bromwich Albion | 38 | 15 | 10 | 13 | 49 | 43 | 40 |
| Bradford City | 38 | 13 | 14 | 11 | 55 | 49 | 40 |
| Middlesbrough | 38 | 13 | 12 | 13 | 62 | 74 | 38 |
| Liverpool | 38 | 14 | 9 | 15 | 65 | 75 | 37 |
| Aston Villa | 38 | 13 | 11 | 14 | 62 | 72 | 37 |
| Newcastle United | 38 | 11 | 10 | 17 | 46 | 48 | 32 |
| Notts County | 38 | 9 | 13 | 16 | 41 | 57 | 31 |
| Bolton Wanderers | 38 | 11 | 8 | 19 | 68 | 84 | 30 |
| Manchester United | 38 | 9 | 12 | 17 | 46 | 62 | 30 |
| Chelsea | 38 | 8 | 13 | 17 | 51 | 65 | 29 |
| *Tottenham Hotspur* | 38 | 8 | 12 | 18 | 57 | 90 | 28 |

## DIVISION TWO 1914-15

| | | | | | | | |
|---|---|---|---|---|---|---|---|
| Derby County | 38 | 23 | 7 | 8 | 71 | 33 | 53 |
| Preston North End | 38 | 20 | 10 | 8 | 61 | 42 | 50 |
| Barnsley | 38 | 22 | 3 | 13 | 51 | 51 | 47 |
| Wolverhampton Wanderers | 38 | 19 | 7 | 12 | 77 | 52 | 45 |
| The Arsenal | 38 | 19 | 5 | 14 | 69 | 41 | 43 |
| Birmingham | 38 | 17 | 9 | 12 | 62 | 39 | 43 |
| Hull City | 38 | 19 | 5 | 14 | 65 | 54 | 43 |
| Huddersfield Town | 38 | 17 | 8 | 13 | 61 | 42 | 42 |
| Clapton Orient | 38 | 16 | 9 | 13 | 50 | 48 | 41 |
| Blackpool | 38 | 17 | 5 | 16 | 58 | 57 | 39 |
| Bury | 38 | 15 | 8 | 15 | 61 | 56 | 38 |
| Fulham | 38 | 15 | 7 | 16 | 53 | 47 | 37 |
| Bristol City | 38 | 15 | 7 | 16 | 62 | 56 | 37 |
| Stockport County | 38 | 15 | 7 | 16 | 54 | 60 | 37 |
| Leeds City | 38 | 14 | 4 | 20 | 65 | 64 | 32 |
| Lincoln City | 38 | 11 | 9 | 18 | 46 | 65 | 31 |
| Grimsby Town | 38 | 11 | 9 | 18 | 48 | 76 | 31 |
| Nottingham Forest | 38 | 10 | 9 | 19 | 43 | 77 | 29 |
| Leicester Fosse | 38 | 10 | 4 | 24 | 47 | 88 | 24 |
| Glossop | 38 | 6 | 6 | 26 | 31 | 87 | 18 |

## 1915 F.A. Cup

**Semi-finals**

| | |
|---|---|
| Sheffield United vs Bolton Wanderers | 2-1 |
| Chelsea vs Everton | 2-0 |

**Final**

Old Trafford, 24th April 1915

**Sheffield United 3** (Simmons, Kitchen, Fazackerley)

**Chelsea 0**

*Attendance 49,557*

## DIVISION ONE 1919-20

| | | | | | | | |
|---|---|---|---|---|---|---|---|
| **WEST BROMWICH ALBION** | 42 | 28 | 4 | 10 | 104 | 47 | 60 |
| Burnley | 42 | 21 | 9 | 12 | 65 | 59 | 51 |
| Chelsea | 42 | 22 | 5 | 15 | 56 | 51 | 49 |
| Liverpool | 42 | 19 | 10 | 13 | 59 | 44 | 48 |
| Sunderland | 42 | 22 | 4 | 16 | 72 | 59 | 48 |
| Bolton Wanderers | 42 | 19 | 9 | 14 | 72 | 65 | 47 |
| Manchester City | 42 | 18 | 9 | 15 | 71 | 62 | 45 |
| Newcastle United | 42 | 17 | 9 | 16 | 44 | 39 | 43 |
| Aston Villa | 42 | 18 | 6 | 18 | 75 | 73 | 42 |
| The Arsenal | 42 | 15 | 12 | 15 | 56 | 58 | 42 |
| Bradford Park Avenue | 42 | 15 | 12 | 15 | 60 | 63 | 42 |
| Manchester United | 42 | 13 | 14 | 15 | 54 | 50 | 40 |
| Middlesbrough | 42 | 15 | 10 | 17 | 61 | 65 | 40 |
| Sheffield United | 42 | 16 | 8 | 18 | 59 | 69 | 40 |
| Bradford City | 42 | 14 | 11 | 17 | 54 | 63 | 39 |
| Everton | 42 | 12 | 14 | 16 | 69 | 68 | 38 |
| Oldham Athletic | 42 | 15 | 8 | 19 | 49 | 52 | 38 |
| Derby County | 42 | 13 | 12 | 17 | 47 | 57 | 38 |
| Preston North End | 42 | 14 | 10 | 18 | 57 | 73 | 38 |
| Blackburn Rovers | 42 | 13 | 11 | 18 | 64 | 77 | 37 |
| *Notts County* | 42 | 12 | 12 | 18 | 56 | 74 | 36 |
| *The Wednesday* | 42 | 7 | 9 | 26 | 28 | 64 | 23 |

## DIVISION ONE 1920-21

| | | | | | | | |
|---|---|---|---|---|---|---|---|
| **BURNLEY** | 42 | 23 | 13 | 6 | 79 | 36 | 59 |
| Manchester City | 42 | 24 | 6 | 12 | 70 | 50 | 54 |
| Bolton Wanderers | 42 | 19 | 14 | 9 | 77 | 53 | 52 |
| Liverpool | 42 | 18 | 15 | 9 | 63 | 35 | 51 |
| Newcastle United | 42 | 20 | 10 | 12 | 66 | 45 | 50 |
| Tottenham Hotspur | 42 | 19 | 9 | 14 | 70 | 48 | 47 |
| Everton | 42 | 17 | 13 | 12 | 66 | 55 | 47 |
| Middlesbrough | 42 | 17 | 12 | 13 | 53 | 53 | 46 |
| The Arsenal | 42 | 15 | 14 | 13 | 59 | 63 | 44 |
| Aston Villa | 42 | 18 | 7 | 17 | 63 | 70 | 43 |
| Blackburn Rovers | 42 | 13 | 15 | 14 | 57 | 59 | 41 |
| Sunderland | 42 | 14 | 13 | 15 | 57 | 60 | 41 |
| Manchester United | 42 | 15 | 10 | 17 | 64 | 68 | 40 |
| West Bromwich Albion | 42 | 13 | 14 | 15 | 54 | 58 | 40 |
| Bradford City | 42 | 12 | 15 | 15 | 61 | 63 | 39 |
| Preston North End | 42 | 15 | 9 | 18 | 61 | 65 | 39 |
| Huddersfield Town | 42 | 15 | 9 | 18 | 42 | 49 | 39 |
| Chelsea | 42 | 13 | 13 | 16 | 48 | 58 | 39 |
| Oldham Athletic | 42 | 9 | 15 | 18 | 49 | 86 | 33 |
| Sheffield United | 42 | 6 | 18 | 18 | 42 | 68 | 30 |
| *Derby County* | 42 | 5 | 16 | 21 | 32 | 58 | 26 |
| *Bradford Park Avenue* | 42 | 8 | 8 | 26 | 43 | 76 | 24 |

## DIVISION TWO 1919-20

| | | | | | | | |
|---|---|---|---|---|---|---|---|
| **Tottenham Hotspur** | 42 | 32 | 6 | 4 | 102 | 32 | 70 |
| **Huddersfield Town** | 42 | 28 | 8 | 6 | 97 | 38 | 64 |
| Birmingham | 42 | 24 | 8 | 10 | 85 | 34 | 56 |
| Blackpool | 42 | 21 | 10 | 11 | 65 | 47 | 52 |
| Bury | 42 | 20 | 8 | 14 | 60 | 44 | 48 |
| Fulham | 42 | 19 | 9 | 14 | 61 | 50 | 47 |
| West Ham United | 42 | 19 | 9 | 14 | 47 | 40 | 47 |
| Bristol City | 42 | 13 | 17 | 12 | 46 | 43 | 43 |
| South Shields | 42 | 15 | 12 | 15 | 58 | 48 | 42 |
| Stoke City | 42 | 18 | 6 | 18 | 60 | 54 | 42 |
| Hull City | 42 | 18 | 6 | 18 | 78 | 72 | 42 |
| Barnsley | 42 | 15 | 10 | 17 | 61 | 55 | 40 |
| Port Vale | 42 | 16 | 8 | 18 | 59 | 62 | 40 |
| Leicester City | 42 | 15 | 10 | 17 | 41 | 61 | 40 |
| Clapton Orient | 42 | 16 | 6 | 20 | 51 | 59 | 38 |
| Stockport County | 42 | 14 | 9 | 19 | 52 | 61 | 37 |
| Rotherham County | 42 | 13 | 8 | 21 | 51 | 83 | 34 |
| Nottingham Forest | 42 | 11 | 9 | 22 | 43 | 73 | 31 |
| Wolverhampton Wanderers | 42 | 10 | 10 | 22 | 55 | 80 | 30 |
| Coventry City | 42 | 9 | 11 | 22 | 35 | 73 | 29 |
| *Lincoln City* | 42 | 9 | 9 | 24 | 44 | 101 | 27 |
| *Grimsby Town* | 42 | 10 | 5 | 27 | 34 | 75 | 25 |

Leeds City were expelled from the League after 8 matches of the season due to financial irregularities. Port Vale took over their fixtures and their final figures include the following statistics from Leeds City　8　4　2　2　17　10　10

## DIVISION TWO 1920-21

| | | | | | | | |
|---|---|---|---|---|---|---|---|
| **Birmingham** | 42 | 24 | 10 | 8 | 79 | 38 | 58 |
| **Cardiff City** | 42 | 24 | 10 | 8 | 59 | 32 | 58 |
| Bristol City | 42 | 19 | 13 | 10 | 49 | 29 | 51 |
| Blackpool | 42 | 20 | 10 | 12 | 54 | 42 | 50 |
| West Ham United | 42 | 19 | 10 | 13 | 51 | 30 | 48 |
| Notts County | 42 | 18 | 11 | 13 | 55 | 40 | 47 |
| Clapton Orient | 42 | 16 | 13 | 13 | 43 | 42 | 45 |
| South Shields | 42 | 17 | 10 | 15 | 61 | 46 | 44 |
| Fulham | 42 | 16 | 10 | 16 | 43 | 47 | 42 |
| The Wednesday | 42 | 15 | 11 | 16 | 48 | 48 | 41 |
| Bury | 42 | 15 | 10 | 17 | 45 | 49 | 40 |
| Leicester City | 42 | 12 | 16 | 14 | 39 | 46 | 40 |
| Hull City | 42 | 10 | 20 | 12 | 43 | 53 | 40 |
| Leeds United | 42 | 14 | 10 | 18 | 40 | 45 | 38 |
| Wolverhampton Wanderers | 42 | 16 | 6 | 20 | 49 | 66 | 38 |
| Barnsley | 42 | 10 | 16 | 16 | 48 | 50 | 36 |
| Port Vale | 42 | 11 | 14 | 17 | 43 | 49 | 36 |
| Nottingham Forest | 42 | 12 | 12 | 18 | 48 | 55 | 36 |
| Rotherham County | 42 | 12 | 12 | 18 | 37 | 53 | 36 |
| Stoke City | 42 | 12 | 11 | 19 | 46 | 56 | 35 |
| Coventry City | 42 | 12 | 11 | 19 | 39 | 70 | 35 |
| *Stockport County* | 42 | 9 | 12 | 21 | 42 | 75 | 30 |

## DIVISION THREE 1920-21

| | | | | | | | |
|---|---|---|---|---|---|---|---|
| **Crystal Palace** | 42 | 24 | 11 | 7 | 70 | 34 | 59 |
| Southampton | 42 | 19 | 16 | 7 | 64 | 28 | 54 |
| Queen's Park Rangers | 42 | 22 | 9 | 11 | 61 | 32 | 53 |
| Swindon Town | 42 | 21 | 10 | 11 | 73 | 49 | 52 |
| Swansea Town | 42 | 18 | 15 | 9 | 56 | 45 | 51 |
| Watford | 42 | 20 | 8 | 14 | 59 | 44 | 48 |
| Millwall Athletic | 42 | 18 | 11 | 13 | 42 | 30 | 47 |
| Merthyr Town | 42 | 15 | 15 | 12 | 60 | 49 | 45 |
| Luton Town | 42 | 16 | 12 | 14 | 61 | 56 | 44 |
| Bristol Rovers | 42 | 18 | 7 | 17 | 68 | 57 | 43 |
| Plymouth Argyle | 42 | 11 | 21 | 10 | 35 | 34 | 43 |
| Portsmouth | 42 | 12 | 15 | 15 | 46 | 48 | 39 |
| Grimsby Town | 42 | 15 | 9 | 18 | 49 | 59 | 39 |
| Northampton Town | 42 | 15 | 8 | 19 | 59 | 75 | 38 |
| Newport County | 42 | 14 | 9 | 19 | 43 | 64 | 37 |
| Norwich City | 42 | 10 | 16 | 16 | 44 | 53 | 36 |
| Southend United | 42 | 14 | 8 | 20 | 44 | 61 | 36 |
| Brighton & Hove Albion | 42 | 14 | 8 | 20 | 42 | 61 | 36 |
| Exeter City | 42 | 10 | 15 | 17 | 39 | 54 | 35 |
| Reading | 42 | 12 | 7 | 23 | 42 | 59 | 31 |
| Brentford | 42 | 9 | 12 | 21 | 42 | 67 | 30 |
| Gillingham | 42 | 8 | 12 | 22 | 34 | 74 | 28 |

## 1920 F.A. Cup

**Semi-finals**

| | |
|---|---|
| Aston Villa vs Chelsea | 3-1 |
| Huddersfield Town vs Bristol City | 2-1 |

**Final**

Stamford Bridge, 24th April 1920

**Aston Villa 1** (Kirton)

**Huddersfield Town 0** (aet.)

*Attendance 50,018*

## 1921 F.A. Cup

**Semi-finals**

| | |
|---|---|
| Tottenham Hotspur vs Preston North End | 2-1 |
| Wolverhampton Wanderers vs Cardiff City | 0-0, 3-1 |

**Final**

Stamford Bridge, 23rd April 1921

**Tottenham Hotspur 1**  (Dimmock)

**Wolverhampton Wanderers 0**

*Attendance 72,805*

## DIVISION ONE 1921-22

| | | | | | | | |
|---|---|---|---|---|---|---|---|
| **LIVERPOOL** | 42 | 22 | 13 | 7 | 63 | 36 | 57 |
| Tottenham Hotspur | 42 | 21 | 9 | 12 | 65 | 39 | 51 |
| Burnley | 42 | 22 | 5 | 15 | 72 | 54 | 49 |
| Cardiff City | 42 | 19 | 10 | 13 | 61 | 53 | 48 |
| Aston Villa | 42 | 22 | 3 | 17 | 74 | 55 | 47 |
| Bolton Wanderers | 42 | 20 | 7 | 15 | 68 | 59 | 47 |
| Newcastle United | 42 | 18 | 10 | 14 | 59 | 45 | 46 |
| Middlesbrough | 42 | 16 | 14 | 12 | 79 | 69 | 46 |
| Chelsea | 42 | 17 | 12 | 13 | 40 | 43 | 46 |
| Manchester City | 42 | 18 | 9 | 15 | 65 | 70 | 45 |
| Sheffield United | 42 | 15 | 10 | 17 | 59 | 54 | 40 |
| Sunderland | 42 | 16 | 8 | 18 | 60 | 62 | 40 |
| West Bromwich Albion | 42 | 15 | 10 | 17 | 51 | 63 | 40 |
| Huddersfield Town | 42 | 15 | 9 | 18 | 53 | 54 | 39 |
| Blackburn Rovers | 42 | 13 | 12 | 17 | 54 | 57 | 38 |
| Preston North End | 42 | 13 | 12 | 17 | 42 | 65 | 38 |
| The Arsenal | 42 | 15 | 7 | 20 | 47 | 56 | 37 |
| Birmingham | 42 | 15 | 7 | 20 | 48 | 60 | 37 |
| Oldham Athletic | 42 | 13 | 11 | 18 | 38 | 50 | 37 |
| Everton | 42 | 12 | 12 | 18 | 57 | 55 | 36 |
| *Bradford City* | *42* | *11* | *10* | *21* | *48* | *72* | *32* |
| *Manchester United* | *42* | *8* | *12* | *22* | *41* | *73* | *28* |

## DIVISION TWO 1921-22

| | | | | | | | |
|---|---|---|---|---|---|---|---|
| **Nottingham Forest** | 42 | 22 | 12 | 8 | 51 | 30 | 56 |
| **Stoke City** | 42 | 18 | 16 | 8 | 60 | 44 | 52 |
| Barnsley | 42 | 22 | 8 | 12 | 67 | 52 | 52 |
| West Ham United | 42 | 20 | 8 | 14 | 52 | 39 | 48 |
| Hull City | 42 | 19 | 10 | 13 | 51 | 41 | 48 |
| South Shields | 42 | 17 | 12 | 13 | 43 | 38 | 46 |
| Fulham | 42 | 18 | 9 | 15 | 57 | 38 | 45 |
| Leeds United | 42 | 16 | 13 | 13 | 48 | 38 | 45 |
| Leicester City | 42 | 14 | 17 | 11 | 39 | 34 | 45 |
| The Wednesday | 42 | 15 | 14 | 13 | 47 | 50 | 44 |
| Bury | 42 | 15 | 10 | 17 | 54 | 55 | 40 |
| Derby County | 42 | 15 | 9 | 18 | 60 | 64 | 39 |
| Notts County | 42 | 12 | 15 | 15 | 47 | 51 | 39 |
| Crystal Palace | 42 | 13 | 13 | 16 | 45 | 51 | 39 |
| Clapton Orient | 42 | 15 | 9 | 18 | 43 | 50 | 39 |
| Rotherham County | 42 | 14 | 11 | 17 | 32 | 43 | 39 |
| Wolverhampton Wanderers | 42 | 13 | 11 | 18 | 44 | 49 | 37 |
| Port Vale | 42 | 14 | 8 | 20 | 43 | 57 | 36 |
| Blackpool | 42 | 15 | 5 | 22 | 44 | 57 | 35 |
| Coventry City | 42 | 12 | 10 | 20 | 51 | 60 | 34 |
| *Bradford Park Avenue* | *42* | *12* | *9* | *21* | *46* | *62* | *33* |
| *Bristol City* | *42* | *12* | *9* | *21* | *37* | *58* | *33* |

## DIVISION THREE (N) 1921-22

| | | | | | | | |
|---|---|---|---|---|---|---|---|
| **Stockport County** | 38 | 24 | 8 | 6 | 60 | 21 | 56 |
| Darlington | 38 | 22 | 6 | 10 | 81 | 37 | 50 |
| Grimsby Town | 38 | 21 | 8 | 9 | 72 | 47 | 50 |
| Hartlepools United | 38 | 17 | 8 | 13 | 52 | 39 | 42 |
| Accrington Stanley | 38 | 19 | 3 | 16 | 73 | 57 | 41 |
| Crewe Alexandra | 38 | 18 | 5 | 15 | 60 | 56 | 41 |
| Stalybridge Celtic | 38 | 18 | 5 | 15 | 62 | 63 | 41 |
| Walsall | 38 | 18 | 3 | 17 | 66 | 65 | 39 |
| Southport | 38 | 14 | 10 | 14 | 55 | 44 | 38 |
| Ashington | 38 | 17 | 4 | 17 | 59 | 66 | 38 |
| Durham City | 38 | 17 | 3 | 18 | 68 | 67 | 37 |
| Wrexham | 38 | 14 | 9 | 15 | 51 | 56 | 37 |
| Chesterfield | 38 | 16 | 3 | 19 | 48 | 67 | 35 |
| Lincoln City | 38 | 14 | 6 | 18 | 48 | 59 | 34 |
| Barrow | 38 | 14 | 5 | 19 | 42 | 54 | 33 |
| Nelson | 38 | 13 | 7 | 18 | 48 | 66 | 33 |
| Wigan Borough | 38 | 11 | 9 | 18 | 46 | 72 | 31 |
| Tranmere Rovers | 38 | 9 | 11 | 18 | 51 | 61 | 29 |
| Halifax Town | 38 | 10 | 9 | 19 | 56 | 76 | 29 |
| Rochdale | 38 | 11 | 4 | 23 | 52 | 77 | 26 |

## DIVISION THREE (S) 1921-22

| | | | | | | | |
|---|---|---|---|---|---|---|---|
| **Southampton** | 42 | 23 | 15 | 4 | 68 | 21 | 61 |
| Plymouth Argyle | 42 | 25 | 11 | 6 | 63 | 24 | 61 |
| Portsmouth | 42 | 18 | 17 | 7 | 62 | 39 | 53 |
| Luton Town | 42 | 22 | 8 | 12 | 64 | 35 | 52 |
| Queen's Park Rangers | 42 | 18 | 13 | 11 | 53 | 44 | 49 |
| Swindon Town | 42 | 16 | 13 | 13 | 72 | 60 | 45 |
| Watford | 42 | 13 | 18 | 11 | 54 | 48 | 44 |
| Aberdare Athletic | 42 | 17 | 10 | 15 | 57 | 51 | 44 |
| Brentford | 42 | 16 | 11 | 15 | 52 | 43 | 43 |
| Swansea Town | 42 | 13 | 15 | 14 | 50 | 47 | 41 |
| Merthyr Town | 42 | 17 | 6 | 19 | 45 | 56 | 40 |
| Millwall Athletic | 42 | 10 | 18 | 14 | 38 | 42 | 38 |
| Reading | 42 | 14 | 10 | 18 | 40 | 47 | 38 |
| Bristol Rovers | 42 | 14 | 10 | 18 | 52 | 67 | 38 |
| Norwich City | 42 | 12 | 13 | 17 | 50 | 62 | 37 |
| Charlton Athletic | 42 | 13 | 11 | 18 | 43 | 56 | 37 |
| Northampton Town | 42 | 13 | 11 | 18 | 47 | 71 | 37 |
| Gillingham | 42 | 14 | 8 | 20 | 47 | 60 | 36 |
| Brighton & Hove Albion | 42 | 13 | 9 | 20 | 45 | 51 | 35 |
| Newport County | 42 | 11 | 12 | 19 | 44 | 61 | 34 |
| Exeter City | 42 | 11 | 12 | 19 | 38 | 59 | 34 |
| Southend United | 42 | 8 | 11 | 23 | 34 | 74 | 27 |

## 1922 F.A. Cup

**Semi-finals**

| | |
|---|---|
| Huddersfield Town vs Notts County | 3-1 |
| Preston North End vs Tottenham Hotspur | 2-1 |

**Final**

Stamford Bridge, 29th April 1922

**Huddersfield Town 1**  (Smith (pen))

**Preston North End 0**

*Attendance 53,000*

## DIVISION ONE 1922-23

| | P | W | D | L | F | A | Pts |
|---|---|---|---|---|---|---|---|
| **LIVERPOOL** | 42 | 26 | 8 | 8 | 70 | 31 | 60 |
| Sunderland | 42 | 22 | 10 | 10 | 72 | 54 | 54 |
| Huddersfield Town | 42 | 21 | 11 | 10 | 60 | 32 | 53 |
| Newcastle United | 42 | 18 | 12 | 12 | 45 | 37 | 48 |
| Everton | 42 | 20 | 7 | 15 | 63 | 59 | 47 |
| Aston Villa | 42 | 18 | 10 | 14 | 64 | 51 | 46 |
| West Bromwich Albion | 42 | 17 | 11 | 14 | 58 | 49 | 45 |
| Manchester City | 42 | 17 | 11 | 14 | 50 | 49 | 45 |
| Cardiff City | 42 | 18 | 7 | 17 | 73 | 59 | 43 |
| Sheffield United | 42 | 16 | 10 | 16 | 68 | 64 | 42 |
| The Arsenal | 42 | 16 | 10 | 16 | 61 | 62 | 42 |
| Tottenham Hotspur | 42 | 17 | 7 | 18 | 50 | 50 | 41 |
| Bolton Wanderers | 42 | 14 | 12 | 16 | 50 | 58 | 40 |
| Blackburn Rovers | 42 | 14 | 12 | 16 | 47 | 62 | 40 |
| Burnley | 42 | 16 | 6 | 20 | 58 | 59 | 38 |
| Preston North End | 42 | 13 | 11 | 18 | 60 | 64 | 37 |
| Birmingham | 42 | 13 | 11 | 18 | 41 | 57 | 37 |
| Middlesbrough | 42 | 13 | 10 | 19 | 57 | 63 | 36 |
| Chelsea | 42 | 9 | 18 | 15 | 45 | 53 | 36 |
| Nottingham Forest | 42 | 13 | 8 | 21 | 41 | 70 | 34 |
| *Stoke City* | *42* | *10* | *10* | *22* | *47* | *67* | *30* |
| *Oldham Athletic* | *42* | *10* | *10* | *22* | *35* | *65* | *30* |

## DIVISION THREE (N) 1922-23

| | P | W | D | L | F | A | Pts |
|---|---|---|---|---|---|---|---|
| **Nelson** | 38 | 24 | 3 | 11 | 61 | 41 | 51 |
| Bradford Park Avenue | 38 | 19 | 9 | 10 | 67 | 38 | 47 |
| Walsall | 38 | 19 | 8 | 11 | 51 | 44 | 46 |
| Chesterfield | 38 | 19 | 7 | 12 | 68 | 52 | 45 |
| Wigan Borough | 38 | 18 | 8 | 12 | 64 | 39 | 44 |
| Crewe Alexandra | 38 | 17 | 9 | 12 | 48 | 38 | 43 |
| Halifax Town | 38 | 17 | 7 | 14 | 53 | 46 | 41 |
| Accrington Stanley | 38 | 17 | 7 | 14 | 59 | 65 | 41 |
| Darlington | 38 | 15 | 10 | 13 | 59 | 46 | 40 |
| Wrexham | 38 | 14 | 10 | 14 | 38 | 48 | 38 |
| *Stalybridge Celtic* | *38* | *15* | *6* | *17* | *42* | *47* | *36* |
| Rochdale | 38 | 13 | 10 | 15 | 42 | 53 | 36 |
| Lincoln City | 38 | 13 | 10 | 15 | 39 | 55 | 36 |
| Grimsby Town | 38 | 14 | 5 | 19 | 55 | 52 | 33 |
| Hartlepools United | 38 | 10 | 12 | 16 | 48 | 54 | 32 |
| Tranmere Rovers | 38 | 12 | 8 | 18 | 49 | 59 | 32 |
| Southport | 38 | 12 | 7 | 19 | 32 | 46 | 31 |
| Barrow | 38 | 13 | 4 | 21 | 50 | 60 | 30 |
| Ashington | 38 | 11 | 8 | 19 | 51 | 77 | 30 |
| Durham City | 38 | 9 | 10 | 19 | 43 | 59 | 28 |

## DIVISION TWO 1922-23

| | P | W | D | L | F | A | Pts |
|---|---|---|---|---|---|---|---|
| **Notts County** | 42 | 23 | 7 | 12 | 46 | 34 | 53 |
| **West Ham United** | 42 | 20 | 11 | 11 | 63 | 38 | 51 |
| Leicester City | 42 | 21 | 9 | 12 | 65 | 44 | 51 |
| Manchester United | 42 | 17 | 14 | 11 | 51 | 36 | 48 |
| Blackpool | 42 | 18 | 11 | 13 | 60 | 43 | 47 |
| Bury | 42 | 18 | 11 | 13 | 55 | 46 | 47 |
| Leeds United | 42 | 18 | 11 | 13 | 43 | 36 | 47 |
| The Wednesday | 42 | 17 | 12 | 13 | 54 | 47 | 46 |
| Barnsley | 42 | 17 | 11 | 14 | 62 | 51 | 45 |
| Fulham | 42 | 16 | 12 | 14 | 43 | 32 | 44 |
| Southampton | 42 | 14 | 14 | 14 | 40 | 40 | 42 |
| Hull City | 42 | 14 | 14 | 14 | 43 | 45 | 42 |
| South Shields | 42 | 15 | 10 | 17 | 35 | 44 | 40 |
| Derby County | 42 | 14 | 11 | 17 | 46 | 50 | 39 |
| Bradford City | 42 | 12 | 13 | 17 | 41 | 45 | 37 |
| Crystal Palace | 42 | 13 | 11 | 18 | 54 | 62 | 37 |
| Port Vale | 42 | 14 | 9 | 19 | 39 | 51 | 37 |
| Coventry City | 42 | 15 | 7 | 20 | 46 | 63 | 37 |
| Clapton Orient | 42 | 12 | 12 | 18 | 40 | 50 | 36 |
| Stockport County | 42 | 14 | 8 | 20 | 43 | 58 | 36 |
| *Rotherham County* | *42* | *13* | *9* | *20* | *44* | *63* | *35* |
| *Wolverhampton Wanderers* | *42* | *9* | *9* | *24* | *42* | *77* | *27* |

## DIVISION THREE (S) 1922-23

| | P | W | D | L | F | A | Pts |
|---|---|---|---|---|---|---|---|
| **Bristol City** | 42 | 24 | 11 | 7 | 66 | 40 | 59 |
| Plymouth Argyle | 42 | 23 | 7 | 12 | 61 | 29 | 53 |
| Swansea Town | 42 | 22 | 9 | 11 | 78 | 45 | 53 |
| Brighton & Hove Albion | 42 | 20 | 11 | 11 | 52 | 34 | 51 |
| Luton Town | 42 | 21 | 7 | 14 | 68 | 49 | 49 |
| Millwall Athletic | 42 | 14 | 18 | 10 | 45 | 40 | 46 |
| Portsmouth | 42 | 19 | 8 | 15 | 58 | 52 | 46 |
| Northampton Town | 42 | 17 | 11 | 14 | 54 | 44 | 45 |
| Swindon Town | 42 | 17 | 11 | 14 | 62 | 56 | 45 |
| Watford | 42 | 17 | 10 | 15 | 57 | 54 | 44 |
| Queen's Park Rangers | 42 | 16 | 10 | 16 | 54 | 49 | 42 |
| Charlton Athletic | 42 | 14 | 14 | 14 | 55 | 51 | 42 |
| Bristol Rovers | 42 | 13 | 16 | 13 | 35 | 36 | 42 |
| Brentford | 42 | 13 | 12 | 17 | 41 | 51 | 38 |
| Southend United | 42 | 12 | 13 | 17 | 49 | 54 | 37 |
| Gillingham | 42 | 15 | 7 | 20 | 51 | 59 | 37 |
| Merthyr Town | 42 | 11 | 14 | 17 | 39 | 48 | 36 |
| Norwich City | 42 | 13 | 10 | 19 | 51 | 71 | 36 |
| Reading | 42 | 10 | 14 | 18 | 36 | 55 | 34 |
| Exeter City | 42 | 13 | 7 | 22 | 47 | 84 | 33 |
| Aberdare Athletic | 42 | 9 | 11 | 22 | 42 | 70 | 29 |
| Newport County | 42 | 8 | 11 | 23 | 40 | 70 | 27 |

## 1923 F.A. Cup

**Semi-finals**

| | |
|---|---|
| Bolton Wanderers vs Sheffield United | 1-0 |
| West Ham United vs Derby County | 5-2 |

**Final**

Wembley, 28th April 1923

**Bolton Wanderers 2**  (Jack, J.R. Smith)

**West Ham United 0**

*Official Attendance 126,047  (the actual attendance could have been as high as 200,000)*

## DIVISION ONE 1923-24

| | | | | | | | |
|---|---|---|---|---|---|---|---|
| HUDDERSFIELD TOWN | 42 | 23 | 11 | 8 | 60 | 33 | 57 |
| Cardiff City | 42 | 22 | 13 | 7 | 61 | 34 | 57 |
| Sunderland | 42 | 22 | 9 | 11 | 71 | 54 | 53 |
| Bolton Wanderers | 42 | 18 | 14 | 10 | 68 | 34 | 50 |
| Sheffield United | 42 | 19 | 12 | 11 | 69 | 49 | 50 |
| Aston Villa | 42 | 18 | 13 | 11 | 52 | 37 | 49 |
| Everton | 42 | 18 | 13 | 11 | 62 | 53 | 49 |
| Blackburn Rovers | 42 | 17 | 11 | 14 | 54 | 50 | 45 |
| Newcastle United | 42 | 17 | 10 | 15 | 60 | 54 | 44 |
| Notts County | 42 | 14 | 14 | 14 | 44 | 49 | 42 |
| Manchester City | 42 | 15 | 12 | 15 | 54 | 71 | 42 |
| Liverpool | 42 | 15 | 11 | 16 | 49 | 48 | 41 |
| West Ham United | 42 | 13 | 15 | 14 | 40 | 43 | 41 |
| Birmingham | 42 | 13 | 13 | 16 | 41 | 49 | 39 |
| Tottenham Hotspur | 42 | 12 | 14 | 16 | 50 | 56 | 38 |
| West Bromwich Albion | 42 | 12 | 14 | 16 | 51 | 62 | 38 |
| Burnley | 42 | 12 | 12 | 18 | 55 | 60 | 36 |
| Preston North End | 42 | 12 | 10 | 20 | 52 | 67 | 34 |
| The Arsenal | 42 | 12 | 9 | 21 | 40 | 63 | 33 |
| Nottingham Forest | 42 | 10 | 12 | 20 | 42 | 64 | 32 |
| *Chelsea* | *42* | *9* | *14* | *19* | *31* | *53* | *32* |
| *Middlesbrough* | *42* | *7* | *8* | *27* | *37* | *60* | *22* |

## DIVISION THREE (N) 1923-24

| | | | | | | | |
|---|---|---|---|---|---|---|---|
| Wolverhampton Wanderers | 42 | 24 | 15 | 3 | 76 | 27 | 63 |
| Rochdale | 42 | 25 | 12 | 5 | 60 | 26 | 62 |
| Chesterfield | 42 | 22 | 10 | 10 | 70 | 39 | 54 |
| Rotherham County | 42 | 23 | 6 | 13 | 70 | 43 | 52 |
| Bradford Park Avenue | 42 | 21 | 10 | 11 | 69 | 43 | 52 |
| Darlington | 42 | 20 | 8 | 14 | 70 | 53 | 48 |
| Southport | 42 | 16 | 14 | 12 | 44 | 42 | 46 |
| Ashington | 42 | 18 | 8 | 16 | 59 | 61 | 44 |
| Doncaster Rovers | 42 | 15 | 12 | 15 | 59 | 53 | 42 |
| Wigan Borough | 42 | 14 | 14 | 14 | 55 | 53 | 42 |
| Grimsby Town | 42 | 14 | 13 | 15 | 49 | 47 | 41 |
| Tranmere Rovers | 42 | 13 | 15 | 14 | 51 | 60 | 41 |
| Accrington Stanley | 42 | 16 | 8 | 18 | 48 | 61 | 40 |
| Halifax Town | 42 | 15 | 10 | 17 | 42 | 59 | 40 |
| Durham City | 42 | 15 | 9 | 18 | 59 | 60 | 39 |
| Wrexham | 42 | 10 | 18 | 14 | 37 | 44 | 38 |
| Walsall | 42 | 14 | 8 | 20 | 44 | 59 | 36 |
| New Brighton | 42 | 11 | 13 | 18 | 40 | 53 | 35 |
| Lincoln City | 42 | 10 | 12 | 20 | 48 | 59 | 32 |
| Crewe Alexandra | 42 | 7 | 13 | 22 | 32 | 58 | 27 |
| Hartlepools United | 42 | 7 | 11 | 24 | 33 | 70 | 25 |
| Barrow | 42 | 8 | 9 | 25 | 35 | 80 | 25 |

## DIVISION TWO 1923-24

| | | | | | | | |
|---|---|---|---|---|---|---|---|
| Leeds United | 42 | 21 | 12 | 9 | 61 | 35 | 54 |
| Bury | 42 | 21 | 9 | 12 | 63 | 35 | 51 |
| Derby County | 42 | 21 | 9 | 12 | 75 | 42 | 51 |
| Blackpool | 42 | 18 | 13 | 11 | 72 | 47 | 49 |
| Southampton | 42 | 17 | 14 | 11 | 52 | 31 | 48 |
| Stoke City | 42 | 14 | 18 | 10 | 44 | 42 | 46 |
| Oldham Athletic | 42 | 14 | 17 | 11 | 45 | 52 | 45 |
| The Wednesday | 42 | 16 | 12 | 14 | 54 | 51 | 44 |
| South Shields | 42 | 17 | 10 | 15 | 49 | 50 | 44 |
| Clapton Orient | 42 | 14 | 15 | 13 | 40 | 36 | 43 |
| Barnsley | 42 | 16 | 11 | 15 | 57 | 61 | 43 |
| Leicester City | 42 | 17 | 8 | 17 | 64 | 54 | 42 |
| Stockport County | 42 | 13 | 16 | 13 | 44 | 52 | 42 |
| Manchester United | 42 | 13 | 14 | 15 | 52 | 44 | 40 |
| Crystal Palace | 42 | 13 | 13 | 16 | 53 | 65 | 39 |
| Port Vale | 42 | 13 | 12 | 17 | 50 | 66 | 38 |
| Hull City | 42 | 10 | 17 | 15 | 46 | 51 | 37 |
| Bradford City | 42 | 11 | 15 | 16 | 35 | 48 | 37 |
| Coventry City | 42 | 11 | 13 | 18 | 52 | 68 | 35 |
| Fulham | 42 | 10 | 14 | 18 | 45 | 56 | 34 |
| *Nelson* | *42* | *10* | *13* | *19* | *40* | *74* | *33* |
| *Bristol City* | *42* | *7* | *15* | *20* | *32* | *65* | *29* |

## DIVISION THREE (S) 1923-24

| | | | | | | | |
|---|---|---|---|---|---|---|---|
| Portsmouth | 42 | 24 | 11 | 7 | 87 | 30 | 59 |
| Plymouth Argyle | 42 | 23 | 9 | 10 | 70 | 34 | 55 |
| Millwall Athletic | 42 | 22 | 10 | 10 | 64 | 38 | 54 |
| Swansea Town | 42 | 22 | 8 | 12 | 60 | 48 | 52 |
| Brighton & Hove Albion | 42 | 21 | 9 | 12 | 68 | 37 | 51 |
| Swindon Town | 42 | 17 | 13 | 12 | 58 | 44 | 47 |
| Luton Town | 42 | 16 | 14 | 12 | 50 | 44 | 46 |
| Northampton Town | 42 | 17 | 11 | 14 | 64 | 47 | 45 |
| Bristol Rovers | 42 | 15 | 13 | 14 | 52 | 46 | 43 |
| Newport County | 42 | 17 | 9 | 16 | 56 | 64 | 43 |
| Norwich City | 42 | 16 | 8 | 18 | 60 | 59 | 40 |
| Aberdare Athletic | 42 | 12 | 14 | 16 | 45 | 58 | 38 |
| Merthyr Town | 42 | 11 | 16 | 15 | 45 | 65 | 38 |
| Charlton Athletic | 42 | 11 | 15 | 16 | 38 | 45 | 37 |
| Gillingham | 42 | 12 | 13 | 17 | 43 | 58 | 37 |
| Exeter City | 42 | 15 | 7 | 20 | 37 | 52 | 37 |
| Brentford | 42 | 14 | 8 | 20 | 54 | 71 | 36 |
| Reading | 42 | 13 | 9 | 20 | 51 | 57 | 35 |
| Southend United | 42 | 12 | 10 | 20 | 53 | 84 | 34 |
| Watford | 42 | 9 | 15 | 18 | 45 | 54 | 33 |
| Bournemouth | 42 | 11 | 11 | 20 | 40 | 65 | 33 |
| Queen's Park Rangers | 42 | 11 | 9 | 22 | 37 | 77 | 31 |

## 1924 F.A. Cup

### Semi-finals

| | |
|---|---|
| Newcastle United vs Manchester City | 2-0 |
| Aston Villa vs Burnley | 3-0 |

### Final

Wembley, 26th April 1924

**Newcastle United 2** (Harris, Seymour)

**Aston Villa 0**

*Attendance 91,695*

## DIVISION ONE 1924-25

| | | | | | | | |
|---|---|---|---|---|---|---|---|
| HUDDERSFIELD TOWN | 42 | 21 | 16 | 5 | 69 | 28 | 58 |
| West Bromwich Albion | 42 | 23 | 10 | 9 | 58 | 34 | 56 |
| Bolton Wanderers | 42 | 22 | 11 | 9 | 76 | 34 | 55 |
| Liverpool | 42 | 20 | 10 | 12 | 63 | 55 | 50 |
| Bury | 42 | 17 | 15 | 10 | 54 | 51 | 49 |
| Newcastle United | 42 | 16 | 16 | 10 | 61 | 42 | 48 |
| Sunderland | 42 | 19 | 10 | 13 | 64 | 51 | 48 |
| Birmingham | 42 | 17 | 12 | 13 | 49 | 53 | 46 |
| Notts County | 42 | 16 | 13 | 13 | 42 | 31 | 45 |
| Manchester City | 42 | 17 | 9 | 16 | 76 | 68 | 43 |
| Cardiff City | 42 | 16 | 11 | 15 | 56 | 51 | 43 |
| Tottenham Hotspur | 42 | 15 | 12 | 15 | 52 | 43 | 42 |
| West Ham United | 42 | 15 | 12 | 15 | 62 | 60 | 42 |
| Sheffield United | 42 | 13 | 13 | 16 | 55 | 63 | 39 |
| Aston Villa | 42 | 13 | 13 | 16 | 58 | 71 | 39 |
| Blackburn Rovers | 42 | 11 | 13 | 18 | 53 | 66 | 35 |
| Everton | 42 | 12 | 11 | 19 | 40 | 60 | 35 |
| Leeds United | 42 | 11 | 12 | 19 | 46 | 59 | 34 |
| Burnley | 42 | 11 | 12 | 19 | 46 | 75 | 34 |
| The Arsenal | 42 | 14 | 5 | 23 | 46 | 58 | 33 |
| *Preston North End* | 42 | 10 | 6 | 26 | 37 | 74 | 26 |
| *Nottingham Forest* | 42 | 6 | 12 | 24 | 29 | 65 | 24 |

## DIVISION TWO 1924-25

| | | | | | | | |
|---|---|---|---|---|---|---|---|
| Leicester City | 42 | 24 | 11 | 7 | 90 | 32 | 59 |
| Manchester United | 42 | 23 | 11 | 8 | 57 | 23 | 57 |
| Derby County | 42 | 22 | 11 | 9 | 71 | 36 | 55 |
| Portsmouth | 42 | 15 | 18 | 9 | 58 | 50 | 48 |
| Chelsea | 42 | 16 | 15 | 11 | 51 | 37 | 47 |
| Wolverhampton Wanderers | 42 | 20 | 6 | 16 | 55 | 51 | 46 |
| Southampton | 42 | 13 | 18 | 11 | 40 | 36 | 44 |
| Port Vale | 42 | 17 | 8 | 17 | 48 | 56 | 42 |
| South Shields | 42 | 12 | 17 | 13 | 42 | 38 | 41 |
| Hull City | 42 | 15 | 11 | 16 | 50 | 49 | 41 |
| Clapton Orient | 42 | 14 | 12 | 16 | 42 | 42 | 40 |
| Fulham | 42 | 15 | 10 | 17 | 41 | 56 | 40 |
| Middlesbrough | 42 | 10 | 19 | 13 | 36 | 44 | 39 |
| The Wednesday | 42 | 15 | 8 | 19 | 50 | 56 | 38 |
| Barnsley | 42 | 13 | 12 | 17 | 46 | 59 | 38 |
| Bradford City | 42 | 13 | 12 | 17 | 37 | 50 | 38 |
| Blackpool | 42 | 14 | 9 | 19 | 65 | 61 | 37 |
| Oldham Athletic | 42 | 13 | 11 | 18 | 35 | 51 | 37 |
| Stockport County | 42 | 13 | 11 | 18 | 37 | 57 | 37 |
| Stoke City | 42 | 12 | 11 | 19 | 34 | 46 | 35 |
| *Crystal Palace* | 42 | 12 | 10 | 20 | 38 | 54 | 34 |
| *Coventry City* | 42 | 11 | 9 | 22 | 45 | 84 | 31 |

## DIVISION THREE (N) 1924-25

| | | | | | | | |
|---|---|---|---|---|---|---|---|
| Darlington | 42 | 24 | 10 | 8 | 78 | 33 | 58 |
| Nelson | 42 | 23 | 7 | 12 | 79 | 50 | 53 |
| New Brighton | 42 | 23 | 7 | 12 | 75 | 50 | 53 |
| Southport | 42 | 22 | 7 | 13 | 59 | 37 | 51 |
| Bradford Park Avenue | 42 | 19 | 12 | 11 | 84 | 42 | 50 |
| Rochdale | 42 | 21 | 7 | 14 | 75 | 53 | 49 |
| Chesterfield | 42 | 17 | 11 | 14 | 60 | 44 | 45 |
| Lincoln City | 42 | 18 | 8 | 16 | 53 | 58 | 44 |
| Halifax Town | 42 | 16 | 11 | 15 | 56 | 52 | 43 |
| Ashington | 42 | 16 | 10 | 16 | 68 | 76 | 42 |
| Wigan Borough | 42 | 15 | 11 | 16 | 62 | 65 | 41 |
| Grimsby Town | 42 | 15 | 9 | 18 | 60 | 60 | 39 |
| Durham City | 42 | 13 | 13 | 16 | 50 | 68 | 39 |
| Barrow | 42 | 16 | 7 | 19 | 51 | 74 | 39 |
| Crewe Alexandra | 42 | 13 | 13 | 16 | 53 | 78 | 39 |
| Wrexham | 42 | 15 | 8 | 19 | 53 | 61 | 38 |
| Accrington Stanley | 42 | 15 | 8 | 19 | 60 | 72 | 38 |
| Doncaster Rovers | 42 | 14 | 10 | 18 | 54 | 65 | 38 |
| Walsall | 42 | 13 | 11 | 18 | 44 | 53 | 37 |
| Hartlepools United | 42 | 12 | 11 | 19 | 45 | 63 | 35 |
| Tranmere Rovers | 42 | 14 | 4 | 24 | 59 | 78 | 32 |
| Rotherham County | 42 | 7 | 7 | 28 | 42 | 88 | 21 |

## DIVISION THREE (S) 1924-25

| | | | | | | | |
|---|---|---|---|---|---|---|---|
| Swansea Town | 42 | 23 | 11 | 8 | 68 | 35 | 57 |
| Plymouth Argyle | 42 | 23 | 10 | 9 | 77 | 38 | 56 |
| Bristol City | 42 | 22 | 9 | 11 | 60 | 41 | 53 |
| Swindon Town | 42 | 20 | 11 | 11 | 66 | 38 | 51 |
| Millwall Athletic | 42 | 18 | 13 | 11 | 58 | 38 | 49 |
| Newport County | 42 | 20 | 9 | 13 | 62 | 42 | 49 |
| Exeter City | 42 | 19 | 9 | 14 | 59 | 48 | 47 |
| Brighton & Hove Albion | 42 | 19 | 8 | 15 | 59 | 45 | 46 |
| Northampton Town | 42 | 20 | 6 | 16 | 51 | 44 | 46 |
| Southend United | 42 | 19 | 5 | 18 | 51 | 61 | 43 |
| Watford | 42 | 17 | 9 | 16 | 38 | 47 | 43 |
| Norwich City | 42 | 14 | 13 | 15 | 53 | 51 | 41 |
| Gillingham | 42 | 13 | 14 | 15 | 35 | 44 | 40 |
| Reading | 42 | 14 | 10 | 18 | 37 | 38 | 38 |
| Charlton Athletic | 42 | 13 | 12 | 17 | 46 | 48 | 38 |
| Luton Town | 42 | 10 | 17 | 15 | 49 | 57 | 37 |
| Bristol Rovers | 42 | 12 | 13 | 17 | 42 | 49 | 37 |
| Aberdare Athletic | 42 | 14 | 9 | 19 | 54 | 67 | 37 |
| Queen's Park Rangers | 42 | 14 | 8 | 20 | 42 | 63 | 36 |
| Bournemouth & Boscombe Ath. | 42 | 13 | 8 | 21 | 40 | 58 | 34 |
| Brentford | 42 | 9 | 7 | 26 | 38 | 91 | 25 |
| Merthyr Town | 42 | 8 | 5 | 29 | 35 | 77 | 21 |

## 1925 F.A. Cup

### Semi-finals

| | |
|---|---|
| Sheffield United vs Southampton | 2-0 |
| Cardiff City vs Blackburn Rovers | 3-1 |

### Final

Wembley, 25th April 1925

**Sheffield United  1**  (Tunstall)
**Cardiff City  0**

*Attendance 91,763*

## DIVISION ONE 1925-26

| | | | | | | | |
|---|---|---|---|---|---|---|---|
| HUDDERSFIELD TOWN | 42 | 23 | 11 | 8 | 92 | 60 | 57 |
| The Arsenal | 42 | 22 | 8 | 12 | 87 | 63 | 52 |
| Sunderland | 42 | 21 | 6 | 15 | 96 | 80 | 48 |
| Bury | 42 | 20 | 7 | 15 | 85 | 77 | 47 |
| Sheffield United | 42 | 19 | 8 | 15 | 102 | 82 | 46 |
| Aston Villa | 42 | 16 | 12 | 14 | 86 | 76 | 44 |
| Liverpool | 42 | 14 | 16 | 12 | 70 | 63 | 44 |
| Bolton Wanderers | 42 | 17 | 10 | 15 | 75 | 76 | 44 |
| Manchester United | 42 | 19 | 6 | 17 | 66 | 73 | 44 |
| Newcastle United | 42 | 16 | 10 | 16 | 84 | 75 | 42 |
| Everton | 42 | 12 | 18 | 12 | 72 | 70 | 42 |
| Blackburn Rovers | 42 | 15 | 11 | 16 | 91 | 80 | 41 |
| West Bromwich Albion | 42 | 16 | 8 | 18 | 79 | 78 | 40 |
| Birmingham | 42 | 16 | 8 | 18 | 66 | 81 | 40 |
| Tottenham Hotspur | 42 | 15 | 9 | 18 | 66 | 79 | 39 |
| Cardiff City | 42 | 16 | 7 | 19 | 61 | 76 | 39 |
| Leicester City | 42 | 14 | 10 | 18 | 70 | 80 | 38 |
| West Ham United | 42 | 15 | 7 | 20 | 63 | 76 | 37 |
| Leeds United | 42 | 14 | 8 | 20 | 64 | 76 | 36 |
| Burnley | 42 | 13 | 10 | 19 | 85 | 108 | 36 |
| *Manchester City* | *42* | *12* | *11* | *19* | *89* | *100* | *35* |
| *Notts County* | *42* | *13* | *7* | *22* | *54* | *74* | *33* |

## DIVISION TWO 1925-26

| | | | | | | | |
|---|---|---|---|---|---|---|---|
| **The Wednesday** | 42 | 27 | 6 | 9 | 88 | 48 | 60 |
| **Derby County** | 42 | 25 | 7 | 10 | 77 | 42 | 57 |
| Chelsea | 42 | 19 | 14 | 9 | 76 | 49 | 52 |
| Wolverhampton Wanderers | 42 | 21 | 7 | 14 | 84 | 60 | 49 |
| Swansea Town | 42 | 19 | 11 | 12 | 77 | 57 | 49 |
| Blackpool | 42 | 17 | 11 | 14 | 76 | 69 | 45 |
| Oldham Athletic | 42 | 18 | 8 | 16 | 74 | 62 | 44 |
| Port Vale | 42 | 19 | 6 | 17 | 79 | 69 | 44 |
| South Shields | 42 | 18 | 8 | 16 | 74 | 65 | 44 |
| Middlesbrough | 42 | 21 | 2 | 19 | 77 | 68 | 44 |
| Portsmouth | 42 | 17 | 10 | 15 | 79 | 74 | 44 |
| Preston North End | 42 | 18 | 7 | 17 | 71 | 84 | 43 |
| Hull City | 42 | 16 | 9 | 17 | 63 | 61 | 41 |
| Southampton | 42 | 15 | 8 | 19 | 63 | 63 | 38 |
| Darlington | 42 | 14 | 10 | 18 | 72 | 77 | 38 |
| Bradford City | 42 | 13 | 10 | 19 | 47 | 66 | 36 |
| Nottingham Forest | 42 | 14 | 8 | 20 | 51 | 73 | 36 |
| Barnsley | 42 | 12 | 12 | 18 | 58 | 84 | 36 |
| Fulham | 42 | 11 | 12 | 19 | 46 | 77 | 34 |
| Clapton Orient | 42 | 12 | 9 | 21 | 50 | 65 | 33 |
| *Stoke City* | *42* | *12* | *8* | *22* | *54* | *77* | *32* |
| *Stockport County* | *42* | *8* | *9* | *25* | *51* | *97* | *25* |

## DIVISION THREE (N) 1925-26

| | | | | | | | |
|---|---|---|---|---|---|---|---|
| Grimsby Town | 42 | 26 | 9 | 7 | 91 | 40 | 61 |
| Bradford Park Avenue | 42 | 26 | 8 | 8 | 101 | 43 | 60 |
| Rochdale | 42 | 27 | 5 | 10 | 104 | 58 | 59 |
| Chesterfield | 42 | 25 | 5 | 12 | 100 | 54 | 55 |
| Halifax Town | 42 | 17 | 11 | 14 | 53 | 50 | 45 |
| Hartlepools United | 42 | 18 | 8 | 16 | 82 | 73 | 44 |
| Tranmere Rovers | 42 | 19 | 6 | 17 | 73 | 83 | 44 |
| Nelson | 42 | 16 | 11 | 15 | 89 | 71 | 43 |
| Ashington | 42 | 16 | 11 | 15 | 70 | 62 | 43 |
| Doncaster Rovers | 42 | 16 | 11 | 15 | 80 | 72 | 43 |
| Crewe Alexandra | 42 | 17 | 9 | 16 | 63 | 61 | 43 |
| New Brighton | 42 | 17 | 8 | 17 | 69 | 67 | 42 |
| Durham City | 42 | 18 | 6 | 18 | 63 | 70 | 42 |
| Rotherham United | 42 | 17 | 7 | 18 | 69 | 92 | 41 |
| Lincoln City | 42 | 17 | 5 | 20 | 66 | 82 | 39 |
| Coventry City | 42 | 16 | 6 | 20 | 73 | 82 | 38 |
| Wigan Borough | 42 | 13 | 11 | 18 | 68 | 74 | 37 |
| Accrington Stanley | 42 | 17 | 3 | 22 | 81 | 105 | 37 |
| Wrexham | 42 | 11 | 10 | 21 | 63 | 92 | 32 |
| Southport | 42 | 11 | 10 | 21 | 62 | 92 | 32 |
| Walsall | 42 | 10 | 6 | 26 | 58 | 107 | 26 |
| Barrow | 42 | 7 | 4 | 31 | 50 | 98 | 18 |

## DIVISION THREE (S) 1925-26

| | | | | | | | |
|---|---|---|---|---|---|---|---|
| Reading | 42 | 23 | 11 | 8 | 77 | 52 | 57 |
| Plymouth Argyle | 42 | 24 | 8 | 10 | 107 | 67 | 56 |
| Millwall | 42 | 21 | 11 | 10 | 73 | 39 | 53 |
| Bristol City | 42 | 21 | 9 | 12 | 72 | 51 | 51 |
| Brighton & Hove Albion | 42 | 19 | 9 | 14 | 84 | 73 | 47 |
| Swindon Town | 42 | 20 | 6 | 16 | 69 | 64 | 46 |
| Luton Town | 42 | 18 | 7 | 17 | 80 | 75 | 43 |
| Bournemouth & Boscombe Ath. | 42 | 17 | 9 | 16 | 75 | 91 | 43 |
| Aberdare Athletic | 42 | 17 | 8 | 17 | 74 | 66 | 42 |
| Gillingham | 42 | 17 | 8 | 17 | 53 | 49 | 42 |
| Southend United | 42 | 19 | 4 | 19 | 78 | 73 | 42 |
| Northampton Town | 42 | 17 | 7 | 18 | 82 | 80 | 41 |
| Crystal Palace | 42 | 19 | 3 | 20 | 75 | 79 | 41 |
| Merthyr Town | 42 | 14 | 11 | 17 | 69 | 75 | 39 |
| Watford | 42 | 15 | 9 | 18 | 73 | 89 | 39 |
| Norwich City | 42 | 15 | 9 | 18 | 58 | 73 | 39 |
| Newport County | 42 | 14 | 10 | 18 | 64 | 74 | 38 |
| Brentford | 42 | 16 | 6 | 20 | 69 | 94 | 38 |
| Bristol Rovers | 42 | 15 | 6 | 21 | 66 | 69 | 36 |
| Exeter City | 42 | 15 | 5 | 22 | 72 | 70 | 35 |
| Charlton Athletic | 42 | 11 | 13 | 18 | 48 | 68 | 35 |
| Queen's Park Rangers | 42 | 6 | 9 | 27 | 37 | 84 | 21 |

## 1926 F.A. Cup

### Semi-finals

| | |
|---|---|
| Bolton Wanderers vs Swansea Town | 3-0 |
| Manchester City vs Manchester United | 3-0 |

### Final

Wembley, 24th April 1926

**Bolton Wanderers 1** (Jack)
**Manchester City 0**

*Attendance 91,447*

## DIVISION ONE 1926-27

| | | | | | | | |
|---|---|---|---|---|---|---|---|
| **NEWCASTLE UNITED** | 42 | 25 | 6 | 11 | 96 | 58 | 56 |
| Huddersfield Town | 42 | 17 | 17 | 8 | 76 | 60 | 51 |
| Sunderland | 42 | 21 | 7 | 14 | 98 | 70 | 49 |
| Bolton Wanderers | 42 | 19 | 10 | 13 | 84 | 62 | 48 |
| Burnley | 42 | 19 | 9 | 14 | 91 | 80 | 47 |
| West Ham United | 42 | 19 | 8 | 15 | 86 | 70 | 46 |
| Leicester City | 42 | 17 | 12 | 13 | 85 | 70 | 46 |
| Sheffield United | 42 | 17 | 10 | 15 | 74 | 86 | 44 |
| Liverpool | 42 | 18 | 7 | 17 | 69 | 61 | 43 |
| Aston Villa | 42 | 18 | 7 | 17 | 81 | 83 | 43 |
| The Arsenal | 42 | 17 | 9 | 16 | 77 | 86 | 43 |
| Derby County | 42 | 17 | 7 | 18 | 86 | 73 | 41 |
| Tottenham Hotspur | 42 | 16 | 9 | 17 | 76 | 78 | 41 |
| Cardiff City | 42 | 16 | 9 | 17 | 55 | 65 | 41 |
| Manchester United | 42 | 13 | 14 | 15 | 52 | 64 | 40 |
| The Wednesday | 42 | 15 | 9 | 18 | 75 | 92 | 39 |
| Birmingham | 42 | 17 | 4 | 21 | 64 | 73 | 38 |
| Blackburn Rovers | 42 | 15 | 8 | 19 | 77 | 96 | 38 |
| Bury | 42 | 12 | 12 | 18 | 68 | 77 | 36 |
| Everton | 42 | 12 | 10 | 20 | 64 | 90 | 34 |
| *Leeds United* | *42* | *11* | *8* | *23* | *69* | *88* | *30* |
| *West Bromwich Albion* | *42* | *11* | *8* | *23* | *65* | *86* | *30* |

## DIVISION THREE (N) 1926-27

| | | | | | | | |
|---|---|---|---|---|---|---|---|
| **Stoke City** | 42 | 27 | 9 | 6 | 92 | 40 | 63 |
| Rochdale | 42 | 26 | 6 | 10 | 105 | 65 | 58 |
| Bradford Park Avenue | 42 | 24 | 7 | 11 | 101 | 59 | 55 |
| Halifax Town | 42 | 21 | 11 | 10 | 70 | 53 | 53 |
| Nelson | 42 | 22 | 7 | 13 | 104 | 75 | 51 |
| Stockport County | 42 | 22 | 7 | 13 | 93 | 69 | 49 |
| Chesterfield | 42 | 21 | 5 | 16 | 92 | 68 | 47 |
| Doncaster Rovers | 42 | 18 | 11 | 13 | 81 | 65 | 47 |
| Tranmere Rovers | 42 | 19 | 8 | 15 | 85 | 67 | 46 |
| New Brighton | 42 | 18 | 10 | 14 | 79 | 67 | 46 |
| Lincoln City | 42 | 15 | 12 | 15 | 90 | 78 | 42 |
| Southport | 42 | 15 | 9 | 18 | 80 | 85 | 39 |
| Wrexham | 42 | 14 | 10 | 18 | 65 | 73 | 38 |
| Walsall | 42 | 14 | 10 | 18 | 68 | 81 | 38 |
| Crewe Alexandra | 42 | 14 | 9 | 19 | 71 | 81 | 37 |
| Ashington | 42 | 12 | 12 | 18 | 60 | 90 | 36 |
| Hartlepools United | 42 | 14 | 6 | 22 | 66 | 81 | 34 |
| Wigan Borough | 42 | 11 | 10 | 21 | 66 | 83 | 32 |
| Rotherham United | 42 | 10 | 12 | 20 | 70 | 92 | 32 |
| Durham City | 42 | 12 | 6 | 24 | 58 | 105 | 30 |
| Accrington Stanley | 42 | 10 | 7 | 25 | 62 | 98 | 27 |
| Barrow | 42 | 7 | 8 | 27 | 34 | 117 | 22 |

Stockport County had two points deducted

## DIVISION TWO 1926-27

| | | | | | | | |
|---|---|---|---|---|---|---|---|
| **Middlesbrough** | 42 | 27 | 8 | 7 | 122 | 60 | 62 |
| **Portsmouth** | 42 | 23 | 8 | 11 | 87 | 49 | 54 |
| Manchester City | 42 | 22 | 10 | 10 | 108 | 61 | 54 |
| Chelsea | 42 | 20 | 12 | 10 | 62 | 52 | 52 |
| Nottingham Forest | 42 | 18 | 14 | 10 | 80 | 55 | 50 |
| Preston North End | 42 | 20 | 9 | 13 | 74 | 72 | 49 |
| Hull City | 42 | 20 | 7 | 15 | 63 | 52 | 47 |
| Port Vale | 42 | 16 | 13 | 13 | 88 | 78 | 45 |
| Blackpool | 42 | 18 | 8 | 16 | 95 | 80 | 44 |
| Oldham Athletic | 42 | 19 | 6 | 17 | 74 | 84 | 44 |
| Barnsley | 42 | 17 | 9 | 16 | 88 | 87 | 43 |
| Swansea Town | 42 | 16 | 11 | 15 | 68 | 72 | 43 |
| Southampton | 42 | 15 | 12 | 15 | 60 | 62 | 42 |
| Reading | 42 | 16 | 8 | 18 | 64 | 72 | 40 |
| Wolverhampton Wanderers | 42 | 14 | 7 | 21 | 73 | 75 | 35 |
| Notts County | 42 | 15 | 5 | 22 | 70 | 96 | 35 |
| Grimsby Town | 42 | 11 | 12 | 19 | 74 | 91 | 34 |
| Fulham | 42 | 13 | 8 | 21 | 58 | 92 | 34 |
| South Shields | 42 | 11 | 11 | 20 | 71 | 96 | 33 |
| Clapton Orient | 42 | 12 | 7 | 23 | 60 | 96 | 31 |
| *Darlington* | *42* | *12* | *6* | *24* | *79* | *98* | *30* |
| *Bradford City* | *42* | *7* | *9* | *26* | *50* | *88* | *23* |

## DIVISION THREE (S) 1926-27

| | | | | | | | |
|---|---|---|---|---|---|---|---|
| **Bristol City** | 42 | 27 | 8 | 7 | 104 | 54 | 62 |
| Plymouth Argyle | 42 | 25 | 10 | 7 | 95 | 61 | 60 |
| Millwall | 42 | 23 | 10 | 9 | 89 | 51 | 56 |
| Brighton & Hove Albion | 42 | 21 | 11 | 10 | 79 | 50 | 53 |
| Swindon Town | 42 | 21 | 9 | 12 | 100 | 85 | 51 |
| Crystal Palace | 42 | 18 | 9 | 15 | 84 | 81 | 45 |
| Bournemouth & Boscombe Ath. | 42 | 18 | 8 | 16 | 78 | 66 | 44 |
| Luton Town | 42 | 15 | 14 | 13 | 68 | 66 | 44 |
| Newport County | 42 | 19 | 6 | 17 | 57 | 71 | 44 |
| Bristol Rovers | 42 | 16 | 9 | 17 | 78 | 80 | 41 |
| Brentford | 42 | 13 | 14 | 15 | 70 | 61 | 40 |
| Exeter City | 42 | 15 | 10 | 17 | 76 | 73 | 40 |
| Charlton Athletic | 42 | 16 | 8 | 18 | 60 | 61 | 40 |
| Queen's Park Rangers | 42 | 15 | 9 | 18 | 65 | 71 | 39 |
| Coventry City | 42 | 15 | 7 | 20 | 71 | 86 | 37 |
| Norwich City | 42 | 12 | 11 | 19 | 59 | 71 | 35 |
| Methyr Town | 42 | 13 | 9 | 20 | 63 | 80 | 35 |
| Northampton Town | 42 | 15 | 5 | 22 | 59 | 87 | 35 |
| Southend United | 42 | 14 | 6 | 22 | 64 | 77 | 34 |
| Gillingham | 42 | 11 | 10 | 21 | 54 | 72 | 32 |
| Watford | 42 | 12 | 8 | 22 | 57 | 87 | 32 |
| *Aberdare Athletic* | *42* | *9* | *7* | *26* | *62* | *101* | *25* |

## 1927 F.A. Cup

### Semi-finals

| | |
|---|---|
| Cardiff City vs Reading | 3-0 |
| Arsenal vs Southampton | 2-1 |

### Final

Wembley, 23rd April 1927

**Cardiff City 1** (Ferguson)

**Arsenal 0**

*Attendance 91,206*

## DIVISION ONE 1927-28

| | | | | | | |
|---|---|---|---|---|---|---|
| **EVERTON** | 42 | 20 | 13 | 9 | 102 | 66 | 53 |
| Huddersfield Town | 42 | 22 | 7 | 13 | 91 | 68 | 51 |
| Leicester City | 42 | 18 | 12 | 12 | 96 | 72 | 48 |
| Derby County | 42 | 17 | 10 | 15 | 96 | 83 | 44 |
| Bury | 42 | 20 | 4 | 18 | 80 | 80 | 44 |
| Cardiff City | 42 | 17 | 10 | 15 | 70 | 80 | 44 |
| Bolton Wanderers | 42 | 16 | 11 | 15 | 81 | 66 | 43 |
| Aston Villa | 42 | 17 | 9 | 16 | 78 | 73 | 43 |
| Newcastle United | 42 | 15 | 13 | 14 | 79 | 81 | 43 |
| Arsenal | 42 | 13 | 15 | 14 | 82 | 86 | 41 |
| Birmingham | 42 | 13 | 15 | 14 | 70 | 75 | 41 |
| Blackburn Rovers | 42 | 16 | 9 | 17 | 66 | 78 | 41 |
| Sheffield United | 42 | 15 | 10 | 17 | 79 | 86 | 40 |
| The Wednesday | 42 | 13 | 13 | 16 | 81 | 78 | 39 |
| Sunderland | 42 | 15 | 9 | 18 | 74 | 76 | 39 |
| Liverpool | 42 | 13 | 13 | 16 | 84 | 87 | 39 |
| West Ham United | 42 | 14 | 11 | 17 | 81 | 88 | 39 |
| Manchester United | 42 | 16 | 7 | 19 | 72 | 80 | 39 |
| Burnley | 42 | 16 | 7 | 19 | 82 | 98 | 39 |
| Portsmouth | 42 | 16 | 7 | 19 | 66 | 90 | 39 |
| *Tottenham Hotspur* | *42* | *15* | *8* | *19* | *74* | *86* | *38* |
| *Middlesbrough* | *42* | *11* | *15* | *16* | *81* | *88* | *37* |

## DIVISION THREE (N) 1927-28

| | | | | | | |
|---|---|---|---|---|---|---|
| **Bradford Park Avenue** | 42 | 27 | 9 | 6 | 101 | 45 | 63 |
| Lincoln City | 42 | 24 | 7 | 11 | 91 | 64 | 55 |
| Stockport County | 42 | 23 | 8 | 11 | 89 | 51 | 54 |
| Doncaster Rovers | 42 | 23 | 7 | 12 | 80 | 44 | 53 |
| Tranmere Rovers | 42 | 22 | 9 | 11 | 105 | 72 | 53 |
| Bradford City | 42 | 18 | 12 | 12 | 85 | 60 | 48 |
| Darlington | 42 | 21 | 5 | 16 | 89 | 74 | 47 |
| Southport | 42 | 20 | 5 | 17 | 79 | 70 | 45 |
| Accrington Stanley | 42 | 18 | 8 | 16 | 76 | 67 | 44 |
| New Brighton | 42 | 14 | 14 | 14 | 72 | 62 | 42 |
| Wrexham | 42 | 18 | 6 | 18 | 64 | 67 | 42 |
| Halifax Town | 42 | 13 | 15 | 14 | 73 | 71 | 41 |
| Rochdale | 42 | 17 | 7 | 18 | 74 | 77 | 41 |
| Rotherham United | 42 | 14 | 11 | 17 | 65 | 69 | 39 |
| Hartlepools United | 42 | 16 | 6 | 20 | 69 | 81 | 38 |
| Chesterfield | 42 | 13 | 10 | 19 | 71 | 78 | 36 |
| Crewe Alexandra | 42 | 12 | 10 | 20 | 77 | 86 | 34 |
| Ashington | 42 | 11 | 11 | 20 | 77 | 103 | 33 |
| Barrow | 42 | 10 | 11 | 21 | 54 | 102 | 31 |
| Wigan Borough | 42 | 10 | 10 | 22 | 56 | 97 | 30 |
| *Durham City* | *42* | *11* | *7* | *24* | *53* | *100* | *29* |
| Nelson | 42 | 10 | 6 | 26 | 76 | 136 | 26 |

## DIVISION TWO 1927-28

| | | | | | | |
|---|---|---|---|---|---|---|
| **Manchester City** | 42 | 25 | 9 | 8 | 100 | 59 | 59 |
| **Leeds United** | 42 | 25 | 7 | 10 | 98 | 49 | 57 |
| Chelsea | 42 | 23 | 8 | 11 | 75 | 45 | 54 |
| Preston North End | 42 | 22 | 9 | 11 | 100 | 66 | 53 |
| Stoke City | 42 | 22 | 8 | 12 | 78 | 59 | 52 |
| Swansea Town | 42 | 18 | 12 | 12 | 75 | 63 | 48 |
| Oldham Athletic | 42 | 19 | 8 | 15 | 75 | 51 | 46 |
| West Bromwich Albion | 42 | 17 | 12 | 13 | 90 | 70 | 46 |
| Port Vale | 42 | 18 | 8 | 16 | 68 | 57 | 44 |
| Nottingham Forest | 42 | 15 | 10 | 17 | 83 | 84 | 40 |
| Grimsby Town | 42 | 14 | 12 | 16 | 69 | 83 | 40 |
| Bristol City | 42 | 15 | 9 | 18 | 76 | 79 | 39 |
| Barnsley | 42 | 14 | 11 | 17 | 65 | 85 | 39 |
| Hull City | 42 | 12 | 15 | 15 | 41 | 54 | 39 |
| Notts County | 42 | 13 | 12 | 17 | 68 | 74 | 38 |
| Wolverhampton Wanderers | 42 | 13 | 10 | 19 | 63 | 91 | 36 |
| Southampton | 42 | 14 | 7 | 21 | 68 | 77 | 35 |
| Reading | 42 | 11 | 13 | 18 | 53 | 75 | 35 |
| Blackpool | 42 | 13 | 8 | 21 | 83 | 101 | 34 |
| Clapton Orient | 42 | 11 | 12 | 19 | 55 | 85 | 34 |
| *Fulham* | *42* | *13* | *7* | *22* | *68* | *89* | *33* |
| *South Shields* | *42* | *7* | *9* | *26* | *56* | *111* | *23* |

## DIVISION THREE (S) 1927-28

| | | | | | | |
|---|---|---|---|---|---|---|
| **Millwall** | 42 | 30 | 5 | 7 | 127 | 50 | 65 |
| Northampton Town | 42 | 23 | 9 | 10 | 102 | 64 | 55 |
| Plymouth Argyle | 42 | 23 | 7 | 12 | 85 | 54 | 53 |
| Brighton & Hove Albion | 42 | 19 | 10 | 13 | 81 | 69 | 48 |
| Crystal Palace | 42 | 18 | 12 | 12 | 79 | 72 | 48 |
| Swindon Town | 42 | 19 | 9 | 14 | 90 | 69 | 47 |
| Southend United | 42 | 20 | 6 | 16 | 80 | 64 | 46 |
| Exeter City | 42 | 17 | 12 | 13 | 70 | 60 | 46 |
| Newport County | 42 | 18 | 9 | 15 | 81 | 84 | 45 |
| Queen's Park Rangers | 42 | 17 | 9 | 16 | 72 | 71 | 43 |
| Charlton Athletic | 42 | 15 | 13 | 14 | 60 | 70 | 43 |
| Brentford | 42 | 16 | 8 | 18 | 76 | 74 | 40 |
| Luton Town | 42 | 16 | 7 | 19 | 94 | 87 | 39 |
| Bournemouth & Boscombe Ath. | 42 | 13 | 12 | 17 | 72 | 79 | 38 |
| Watford | 42 | 14 | 10 | 18 | 68 | 78 | 38 |
| Gillingham | 42 | 13 | 11 | 18 | 62 | 81 | 37 |
| Norwich City | 42 | 10 | 16 | 16 | 66 | 70 | 36 |
| Walsall | 42 | 12 | 9 | 21 | 75 | 101 | 33 |
| Bristol Rovers | 42 | 14 | 4 | 24 | 67 | 93 | 32 |
| Coventry City | 42 | 11 | 9 | 22 | 67 | 96 | 31 |
| Merthyr Town | 42 | 9 | 13 | 20 | 53 | 91 | 31 |
| Torquay United | 42 | 8 | 14 | 20 | 53 | 103 | 30 |

## 1928 F.A. Cup

### Semi-finals

| | |
|---|---|
| Blackburn Rovers vs Arsenal | 1-0 |
| Huddersfield Town vs Sheffield United | 2-2, 0-0, 1-0 |

### Final

Wembley, 21st April 1928

**Blackburn Rovers 3**  (Roscamp 2, McLean)
**Huddersfield Town 1**  (Jackson)

*Attendance 92,041*

## DIVISION ONE 1928-29

| | | | | | | | |
|---|---|---|---|---|---|---|---|
| **THE WEDNESDAY** | 42 | 21 | 10 | 11 | 86 | 62 | 52 |
| Leicester City | 42 | 21 | 9 | 12 | 96 | 67 | 51 |
| Aston Villa | 42 | 23 | 4 | 15 | 98 | 81 | 50 |
| Sunderland | 42 | 20 | 7 | 15 | 93 | 75 | 47 |
| Liverpool | 42 | 17 | 12 | 13 | 90 | 64 | 46 |
| Derby County | 42 | 18 | 10 | 14 | 86 | 71 | 46 |
| Blackburn Rovers | 42 | 17 | 11 | 14 | 72 | 63 | 45 |
| Manchester City | 42 | 18 | 9 | 15 | 95 | 86 | 45 |
| Arsenal | 42 | 16 | 13 | 13 | 77 | 72 | 45 |
| Newcastle United | 42 | 19 | 6 | 17 | 70 | 72 | 44 |
| Sheffield United | 42 | 15 | 11 | 16 | 86 | 85 | 41 |
| Manchester United | 42 | 14 | 13 | 15 | 66 | 76 | 41 |
| Leeds United | 42 | 16 | 9 | 17 | 71 | 84 | 41 |
| Bolton Wanderers | 42 | 14 | 12 | 16 | 73 | 80 | 40 |
| Birmingham | 42 | 15 | 10 | 17 | 68 | 77 | 40 |
| Huddersfield Town | 42 | 14 | 11 | 17 | 70 | 61 | 39 |
| West Ham United | 42 | 15 | 9 | 18 | 86 | 96 | 39 |
| Everton | 42 | 17 | 4 | 21 | 63 | 75 | 38 |
| Burnley | 42 | 15 | 8 | 19 | 81 | 103 | 38 |
| Portsmouth | 42 | 15 | 6 | 21 | 56 | 80 | 36 |
| *Bury* | *42* | *12* | *7* | *23* | *62* | *99* | *31* |
| *Cardiff City* | *42* | *8* | *13* | *21* | *43* | *59* | *29* |

## DIVISION TWO 1928-29

| | | | | | | | |
|---|---|---|---|---|---|---|---|
| **Middlesbrough** | 42 | 22 | 11 | 9 | 92 | 57 | 55 |
| **Grimsby Town** | 42 | 24 | 5 | 13 | 82 | 61 | 53 |
| Bradford Park Avenue | 42 | 22 | 4 | 16 | 88 | 70 | 48 |
| Southampton | 42 | 17 | 14 | 11 | 74 | 60 | 48 |
| Notts County | 42 | 19 | 9 | 14 | 78 | 65 | 47 |
| Stoke City | 42 | 17 | 12 | 13 | 74 | 51 | 46 |
| West Bromwich Albion | 42 | 19 | 8 | 15 | 80 | 79 | 46 |
| Blackpool | 42 | 19 | 7 | 16 | 92 | 76 | 45 |
| Chelsea | 42 | 17 | 10 | 15 | 64 | 65 | 44 |
| Tottenham Hotspur | 42 | 17 | 9 | 16 | 75 | 81 | 43 |
| Nottingham Forest | 42 | 15 | 12 | 15 | 71 | 70 | 42 |
| Hull City | 42 | 13 | 14 | 15 | 58 | 63 | 40 |
| Preston North End | 42 | 15 | 9 | 18 | 78 | 79 | 39 |
| Millwall | 42 | 16 | 7 | 19 | 71 | 86 | 39 |
| Reading | 42 | 15 | 9 | 18 | 63 | 86 | 39 |
| Barnsley | 42 | 16 | 6 | 20 | 69 | 66 | 38 |
| Wolverhampton Wanderers | 42 | 15 | 7 | 20 | 77 | 81 | 37 |
| Oldham Athletic | 42 | 16 | 5 | 21 | 54 | 75 | 37 |
| Swansea Town | 42 | 13 | 10 | 19 | 62 | 75 | 36 |
| Bristol City | 42 | 13 | 10 | 19 | 58 | 72 | 36 |
| *Port Vale* | *42* | *15* | *4* | *23* | *71* | *86* | *34* |
| *Clapton Orient* | *42* | *12* | *8* | *22* | *45* | *72* | *32* |

## DIVISION THREE (N) 1928-29

| | | | | | | | |
|---|---|---|---|---|---|---|---|
| **Bradford City** | 42 | 27 | 9 | 6 | 128 | 43 | 63 |
| Stockport County | 42 | 28 | 6 | 8 | 111 | 58 | 62 |
| Wrexham | 42 | 21 | 10 | 11 | 91 | 69 | 52 |
| Wigan Borough | 42 | 21 | 9 | 12 | 82 | 49 | 51 |
| Doncaster Rovers | 42 | 20 | 10 | 12 | 76 | 66 | 50 |
| Lincoln City | 42 | 21 | 6 | 15 | 91 | 67 | 48 |
| Tranmere Rovers | 42 | 22 | 3 | 17 | 79 | 77 | 47 |
| Carlisle United | 42 | 19 | 8 | 15 | 86 | 77 | 46 |
| Crewe Alexandra | 42 | 18 | 8 | 16 | 80 | 68 | 44 |
| South Shields | 42 | 18 | 8 | 16 | 83 | 74 | 44 |
| Chesterfield | 42 | 18 | 5 | 19 | 71 | 77 | 41 |
| Southport | 42 | 16 | 8 | 18 | 75 | 85 | 40 |
| Halifax Town | 42 | 13 | 13 | 16 | 63 | 62 | 39 |
| New Brighton | 42 | 15 | 9 | 18 | 64 | 71 | 39 |
| Nelson | 42 | 17 | 5 | 20 | 77 | 90 | 39 |
| Rotherham United | 42 | 15 | 9 | 18 | 60 | 77 | 39 |
| Rochdale | 42 | 13 | 10 | 19 | 79 | 96 | 36 |
| Accrington Stanley | 42 | 13 | 8 | 21 | 68 | 82 | 34 |
| Darlington | 42 | 13 | 7 | 22 | 64 | 88 | 33 |
| Barrow | 42 | 10 | 8 | 24 | 64 | 93 | 28 |
| Hartlepools United | 42 | 10 | 6 | 26 | 59 | 112 | 26 |
| *Ashington* | *42* | *8* | *7* | *27* | *45* | *115* | *23* |

## DIVISION THREE (S) 1928-29

| | | | | | | | |
|---|---|---|---|---|---|---|---|
| **Charlton Athletic** | 42 | 23 | 8 | 11 | 86 | 60 | 54 |
| Crystal Palace | 42 | 23 | 8 | 11 | 81 | 67 | 54 |
| Northampton Town | 42 | 20 | 12 | 10 | 96 | 57 | 52 |
| Plymouth Argyle | 42 | 20 | 12 | 10 | 83 | 51 | 52 |
| Fulham | 42 | 21 | 10 | 11 | 101 | 71 | 52 |
| Queen's Park Rangers | 42 | 19 | 14 | 9 | 82 | 61 | 52 |
| Luton Town | 42 | 19 | 11 | 12 | 89 | 73 | 49 |
| Watford | 42 | 19 | 10 | 13 | 79 | 74 | 48 |
| Bournemouth & Boscombe Ath. | 42 | 19 | 9 | 14 | 84 | 77 | 47 |
| Swindon Town | 42 | 15 | 13 | 14 | 75 | 72 | 43 |
| Coventry City | 42 | 14 | 14 | 14 | 62 | 57 | 42 |
| Southend United | 42 | 15 | 11 | 16 | 80 | 75 | 41 |
| Brentford | 42 | 14 | 10 | 18 | 56 | 60 | 38 |
| Walsall | 42 | 13 | 12 | 17 | 73 | 79 | 38 |
| Brighton & Hove Albion | 42 | 16 | 6 | 20 | 58 | 76 | 38 |
| Newport County | 42 | 13 | 9 | 20 | 69 | 86 | 35 |
| Norwich City | 42 | 14 | 6 | 22 | 69 | 81 | 34 |
| Torquay United | 42 | 14 | 6 | 22 | 66 | 84 | 34 |
| Bristol Rovers | 42 | 13 | 7 | 22 | 60 | 79 | 33 |
| Merthyr Town | 42 | 11 | 8 | 23 | 55 | 103 | 30 |
| Exeter City | 42 | 9 | 11 | 22 | 67 | 88 | 29 |
| Gillingham | 42 | 10 | 9 | 23 | 43 | 83 | 29 |

## 1929 F.A. Cup

**Semi-finals**

| | |
|---|---|
| Bolton Wanderers vs Huddersfield Town | 3-1 |
| Portsmouth vs Aston Villa | 1-0 |

**Final**

Wembley, 27th April 1929

**Bolton Wanderers 2**  (Butler, Blackmore)

**Portsmouth 0**

*Attendance 92,576*

## DIVISION ONE 1929-30

| | | | | | | | |
|---|---|---|---|---|---|---|---|
| SHEFFIELD WEDNESDAY | 42 | 26 | 8 | 8 | 105 | 57 | 60 |
| Derby County | 42 | 21 | 8 | 13 | 90 | 82 | 50 |
| Manchester City | 42 | 19 | 9 | 14 | 91 | 81 | 47 |
| Aston Villa | 42 | 21 | 5 | 16 | 92 | 83 | 47 |
| Leeds United | 42 | 20 | 6 | 16 | 79 | 63 | 46 |
| Blackburn Rovers | 42 | 19 | 7 | 16 | 99 | 93 | 45 |
| West Ham United | 42 | 19 | 5 | 18 | 86 | 79 | 43 |
| Leicester City | 42 | 17 | 9 | 16 | 86 | 90 | 43 |
| Sunderland | 42 | 18 | 7 | 17 | 76 | 80 | 43 |
| Huddersfield Town | 42 | 17 | 9 | 16 | 63 | 69 | 43 |
| Birmingham | 42 | 16 | 9 | 17 | 67 | 62 | 41 |
| Liverpool | 42 | 16 | 9 | 17 | 63 | 79 | 41 |
| Portsmouth | 42 | 15 | 10 | 17 | 66 | 62 | 40 |
| Arsenal | 42 | 14 | 11 | 17 | 78 | 66 | 39 |
| Bolton Wanderers | 42 | 15 | 9 | 18 | 74 | 74 | 39 |
| Middlesbrough | 42 | 16 | 6 | 20 | 82 | 84 | 38 |
| Manchester United | 42 | 15 | 8 | 19 | 67 | 88 | 38 |
| Grimsby Town | 42 | 15 | 7 | 20 | 73 | 89 | 37 |
| Newcastle United | 42 | 15 | 7 | 20 | 71 | 92 | 37 |
| Sheffield United | 42 | 15 | 6 | 21 | 91 | 96 | 36 |
| *Burnley* | *42* | *14* | *8* | *20* | *79* | *97* | *36* |
| *Everton* | *42* | *12* | *11* | *19* | *80* | *92* | *35* |

## DIVISION TWO 1929-30

| | | | | | | | |
|---|---|---|---|---|---|---|---|
| **Blackpool** | 42 | 27 | 4 | 11 | 98 | 67 | 58 |
| **Chelsea** | 42 | 22 | 11 | 9 | 74 | 46 | 55 |
| Oldham Athletic | 42 | 21 | 11 | 10 | 90 | 51 | 53 |
| Bradford Park Avenue | 42 | 19 | 12 | 11 | 91 | 70 | 50 |
| Bury | 42 | 22 | 5 | 15 | 78 | 67 | 49 |
| West Bromwich Albion | 42 | 21 | 5 | 16 | 105 | 73 | 47 |
| Southampton | 42 | 17 | 11 | 14 | 77 | 76 | 45 |
| Cardiff City | 42 | 18 | 8 | 16 | 61 | 59 | 44 |
| Wolverhampton Wanderers | 42 | 16 | 9 | 17 | 77 | 79 | 41 |
| Nottingham Forest | 42 | 13 | 15 | 14 | 55 | 69 | 41 |
| Stoke City | 42 | 16 | 8 | 18 | 74 | 72 | 40 |
| Tottenham Hotspur | 42 | 15 | 9 | 18 | 59 | 61 | 39 |
| Charlton Athletic | 42 | 14 | 11 | 17 | 59 | 63 | 39 |
| Millwall | 42 | 12 | 15 | 15 | 57 | 73 | 39 |
| Swansea Town | 42 | 14 | 9 | 19 | 57 | 61 | 37 |
| Preston North End | 42 | 13 | 11 | 18 | 65 | 80 | 37 |
| Barnsley | 42 | 14 | 8 | 20 | 56 | 71 | 36 |
| Bradford City | 42 | 12 | 12 | 18 | 60 | 77 | 36 |
| Reading | 42 | 12 | 11 | 19 | 54 | 67 | 35 |
| Bristol City | 42 | 13 | 9 | 20 | 61 | 83 | 35 |
| *Hull City* | *42* | *14* | *7* | *21* | *51* | *78* | *35* |
| *Notts County* | *42* | *9* | *15* | *18* | *54* | *70* | *33* |

## DIVISION THREE (N) 1929-30

| | | | | | | | |
|---|---|---|---|---|---|---|---|
| Port Vale | 42 | 30 | 7 | 5 | 103 | 37 | 67 |
| Stockport County | 42 | 28 | 7 | 7 | 106 | 44 | 63 |
| Darlington | 42 | 22 | 6 | 14 | 108 | 73 | 50 |
| Chesterfield | 42 | 22 | 6 | 14 | 76 | 56 | 50 |
| Lincoln City | 42 | 17 | 14 | 11 | 83 | 61 | 48 |
| York City | 42 | 15 | 16 | 11 | 77 | 64 | 46 |
| South Shields | 42 | 18 | 10 | 14 | 77 | 74 | 46 |
| Hartlepools United | 42 | 17 | 11 | 14 | 81 | 74 | 45 |
| Southport | 42 | 15 | 13 | 14 | 81 | 74 | 43 |
| Rochdale | 42 | 18 | 7 | 17 | 89 | 91 | 43 |
| Crewe Alexandra | 42 | 17 | 8 | 17 | 82 | 71 | 42 |
| Tranmere Rovers | 42 | 16 | 9 | 17 | 83 | 86 | 41 |
| New Brighton | 42 | 16 | 8 | 18 | 69 | 79 | 40 |
| Doncaster Rovers | 42 | 15 | 9 | 18 | 62 | 69 | 39 |
| Carlisle United | 42 | 16 | 7 | 19 | 90 | 101 | 39 |
| Accrington Stanley | 42 | 14 | 9 | 19 | 84 | 81 | 37 |
| Wrexham | 42 | 13 | 8 | 21 | 67 | 88 | 34 |
| Wigan Borough | 42 | 13 | 7 | 22 | 60 | 88 | 33 |
| Nelson | 42 | 13 | 7 | 22 | 51 | 80 | 33 |
| Rotherham United | 42 | 11 | 8 | 23 | 67 | 113 | 30 |
| Halifax Town | 42 | 10 | 8 | 24 | 44 | 79 | 28 |
| Barrow | 42 | 11 | 5 | 26 | 41 | 98 | 27 |

## DIVISION THREE (S) 1929-30

| | | | | | | | |
|---|---|---|---|---|---|---|---|
| Plymouth Argyle | 42 | 30 | 8 | 4 | 98 | 38 | 68 |
| Brentford | 42 | 28 | 5 | 9 | 94 | 44 | 61 |
| Queen's Park Rangers | 42 | 21 | 9 | 12 | 80 | 68 | 51 |
| Northampton Town | 42 | 21 | 8 | 13 | 82 | 58 | 50 |
| Brighton & Hove Albion | 42 | 21 | 8 | 13 | 87 | 63 | 50 |
| Coventry City | 42 | 19 | 9 | 14 | 88 | 73 | 47 |
| Fulham | 42 | 18 | 11 | 13 | 87 | 83 | 47 |
| Norwich City | 42 | 18 | 10 | 14 | 88 | 77 | 46 |
| Crystal Palace | 42 | 17 | 12 | 13 | 81 | 74 | 46 |
| Bournemouth & Boscombe Ath. | 42 | 15 | 13 | 14 | 72 | 61 | 43 |
| Southend United | 42 | 15 | 13 | 14 | 69 | 59 | 43 |
| Clapton Orient | 42 | 14 | 13 | 15 | 55 | 62 | 41 |
| Luton Town | 42 | 14 | 12 | 16 | 64 | 78 | 40 |
| Swindon Town | 42 | 13 | 12 | 17 | 73 | 83 | 38 |
| Watford | 42 | 15 | 8 | 19 | 60 | 73 | 38 |
| Exeter City | 42 | 12 | 11 | 19 | 67 | 73 | 35 |
| Walsall | 42 | 13 | 8 | 21 | 71 | 78 | 34 |
| Newport County | 42 | 12 | 10 | 20 | 74 | 85 | 34 |
| Torquay United | 42 | 10 | 11 | 21 | 64 | 94 | 31 |
| Bristol Rovers | 42 | 11 | 8 | 23 | 67 | 93 | 30 |
| Gillingham | 42 | 11 | 8 | 23 | 51 | 80 | 30 |
| *Merthyr Town* | *42* | *6* | *9* | *27* | *60* | *135* | *21* |

## 1930 F.A. Cup

### Semi-finals

| | |
|---|---|
| Arsenal vs Hull City | 2-2, 1-0 |
| Huddersfield Town vs Sheffield Wednesday | 2-1 |

### Final

Wembley, 26th April 1930

**Arsenal 2**   (James, Lambert)
**Huddersfield Town  0**

*Attendance 92,448*

## DIVISION ONE 1930-31

| | | | | | | | |
|---|---|---|---|---|---|---|---|
| ARSENAL | 42 | 28 | 10 | 4 | 127 | 59 | 66 |
| Aston Villa | 42 | 25 | 9 | 8 | 128 | 78 | 59 |
| Sheffield Wednesday | 42 | 22 | 8 | 12 | 102 | 75 | 52 |
| Portsmouth | 42 | 18 | 13 | 11 | 84 | 67 | 49 |
| Huddersfield Town | 42 | 18 | 12 | 12 | 81 | 65 | 48 |
| Derby County | 42 | 18 | 10 | 14 | 94 | 79 | 46 |
| Middlesbrough | 42 | 19 | 8 | 15 | 98 | 90 | 46 |
| Manchester City | 42 | 18 | 10 | 14 | 75 | 70 | 46 |
| Liverpool | 42 | 15 | 12 | 15 | 86 | 85 | 42 |
| Blackburn Rovers | 42 | 17 | 8 | 17 | 83 | 84 | 42 |
| Sunderland | 42 | 16 | 9 | 17 | 89 | 85 | 41 |
| Chelsea | 42 | 15 | 10 | 17 | 64 | 67 | 40 |
| Grimsby Town | 42 | 17 | 5 | 20 | 82 | 87 | 39 |
| Bolton Wanderers | 42 | 15 | 9 | 18 | 68 | 81 | 39 |
| Sheffield United | 42 | 14 | 10 | 18 | 78 | 84 | 38 |
| Leicester City | 42 | 16 | 6 | 20 | 80 | 95 | 38 |
| Newcastle United | 42 | 15 | 6 | 21 | 78 | 87 | 36 |
| West Ham United | 42 | 14 | 8 | 20 | 79 | 94 | 36 |
| Birmingham | 42 | 13 | 10 | 19 | 55 | 70 | 36 |
| Blackpool | 42 | 11 | 10 | 21 | 71 | 125 | 32 |
| *Leeds United* | *42* | *12* | *7* | *23* | *68* | *81* | *31* |
| *Manchester United* | *42* | *7* | *8* | *27* | *53* | *115* | *22* |

## DIVISION TWO 1930-31

| | | | | | | | |
|---|---|---|---|---|---|---|---|
| Everton | 42 | 28 | 5 | 9 | 121 | 66 | 61 |
| **West Bromwich Albion** | 42 | 22 | 10 | 10 | 83 | 49 | 54 |
| Tottenham Hotspur | 42 | 22 | 7 | 13 | 88 | 55 | 51 |
| Wolverhampton Wanderers | 42 | 21 | 5 | 16 | 84 | 67 | 47 |
| Port Vale | 42 | 21 | 5 | 16 | 67 | 61 | 47 |
| Bradford Park Avenue | 42 | 18 | 10 | 14 | 97 | 66 | 46 |
| Preston North End | 42 | 17 | 11 | 14 | 83 | 64 | 45 |
| Burnley | 42 | 17 | 11 | 14 | 81 | 77 | 45 |
| Southampton | 42 | 19 | 6 | 17 | 74 | 62 | 44 |
| Bradford City | 42 | 17 | 10 | 15 | 61 | 63 | 44 |
| Stoke City | 42 | 17 | 10 | 15 | 64 | 71 | 44 |
| Oldham Athletic | 42 | 16 | 10 | 16 | 61 | 72 | 42 |
| Bury | 42 | 19 | 3 | 20 | 75 | 82 | 41 |
| Millwall | 42 | 16 | 7 | 19 | 71 | 80 | 39 |
| Charlton Athletic | 42 | 15 | 9 | 18 | 59 | 86 | 39 |
| Bristol City | 42 | 15 | 8 | 19 | 54 | 82 | 38 |
| Nottingham Forest | 42 | 14 | 9 | 19 | 80 | 85 | 37 |
| Plymouth Argyle | 42 | 14 | 8 | 20 | 76 | 84 | 36 |
| Barnsley | 42 | 13 | 9 | 20 | 59 | 79 | 35 |
| Swansea Town | 42 | 12 | 10 | 20 | 51 | 74 | 34 |
| *Reading* | *42* | *12* | *6* | *24* | *72* | *96* | *30* |
| *Cardiff City* | *42* | *8* | *9* | *25* | *47* | *87* | *25* |

## DIVISION THREE (N) 1930-31

| | | | | | | | |
|---|---|---|---|---|---|---|---|
| Chesterfield | 42 | 26 | 6 | 10 | 102 | 57 | 58 |
| Lincoln City | 42 | 25 | 7 | 10 | 102 | 59 | 57 |
| Wrexham | 42 | 21 | 12 | 9 | 94 | 62 | 54 |
| Tranmere Rovers | 42 | 24 | 6 | 12 | 111 | 74 | 54 |
| Southport | 42 | 22 | 9 | 11 | 88 | 56 | 53 |
| Hull City | 42 | 20 | 10 | 12 | 99 | 55 | 50 |
| Stockport County | 42 | 20 | 9 | 13 | 77 | 61 | 49 |
| Carlisle United | 42 | 20 | 5 | 17 | 98 | 81 | 45 |
| Gateshead | 42 | 16 | 13 | 13 | 71 | 73 | 45 |
| Wigan Borough | 42 | 19 | 5 | 18 | 76 | 86 | 43 |
| Darlington | 42 | 16 | 10 | 16 | 71 | 59 | 42 |
| York City | 42 | 18 | 6 | 18 | 85 | 82 | 42 |
| Accrington Stanley | 42 | 15 | 9 | 18 | 84 | 108 | 39 |
| Rotherham United | 42 | 13 | 12 | 17 | 81 | 83 | 38 |
| Doncaster Rovers | 42 | 13 | 11 | 18 | 65 | 65 | 37 |
| Barrow | 42 | 15 | 7 | 20 | 68 | 89 | 37 |
| Halifax Town | 42 | 13 | 9 | 20 | 55 | 89 | 35 |
| Crewe Alexandra | 42 | 14 | 6 | 22 | 66 | 93 | 34 |
| New Brighton | 42 | 13 | 7 | 22 | 49 | 76 | 33 |
| Hartlepools United | 42 | 12 | 6 | 24 | 67 | 86 | 30 |
| Rochdale | 42 | 12 | 6 | 24 | 62 | 107 | 30 |
| *Nelson* | *42* | *6* | *7* | *29* | *43* | *113* | *19* |

## DIVISION THREE (S) 1930-31

| | | | | | | | |
|---|---|---|---|---|---|---|---|
| Notts County | 42 | 24 | 11 | 7 | 97 | 46 | 59 |
| Crystal Palace | 42 | 22 | 7 | 13 | 107 | 71 | 51 |
| Brentford | 42 | 22 | 6 | 14 | 90 | 64 | 50 |
| Brighton & Hove Albion | 42 | 17 | 15 | 10 | 68 | 53 | 49 |
| Southend United | 42 | 22 | 5 | 15 | 76 | 60 | 49 |
| Northampton Town | 42 | 18 | 12 | 12 | 77 | 59 | 48 |
| Luton Town | 42 | 19 | 8 | 15 | 76 | 51 | 46 |
| Queen's Park Rangers | 42 | 20 | 3 | 19 | 82 | 75 | 43 |
| Fulham | 42 | 18 | 7 | 17 | 77 | 75 | 43 |
| Bournemouth & Boscombe Ath. | 42 | 15 | 13 | 14 | 72 | 73 | 43 |
| Torquay United | 42 | 17 | 9 | 16 | 80 | 84 | 43 |
| Swindon Town | 42 | 18 | 6 | 18 | 89 | 94 | 42 |
| Exeter City | 42 | 17 | 8 | 17 | 84 | 90 | 42 |
| Coventry City | 42 | 16 | 9 | 17 | 75 | 65 | 41 |
| Bristol Rovers | 42 | 16 | 8 | 18 | 75 | 92 | 40 |
| Gillingham | 42 | 14 | 10 | 18 | 61 | 76 | 38 |
| Walsall | 42 | 14 | 9 | 19 | 78 | 95 | 37 |
| Watford | 42 | 14 | 7 | 21 | 72 | 75 | 35 |
| Clapton Orient | 42 | 14 | 7 | 21 | 63 | 91 | 35 |
| Thames Association | 42 | 13 | 8 | 21 | 54 | 93 | 34 |
| *Newport County* | *42* | *11* | *6* | *25* | *69* | *111* | *28* |
| Norwich City | 42 | 10 | 8 | 24 | 47 | 76 | 28 |

## 1931 F.A. Cup

**Semi-finals**

| | |
|---|---|
| Everton vs West Bromwich Albion | 0-1 |
| Birmingham vs Sunderland | 2-0 |

**Final**

Wembley, 25th April 1931

**West Bromwich Albion 2**  (W.G. Richardson 2)

**Birmingham 1**  (Bradford)

*Attendance 92,406*

## DIVISION ONE 1931-32

| | | | | | | | |
|---|---|---|---|---|---|---|---|
| **EVERTON** | 42 | 26 | 4 | 12 | 116 | 64 | 56 |
| Arsenal | 42 | 22 | 10 | 10 | 90 | 48 | 54 |
| Sheffield Wednesday | 42 | 22 | 6 | 14 | 96 | 82 | 50 |
| Huddersfield Town | 42 | 19 | 10 | 13 | 80 | 63 | 48 |
| Aston Villa | 42 | 19 | 8 | 15 | 104 | 72 | 46 |
| West Bromwich Albion | 42 | 20 | 6 | 16 | 77 | 55 | 46 |
| Sheffield United | 42 | 20 | 6 | 16 | 80 | 75 | 46 |
| Portsmouth | 42 | 19 | 7 | 16 | 62 | 62 | 45 |
| Birmingham | 42 | 18 | 8 | 16 | 78 | 67 | 44 |
| Liverpool | 42 | 19 | 6 | 17 | 81 | 93 | 44 |
| Newcastle United | 42 | 18 | 6 | 18 | 80 | 87 | 42 |
| Chelsea | 42 | 16 | 8 | 18 | 69 | 73 | 40 |
| Sunderland | 42 | 15 | 10 | 17 | 67 | 73 | 40 |
| Manchester City | 42 | 13 | 12 | 17 | 83 | 73 | 38 |
| Derby County | 42 | 14 | 10 | 18 | 71 | 75 | 38 |
| Blackburn Rovers | 42 | 16 | 6 | 20 | 89 | 95 | 38 |
| Bolton Wanderers | 42 | 17 | 4 | 21 | 72 | 80 | 38 |
| Middlesbrough | 42 | 15 | 8 | 19 | 64 | 89 | 38 |
| Leicester City | 42 | 15 | 7 | 20 | 74 | 94 | 37 |
| Blackpool | 42 | 12 | 9 | 21 | 65 | 102 | 33 |
| *Grimsby Town* | *42* | *13* | *6* | *23* | *67* | *98* | *32* |
| *West Ham United* | *42* | *12* | *7* | *23* | *62* | *107* | *31* |

## DIVISION THREE (N) 1931-32

| | | | | | | | |
|---|---|---|---|---|---|---|---|
| **Lincoln City** | 40 | 26 | 5 | 9 | 106 | 47 | 57 |
| Gateshead | 40 | 25 | 7 | 8 | 94 | 48 | 57 |
| Chester | 40 | 21 | 8 | 11 | 78 | 60 | 50 |
| Tranmere Rovers | 40 | 19 | 11 | 10 | 107 | 58 | 49 |
| Barrow | 40 | 24 | 1 | 15 | 86 | 59 | 49 |
| Crewe Alexandra | 40 | 21 | 6 | 13 | 95 | 66 | 48 |
| Southport | 40 | 18 | 10 | 12 | 58 | 53 | 46 |
| Hull City | 40 | 20 | 5 | 15 | 82 | 53 | 45 |
| York City | 40 | 18 | 7 | 15 | 76 | 81 | 43 |
| Wrexham | 40 | 18 | 7 | 15 | 64 | 69 | 43 |
| Darlington | 40 | 17 | 4 | 19 | 66 | 69 | 38 |
| Stockport County | 40 | 13 | 11 | 16 | 55 | 53 | 37 |
| Hartlepools United | 40 | 16 | 5 | 19 | 78 | 100 | 37 |
| Accrington Stanley | 40 | 15 | 6 | 19 | 75 | 80 | 36 |
| Doncaster Rovers | 40 | 16 | 4 | 20 | 59 | 80 | 36 |
| Walsall | 40 | 16 | 3 | 21 | 57 | 85 | 35 |
| Halifax Town | 40 | 13 | 8 | 19 | 61 | 87 | 34 |
| Carlisle United | 40 | 11 | 11 | 18 | 64 | 79 | 33 |
| Rotherham United | 40 | 14 | 4 | 22 | 63 | 72 | 32 |
| New Brighton | 40 | 8 | 8 | 24 | 38 | 76 | 24 |
| Rochdale | 40 | 4 | 3 | 33 | 48 | 135 | 11 |

Wigan Borough resigned from the League during the season and their record was expunged

## DIVISION TWO 1931-32

| | | | | | | | |
|---|---|---|---|---|---|---|---|
| **Wolverhampton Wanderers** | 42 | 24 | 8 | 10 | 115 | 49 | 56 |
| **Leeds United** | 42 | 22 | 10 | 10 | 78 | 54 | 54 |
| Stoke City | 42 | 19 | 14 | 9 | 69 | 48 | 52 |
| Plymouth Argyle | 42 | 20 | 9 | 13 | 100 | 66 | 49 |
| Bury | 42 | 21 | 7 | 14 | 70 | 58 | 49 |
| Bradford Park Avenue | 42 | 21 | 7 | 14 | 72 | 63 | 49 |
| Bradford City | 42 | 16 | 13 | 13 | 80 | 61 | 45 |
| Tottenham Hotspur | 42 | 16 | 11 | 15 | 87 | 78 | 43 |
| Millwall | 42 | 17 | 9 | 16 | 61 | 61 | 43 |
| Charlton Athletic | 42 | 17 | 9 | 16 | 61 | 66 | 43 |
| Nottingham Forest | 42 | 16 | 10 | 16 | 77 | 72 | 42 |
| Manchester United | 42 | 17 | 8 | 17 | 71 | 72 | 42 |
| Preston North End | 42 | 16 | 10 | 16 | 75 | 77 | 42 |
| Southampton | 42 | 17 | 7 | 18 | 66 | 77 | 41 |
| Swansea Town | 42 | 16 | 7 | 19 | 73 | 75 | 39 |
| Notts County | 42 | 13 | 12 | 17 | 75 | 75 | 38 |
| Chesterfield | 42 | 13 | 11 | 18 | 64 | 86 | 37 |
| Oldham Athletic | 42 | 13 | 10 | 19 | 62 | 84 | 36 |
| Burnley | 42 | 13 | 9 | 20 | 59 | 87 | 35 |
| Port Vale | 42 | 13 | 7 | 22 | 58 | 89 | 33 |
| *Barnsley* | *42* | *12* | *9* | *21* | *55* | *91* | *33* |
| *Bristol City* | *42* | *6* | *11* | *25* | *39* | *78* | *23* |

## DIVISION THREE (S) 1931-32

| | | | | | | | |
|---|---|---|---|---|---|---|---|
| **Fulham** | 42 | 24 | 9 | 9 | 111 | 62 | 57 |
| Reading | 42 | 23 | 9 | 10 | 97 | 67 | 55 |
| Southend United | 42 | 21 | 11 | 10 | 77 | 53 | 53 |
| Crystal Palace | 42 | 20 | 11 | 11 | 74 | 63 | 51 |
| Brentford | 42 | 19 | 10 | 13 | 68 | 52 | 48 |
| Luton Town | 42 | 20 | 7 | 15 | 95 | 70 | 47 |
| Exeter City | 42 | 20 | 7 | 15 | 77 | 62 | 47 |
| Brighton & Hove Albion | 42 | 17 | 12 | 13 | 73 | 58 | 46 |
| Cardiff City | 42 | 19 | 8 | 15 | 87 | 73 | 46 |
| Norwich City | 42 | 17 | 12 | 13 | 76 | 67 | 46 |
| Watford | 42 | 19 | 8 | 15 | 81 | 79 | 46 |
| Coventry City | 42 | 18 | 8 | 16 | 108 | 97 | 44 |
| Queen's Park Rangers | 42 | 15 | 12 | 15 | 79 | 73 | 42 |
| Northampton Town | 42 | 16 | 7 | 19 | 69 | 69 | 39 |
| Bournemouth & Boscombe Ath. | 42 | 13 | 12 | 17 | 70 | 78 | 38 |
| Clapton Orient | 42 | 12 | 11 | 19 | 77 | 90 | 35 |
| Swindon Town | 42 | 14 | 6 | 22 | 70 | 84 | 34 |
| Bristol Rovers | 42 | 13 | 8 | 21 | 65 | 92 | 34 |
| Torquay United | 42 | 12 | 9 | 21 | 72 | 106 | 33 |
| Mansfield Town | 42 | 11 | 10 | 21 | 75 | 108 | 32 |
| Gillingham | 42 | 10 | 8 | 24 | 40 | 82 | 28 |
| *Thames Association* | *42* | *7* | *9* | *26* | *53* | *109* | *23* |

## 1932 F.A. Cup

**Semi-finals**

| | |
|---|---|
| Chelsea vs Newcastle United | 1-2 |
| Arsenal vs Manchester City | 1-0 |

**Final**

Wembley, 23rd April 1932

**Newcastle United 2**  (Allen 2)

**Arsenal 1**  (John)

*Attendance 92,298*

## DIVISION ONE 1932-33

| | | | | | | | |
|---|---|---|---|---|---|---|---|
| **ARSENAL** | 42 | 25 | 8 | 9 | 118 | 61 | 58 |
| Aston Villa | 42 | 23 | 8 | 11 | 92 | 67 | 54 |
| Sheffield Wednesday | 42 | 21 | 9 | 12 | 80 | 68 | 51 |
| West Bromwich Albion | 42 | 20 | 9 | 13 | 83 | 70 | 49 |
| Newcastle United | 42 | 22 | 5 | 15 | 71 | 63 | 49 |
| Huddersfield Town | 42 | 18 | 11 | 13 | 66 | 53 | 47 |
| Derby County | 42 | 15 | 14 | 13 | 76 | 69 | 44 |
| Leeds United | 42 | 15 | 14 | 13 | 59 | 62 | 44 |
| Portsmouth | 42 | 18 | 7 | 17 | 74 | 76 | 43 |
| Sheffield United | 42 | 17 | 9 | 16 | 74 | 80 | 43 |
| Everton | 42 | 16 | 9 | 17 | 81 | 74 | 41 |
| Sunderland | 42 | 15 | 10 | 17 | 63 | 80 | 40 |
| Birmingham | 42 | 14 | 11 | 17 | 57 | 57 | 39 |
| Liverpool | 42 | 14 | 11 | 17 | 79 | 84 | 39 |
| Blackburn Rovers | 42 | 14 | 10 | 18 | 76 | 102 | 38 |
| Manchester City | 42 | 16 | 5 | 21 | 68 | 71 | 37 |
| Middlesbrough | 42 | 14 | 9 | 19 | 63 | 73 | 37 |
| Chelsea | 42 | 14 | 7 | 21 | 63 | 73 | 35 |
| Leicester City | 42 | 11 | 13 | 18 | 75 | 89 | 35 |
| Wolverhampton Wanderers | 42 | 13 | 9 | 20 | 80 | 96 | 35 |
| *Bolton Wanderers* | *42* | *12* | *9* | *21* | *78* | *92* | *33* |
| *Blackpool* | *42* | *14* | *5* | *23* | *69* | *85* | *33* |

## DIVISION THREE (N) 1932-33

| | | | | | | | |
|---|---|---|---|---|---|---|---|
| **Hull City** | 42 | 26 | 7 | 9 | 100 | 45 | 59 |
| Wrexham | 42 | 24 | 9 | 9 | 106 | 51 | 57 |
| Stockport County | 42 | 21 | 12 | 9 | 99 | 58 | 54 |
| Chester | 42 | 22 | 8 | 12 | 94 | 66 | 52 |
| Walsall | 42 | 19 | 10 | 13 | 75 | 58 | 48 |
| Doncaster Rovers | 42 | 17 | 14 | 11 | 77 | 79 | 48 |
| Gateshead | 42 | 19 | 9 | 14 | 78 | 67 | 47 |
| Barnsley | 42 | 19 | 8 | 15 | 92 | 80 | 46 |
| Barrow | 42 | 18 | 7 | 17 | 60 | 60 | 43 |
| Crewe Alexandra | 42 | 20 | 3 | 19 | 80 | 84 | 43 |
| Tranmere Rovers | 42 | 17 | 8 | 17 | 70 | 66 | 42 |
| Southport | 42 | 17 | 7 | 18 | 70 | 67 | 41 |
| Accrington Stanley | 42 | 15 | 10 | 17 | 78 | 76 | 40 |
| Hartlepools United | 42 | 16 | 7 | 19 | 87 | 116 | 39 |
| Halifax Town | 42 | 15 | 8 | 19 | 71 | 90 | 38 |
| Mansfield Town | 42 | 14 | 7 | 21 | 84 | 100 | 35 |
| Rotherham United | 42 | 14 | 6 | 22 | 60 | 84 | 34 |
| Rochdale | 42 | 13 | 7 | 22 | 58 | 80 | 33 |
| Carlisle United | 42 | 13 | 7 | 22 | 51 | 75 | 33 |
| York City | 42 | 13 | 6 | 23 | 72 | 92 | 32 |
| New Brighton | 42 | 11 | 10 | 21 | 63 | 88 | 32 |
| Darlington | 42 | 10 | 8 | 24 | 66 | 109 | 28 |

## DIVISION TWO 1932-33

| | | | | | | | |
|---|---|---|---|---|---|---|---|
| **Stoke City** | 42 | 25 | 6 | 11 | 78 | 39 | 56 |
| **Tottenham Hotspur** | 42 | 20 | 15 | 7 | 96 | 51 | 55 |
| Fulham | 42 | 20 | 10 | 12 | 78 | 65 | 50 |
| Bury | 42 | 20 | 9 | 13 | 84 | 59 | 49 |
| Nottingham Forest | 42 | 17 | 15 | 10 | 67 | 59 | 49 |
| Manchester United | 42 | 15 | 13 | 14 | 71 | 68 | 43 |
| Millwall | 42 | 16 | 11 | 15 | 59 | 57 | 43 |
| Bradford Park Avenue | 42 | 17 | 8 | 17 | 77 | 71 | 42 |
| Preston North End | 42 | 16 | 10 | 16 | 74 | 70 | 42 |
| Swansea Town | 42 | 19 | 4 | 19 | 50 | 54 | 42 |
| Bradford City | 42 | 14 | 13 | 15 | 65 | 61 | 41 |
| Southampton | 42 | 18 | 5 | 19 | 66 | 66 | 41 |
| Grimsby Town | 42 | 14 | 13 | 15 | 79 | 84 | 41 |
| Plymouth Argyle | 42 | 16 | 9 | 17 | 63 | 67 | 41 |
| Notts County | 42 | 15 | 10 | 17 | 67 | 78 | 40 |
| Oldham Athletic | 42 | 15 | 8 | 19 | 67 | 80 | 38 |
| Port Vale | 42 | 14 | 10 | 18 | 66 | 79 | 38 |
| Lincoln City | 42 | 12 | 13 | 17 | 72 | 87 | 37 |
| Burnley | 42 | 11 | 14 | 17 | 67 | 79 | 36 |
| West Ham United | 42 | 13 | 9 | 20 | 75 | 93 | 35 |
| *Chesterfield* | *42* | *12* | *10* | *20* | *61* | *84* | *34* |
| *Charlton Athletic* | *42* | *12* | *7* | *23* | *60* | *91* | *31* |

## DIVISION THREE (S) 1932-33

| | | | | | | | |
|---|---|---|---|---|---|---|---|
| **Brentford** | 42 | 26 | 10 | 6 | 90 | 49 | 62 |
| Exeter City | 42 | 24 | 10 | 8 | 88 | 48 | 58 |
| Norwich City | 42 | 22 | 13 | 7 | 88 | 55 | 57 |
| Reading | 42 | 19 | 13 | 10 | 103 | 71 | 51 |
| Crystal Palace | 42 | 19 | 8 | 15 | 78 | 64 | 46 |
| Coventry City | 42 | 19 | 6 | 17 | 106 | 77 | 44 |
| Gillingham | 42 | 18 | 8 | 16 | 72 | 61 | 44 |
| Northampton Town | 42 | 18 | 8 | 16 | 76 | 66 | 44 |
| Bristol Rovers | 42 | 15 | 14 | 13 | 61 | 56 | 44 |
| Torquay United | 42 | 16 | 12 | 14 | 72 | 67 | 44 |
| Watford | 42 | 16 | 12 | 14 | 66 | 63 | 44 |
| Brighton & Hove Albion | 42 | 17 | 8 | 17 | 66 | 65 | 42 |
| Southend United | 42 | 15 | 11 | 16 | 65 | 82 | 41 |
| Luton Town | 42 | 13 | 13 | 16 | 78 | 78 | 39 |
| Bristol City | 42 | 12 | 13 | 17 | 83 | 90 | 37 |
| Queen's Park Rangers | 42 | 13 | 11 | 18 | 72 | 87 | 37 |
| Aldershot | 42 | 13 | 10 | 19 | 61 | 72 | 36 |
| Bournemouth & Boscombe Ath. | 42 | 12 | 12 | 18 | 60 | 81 | 36 |
| Cardiff City | 42 | 12 | 7 | 23 | 69 | 99 | 31 |
| Clapton Orient | 42 | 8 | 13 | 21 | 59 | 93 | 29 |
| Newport County | 42 | 11 | 7 | 24 | 61 | 105 | 29 |
| Swindon Town | 42 | 9 | 11 | 22 | 60 | 105 | 29 |

## 1933 F.A. Cup

### Semi-finals

| | |
|---|---|
| Everton vs West Ham United | 2-1 |
| Manchester City vs Derby County | 3-2 |

### Final

Wembley, 29th April 1933

**Everton 3**   (Stein, Dean, Dunn)

**Manchester City 0**

*Attendance 92,950*

## DIVISION ONE 1933-34

| | | | | | | | |
|---|---|---|---|---|---|---|---|
| ARSENAL | 42 | 25 | 9 | 8 | 75 | 47 | 59 |
| Huddersfield Town | 42 | 23 | 10 | 9 | 90 | 61 | 56 |
| Tottenham Hotspur | 42 | 21 | 7 | 14 | 79 | 56 | 49 |
| Derby County | 42 | 17 | 11 | 14 | 68 | 54 | 45 |
| Manchester City | 42 | 17 | 11 | 14 | 65 | 72 | 45 |
| Sunderland | 42 | 16 | 12 | 14 | 81 | 56 | 44 |
| West Bromwich Albion | 42 | 17 | 10 | 15 | 78 | 70 | 44 |
| Blackburn Rovers | 42 | 18 | 7 | 17 | 74 | 81 | 43 |
| Leeds United | 42 | 17 | 8 | 17 | 75 | 66 | 42 |
| Portsmouth | 42 | 15 | 12 | 15 | 52 | 55 | 42 |
| Sheffield Wednesday | 42 | 16 | 9 | 17 | 62 | 67 | 41 |
| Stoke City | 42 | 15 | 11 | 16 | 58 | 71 | 41 |
| Aston Villa | 42 | 14 | 12 | 16 | 78 | 75 | 40 |
| Everton | 42 | 12 | 16 | 14 | 62 | 63 | 40 |
| Wolverhampton Wanderers | 42 | 14 | 12 | 16 | 74 | 86 | 40 |
| Middlesbrough | 42 | 16 | 7 | 19 | 68 | 80 | 39 |
| Leicester City | 42 | 14 | 11 | 17 | 59 | 74 | 39 |
| Liverpool | 42 | 14 | 10 | 18 | 79 | 87 | 38 |
| Chelsea | 42 | 14 | 8 | 20 | 67 | 69 | 36 |
| Birmingham | 42 | 12 | 12 | 18 | 54 | 56 | 36 |
| *Newcastle United* | *42* | *10* | *14* | *18* | *68* | *77* | *34* |
| *Sheffield United* | *42* | *12* | *7* | *23* | *58* | *101* | *31* |

## DIVISION TWO 1933-34

| | | | | | | | |
|---|---|---|---|---|---|---|---|
| **Grimsby Town** | 42 | 27 | 5 | 10 | 103 | 59 | 59 |
| **Preston North End** | 42 | 23 | 6 | 13 | 71 | 52 | 52 |
| Bolton Wanderers | 42 | 21 | 9 | 12 | 79 | 55 | 51 |
| Brentford | 42 | 22 | 7 | 13 | 85 | 60 | 51 |
| Bradford Park Avenue | 42 | 23 | 3 | 16 | 86 | 67 | 49 |
| Bradford City | 42 | 20 | 6 | 16 | 73 | 67 | 46 |
| West Ham United | 42 | 17 | 11 | 14 | 78 | 70 | 45 |
| Port Vale | 42 | 19 | 7 | 16 | 60 | 55 | 45 |
| Oldham Athletic | 42 | 17 | 10 | 15 | 72 | 60 | 44 |
| Plymouth Argyle | 42 | 15 | 13 | 14 | 69 | 70 | 43 |
| Blackpool | 42 | 15 | 13 | 14 | 62 | 64 | 43 |
| Bury | 42 | 17 | 9 | 16 | 70 | 73 | 43 |
| Burnley | 42 | 18 | 6 | 18 | 60 | 72 | 42 |
| Southampton | 42 | 15 | 8 | 19 | 54 | 58 | 38 |
| Hull City | 42 | 13 | 12 | 17 | 52 | 68 | 38 |
| Fulham | 42 | 15 | 7 | 20 | 48 | 67 | 37 |
| Nottingham Forest | 42 | 13 | 9 | 20 | 73 | 74 | 35 |
| Notts County | 42 | 12 | 11 | 19 | 53 | 62 | 35 |
| Swansea Town | 42 | 10 | 15 | 17 | 51 | 60 | 35 |
| Manchester United | 42 | 14 | 6 | 22 | 59 | 85 | 34 |
| *Millwall* | *42* | *11* | *11* | *20* | *39* | *68* | *33* |
| *Lincoln City* | *42* | *9* | *8* | *25* | *44* | *75* | *26* |

## DIVISION THREE (N) 1933-34

| | | | | | | | |
|---|---|---|---|---|---|---|---|
| **Barnsley** | 42 | 27 | 8 | 7 | 118 | 61 | 62 |
| Chesterfield | 42 | 27 | 7 | 8 | 86 | 43 | 61 |
| Stockport County | 42 | 24 | 11 | 7 | 115 | 52 | 59 |
| Walsall | 42 | 23 | 7 | 12 | 97 | 60 | 53 |
| Doncaster Rovers | 42 | 22 | 9 | 11 | 83 | 61 | 53 |
| Wrexham | 42 | 23 | 5 | 14 | 102 | 73 | 51 |
| Tranmere Rovers | 42 | 20 | 7 | 15 | 84 | 63 | 47 |
| Barrow | 42 | 19 | 9 | 14 | 116 | 94 | 47 |
| Halifax Town | 42 | 20 | 4 | 18 | 80 | 91 | 44 |
| Chester | 42 | 17 | 6 | 19 | 89 | 86 | 40 |
| Hartlepools United | 42 | 16 | 7 | 19 | 89 | 93 | 39 |
| York City | 42 | 15 | 8 | 19 | 71 | 74 | 38 |
| Carlisle United | 42 | 15 | 8 | 19 | 66 | 81 | 38 |
| Crewe Alexandra | 42 | 15 | 6 | 21 | 81 | 97 | 36 |
| New Brighton | 42 | 14 | 8 | 20 | 62 | 87 | 36 |
| Darlington | 42 | 13 | 9 | 20 | 70 | 101 | 35 |
| Mansfield Town | 42 | 11 | 12 | 19 | 81 | 88 | 34 |
| Southport | 42 | 8 | 17 | 17 | 63 | 90 | 33 |
| Gateshead | 42 | 12 | 9 | 21 | 76 | 110 | 33 |
| Accrington Stanley | 42 | 13 | 7 | 22 | 65 | 101 | 33 |
| Rotherham United | 42 | 10 | 8 | 24 | 53 | 91 | 28 |
| Rochdale | 42 | 9 | 6 | 27 | 53 | 103 | 24 |

## DIVISION THREE (S) 1933-34

| | | | | | | | |
|---|---|---|---|---|---|---|---|
| **Norwich City** | 42 | 25 | 11 | 6 | 88 | 49 | 61 |
| Coventry City | 42 | 21 | 12 | 9 | 100 | 54 | 54 |
| Reading | 42 | 21 | 12 | 9 | 82 | 50 | 54 |
| Queen's Park Rangers | 42 | 24 | 6 | 12 | 70 | 51 | 54 |
| Charlton Athletic | 42 | 22 | 8 | 12 | 83 | 56 | 52 |
| Luton Town | 42 | 21 | 10 | 11 | 83 | 61 | 52 |
| Bristol Rovers | 42 | 20 | 11 | 11 | 77 | 47 | 51 |
| Swindon Town | 42 | 17 | 11 | 14 | 64 | 68 | 45 |
| Exeter City | 42 | 16 | 11 | 15 | 68 | 57 | 43 |
| Brighton & Hove Albion | 42 | 15 | 13 | 14 | 68 | 60 | 43 |
| Clapton Orient | 42 | 16 | 10 | 16 | 75 | 69 | 42 |
| Crystal Palace | 42 | 16 | 9 | 17 | 71 | 67 | 41 |
| Northampton Town | 42 | 14 | 12 | 16 | 71 | 78 | 40 |
| Aldershot | 42 | 13 | 12 | 17 | 52 | 71 | 38 |
| Watford | 42 | 15 | 7 | 20 | 71 | 63 | 37 |
| Southend United | 42 | 12 | 10 | 20 | 51 | 74 | 34 |
| Gillingham | 42 | 11 | 11 | 20 | 75 | 96 | 33 |
| Newport County | 42 | 8 | 17 | 17 | 49 | 70 | 33 |
| Bristol City | 42 | 10 | 13 | 19 | 58 | 85 | 33 |
| Torquay United | 42 | 13 | 7 | 22 | 53 | 93 | 33 |
| Bournemouth & Boscombe Ath. | 42 | 9 | 9 | 24 | 60 | 102 | 27 |
| Cardiff City | 42 | 9 | 6 | 27 | 57 | 105 | 24 |

## 1934 F.A. Cup

### Semi-finals

| | |
|---|---|
| Manchester City vs Aston Villa | 6-1 |
| Portsmouth vs Leicester City | 4-1 |

### Final

Wembley, 28th April 1934

**Manchester City 2**  (Tilson 2)
**Portsmouth 1**  (Rutherford)

*Attendance 93,258*

## DIVISION ONE 1934-35

| | | | | | | | |
|---|---|---|---|---|---|---|---|
| **ARSENAL** | 42 | 23 | 12 | 7 | 115 | 46 | 58 |
| Sunderland | 42 | 19 | 16 | 7 | 90 | 51 | 54 |
| Sheffield Wednesday | 42 | 18 | 13 | 11 | 70 | 64 | 49 |
| Manchester City | 42 | 20 | 8 | 14 | 82 | 67 | 48 |
| Grimsby Town | 42 | 17 | 11 | 14 | 78 | 60 | 45 |
| Derby County | 42 | 18 | 9 | 15 | 81 | 66 | 45 |
| Liverpool | 42 | 19 | 7 | 16 | 85 | 88 | 45 |
| Everton | 42 | 16 | 12 | 14 | 89 | 88 | 44 |
| West Bromwich Albion | 42 | 17 | 10 | 15 | 83 | 83 | 44 |
| Stoke City | 42 | 18 | 6 | 18 | 71 | 70 | 42 |
| Preston North End | 42 | 15 | 12 | 15 | 62 | 67 | 42 |
| Chelsea | 42 | 16 | 9 | 17 | 73 | 82 | 41 |
| Aston Villa | 42 | 14 | 13 | 15 | 74 | 88 | 41 |
| Portsmouth | 42 | 15 | 10 | 17 | 71 | 72 | 40 |
| Blackburn Rovers | 42 | 14 | 11 | 17 | 66 | 78 | 39 |
| Huddersfield Town | 42 | 14 | 10 | 18 | 76 | 71 | 38 |
| Wolverhampton Wanderers | 42 | 15 | 8 | 19 | 88 | 94 | 38 |
| Leeds United | 42 | 13 | 12 | 17 | 75 | 92 | 38 |
| Birmingham | 42 | 13 | 10 | 19 | 63 | 81 | 36 |
| Middlesbrough | 42 | 10 | 14 | 18 | 70 | 90 | 34 |
| *Leicester City* | *42* | *12* | *9* | *21* | *61* | *86* | *33* |
| *Tottenham Hotspur* | *42* | *10* | *10* | *22* | *54* | *93* | *30* |

## DIVISION TWO 1934-35

| | | | | | | | |
|---|---|---|---|---|---|---|---|
| **Brentford** | 42 | 26 | 9 | 7 | 93 | 48 | 61 |
| **Bolton Wanderers** | 42 | 26 | 4 | 12 | 96 | 48 | 56 |
| West Ham United | 42 | 26 | 4 | 12 | 80 | 63 | 56 |
| Blackpool | 42 | 21 | 11 | 10 | 79 | 57 | 53 |
| Manchester United | 42 | 23 | 4 | 15 | 76 | 55 | 50 |
| Newcastle United | 42 | 22 | 4 | 16 | 89 | 68 | 48 |
| Fulham | 42 | 17 | 12 | 13 | 76 | 56 | 46 |
| Plymouth Argyle | 42 | 19 | 8 | 15 | 75 | 64 | 46 |
| Nottingham Forest | 42 | 17 | 8 | 17 | 76 | 70 | 42 |
| Bury | 42 | 19 | 4 | 19 | 62 | 73 | 42 |
| Sheffield United | 42 | 16 | 9 | 17 | 79 | 70 | 41 |
| Burnley | 42 | 16 | 9 | 17 | 63 | 73 | 41 |
| Hull City | 42 | 16 | 8 | 18 | 63 | 74 | 40 |
| Norwich City | 42 | 14 | 11 | 17 | 71 | 61 | 39 |
| Bradford Park Avenue | 42 | 11 | 16 | 15 | 55 | 63 | 38 |
| Barnsley | 42 | 13 | 12 | 17 | 60 | 83 | 38 |
| Swansea Town | 42 | 14 | 8 | 20 | 56 | 67 | 36 |
| Port Vale | 42 | 11 | 12 | 19 | 55 | 74 | 34 |
| Southampton | 42 | 11 | 12 | 19 | 46 | 75 | 34 |
| Bradford City | 42 | 12 | 8 | 22 | 50 | 68 | 32 |
| *Oldham Athletic* | *42* | *10* | *6* | *26* | *56* | *95* | *26* |
| *Notts County* | *42* | *9* | *7* | *26* | *46* | *97* | *25* |

## DIVISION THREE (N) 1934-35

| | | | | | | | |
|---|---|---|---|---|---|---|---|
| **Doncaster Rovers** | 42 | 26 | 5 | 11 | 87 | 44 | 57 |
| Halifax Town | 42 | 25 | 5 | 12 | 76 | 67 | 55 |
| Chester | 42 | 20 | 14 | 8 | 91 | 58 | 54 |
| Lincoln City | 42 | 22 | 7 | 13 | 87 | 58 | 51 |
| Darlington | 42 | 21 | 9 | 12 | 80 | 59 | 51 |
| Tranmere Rovers | 42 | 20 | 11 | 11 | 74 | 55 | 51 |
| Stockport County | 42 | 22 | 3 | 17 | 90 | 72 | 47 |
| Mansfield Town | 42 | 19 | 9 | 14 | 75 | 62 | 47 |
| Rotherham United | 42 | 19 | 7 | 16 | 86 | 73 | 45 |
| Chesterfield | 42 | 17 | 10 | 15 | 71 | 52 | 44 |
| Wrexham | 42 | 16 | 11 | 15 | 76 | 69 | 43 |
| Hartlepools United | 42 | 17 | 7 | 18 | 80 | 78 | 41 |
| Crewe Alexandra | 42 | 14 | 11 | 17 | 66 | 86 | 39 |
| Walsall | 42 | 13 | 10 | 19 | 81 | 72 | 36 |
| York City | 42 | 15 | 6 | 21 | 76 | 82 | 36 |
| New Brighton | 42 | 14 | 8 | 20 | 59 | 76 | 36 |
| Barrow | 42 | 13 | 9 | 20 | 58 | 87 | 35 |
| Accrington Stanley | 42 | 12 | 10 | 20 | 63 | 89 | 34 |
| Gateshead | 42 | 13 | 8 | 21 | 58 | 96 | 34 |
| Rochdale | 42 | 11 | 11 | 20 | 53 | 71 | 33 |
| Southport | 42 | 10 | 12 | 20 | 55 | 85 | 32 |
| Carlisle United | 42 | 8 | 7 | 27 | 51 | 102 | 23 |

## DIVISION THREE (S) 1934-35

| | | | | | | | |
|---|---|---|---|---|---|---|---|
| **Charlton Athletic** | 42 | 27 | 7 | 8 | 103 | 52 | 61 |
| Reading | 42 | 21 | 11 | 10 | 89 | 65 | 53 |
| Coventry City | 42 | 21 | 9 | 12 | 86 | 50 | 51 |
| Luton Town | 42 | 19 | 12 | 11 | 92 | 60 | 50 |
| Crystal Palace | 42 | 19 | 10 | 13 | 86 | 64 | 48 |
| Watford | 42 | 19 | 9 | 14 | 76 | 49 | 47 |
| Northampton Town | 42 | 19 | 8 | 15 | 65 | 67 | 46 |
| Bristol Rovers | 42 | 17 | 10 | 15 | 73 | 77 | 44 |
| Brighton & Hove Albion | 42 | 17 | 9 | 16 | 69 | 62 | 43 |
| Torquay United | 42 | 18 | 6 | 18 | 81 | 75 | 42 |
| Exeter City | 42 | 16 | 9 | 17 | 70 | 75 | 41 |
| Millwall | 42 | 17 | 7 | 18 | 57 | 62 | 41 |
| Queen's Park Rangers | 42 | 16 | 9 | 17 | 63 | 72 | 41 |
| Clapton Orient | 42 | 15 | 10 | 17 | 65 | 65 | 40 |
| Bristol City | 42 | 15 | 5 | 18 | 52 | 68 | 39 |
| Swindon Town | 42 | 13 | 12 | 17 | 67 | 78 | 38 |
| Bournemouth & Boscombe Ath. | 42 | 15 | 7 | 20 | 54 | 71 | 37 |
| Aldershot | 42 | 13 | 10 | 19 | 50 | 75 | 36 |
| Cardiff City | 42 | 13 | 9 | 20 | 62 | 82 | 35 |
| Gillingham | 42 | 11 | 13 | 18 | 55 | 75 | 35 |
| Southend United | 42 | 11 | 9 | 22 | 65 | 78 | 31 |
| Newport County | 42 | 10 | 5 | 27 | 54 | 112 | 25 |

## 1935 F.A. Cup

**Semi-finals**

Sheffield Wednesday vs Burnley 3-0
Bolton Wanderers vs West Bromwich Albion 1-1, 0-2

**Final**

Wembley, 27th April 1935

**Sheffield Wednesday 4** (Rimmer 2, Palethorpe, Hooper)

**West Bromwich Albion 2** (Boyes, Sandford)

*Attendance 93,204*

## DIVISION ONE 1935-36

| | | | | | | | |
|---|---|---|---|---|---|---|---|
| SUNDERLAND | 42 | 25 | 6 | 11 | 109 | 74 | 56 |
| Derby County | 42 | 18 | 12 | 12 | 61 | 52 | 48 |
| Huddersfield Town | 42 | 18 | 12 | 12 | 59 | 56 | 48 |
| Stoke City | 42 | 20 | 7 | 15 | 57 | 57 | 47 |
| Brentford | 42 | 17 | 12 | 13 | 81 | 60 | 46 |
| Arsenal | 42 | 15 | 15 | 12 | 78 | 48 | 45 |
| Preston North End | 42 | 18 | 8 | 16 | 67 | 64 | 44 |
| Chelsea | 42 | 15 | 13 | 14 | 65 | 72 | 43 |
| Manchester City | 42 | 17 | 8 | 17 | 68 | 60 | 42 |
| Portsmouth | 42 | 17 | 8 | 17 | 54 | 67 | 42 |
| Leeds United | 42 | 15 | 11 | 16 | 66 | 64 | 41 |
| Birmingham | 42 | 15 | 11 | 16 | 61 | 63 | 41 |
| Bolton Wanderers | 42 | 14 | 13 | 15 | 67 | 76 | 41 |
| Middlesbrough | 42 | 15 | 10 | 17 | 84 | 70 | 40 |
| Wolverhampton Wanderers | 42 | 15 | 10 | 17 | 77 | 76 | 40 |
| Everton | 42 | 13 | 13 | 16 | 89 | 89 | 39 |
| Grimsby Town | 42 | 17 | 5 | 20 | 65 | 73 | 39 |
| West Bromwich Albion | 42 | 16 | 6 | 20 | 89 | 88 | 38 |
| Liverpool | 42 | 13 | 12 | 17 | 60 | 64 | 38 |
| Sheffield Wednesday | 42 | 13 | 12 | 17 | 63 | 77 | 38 |
| *Aston Villa* | *42* | *13* | *9* | *20* | *81* | *110* | *35* |
| *Blackburn Rovers* | *42* | *12* | *9* | *21* | *55* | *96* | *33* |

## DIVISION TWO 1935-36

| | | | | | | | |
|---|---|---|---|---|---|---|---|
| **Manchester United** | 42 | 22 | 12 | 8 | 85 | 43 | 56 |
| **Charlton Athletic** | 42 | 22 | 11 | 9 | 85 | 58 | 55 |
| Sheffield United | 42 | 20 | 12 | 10 | 79 | 50 | 52 |
| West Ham United | 42 | 22 | 8 | 12 | 90 | 68 | 52 |
| Tottenham Hotspur | 42 | 18 | 13 | 11 | 91 | 55 | 49 |
| Leicester City | 42 | 19 | 10 | 13 | 79 | 57 | 48 |
| Plymouth Argyle | 42 | 20 | 8 | 14 | 71 | 57 | 48 |
| Newcastle United | 42 | 20 | 6 | 16 | 88 | 79 | 46 |
| Fulham | 42 | 15 | 14 | 13 | 76 | 52 | 44 |
| Blackpool | 42 | 18 | 7 | 17 | 93 | 72 | 43 |
| Norwich City | 42 | 17 | 9 | 16 | 72 | 65 | 43 |
| Bradford City | 42 | 15 | 13 | 14 | 55 | 65 | 43 |
| Swansea Town | 42 | 15 | 9 | 18 | 67 | 76 | 39 |
| Bury | 42 | 13 | 12 | 17 | 66 | 84 | 38 |
| Burnley | 42 | 12 | 13 | 17 | 50 | 59 | 37 |
| Bradford Park Avenue | 42 | 14 | 9 | 19 | 62 | 84 | 37 |
| Southampton | 42 | 14 | 9 | 19 | 47 | 65 | 37 |
| Doncaster Rovers | 42 | 14 | 9 | 19 | 51 | 71 | 37 |
| Nottingham Forest | 42 | 12 | 11 | 19 | 69 | 76 | 35 |
| Barnsley | 42 | 12 | 9 | 21 | 54 | 80 | 33 |
| *Port Vale* | *42* | *12* | *8* | *22* | *56* | *106* | *32* |
| *Hull City* | *42* | *5* | *10* | *27* | *47* | *111* | *20* |

## DIVISION THREE (N) 1935-36

| | | | | | | | |
|---|---|---|---|---|---|---|---|
| **Chesterfield** | 42 | 24 | 12 | 6 | 92 | 39 | 60 |
| Chester | 42 | 22 | 11 | 9 | 100 | 45 | 55 |
| Tranmere Rovers | 42 | 22 | 11 | 9 | 93 | 58 | 55 |
| Lincoln City | 42 | 22 | 9 | 11 | 91 | 51 | 53 |
| Stockport County | 42 | 20 | 8 | 14 | 65 | 49 | 48 |
| Crewe Alexandra | 42 | 19 | 9 | 14 | 80 | 76 | 47 |
| Oldham Athletic | 42 | 18 | 9 | 15 | 86 | 73 | 45 |
| Hartlepools United | 42 | 15 | 12 | 15 | 57 | 61 | 42 |
| Accrington Stanley | 42 | 17 | 8 | 17 | 63 | 72 | 42 |
| Walsall | 42 | 16 | 9 | 17 | 79 | 59 | 41 |
| Rotherham United | 42 | 16 | 9 | 17 | 69 | 66 | 41 |
| Darlington | 42 | 17 | 6 | 19 | 74 | 79 | 40 |
| Carlisle United | 42 | 14 | 12 | 16 | 56 | 62 | 40 |
| Gateshead | 42 | 13 | 14 | 15 | 56 | 76 | 40 |
| Barrow | 42 | 13 | 12 | 17 | 58 | 65 | 38 |
| York City | 42 | 13 | 12 | 17 | 62 | 95 | 38 |
| Halifax Town | 42 | 15 | 7 | 20 | 57 | 61 | 37 |
| Wrexham | 42 | 15 | 7 | 20 | 66 | 75 | 37 |
| Mansfield Town | 42 | 14 | 9 | 19 | 80 | 91 | 37 |
| Rochdale | 42 | 10 | 13 | 19 | 58 | 88 | 33 |
| Southport | 42 | 11 | 9 | 22 | 48 | 90 | 31 |
| New Brighton | 42 | 9 | 6 | 27 | 43 | 102 | 24 |

## DIVISION THREE (S) 1935-36

| | | | | | | | |
|---|---|---|---|---|---|---|---|
| **Coventry City** | 42 | 24 | 9 | 9 | 102 | 45 | 57 |
| Luton Town | 42 | 22 | 12 | 8 | 81 | 45 | 56 |
| Reading | 42 | 26 | 2 | 14 | 87 | 62 | 54 |
| Queen's Park Rangers | 42 | 22 | 9 | 11 | 84 | 53 | 53 |
| Watford | 42 | 20 | 9 | 13 | 80 | 54 | 49 |
| Crystal Palace | 42 | 22 | 5 | 15 | 96 | 74 | 49 |
| Brighton & Hove Albion | 42 | 18 | 8 | 16 | 70 | 63 | 44 |
| Bournemouth & Boscombe Ath. | 42 | 16 | 11 | 15 | 60 | 56 | 43 |
| Notts County | 42 | 15 | 12 | 15 | 60 | 57 | 42 |
| Torquay United | 42 | 16 | 9 | 17 | 62 | 62 | 41 |
| Aldershot | 42 | 14 | 12 | 16 | 53 | 61 | 40 |
| Millwall | 42 | 14 | 12 | 16 | 58 | 71 | 40 |
| Bristol City | 42 | 15 | 10 | 17 | 48 | 59 | 40 |
| Clapton Orient | 42 | 16 | 6 | 20 | 55 | 61 | 38 |
| Northampton Town | 42 | 15 | 8 | 19 | 62 | 90 | 38 |
| Gillingham | 42 | 14 | 9 | 19 | 66 | 77 | 37 |
| Bristol Rovers | 42 | 14 | 9 | 19 | 69 | 95 | 37 |
| Southend United | 42 | 13 | 10 | 19 | 61 | 62 | 36 |
| Swindon Town | 42 | 14 | 8 | 20 | 64 | 73 | 36 |
| Cardiff City | 42 | 13 | 10 | 19 | 60 | 73 | 36 |
| Newport County | 42 | 11 | 9 | 22 | 60 | 111 | 31 |
| Exeter City | 42 | 8 | 11 | 23 | 59 | 93 | 27 |

## 1936 F.A. Cup

**Semi-finals**

| | |
|---|---|
| Arsenal vs Grimsby Town | 1-0 |
| Fulham vs Sheffield United | 1-2 |

**Final**

Wembley, 25th April 1936

**Arsenal 1**  (Drake)

**Sheffield United 0**

*Attendance 93,384*

## DIVISION ONE 1936-37

| | | | | | | | |
|---|---|---|---|---|---|---|---|
| MANCHESTER CITY | 42 | 22 | 13 | 7 | 107 | 61 | 57 |
| Charlton Athletic | 42 | 21 | 12 | 9 | 58 | 49 | 54 |
| Arsenal | 42 | 18 | 16 | 8 | 80 | 49 | 52 |
| Derby County | 42 | 21 | 7 | 14 | 96 | 90 | 49 |
| Wolverhampton Wanderers | 42 | 21 | 5 | 16 | 84 | 67 | 47 |
| Brentford | 42 | 18 | 10 | 14 | 82 | 78 | 46 |
| Middlesbrough | 42 | 19 | 8 | 15 | 74 | 71 | 46 |
| Sunderland | 42 | 19 | 6 | 17 | 89 | 87 | 44 |
| Portsmouth | 42 | 17 | 10 | 15 | 62 | 66 | 44 |
| Stoke City | 42 | 15 | 12 | 15 | 72 | 57 | 42 |
| Birmingham | 42 | 13 | 15 | 14 | 64 | 60 | 41 |
| Grimsby Town | 42 | 17 | 7 | 18 | 86 | 81 | 41 |
| Chelsea | 42 | 14 | 13 | 15 | 52 | 55 | 41 |
| Preston North End | 42 | 14 | 13 | 15 | 56 | 67 | 41 |
| Huddersfield Town | 42 | 12 | 15 | 15 | 62 | 64 | 39 |
| West Bromwich Albion | 42 | 16 | 6 | 20 | 77 | 98 | 38 |
| Everton | 42 | 14 | 9 | 19 | 81 | 78 | 37 |
| Liverpool | 42 | 12 | 11 | 19 | 62 | 84 | 35 |
| Leeds United | 42 | 15 | 4 | 23 | 60 | 80 | 34 |
| Bolton Wanderers | 42 | 10 | 14 | 18 | 43 | 66 | 34 |
| *Manchester United* | *42* | *10* | *12* | *20* | *55* | *78* | *32* |
| *Sheffield Wednesday* | *42* | *9* | *12* | *21* | *53* | *69* | *30* |

## DIVISION THREE (N) 1936-37

| | | | | | | | |
|---|---|---|---|---|---|---|---|
| Stockport County | 42 | 23 | 14 | 5 | 84 | 39 | 60 |
| Lincoln City | 42 | 25 | 7 | 10 | 103 | 57 | 57 |
| Chester | 42 | 22 | 9 | 11 | 87 | 57 | 53 |
| Oldham Athletic | 42 | 20 | 11 | 11 | 77 | 59 | 51 |
| Hull City | 42 | 17 | 12 | 13 | 68 | 69 | 46 |
| Hartlepools United | 42 | 19 | 7 | 16 | 75 | 69 | 45 |
| Halifax Town | 42 | 18 | 9 | 15 | 68 | 63 | 45 |
| Wrexham | 42 | 16 | 12 | 14 | 71 | 57 | 44 |
| Mansfield Town | 42 | 18 | 8 | 16 | 91 | 76 | 44 |
| Carlisle United | 42 | 18 | 8 | 16 | 65 | 68 | 44 |
| Port Vale | 42 | 17 | 10 | 15 | 58 | 64 | 44 |
| York City | 42 | 16 | 11 | 15 | 79 | 70 | 43 |
| Accrington Stanley | 42 | 16 | 9 | 17 | 76 | 69 | 41 |
| Southport | 42 | 12 | 13 | 17 | 73 | 87 | 37 |
| New Brighton | 42 | 13 | 11 | 18 | 55 | 70 | 37 |
| Barrow | 42 | 13 | 10 | 19 | 70 | 86 | 36 |
| Rotherham United | 42 | 14 | 7 | 21 | 78 | 91 | 35 |
| Rochdale | 42 | 13 | 9 | 20 | 69 | 86 | 35 |
| Tranmere Rovers | 42 | 12 | 9 | 21 | 71 | 88 | 33 |
| Crewe Alexandra | 42 | 10 | 12 | 20 | 55 | 83 | 32 |
| Gateshead | 42 | 11 | 10 | 21 | 63 | 98 | 32 |
| Darlington | 42 | 8 | 14 | 20 | 66 | 96 | 30 |

## DIVISION TWO 1936-37

| | | | | | | | |
|---|---|---|---|---|---|---|---|
| Leicester City | 42 | 24 | 8 | 10 | 89 | 57 | 56 |
| Blackpool | 42 | 24 | 7 | 11 | 88 | 53 | 55 |
| Bury | 42 | 22 | 8 | 12 | 74 | 55 | 52 |
| Newcastle United | 42 | 22 | 5 | 15 | 80 | 56 | 49 |
| Plymouth Argyle | 42 | 18 | 13 | 11 | 71 | 53 | 49 |
| West Ham United | 42 | 19 | 11 | 12 | 73 | 55 | 49 |
| Sheffield United | 42 | 18 | 10 | 14 | 66 | 54 | 46 |
| Coventry City | 42 | 17 | 11 | 14 | 66 | 54 | 45 |
| Aston Villa | 42 | 16 | 12 | 14 | 82 | 70 | 44 |
| Tottenham Hotspur | 42 | 17 | 9 | 16 | 88 | 66 | 43 |
| Fulham | 42 | 15 | 13 | 14 | 71 | 61 | 43 |
| Blackburn Rovers | 42 | 16 | 10 | 16 | 70 | 62 | 42 |
| Burnley | 42 | 16 | 10 | 16 | 57 | 61 | 42 |
| Barnsley | 42 | 16 | 9 | 17 | 50 | 64 | 41 |
| Chesterfield | 42 | 16 | 8 | 18 | 84 | 89 | 40 |
| Swansea Town | 42 | 15 | 7 | 20 | 50 | 65 | 37 |
| Norwich City | 42 | 14 | 8 | 20 | 63 | 71 | 36 |
| Nottingham Forest | 42 | 12 | 10 | 20 | 68 | 90 | 34 |
| Southampton | 42 | 11 | 12 | 19 | 53 | 77 | 34 |
| Bradford Park Avenue | 42 | 12 | 9 | 21 | 52 | 88 | 33 |
| *Bradford City* | *42* | *9* | *12* | *21* | *54* | *94* | *30* |
| *Doncaster Rovers* | *42* | *7* | *10* | *25* | *30* | *84* | *24* |

## DIVISION THREE (S) 1936-37

| | | | | | | | |
|---|---|---|---|---|---|---|---|
| Luton Town | 42 | 27 | 4 | 11 | 103 | 53 | 58 |
| Notts County | 42 | 23 | 10 | 9 | 74 | 52 | 56 |
| Brighton & Hove Albion | 42 | 24 | 5 | 13 | 74 | 43 | 53 |
| Watford | 42 | 19 | 11 | 12 | 85 | 60 | 49 |
| Reading | 42 | 19 | 11 | 12 | 76 | 60 | 49 |
| Bournemouth & Boscombe Ath. | 42 | 20 | 9 | 13 | 65 | 59 | 49 |
| Northampton Town | 42 | 20 | 6 | 16 | 85 | 68 | 46 |
| Millwall | 42 | 18 | 10 | 14 | 64 | 54 | 46 |
| Queen's Park Rangers | 42 | 18 | 9 | 15 | 73 | 52 | 45 |
| Southend United | 42 | 17 | 11 | 14 | 78 | 67 | 45 |
| Gillingham | 42 | 18 | 8 | 16 | 52 | 66 | 44 |
| Clapton Orient | 42 | 14 | 15 | 13 | 52 | 52 | 43 |
| Swindon Town | 42 | 14 | 11 | 17 | 75 | 73 | 39 |
| Crystal Palace | 42 | 13 | 12 | 17 | 62 | 61 | 38 |
| Bristol Rovers | 42 | 16 | 4 | 22 | 71 | 80 | 36 |
| Bristol City | 42 | 15 | 6 | 21 | 58 | 70 | 36 |
| Walsall | 42 | 13 | 10 | 19 | 62 | 84 | 36 |
| Cardiff City | 42 | 14 | 7 | 21 | 54 | 87 | 35 |
| Newport County | 42 | 12 | 10 | 20 | 67 | 98 | 34 |
| Torquay United | 42 | 11 | 10 | 21 | 57 | 80 | 32 |
| Exeter City | 42 | 10 | 12 | 20 | 59 | 88 | 32 |
| Aldershot | 42 | 7 | 9 | 26 | 50 | 89 | 23 |

## 1937 F.A. Cup

**Semi-finals**

| | |
|---|---|
| Sunderland vs Millwall | 2-1 |
| Preston North End vs West Bromwich Albion | 4-1 |

**Final**

Wembley, 1st May 1937

**Sunderland 3** (Gurney, Carter, Burbanks)

**Preston North End 1** (F. O'Donnell)

*Attendance 93,495*

## DIVISION ONE 1937-38

| | | | | | | | |
|---|---|---|---|---|---|---|---|
| **ARSENAL** | 42 | 21 | 10 | 11 | 77 | 44 | 52 |
| Wolverhampton Wanderers | 42 | 20 | 11 | 11 | 72 | 49 | 51 |
| Preston North End | 42 | 16 | 17 | 9 | 64 | 44 | 49 |
| Charlton Athletic | 42 | 16 | 14 | 12 | 65 | 51 | 46 |
| Middlesbrough | 42 | 19 | 8 | 15 | 72 | 65 | 46 |
| Brentford | 42 | 18 | 9 | 15 | 69 | 59 | 45 |
| Bolton Wanderers | 42 | 15 | 15 | 12 | 64 | 60 | 45 |
| Sunderland | 42 | 14 | 16 | 12 | 55 | 57 | 44 |
| Leeds United | 42 | 14 | 15 | 13 | 64 | 69 | 43 |
| Chelsea | 42 | 14 | 13 | 15 | 65 | 65 | 41 |
| Liverpool | 42 | 15 | 11 | 16 | 65 | 71 | 41 |
| Blackpool | 42 | 16 | 8 | 18 | 61 | 66 | 40 |
| Derby County | 42 | 15 | 10 | 17 | 66 | 87 | 40 |
| Everton | 42 | 16 | 7 | 19 | 79 | 75 | 39 |
| Huddersfield Town | 42 | 17 | 5 | 20 | 55 | 68 | 39 |
| Leicester City | 42 | 14 | 11 | 17 | 54 | 75 | 39 |
| Stoke City | 42 | 13 | 12 | 17 | 58 | 59 | 38 |
| Birmingham | 42 | 10 | 18 | 14 | 58 | 62 | 38 |
| Portsmouth | 42 | 13 | 12 | 17 | 62 | 68 | 38 |
| Grimsby Town | 42 | 13 | 12 | 17 | 51 | 68 | 38 |
| *Manchester City* | *42* | *14* | *8* | *20* | *80* | *77* | *36* |
| *West Bromwich Albion* | *42* | *14* | *8* | *20* | *74* | *91* | *36* |

## DIVISION THREE (N) 1937-38

| | | | | | | | |
|---|---|---|---|---|---|---|---|
| **Tranmere Rovers** | 42 | 23 | 10 | 9 | 81 | 41 | 56 |
| Doncaster Rovers | 42 | 21 | 12 | 9 | 74 | 49 | 54 |
| Hull City | 42 | 20 | 13 | 9 | 80 | 43 | 53 |
| Oldham Athletic | 42 | 19 | 13 | 10 | 67 | 46 | 51 |
| Gateshead | 42 | 20 | 11 | 11 | 84 | 59 | 51 |
| Rotherham United | 42 | 20 | 10 | 12 | 68 | 56 | 50 |
| Lincoln City | 42 | 19 | 8 | 15 | 66 | 50 | 46 |
| Crewe Alexandra | 42 | 18 | 9 | 15 | 71 | 53 | 45 |
| Chester | 42 | 16 | 12 | 14 | 77 | 72 | 44 |
| Wrexham | 42 | 16 | 11 | 15 | 58 | 63 | 43 |
| York City | 42 | 16 | 10 | 16 | 70 | 68 | 42 |
| Carlisle United | 42 | 15 | 9 | 18 | 57 | 67 | 39 |
| New Brighton | 42 | 15 | 8 | 19 | 60 | 61 | 38 |
| Bradford City | 42 | 14 | 10 | 18 | 66 | 69 | 38 |
| Port Vale | 42 | 12 | 14 | 16 | 65 | 73 | 38 |
| Southport | 42 | 12 | 14 | 16 | 53 | 82 | 38 |
| Rochdale | 42 | 13 | 11 | 18 | 67 | 78 | 37 |
| Halifax Town | 42 | 12 | 12 | 18 | 44 | 66 | 36 |
| Darlington | 42 | 11 | 10 | 21 | 54 | 79 | 32 |
| Hartlepools United | 42 | 10 | 12 | 20 | 53 | 80 | 32 |
| Barrow | 42 | 11 | 10 | 21 | 41 | 71 | 32 |
| Accrington Stanley | 42 | 11 | 7 | 24 | 45 | 75 | 29 |

## DIVISION TWO 1937-38

| | | | | | | | |
|---|---|---|---|---|---|---|---|
| **Aston Villa** | 42 | 25 | 7 | 10 | 73 | 35 | 57 |
| **Manchester United** | 42 | 22 | 9 | 11 | 82 | 50 | 53 |
| Sheffield United | 42 | 22 | 9 | 11 | 73 | 56 | 53 |
| Coventry City | 42 | 20 | 12 | 10 | 66 | 45 | 52 |
| Tottenham Hotspur | 42 | 19 | 6 | 17 | 76 | 54 | 44 |
| Burnley | 42 | 17 | 10 | 15 | 54 | 54 | 44 |
| Bradford Park Avenue | 42 | 17 | 9 | 16 | 69 | 56 | 43 |
| Fulham | 42 | 16 | 11 | 15 | 61 | 57 | 43 |
| West Ham United | 42 | 14 | 14 | 14 | 53 | 52 | 42 |
| Bury | 42 | 18 | 5 | 19 | 63 | 60 | 41 |
| Chesterfield | 42 | 16 | 9 | 17 | 63 | 63 | 41 |
| Luton Town | 42 | 15 | 10 | 17 | 89 | 86 | 40 |
| Plymouth Argyle | 42 | 14 | 12 | 16 | 57 | 65 | 40 |
| Norwich City | 42 | 14 | 11 | 17 | 56 | 75 | 39 |
| Southampton | 42 | 15 | 9 | 18 | 55 | 77 | 39 |
| Blackburn Rovers | 42 | 14 | 10 | 18 | 71 | 80 | 38 |
| Sheffield Wednesday | 42 | 14 | 10 | 18 | 49 | 56 | 38 |
| Swansea Town | 42 | 13 | 12 | 17 | 45 | 73 | 38 |
| Newcastle United | 42 | 14 | 8 | 20 | 51 | 58 | 36 |
| Nottingham Forest | 42 | 14 | 8 | 20 | 47 | 60 | 36 |
| *Barnsley* | *42* | *11* | *14* | *17* | *50* | *64* | *36* |
| *Stockport County* | *42* | *11* | *9* | *22* | *43* | *70* | *31* |

## DIVISION THREE (S) 1937-38

| | | | | | | | |
|---|---|---|---|---|---|---|---|
| **Millwall** | 42 | 23 | 10 | 9 | 83 | 37 | 56 |
| Bristol City | 42 | 21 | 13 | 8 | 68 | 40 | 55 |
| Queen's Park Rangers | 42 | 22 | 9 | 11 | 80 | 47 | 53 |
| Watford | 42 | 21 | 11 | 10 | 73 | 43 | 53 |
| Brighton & Hove Albion | 42 | 21 | 9 | 12 | 64 | 44 | 51 |
| Reading | 42 | 20 | 11 | 11 | 71 | 63 | 51 |
| Crystal Palace | 42 | 18 | 12 | 12 | 67 | 47 | 48 |
| Swindon Town | 42 | 17 | 10 | 15 | 49 | 49 | 44 |
| Northampton Town | 42 | 17 | 9 | 16 | 51 | 57 | 43 |
| Cardiff City | 42 | 15 | 12 | 15 | 67 | 54 | 42 |
| Notts County | 42 | 16 | 9 | 17 | 50 | 50 | 41 |
| Southend United | 42 | 15 | 10 | 17 | 70 | 68 | 40 |
| Bournemouth & Boscombe Ath. | 42 | 14 | 12 | 16 | 56 | 57 | 40 |
| Mansfield Town | 42 | 15 | 9 | 18 | 62 | 67 | 39 |
| Bristol Rovers | 42 | 13 | 13 | 16 | 46 | 61 | 39 |
| Newport County | 42 | 11 | 16 | 15 | 43 | 52 | 38 |
| Exeter City | 42 | 13 | 12 | 17 | 57 | 70 | 38 |
| Aldershot | 42 | 15 | 5 | 22 | 39 | 59 | 35 |
| Clapton Orient | 42 | 13 | 7 | 22 | 42 | 61 | 33 |
| Torquay United | 42 | 9 | 12 | 21 | 38 | 73 | 30 |
| Walsall | 42 | 11 | 7 | 24 | 52 | 88 | 29 |
| *Gillingham* | *42* | *10* | *6* | *26* | *36* | *77* | *26* |

## 1938 F.A. Cup

### Semi-finals

| | |
|---|---|
| Preston North End vs Aston Villa | 2-1 |
| Sunderland vs Huddersfield Town | 1-3 |

### Final

Wembley, 30th April 1938

**Preston North End  1**  (Mutch (pen))
**Huddersfield Town  0  (aet.)**

*Attendance 93,497*

## DIVISION ONE 1938-39

| | | | | | | | |
|---|---|---|---|---|---|---|---|
| **EVERTON** | 42 | 27 | 5 | 10 | 88 | 52 | 59 |
| Wolverhampton Wanderers | 42 | 22 | 11 | 9 | 88 | 39 | 55 |
| Charlton Athletic | 42 | 22 | 6 | 14 | 75 | 59 | 50 |
| Middlesbrough | 42 | 20 | 9 | 13 | 93 | 74 | 49 |
| Arsenal | 42 | 19 | 9 | 14 | 55 | 41 | 47 |
| Derby County | 42 | 19 | 8 | 15 | 66 | 55 | 46 |
| Stoke City | 42 | 17 | 12 | 13 | 71 | 68 | 46 |
| Bolton Wanderers | 42 | 15 | 15 | 12 | 67 | 58 | 45 |
| Preston North End | 42 | 16 | 12 | 14 | 63 | 59 | 44 |
| Grimsby Town | 42 | 16 | 11 | 15 | 61 | 69 | 43 |
| Liverpool | 42 | 14 | 14 | 14 | 62 | 63 | 42 |
| Aston Villa | 42 | 15 | 11 | 16 | 71 | 60 | 41 |
| Leeds United | 42 | 16 | 9 | 17 | 59 | 67 | 41 |
| Manchester United | 42 | 11 | 16 | 15 | 57 | 65 | 38 |
| Blackpool | 42 | 12 | 14 | 16 | 56 | 68 | 38 |
| Sunderland | 42 | 13 | 12 | 17 | 54 | 67 | 38 |
| Portsmouth | 42 | 12 | 13 | 17 | 47 | 70 | 37 |
| Brentford | 42 | 14 | 8 | 20 | 53 | 74 | 36 |
| Huddersfield Town | 42 | 12 | 11 | 19 | 58 | 64 | 35 |
| Chelsea | 42 | 12 | 9 | 21 | 64 | 80 | 33 |
| *Birmingham* | *42* | *12* | *8* | *22* | *62* | *84* | *32* |
| *Leicester City* | *42* | *9* | *11* | *22* | *48* | *82* | *29* |

## DIVISION THREE (N) 1938-39

| | | | | | | | |
|---|---|---|---|---|---|---|---|
| **Barnsley** | 42 | 30 | 7 | 5 | 94 | 34 | 67 |
| Doncaster Rovers | 42 | 21 | 14 | 7 | 87 | 47 | 56 |
| Bradford City | 42 | 22 | 8 | 12 | 89 | 56 | 52 |
| Southport | 42 | 20 | 10 | 12 | 75 | 54 | 50 |
| Oldham Athletic | 42 | 22 | 5 | 15 | 76 | 59 | 49 |
| Chester | 42 | 20 | 9 | 13 | 88 | 70 | 49 |
| Hull City | 42 | 18 | 10 | 14 | 83 | 74 | 46 |
| Crewe Alexandra | 42 | 19 | 6 | 17 | 82 | 70 | 44 |
| Stockport County | 42 | 17 | 9 | 16 | 91 | 77 | 43 |
| Gateshead | 42 | 14 | 14 | 14 | 74 | 67 | 42 |
| Rotherham United | 42 | 17 | 8 | 17 | 64 | 64 | 42 |
| Halifax Town | 42 | 13 | 16 | 13 | 52 | 54 | 42 |
| Barrow | 42 | 16 | 9 | 17 | 66 | 65 | 41 |
| Wrexham | 42 | 17 | 7 | 18 | 66 | 79 | 41 |
| Rochdale | 42 | 15 | 9 | 18 | 92 | 82 | 39 |
| New Brighton | 42 | 15 | 9 | 18 | 68 | 73 | 39 |
| Lincoln City | 42 | 12 | 9 | 21 | 66 | 92 | 33 |
| Darlington | 42 | 13 | 7 | 22 | 62 | 92 | 33 |
| Carlisle United | 42 | 13 | 7 | 22 | 64 | 111 | 33 |
| York City | 42 | 12 | 8 | 22 | 66 | 92 | 32 |
| Hartlepools United | 42 | 12 | 7 | 23 | 55 | 94 | 31 |
| Accrington Stanley | 42 | 7 | 6 | 29 | 49 | 103 | 20 |

## DIVISION TWO 1938-39

| | | | | | | | |
|---|---|---|---|---|---|---|---|
| **Blackburn Rovers** | 42 | 25 | 5 | 12 | 94 | 60 | 55 |
| **Sheffield United** | 42 | 20 | 14 | 8 | 69 | 41 | 54 |
| Sheffield Wednesday | 42 | 21 | 11 | 10 | 88 | 59 | 53 |
| Coventry City | 42 | 21 | 8 | 13 | 62 | 45 | 50 |
| Manchester City | 42 | 21 | 7 | 14 | 96 | 72 | 49 |
| Chesterfield | 42 | 20 | 9 | 13 | 69 | 52 | 49 |
| Luton Town | 42 | 22 | 5 | 15 | 82 | 66 | 49 |
| Tottenham Hotspur | 42 | 19 | 9 | 14 | 67 | 62 | 47 |
| Newcastle United | 42 | 18 | 10 | 14 | 61 | 48 | 46 |
| West Bromwich Albion | 42 | 18 | 9 | 15 | 89 | 72 | 45 |
| West Ham United | 42 | 17 | 10 | 15 | 70 | 52 | 44 |
| Fulham | 42 | 17 | 10 | 15 | 61 | 55 | 44 |
| Millwall | 42 | 14 | 14 | 14 | 64 | 53 | 42 |
| Burnley | 42 | 15 | 9 | 18 | 50 | 56 | 39 |
| Plymouth Argyle | 42 | 15 | 8 | 19 | 49 | 55 | 38 |
| Bury | 42 | 12 | 13 | 17 | 65 | 74 | 37 |
| Bradford Park Avenue | 42 | 12 | 11 | 19 | 61 | 82 | 35 |
| Southampton | 42 | 13 | 9 | 20 | 56 | 82 | 35 |
| Swansea Town | 42 | 11 | 12 | 19 | 50 | 83 | 34 |
| Nottingham Forest | 42 | 10 | 11 | 21 | 49 | 82 | 31 |
| *Norwich City* | *42* | *13* | *5* | *24* | *50* | *91* | *31* |
| *Tranmere Rovers* | *42* | *6* | *5* | *31* | *39* | *99* | *17* |

## DIVISION THREE (S) 1938-39

| | | | | | | | |
|---|---|---|---|---|---|---|---|
| **Newport County** | 42 | 22 | 11 | 9 | 58 | 45 | 55 |
| Crystal Palace | 42 | 20 | 12 | 10 | 71 | 52 | 52 |
| Brighton & Hove Albion | 42 | 19 | 11 | 12 | 68 | 49 | 49 |
| Watford | 42 | 17 | 12 | 13 | 62 | 51 | 46 |
| Reading | 42 | 16 | 14 | 12 | 69 | 59 | 46 |
| Queen's Park Rangers | 42 | 15 | 14 | 13 | 68 | 49 | 44 |
| Ipswich Town | 42 | 16 | 12 | 14 | 62 | 52 | 44 |
| Bristol City | 42 | 16 | 12 | 14 | 61 | 63 | 44 |
| Swindon Town | 42 | 18 | 8 | 16 | 72 | 77 | 44 |
| Aldershot | 42 | 16 | 12 | 14 | 53 | 66 | 44 |
| Notts County | 42 | 17 | 9 | 16 | 59 | 54 | 43 |
| Southend United | 42 | 16 | 9 | 17 | 61 | 64 | 41 |
| Cardiff City | 42 | 15 | 11 | 16 | 61 | 65 | 41 |
| Exeter City | 42 | 13 | 14 | 15 | 65 | 82 | 40 |
| Bournemouth & Boscombe Ath. | 42 | 13 | 13 | 16 | 52 | 58 | 39 |
| Mansfield Town | 42 | 12 | 15 | 15 | 44 | 62 | 39 |
| Northampton Town | 42 | 15 | 8 | 19 | 51 | 58 | 38 |
| Port Vale | 42 | 14 | 9 | 19 | 52 | 58 | 37 |
| Torquay United | 42 | 14 | 9 | 19 | 54 | 70 | 37 |
| Clapton Orient | 42 | 11 | 13 | 18 | 53 | 55 | 35 |
| Walsall | 42 | 11 | 11 | 20 | 68 | 69 | 33 |
| Bristol Rovers | 42 | 10 | 13 | 19 | 55 | 61 | 33 |

## 1939 F.A. Cup

**Semi-finals**

| | |
|---|---|
| Portsmouth vs Huddersfield Town | 2-1 |
| Wolverhampton Wanderers vs Grimsby Town | 5-0 |

**Final**

Wembley, 29th April 1939

**Portsmouth 4**  (Parker 2, Barlow, Anderson)
**Wolverhampton Wanderers 1**  (Dorsett)

*Attendance 99,370*

## 1946 F.A. Cup

**Semi-finals**

| | |
|---|---|
| Bolton Wanderers vs Charlton Athletic | 0-2 |
| Derby County vs Birmingham City | 1-1,4-0 |

**Final**

Wembley, 27th April 1946

**Derby County 4**  (H. Turner (og), Doherty, Stamps 2)
**Charlton Athletic 1**  (H. Turner)

*Attendance 98,000*

## DIVISION ONE 1946-47

| | | | | | | | |
|---|---|---|---|---|---|---|---|
| LIVERPOOL | 42 | 25 | 7 | 10 | 84 | 52 | 57 |
| Manchester United | 42 | 22 | 12 | 8 | 95 | 54 | 56 |
| Wolverhampton Wanderers | 42 | 25 | 6 | 11 | 98 | 56 | 56 |
| Stoke City | 42 | 24 | 7 | 11 | 90 | 53 | 55 |
| Blackpool | 42 | 22 | 6 | 14 | 71 | 70 | 50 |
| Sheffield United | 42 | 21 | 7 | 14 | 89 | 75 | 49 |
| Preston North End | 42 | 18 | 11 | 13 | 76 | 74 | 47 |
| Aston Villa | 42 | 18 | 9 | 15 | 67 | 53 | 45 |
| Sunderland | 42 | 18 | 8 | 16 | 65 | 66 | 44 |
| Everton | 42 | 17 | 9 | 16 | 62 | 67 | 43 |
| Middlesbrough | 42 | 17 | 8 | 17 | 73 | 68 | 42 |
| Portsmouth | 42 | 16 | 9 | 17 | 66 | 60 | 41 |
| Arsenal | 42 | 16 | 9 | 17 | 72 | 70 | 41 |
| Derby County | 42 | 18 | 5 | 19 | 73 | 79 | 41 |
| Chelsea | 42 | 16 | 7 | 19 | 69 | 84 | 39 |
| Grimsby Town | 42 | 13 | 12 | 17 | 61 | 82 | 38 |
| Blackburn Rovers | 42 | 14 | 8 | 20 | 45 | 53 | 36 |
| Bolton Wanderers | 42 | 13 | 8 | 21 | 57 | 69 | 34 |
| Charlton Athletic | 42 | 11 | 12 | 19 | 57 | 71 | 34 |
| Huddersfield Town | 42 | 13 | 7 | 22 | 53 | 79 | 33 |
| *Brentford* | 42 | 9 | 7 | 26 | 45 | 88 | 25 |
| *Leeds United* | 42 | 6 | 6 | 30 | 45 | 90 | 18 |

## DIVISION THREE (N) 1946-47

| | | | | | | | |
|---|---|---|---|---|---|---|---|
| Doncaster Rovers | 42 | 33 | 6 | 3 | 123 | 40 | 72 |
| Rotherham United | 42 | 29 | 6 | 7 | 114 | 53 | 64 |
| Chester | 42 | 25 | 6 | 11 | 95 | 51 | 56 |
| Stockport County | 42 | 24 | 2 | 16 | 78 | 53 | 50 |
| Bradford City | 42 | 20 | 10 | 12 | 62 | 47 | 50 |
| Rochdale | 42 | 19 | 10 | 13 | 80 | 64 | 48 |
| Wrexham | 42 | 17 | 12 | 13 | 65 | 51 | 46 |
| Crewe Alexandra | 42 | 17 | 9 | 16 | 70 | 74 | 43 |
| Barrow | 42 | 17 | 7 | 18 | 54 | 62 | 41 |
| Tranmere Rovers | 42 | 17 | 7 | 18 | 66 | 77 | 41 |
| Hull City | 42 | 16 | 8 | 18 | 49 | 53 | 40 |
| Lincoln City | 42 | 17 | 5 | 20 | 86 | 87 | 39 |
| Hartlepools United | 42 | 15 | 9 | 18 | 64 | 73 | 39 |
| Gateshead | 42 | 16 | 6 | 20 | 62 | 72 | 38 |
| York City | 42 | 14 | 9 | 19 | 67 | 81 | 37 |
| Carlisle United | 42 | 14 | 9 | 19 | 70 | 93 | 37 |
| Darlington | 42 | 15 | 6 | 21 | 68 | 80 | 36 |
| New Brighton | 42 | 14 | 8 | 20 | 57 | 77 | 36 |
| Oldham Athletic | 42 | 12 | 8 | 22 | 55 | 80 | 32 |
| Accrington Stanley | 42 | 14 | 4 | 24 | 56 | 92 | 32 |
| Southport | 42 | 7 | 11 | 24 | 53 | 85 | 25 |
| Halifax Town | 42 | 8 | 6 | 28 | 43 | 92 | 22 |

## DIVISION TWO 1946-47

| | | | | | | | |
|---|---|---|---|---|---|---|---|
| Manchester City | 42 | 26 | 10 | 6 | 78 | 35 | 62 |
| Burnley | 42 | 22 | 14 | 6 | 65 | 29 | 58 |
| Birmingham City | 42 | 25 | 5 | 12 | 74 | 33 | 55 |
| Chesterfield | 42 | 18 | 14 | 10 | 58 | 44 | 50 |
| Newcastle United | 42 | 19 | 10 | 13 | 95 | 62 | 48 |
| Tottenham Hotspur | 42 | 17 | 14 | 11 | 65 | 53 | 48 |
| West Bromwich Albion | 42 | 20 | 8 | 14 | 88 | 75 | 48 |
| Coventry City | 42 | 16 | 13 | 13 | 66 | 59 | 45 |
| Leicester City | 42 | 18 | 7 | 17 | 69 | 64 | 43 |
| Barnsley | 42 | 17 | 8 | 17 | 84 | 86 | 42 |
| Nottingham Forest | 42 | 15 | 10 | 17 | 69 | 74 | 40 |
| West Ham United | 42 | 16 | 8 | 18 | 70 | 76 | 40 |
| Luton Town | 42 | 16 | 7 | 19 | 71 | 73 | 39 |
| Southampton | 42 | 15 | 9 | 18 | 69 | 76 | 39 |
| Fulham | 42 | 15 | 9 | 18 | 63 | 74 | 39 |
| Bradford Park Avenue | 42 | 14 | 11 | 17 | 65 | 77 | 39 |
| Bury | 42 | 12 | 12 | 18 | 80 | 78 | 36 |
| Millwall | 42 | 14 | 8 | 20 | 56 | 79 | 36 |
| Plymouth Argyle | 42 | 14 | 5 | 23 | 79 | 96 | 33 |
| Sheffield Wednesday | 42 | 12 | 8 | 22 | 67 | 88 | 32 |
| *Swansea Town* | 42 | 11 | 7 | 24 | 55 | 83 | 29 |
| *Newport County* | 42 | 10 | 3 | 29 | 61 | 133 | 23 |

## DIVISION THREE (S) 1946-47

| | | | | | | | |
|---|---|---|---|---|---|---|---|
| Cardiff City | 42 | 30 | 6 | 6 | 93 | 30 | 66 |
| Queen's Park Rangers | 42 | 23 | 11 | 8 | 74 | 40 | 57 |
| Bristol City | 42 | 20 | 11 | 11 | 94 | 56 | 51 |
| Swindon Town | 42 | 19 | 11 | 12 | 84 | 73 | 49 |
| Walsall | 42 | 17 | 12 | 13 | 74 | 59 | 46 |
| Ipswich Town | 42 | 16 | 14 | 12 | 61 | 53 | 46 |
| Bournemouth & Boscombe Ath. | 42 | 18 | 8 | 16 | 72 | 54 | 44 |
| Southend United | 42 | 17 | 10 | 15 | 71 | 60 | 44 |
| Reading | 42 | 16 | 11 | 15 | 83 | 74 | 43 |
| Port Vale | 42 | 17 | 9 | 16 | 68 | 63 | 43 |
| Torquay United | 42 | 15 | 12 | 15 | 52 | 61 | 42 |
| Notts County | 42 | 15 | 10 | 17 | 63 | 63 | 40 |
| Northampton Town | 42 | 15 | 10 | 17 | 72 | 75 | 40 |
| Bristol Rovers | 42 | 16 | 8 | 18 | 59 | 69 | 40 |
| Exeter City | 42 | 15 | 9 | 18 | 60 | 69 | 39 |
| Watford | 42 | 17 | 5 | 20 | 61 | 76 | 39 |
| Brighton & Hove Albion | 42 | 13 | 13 | 16 | 54 | 72 | 38 |
| Crystal Palace | 42 | 13 | 11 | 18 | 49 | 62 | 37 |
| Leyton Orient | 42 | 12 | 8 | 22 | 54 | 75 | 32 |
| Aldershot | 42 | 10 | 12 | 20 | 48 | 78 | 32 |
| Norwich City | 42 | 10 | 8 | 24 | 64 | 100 | 28 |
| Mansfield Town | 42 | 9 | 10 | 23 | 48 | 96 | 28 |

## 1947 F.A. Cup

**Semi-finals**

| | |
|---|---|
| Charlton Athletic vs Newcastle United | 4-0 |
| Burnley vs Liverpool | 0-0, 1-0 |

**Final**

Wembley, 26th April 1947

**Charlton Athletic 1** (Duffy)
**Burnley 0 (aet.)**

*Attendance 99,000*

## DIVISION ONE 1947-48

| | | | | | | | |
|---|---|---|---|---|---|---|---|
| **ARSENAL** | 42 | 23 | 13 | 6 | 81 | 32 | 59 |
| Manchester United | 42 | 19 | 14 | 9 | 81 | 48 | 52 |
| Burnley | 42 | 20 | 12 | 10 | 56 | 43 | 52 |
| Derby County | 42 | 19 | 12 | 11 | 77 | 57 | 50 |
| Wolverhampton Wanderers | 42 | 19 | 9 | 14 | 83 | 70 | 47 |
| Aston Villa | 42 | 19 | 9 | 14 | 65 | 57 | 47 |
| Preston North End | 42 | 20 | 7 | 15 | 67 | 68 | 47 |
| Portsmouth | 42 | 19 | 7 | 16 | 68 | 50 | 45 |
| Blackpool | 42 | 17 | 10 | 15 | 57 | 41 | 44 |
| Manchester City | 42 | 15 | 12 | 15 | 52 | 47 | 42 |
| Liverpool | 42 | 16 | 10 | 16 | 65 | 61 | 42 |
| Sheffield United | 42 | 16 | 10 | 16 | 65 | 70 | 42 |
| Charlton Athletic | 42 | 17 | 6 | 19 | 57 | 66 | 40 |
| Everton | 42 | 17 | 6 | 19 | 52 | 66 | 40 |
| Stoke City | 42 | 14 | 10 | 18 | 41 | 55 | 38 |
| Middlesbrough | 42 | 14 | 9 | 19 | 71 | 73 | 37 |
| Bolton Wanderers | 42 | 16 | 5 | 21 | 46 | 58 | 37 |
| Chelsea | 42 | 14 | 9 | 19 | 53 | 71 | 37 |
| Huddersfield Town | 42 | 12 | 12 | 18 | 51 | 60 | 36 |
| Sunderland | 42 | 13 | 10 | 19 | 56 | 67 | 36 |
| *Blackburn Rovers* | *42* | *11* | *10* | *21* | *54* | *72* | *32* |
| *Grimsby Town* | *42* | *8* | *6* | *28* | *45* | *111* | *22* |

## DIVISION TWO 1947-48

| | | | | | | | |
|---|---|---|---|---|---|---|---|
| **Birmingham City** | 42 | 22 | 15 | 5 | 55 | 24 | 59 |
| **Newcastle United** | 42 | 24 | 8 | 10 | 72 | 41 | 56 |
| Southampton | 42 | 21 | 10 | 11 | 71 | 53 | 52 |
| Sheffield Wednesday | 42 | 20 | 11 | 11 | 66 | 53 | 51 |
| Cardiff City | 42 | 18 | 11 | 13 | 61 | 58 | 47 |
| West Ham United | 42 | 16 | 14 | 12 | 55 | 53 | 46 |
| West Bromwich Albion | 42 | 18 | 9 | 15 | 63 | 58 | 45 |
| Tottenham Hotspur | 42 | 15 | 14 | 13 | 56 | 43 | 44 |
| Leicester City | 42 | 16 | 11 | 15 | 60 | 57 | 43 |
| Coventry City | 42 | 14 | 13 | 15 | 59 | 52 | 41 |
| Fulham | 42 | 15 | 10 | 17 | 47 | 46 | 40 |
| Barnsley | 42 | 15 | 10 | 17 | 62 | 64 | 40 |
| Luton Town | 42 | 14 | 12 | 16 | 56 | 59 | 40 |
| Bradford Park Avenue | 42 | 16 | 8 | 18 | 68 | 72 | 40 |
| Brentford | 42 | 13 | 14 | 15 | 44 | 61 | 40 |
| Chesterfield | 42 | 16 | 7 | 19 | 54 | 55 | 39 |
| Plymouth Argyle | 42 | 9 | 20 | 13 | 40 | 58 | 38 |
| Leeds United | 42 | 14 | 8 | 20 | 62 | 72 | 36 |
| Nottingham Forest | 42 | 12 | 11 | 19 | 54 | 60 | 35 |
| Bury | 42 | 9 | 16 | 17 | 58 | 68 | 34 |
| *Doncaster Rovers* | *42* | *9* | *11* | *22* | *40* | *66* | *29* |
| *Millwall* | *42* | *9* | *11* | *22* | *44* | *74* | *29* |

## DIVISION THREE (N) 1947-48

| | | | | | | | |
|---|---|---|---|---|---|---|---|
| **Lincoln City** | 42 | 26 | 8 | 8 | 81 | 40 | 60 |
| Rotherham United | 42 | 25 | 9 | 8 | 95 | 49 | 59 |
| Wrexham | 42 | 21 | 8 | 13 | 74 | 54 | 50 |
| Gateshead | 42 | 19 | 11 | 12 | 75 | 57 | 49 |
| Hull City | 42 | 18 | 11 | 13 | 59 | 48 | 47 |
| Accrington Stanley | 42 | 20 | 6 | 16 | 62 | 59 | 46 |
| Barrow | 42 | 16 | 13 | 13 | 49 | 40 | 45 |
| Mansfield Town | 42 | 17 | 11 | 14 | 57 | 51 | 45 |
| Carlisle United | 42 | 18 | 7 | 17 | 88 | 77 | 43 |
| Crewe Alexandra | 42 | 18 | 7 | 17 | 61 | 63 | 43 |
| Oldham Athletic | 42 | 14 | 13 | 15 | 63 | 64 | 41 |
| Rochdale | 42 | 15 | 11 | 16 | 48 | 72 | 41 |
| York City | 42 | 13 | 14 | 15 | 65 | 60 | 40 |
| Bradford City | 42 | 15 | 10 | 17 | 65 | 66 | 40 |
| Southport | 42 | 14 | 11 | 17 | 60 | 63 | 39 |
| Darlington | 42 | 13 | 13 | 16 | 54 | 70 | 39 |
| Stockport County | 42 | 13 | 12 | 17 | 63 | 67 | 38 |
| Tranmere Rovers | 42 | 16 | 4 | 22 | 54 | 72 | 36 |
| Hartlepools United | 42 | 14 | 8 | 20 | 51 | 73 | 36 |
| Chester | 42 | 13 | 9 | 20 | 64 | 67 | 35 |
| Halifax Town | 42 | 7 | 13 | 22 | 43 | 76 | 27 |
| New Brighton | 42 | 8 | 9 | 25 | 38 | 81 | 25 |

## DIVISION THREE (S) 1947-48

| | | | | | | | |
|---|---|---|---|---|---|---|---|
| **Queen's Park Rangers** | 42 | 26 | 9 | 7 | 74 | 37 | 61 |
| Bournemouth & Boscombe Ath. | 42 | 24 | 9 | 9 | 76 | 35 | 57 |
| Walsall | 42 | 21 | 9 | 12 | 70 | 40 | 51 |
| Ipswich Town | 42 | 23 | 3 | 16 | 67 | 61 | 49 |
| Swansea Town | 42 | 18 | 12 | 12 | 70 | 52 | 48 |
| Notts County | 42 | 19 | 8 | 15 | 68 | 59 | 46 |
| Bristol City | 42 | 18 | 7 | 17 | 77 | 65 | 43 |
| Port Vale | 42 | 16 | 11 | 15 | 63 | 54 | 43 |
| Southend United | 42 | 15 | 13 | 14 | 51 | 58 | 43 |
| Reading | 42 | 15 | 11 | 16 | 56 | 58 | 41 |
| Exeter City | 42 | 15 | 11 | 16 | 55 | 63 | 41 |
| Newport County | 42 | 14 | 13 | 15 | 61 | 73 | 41 |
| Crystal Palace | 42 | 13 | 13 | 16 | 49 | 49 | 39 |
| Northampton Town | 42 | 14 | 11 | 17 | 58 | 72 | 39 |
| Watford | 42 | 14 | 10 | 18 | 57 | 79 | 38 |
| Swindon Town | 42 | 10 | 16 | 16 | 41 | 46 | 36 |
| Leyton Orient | 42 | 13 | 10 | 19 | 51 | 73 | 36 |
| Torquay United | 42 | 11 | 13 | 18 | 63 | 62 | 35 |
| Aldershot | 42 | 10 | 15 | 17 | 45 | 67 | 35 |
| Bristol Rovers | 42 | 13 | 8 | 21 | 71 | 75 | 34 |
| Norwich City | 42 | 13 | 8 | 21 | 61 | 76 | 34 |
| Brighton & Hove Albion | 42 | 11 | 12 | 19 | 43 | 73 | 34 |

## 1948 F.A. Cup

**Semi-finals**

| | |
|---|---|
| Derby County vs Manchester United | 1-3 |
| Blackpool vs Tottenham Hotspur | 3-1 |

**Final**

Wembley, 24th April 1948

**Manchester United 4**   (Rowley 2, Pearson, Anderson)

**Blackpool 2**   (Shimwell (pen), Mortensen)

*Attendance 99,000*

## DIVISION ONE 1948-49

| | | | | | | | |
|---|---|---|---|---|---|---|---|
| **PORTSMOUTH** | 42 | 25 | 8 | 9 | 84 | 42 | 58 |
| Manchester United | 42 | 21 | 11 | 10 | 77 | 44 | 53 |
| Derby County | 42 | 22 | 9 | 11 | 74 | 55 | 53 |
| Newcastle United | 42 | 20 | 12 | 10 | 70 | 56 | 52 |
| Arsenal | 42 | 18 | 13 | 11 | 74 | 44 | 49 |
| Wolverhampton Wanderers | 42 | 17 | 12 | 13 | 79 | 66 | 46 |
| Manchester City | 42 | 15 | 15 | 12 | 47 | 51 | 45 |
| Sunderland | 42 | 13 | 17 | 12 | 49 | 58 | 43 |
| Charlton Athletic | 42 | 15 | 12 | 15 | 63 | 67 | 42 |
| Aston Villa | 42 | 16 | 10 | 16 | 60 | 76 | 42 |
| Stoke City | 42 | 16 | 9 | 17 | 66 | 68 | 41 |
| Liverpool | 42 | 13 | 14 | 15 | 53 | 43 | 40 |
| Chelsea | 42 | 12 | 14 | 16 | 69 | 68 | 38 |
| Bolton Wanderers | 42 | 14 | 10 | 18 | 59 | 68 | 38 |
| Burnley | 42 | 12 | 14 | 16 | 43 | 50 | 38 |
| Blackpool | 42 | 11 | 16 | 15 | 54 | 67 | 38 |
| Birmingham City | 42 | 11 | 15 | 16 | 36 | 38 | 37 |
| Everton | 42 | 13 | 11 | 18 | 41 | 63 | 37 |
| Middlesbrough | 42 | 11 | 12 | 19 | 46 | 57 | 34 |
| Huddersfield Town | 42 | 12 | 10 | 20 | 40 | 69 | 34 |
| *Preston North End* | *42* | *11* | *11* | *20* | *62* | *75* | *33* |
| *Sheffield United* | *42* | *11* | *11* | *20* | *57* | *78* | *33* |

## DIVISION TWO 1948-49

| | | | | | | | |
|---|---|---|---|---|---|---|---|
| **Fulham** | 42 | 24 | 9 | 9 | 77 | 37 | 57 |
| **West Bromwich Albion** | 42 | 24 | 8 | 10 | 69 | 39 | 56 |
| Southampton | 42 | 23 | 9 | 10 | 69 | 36 | 55 |
| Cardiff City | 42 | 19 | 13 | 10 | 62 | 47 | 51 |
| Tottenham Hotspur | 42 | 17 | 16 | 9 | 72 | 44 | 50 |
| Chesterfield | 42 | 15 | 17 | 10 | 51 | 45 | 47 |
| West Ham United | 42 | 18 | 10 | 14 | 56 | 58 | 46 |
| Sheffield Wednesday | 42 | 15 | 13 | 14 | 63 | 56 | 43 |
| Barnsley | 42 | 14 | 12 | 16 | 62 | 61 | 40 |
| Luton Town | 42 | 14 | 12 | 16 | 55 | 57 | 40 |
| Grimsby Town | 42 | 15 | 10 | 17 | 72 | 76 | 40 |
| Bury | 42 | 17 | 6 | 19 | 67 | 76 | 40 |
| Queen's Park Rangers | 42 | 14 | 11 | 17 | 44 | 62 | 39 |
| Blackburn Rovers | 42 | 15 | 8 | 19 | 53 | 63 | 38 |
| Leeds United | 42 | 12 | 13 | 17 | 55 | 63 | 37 |
| Coventry City | 42 | 15 | 7 | 20 | 55 | 64 | 37 |
| Bradford Park Avenue | 42 | 13 | 11 | 18 | 65 | 78 | 37 |
| Brentford | 42 | 11 | 14 | 17 | 42 | 53 | 36 |
| Leicester City | 42 | 10 | 16 | 16 | 62 | 79 | 36 |
| Plymouth Argyle | 42 | 12 | 12 | 18 | 49 | 64 | 36 |
| *Nottingham Forest* | *42* | *14* | *7* | *21* | *50* | *54* | *35* |
| *Lincoln City* | *42* | *8* | *12* | *22* | *53* | *91* | *28* |

## DIVISION THREE (N) 1948-49

| | | | | | | | |
|---|---|---|---|---|---|---|---|
| **Hull City** | 42 | 27 | 11 | 4 | 93 | 28 | 65 |
| Rotherham United | 42 | 28 | 6 | 8 | 90 | 46 | 62 |
| Doncaster Rovers | 42 | 20 | 10 | 12 | 53 | 40 | 50 |
| Darlington | 42 | 20 | 6 | 16 | 83 | 74 | 46 |
| Gateshead | 42 | 16 | 13 | 13 | 69 | 58 | 45 |
| Oldham Athletic | 42 | 18 | 9 | 15 | 75 | 67 | 45 |
| Rochdale | 42 | 18 | 9 | 15 | 55 | 53 | 45 |
| Stockport County | 42 | 16 | 11 | 15 | 61 | 56 | 43 |
| Wrexham | 42 | 17 | 9 | 16 | 56 | 62 | 43 |
| Mansfield Town | 42 | 14 | 14 | 14 | 52 | 48 | 42 |
| Tranmere Rovers | 42 | 13 | 15 | 14 | 46 | 57 | 41 |
| Crewe Alexandra | 42 | 16 | 9 | 17 | 52 | 74 | 41 |
| Barrow | 42 | 14 | 12 | 16 | 41 | 48 | 40 |
| York City | 42 | 15 | 9 | 18 | 74 | 74 | 39 |
| Carlisle United | 42 | 14 | 11 | 17 | 60 | 77 | 39 |
| Hartlepools United | 42 | 14 | 10 | 18 | 45 | 58 | 38 |
| New Brighton | 42 | 14 | 8 | 20 | 46 | 58 | 36 |
| Chester | 42 | 11 | 13 | 18 | 57 | 56 | 35 |
| Halifax Town | 42 | 12 | 11 | 19 | 45 | 62 | 35 |
| Accrington Stanley | 42 | 12 | 10 | 20 | 55 | 64 | 34 |
| Southport | 42 | 11 | 9 | 22 | 45 | 64 | 31 |
| Bradford City | 42 | 10 | 9 | 23 | 48 | 77 | 29 |

## DIVISION THREE (S) 1948-49

| | | | | | | | |
|---|---|---|---|---|---|---|---|
| **Swansea Town** | 42 | 27 | 8 | 7 | 87 | 34 | 62 |
| Reading | 42 | 25 | 5 | 12 | 77 | 50 | 55 |
| Bournemouth & Boscombe Ath. | 42 | 22 | 8 | 12 | 69 | 48 | 52 |
| Swindon Town | 42 | 18 | 15 | 9 | 64 | 56 | 51 |
| Bristol Rovers | 42 | 19 | 10 | 13 | 61 | 51 | 48 |
| Brighton & Hove Albion | 42 | 15 | 18 | 9 | 55 | 55 | 48 |
| Ipswich Town | 42 | 18 | 9 | 15 | 78 | 77 | 45 |
| Millwall | 42 | 17 | 11 | 14 | 63 | 64 | 45 |
| Torquay United | 42 | 17 | 11 | 14 | 65 | 70 | 45 |
| Norwich City | 42 | 16 | 12 | 14 | 67 | 49 | 44 |
| Notts County | 42 | 19 | 5 | 18 | 102 | 68 | 43 |
| Exeter City | 42 | 15 | 10 | 17 | 63 | 76 | 40 |
| Port Vale | 42 | 14 | 11 | 17 | 51 | 54 | 39 |
| Walsall | 42 | 15 | 8 | 19 | 56 | 64 | 38 |
| Newport County | 42 | 14 | 9 | 19 | 68 | 92 | 37 |
| Bristol City | 42 | 11 | 14 | 17 | 44 | 62 | 36 |
| Watford | 42 | 10 | 15 | 17 | 41 | 54 | 35 |
| Southend United | 42 | 9 | 16 | 17 | 41 | 46 | 34 |
| Leyton Orient | 42 | 11 | 12 | 19 | 58 | 80 | 34 |
| Northampton Town | 42 | 12 | 9 | 21 | 51 | 62 | 33 |
| Aldershot | 42 | 11 | 11 | 20 | 48 | 59 | 33 |
| Crystal Palace | 42 | 8 | 11 | 23 | 38 | 76 | 27 |

## 1949 F.A. Cup

**Semi-finals**

| | |
|---|---|
| Manchester Utd. vs Wolverhampton Wanderers | 1-1, 0-1 |
| Leicester City vs Portsmouth | 3-1 |

**Final**

Wembley, 30th April 1949

**Wolverhampton Wanderers 3**  (Pye 2, Smyth)
**Leicester City 1**  (Griffiths)

*Attendance 99,500*

## DIVISION ONE 1949-50

| | | | | | | | |
|---|---|---|---|---|---|---|---|
| **PORTSMOUTH** | 42 | 22 | 9 | 11 | 74 | 38 | 53 |
| Wolverhampton Wanderers | 42 | 20 | 13 | 9 | 76 | 49 | 53 |
| Sunderland | 42 | 21 | 10 | 11 | 83 | 62 | 52 |
| Manchester United | 42 | 18 | 14 | 10 | 69 | 44 | 50 |
| Newcastle United | 42 | 19 | 12 | 11 | 77 | 55 | 50 |
| Arsenal | 42 | 19 | 11 | 12 | 79 | 55 | 49 |
| Blackpool | 42 | 17 | 15 | 10 | 46 | 35 | 49 |
| Liverpool | 42 | 17 | 14 | 11 | 64 | 54 | 48 |
| Middlesbrough | 42 | 20 | 7 | 15 | 59 | 48 | 47 |
| Burnley | 42 | 16 | 13 | 13 | 40 | 40 | 45 |
| Derby County | 42 | 17 | 10 | 15 | 69 | 61 | 44 |
| Aston Villa | 42 | 15 | 12 | 15 | 61 | 61 | 42 |
| Chelsea | 42 | 12 | 16 | 14 | 58 | 65 | 40 |
| West Bromwich Albion | 42 | 14 | 12 | 16 | 47 | 53 | 40 |
| Huddersfield Town | 42 | 14 | 9 | 19 | 52 | 73 | 37 |
| Bolton Wanderers | 42 | 10 | 14 | 18 | 45 | 59 | 34 |
| Fulham | 42 | 10 | 14 | 18 | 41 | 54 | 34 |
| Everton | 42 | 10 | 14 | 18 | 42 | 66 | 34 |
| Stoke City | 42 | 11 | 12 | 19 | 45 | 75 | 34 |
| Charlton Athletic | 42 | 13 | 6 | 23 | 53 | 65 | 32 |
| *Manchester City* | *42* | *8* | *13* | *21* | *36* | *68* | *29* |
| *Birmingham City* | *42* | *7* | *14* | *21* | *31* | *67* | *28* |

## DIVISION THREE (N) 1949-50

| | | | | | | | |
|---|---|---|---|---|---|---|---|
| **Doncaster Rovers** | 42 | 19 | 17 | 6 | 66 | 38 | 55 |
| Gateshead | 42 | 23 | 7 | 12 | 87 | 54 | 53 |
| Rochdale | 42 | 21 | 9 | 12 | 68 | 41 | 51 |
| Lincoln City | 42 | 21 | 9 | 12 | 60 | 39 | 51 |
| Tranmere Rovers | 42 | 19 | 11 | 12 | 51 | 48 | 49 |
| Rotherham United | 42 | 19 | 10 | 13 | 80 | 59 | 48 |
| Crewe Alexandra | 42 | 17 | 14 | 11 | 68 | 55 | 48 |
| Mansfield Town | 42 | 18 | 12 | 12 | 66 | 54 | 48 |
| Carlisle United | 42 | 16 | 15 | 11 | 68 | 51 | 47 |
| Stockport County | 42 | 19 | 7 | 16 | 55 | 52 | 45 |
| Oldham Athletic | 42 | 16 | 11 | 15 | 58 | 63 | 43 |
| Chester | 42 | 17 | 6 | 19 | 70 | 79 | 40 |
| Accrington Stanley | 42 | 16 | 7 | 19 | 57 | 62 | 39 |
| New Brighton | 42 | 14 | 10 | 18 | 45 | 63 | 38 |
| Barrow | 42 | 14 | 9 | 19 | 47 | 53 | 37 |
| Southport | 42 | 12 | 13 | 17 | 51 | 71 | 37 |
| Darlington | 42 | 11 | 13 | 18 | 56 | 69 | 35 |
| Hartlepools United | 42 | 14 | 5 | 23 | 52 | 79 | 33 |
| Bradford City | 42 | 12 | 8 | 22 | 61 | 76 | 32 |
| Wrexham | 42 | 10 | 12 | 20 | 39 | 54 | 32 |
| Halifax Town | 42 | 12 | 8 | 22 | 58 | 85 | 32 |
| York City | 42 | 9 | 13 | 20 | 52 | 70 | 31 |

## DIVISION TWO 1949-50

| | | | | | | | |
|---|---|---|---|---|---|---|---|
| **Tottenham Hotspur** | 42 | 27 | 7 | 8 | 81 | 35 | 61 |
| **Sheffield Wednesday** | 42 | 18 | 16 | 8 | 67 | 48 | 52 |
| Sheffield United | 42 | 19 | 14 | 9 | 68 | 49 | 52 |
| Southampton | 42 | 19 | 14 | 9 | 64 | 48 | 52 |
| Leeds United | 42 | 17 | 13 | 12 | 54 | 45 | 47 |
| Preston North End | 42 | 18 | 9 | 15 | 60 | 49 | 45 |
| Hull City | 42 | 17 | 11 | 14 | 64 | 72 | 45 |
| Swansea Town | 42 | 17 | 9 | 16 | 53 | 49 | 43 |
| Brentford | 42 | 15 | 13 | 14 | 44 | 49 | 43 |
| Cardiff City | 42 | 16 | 10 | 16 | 41 | 44 | 42 |
| Grimsby Town | 42 | 16 | 8 | 18 | 74 | 73 | 40 |
| Coventry City | 42 | 13 | 13 | 16 | 55 | 55 | 39 |
| Barnsley | 42 | 13 | 13 | 16 | 64 | 67 | 39 |
| Chesterfield | 42 | 15 | 9 | 18 | 43 | 47 | 39 |
| Leicester City | 42 | 12 | 15 | 15 | 55 | 65 | 39 |
| Blackburn Rovers | 42 | 14 | 10 | 18 | 55 | 60 | 38 |
| Luton Town | 42 | 10 | 18 | 14 | 41 | 51 | 38 |
| Bury | 42 | 14 | 9 | 19 | 60 | 65 | 37 |
| West Ham United | 42 | 12 | 12 | 18 | 53 | 61 | 36 |
| Queen's Park Rangers | 42 | 11 | 12 | 19 | 40 | 57 | 34 |
| *Plymouth Argyle* | *42* | *8* | *16* | *18* | *44* | *65* | *32* |
| *Bradford Park Avenue* | *42* | *10* | *11* | *21* | *51* | *77* | *31* |

## DIVISION THREE (S) 1949-50

| | | | | | | | |
|---|---|---|---|---|---|---|---|
| **Notts County** | 42 | 25 | 8 | 9 | 95 | 50 | 58 |
| Northampton Town | 42 | 20 | 11 | 11 | 72 | 50 | 51 |
| Southend United | 42 | 19 | 13 | 10 | 66 | 48 | 51 |
| Nottingham Forest | 42 | 20 | 9 | 13 | 67 | 39 | 49 |
| Torquay United | 42 | 19 | 10 | 13 | 66 | 63 | 48 |
| Watford | 42 | 16 | 13 | 13 | 45 | 35 | 45 |
| Crystal Palace | 42 | 15 | 14 | 13 | 55 | 54 | 44 |
| Brighton & Hove Albion | 42 | 16 | 12 | 14 | 57 | 69 | 44 |
| Bristol Rovers | 42 | 19 | 5 | 18 | 51 | 51 | 43 |
| Reading | 42 | 17 | 8 | 17 | 70 | 64 | 42 |
| Norwich City | 42 | 16 | 10 | 16 | 65 | 63 | 42 |
| Bournemouth & Boscombe Ath. | 42 | 16 | 10 | 16 | 57 | 56 | 42 |
| Port Vale | 42 | 15 | 11 | 16 | 47 | 42 | 41 |
| Swindon Town | 42 | 15 | 11 | 16 | 59 | 62 | 41 |
| Bristol City | 42 | 15 | 10 | 17 | 60 | 61 | 40 |
| Exeter City | 42 | 14 | 11 | 17 | 63 | 75 | 39 |
| Ipswich Town | 42 | 12 | 11 | 19 | 57 | 86 | 35 |
| Leyton Orient | 42 | 12 | 11 | 19 | 53 | 85 | 35 |
| Walsall | 42 | 9 | 16 | 17 | 61 | 62 | 34 |
| Aldershot | 42 | 13 | 8 | 21 | 48 | 60 | 34 |
| Newport County | 42 | 13 | 8 | 21 | 67 | 98 | 34 |
| Millwall | 42 | 14 | 4 | 24 | 55 | 63 | 32 |

## 1950 F.A. Cup

**Semi-final**

| | |
|---|---|
| Arsenal vs Chelsea | 2-2, 1-0 |
| Liverpool vs Everton | 2-0 |

**Final**

Wembley, 29th April 1950

**Arsenal 2**    (Lewis 2)

**Liverpool 0**

*Attendance 100,000*

## DIVISION ONE 1950-51

| | | | | | | | |
|---|---|---|---|---|---|---|---|
| TOTTENHAM HOTSPUR | 42 | 25 | 10 | 7 | 82 | 44 | 60 |
| Manchester United | 42 | 24 | 8 | 10 | 74 | 40 | 56 |
| Blackpool | 42 | 20 | 10 | 12 | 79 | 53 | 50 |
| Newcastle United | 42 | 18 | 13 | 11 | 62 | 53 | 49 |
| Arsenal | 42 | 19 | 9 | 14 | 73 | 56 | 47 |
| Middlesbrough | 42 | 18 | 11 | 13 | 76 | 65 | 47 |
| Portsmouth | 42 | 16 | 15 | 11 | 71 | 68 | 47 |
| Bolton Wanderers | 42 | 19 | 7 | 16 | 64 | 61 | 45 |
| Liverpool | 42 | 16 | 11 | 15 | 53 | 59 | 43 |
| Burnley | 42 | 14 | 14 | 14 | 48 | 43 | 42 |
| Derby County | 42 | 16 | 8 | 18 | 81 | 75 | 40 |
| Sunderland | 42 | 12 | 16 | 14 | 63 | 73 | 40 |
| Stoke City | 42 | 13 | 14 | 15 | 50 | 59 | 40 |
| Wolverhampton Wanderers | 42 | 15 | 8 | 19 | 74 | 61 | 38 |
| Aston Villa | 42 | 12 | 13 | 17 | 66 | 68 | 37 |
| West Bromwich Albion | 42 | 13 | 11 | 18 | 53 | 61 | 37 |
| Charlton Athletic | 42 | 14 | 9 | 19 | 63 | 80 | 37 |
| Fulham | 42 | 13 | 11 | 18 | 52 | 68 | 37 |
| Huddersfield Town | 42 | 15 | 6 | 21 | 64 | 92 | 36 |
| Chelsea | 42 | 12 | 8 | 22 | 53 | 65 | 32 |
| *Sheffield Wednesday* | *42* | *12* | *8* | *22* | *64* | *83* | *32* |
| *Everton* | *42* | *12* | *8* | *22* | *48* | *86* | *32* |

## DIVISION TWO 1950-51

| | | | | | | | |
|---|---|---|---|---|---|---|---|
| Preston North End | 42 | 26 | 5 | 11 | 91 | 49 | 57 |
| Manchester City | 42 | 19 | 14 | 9 | 89 | 61 | 52 |
| Cardiff City | 42 | 17 | 16 | 9 | 53 | 45 | 50 |
| Birmingham City | 42 | 20 | 9 | 13 | 64 | 53 | 49 |
| Leeds United | 42 | 20 | 8 | 14 | 63 | 55 | 48 |
| Blackburn Rovers | 42 | 19 | 8 | 15 | 65 | 66 | 46 |
| Coventry City | 42 | 19 | 7 | 16 | 75 | 59 | 45 |
| Sheffield United | 42 | 16 | 12 | 14 | 72 | 62 | 44 |
| Brentford | 42 | 18 | 8 | 16 | 75 | 74 | 44 |
| Hull City | 42 | 16 | 11 | 15 | 74 | 70 | 43 |
| Doncaster Rovers | 42 | 15 | 13 | 14 | 64 | 68 | 43 |
| Southampton | 42 | 15 | 13 | 14 | 66 | 73 | 43 |
| West Ham United | 42 | 16 | 10 | 16 | 68 | 69 | 42 |
| Leicester City | 42 | 15 | 11 | 16 | 68 | 58 | 41 |
| Barnsley | 42 | 15 | 10 | 17 | 74 | 68 | 40 |
| Queen's Park Rangers | 42 | 15 | 10 | 17 | 71 | 82 | 40 |
| Notts County | 42 | 13 | 13 | 16 | 61 | 60 | 39 |
| Swansea Town | 42 | 16 | 4 | 22 | 54 | 77 | 36 |
| Luton Town | 42 | 9 | 14 | 19 | 57 | 70 | 32 |
| Bury | 42 | 12 | 8 | 22 | 60 | 86 | 32 |
| *Chesterfield* | *42* | *9* | *12* | *21* | *44* | *69* | *30* |
| *Grimsby Town* | *42* | *8* | *12* | *22* | *61* | *95* | *28* |

## DIVISION THREE (N) 1950-51

| | | | | | | | |
|---|---|---|---|---|---|---|---|
| Rotherham United | 46 | 31 | 9 | 6 | 103 | 41 | 71 |
| Mansfield Town | 46 | 26 | 12 | 8 | 78 | 48 | 64 |
| Carlisle United | 46 | 25 | 12 | 9 | 79 | 50 | 62 |
| Tranmere Rovers | 46 | 24 | 11 | 11 | 83 | 62 | 59 |
| Lincoln City | 46 | 25 | 8 | 13 | 89 | 58 | 58 |
| Bradford Park Avenue | 46 | 23 | 8 | 15 | 90 | 72 | 54 |
| Bradford City | 46 | 21 | 10 | 15 | 90 | 63 | 52 |
| Gateshead | 46 | 21 | 8 | 17 | 84 | 62 | 50 |
| Crewe Alexandra | 46 | 19 | 10 | 17 | 61 | 60 | 48 |
| Stockport County | 46 | 20 | 8 | 18 | 63 | 63 | 48 |
| Rochdale | 46 | 17 | 11 | 18 | 69 | 62 | 45 |
| Scunthorpe United | 46 | 13 | 18 | 15 | 58 | 57 | 44 |
| Chester | 46 | 17 | 9 | 20 | 62 | 64 | 43 |
| Wrexham | 46 | 15 | 12 | 19 | 55 | 71 | 42 |
| Oldham Athletic | 46 | 16 | 8 | 22 | 73 | 73 | 40 |
| Hartlepools United | 46 | 16 | 7 | 23 | 64 | 66 | 39 |
| York City | 46 | 12 | 15 | 19 | 66 | 77 | 39 |
| Darlington | 46 | 13 | 13 | 20 | 59 | 77 | 39 |
| Barrow | 46 | 16 | 6 | 24 | 51 | 76 | 38 |
| Shrewsbury Town | 46 | 15 | 7 | 24 | 43 | 74 | 37 |
| Southport | 46 | 13 | 10 | 23 | 56 | 72 | 36 |
| Halifax Town | 46 | 11 | 12 | 23 | 50 | 69 | 34 |
| Accrington Stanley | 46 | 11 | 10 | 25 | 42 | 101 | 32 |
| *New Brighton* | *46* | *11* | *8* | *27* | *40* | *90* | *30* |

## DIVISION THREE (S) 1950-51

| | | | | | | | |
|---|---|---|---|---|---|---|---|
| Nottingham Forest | 46 | 30 | 10 | 6 | 110 | 40 | 70 |
| Norwich City | 46 | 25 | 14 | 7 | 82 | 45 | 64 |
| Reading | 46 | 21 | 15 | 10 | 88 | 53 | 57 |
| Plymouth Argyle | 46 | 24 | 9 | 13 | 85 | 55 | 57 |
| Millwall | 46 | 23 | 10 | 13 | 80 | 57 | 56 |
| Bristol Rovers | 46 | 20 | 15 | 11 | 64 | 42 | 55 |
| Southend United | 46 | 21 | 10 | 15 | 92 | 69 | 52 |
| Ipswich Town | 46 | 23 | 6 | 17 | 69 | 58 | 52 |
| Bournemouth & Boscombe Ath. | 46 | 22 | 7 | 17 | 65 | 57 | 51 |
| Bristol City | 46 | 20 | 11 | 15 | 64 | 59 | 51 |
| Newport County | 46 | 19 | 9 | 18 | 77 | 70 | 47 |
| Port Vale | 46 | 16 | 13 | 17 | 60 | 65 | 45 |
| Brighton & Hove Albion | 46 | 13 | 17 | 16 | 71 | 79 | 43 |
| Exeter City | 46 | 18 | 6 | 22 | 62 | 85 | 42 |
| Walsall | 46 | 15 | 10 | 21 | 52 | 62 | 40 |
| Colchester United | 46 | 14 | 12 | 20 | 63 | 76 | 40 |
| Swindon Town | 46 | 18 | 4 | 24 | 55 | 67 | 40 |
| Aldershot | 46 | 15 | 10 | 21 | 56 | 88 | 40 |
| Leyton Orient | 46 | 15 | 8 | 23 | 53 | 75 | 38 |
| Torquay United | 46 | 14 | 9 | 23 | 64 | 81 | 37 |
| Northampton Town | 46 | 10 | 16 | 20 | 55 | 67 | 36 |
| Gillingham | 46 | 13 | 9 | 24 | 69 | 101 | 35 |
| Watford | 46 | 9 | 11 | 26 | 54 | 88 | 29 |
| Crystal Palace | 46 | 8 | 11 | 27 | 33 | 84 | 27 |

## 1951 F.A. Cup

**Semi-final**

| | |
|---|---|
| Newcastle Utd. vs Wolverhampton Wanderers | 0-0, 2-1 |
| Blackpool vs Birmingham City | 0-0, 2-1 |

**Final**

Wembley, 28th April 1951

**Newcastle United 2**  (Milburn 2)

**Blackpool 0**

*Attendance 100,000*

## DIVISION ONE 1951-52

| | | | | | | | |
|---|---|---|---|---|---|---|---|
| **MANCHESTER UNITED** | 42 | 23 | 11 | 8 | 95 | 52 | 57 |
| Tottenham Hotspur | 42 | 22 | 9 | 11 | 76 | 51 | 53 |
| Arsenal | 42 | 21 | 11 | 10 | 80 | 61 | 53 |
| Portsmouth | 42 | 20 | 8 | 14 | 68 | 58 | 48 |
| Bolton Wanderers | 42 | 19 | 10 | 13 | 65 | 61 | 48 |
| Aston Villa | 42 | 19 | 9 | 14 | 79 | 70 | 47 |
| Preston North End | 42 | 17 | 12 | 13 | 74 | 54 | 46 |
| Newcastle United | 42 | 18 | 9 | 15 | 98 | 73 | 45 |
| Blackpool | 42 | 18 | 9 | 15 | 64 | 64 | 45 |
| Charlton Athletic | 42 | 17 | 10 | 15 | 68 | 63 | 44 |
| Liverpool | 42 | 12 | 19 | 11 | 57 | 61 | 43 |
| Sunderland | 42 | 15 | 12 | 15 | 70 | 61 | 42 |
| West Bromwich Albion | 42 | 14 | 13 | 15 | 74 | 77 | 41 |
| Burnley | 42 | 15 | 10 | 17 | 56 | 63 | 40 |
| Manchester City | 42 | 13 | 13 | 16 | 58 | 61 | 39 |
| Wolverhampton Wanderers | 42 | 12 | 14 | 16 | 73 | 73 | 38 |
| Derby County | 42 | 15 | 7 | 20 | 63 | 80 | 37 |
| Middlesbrough | 42 | 15 | 6 | 21 | 64 | 88 | 36 |
| Chelsea | 42 | 14 | 8 | 20 | 52 | 72 | 36 |
| Stoke City | 42 | 12 | 7 | 23 | 49 | 88 | 31 |
| *Huddersfield Town* | 42 | 10 | 8 | 24 | 49 | 82 | 28 |
| *Fulham* | 42 | 8 | 11 | 23 | 58 | 77 | 27 |

## DIVISION TWO 1951-52

| | | | | | | | |
|---|---|---|---|---|---|---|---|
| **Sheffield Wednesday** | 42 | 21 | 11 | 10 | 100 | 66 | 53 |
| **Cardiff City** | 42 | 20 | 11 | 11 | 72 | 54 | 51 |
| Birmingham City | 42 | 21 | 9 | 12 | 67 | 56 | 51 |
| Nottingham Forest | 42 | 18 | 13 | 11 | 77 | 62 | 49 |
| Leicester City | 42 | 19 | 9 | 14 | 78 | 64 | 47 |
| Leeds United | 42 | 18 | 11 | 13 | 59 | 57 | 47 |
| Everton | 42 | 17 | 10 | 15 | 64 | 58 | 44 |
| Luton Town | 42 | 16 | 12 | 14 | 77 | 78 | 44 |
| Rotherham United | 42 | 17 | 8 | 17 | 73 | 71 | 42 |
| Brentford | 42 | 15 | 12 | 15 | 54 | 55 | 42 |
| Sheffield United | 42 | 18 | 5 | 19 | 90 | 76 | 41 |
| West Ham United | 42 | 15 | 11 | 16 | 67 | 77 | 41 |
| Southampton | 42 | 15 | 11 | 16 | 61 | 73 | 41 |
| Blackburn Rovers | 42 | 17 | 6 | 19 | 54 | 63 | 40 |
| Notts County | 42 | 16 | 7 | 19 | 71 | 68 | 39 |
| Doncaster Rovers | 42 | 13 | 12 | 17 | 55 | 60 | 38 |
| Bury | 42 | 15 | 7 | 20 | 67 | 69 | 37 |
| Hull City | 42 | 13 | 11 | 18 | 60 | 70 | 37 |
| Swansea Town | 42 | 12 | 12 | 18 | 72 | 76 | 36 |
| Barnsley | 42 | 11 | 14 | 17 | 59 | 72 | 36 |
| *Coventry City* | 42 | 14 | 6 | 22 | 59 | 82 | 34 |
| *Queen's Park Rangers* | 42 | 11 | 12 | 19 | 52 | 81 | 34 |

## DIVISION THREE (N) 1951-52

| | | | | | | | |
|---|---|---|---|---|---|---|---|
| **Lincoln City** | 46 | 30 | 9 | 7 | 121 | 52 | 69 |
| Grimsby Town | 46 | 29 | 8 | 9 | 96 | 45 | 66 |
| Stockport County | 46 | 23 | 13 | 10 | 74 | 40 | 59 |
| Oldham Athletic | 46 | 24 | 9 | 13 | 90 | 61 | 57 |
| Gateshead | 46 | 21 | 11 | 14 | 66 | 49 | 53 |
| Mansfield Town | 46 | 22 | 8 | 16 | 73 | 60 | 52 |
| Carlisle United | 46 | 19 | 13 | 14 | 62 | 57 | 51 |
| Bradford Park Avenue | 46 | 19 | 12 | 15 | 74 | 64 | 50 |
| Hartlepools United | 46 | 21 | 8 | 17 | 71 | 65 | 50 |
| York City | 46 | 18 | 13 | 15 | 73 | 52 | 49 |
| Tranmere Rovers | 46 | 21 | 6 | 19 | 76 | 71 | 48 |
| Barrow | 46 | 17 | 12 | 17 | 57 | 61 | 46 |
| Chesterfield | 46 | 17 | 11 | 18 | 65 | 66 | 45 |
| Scunthorpe United | 46 | 14 | 16 | 16 | 65 | 74 | 44 |
| Bradford City | 46 | 16 | 10 | 20 | 61 | 68 | 42 |
| Crewe Alexandra | 46 | 17 | 8 | 21 | 63 | 82 | 42 |
| Southport | 46 | 15 | 11 | 20 | 53 | 71 | 41 |
| Wrexham | 46 | 15 | 9 | 22 | 63 | 73 | 39 |
| Chester | 46 | 15 | 9 | 22 | 72 | 85 | 39 |
| Halifax Town | 46 | 14 | 7 | 25 | 61 | 97 | 35 |
| Rochdale | 46 | 11 | 13 | 22 | 47 | 79 | 35 |
| Accrington Stanley | 46 | 10 | 12 | 24 | 61 | 92 | 32 |
| Darlington | 46 | 11 | 9 | 26 | 64 | 103 | 31 |
| Workington | 46 | 11 | 7 | 28 | 50 | 91 | 29 |

## DIVISION THREE (S) 1951-52

| | | | | | | | |
|---|---|---|---|---|---|---|---|
| **Plymouth Argyle** | 46 | 29 | 8 | 9 | 107 | 53 | 66 |
| Reading | 46 | 29 | 3 | 14 | 112 | 60 | 61 |
| Norwich City | 46 | 26 | 9 | 11 | 89 | 50 | 61 |
| Millwall | 46 | 23 | 12 | 11 | 74 | 53 | 58 |
| Brighton & Hove Albion | 46 | 24 | 10 | 12 | 87 | 63 | 58 |
| Newport County | 46 | 21 | 12 | 13 | 77 | 76 | 54 |
| Bristol Rovers | 46 | 20 | 12 | 14 | 89 | 53 | 52 |
| Northampton Town | 46 | 22 | 5 | 19 | 93 | 74 | 49 |
| Southend United | 46 | 19 | 10 | 17 | 75 | 66 | 48 |
| Colchester United | 46 | 17 | 12 | 17 | 56 | 77 | 46 |
| Torquay United | 46 | 17 | 10 | 19 | 86 | 98 | 44 |
| Aldershot | 46 | 18 | 8 | 20 | 78 | 89 | 44 |
| Port Vale | 46 | 14 | 15 | 17 | 50 | 66 | 43 |
| Bournemouth & Boscombe Ath. | 46 | 16 | 10 | 20 | 69 | 75 | 42 |
| Bristol City | 46 | 15 | 12 | 19 | 58 | 69 | 42 |
| Swindon Town | 46 | 14 | 14 | 18 | 51 | 68 | 42 |
| Ipswich Town | 46 | 16 | 9 | 21 | 63 | 74 | 41 |
| Leyton Orient | 46 | 16 | 9 | 21 | 55 | 68 | 41 |
| Crystal Palace | 46 | 15 | 9 | 22 | 61 | 80 | 39 |
| Shrewsbury Town | 46 | 13 | 10 | 23 | 62 | 86 | 36 |
| Watford | 46 | 13 | 10 | 23 | 57 | 81 | 36 |
| Gillingham | 46 | 11 | 13 | 22 | 71 | 81 | 35 |
| Exeter City | 46 | 13 | 9 | 24 | 65 | 86 | 35 |
| Walsall | 46 | 13 | 5 | 28 | 55 | 94 | 31 |

## 1952 F.A. Cup

**Semi-finals**

| | |
|---|---|
| Newcastle United vs Blackburn Rovers | 0-0, 2-1 |
| Arsenal vs Chelsea | 1-1, 3-0 |

**Final**

Wembley, 3rd May 1952

**Newcastle United 1**  (G. Robledo)

**Arsenal 0**

*Attendance 100,000*

## DIVISION ONE 1952-53

| | | | | | | | |
|---|---|---|---|---|---|---|---|
| **ARSENAL** | 42 | 21 | 12 | 9 | 97 | 64 | 54 |
| Preston North End | 42 | 21 | 12 | 9 | 85 | 60 | 54 |
| Wolverhampton Wanderers | 42 | 19 | 13 | 10 | 86 | 63 | 51 |
| West Bromwich Albion | 42 | 21 | 8 | 13 | 66 | 60 | 50 |
| Charlton Athletic | 42 | 19 | 11 | 12 | 77 | 63 | 49 |
| Burnley | 42 | 18 | 12 | 12 | 67 | 52 | 48 |
| Blackpool | 42 | 19 | 9 | 14 | 71 | 70 | 47 |
| Manchester United | 42 | 18 | 10 | 14 | 69 | 72 | 46 |
| Sunderland | 42 | 15 | 13 | 14 | 68 | 82 | 43 |
| Tottenham Hotspur | 42 | 15 | 11 | 16 | 78 | 69 | 41 |
| Aston Villa | 42 | 14 | 13 | 15 | 63 | 61 | 41 |
| Cardiff City | 42 | 14 | 12 | 16 | 54 | 46 | 40 |
| Middlesbrough | 42 | 14 | 11 | 17 | 70 | 77 | 39 |
| Bolton Wanderers | 42 | 15 | 9 | 18 | 61 | 69 | 39 |
| Portsmouth | 42 | 14 | 10 | 18 | 74 | 83 | 38 |
| Newcastle United | 42 | 14 | 9 | 19 | 59 | 70 | 37 |
| Liverpool | 42 | 14 | 8 | 20 | 61 | 82 | 36 |
| Sheffield Wednesday | 42 | 12 | 11 | 19 | 62 | 72 | 35 |
| Chelsea | 42 | 12 | 11 | 19 | 56 | 66 | 35 |
| Manchester City | 42 | 14 | 7 | 21 | 72 | 87 | 35 |
| *Stoke City* | 42 | 12 | 10 | 20 | 53 | 66 | 34 |
| *Derby County* | 42 | 11 | 10 | 21 | 59 | 74 | 32 |

## DIVISION THREE (N) 1952-53

| | | | | | | | |
|---|---|---|---|---|---|---|---|
| **Oldham Athletic** | 46 | 22 | 15 | 9 | 77 | 45 | 59 |
| Port Vale | 46 | 20 | 18 | 8 | 67 | 35 | 58 |
| Wrexham | 46 | 24 | 8 | 14 | 86 | 66 | 56 |
| York City | 46 | 20 | 13 | 13 | 60 | 45 | 53 |
| Grimsby Town | 46 | 21 | 10 | 15 | 75 | 59 | 52 |
| Southport | 46 | 20 | 11 | 15 | 63 | 60 | 51 |
| Bradford Park Avenue | 46 | 19 | 12 | 15 | 75 | 61 | 50 |
| Gateshead | 46 | 17 | 15 | 14 | 76 | 60 | 49 |
| Carlisle United | 46 | 18 | 13 | 15 | 82 | 68 | 49 |
| Crewe Alexandra | 46 | 20 | 8 | 18 | 70 | 68 | 48 |
| Stockport County | 46 | 17 | 13 | 16 | 82 | 69 | 47 |
| Chesterfield | 46 | 18 | 11 | 17 | 65 | 63 | 47 |
| Tranmere Rovers | 46 | 21 | 5 | 20 | 65 | 63 | 47 |
| Halifax Town | 46 | 16 | 15 | 15 | 68 | 68 | 47 |
| Scunthorpe United | 46 | 16 | 14 | 16 | 62 | 56 | 46 |
| Bradford City | 46 | 14 | 18 | 14 | 75 | 80 | 46 |
| Hartlepools United | 46 | 16 | 14 | 16 | 57 | 61 | 46 |
| Mansfield Town | 46 | 16 | 14 | 16 | 55 | 62 | 46 |
| Barrow | 46 | 16 | 12 | 18 | 66 | 71 | 44 |
| Chester | 46 | 11 | 15 | 20 | 64 | 85 | 37 |
| Darlington | 46 | 14 | 6 | 26 | 58 | 96 | 34 |
| Rochdale | 46 | 14 | 5 | 27 | 62 | 83 | 33 |
| Workington | 46 | 11 | 10 | 25 | 55 | 91 | 32 |
| Accrington Stanley | 46 | 8 | 11 | 27 | 39 | 89 | 27 |

## DIVISION TWO 1952-53

| | | | | | | | |
|---|---|---|---|---|---|---|---|
| **Sheffield United** | 42 | 25 | 10 | 7 | 97 | 55 | 60 |
| **Huddersfield Town** | 42 | 24 | 10 | 8 | 84 | 33 | 58 |
| Luton Town | 42 | 22 | 8 | 12 | 84 | 49 | 52 |
| Plymouth Argyle | 42 | 20 | 9 | 13 | 65 | 60 | 49 |
| Leicester City | 42 | 18 | 12 | 12 | 89 | 74 | 48 |
| Birmingham City | 42 | 19 | 10 | 13 | 71 | 66 | 48 |
| Nottingham Forest | 42 | 18 | 8 | 16 | 77 | 67 | 44 |
| Fulham | 42 | 17 | 10 | 15 | 81 | 71 | 44 |
| Blackburn Rovers | 42 | 18 | 8 | 16 | 68 | 65 | 44 |
| Leeds United | 42 | 14 | 15 | 13 | 71 | 63 | 43 |
| Swansea Town | 42 | 15 | 12 | 15 | 78 | 81 | 42 |
| Rotherham United | 42 | 16 | 9 | 17 | 75 | 74 | 41 |
| Doncaster Rovers | 42 | 12 | 16 | 14 | 58 | 64 | 40 |
| West Ham United | 42 | 13 | 13 | 16 | 58 | 60 | 39 |
| Lincoln City | 42 | 11 | 17 | 14 | 64 | 71 | 39 |
| Everton | 42 | 12 | 14 | 16 | 71 | 75 | 38 |
| Brentford | 42 | 13 | 11 | 18 | 59 | 76 | 37 |
| Hull City | 42 | 14 | 8 | 20 | 57 | 69 | 36 |
| Notts County | 42 | 14 | 8 | 20 | 60 | 88 | 36 |
| Bury | 42 | 13 | 9 | 20 | 53 | 81 | 35 |
| *Southampton* | 42 | 10 | 13 | 19 | 68 | 85 | 33 |
| *Barnsley* | 42 | 5 | 8 | 29 | 47 | 108 | 18 |

## DIVISION THREE (S) 1952-53

| | | | | | | | |
|---|---|---|---|---|---|---|---|
| **Bristol Rovers** | 46 | 26 | 12 | 8 | 92 | 46 | 64 |
| Millwall | 46 | 24 | 14 | 8 | 82 | 44 | 62 |
| Northampton Town | 46 | 26 | 10 | 10 | 109 | 70 | 62 |
| Norwich City | 46 | 25 | 10 | 11 | 99 | 55 | 60 |
| Bristol City | 46 | 22 | 15 | 9 | 95 | 61 | 59 |
| Coventry City | 46 | 19 | 12 | 15 | 77 | 62 | 50 |
| Brighton & Hove Albion | 46 | 19 | 12 | 15 | 81 | 75 | 50 |
| Southend United | 46 | 18 | 13 | 15 | 69 | 74 | 49 |
| Bournemouth & Boscombe Ath. | 46 | 19 | 9 | 18 | 74 | 69 | 47 |
| Watford | 46 | 15 | 17 | 14 | 62 | 63 | 47 |
| Reading | 46 | 19 | 8 | 19 | 69 | 64 | 46 |
| Torquay United | 46 | 18 | 9 | 19 | 87 | 88 | 45 |
| Crystal Palace | 46 | 15 | 13 | 18 | 66 | 82 | 43 |
| Leyton Orient | 46 | 16 | 10 | 20 | 68 | 73 | 42 |
| Newport County | 46 | 16 | 10 | 20 | 70 | 82 | 42 |
| Ipswich Town | 46 | 13 | 15 | 18 | 60 | 69 | 41 |
| Exeter City | 46 | 13 | 14 | 19 | 61 | 71 | 40 |
| Swindon Town | 46 | 14 | 12 | 20 | 64 | 79 | 40 |
| Aldershot | 46 | 12 | 15 | 19 | 61 | 77 | 39 |
| Queen's Park Rangers | 46 | 12 | 15 | 19 | 61 | 82 | 39 |
| Gillingham | 46 | 12 | 15 | 19 | 55 | 74 | 39 |
| Colchester United | 46 | 12 | 14 | 20 | 59 | 76 | 38 |
| Shrewsbury Town | 46 | 12 | 12 | 22 | 68 | 91 | 36 |
| Walsall | 46 | 7 | 10 | 29 | 56 | 118 | 24 |

## 1953 F.A. Cup

**Semi-finals**

| | |
|---|---|
| Blackpool vs Tottenham Hotspur | 2-1 |
| Bolton Wanderers vs Everton | 4-3 |

**Final**

Wembley, 2nd May 1953

**Blackpool 4**   (Mortensen 3, Perry)

**Bolton Wanderers 3**   (Lofthouse, Moir, Bell)

*Attendance 100,000*

## DIVISION ONE 1953-54

| | | | | | | | |
|---|---|---|---|---|---|---|---|
| WOLVERHAMPTON WANDS. | 42 | 25 | 7 | 10 | 96 | 56 | 57 |
| West Bromwich Albion | 42 | 22 | 9 | 11 | 86 | 63 | 53 |
| Huddersfield Town | 42 | 20 | 11 | 11 | 78 | 61 | 51 |
| Manchester United | 42 | 18 | 12 | 12 | 73 | 58 | 48 |
| Bolton Wanderers | 42 | 18 | 12 | 12 | 75 | 60 | 48 |
| Blackpool | 42 | 19 | 10 | 13 | 80 | 69 | 48 |
| Burnley | 42 | 21 | 4 | 17 | 78 | 67 | 46 |
| Chelsea | 42 | 16 | 12 | 14 | 74 | 68 | 44 |
| Charlton Athletic | 42 | 19 | 6 | 17 | 75 | 77 | 44 |
| Cardiff City | 42 | 18 | 8 | 16 | 51 | 71 | 44 |
| Preston North End | 42 | 19 | 5 | 18 | 87 | 58 | 43 |
| Arsenal | 42 | 15 | 13 | 14 | 75 | 73 | 43 |
| Aston Villa | 42 | 16 | 9 | 17 | 70 | 68 | 41 |
| Portsmouth | 42 | 14 | 11 | 17 | 81 | 89 | 39 |
| Newcastle United | 42 | 14 | 10 | 18 | 72 | 77 | 38 |
| Tottenham Hotspur | 42 | 16 | 5 | 21 | 65 | 76 | 37 |
| Manchester City | 42 | 14 | 9 | 19 | 62 | 77 | 37 |
| Sunderland | 42 | 14 | 8 | 20 | 81 | 89 | 36 |
| Sheffield Wednesday | 42 | 15 | 6 | 21 | 70 | 91 | 36 |
| Sheffield United | 42 | 11 | 11 | 20 | 69 | 90 | 33 |
| *Middlesbrough* | *42* | *10* | *10* | *22* | *60* | *91* | *30* |
| *Liverpool* | *42* | *9* | *10* | *23* | *68* | *97* | *28* |

## DIVISION TWO 1953-54

| | | | | | | | |
|---|---|---|---|---|---|---|---|
| Leicester City | 42 | 23 | 10 | 9 | 97 | 60 | 56 |
| Everton | 42 | 20 | 16 | 6 | 92 | 58 | 56 |
| Blackburn Rovers | 42 | 23 | 9 | 10 | 86 | 50 | 55 |
| Nottingham Forest | 42 | 20 | 12 | 10 | 86 | 59 | 52 |
| Rotherham United | 42 | 21 | 7 | 14 | 80 | 67 | 49 |
| Luton Town | 42 | 18 | 12 | 12 | 64 | 59 | 48 |
| Birmingham City | 42 | 18 | 11 | 13 | 78 | 58 | 47 |
| Fulham | 42 | 17 | 10 | 15 | 98 | 85 | 44 |
| Bristol Rovers | 42 | 14 | 16 | 12 | 64 | 58 | 44 |
| Leeds United | 42 | 15 | 13 | 14 | 89 | 81 | 43 |
| Stoke City | 42 | 12 | 17 | 13 | 71 | 60 | 41 |
| Doncaster Rovers | 42 | 16 | 9 | 17 | 59 | 63 | 41 |
| West Ham United | 42 | 15 | 9 | 18 | 67 | 69 | 39 |
| Notts County | 42 | 13 | 13 | 16 | 54 | 74 | 39 |
| Hull City | 42 | 16 | 6 | 20 | 64 | 66 | 38 |
| Lincoln City | 42 | 14 | 9 | 19 | 65 | 83 | 37 |
| Bury | 42 | 11 | 14 | 17 | 54 | 72 | 36 |
| Derby County | 42 | 12 | 11 | 19 | 64 | 82 | 35 |
| Plymouth Argyle | 42 | 9 | 16 | 17 | 65 | 82 | 34 |
| Swansea Town | 42 | 13 | 8 | 21 | 58 | 82 | 34 |
| *Brentford* | *42* | *10* | *11* | *21* | *40* | *78* | *31* |
| *Oldham Athletic* | *42* | *8* | *9* | *25* | *40* | *89* | *25* |

## DIVISION THREE (N) 1953-54

| | | | | | | | |
|---|---|---|---|---|---|---|---|
| Port Vale | 46 | 26 | 17 | 3 | 74 | 21 | 69 |
| Barnsley | 46 | 24 | 10 | 12 | 77 | 57 | 58 |
| Scunthorpe United | 46 | 21 | 15 | 10 | 77 | 56 | 57 |
| Gateshead | 46 | 21 | 13 | 12 | 74 | 55 | 55 |
| Bradford City | 46 | 22 | 9 | 15 | 60 | 55 | 53 |
| Chesterfield | 46 | 19 | 14 | 13 | 76 | 64 | 52 |
| Mansfield Town | 46 | 20 | 11 | 15 | 88 | 67 | 51 |
| Wrexham | 46 | 21 | 9 | 16 | 81 | 68 | 51 |
| Bradford Park Avenue | 46 | 18 | 14 | 14 | 77 | 68 | 50 |
| Stockport County | 46 | 18 | 11 | 17 | 77 | 67 | 47 |
| Southport | 46 | 17 | 12 | 17 | 63 | 60 | 46 |
| Barrow | 46 | 16 | 12 | 18 | 72 | 71 | 44 |
| Carlisle United | 46 | 14 | 15 | 17 | 83 | 71 | 43 |
| Tranmere Rovers | 46 | 18 | 7 | 21 | 59 | 70 | 43 |
| Accrington Stanley | 46 | 16 | 10 | 20 | 66 | 74 | 42 |
| Crewe Alexandra | 46 | 14 | 13 | 19 | 49 | 67 | 41 |
| Grimsby Town | 46 | 16 | 9 | 21 | 51 | 77 | 41 |
| Hartlepools United | 46 | 13 | 14 | 19 | 59 | 65 | 40 |
| Rochdale | 46 | 15 | 10 | 21 | 59 | 77 | 40 |
| Workington | 46 | 13 | 14 | 19 | 59 | 80 | 40 |
| Darlington | 46 | 12 | 14 | 20 | 50 | 71 | 38 |
| York City | 46 | 12 | 13 | 21 | 64 | 86 | 37 |
| Halifax Town | 46 | 12 | 10 | 24 | 44 | 73 | 34 |
| Chester | 46 | 11 | 10 | 25 | 48 | 67 | 32 |

## DIVISION THREE (S) 1953-54

| | | | | | | | |
|---|---|---|---|---|---|---|---|
| Ipswich Town | 46 | 27 | 10 | 9 | 82 | 51 | 64 |
| Brighton & Hove Albion | 46 | 26 | 9 | 11 | 86 | 61 | 61 |
| Bristol City | 46 | 25 | 6 | 15 | 88 | 66 | 56 |
| Watford | 46 | 21 | 10 | 15 | 85 | 69 | 52 |
| Northampton Town | 46 | 20 | 11 | 15 | 82 | 55 | 51 |
| Southampton | 46 | 22 | 7 | 17 | 76 | 63 | 51 |
| Norwich City | 46 | 20 | 11 | 15 | 73 | 66 | 51 |
| Reading | 46 | 20 | 9 | 17 | 86 | 73 | 49 |
| Exeter City | 46 | 20 | 8 | 18 | 68 | 58 | 48 |
| Gillingham | 46 | 19 | 10 | 17 | 61 | 66 | 48 |
| Leyton Orient | 46 | 18 | 11 | 17 | 79 | 73 | 47 |
| Millwall | 46 | 19 | 9 | 18 | 74 | 77 | 47 |
| Torquay United | 46 | 17 | 12 | 17 | 81 | 88 | 46 |
| Coventry City | 46 | 18 | 9 | 19 | 61 | 56 | 45 |
| Newport County | 46 | 19 | 6 | 21 | 61 | 81 | 44 |
| Southend United | 46 | 18 | 7 | 21 | 69 | 71 | 43 |
| Aldershot | 46 | 17 | 9 | 20 | 74 | 86 | 43 |
| Queen's Park Rangers | 46 | 16 | 10 | 20 | 60 | 68 | 42 |
| Bournemouth & Boscombe Ath. | 46 | 16 | 8 | 22 | 67 | 70 | 40 |
| Swindon Town | 46 | 15 | 10 | 21 | 67 | 70 | 40 |
| Shrewsbury Town | 46 | 14 | 12 | 20 | 65 | 76 | 40 |
| Crystal Palace | 46 | 14 | 12 | 20 | 60 | 86 | 40 |
| Colchester United | 46 | 10 | 10 | 26 | 50 | 78 | 30 |
| Walsall | 46 | 9 | 8 | 29 | 40 | 87 | 26 |

## 1954 F.A. Cup

### Semi-finals

| | |
|---|---|
| West Bromwich Albion vs Port Vale | 2-1 |
| Sheffield Wednesday vs Preston North End | 0-2 |

### Final

Wembley, 1st May 1954

**West Bromwich Albion 3**   (Allen 2 (1 pen), Griffin)
**Preston North End 2**   (Morrison, Wayman)

*Attendance 100,000*

## DIVISION ONE 1954-55

| | | | | | | | |
|---|---|---|---|---|---|---|---|
| **CHELSEA** | 42 | 20 | 12 | 10 | 81 | 57 | 52 |
| Wolverhampton Wanderers | 42 | 19 | 10 | 13 | 89 | 70 | 48 |
| Portsmouth | 42 | 18 | 12 | 12 | 74 | 62 | 48 |
| Sunderland | 42 | 15 | 18 | 9 | 64 | 54 | 48 |
| Manchester United | 42 | 20 | 7 | 15 | 84 | 74 | 47 |
| Aston Villa | 42 | 20 | 7 | 15 | 72 | 73 | 47 |
| Manchester City | 42 | 18 | 10 | 14 | 76 | 69 | 46 |
| Newcastle United | 42 | 17 | 9 | 16 | 89 | 77 | 43 |
| Arsenal | 42 | 17 | 9 | 16 | 69 | 63 | 43 |
| Burnley | 42 | 17 | 9 | 16 | 51 | 48 | 43 |
| Everton | 42 | 16 | 10 | 16 | 62 | 68 | 42 |
| Huddersfield Town | 42 | 14 | 13 | 15 | 63 | 68 | 41 |
| Sheffield United | 42 | 17 | 7 | 18 | 70 | 86 | 41 |
| Preston North End | 42 | 16 | 8 | 18 | 83 | 64 | 40 |
| Charlton Athletic | 42 | 15 | 10 | 17 | 76 | 75 | 40 |
| Tottenham Hotspur | 42 | 16 | 8 | 18 | 72 | 73 | 40 |
| West Bromwich Albion | 42 | 16 | 8 | 18 | 76 | 96 | 40 |
| Bolton Wanderers | 42 | 13 | 13 | 16 | 62 | 69 | 39 |
| Blackpool | 42 | 14 | 10 | 18 | 60 | 64 | 38 |
| Cardiff City | 42 | 13 | 11 | 18 | 62 | 76 | 37 |
| *Leicester City* | *42* | *12* | *11* | *19* | *74* | *86* | *35* |
| *Sheffield Wednesday* | *42* | *8* | *10* | *24* | *63* | *100* | *26* |

## DIVISION TWO 1954-55

| | | | | | | | |
|---|---|---|---|---|---|---|---|
| **Birmingham City** | 42 | 22 | 10 | 10 | 92 | 47 | 54 |
| **Luton Town** | 42 | 23 | 8 | 11 | 88 | 53 | 54 |
| Rotherham United | 42 | 25 | 4 | 13 | 94 | 64 | 54 |
| Leeds United | 42 | 23 | 7 | 12 | 70 | 53 | 53 |
| Stoke City | 42 | 21 | 10 | 11 | 69 | 46 | 52 |
| Blackburn Rovers | 42 | 22 | 6 | 14 | 114 | 79 | 50 |
| Notts County | 42 | 21 | 6 | 15 | 74 | 71 | 48 |
| West Ham United | 42 | 18 | 10 | 14 | 74 | 70 | 46 |
| Bristol Rovers | 42 | 19 | 7 | 16 | 75 | 70 | 45 |
| Swansea Town | 42 | 17 | 9 | 16 | 86 | 83 | 43 |
| Liverpool | 42 | 16 | 10 | 16 | 92 | 96 | 42 |
| Middlesbrough | 42 | 18 | 6 | 18 | 73 | 82 | 42 |
| Bury | 42 | 15 | 11 | 16 | 77 | 72 | 41 |
| Fulham | 42 | 14 | 11 | 17 | 76 | 79 | 39 |
| Nottingham Forest | 42 | 16 | 7 | 19 | 58 | 62 | 39 |
| Lincoln City | 42 | 13 | 10 | 19 | 68 | 79 | 36 |
| Port Vale | 42 | 12 | 11 | 19 | 48 | 71 | 35 |
| Doncaster Rovers | 42 | 14 | 7 | 21 | 58 | 95 | 35 |
| Hull City | 42 | 12 | 10 | 20 | 44 | 69 | 34 |
| Plymouth Argyle | 42 | 12 | 7 | 23 | 57 | 82 | 31 |
| *Ipswich Town* | *42* | *11* | *6* | *25* | *57* | *92* | *28* |
| *Derby County* | *42* | *7* | *9* | *26* | *53* | *82* | *23* |

## DIVISION THREE (N) 1954-55

| | | | | | | | |
|---|---|---|---|---|---|---|---|
| **Barnsley** | 46 | 30 | 5 | 11 | 86 | 46 | 65 |
| Accrington Stanley | 46 | 25 | 11 | 10 | 96 | 67 | 61 |
| Scunthorpe United | 46 | 23 | 12 | 11 | 81 | 53 | 58 |
| York City | 46 | 24 | 10 | 12 | 92 | 63 | 58 |
| Hartlepools United | 46 | 25 | 5 | 16 | 64 | 49 | 55 |
| Chesterfield | 46 | 24 | 6 | 16 | 81 | 70 | 54 |
| Gateshead | 46 | 20 | 12 | 14 | 65 | 69 | 52 |
| Workington | 46 | 18 | 14 | 14 | 68 | 55 | 50 |
| Stockport County | 46 | 18 | 12 | 16 | 84 | 70 | 48 |
| Oldham Athletic | 46 | 19 | 10 | 17 | 74 | 68 | 48 |
| Southport | 46 | 16 | 16 | 14 | 47 | 44 | 48 |
| Rochdale | 46 | 17 | 14 | 15 | 69 | 66 | 48 |
| Mansfield Town | 46 | 18 | 9 | 19 | 65 | 71 | 45 |
| Halifax Town | 46 | 15 | 13 | 18 | 63 | 67 | 43 |
| Darlington | 46 | 14 | 14 | 18 | 62 | 73 | 42 |
| Bradford Park Avenue | 46 | 15 | 11 | 20 | 56 | 70 | 41 |
| Barrow | 46 | 17 | 6 | 23 | 70 | 89 | 40 |
| Wrexham | 46 | 13 | 12 | 21 | 65 | 77 | 38 |
| Tranmere Rovers | 46 | 13 | 11 | 22 | 55 | 70 | 37 |
| Carlisle United | 46 | 15 | 6 | 25 | 78 | 89 | 36 |
| Bradford City | 46 | 13 | 10 | 23 | 47 | 55 | 36 |
| Crewe Alexandra | 46 | 10 | 14 | 22 | 68 | 91 | 34 |
| Grimsby Town | 46 | 13 | 8 | 25 | 47 | 78 | 34 |
| Chester | 46 | 12 | 9 | 25 | 44 | 77 | 33 |

## DIVISION THREE (S) 1954-55

| | | | | | | | |
|---|---|---|---|---|---|---|---|
| **Bristol City** | 46 | 30 | 10 | 6 | 101 | 47 | 70 |
| Leyton Orient | 46 | 26 | 9 | 11 | 89 | 47 | 61 |
| Southampton | 46 | 24 | 11 | 11 | 75 | 51 | 59 |
| Gillingham | 46 | 20 | 15 | 11 | 77 | 66 | 55 |
| Millwall | 46 | 20 | 11 | 15 | 72 | 68 | 51 |
| Brighton & Hove Albion | 46 | 20 | 10 | 16 | 76 | 63 | 50 |
| Watford | 46 | 18 | 14 | 14 | 71 | 62 | 50 |
| Torquay United | 46 | 18 | 12 | 16 | 82 | 82 | 48 |
| Coventry City | 46 | 18 | 11 | 17 | 67 | 59 | 47 |
| Southend United | 46 | 17 | 12 | 17 | 83 | 80 | 46 |
| Brentford | 46 | 16 | 14 | 16 | 82 | 82 | 46 |
| Norwich City | 46 | 18 | 10 | 18 | 60 | 60 | 46 |
| Northampton Town | 46 | 19 | 8 | 19 | 73 | 81 | 46 |
| Aldershot | 46 | 16 | 13 | 17 | 75 | 71 | 45 |
| Queen's Park Rangers | 46 | 15 | 14 | 17 | 69 | 75 | 44 |
| Shrewsbury Town | 46 | 16 | 10 | 20 | 70 | 78 | 42 |
| Bournemouth & Boscombe Ath. | 46 | 12 | 18 | 16 | 57 | 65 | 42 |
| Reading | 46 | 13 | 15 | 18 | 65 | 73 | 41 |
| Newport County | 46 | 11 | 16 | 19 | 60 | 73 | 38 |
| Crystal Palace | 46 | 11 | 16 | 19 | 52 | 80 | 38 |
| Swindon Town | 46 | 11 | 15 | 20 | 46 | 64 | 37 |
| Exeter City | 46 | 11 | 15 | 20 | 47 | 73 | 37 |
| Walsall | 46 | 10 | 14 | 22 | 75 | 86 | 34 |
| Colchester United | 46 | 9 | 13 | 24 | 53 | 91 | 31 |

## 1955 F.A. Cup

**Semi-finals**

| | |
|---|---|
| Newcastle United vs York City | 1-1, 2-0 |
| Sunderland vs Manchester City | 0-1 |

**Final**

Wembley, 7th May 1955

**Newcastle United 3** (Milburn, Mitchell, Hannah)
**Manchester City 1** (Johnstone)

*Attendance 100,000*

## DIVISION ONE 1955-56

| | | | | | | | |
|---|---|---|---|---|---|---|---|
| **MANCHESTER UNITED** | 42 | 25 | 10 | 7 | 83 | 51 | 60 |
| Blackpool | 42 | 20 | 9 | 13 | 86 | 62 | 49 |
| Wolverhampton Wanderers | 42 | 20 | 9 | 13 | 89 | 65 | 49 |
| Manchester City | 42 | 18 | 10 | 14 | 82 | 69 | 46 |
| Arsenal | 42 | 18 | 10 | 14 | 60 | 61 | 46 |
| Birmingham City | 42 | 18 | 9 | 15 | 75 | 57 | 45 |
| Burnley | 42 | 18 | 8 | 16 | 64 | 54 | 44 |
| Bolton Wanderers | 42 | 18 | 7 | 17 | 71 | 58 | 43 |
| Sunderland | 42 | 17 | 9 | 16 | 80 | 95 | 43 |
| Luton Town | 42 | 17 | 8 | 17 | 66 | 64 | 42 |
| Newcastle United | 42 | 17 | 7 | 18 | 85 | 70 | 41 |
| Portsmouth | 42 | 16 | 9 | 17 | 78 | 85 | 41 |
| West Bromwich Albion | 42 | 18 | 5 | 19 | 58 | 70 | 41 |
| Charlton Athletic | 42 | 17 | 6 | 19 | 75 | 81 | 40 |
| Everton | 42 | 15 | 10 | 17 | 55 | 69 | 40 |
| Chelsea | 42 | 14 | 11 | 17 | 64 | 77 | 39 |
| Cardiff City | 42 | 15 | 9 | 18 | 55 | 69 | 39 |
| Tottenham Hotspur | 42 | 15 | 7 | 20 | 61 | 71 | 37 |
| Preston North End | 42 | 14 | 8 | 20 | 73 | 72 | 36 |
| Aston Villa | 42 | 11 | 13 | 18 | 52 | 69 | 35 |
| *Huddersfield Town* | *42* | *14* | *7* | *21* | *54* | *83* | *35* |
| *Sheffield United* | *42* | *12* | *9* | *21* | *63* | *77* | *33* |

## DIVISION TWO 1955-56

| | | | | | | | |
|---|---|---|---|---|---|---|---|
| **Sheffield Wednesday** | 42 | 21 | 13 | 8 | 101 | 62 | 55 |
| **Leeds United** | 42 | 23 | 6 | 13 | 80 | 60 | 52 |
| Liverpool | 42 | 21 | 6 | 15 | 85 | 63 | 48 |
| Blackburn Rovers | 42 | 21 | 6 | 15 | 84 | 65 | 48 |
| Leicester City | 42 | 21 | 6 | 15 | 94 | 78 | 48 |
| Bristol Rovers | 42 | 21 | 6 | 15 | 84 | 70 | 48 |
| Nottingham Forest | 42 | 19 | 9 | 14 | 68 | 63 | 47 |
| Lincoln City | 42 | 18 | 10 | 14 | 79 | 65 | 46 |
| Fulham | 42 | 20 | 6 | 16 | 89 | 79 | 46 |
| Swansea Town | 42 | 20 | 6 | 16 | 83 | 81 | 46 |
| Bristol City | 42 | 19 | 7 | 16 | 80 | 64 | 45 |
| Port Vale | 42 | 16 | 13 | 13 | 60 | 58 | 45 |
| Stoke City | 42 | 20 | 4 | 18 | 71 | 62 | 44 |
| Middlesbrough | 42 | 16 | 8 | 18 | 76 | 78 | 40 |
| Bury | 42 | 16 | 8 | 18 | 86 | 90 | 40 |
| West Ham United | 42 | 14 | 11 | 17 | 74 | 69 | 39 |
| Doncaster Rovers | 42 | 12 | 11 | 19 | 69 | 96 | 35 |
| Barnsley | 42 | 11 | 12 | 19 | 47 | 84 | 34 |
| Rotherham United | 42 | 12 | 9 | 21 | 56 | 75 | 33 |
| Notts County | 42 | 11 | 9 | 22 | 55 | 82 | 31 |
| *Plymouth Argyle* | *42* | *10* | *8* | *24* | *54* | *87* | *28* |
| *Hull City* | *42* | *10* | *6* | *26* | *53* | *97* | *26* |

## DIVISION THREE (N) 1955-56

| | | | | | | | |
|---|---|---|---|---|---|---|---|
| **Grimsby Town** | 46 | 31 | 6 | 9 | 76 | 29 | 68 |
| Derby County | 46 | 28 | 7 | 11 | 110 | 55 | 63 |
| Accrington Stanley | 46 | 25 | 9 | 12 | 92 | 57 | 59 |
| Hartlepools United | 46 | 26 | 5 | 15 | 81 | 60 | 57 |
| Southport | 46 | 23 | 11 | 12 | 66 | 53 | 57 |
| Chesterfield | 46 | 25 | 4 | 17 | 94 | 66 | 54 |
| Stockport County | 46 | 21 | 9 | 16 | 90 | 61 | 51 |
| Bradford City | 46 | 18 | 13 | 15 | 78 | 64 | 49 |
| Scunthorpe United | 46 | 20 | 8 | 18 | 75 | 63 | 48 |
| Workington | 46 | 19 | 9 | 18 | 75 | 63 | 47 |
| York City | 46 | 19 | 9 | 18 | 85 | 72 | 47 |
| Rochdale | 46 | 17 | 13 | 16 | 66 | 84 | 47 |
| Gateshead | 46 | 17 | 11 | 18 | 77 | 84 | 45 |
| Wrexham | 46 | 16 | 10 | 20 | 66 | 73 | 42 |
| Darlington | 46 | 16 | 9 | 21 | 60 | 73 | 41 |
| Tranmere Rovers | 46 | 16 | 9 | 21 | 59 | 84 | 41 |
| Chester | 46 | 13 | 14 | 19 | 52 | 82 | 40 |
| Mansfield Town | 46 | 14 | 11 | 21 | 84 | 81 | 39 |
| Halifax Town | 46 | 14 | 11 | 21 | 66 | 76 | 39 |
| Oldham Athletic | 46 | 10 | 18 | 18 | 76 | 86 | 38 |
| Carlisle United | 46 | 15 | 8 | 23 | 71 | 95 | 38 |
| Barrow | 46 | 12 | 9 | 25 | 61 | 83 | 33 |
| Bradford Park Avenue | 46 | 13 | 7 | 26 | 61 | 122 | 33 |
| Crewe Alexandra | 46 | 9 | 10 | 27 | 50 | 105 | 28 |

## DIVISION THREE (S) 1955-56

| | | | | | | | |
|---|---|---|---|---|---|---|---|
| **Leyton Orient** | 46 | 29 | 8 | 9 | 106 | 49 | 66 |
| Brighton & Hove Albion | 46 | 29 | 7 | 10 | 112 | 50 | 65 |
| Ipswich Town | 46 | 25 | 14 | 7 | 106 | 60 | 64 |
| Southend United | 46 | 21 | 11 | 14 | 88 | 80 | 53 |
| Torquay United | 46 | 20 | 12 | 14 | 86 | 63 | 52 |
| Brentford | 46 | 19 | 14 | 13 | 69 | 66 | 52 |
| Norwich City | 46 | 19 | 13 | 14 | 86 | 82 | 51 |
| Coventry City | 46 | 20 | 9 | 17 | 73 | 60 | 49 |
| Bournemouth & Boscombe Ath. | 46 | 19 | 10 | 17 | 63 | 51 | 48 |
| Gillingham | 46 | 19 | 10 | 17 | 69 | 71 | 48 |
| Northampton Town | 46 | 20 | 7 | 19 | 67 | 71 | 47 |
| Colchester United | 46 | 18 | 11 | 17 | 76 | 81 | 47 |
| Shrewsbury Town | 46 | 17 | 12 | 17 | 69 | 66 | 46 |
| Southampton | 46 | 18 | 8 | 20 | 91 | 81 | 44 |
| Aldershot | 46 | 12 | 16 | 18 | 70 | 90 | 40 |
| Exeter City | 46 | 15 | 10 | 21 | 58 | 77 | 40 |
| Reading | 46 | 15 | 9 | 22 | 70 | 79 | 39 |
| Queen's Park Rangers | 46 | 14 | 11 | 21 | 64 | 86 | 39 |
| Newport County | 46 | 15 | 9 | 22 | 58 | 79 | 39 |
| Walsall | 46 | 15 | 8 | 23 | 68 | 84 | 38 |
| Watford | 46 | 13 | 11 | 22 | 52 | 85 | 37 |
| Millwall | 46 | 15 | 6 | 25 | 83 | 100 | 36 |
| Crystal Palace | 46 | 12 | 10 | 24 | 54 | 83 | 34 |
| Swindon Town | 46 | 8 | 14 | 24 | 34 | 78 | 30 |

## 1956 F.A. Cup

### Semi-finals

| | |
|---|---|
| Tottenham Hotspur vs Manchester City | 0-1 |
| Birmingham City vs Sunderland | 3-0 |

### Final

Wembley, 5th May 1956

**Manchester City 3** (Hayes, Dyson, Johnstone)

**Birmingham City 1** (Kinsey)

*Attendance 100,000*

## DIVISION ONE 1956-57

| | | | | | | | |
|---|---|---|---|---|---|---|---|
| MANCHESTER UNITED | 42 | 28 | 8 | 6 | 103 | 54 | 64 |
| Tottenham Hotspur | 42 | 22 | 12 | 8 | 104 | 56 | 56 |
| Preston North End | 42 | 23 | 10 | 9 | 84 | 56 | 56 |
| Blackpool | 42 | 22 | 9 | 11 | 93 | 65 | 53 |
| Arsenal | 42 | 21 | 8 | 13 | 85 | 69 | 50 |
| Wolverhampton Wanderers | 42 | 20 | 8 | 14 | 94 | 70 | 48 |
| Burnley | 42 | 18 | 10 | 14 | 56 | 50 | 46 |
| Leeds United | 42 | 15 | 14 | 13 | 72 | 63 | 44 |
| Bolton Wanderers | 42 | 16 | 12 | 14 | 65 | 65 | 44 |
| Aston Villa | 42 | 14 | 15 | 13 | 65 | 55 | 43 |
| West Bromwich Albion | 42 | 14 | 14 | 14 | 59 | 61 | 42 |
| Birmingham City | 42 | 15 | 9 | 18 | 69 | 69 | 39 |
| Chelsea | 42 | 13 | 13 | 16 | 73 | 73 | 39 |
| Sheffield Wednesday | 42 | 16 | 6 | 20 | 82 | 88 | 38 |
| Everton | 42 | 14 | 10 | 18 | 61 | 79 | 38 |
| Luton Town | 42 | 14 | 9 | 19 | 58 | 76 | 37 |
| Newcastle United | 42 | 14 | 8 | 20 | 67 | 87 | 36 |
| Manchester City | 42 | 13 | 9 | 20 | 78 | 88 | 35 |
| Portsmouth | 42 | 10 | 13 | 19 | 62 | 92 | 33 |
| Sunderland | 42 | 12 | 8 | 22 | 67 | 88 | 32 |
| *Cardiff City* | *42* | *10* | *9* | *23* | *53* | *88* | *29* |
| *Charlton Athletic* | *42* | *9* | *4* | *29* | *62* | *120* | *22* |

## DIVISION TWO 1956-57

| | | | | | | | |
|---|---|---|---|---|---|---|---|
| Leicester City | 42 | 25 | 11 | 6 | 109 | 67 | 61 |
| Nottingham Forest | 42 | 22 | 10 | 10 | 94 | 55 | 54 |
| Liverpool | 42 | 21 | 11 | 10 | 82 | 54 | 53 |
| Blackburn Rovers | 42 | 21 | 10 | 11 | 83 | 75 | 52 |
| Stoke City | 42 | 20 | 8 | 14 | 83 | 58 | 48 |
| Middlesbrough | 42 | 19 | 10 | 13 | 84 | 60 | 48 |
| Sheffield United | 42 | 19 | 8 | 15 | 87 | 76 | 46 |
| West Ham United | 42 | 19 | 8 | 15 | 59 | 63 | 46 |
| Bristol Rovers | 42 | 18 | 9 | 15 | 81 | 67 | 45 |
| Swansea Town | 42 | 19 | 7 | 16 | 90 | 90 | 45 |
| Fulham | 42 | 19 | 4 | 19 | 84 | 76 | 42 |
| Huddersfield Town | 42 | 18 | 6 | 18 | 68 | 74 | 42 |
| Bristol City | 42 | 16 | 9 | 17 | 74 | 79 | 41 |
| Doncaster Rovers | 42 | 15 | 10 | 17 | 77 | 77 | 40 |
| Leyton Orient | 42 | 15 | 10 | 17 | 66 | 84 | 40 |
| Grimsby Town | 42 | 17 | 5 | 20 | 61 | 62 | 39 |
| Rotherham United | 42 | 13 | 11 | 18 | 74 | 75 | 37 |
| Lincoln City | 42 | 14 | 6 | 22 | 54 | 80 | 34 |
| Barnsley | 42 | 12 | 10 | 20 | 59 | 89 | 34 |
| Notts County | 42 | 9 | 12 | 21 | 58 | 86 | 30 |
| *Bury* | *42* | *8* | *9* | *25* | *60* | *96* | *25* |
| *Port Vale* | *42* | *8* | *6* | *28* | *57* | *101* | *22* |

## DIVISION THREE (N) 1956-57

| | | | | | | | |
|---|---|---|---|---|---|---|---|
| Derby County | 46 | 26 | 11 | 9 | 111 | 53 | 63 |
| Hartlepools United | 46 | 25 | 9 | 12 | 90 | 63 | 59 |
| Accrington Stanley | 46 | 25 | 8 | 13 | 95 | 64 | 58 |
| Workington | 46 | 24 | 10 | 12 | 93 | 63 | 58 |
| Stockport County | 46 | 23 | 8 | 15 | 91 | 75 | 54 |
| Chesterfield | 46 | 22 | 9 | 15 | 96 | 79 | 53 |
| York City | 46 | 21 | 10 | 15 | 75 | 61 | 52 |
| Hull City | 46 | 21 | 10 | 15 | 84 | 69 | 52 |
| Bradford City | 46 | 22 | 8 | 16 | 78 | 68 | 52 |
| Barrow | 46 | 21 | 9 | 16 | 76 | 62 | 51 |
| Halifax Town | 46 | 21 | 7 | 18 | 65 | 70 | 49 |
| Wrexham | 46 | 19 | 10 | 17 | 97 | 74 | 48 |
| Rochdale | 46 | 18 | 12 | 16 | 65 | 65 | 48 |
| Scunthorpe United | 46 | 15 | 15 | 16 | 71 | 69 | 45 |
| Carlisle United | 46 | 16 | 13 | 17 | 76 | 85 | 45 |
| Mansfield Town | 46 | 17 | 10 | 19 | 91 | 90 | 44 |
| Gateshead | 46 | 17 | 10 | 19 | 72 | 90 | 44 |
| Darlington | 46 | 17 | 8 | 21 | 82 | 95 | 42 |
| Oldham Athletic | 46 | 12 | 15 | 19 | 66 | 74 | 39 |
| Bradford Park Avenue | 46 | 16 | 3 | 27 | 66 | 93 | 35 |
| Chester | 46 | 10 | 13 | 23 | 55 | 84 | 33 |
| Southport | 46 | 10 | 12 | 24 | 52 | 94 | 32 |
| Tranmere Rovers | 46 | 7 | 13 | 26 | 51 | 91 | 27 |
| Crewe Alexandra | 46 | 6 | 9 | 31 | 43 | 110 | 21 |

## DIVISION THREE (S) 1956-57

| | | | | | | | |
|---|---|---|---|---|---|---|---|
| Ipswich Town | 46 | 25 | 9 | 12 | 101 | 54 | 59 |
| Torquay United | 46 | 24 | 11 | 11 | 89 | 64 | 59 |
| Colchester United | 46 | 22 | 14 | 10 | 84 | 56 | 58 |
| Southampton | 46 | 22 | 10 | 14 | 76 | 52 | 54 |
| Bournemouth & Boscombe Ath. | 46 | 19 | 14 | 13 | 88 | 62 | 52 |
| Brighton & Hove Albion | 46 | 19 | 14 | 13 | 86 | 65 | 52 |
| Southend United | 46 | 18 | 12 | 16 | 73 | 65 | 48 |
| Brentford | 46 | 16 | 16 | 14 | 78 | 76 | 48 |
| Shrewsbury Town | 46 | 15 | 18 | 13 | 72 | 79 | 48 |
| Queen's Park Rangers | 46 | 18 | 11 | 17 | 61 | 60 | 47 |
| Watford | 46 | 18 | 10 | 18 | 72 | 75 | 46 |
| Newport County | 46 | 16 | 13 | 17 | 65 | 62 | 45 |
| Reading | 46 | 18 | 9 | 19 | 80 | 81 | 45 |
| Northampton Town | 46 | 18 | 9 | 19 | 66 | 73 | 45 |
| Walsall | 46 | 16 | 12 | 18 | 80 | 74 | 44 |
| Coventry City | 46 | 16 | 12 | 18 | 74 | 84 | 44 |
| Millwall | 46 | 16 | 12 | 18 | 64 | 84 | 44 |
| Plymouth Argyle | 46 | 16 | 11 | 19 | 68 | 73 | 43 |
| Aldershot | 46 | 15 | 12 | 19 | 79 | 92 | 42 |
| Crystal Palace | 46 | 11 | 18 | 17 | 62 | 75 | 40 |
| Exeter City | 46 | 12 | 13 | 21 | 61 | 79 | 37 |
| Gillingham | 46 | 12 | 13 | 21 | 54 | 85 | 37 |
| Swindon Town | 46 | 15 | 6 | 25 | 66 | 96 | 36 |
| Norwich City | 46 | 8 | 15 | 23 | 61 | 94 | 31 |

## 1957 F.A. Cup

**Semi-finals**

| | |
|---|---|
| Aston Villa vs West Bromwich Albion | 2-2, 1-0 |
| Manchester United vs Birmingham City | 2-0 |

**Final**

Wembley, 4th May 1957

**Aston Villa 2**   (McParland 2)
**Manchester United 1**   (Taylor)

*Attendance 100,000*

## DIVISION ONE 1957-58

| | | | | | | | |
|---|---|---|---|---|---|---|---|
| **WOLVERHAMPTON WANDS.** | 42 | 28 | 8 | 6 | 103 | 47 | 64 |
| Preston North End | 42 | 26 | 7 | 9 | 100 | 51 | 59 |
| Tottenham Hotspur | 42 | 21 | 9 | 12 | 93 | 77 | 51 |
| West Bromwich Albion | 42 | 18 | 14 | 10 | 92 | 70 | 50 |
| Manchester City | 42 | 22 | 5 | 15 | 104 | 100 | 49 |
| Burnley | 42 | 21 | 5 | 16 | 80 | 74 | 47 |
| Blackpool | 42 | 19 | 6 | 17 | 80 | 67 | 44 |
| Luton Town | 42 | 19 | 6 | 17 | 69 | 63 | 44 |
| Manchester United | 42 | 16 | 11 | 15 | 85 | 75 | 43 |
| Nottingham Forest | 42 | 16 | 10 | 16 | 69 | 63 | 42 |
| Chelsea | 42 | 15 | 12 | 15 | 83 | 79 | 42 |
| Arsenal | 42 | 16 | 7 | 19 | 73 | 85 | 39 |
| Birmingham City | 42 | 14 | 11 | 17 | 76 | 89 | 39 |
| Aston Villa | 42 | 16 | 7 | 19 | 73 | 86 | 39 |
| Bolton Wanderers | 42 | 14 | 10 | 18 | 65 | 87 | 38 |
| Everton | 42 | 13 | 11 | 18 | 65 | 75 | 37 |
| Leeds United | 42 | 14 | 9 | 19 | 51 | 63 | 37 |
| Leicester City | 42 | 14 | 5 | 23 | 91 | 112 | 33 |
| Newcastle United | 42 | 12 | 8 | 22 | 73 | 81 | 32 |
| Portsmouth | 42 | 12 | 8 | 22 | 73 | 88 | 32 |
| *Sunderland* | *42* | *10* | *12* | *20* | *54* | *97* | *32* |
| *Sheffield Wednesday* | *42* | *12* | *7* | *23* | *69* | *92* | *31* |

## DIVISION TWO 1957-58

| | | | | | | | |
|---|---|---|---|---|---|---|---|
| **West Ham United** | 42 | 23 | 11 | 8 | 101 | 54 | 57 |
| **Blackburn Rovers** | 42 | 22 | 12 | 8 | 93 | 57 | 56 |
| Charlton Athletic | 42 | 24 | 7 | 11 | 107 | 69 | 55 |
| Liverpool | 42 | 22 | 10 | 10 | 79 | 54 | 54 |
| Fulham | 42 | 20 | 12 | 10 | 97 | 59 | 52 |
| Sheffield United | 42 | 21 | 10 | 11 | 75 | 50 | 52 |
| Middlesbrough | 42 | 19 | 7 | 16 | 83 | 74 | 45 |
| Ipswich Town | 42 | 16 | 12 | 14 | 68 | 69 | 44 |
| Huddersfield Town | 42 | 14 | 16 | 12 | 63 | 66 | 44 |
| Bristol Rovers | 42 | 17 | 8 | 17 | 85 | 80 | 42 |
| Stoke City | 42 | 18 | 6 | 18 | 75 | 73 | 42 |
| Leyton Orient | 42 | 18 | 5 | 19 | 77 | 79 | 41 |
| Grimsby Town | 42 | 17 | 6 | 19 | 86 | 83 | 40 |
| Barnsley | 42 | 14 | 12 | 16 | 70 | 74 | 40 |
| Cardiff City | 42 | 14 | 9 | 19 | 63 | 77 | 37 |
| Derby County | 42 | 14 | 8 | 20 | 60 | 81 | 36 |
| Bristol City | 42 | 13 | 9 | 20 | 63 | 88 | 35 |
| Rotherham United | 42 | 14 | 5 | 23 | 65 | 101 | 33 |
| Swansea Town | 42 | 11 | 9 | 22 | 72 | 99 | 31 |
| Lincoln City | 42 | 11 | 9 | 22 | 55 | 82 | 31 |
| *Notts County* | *42* | *12* | *6* | *24* | *44* | *80* | *30* |
| *Doncaster Rovers* | *42* | *8* | *11* | *23* | *56* | *88* | *27* |

## DIVISION THREE (N) 1957-58

| | | | | | | | |
|---|---|---|---|---|---|---|---|
| **Scunthorpe United** | 46 | 29 | 8 | 9 | 88 | 50 | 66 |
| Accrington Stanley | 46 | 25 | 9 | 12 | 83 | 61 | 59 |
| Bradford City | 46 | 21 | 15 | 10 | 73 | 49 | 57 |
| Bury | 46 | 23 | 10 | 13 | 94 | 62 | 56 |
| Hull City | 46 | 19 | 15 | 12 | 78 | 67 | 53 |
| Mansfield Town | 46 | 22 | 8 | 16 | 100 | 92 | 52 |
| Halifax Town | 46 | 20 | 11 | 15 | 83 | 69 | 51 |
| Chesterfield | 46 | 18 | 15 | 13 | 71 | 69 | 51 |
| Stockport County | 46 | 18 | 11 | 17 | 74 | 67 | 47 |
| Rochdale | 46 | 19 | 8 | 19 | 79 | 67 | 46 |
| Tranmere Rovers | 46 | 18 | 10 | 18 | 82 | 76 | 46 |
| Wrexham | 46 | 17 | 12 | 17 | 61 | 63 | 46 |
| York City | 46 | 17 | 12 | 17 | 68 | 76 | 46 |
| Gateshead | 46 | 15 | 15 | 16 | 68 | 76 | 45 |
| Oldham Athletic | 46 | 14 | 17 | 15 | 72 | 84 | 45 |
| Carlisle United | 46 | 19 | 6 | 21 | 80 | 78 | 44 |
| Hartlepools United | 46 | 16 | 12 | 18 | 73 | 76 | 44 |
| Barrow | 46 | 13 | 15 | 18 | 66 | 74 | 41 |
| Workington | 46 | 14 | 13 | 19 | 72 | 81 | 41 |
| Darlington | 46 | 17 | 7 | 22 | 78 | 89 | 41 |
| Chester | 46 | 13 | 13 | 20 | 73 | 81 | 39 |
| Bradford Park Avenue | 46 | 13 | 11 | 22 | 68 | 95 | 37 |
| Southport | 46 | 11 | 6 | 29 | 52 | 88 | 28 |
| Crewe Alexandra | 46 | 8 | 7 | 31 | 47 | 93 | 23 |

## DIVISION THREE (S) 1957-58

| | | | | | | | |
|---|---|---|---|---|---|---|---|
| **Brighton & Hove Albion** | 46 | 24 | 12 | 10 | 88 | 64 | 60 |
| Brentford | 46 | 24 | 10 | 12 | 82 | 56 | 58 |
| Plymouth Argyle | 46 | 25 | 8 | 13 | 67 | 48 | 58 |
| Swindon Town | 46 | 21 | 15 | 10 | 79 | 50 | 57 |
| Reading | 46 | 21 | 13 | 12 | 79 | 51 | 55 |
| Southampton | 46 | 22 | 10 | 14 | 112 | 72 | 54 |
| Southend United | 46 | 21 | 12 | 13 | 90 | 58 | 54 |
| Norwich City | 46 | 19 | 15 | 12 | 75 | 70 | 53 |
| Bournemouth & Boscombe Ath. | 46 | 21 | 9 | 16 | 81 | 74 | 51 |
| Queen's Park Rangers | 46 | 18 | 14 | 14 | 64 | 65 | 50 |
| Newport County | 46 | 17 | 14 | 15 | 73 | 67 | 48 |
| Colchester United | 46 | 17 | 13 | 16 | 77 | 79 | 47 |
| Northampton Town | 46 | 19 | 6 | 21 | 87 | 79 | 44 |
| Crystal Palace | 46 | 15 | 13 | 18 | 70 | 72 | 43 |
| Port Vale | 46 | 16 | 10 | 20 | 67 | 58 | 42 |
| Watford | 46 | 13 | 16 | 17 | 59 | 77 | 42 |
| Shrewsbury Town | 46 | 15 | 10 | 21 | 49 | 71 | 40 |
| Aldershot | 46 | 12 | 16 | 18 | 59 | 89 | 40 |
| Coventry City | 46 | 13 | 13 | 20 | 61 | 81 | 39 |
| Walsall | 46 | 14 | 9 | 23 | 61 | 75 | 37 |
| Torquay United | 46 | 11 | 13 | 22 | 49 | 74 | 35 |
| Gillingham | 46 | 13 | 9 | 24 | 52 | 81 | 35 |
| Millwall | 46 | 11 | 9 | 26 | 63 | 91 | 31 |
| Exeter City | 46 | 11 | 9 | 26 | 57 | 99 | 31 |

## 1958 F.A. Cup

### Semi-finals

| | |
|---|---|
| Blackburn Rovers vs Bolton Wanderers | 1-2 |
| Manchester United vs Fulham | 2-2, 5-3 |

### Final

Wembley, 3rd May 1958

**Bolton Wanderers 2**   (Lofthouse 2)

**Manchester United 0**

*Attendance 100,000*

## DIVISION ONE 1958-59

| | P | W | D | L | F | A | Pts |
|---|---|---|---|---|---|---|---|
| WOLVERHAMPTON WANDS. | 42 | 28 | 5 | 9 | 110 | 49 | 61 |
| Manchester United | 42 | 24 | 7 | 11 | 103 | 66 | 55 |
| Arsenal | 42 | 21 | 8 | 13 | 88 | 68 | 50 |
| Bolton Wanderers | 42 | 20 | 10 | 12 | 79 | 66 | 50 |
| West Bromwich Albion | 42 | 18 | 13 | 11 | 88 | 68 | 49 |
| West Ham United | 42 | 21 | 6 | 15 | 85 | 70 | 48 |
| Burnley | 42 | 19 | 10 | 13 | 81 | 70 | 48 |
| Blackpool | 42 | 18 | 11 | 13 | 66 | 49 | 47 |
| Birmingham City | 42 | 20 | 6 | 16 | 84 | 68 | 46 |
| Blackburn Rovers | 42 | 17 | 10 | 15 | 76 | 70 | 44 |
| Newcastle United | 42 | 17 | 7 | 18 | 80 | 80 | 41 |
| Preston North End | 42 | 17 | 7 | 18 | 70 | 77 | 41 |
| Nottingham Forest | 42 | 17 | 6 | 19 | 71 | 74 | 40 |
| Chelsea | 42 | 18 | 4 | 20 | 77 | 98 | 40 |
| Leeds United | 42 | 15 | 9 | 18 | 57 | 74 | 39 |
| Everton | 42 | 17 | 4 | 21 | 71 | 87 | 38 |
| Luton Town | 42 | 12 | 13 | 17 | 68 | 71 | 37 |
| Tottenham Hotspur | 42 | 13 | 10 | 19 | 85 | 95 | 36 |
| Leicester City | 42 | 11 | 10 | 21 | 67 | 98 | 32 |
| Manchester City | 42 | 11 | 9 | 22 | 64 | 95 | 31 |
| *Aston Villa* | 42 | 11 | 8 | 23 | 58 | 87 | 30 |
| *Portsmouth* | 42 | 6 | 9 | 27 | 64 | 112 | 21 |

## DIVSION 2 1958-59

| | P | W | D | L | F | A | Pts |
|---|---|---|---|---|---|---|---|
| **Sheffield Wednesday** | 42 | 28 | 6 | 8 | 106 | 48 | 62 |
| **Fulham** | 42 | 27 | 6 | 9 | 96 | 61 | 60 |
| Sheffield United | 42 | 23 | 7 | 12 | 82 | 48 | 53 |
| Liverpool | 42 | 24 | 5 | 13 | 87 | 62 | 53 |
| Stoke City | 42 | 21 | 7 | 14 | 72 | 58 | 49 |
| Bristol Rovers | 42 | 18 | 12 | 12 | 80 | 64 | 48 |
| Derby County | 42 | 20 | 8 | 14 | 74 | 71 | 48 |
| Charlton Athletic | 42 | 18 | 7 | 17 | 92 | 90 | 43 |
| Cardiff City | 42 | 18 | 7 | 17 | 65 | 65 | 43 |
| Bristol City | 42 | 17 | 7 | 18 | 74 | 70 | 41 |
| Swansea Town | 42 | 16 | 9 | 17 | 79 | 81 | 41 |
| Brighton & Hove Albion | 42 | 15 | 11 | 16 | 74 | 90 | 41 |
| Middlesbrough | 42 | 15 | 10 | 17 | 87 | 71 | 40 |
| Huddersfield Town | 42 | 16 | 8 | 18 | 62 | 55 | 40 |
| Sunderland | 42 | 16 | 8 | 18 | 64 | 75 | 40 |
| Ipswich Town | 42 | 17 | 6 | 19 | 62 | 77 | 40 |
| Leyton Orient | 42 | 14 | 8 | 20 | 71 | 78 | 36 |
| Scunthorpe United | 42 | 12 | 9 | 21 | 55 | 84 | 33 |
| Lincoln City | 42 | 11 | 7 | 24 | 63 | 93 | 29 |
| Rotherham United | 42 | 10 | 9 | 23 | 42 | 82 | 29 |
| *Grimsby Town* | 42 | 9 | 10 | 23 | 62 | 90 | 28 |
| *Barnsley* | 42 | 10 | 7 | 25 | 55 | 91 | 27 |

## DIVISION THREE 1958-59

| | P | W | D | L | F | A | Pts |
|---|---|---|---|---|---|---|---|
| Plymouth Argyle | 46 | 23 | 16 | 7 | 89 | 59 | 62 |
| Hull City | 46 | 26 | 9 | 11 | 90 | 55 | 61 |
| Brentford | 46 | 21 | 15 | 10 | 76 | 49 | 57 |
| Norwich City | 46 | 22 | 13 | 11 | 89 | 62 | 57 |
| Colchester United | 46 | 21 | 10 | 15 | 71 | 67 | 52 |
| Reading | 46 | 21 | 8 | 17 | 78 | 63 | 50 |
| Tranmere Rovers | 46 | 21 | 8 | 17 | 82 | 67 | 50 |
| Southend United | 46 | 21 | 8 | 17 | 85 | 80 | 50 |
| Halifax Town | 46 | 21 | 8 | 17 | 80 | 77 | 50 |
| Bury | 46 | 17 | 14 | 15 | 69 | 58 | 48 |
| Bradford City | 46 | 18 | 11 | 17 | 84 | 76 | 47 |
| Bournemouth & Boscombe Ath. | 46 | 17 | 12 | 17 | 69 | 69 | 46 |
| Queen's Park Rangers | 46 | 19 | 8 | 19 | 74 | 77 | 46 |
| Southampton | 46 | 17 | 11 | 18 | 88 | 80 | 45 |
| Swindon Town | 46 | 16 | 13 | 17 | 59 | 57 | 45 |
| Chesterfield | 46 | 17 | 10 | 19 | 67 | 64 | 44 |
| Newport County | 46 | 17 | 9 | 20 | 69 | 68 | 43 |
| Wrexham | 46 | 14 | 14 | 18 | 63 | 77 | 42 |
| Accrington Stanley | 46 | 15 | 12 | 19 | 71 | 87 | 42 |
| Mansfield Town | 46 | 14 | 13 | 19 | 73 | 98 | 41 |
| *Stockport County* | 46 | 13 | 10 | 23 | 65 | 78 | 36 |
| *Doncaster Rovers* | 46 | 14 | 5 | 27 | 50 | 90 | 33 |
| *Notts County* | 46 | 8 | 13 | 25 | 55 | 96 | 29 |
| *Rochdale* | 46 | 8 | 12 | 26 | 37 | 79 | 28 |

## DIVISION FOUR 1958-59

| | P | W | D | L | F | A | Pts |
|---|---|---|---|---|---|---|---|
| **Port Vale** | 46 | 26 | 12 | 8 | 110 | 58 | 64 |
| **Coventry City** | 46 | 24 | 12 | 10 | 84 | 47 | 60 |
| **York City** | 46 | 21 | 18 | 7 | 73 | 52 | 60 |
| **Shrewsbury Town** | 46 | 24 | 10 | 12 | 101 | 63 | 58 |
| Exeter City | 46 | 23 | 11 | 12 | 87 | 61 | 57 |
| Walsall | 46 | 21 | 10 | 15 | 95 | 64 | 52 |
| Crystal Palace | 46 | 20 | 12 | 14 | 90 | 71 | 52 |
| Northampton Town | 46 | 21 | 9 | 16 | 85 | 78 | 51 |
| Millwall | 46 | 20 | 10 | 16 | 76 | 69 | 50 |
| Carlisle United | 46 | 19 | 12 | 15 | 62 | 65 | 50 |
| Gillingham | 46 | 20 | 9 | 17 | 82 | 77 | 49 |
| Torquay United | 46 | 16 | 12 | 18 | 78 | 77 | 44 |
| Chester | 46 | 16 | 12 | 18 | 72 | 84 | 44 |
| Bradford Park Avenue | 46 | 18 | 7 | 21 | 75 | 77 | 43 |
| Watford | 46 | 16 | 10 | 20 | 81 | 79 | 42 |
| Darlington | 46 | 13 | 16 | 17 | 66 | 68 | 42 |
| Workington | 46 | 12 | 17 | 17 | 63 | 78 | 41 |
| Crewe Alexandra | 46 | 15 | 10 | 21 | 70 | 82 | 40 |
| Hartlepools United | 46 | 15 | 10 | 21 | 74 | 88 | 40 |
| Gateshead | 46 | 16 | 8 | 22 | 56 | 85 | 40 |
| Oldham Athletic | 46 | 16 | 4 | 26 | 59 | 84 | 36 |
| Aldershot | 46 | 14 | 7 | 25 | 63 | 97 | 35 |
| Barrow | 46 | 9 | 10 | 27 | 51 | 104 | 28 |
| Southport | 46 | 7 | 12 | 27 | 41 | 86 | 26 |

## 1959 F.A. Cup

**Semi-finals**

| | |
|---|---|
| Nottingham Forest vs Aston Villa | 1-0 |
| Norwich City vs Luton Town | 1-1, 0-1 |

**Final**

Wembley, 2nd May 1959

**Nottingham Forest 2**   (Dwight, Wilson)

**Luton Town 1**   (Pacey)

*Attendance 100,000*

## DIVISION ONE 1959-60

| | | | | | | | |
|---|---|---|---|---|---|---|---|
| **BURNLEY** | 42 | 24 | 7 | 11 | 85 | 61 | 55 |
| Wolverhampton Wanderers | 42 | 24 | 6 | 12 | 106 | 67 | 54 |
| Tottenham Hotspur | 42 | 21 | 11 | 10 | 86 | 50 | 53 |
| West Bromwich Albion | 42 | 19 | 11 | 12 | 83 | 57 | 49 |
| Sheffield Wednesday | 42 | 19 | 11 | 12 | 80 | 59 | 49 |
| Bolton Wanderers | 42 | 20 | 8 | 14 | 59 | 51 | 48 |
| Manchester United | 42 | 19 | 7 | 16 | 102 | 80 | 45 |
| Newcastle United | 42 | 18 | 8 | 16 | 82 | 78 | 44 |
| Preston North End | 42 | 16 | 12 | 14 | 79 | 76 | 44 |
| Fulham | 42 | 17 | 10 | 15 | 73 | 80 | 44 |
| Blackpool | 42 | 15 | 10 | 17 | 59 | 71 | 40 |
| Leicester City | 42 | 13 | 13 | 16 | 66 | 75 | 39 |
| Arsenal | 42 | 15 | 9 | 18 | 68 | 80 | 39 |
| West Ham United | 42 | 16 | 6 | 20 | 75 | 91 | 38 |
| Everton | 42 | 13 | 11 | 18 | 73 | 78 | 37 |
| Manchester City | 42 | 17 | 3 | 22 | 78 | 84 | 37 |
| Blackburn Rovers | 42 | 16 | 5 | 21 | 60 | 70 | 37 |
| Chelsea | 42 | 14 | 9 | 19 | 76 | 91 | 37 |
| Birmingham City | 42 | 13 | 10 | 19 | 63 | 80 | 36 |
| Nottingham Forest | 42 | 13 | 9 | 20 | 50 | 74 | 35 |
| *Leeds United* | *42* | *12* | *10* | *20* | *65* | *92* | *34* |
| *Luton Town* | *42* | *9* | *12* | *21* | *50* | *73* | *30* |

## DIVISION TWO 1959-60

| | | | | | | | |
|---|---|---|---|---|---|---|---|
| **Aston Villa** | 42 | 25 | 9 | 8 | 89 | 43 | 59 |
| **Cardiff City** | 42 | 23 | 12 | 7 | 90 | 62 | 58 |
| Liverpool | 42 | 20 | 10 | 12 | 90 | 66 | 50 |
| Sheffield United | 42 | 19 | 12 | 11 | 68 | 51 | 50 |
| Middlesbrough | 42 | 19 | 10 | 13 | 90 | 64 | 48 |
| Huddersfield Town | 42 | 19 | 9 | 14 | 73 | 52 | 47 |
| Charlton Athletic | 42 | 17 | 13 | 12 | 90 | 87 | 47 |
| Rotherham United | 42 | 17 | 13 | 12 | 61 | 60 | 47 |
| Bristol Rovers | 42 | 18 | 11 | 13 | 72 | 78 | 47 |
| Leyton Orient | 42 | 15 | 14 | 13 | 76 | 61 | 44 |
| Ipswich Town | 42 | 19 | 6 | 17 | 78 | 68 | 44 |
| Swansea Town | 42 | 15 | 10 | 17 | 82 | 84 | 40 |
| Lincoln City | 42 | 16 | 7 | 19 | 75 | 78 | 39 |
| Brighton & Hove Albion | 42 | 13 | 12 | 17 | 67 | 76 | 38 |
| Scunthorpe United | 42 | 13 | 10 | 19 | 57 | 71 | 36 |
| Sunderland | 42 | 12 | 12 | 18 | 52 | 65 | 36 |
| Stoke City | 42 | 14 | 7 | 21 | 66 | 83 | 35 |
| Derby County | 42 | 14 | 7 | 21 | 61 | 77 | 35 |
| Plymouth Argyle | 42 | 13 | 9 | 20 | 61 | 89 | 35 |
| Portsmouth | 42 | 10 | 12 | 20 | 59 | 77 | 32 |
| *Hull City* | *42* | *10* | *10* | *22* | *48* | *76* | *30* |
| *Bristol City* | *42* | *11* | *5* | *26* | *60* | *97* | *27* |

## DIVISION THREE 1959-60

| | | | | | | | |
|---|---|---|---|---|---|---|---|
| **Southampton** | 46 | 26 | 9 | 11 | 106 | 75 | 61 |
| **Norwich City** | 46 | 24 | 11 | 11 | 82 | 54 | 59 |
| Shrewsbury Town | 46 | 18 | 16 | 12 | 97 | 75 | 52 |
| Grimsby Town | 46 | 18 | 16 | 12 | 87 | 70 | 52 |
| Coventry City | 46 | 21 | 10 | 15 | 78 | 63 | 52 |
| Brentford | 46 | 21 | 9 | 16 | 78 | 61 | 51 |
| Bury | 46 | 21 | 9 | 16 | 64 | 51 | 51 |
| Queen's Park Rangers | 46 | 18 | 13 | 15 | 73 | 54 | 49 |
| Colchester United | 46 | 18 | 11 | 17 | 83 | 74 | 47 |
| Bournemouth & Boscombe Ath. | 46 | 17 | 13 | 16 | 72 | 72 | 47 |
| Reading | 46 | 18 | 10 | 18 | 84 | 77 | 46 |
| Southend United | 46 | 19 | 8 | 19 | 76 | 74 | 46 |
| Newport County | 46 | 20 | 6 | 20 | 80 | 79 | 46 |
| Port Vale | 46 | 19 | 8 | 19 | 80 | 79 | 46 |
| Halifax Town | 46 | 18 | 10 | 18 | 70 | 72 | 46 |
| Swindon Town | 46 | 19 | 8 | 19 | 69 | 78 | 46 |
| Barnsley | 46 | 15 | 14 | 17 | 65 | 66 | 44 |
| Chesterfield | 46 | 18 | 7 | 21 | 71 | 84 | 43 |
| Bradford City | 46 | 15 | 12 | 19 | 66 | 74 | 42 |
| Tranmere Rovers | 46 | 14 | 13 | 19 | 72 | 75 | 41 |
| *York City* | *46* | *13* | *12* | *21* | *57* | *73* | *38* |
| *Mansfield Town* | *46* | *15* | *6* | *25* | *81* | *112* | *36* |
| *Wrexham* | *46* | *14* | *8* | *24* | *68* | *101* | *36* |
| *Accrington Stanley* | *46* | *11* | *5* | *30* | *57* | *123* | *27* |

## DIVISION FOUR 1959-60

| | | | | | | | |
|---|---|---|---|---|---|---|---|
| **Walsall** | 46 | 28 | 9 | 9 | 102 | 60 | 65 |
| **Notts County** | 46 | 26 | 8 | 12 | 107 | 69 | 60 |
| **Torquay United** | 46 | 26 | 8 | 12 | 84 | 58 | 60 |
| **Watford** | 46 | 24 | 9 | 13 | 92 | 67 | 57 |
| Millwall | 46 | 18 | 17 | 11 | 84 | 61 | 53 |
| Northampton Town | 46 | 22 | 9 | 15 | 85 | 63 | 53 |
| Gillingham | 46 | 21 | 10 | 15 | 74 | 69 | 52 |
| Crystal Palace | 46 | 19 | 12 | 15 | 84 | 64 | 50 |
| Exeter City | 46 | 19 | 11 | 16 | 80 | 70 | 49 |
| Stockport County | 46 | 19 | 11 | 16 | 58 | 54 | 49 |
| Bradford Park Avenue | 46 | 17 | 15 | 14 | 70 | 68 | 49 |
| Rochdale | 46 | 18 | 10 | 18 | 65 | 60 | 46 |
| Aldershot | 46 | 18 | 9 | 19 | 77 | 74 | 45 |
| Crewe Alexandra | 46 | 18 | 9 | 19 | 79 | 88 | 45 |
| Darlington | 46 | 17 | 9 | 20 | 63 | 73 | 43 |
| Workington | 46 | 14 | 14 | 18 | 68 | 60 | 42 |
| Doncaster Rovers | 46 | 16 | 10 | 20 | 69 | 76 | 42 |
| Barrow | 46 | 15 | 11 | 20 | 77 | 87 | 41 |
| Carlisle United | 46 | 15 | 11 | 20 | 51 | 66 | 41 |
| Chester | 46 | 14 | 12 | 20 | 59 | 77 | 40 |
| Southport | 46 | 10 | 14 | 22 | 48 | 92 | 34 |
| *Gateshead* | *46* | *12* | *9* | *25* | *58* | *86* | *33* |
| Oldham Athletic | 46 | 8 | 12 | 26 | 41 | 83 | 28 |
| Hartlepools United | 46 | 10 | 7 | 29 | 59 | 109 | 27 |

## 1960 F.A. Cup

**Semi-finals**

| | |
|---|---|
| Wolverhampton Wanderers vs Aston Villa | 1-0 |
| Sheffield Wednesday vs Blackburn Rovers | 1-2 |

**Final**

Wembley, 7th May 1960

**Wolverhampton Wands. 3**   (McGrath (og), Deeley 2)
**Blackburn Rovers 0**

*Attendance 100,000*

## DIVISION ONE 1960-61

| | | | | | | | |
|---|---|---|---|---|---|---|---|
| TOTTENHAM HOTSPUR | 42 | 31 | 4 | 7 | 115 | 55 | 66 |
| Sheffield Wednesday | 42 | 23 | 12 | 7 | 78 | 47 | 58 |
| Wolverhampton Wanderers | 42 | 25 | 7 | 10 | 103 | 75 | 57 |
| Burnley | 42 | 22 | 7 | 13 | 102 | 77 | 51 |
| Everton | 42 | 22 | 6 | 14 | 87 | 69 | 50 |
| Leicester City | 42 | 18 | 9 | 15 | 87 | 70 | 45 |
| Manchester United | 42 | 18 | 9 | 15 | 88 | 76 | 45 |
| Blackburn Rovers | 42 | 15 | 13 | 14 | 77 | 76 | 43 |
| Aston Villa | 42 | 17 | 9 | 16 | 78 | 77 | 43 |
| West Bromwich Albion | 42 | 18 | 5 | 19 | 67 | 71 | 41 |
| Arsenal | 42 | 15 | 11 | 16 | 77 | 85 | 41 |
| Chelsea | 42 | 15 | 7 | 20 | 98 | 100 | 37 |
| Manchester City | 42 | 13 | 11 | 18 | 79 | 90 | 37 |
| Nottingham Forest | 42 | 14 | 9 | 19 | 62 | 78 | 37 |
| Cardiff City | 42 | 13 | 11 | 18 | 60 | 85 | 37 |
| West Ham United | 42 | 13 | 10 | 19 | 77 | 88 | 36 |
| Fulham | 42 | 14 | 8 | 20 | 72 | 95 | 36 |
| Bolton Wanderers | 42 | 12 | 11 | 19 | 58 | 73 | 35 |
| Birmingham City | 42 | 14 | 6 | 22 | 62 | 84 | 34 |
| Blackpool | 42 | 12 | 9 | 21 | 68 | 73 | 33 |
| *Newcastle United* | *42* | *11* | *10* | *21* | *86* | *109* | *32* |
| *Preston North End* | *42* | *10* | *10* | *22* | *43* | *71* | *30* |

## DIVISION TWO 1960-61

| | | | | | | | |
|---|---|---|---|---|---|---|---|
| Ipswich Town | 42 | 26 | 7 | 9 | 100 | 55 | 59 |
| Sheffield United | 42 | 26 | 6 | 10 | 81 | 51 | 58 |
| Liverpool | 42 | 21 | 10 | 11 | 87 | 58 | 52 |
| Norwich City | 42 | 20 | 9 | 13 | 70 | 53 | 49 |
| Middlesbrough | 42 | 18 | 12 | 12 | 83 | 74 | 48 |
| Sunderland | 42 | 17 | 13 | 12 | 75 | 60 | 47 |
| Swansea Town | 42 | 18 | 11 | 13 | 77 | 73 | 47 |
| Southampton | 42 | 18 | 8 | 16 | 84 | 81 | 44 |
| Scunthorpe United | 42 | 14 | 15 | 13 | 69 | 64 | 43 |
| Charlton Athletic | 42 | 16 | 11 | 15 | 97 | 91 | 43 |
| Plymouth Argyle | 42 | 17 | 8 | 17 | 81 | 82 | 42 |
| Derby County | 42 | 15 | 10 | 17 | 80 | 80 | 40 |
| Luton Town | 42 | 15 | 9 | 18 | 71 | 79 | 39 |
| Leeds United | 42 | 14 | 10 | 18 | 75 | 83 | 38 |
| Rotherham United | 42 | 12 | 13 | 17 | 65 | 64 | 37 |
| Brighton & Hove Albion | 42 | 14 | 9 | 19 | 61 | 75 | 37 |
| Bristol Rovers | 42 | 15 | 7 | 20 | 73 | 92 | 37 |
| Stoke City | 42 | 12 | 12 | 18 | 51 | 59 | 36 |
| Leyton Orient | 42 | 14 | 8 | 20 | 55 | 78 | 36 |
| Huddersfield Town | 42 | 13 | 9 | 20 | 62 | 71 | 35 |
| *Portsmouth* | *42* | *11* | *11* | *20* | *64* | *91* | *33* |
| *Lincoln City* | *42* | *8* | *8* | *26* | *48* | *95* | *24* |

## DIVISION THREE 1960-61

| | | | | | | | |
|---|---|---|---|---|---|---|---|
| Bury | 46 | 30 | 8 | 8 | 108 | 45 | 68 |
| Walsall | 46 | 28 | 6 | 12 | 98 | 60 | 62 |
| Queen's Park Rangers | 46 | 25 | 10 | 11 | 93 | 60 | 60 |
| Watford | 46 | 20 | 12 | 14 | 85 | 72 | 52 |
| Notts County | 46 | 21 | 9 | 16 | 82 | 77 | 51 |
| Grimsby Town | 46 | 20 | 10 | 16 | 77 | 69 | 50 |
| Port Vale | 46 | 17 | 15 | 14 | 96 | 79 | 49 |
| Barnsley | 46 | 21 | 7 | 18 | 83 | 80 | 49 |
| Halifax Town | 46 | 16 | 17 | 13 | 71 | 78 | 49 |
| Shrewsbury Town | 46 | 15 | 16 | 15 | 83 | 75 | 46 |
| Hull City | 46 | 17 | 12 | 17 | 73 | 73 | 46 |
| Torquay United | 46 | 14 | 17 | 15 | 75 | 83 | 45 |
| Newport County | 46 | 17 | 11 | 18 | 81 | 90 | 45 |
| Bristol City | 46 | 17 | 10 | 19 | 70 | 68 | 44 |
| Coventry City | 46 | 16 | 12 | 18 | 80 | 83 | 44 |
| Swindon Town | 46 | 14 | 15 | 17 | 62 | 55 | 43 |
| Brentford | 46 | 13 | 17 | 16 | 56 | 70 | 43 |
| Reading | 46 | 14 | 12 | 20 | 72 | 83 | 40 |
| Bournemouth & Boscombe Ath. | 46 | 15 | 10 | 21 | 58 | 76 | 40 |
| Southend United | 46 | 14 | 11 | 21 | 60 | 76 | 39 |
| *Tranmere Rovers* | *46* | *15* | *8* | *23* | *79* | *115* | *38* |
| *Bradford City* | *46* | *11* | *14* | *21* | *65* | *87* | *36* |
| *Colchester United* | *46* | *11* | *11* | *24* | *68* | *101* | *33* |
| *Chesterfield* | *46* | *10* | *12* | *24* | *67* | *87* | *32* |

## DIVISION FOUR 1960-61

| | | | | | | | |
|---|---|---|---|---|---|---|---|
| Peterborough United | 46 | 28 | 10 | 8 | 134 | 65 | 66 |
| Crystal Palace | 46 | 29 | 6 | 11 | 110 | 69 | 64 |
| Northampton Town | 46 | 25 | 10 | 11 | 90 | 62 | 60 |
| Bradford Park Avenue | 46 | 26 | 8 | 12 | 84 | 74 | 60 |
| York City | 46 | 21 | 9 | 16 | 80 | 60 | 51 |
| Millwall | 46 | 21 | 8 | 17 | 97 | 86 | 50 |
| Darlington | 46 | 18 | 13 | 15 | 78 | 70 | 49 |
| Workington | 46 | 21 | 7 | 18 | 74 | 76 | 49 |
| Crewe Alexandra | 46 | 20 | 9 | 17 | 61 | 67 | 49 |
| Aldershot | 46 | 18 | 9 | 19 | 79 | 69 | 45 |
| Doncaster Rovers | 46 | 19 | 7 | 20 | 76 | 78 | 45 |
| Oldham Athletic | 46 | 19 | 7 | 20 | 79 | 88 | 45 |
| Stockport County | 46 | 18 | 9 | 19 | 57 | 66 | 45 |
| Southport | 46 | 19 | 6 | 21 | 69 | 67 | 44 |
| Gillingham | 46 | 15 | 13 | 18 | 64 | 66 | 43 |
| Wrexham | 46 | 17 | 8 | 21 | 62 | 56 | 42 |
| Rochdale | 46 | 17 | 8 | 21 | 60 | 66 | 42 |
| Accrington Stanley | 46 | 16 | 8 | 22 | 74 | 88 | 40 |
| Carlisle United | 46 | 13 | 13 | 20 | 61 | 79 | 39 |
| Mansfield Town | 46 | 16 | 6 | 24 | 71 | 78 | 38 |
| Exeter City | 46 | 14 | 10 | 22 | 66 | 94 | 38 |
| Barrow | 46 | 13 | 11 | 22 | 52 | 79 | 37 |
| Hartlepools United | 46 | 12 | 8 | 26 | 71 | 103 | 32 |
| Chester | 46 | 11 | 9 | 26 | 61 | 104 | 31 |

## 1961 F.A. Cup

### Semi-finals
| | |
|---|---|
| Burnley vs Tottenham Hotspur | 0-3 |
| Leicester City vs Sheffield United | 0-0, 0-0, 2-0 |

### Final
Wembley, 6th May 1961

**Tottenham Hotspur 2** (Smith, Dyson)
**Leicester City 0**

*Attendance 100,000*

## 1961 Football League Cup

### Semi-finals
| | |
|---|---|
| Rotherham United vs Shrewsbury Town (3-2, 1-1) | 4-3 |
| Burnley vs Aston Villa (1-1, 2-2) | 3-3 |

### Play-off
| | |
|---|---|
| Burnley vs Aston Villa | 2-1 |

### Final (1st leg)
Rotherham, 22nd August 1961

**Rotherham United 2** (Webster, Kirkman)
**Aston Villa 0**

*Attendance 12,226*

### Final (2nd leg)
Villa Park, 5th September 1961

**Aston Villa 3** (O'Neill, Burrows, McParland)
**Rotherham United 0 (aet.)**

*Attendance 27,000*

*Aston Villa won 3-2 on aggregate*

## DIVISION ONE 1961-62

| IPSWICH TOWN | 42 | 24 | 8 | 10 | 93 | 67 | 56 |
|---|---|---|---|---|---|---|---|
| Burnley | 42 | 21 | 11 | 10 | 101 | 67 | 53 |
| Tottenham Hotspur | 42 | 21 | 10 | 11 | 88 | 69 | 52 |
| Everton | 42 | 20 | 11 | 11 | 88 | 54 | 51 |
| Sheffield United | 42 | 19 | 9 | 14 | 61 | 69 | 47 |
| Sheffield Wednesday | 42 | 20 | 6 | 16 | 72 | 58 | 46 |
| Aston Villa | 42 | 18 | 8 | 16 | 65 | 56 | 44 |
| West Ham United | 42 | 17 | 10 | 15 | 76 | 82 | 44 |
| West Bromwich Albion | 42 | 15 | 13 | 14 | 83 | 67 | 43 |
| Arsenal | 42 | 16 | 11 | 15 | 71 | 72 | 43 |
| Bolton Wanderers | 42 | 16 | 10 | 16 | 62 | 66 | 42 |
| Manchester City | 42 | 17 | 7 | 18 | 78 | 81 | 41 |
| Blackpool | 42 | 15 | 11 | 16 | 70 | 75 | 41 |
| Leicester City | 42 | 17 | 6 | 19 | 72 | 71 | 40 |
| Manchester United | 42 | 15 | 9 | 18 | 72 | 75 | 39 |
| Blackburn Rovers | 42 | 14 | 11 | 17 | 50 | 58 | 39 |
| Birmingham City | 42 | 14 | 10 | 18 | 65 | 81 | 38 |
| Wolverhampton Wanderers | 42 | 13 | 10 | 19 | 73 | 86 | 36 |
| Nottingham Forest | 42 | 13 | 10 | 19 | 63 | 79 | 36 |
| Fulham | 42 | 13 | 7 | 22 | 66 | 74 | 33 |
| *Cardiff City* | *42* | *9* | *14* | *19* | *50* | *81* | *32* |
| *Chelsea* | *42* | *9* | *10* | *23* | *63* | *94* | *28* |

## DIVISION TWO 1961-62

| Liverpool | 42 | 27 | 8 | 7 | 99 | 43 | 62 |
|---|---|---|---|---|---|---|---|
| Leyton Orient | 42 | 22 | 10 | 10 | 69 | 40 | 54 |
| Sunderland | 42 | 22 | 9 | 11 | 85 | 50 | 53 |
| Scunthorpe United | 42 | 21 | 7 | 14 | 86 | 71 | 49 |
| Plymouth Argyle | 42 | 19 | 8 | 15 | 75 | 75 | 46 |
| Southampton | 42 | 18 | 9 | 15 | 77 | 62 | 45 |
| Huddersfield Town | 42 | 16 | 12 | 14 | 67 | 59 | 44 |
| Stoke City | 42 | 17 | 8 | 17 | 55 | 57 | 42 |
| Rotherham United | 42 | 16 | 9 | 17 | 70 | 76 | 41 |
| Preston North End | 42 | 15 | 10 | 17 | 55 | 57 | 40 |
| Newcastle United | 42 | 15 | 9 | 18 | 64 | 58 | 39 |
| Middlesbrough | 42 | 16 | 7 | 19 | 76 | 72 | 39 |
| Luton Town | 42 | 17 | 5 | 20 | 69 | 71 | 39 |
| Walsall | 42 | 14 | 11 | 17 | 70 | 75 | 39 |
| Charlton Athletic | 42 | 15 | 9 | 18 | 69 | 75 | 39 |
| Derby County | 42 | 14 | 11 | 17 | 68 | 75 | 39 |
| Norwich City | 42 | 14 | 11 | 17 | 61 | 70 | 39 |
| Bury | 42 | 17 | 5 | 20 | 52 | 76 | 39 |
| Leeds United | 42 | 12 | 12 | 18 | 50 | 61 | 36 |
| Swansea Town | 42 | 12 | 12 | 18 | 61 | 83 | 36 |
| *Bristol Rovers* | *42* | *13* | *7* | *22* | *53* | *81* | *33* |
| *Brighton & Hove Albion* | *42* | *10* | *11* | *21* | *42* | *86* | *31* |

## DIVISION THREE 1961-62

| Portsmouth | 46 | 27 | 11 | 8 | 87 | 47 | 65 |
|---|---|---|---|---|---|---|---|
| **Grimsby Town** | **46** | **28** | **6** | **12** | **80** | **56** | **62** |
| Bournemouth & Boscombe Ath. | 46 | 21 | 17 | 8 | 69 | 45 | 59 |
| Queen's Park Rangers | 46 | 24 | 11 | 11 | 111 | 73 | 59 |
| Peterborough United | 46 | 26 | 6 | 14 | 107 | 82 | 58 |
| Bristol City | 46 | 23 | 8 | 15 | 94 | 72 | 54 |
| Reading | 46 | 22 | 9 | 15 | 77 | 66 | 53 |
| Northampton Town | 46 | 20 | 11 | 15 | 85 | 57 | 51 |
| Swindon Town | 46 | 17 | 15 | 14 | 78 | 71 | 49 |
| Hull City | 46 | 20 | 8 | 18 | 67 | 54 | 48 |
| Bradford Park Avenue | 46 | 20 | 7 | 19 | 80 | 78 | 47 |
| Port Vale | 46 | 17 | 11 | 18 | 65 | 58 | 45 |
| Notts County | 46 | 17 | 9 | 20 | 67 | 74 | 43 |
| Coventry City | 46 | 16 | 11 | 19 | 64 | 71 | 43 |
| Crystal Palace | 46 | 14 | 14 | 18 | 83 | 80 | 42 |
| Southend United | 46 | 13 | 16 | 17 | 57 | 69 | 42 |
| Watford | 46 | 14 | 13 | 19 | 63 | 74 | 41 |
| Halifax Town | 46 | 15 | 10 | 21 | 62 | 84 | 40 |
| Shrewsbury Town | 46 | 13 | 12 | 21 | 73 | 84 | 38 |
| Barnsley | 46 | 13 | 12 | 21 | 71 | 95 | 38 |
| *Torquay United* | *46* | *15* | *6* | *25* | *76* | *100* | *36* |
| *Lincoln City* | *46* | *9* | *17* | *20* | *57* | *87* | *35* |
| *Brentford* | *46* | *13* | *8* | *25* | *53* | *93* | *34* |
| *Newport County* | *46* | *7* | *8* | *31* | *46* | *102* | *22* |

## DIVISION FOUR 1961-62

| **Millwall** | **44** | **23** | **10** | **11** | **87** | **62** | **56** |
|---|---|---|---|---|---|---|---|
| **Colchester United** | **44** | **23** | **9** | **12** | **104** | **71** | **55** |
| **Wrexham** | **44** | **22** | **9** | **13** | **96** | **56** | **53** |
| **Carlisle United** | **44** | **22** | **8** | **14** | **64** | **63** | **52** |
| Bradford City | 44 | 21 | 9 | 14 | 94 | 86 | 51 |
| York City | 44 | 20 | 10 | 14 | 84 | 53 | 50 |
| Aldershot | 44 | 22 | 5 | 17 | 81 | 60 | 49 |
| Workington | 44 | 19 | 11 | 14 | 69 | 70 | 49 |
| Barrow | 44 | 17 | 14 | 13 | 74 | 58 | 48 |
| Crewe Alexandra | 44 | 20 | 6 | 18 | 79 | 70 | 46 |
| Oldham Athletic | 44 | 17 | 12 | 15 | 77 | 70 | 46 |
| Rochdale | 44 | 19 | 7 | 18 | 71 | 71 | 45 |
| Darlington | 44 | 18 | 9 | 17 | 61 | 73 | 45 |
| Mansfield Town | 44 | 19 | 6 | 19 | 77 | 66 | 44 |
| Tranmere Rovers | 44 | 20 | 4 | 20 | 70 | 81 | 44 |
| Stockport County | 44 | 17 | 9 | 18 | 70 | 69 | 43 |
| Southport | 44 | 17 | 9 | 18 | 61 | 71 | 43 |
| Exeter City | 44 | 13 | 11 | 20 | 62 | 77 | 37 |
| Chesterfield | 44 | 14 | 9 | 21 | 70 | 87 | 37 |
| Gillingham | 44 | 13 | 11 | 20 | 73 | 94 | 37 |
| Doncaster Rovers | 44 | 11 | 7 | 26 | 60 | 85 | 29 |
| Hartlepools United | 44 | 8 | 11 | 25 | 52 | 101 | 27 |
| Chester | 44 | 7 | 12 | 25 | 54 | 96 | 26 |

Accrington Stanley resigned from the League after 33 matches

# 1962 F.A. Cup

**Semi-finals**

| Manchester United vs Tottenham Hotspur | 1-3 |
|---|---|
| Burnley vs Fulham | 1-1, 2-1 |

**Final**

Wembley, 5th May 1962

**Tottenham Hotspur 3** (Greaves, Smith, Blanchflower (pen))

**Burnley 1** (Robson)

*Attendance 100,000*

# 1962 Football League Cup

**Semi-finals**

| Norwich City vs Blackpool (4-1, 0-2) | 4-3 |
|---|---|
| Rochdale vs Blackburn Rovers (3-1, 1-2) | 4-3 |

**Final (1st leg)**

Rochdale, 26th April 1962

**Rochdale 0**

**Norwich City 3** (Lythgoe 2, Punton)

*Attendance 11,123*

**Final (2nd leg)**

Norwich, 1st May 1962

**Norwich City 1** (Hill)

**Rochdale 0**

*Attendance 19,708*

*Norwich City won 4-0 on aggregate*

## DIVISION ONE 1962-63

| | | | | | | | |
|---|---|---|---|---|---|---|---|
| **EVERTON** | 42 | 25 | 11 | 6 | 84 | 42 | 61 |
| Tottenham Hotspur | 42 | 23 | 9 | 10 | 111 | 62 | 55 |
| Burnley | 42 | 22 | 10 | 10 | 78 | 57 | 54 |
| Leicester City | 42 | 20 | 12 | 10 | 79 | 53 | 52 |
| Wolverhampton Wanderers | 42 | 20 | 10 | 12 | 93 | 65 | 50 |
| Sheffield Wednesday | 42 | 19 | 10 | 13 | 77 | 63 | 48 |
| Arsenal | 42 | 18 | 10 | 14 | 86 | 77 | 46 |
| Liverpool | 42 | 17 | 10 | 15 | 71 | 59 | 44 |
| Nottingham Forest | 42 | 17 | 10 | 15 | 67 | 69 | 44 |
| Sheffield United | 42 | 16 | 12 | 14 | 58 | 60 | 44 |
| Blackburn Rovers | 42 | 15 | 12 | 15 | 79 | 71 | 42 |
| West Ham United | 42 | 14 | 12 | 16 | 73 | 69 | 40 |
| Blackpool | 42 | 13 | 14 | 15 | 58 | 64 | 40 |
| West Bromwich Albion | 42 | 16 | 7 | 19 | 71 | 79 | 39 |
| Aston Villa | 42 | 15 | 8 | 19 | 62 | 68 | 38 |
| Fulham | 42 | 14 | 10 | 18 | 50 | 71 | 38 |
| Ipswich Town | 42 | 12 | 11 | 19 | 59 | 78 | 35 |
| Bolton Wanderers | 42 | 15 | 5 | 22 | 55 | 75 | 35 |
| Manchester United | 42 | 12 | 10 | 20 | 67 | 81 | 34 |
| Birmingham City | 42 | 10 | 13 | 19 | 63 | 90 | 33 |
| *Manchester City* | *42* | *10* | *11* | *21* | *58* | *102* | *31* |
| *Leyton Orient* | *42* | *6* | *9* | *27* | *37* | *81* | *21* |

## DIVISION TWO 1962-63

| | | | | | | | |
|---|---|---|---|---|---|---|---|
| **Stoke City** | 42 | 20 | 13 | 9 | 73 | 50 | 53 |
| **Chelsea** | 42 | 24 | 4 | 14 | 81 | 42 | 52 |
| Sunderland | 42 | 20 | 12 | 10 | 84 | 55 | 52 |
| Middlesbrough | 42 | 20 | 9 | 13 | 86 | 85 | 49 |
| Leeds United | 42 | 19 | 10 | 13 | 79 | 53 | 48 |
| Huddersfield Town | 42 | 17 | 14 | 11 | 63 | 50 | 48 |
| Newcastle United | 42 | 18 | 11 | 13 | 79 | 59 | 47 |
| Bury | 42 | 18 | 11 | 13 | 51 | 47 | 47 |
| Scunthorpe United | 42 | 16 | 12 | 14 | 57 | 59 | 44 |
| Cardiff City | 42 | 18 | 7 | 17 | 83 | 73 | 43 |
| Southampton | 42 | 17 | 8 | 17 | 72 | 67 | 42 |
| Plymouth Argyle | 42 | 15 | 12 | 15 | 76 | 73 | 42 |
| Norwich City | 42 | 17 | 8 | 17 | 80 | 79 | 42 |
| Rotherham United | 42 | 17 | 6 | 19 | 67 | 74 | 40 |
| Swansea Town | 42 | 15 | 9 | 18 | 51 | 72 | 39 |
| Portsmouth | 42 | 13 | 11 | 18 | 63 | 79 | 37 |
| Preston North End | 42 | 13 | 11 | 18 | 59 | 74 | 37 |
| Derby County | 42 | 12 | 12 | 18 | 61 | 72 | 36 |
| Grimsby Town | 42 | 11 | 13 | 18 | 55 | 66 | 35 |
| Charlton Athletic | 42 | 13 | 5 | 24 | 62 | 94 | 31 |
| *Walsall* | *42* | *11* | *9* | *22* | *53* | *89* | *31* |
| *Luton Town* | *42* | *11* | *7* | *24* | *61* | *84* | *29* |

## DIVISION THREE 1962-63

| | | | | | | | |
|---|---|---|---|---|---|---|---|
| **Northampton Town** | 46 | 26 | 10 | 10 | 109 | 60 | 62 |
| **Swindon Town** | 46 | 22 | 14 | 10 | 87 | 56 | 58 |
| Port Vale | 46 | 23 | 8 | 15 | 72 | 58 | 54 |
| Coventry City | 46 | 18 | 17 | 11 | 83 | 69 | 53 |
| Bournemouth & Boscombe Ath. | 46 | 18 | 16 | 12 | 63 | 46 | 52 |
| Peterborough United | 46 | 20 | 11 | 15 | 93 | 75 | 51 |
| Notts County | 46 | 19 | 13 | 14 | 73 | 74 | 51 |
| Southend United | 46 | 19 | 12 | 15 | 75 | 77 | 50 |
| Wrexham | 46 | 20 | 9 | 17 | 84 | 83 | 49 |
| Hull City | 46 | 19 | 10 | 17 | 74 | 69 | 48 |
| Crystal Palace | 46 | 17 | 13 | 16 | 68 | 58 | 47 |
| Colchester United | 46 | 18 | 11 | 17 | 73 | 93 | 47 |
| Queen's Park Rangers | 46 | 17 | 11 | 18 | 85 | 76 | 45 |
| Bristol City | 46 | 16 | 13 | 17 | 100 | 92 | 45 |
| Shrewsbury Town | 46 | 16 | 12 | 18 | 83 | 81 | 44 |
| Millwall | 46 | 15 | 13 | 18 | 82 | 87 | 43 |
| Watford | 46 | 17 | 8 | 21 | 82 | 85 | 42 |
| Barnsley | 46 | 15 | 11 | 20 | 63 | 74 | 41 |
| Bristol Rovers | 46 | 15 | 11 | 20 | 70 | 88 | 41 |
| Reading | 46 | 16 | 8 | 22 | 74 | 78 | 40 |
| *Bradford Park Avenue* | *46* | *14* | *12* | *20* | *79* | *97* | *40* |
| *Brighton & Hove Albion* | *46* | *12* | *12* | *22* | *58* | *84* | *36* |
| *Carlisle United* | *46* | *13* | *9* | *24* | *61* | *89* | *35* |
| *Halifax Town* | *46* | *9* | *12* | *25* | *64* | *106* | *30* |

## DIVISION FOUR 1962-63

| | | | | | | | |
|---|---|---|---|---|---|---|---|
| **Brentford** | 46 | 27 | 8 | 11 | 98 | 64 | 62 |
| **Oldham Athletic** | 46 | 24 | 11 | 11 | 95 | 60 | 59 |
| **Crewe Alexandra** | 46 | 24 | 11 | 11 | 86 | 58 | 59 |
| **Mansfield Town** | 46 | 24 | 9 | 13 | 108 | 69 | 57 |
| Gillingham | 46 | 22 | 13 | 11 | 71 | 49 | 57 |
| Torquay United | 46 | 20 | 16 | 10 | 75 | 56 | 56 |
| Rochdale | 46 | 20 | 11 | 15 | 67 | 59 | 51 |
| Tranmere Rovers | 46 | 20 | 10 | 16 | 81 | 67 | 50 |
| Barrow | 46 | 19 | 12 | 15 | 82 | 80 | 50 |
| Workington | 46 | 17 | 13 | 16 | 76 | 68 | 47 |
| Aldershot | 46 | 15 | 17 | 14 | 73 | 69 | 47 |
| Darlington | 46 | 19 | 6 | 21 | 72 | 87 | 44 |
| Southport | 46 | 15 | 14 | 17 | 72 | 106 | 44 |
| York City | 46 | 16 | 11 | 19 | 67 | 62 | 43 |
| Chesterfield | 46 | 13 | 16 | 17 | 70 | 64 | 42 |
| Doncaster Rovers | 46 | 14 | 14 | 18 | 64 | 77 | 42 |
| Exeter City | 46 | 16 | 10 | 20 | 57 | 77 | 42 |
| Oxford United | 46 | 13 | 15 | 18 | 70 | 71 | 41 |
| Stockport County | 46 | 15 | 11 | 20 | 56 | 70 | 41 |
| Newport County | 46 | 14 | 11 | 21 | 76 | 90 | 39 |
| Chester | 46 | 15 | 9 | 22 | 51 | 66 | 39 |
| Lincoln City | 46 | 13 | 9 | 24 | 68 | 89 | 35 |
| Bradford City | 46 | 11 | 10 | 25 | 64 | 93 | 32 |
| Hartlepools United | 46 | 7 | 11 | 28 | 56 | 104 | 25 |

## 1963 F.A. Cup

**Semi-finals**

| | |
|---|---|
| Leicester City vs Liverpool | 1-0 |
| Southampton vs Manchester United | 0-1 |

**Final**

Wembley, 25th May 1963

**Manchester United 3**  (Law, Herd 2)
**Leicester City 1**  (Keyworth)

*Attendance 100,000*

## 1963 Football League Cup

**Semi-finals**

| | |
|---|---|
| Birmingham City vs Bury (3-2, 1-1) | 4-3 |
| Sunderland vs Aston Villa (1-3, 0-0) | 1-3 |

**Final (1st leg)**

St. Andrews, 23rd May 1963

**Birmingham City 3**  (Leek 2, Bloomfield)
**Aston Villa 1**  (Thomson)

*Attendance 31,850*

**Final (2nd leg)**

Villa Park, 27th May 1963

**Aston Villa 0**
**Birmingham City 0**

*Attendance 37,920*

*Birmingham City won 3-1 on aggregate*

## DIVISION ONE 1963-64

| | | | | | | | |
|---|---|---|---|---|---|---|---|
| LIVERPOOL | 42 | 26 | 5 | 11 | 92 | 45 | 57 |
| Manchester United | 42 | 23 | 7 | 12 | 90 | 62 | 53 |
| Everton | 42 | 21 | 10 | 11 | 84 | 64 | 52 |
| Tottenham Hotspur | 42 | 22 | 7 | 13 | 97 | 81 | 51 |
| Chelsea | 42 | 20 | 10 | 12 | 72 | 56 | 50 |
| Sheffield Wednesday | 42 | 19 | 11 | 12 | 84 | 67 | 49 |
| Blackburn Rovers | 42 | 18 | 10 | 14 | 89 | 65 | 46 |
| Arsenal | 42 | 17 | 11 | 14 | 90 | 82 | 45 |
| Burnley | 42 | 17 | 10 | 15 | 71 | 64 | 44 |
| West Bromwich Albion | 42 | 16 | 11 | 15 | 70 | 61 | 43 |
| Leicester City | 42 | 16 | 11 | 15 | 61 | 58 | 43 |
| Sheffield United | 42 | 16 | 11 | 15 | 61 | 64 | 43 |
| Nottingham Forest | 42 | 16 | 9 | 17 | 64 | 68 | 41 |
| West Ham United | 42 | 14 | 12 | 16 | 69 | 74 | 40 |
| Fulham | 42 | 13 | 13 | 16 | 58 | 65 | 39 |
| Wolverhampton Wanderers | 42 | 12 | 15 | 15 | 70 | 80 | 39 |
| Stoke City | 42 | 14 | 10 | 18 | 77 | 78 | 38 |
| Blackpool | 42 | 13 | 9 | 20 | 52 | 73 | 35 |
| Aston Villa | 42 | 11 | 12 | 19 | 62 | 71 | 34 |
| Birmingham City | 42 | 11 | 7 | 24 | 54 | 92 | 29 |
| *Bolton Wanderers* | *42* | *10* | *8* | *24* | *48* | *80* | *28* |
| *Ipswich Town* | *42* | *9* | *7* | *26* | *56* | *121* | *25* |

## DIVISION TWO 1963-64

| | | | | | | | |
|---|---|---|---|---|---|---|---|
| Leeds United | 42 | 24 | 15 | 3 | 71 | 34 | 63 |
| Sunderland | 42 | 25 | 11 | 6 | 81 | 37 | 61 |
| Preston North End | 42 | 23 | 10 | 9 | 79 | 54 | 56 |
| Charlton Athletic | 42 | 19 | 10 | 13 | 76 | 70 | 48 |
| Southampton | 42 | 19 | 9 | 14 | 100 | 73 | 47 |
| Manchester City | 42 | 18 | 10 | 14 | 84 | 66 | 46 |
| Rotherham United | 42 | 19 | 7 | 16 | 90 | 78 | 45 |
| Newcastle United | 42 | 20 | 5 | 17 | 74 | 69 | 45 |
| Portsmouth | 42 | 16 | 11 | 15 | 79 | 70 | 43 |
| Middlesbrough | 42 | 15 | 11 | 16 | 67 | 52 | 41 |
| Northampton Town | 42 | 16 | 9 | 17 | 58 | 60 | 41 |
| Huddersfield Town | 42 | 15 | 10 | 17 | 57 | 64 | 40 |
| Derby County | 42 | 14 | 11 | 17 | 56 | 67 | 39 |
| Swindon Town | 42 | 14 | 10 | 18 | 57 | 69 | 38 |
| Cardiff City | 42 | 14 | 10 | 18 | 56 | 81 | 38 |
| Leyton Orient | 42 | 13 | 10 | 19 | 54 | 72 | 36 |
| Norwich City | 42 | 11 | 13 | 18 | 64 | 80 | 35 |
| Bury | 42 | 13 | 9 | 20 | 57 | 73 | 35 |
| Swansea Town | 42 | 12 | 9 | 21 | 63 | 74 | 33 |
| Plymouth Argyle | 42 | 8 | 16 | 18 | 45 | 67 | 32 |
| *Grimsby Town* | *42* | *9* | *14* | *19* | *47* | *75* | *32* |
| *Scunthorpe United* | *42* | *10* | *10* | *22* | *52* | *82* | *30* |

## DIVISION THREE 1963-64

| | | | | | | | |
|---|---|---|---|---|---|---|---|
| Coventry City | 46 | 22 | 16 | 8 | 98 | 61 | 60 |
| Crystal Palace | 46 | 23 | 14 | 9 | 73 | 51 | 60 |
| Watford | 46 | 23 | 12 | 11 | 79 | 59 | 58 |
| Bournemouth & Boscombe Ath. | 46 | 24 | 8 | 14 | 79 | 58 | 56 |
| Bristol City | 46 | 20 | 15 | 11 | 84 | 64 | 55 |
| Reading | 46 | 21 | 10 | 15 | 79 | 62 | 52 |
| Mansfield Town | 46 | 20 | 11 | 15 | 76 | 62 | 51 |
| Hull City | 46 | 16 | 17 | 13 | 73 | 68 | 49 |
| Oldham Athletic | 46 | 20 | 8 | 18 | 73 | 70 | 48 |
| Peterborough United | 46 | 18 | 11 | 17 | 75 | 70 | 47 |
| Shrewsbury Town | 46 | 18 | 11 | 17 | 73 | 80 | 47 |
| Bristol Rovers | 46 | 19 | 8 | 19 | 91 | 79 | 46 |
| Port Vale | 46 | 16 | 14 | 16 | 53 | 49 | 46 |
| Southend United | 46 | 15 | 15 | 16 | 77 | 78 | 45 |
| Queen's Park Rangers | 46 | 18 | 9 | 19 | 76 | 78 | 45 |
| Brentford | 46 | 15 | 14 | 17 | 87 | 80 | 44 |
| Colchester United | 46 | 12 | 19 | 15 | 70 | 68 | 43 |
| Luton Town | 46 | 16 | 10 | 20 | 64 | 80 | 42 |
| Walsall | 46 | 13 | 14 | 19 | 59 | 76 | 40 |
| Barnsley | 46 | 12 | 15 | 19 | 68 | 94 | 39 |
| *Millwall* | *46* | *14* | *10* | *22* | *53* | *67* | *38* |
| *Crewe Alexandra* | *46* | *11* | *12* | *23* | *50* | *77* | *34* |
| *Wrexham* | *46* | *13* | *6* | *27* | *75* | *107* | *32* |
| *Notts County* | *46* | *9* | *9* | *28* | *45* | *92* | *27* |

## DIVISION FOUR 1963-64

| | | | | | | | |
|---|---|---|---|---|---|---|---|
| Gillingham | 46 | 23 | 14 | 9 | 59 | 30 | 60 |
| Carlisle United | 46 | 25 | 10 | 11 | 113 | 58 | 60 |
| Workington | 46 | 24 | 11 | 11 | 76 | 52 | 59 |
| Exeter City | 46 | 20 | 18 | 8 | 62 | 37 | 58 |
| Bradford City | 46 | 25 | 6 | 15 | 76 | 62 | 56 |
| Torquay United | 46 | 20 | 11 | 15 | 80 | 54 | 51 |
| Tranmere Rovers | 46 | 20 | 11 | 15 | 85 | 73 | 51 |
| Brighton & Hove Albion | 46 | 19 | 12 | 15 | 71 | 52 | 50 |
| Aldershot | 46 | 19 | 10 | 17 | 83 | 78 | 48 |
| Halifax Town | 46 | 17 | 14 | 15 | 77 | 77 | 48 |
| Lincoln City | 46 | 19 | 9 | 18 | 67 | 75 | 47 |
| Chester | 46 | 19 | 9 | 18 | 65 | 60 | 46 |
| Bradford Park Avenue | 46 | 18 | 9 | 19 | 75 | 81 | 45 |
| Doncaster Rovers | 46 | 15 | 12 | 19 | 70 | 75 | 42 |
| Newport County | 46 | 17 | 8 | 21 | 64 | 73 | 42 |
| Chesterfield | 46 | 15 | 12 | 19 | 57 | 71 | 42 |
| Stockport County | 46 | 15 | 12 | 19 | 50 | 68 | 42 |
| Oxford United | 46 | 14 | 13 | 19 | 59 | 63 | 41 |
| Darlington | 46 | 14 | 12 | 20 | 66 | 93 | 40 |
| Rochdale | 46 | 12 | 15 | 19 | 56 | 59 | 39 |
| Southport | 46 | 15 | 9 | 22 | 63 | 88 | 39 |
| York City | 46 | 14 | 7 | 25 | 52 | 66 | 35 |
| Hartlepools United | 46 | 12 | 9 | 25 | 54 | 93 | 33 |
| Barrow | 46 | 6 | 18 | 22 | 51 | 93 | 30 |

## 1964 F.A. Cup

### Semi-finals

| | |
|---|---|
| West Ham United vs Manchester United | 3-1 |
| Swansea Town vs Preston North End | 1-2 |

### Final

Wembley, 2nd May 1964

**West Ham United 3** (Sissons, Hurst, Boyce)
**Preston North End 2** (Holden, Dawson)

*Attendance 100,000*

## 1964 Football League Cup

### Semi-finals

| | |
|---|---|
| Leicester City vs West Ham United (4-3, 2-0) | 6-3 |
| Stoke City vs Manchester City (2-0, 0-1) | 2-1 |

### Final (1st leg)

Stoke, 15th April 1964

**Stoke City 1** (Bebbington)
**Leicester City 1** (Gibson)

*Attendance 22,309*

### Final (2nd leg)

Leicester, 22nd April 1964

**Leicester City 3** (Stringfellow, Gibson, Riley)
**Stoke City 2** (Viollet, Kinnell)

*Attendance 25,372*

*Leicester City won 4-3 on aggregate*

## DIVISION ONE 1964-65

| | | | | | | | |
|---|---|---|---|---|---|---|---|
| **MANCHESTER UNITED** | 42 | 26 | 9 | 7 | 89 | 39 | 61 |
| Leeds United | 42 | 26 | 9 | 7 | 83 | 52 | 61 |
| Chelsea | 42 | 24 | 8 | 10 | 89 | 54 | 56 |
| Everton | 42 | 17 | 15 | 10 | 69 | 60 | 49 |
| Nottingham Forest | 42 | 17 | 13 | 12 | 71 | 67 | 47 |
| Tottenham Hotspur | 42 | 19 | 7 | 16 | 87 | 71 | 45 |
| Liverpool | 42 | 17 | 10 | 15 | 67 | 73 | 44 |
| Sheffield Wednesday | 42 | 16 | 11 | 15 | 57 | 55 | 43 |
| West Ham United | 42 | 19 | 4 | 19 | 82 | 71 | 42 |
| Blackburn Rovers | 42 | 16 | 10 | 16 | 83 | 79 | 42 |
| Stoke City | 42 | 16 | 10 | 16 | 67 | 66 | 42 |
| Burnley | 42 | 16 | 10 | 16 | 70 | 70 | 42 |
| Arsenal | 42 | 17 | 7 | 18 | 69 | 75 | 41 |
| West Bromwich Albion | 42 | 13 | 13 | 16 | 70 | 65 | 39 |
| Sunderland | 42 | 14 | 9 | 19 | 64 | 74 | 37 |
| Aston Villa | 42 | 16 | 5 | 21 | 57 | 82 | 37 |
| Blackpool | 42 | 12 | 11 | 19 | 67 | 78 | 35 |
| Leicester City | 42 | 11 | 13 | 18 | 69 | 85 | 35 |
| Sheffield United | 42 | 12 | 11 | 19 | 50 | 64 | 35 |
| Fulham | 42 | 11 | 12 | 19 | 60 | 78 | 34 |
| *Wolverhampton Wanderers* | *42* | *13* | *4* | *25* | *59* | *89* | *30* |
| *Birmingham City* | *42* | *8* | *11* | *23* | *64* | *96* | *27* |

## DIVISION TWO 1964-65

| | | | | | | | |
|---|---|---|---|---|---|---|---|
| **Newcastle United** | 42 | 24 | 9 | 9 | 81 | 45 | 57 |
| **Northampton Town** | 42 | 20 | 16 | 6 | 66 | 50 | 56 |
| Bolton Wanderers | 42 | 20 | 10 | 12 | 80 | 58 | 50 |
| Southampton | 42 | 17 | 14 | 11 | 83 | 63 | 48 |
| Ipswich Town | 42 | 15 | 17 | 10 | 74 | 67 | 47 |
| Norwich City | 42 | 20 | 7 | 15 | 61 | 57 | 47 |
| Crystal Palace | 42 | 16 | 13 | 13 | 55 | 51 | 45 |
| Huddersfield Town | 42 | 17 | 10 | 15 | 53 | 51 | 44 |
| Derby County | 42 | 16 | 11 | 15 | 84 | 79 | 43 |
| Coventry City | 42 | 17 | 9 | 16 | 72 | 70 | 43 |
| Manchester City | 42 | 16 | 9 | 17 | 63 | 62 | 41 |
| Preston North End | 42 | 14 | 13 | 15 | 76 | 81 | 41 |
| Cardiff City | 42 | 13 | 14 | 15 | 64 | 57 | 40 |
| Rotherham United | 42 | 14 | 12 | 16 | 70 | 69 | 40 |
| Plymouth Argyle | 42 | 16 | 8 | 18 | 63 | 79 | 40 |
| Bury | 42 | 14 | 10 | 18 | 60 | 66 | 38 |
| Middlesbrough | 42 | 13 | 9 | 20 | 70 | 76 | 35 |
| Charlton Athletic | 42 | 13 | 9 | 20 | 64 | 75 | 35 |
| Leyton Orient | 42 | 12 | 11 | 19 | 50 | 72 | 35 |
| Portsmouth | 42 | 12 | 10 | 20 | 56 | 77 | 34 |
| *Swindon Town* | *42* | *14* | *5* | *23* | *63* | *81* | *33* |
| *Swansea Town* | *42* | *11* | *10* | *21* | *62* | *84* | *32* |

## DIVISION THREE 1964-65

| | | | | | | | |
|---|---|---|---|---|---|---|---|
| **Carlisle United** | 46 | 25 | 10 | 11 | 76 | 53 | 60 |
| **Bristol City** | 46 | 24 | 11 | 11 | 92 | 55 | 59 |
| Mansfield Town | 46 | 24 | 11 | 11 | 95 | 61 | 59 |
| Hull City | 46 | 23 | 12 | 11 | 91 | 57 | 58 |
| Brentford | 46 | 24 | 9 | 13 | 83 | 55 | 57 |
| Bristol Rovers | 46 | 20 | 15 | 11 | 82 | 58 | 55 |
| Gillingham | 46 | 23 | 9 | 14 | 70 | 50 | 55 |
| Peterborough United | 46 | 22 | 7 | 17 | 85 | 74 | 51 |
| Watford | 46 | 17 | 16 | 13 | 71 | 64 | 50 |
| Grimsby Town | 46 | 16 | 17 | 13 | 68 | 67 | 49 |
| Bournemouth & Boscombe Ath. | 46 | 18 | 11 | 17 | 72 | 63 | 47 |
| Southend United | 46 | 19 | 8 | 19 | 78 | 71 | 46 |
| Reading | 46 | 16 | 14 | 16 | 70 | 70 | 46 |
| Queen's Park Rangers | 46 | 17 | 12 | 17 | 72 | 80 | 46 |
| Workington | 46 | 17 | 12 | 17 | 58 | 69 | 46 |
| Shrewsbury Town | 46 | 15 | 12 | 19 | 76 | 84 | 42 |
| Exeter City | 46 | 12 | 17 | 17 | 51 | 52 | 41 |
| Scunthorpe United | 46 | 14 | 12 | 20 | 65 | 72 | 40 |
| Walsall | 46 | 15 | 7 | 24 | 55 | 80 | 37 |
| Oldham Athletic | 46 | 13 | 10 | 23 | 61 | 83 | 36 |
| *Luton Town* | *46* | *11* | *11* | *24* | *51* | *94* | *33* |
| *Port Vale* | *46* | *9* | *14* | *23* | *41* | *76* | *32* |
| *Colchester United* | *46* | *10* | *10* | *26* | *50* | *89* | *30* |
| *Barnsley* | *46* | *9* | *11* | *26* | *54* | *90* | *29* |

## DIVISION FOUR 1964-65

| | | | | | | | |
|---|---|---|---|---|---|---|---|
| **Brighton & Hove Albion** | 46 | 26 | 11 | 9 | 102 | 57 | 63 |
| **Millwall** | 46 | 23 | 16 | 7 | 78 | 45 | 62 |
| **York City** | 46 | 28 | 6 | 12 | 91 | 56 | 62 |
| **Oxford United** | 46 | 23 | 15 | 8 | 87 | 44 | 61 |
| Tranmere Rovers | 46 | 27 | 6 | 13 | 99 | 56 | 60 |
| Rochdale | 46 | 22 | 14 | 10 | 74 | 53 | 58 |
| Bradford Park Avenue | 46 | 20 | 17 | 9 | 86 | 62 | 57 |
| Chester | 46 | 25 | 6 | 15 | 119 | 81 | 56 |
| Doncaster Rovers | 46 | 20 | 11 | 15 | 84 | 72 | 51 |
| Crewe Alexandra | 46 | 18 | 13 | 15 | 90 | 81 | 49 |
| Torquay United | 46 | 21 | 7 | 18 | 70 | 70 | 49 |
| Chesterfield | 46 | 20 | 8 | 18 | 58 | 70 | 48 |
| Notts County | 46 | 15 | 14 | 17 | 61 | 73 | 44 |
| Wrexham | 46 | 17 | 9 | 20 | 84 | 92 | 43 |
| Hartlepools United | 46 | 15 | 13 | 18 | 61 | 85 | 43 |
| Newport County | 46 | 17 | 8 | 21 | 85 | 81 | 42 |
| Darlington | 46 | 18 | 6 | 22 | 84 | 87 | 42 |
| Aldershot | 46 | 15 | 7 | 24 | 64 | 84 | 37 |
| Bradford City | 46 | 12 | 8 | 26 | 70 | 88 | 32 |
| Southport | 46 | 8 | 16 | 22 | 58 | 89 | 32 |
| Barrow | 46 | 12 | 6 | 28 | 59 | 105 | 30 |
| Lincoln City | 46 | 11 | 6 | 29 | 58 | 99 | 28 |
| Halifax | 46 | 11 | 6 | 29 | 54 | 103 | 28 |
| Stockport County | 46 | 10 | 7 | 29 | 44 | 87 | 27 |

## 1965 F.A. Cup

**Semi-finals**

| | |
|---|---|
| Liverpool vs Chelsea | 2-0 |
| Manchester United vs Leeds United | 0-0, 0-1 |

**Final**

Wembley, 1st May 1965

**Liverpool 2**   (Hunt, St. John)
**Leeds United 1 (aet.)**   (Bremner)

*Attendance 100,000*

## 1965 Football League Cup

**Semi-finals**

| | |
|---|---|
| Aston Villa vs Chelsea (2-3, 1-1) | 3-4 |
| Leicester City vs Plymouth Argyle (3-2, 1-0) | 4-2 |

**Final (1st leg)**

Stamford Bridge, 15th March 1965

**Chelsea 3**   (Tambling, Venables (pen), McCreadie)
**Leicester City 2**   (Appleton, Goodfellow)

*Attendance 20,690*

**Final (2nd leg)**

Leicester, 5th April 1965

**Leicester City 0**
**Chelsea 0**

*Attendance 26,958*

*Chelsea won 3-2 on aggregate*

## DIVISION ONE 1965-66

| | | | | | | | |
|---|---|---|---|---|---|---|---|
| **LIVERPOOL** | 42 | 26 | 9 | 7 | 79 | 34 | 61 |
| Leeds United | 42 | 23 | 9 | 10 | 79 | 38 | 55 |
| Burnley | 42 | 24 | 7 | 11 | 79 | 47 | 55 |
| Manchester United | 42 | 18 | 15 | 9 | 84 | 59 | 51 |
| Chelsea | 42 | 22 | 7 | 13 | 65 | 53 | 51 |
| West Bromwich Albion | 42 | 19 | 12 | 11 | 91 | 69 | 50 |
| Leicester City | 42 | 21 | 7 | 14 | 80 | 65 | 49 |
| Tottenham Hotspur | 42 | 16 | 12 | 14 | 75 | 66 | 44 |
| Sheffield United | 42 | 16 | 11 | 15 | 56 | 59 | 43 |
| Stoke City | 42 | 15 | 12 | 15 | 65 | 64 | 42 |
| Everton | 42 | 15 | 11 | 16 | 56 | 62 | 41 |
| West Ham United | 42 | 15 | 9 | 18 | 70 | 83 | 39 |
| Blackpool | 42 | 14 | 9 | 19 | 55 | 65 | 37 |
| Arsenal | 42 | 12 | 13 | 17 | 62 | 75 | 37 |
| Newcastle United | 42 | 14 | 9 | 19 | 50 | 63 | 37 |
| Aston Villa | 42 | 15 | 6 | 21 | 69 | 80 | 36 |
| Sheffield Wednesday | 42 | 14 | 8 | 20 | 56 | 66 | 36 |
| Nottingham Forest | 42 | 14 | 8 | 20 | 56 | 72 | 36 |
| Sunderland | 42 | 14 | 8 | 20 | 51 | 72 | 36 |
| Fulham | 42 | 14 | 7 | 21 | 67 | 85 | 35 |
| *Northampton Town* | *42* | *10* | *13* | *19* | *55* | *92* | *33* |
| *Blackburn Rovers* | *42* | *8* | *4* | *30* | *57* | *88* | *20* |

## DIVISION TWO 1965-66

| | | | | | | | |
|---|---|---|---|---|---|---|---|
| **Manchester City** | 42 | 22 | 15 | 5 | 76 | 44 | 59 |
| **Southampton** | 42 | 22 | 10 | 10 | 85 | 56 | 54 |
| Coventry City | 42 | 20 | 13 | 9 | 73 | 53 | 53 |
| Huddersfield Town | 42 | 19 | 13 | 10 | 62 | 36 | 51 |
| Bristol City | 42 | 17 | 17 | 8 | 63 | 48 | 51 |
| Wolverhampton Wanderers | 42 | 20 | 10 | 12 | 87 | 61 | 50 |
| Rotherham United | 42 | 16 | 14 | 12 | 75 | 74 | 46 |
| Derby County | 42 | 16 | 11 | 15 | 71 | 68 | 43 |
| Bolton Wanderers | 42 | 16 | 9 | 17 | 62 | 59 | 41 |
| Birmingham City | 42 | 16 | 9 | 17 | 70 | 75 | 41 |
| Crystal Palace | 42 | 14 | 13 | 15 | 47 | 52 | 41 |
| Portsmouth | 42 | 16 | 8 | 18 | 74 | 78 | 40 |
| Norwich City | 42 | 12 | 15 | 15 | 52 | 52 | 39 |
| Carlisle United | 42 | 17 | 5 | 20 | 60 | 63 | 39 |
| Ipswich Town | 42 | 15 | 9 | 18 | 58 | 66 | 39 |
| Charlton Athletic | 42 | 12 | 14 | 16 | 61 | 70 | 38 |
| Preston North End | 42 | 11 | 15 | 16 | 62 | 70 | 37 |
| Plymouth Argyle | 42 | 12 | 13 | 17 | 54 | 63 | 37 |
| Bury | 42 | 14 | 7 | 21 | 62 | 76 | 35 |
| Cardiff City | 42 | 12 | 10 | 20 | 71 | 91 | 34 |
| *Middlesbrough* | *42* | *10* | *13* | *19* | *58* | *86* | *33* |
| *Leyton Orient* | *42* | *5* | *13* | *24* | *38* | *80* | *23* |

## DIVISION THREE 1965-66

| | | | | | | | |
|---|---|---|---|---|---|---|---|
| **Hull City** | 46 | 31 | 7 | 8 | 109 | 62 | 69 |
| **Millwall** | 46 | 27 | 11 | 8 | 76 | 43 | 65 |
| Queen's Park Rangers | 46 | 24 | 9 | 13 | 95 | 65 | 57 |
| Scunthorpe United | 46 | 21 | 11 | 14 | 80 | 67 | 53 |
| Workington | 46 | 19 | 14 | 13 | 67 | 57 | 52 |
| Gillingham | 46 | 22 | 8 | 16 | 62 | 54 | 52 |
| Swindon Town | 46 | 19 | 13 | 14 | 74 | 48 | 51 |
| Reading | 46 | 19 | 13 | 14 | 70 | 63 | 51 |
| Walsall | 46 | 20 | 10 | 16 | 77 | 64 | 50 |
| Shrewsbury Town | 46 | 19 | 11 | 16 | 73 | 64 | 49 |
| Grimsby Town | 46 | 17 | 13 | 16 | 68 | 62 | 47 |
| Watford | 46 | 17 | 13 | 16 | 55 | 51 | 47 |
| Peterborough United | 46 | 17 | 12 | 17 | 80 | 66 | 46 |
| Oxford United | 46 | 19 | 8 | 19 | 70 | 74 | 46 |
| Brighton & Hove Albion | 46 | 16 | 11 | 19 | 67 | 65 | 43 |
| Bristol Rovers | 46 | 14 | 14 | 18 | 64 | 64 | 42 |
| Swansea Town | 46 | 15 | 11 | 20 | 81 | 96 | 41 |
| Bournemouth & Boscombe Ath. | 46 | 13 | 12 | 21 | 38 | 56 | 38 |
| Mansfield Town | 46 | 15 | 8 | 23 | 59 | 89 | 38 |
| Oldham Athletic | 46 | 12 | 13 | 21 | 55 | 81 | 37 |
| *Southend United* | *46* | *16* | *4* | *26* | *54* | *83* | *36* |
| *Exeter City* | *46* | *12* | *11* | *23* | *53* | *79* | *35* |
| *Brentford* | *46* | *10* | *12* | *24* | *48* | *69* | *32* |
| *York City* | *46* | *9* | *9* | *28* | *53* | *106* | *27* |

## DIVISION FOUR 1965-66

| | | | | | | | |
|---|---|---|---|---|---|---|---|
| **Doncaster Rovers** | 46 | 24 | 11 | 11 | 85 | 54 | 59 |
| **Darlington** | 46 | 25 | 9 | 12 | 72 | 53 | 59 |
| **Torquay United** | 46 | 24 | 10 | 12 | 72 | 49 | 58 |
| **Colchester United** | 46 | 23 | 10 | 13 | 70 | 47 | 56 |
| Tranmere Rovers | 46 | 24 | 8 | 14 | 93 | 66 | 56 |
| Luton Town | 46 | 24 | 8 | 14 | 90 | 70 | 56 |
| Chester | 46 | 20 | 12 | 14 | 79 | 70 | 52 |
| Notts County | 46 | 19 | 12 | 15 | 61 | 53 | 50 |
| Newport County | 46 | 18 | 12 | 16 | 75 | 75 | 48 |
| Southport | 46 | 18 | 12 | 16 | 68 | 69 | 48 |
| Bradford Park Avenue | 46 | 21 | 5 | 20 | 102 | 92 | 47 |
| Barrow | 46 | 16 | 15 | 15 | 72 | 76 | 47 |
| Stockport County | 46 | 18 | 6 | 22 | 71 | 70 | 42 |
| Crewe Alexandra | 46 | 16 | 9 | 21 | 61 | 63 | 41 |
| Halifax Town | 46 | 15 | 11 | 20 | 67 | 75 | 41 |
| Barnsley | 46 | 15 | 10 | 21 | 74 | 78 | 40 |
| Aldershot | 46 | 15 | 10 | 21 | 75 | 84 | 40 |
| Hartlepools United | 46 | 16 | 8 | 22 | 63 | 75 | 40 |
| Port Vale | 46 | 15 | 9 | 22 | 48 | 59 | 39 |
| Chesterfield | 46 | 13 | 13 | 20 | 62 | 78 | 39 |
| Rochdale | 46 | 16 | 5 | 25 | 71 | 87 | 37 |
| Lincoln City | 46 | 13 | 11 | 22 | 57 | 82 | 37 |
| Bradford City | 46 | 12 | 13 | 21 | 63 | 94 | 37 |
| Wrexham | 46 | 13 | 9 | 24 | 72 | 104 | 35 |

## 1966 F.A. Cup

**Semi-finals**

| | |
|---|---|
| Everton vs Manchester United | 1-0 |
| Sheffield Wednesday vs Chelsea | 2-0 |

**Final**

Wembley, 14th May 1966

**Everton 3**   (Trebilcock 2, Temple)
**Sheffield Wednesday 2**   (McCalliog, Ford)

*Attendance 100,000*

## 1966 Football League Cup

**Semi-finals**

| | |
|---|---|
| West Brom. Albion vs Peterborough Utd. (2-1, 4-2) | 6-3 |
| West Ham United vs Cardiff City (5-2, 5-1) | 10-3 |

**Final (1st leg)**

Upton Park, 9th March 1966

**West Ham United 2**   (Moore, Byrne)
**West Bromwich Albion 1**   (Astle)

*Attendance 28,341*

**Final (2nd leg)**

The Hawthorns, 23rd March 1966

**West Bromwich Albion 4**   (Kaye, Brown, Clark, Williams)
**West Ham United 1**   (Peters)

*Attendance 31,925*

*West Bromwich Albion won 5-3 on aggregate*

## DIVISION ONE 1966-67

| MANCHESTER UNITED | 42 | 24 | 12 | 6 | 84 | 45 | 60 |
|---|---|---|---|---|---|---|---|
| Nottingham Forest | 42 | 23 | 10 | 9 | 64 | 41 | 56 |
| Tottenham Hotspur | 42 | 24 | 8 | 10 | 71 | 48 | 56 |
| Leeds United | 42 | 22 | 11 | 9 | 62 | 42 | 55 |
| Liverpool | 42 | 19 | 13 | 10 | 64 | 47 | 51 |
| Everton | 42 | 19 | 10 | 13 | 65 | 46 | 48 |
| Arsenal | 42 | 16 | 14 | 12 | 58 | 47 | 46 |
| Leicester City | 42 | 18 | 8 | 16 | 78 | 71 | 44 |
| Chelsea | 42 | 15 | 14 | 13 | 67 | 62 | 44 |
| Sheffield United | 42 | 16 | 10 | 16 | 52 | 59 | 42 |
| Sheffield Wednesday | 42 | 14 | 13 | 15 | 56 | 47 | 41 |
| Stoke City | 42 | 17 | 7 | 18 | 63 | 58 | 41 |
| West Bromwich Albion | 42 | 16 | 7 | 19 | 77 | 73 | 39 |
| Burnley | 42 | 15 | 9 | 18 | 66 | 76 | 39 |
| Manchester City | 42 | 12 | 15 | 15 | 43 | 52 | 39 |
| West Ham United | 42 | 14 | 8 | 20 | 80 | 84 | 36 |
| Sunderland | 42 | 14 | 8 | 20 | 58 | 72 | 36 |
| Fulham | 42 | 11 | 12 | 19 | 71 | 83 | 34 |
| Southampton | 42 | 14 | 6 | 22 | 74 | 92 | 34 |
| Newcastle United | 42 | 12 | 9 | 21 | 39 | 81 | 33 |
| *Aston Villa* | *42* | *11* | *7* | *24* | *54* | *85* | *29* |
| *Blackpool* | *42* | *6* | *9* | *27* | *41* | *76* | *21* |

## DIVISION THREE 1966-67

| Queen's Park Rangers | 46 | 26 | 15 | 5 | 103 | 38 | 67 |
|---|---|---|---|---|---|---|---|
| **Middlesbrough** | 46 | 23 | 9 | 14 | 87 | 64 | 55 |
| Watford | 46 | 20 | 14 | 12 | 61 | 46 | 54 |
| Reading | 46 | 22 | 9 | 15 | 76 | 57 | 53 |
| Bristol Rovers | 46 | 20 | 13 | 13 | 76 | 67 | 53 |
| Shrewsbury Town | 46 | 20 | 12 | 14 | 77 | 62 | 52 |
| Torquay United | 46 | 21 | 9 | 16 | 73 | 54 | 51 |
| Swindon Town | 46 | 20 | 10 | 16 | 81 | 59 | 50 |
| Mansfield Town | 46 | 20 | 9 | 17 | 84 | 79 | 49 |
| Oldham Athletic | 46 | 19 | 10 | 17 | 80 | 63 | 48 |
| Gillingham | 46 | 15 | 16 | 15 | 58 | 62 | 46 |
| Walsall | 46 | 18 | 10 | 18 | 65 | 72 | 46 |
| Colchester United | 46 | 17 | 10 | 19 | 76 | 73 | 44 |
| Leyton Orient | 46 | 13 | 18 | 15 | 58 | 68 | 44 |
| Peterborough United | 46 | 14 | 15 | 17 | 66 | 71 | 43 |
| Oxford United | 46 | 15 | 13 | 18 | 61 | 66 | 43 |
| Grimsby Town | 46 | 17 | 9 | 20 | 61 | 68 | 43 |
| Scunthorpe United | 46 | 17 | 8 | 21 | 58 | 73 | 42 |
| Brighton & Hove Albion | 46 | 13 | 15 | 18 | 61 | 71 | 41 |
| Bournemouth & Boscombe Ath. | 46 | 12 | 17 | 17 | 39 | 57 | 41 |
| *Swansea Town* | *46* | *12* | *15* | *19* | *85* | *89* | *39* |
| *Darlington* | *46* | *13* | *11* | *22* | *47* | *81* | *37* |
| *Doncaster Rovers* | *46* | *12* | *8* | *26* | *58* | *117* | *32* |
| *Workington* | *46* | *12* | *7* | *27* | *55* | *89* | *31* |

## DIVISION TWO 1966-67

| Coventry City | 42 | 23 | 13 | 6 | 74 | 43 | 59 |
|---|---|---|---|---|---|---|---|
| **Wolverhampton Wanderers** | 42 | 25 | 8 | 9 | 88 | 48 | 58 |
| Carlisle United | 42 | 23 | 6 | 13 | 71 | 54 | 52 |
| Blackburn Rovers | 42 | 19 | 13 | 10 | 56 | 46 | 51 |
| Ipswich Town | 42 | 17 | 16 | 9 | 70 | 54 | 50 |
| Huddersfield Town | 42 | 20 | 9 | 13 | 58 | 46 | 49 |
| Crystal Palace | 42 | 19 | 10 | 13 | 61 | 55 | 48 |
| Millwall | 42 | 18 | 9 | 15 | 49 | 58 | 45 |
| Bolton Wanderers | 42 | 14 | 14 | 14 | 64 | 58 | 42 |
| Birmingham City | 42 | 16 | 8 | 18 | 70 | 66 | 40 |
| Norwich City | 42 | 13 | 14 | 15 | 49 | 55 | 40 |
| Hull City | 42 | 16 | 7 | 19 | 77 | 72 | 39 |
| Preston North End | 42 | 16 | 7 | 19 | 65 | 67 | 39 |
| Portsmouth | 42 | 13 | 13 | 16 | 59 | 70 | 39 |
| Bristol City | 42 | 12 | 14 | 16 | 56 | 62 | 38 |
| Plymouth Argyle | 42 | 14 | 9 | 19 | 59 | 58 | 37 |
| Derby County | 42 | 12 | 12 | 18 | 68 | 72 | 36 |
| Rotherham United | 42 | 13 | 10 | 19 | 61 | 70 | 36 |
| Charlton Athletic | 42 | 13 | 9 | 20 | 49 | 53 | 35 |
| Cardiff City | 42 | 12 | 9 | 21 | 61 | 87 | 33 |
| *Northampton Town* | *42* | *12* | *6* | *24* | *47* | *84* | *30* |
| *Bury* | *42* | *11* | *6* | *25* | *49* | *83* | *28* |

## DIVISION FOUR 1966-67

| Stockport County | 46 | 26 | 12 | 8 | 69 | 42 | 64 |
|---|---|---|---|---|---|---|---|
| **Southport** | 46 | 23 | 13 | 10 | 69 | 42 | 59 |
| **Barrow** | 46 | 24 | 11 | 11 | 76 | 54 | 59 |
| **Tranmere Rovers** | 46 | 22 | 14 | 10 | 66 | 43 | 58 |
| Crewe Alexandra | 46 | 21 | 12 | 13 | 70 | 55 | 54 |
| Southend United | 46 | 22 | 9 | 15 | 70 | 49 | 53 |
| Wrexham | 46 | 16 | 20 | 10 | 76 | 62 | 52 |
| Hartlepools United | 46 | 22 | 7 | 17 | 66 | 64 | 51 |
| Brentford | 46 | 18 | 13 | 15 | 58 | 56 | 49 |
| Aldershot | 46 | 18 | 12 | 16 | 72 | 57 | 48 |
| Bradford City | 46 | 19 | 10 | 17 | 74 | 62 | 48 |
| Halifax Town | 46 | 15 | 14 | 17 | 59 | 68 | 44 |
| Port Vale | 46 | 14 | 15 | 17 | 55 | 58 | 43 |
| Exeter City | 46 | 14 | 15 | 17 | 50 | 60 | 43 |
| Chesterfield | 46 | 17 | 8 | 21 | 60 | 63 | 42 |
| Barnsley | 46 | 13 | 15 | 16 | 60 | 64 | 41 |
| Luton Town | 46 | 16 | 9 | 21 | 59 | 73 | 41 |
| Newport County | 46 | 12 | 16 | 18 | 56 | 63 | 40 |
| Chester | 46 | 15 | 10 | 21 | 54 | 78 | 40 |
| Notts County | 46 | 13 | 11 | 22 | 53 | 72 | 37 |
| Rochdale | 46 | 13 | 11 | 22 | 53 | 75 | 37 |
| York City | 46 | 12 | 11 | 23 | 65 | 79 | 35 |
| Bradford Park Avenue | 46 | 11 | 13 | 22 | 52 | 79 | 35 |
| Lincoln City | 46 | 9 | 13 | 24 | 58 | 82 | 31 |

## 1967 F.A. Cup

**Semi-finals**

| Tottenham Hotspur vs Nottingham Forest | 2-1 |
|---|---|
| Chelsea vs Leeds United | 1-0 |

**Final**

Wembley, 20th May 1967

**Tottenham Hotspur 2** (Robertson, Saul)
**Chelsea 1** (Tambling)

*Attendance 100,000*

## 1967 Football League Cup

**Semi-finals**

| Birmingham City vs Queen's Park Rangers (1-4, 1-3) | 2-7 |
|---|---|
| West Bromwich Albion vs West Ham Utd. (4-0, 2-2) | 6-2 |

**Final**

Wembley, 4th March 1967

**Queen's Park Rangers 3** (R. Morgan, Marsh, Lazarus)
**West Bromwich Albion 2** (Clark 2)

*Attendance 97,952*

## DIVISION ONE 1967-68

| | | | | | | | |
|---|---|---|---|---|---|---|---|
| **MANCHESTER CITY** | 42 | 26 | 6 | 10 | 86 | 43 | 58 |
| Manchester United | 42 | 24 | 8 | 10 | 89 | 55 | 56 |
| Liverpool | 42 | 22 | 11 | 9 | 71 | 40 | 55 |
| Leeds United | 42 | 22 | 9 | 11 | 71 | 41 | 53 |
| Everton | 42 | 23 | 6 | 13 | 67 | 40 | 52 |
| Chelsea | 42 | 18 | 12 | 12 | 62 | 68 | 48 |
| Tottenham Hotspur | 42 | 19 | 9 | 14 | 70 | 59 | 47 |
| West Bromwich Albion | 42 | 17 | 12 | 13 | 75 | 62 | 46 |
| Arsenal | 42 | 17 | 10 | 15 | 60 | 56 | 44 |
| Newcastle United | 42 | 13 | 15 | 14 | 54 | 67 | 41 |
| Nottingham Forest | 42 | 14 | 11 | 17 | 52 | 64 | 39 |
| West Ham United | 42 | 14 | 10 | 18 | 73 | 69 | 38 |
| Leicester City | 42 | 13 | 12 | 17 | 64 | 69 | 38 |
| Burnley | 42 | 14 | 10 | 18 | 64 | 71 | 38 |
| Sunderland | 42 | 13 | 11 | 18 | 51 | 61 | 37 |
| Southampton | 42 | 13 | 11 | 18 | 66 | 83 | 37 |
| Wolverhampton Wanderers | 42 | 14 | 8 | 20 | 66 | 75 | 36 |
| Stoke City | 42 | 14 | 7 | 21 | 50 | 73 | 35 |
| Sheffield Wednesday | 42 | 11 | 12 | 19 | 51 | 63 | 34 |
| Coventry City | 42 | 9 | 15 | 18 | 51 | 71 | 33 |
| *Sheffield United* | *42* | *11* | *10* | *21* | *49* | *70* | *32* |
| *Fulham* | *42* | *10* | *7* | *25* | *56* | *98* | *27* |

## DIVISION TWO 1967-68

| | | | | | | | |
|---|---|---|---|---|---|---|---|
| **Ipswich Town** | 42 | 22 | 15 | 5 | 79 | 44 | 59 |
| **Queen's Park Rangers** | 42 | 25 | 8 | 9 | 67 | 36 | 58 |
| Blackpool | 42 | 24 | 10 | 8 | 71 | 43 | 58 |
| Birmingham City | 42 | 19 | 14 | 9 | 83 | 51 | 52 |
| Portsmouth | 42 | 18 | 13 | 11 | 68 | 55 | 49 |
| Middlesbrough | 42 | 17 | 12 | 13 | 60 | 54 | 46 |
| Millwall | 42 | 14 | 17 | 11 | 62 | 50 | 45 |
| Blackburn Rovers | 42 | 16 | 11 | 15 | 56 | 49 | 43 |
| Norwich City | 42 | 16 | 11 | 15 | 60 | 65 | 43 |
| Carlisle United | 42 | 14 | 13 | 15 | 58 | 52 | 41 |
| Crystal Palace | 42 | 14 | 11 | 17 | 56 | 56 | 39 |
| Bolton Wanderers | 42 | 13 | 13 | 16 | 60 | 63 | 39 |
| Cardiff City | 42 | 13 | 12 | 17 | 60 | 66 | 38 |
| Huddersfield Town | 42 | 13 | 12 | 17 | 46 | 61 | 38 |
| Charlton Athletic | 42 | 12 | 13 | 17 | 63 | 68 | 37 |
| Aston Villa | 42 | 15 | 7 | 20 | 54 | 64 | 37 |
| Hull City | 42 | 12 | 13 | 17 | 58 | 73 | 37 |
| Derby County | 42 | 13 | 10 | 19 | 71 | 78 | 36 |
| Bristol City | 42 | 13 | 10 | 19 | 48 | 62 | 36 |
| Preston North End | 42 | 12 | 11 | 19 | 43 | 65 | 35 |
| *Rotherham United* | *42* | *10* | *11* | *21* | *42* | *76* | *31* |
| *Plymouth Argyle* | *42* | *9* | *9* | *24* | *38* | *72* | *27* |

## DIVISION THREE 1967-68

| | | | | | | | |
|---|---|---|---|---|---|---|---|
| **Oxford United** | 46 | 22 | 13 | 11 | 69 | 47 | 57 |
| **Bury** | 46 | 24 | 8 | 14 | 91 | 66 | 56 |
| Shrewsbury Town | 46 | 20 | 15 | 11 | 61 | 49 | 55 |
| Torquay United | 46 | 21 | 11 | 14 | 60 | 56 | 53 |
| Reading | 46 | 21 | 9 | 16 | 70 | 60 | 51 |
| Watford | 46 | 21 | 8 | 17 | 74 | 50 | 50 |
| Walsall | 46 | 19 | 12 | 15 | 74 | 61 | 50 |
| Barrow | 46 | 18 | 12 | 16 | 65 | 54 | 48 |
| Swindon Town | 46 | 16 | 17 | 13 | 74 | 51 | 49 |
| Brighton & Hove Albion | 46 | 16 | 16 | 14 | 57 | 55 | 48 |
| Gillingham | 46 | 18 | 12 | 16 | 59 | 63 | 48 |
| Bournemouth & Boscombe Ath. | 46 | 16 | 15 | 15 | 56 | 51 | 47 |
| Stockport County | 46 | 19 | 9 | 18 | 70 | 75 | 47 |
| Southport | 46 | 17 | 12 | 17 | 65 | 65 | 46 |
| Bristol Rovers | 46 | 17 | 9 | 20 | 72 | 78 | 43 |
| Oldham Athletic | 46 | 18 | 7 | 21 | 60 | 65 | 43 |
| Northampton Town | 46 | 14 | 13 | 19 | 58 | 72 | 41 |
| Orient | 46 | 12 | 17 | 17 | 46 | 62 | 41 |
| Tranmere Rovers | 46 | 14 | 12 | 20 | 62 | 74 | 40 |
| Mansfield Town | 46 | 12 | 13 | 21 | 51 | 67 | 37 |
| *Grimsby Town* | *46* | *14* | *9* | *23* | *52* | *69* | *37* |
| *Colchester United* | *46* | *9* | *15* | *22* | *50* | *87* | *33* |
| *Scunthorpe United* | *46* | *10* | *12* | *24* | *56* | *87* | *32* |
| *Peterborough United* | *46* | *20* | *10* | *16* | *79* | *67* | *31†* |

† Peterborough United were 'fined' 19 points and relegated for offering illegal bonuses.

## DIVISION FOUR 1967-68

| | | | | | | | |
|---|---|---|---|---|---|---|---|
| **Luton Town** | 46 | 27 | 12 | 7 | 87 | 44 | 66 |
| **Barnsley** | 46 | 24 | 13 | 9 | 68 | 46 | 61 |
| **Hartlepools United** | 46 | 25 | 10 | 11 | 60 | 46 | 60 |
| **Crewe Alexandra** | 46 | 20 | 18 | 8 | 74 | 49 | 58 |
| Bradford City | 46 | 23 | 11 | 12 | 72 | 51 | 57 |
| Southend United | 46 | 20 | 14 | 12 | 77 | 58 | 54 |
| Chesterfield | 46 | 21 | 11 | 14 | 71 | 50 | 53 |
| Wrexham | 46 | 20 | 13 | 13 | 72 | 53 | 53 |
| Aldershot | 46 | 18 | 17 | 11 | 70 | 55 | 53 |
| Doncaster Rovers | 46 | 18 | 15 | 13 | 66 | 56 | 51 |
| Halifax Town | 46 | 15 | 16 | 15 | 52 | 49 | 46 |
| Newport County | 46 | 16 | 13 | 17 | 58 | 63 | 45 |
| Lincoln City | 46 | 17 | 9 | 20 | 71 | 68 | 43 |
| Brentford | 46 | 18 | 7 | 21 | 61 | 64 | 43 |
| Swansea Town | 46 | 16 | 10 | 20 | 63 | 77 | 42 |
| Darlington | 46 | 12 | 17 | 17 | 47 | 53 | 41 |
| Notts County | 46 | 15 | 11 | 20 | 53 | 79 | 41 |
| Port Vale | 46 | 12 | 15 | 19 | 61 | 72 | 39 |
| Rochdale | 46 | 12 | 14 | 20 | 51 | 72 | 38 |
| Exeter City | 46 | 11 | 16 | 19 | 45 | 65 | 38 |
| York City | 46 | 11 | 14 | 21 | 65 | 68 | 36 |
| Chester | 46 | 9 | 14 | 23 | 57 | 78 | 32 |
| Workington | 46 | 10 | 11 | 25 | 54 | 87 | 31 |
| Bradford Park Avenue | 46 | 4 | 15 | 27 | 30 | 82 | 23 |

Port Vale was expelled from the League for financial irregularities but successfully applied for re-election for the 1968/69 season.

## 1968 F.A. Cup

**Semi-finals**

| | |
|---|---|
| West Bromwich Albion vs Birmingham City | 2-0 |
| Everton vs Leeds United | 1-0 |

**Final**

Wembley, 18th May 1968

**West Bromwich Albion 1**  (Astle)

**Everton 0  (aet.)**

*Attendance 100,000*

## 1968 Football League Cup

**Semi-finals**

| | |
|---|---|
| Derby County vs Leeds United  (0-1, 2-3) | 2-4 |
| Arsenal vs Huddersfield Town  (3-2, 3-1) | 6-3 |

**Final**

Wembley, 2nd March 1968

**Leeds United 1**  (Cooper)

**Arsenal 0**

*Attendance 97,887*

## DIVISION ONE 1968-69

| | | | | | | | |
|---|---|---|---|---|---|---|---|
| **LEEDS UNITED** | 42 | 27 | 13 | 2 | 66 | 26 | 67 |
| Liverpool | 42 | 25 | 11 | 6 | 63 | 24 | 61 |
| Everton | 42 | 21 | 15 | 6 | 77 | 36 | 57 |
| Arsenal | 42 | 22 | 12 | 8 | 56 | 27 | 56 |
| Chelsea | 42 | 20 | 10 | 12 | 73 | 53 | 50 |
| Tottenham Hotspur | 42 | 14 | 17 | 11 | 61 | 51 | 45 |
| Southampton | 42 | 16 | 13 | 13 | 57 | 48 | 45 |
| West Ham United | 42 | 13 | 18 | 11 | 66 | 50 | 44 |
| Newcastle United | 42 | 15 | 14 | 13 | 61 | 55 | 44 |
| West Bromwich Albion | 42 | 16 | 11 | 15 | 64 | 67 | 43 |
| Manchester United | 42 | 15 | 12 | 15 | 57 | 53 | 42 |
| Ipswich Town | 42 | 15 | 11 | 16 | 59 | 60 | 41 |
| Manchester City | 42 | 15 | 10 | 17 | 64 | 55 | 40 |
| Burnley | 42 | 15 | 9 | 18 | 55 | 82 | 39 |
| Sheffield Wednesday | 42 | 10 | 16 | 16 | 41 | 54 | 36 |
| Wolverhampton Wanderers | 42 | 10 | 15 | 17 | 41 | 58 | 35 |
| Sunderland | 42 | 11 | 12 | 19 | 43 | 67 | 34 |
| Nottingham Forest | 42 | 10 | 13 | 19 | 45 | 57 | 33 |
| Stoke City | 42 | 9 | 15 | 18 | 40 | 63 | 33 |
| Coventry City | 42 | 10 | 11 | 21 | 46 | 64 | 31 |
| *Leicester City* | 42 | 9 | 12 | 21 | 39 | 68 | 30 |
| *Queen's Park Rangers* | 42 | 4 | 10 | 28 | 39 | 95 | 18 |

## DIVISION TWO 1968-69

| | | | | | | | |
|---|---|---|---|---|---|---|---|
| **Derby County** | 42 | 26 | 11 | 5 | 65 | 32 | 63 |
| **Crystal Palace** | 42 | 22 | 12 | 8 | 70 | 47 | 56 |
| Charlton Athletic | 42 | 18 | 14 | 10 | 61 | 52 | 50 |
| Middlesbrough | 42 | 19 | 11 | 12 | 58 | 49 | 49 |
| Cardiff City | 42 | 20 | 7 | 15 | 67 | 54 | 47 |
| Huddersfield Town | 42 | 17 | 12 | 13 | 53 | 46 | 46 |
| Birmingham City | 42 | 18 | 8 | 16 | 73 | 59 | 44 |
| Blackpool | 42 | 14 | 15 | 13 | 51 | 41 | 43 |
| Sheffield United | 42 | 16 | 11 | 15 | 61 | 50 | 43 |
| Millwall | 42 | 17 | 9 | 16 | 57 | 49 | 43 |
| Hull City | 42 | 13 | 16 | 13 | 59 | 52 | 42 |
| Carlisle United | 42 | 16 | 10 | 16 | 46 | 49 | 42 |
| Norwich City | 42 | 15 | 10 | 17 | 53 | 56 | 40 |
| Preston North End | 42 | 12 | 15 | 15 | 38 | 44 | 39 |
| Portsmouth | 42 | 12 | 14 | 16 | 58 | 58 | 38 |
| Bristol City | 42 | 11 | 16 | 15 | 46 | 53 | 38 |
| Bolton Wanderers | 42 | 12 | 14 | 16 | 55 | 67 | 38 |
| Aston Villa | 42 | 12 | 14 | 16 | 37 | 48 | 38 |
| Blackburn Rovers | 42 | 13 | 11 | 18 | 52 | 63 | 37 |
| Oxford United | 42 | 12 | 9 | 21 | 34 | 55 | 33 |
| *Bury* | 42 | 11 | 8 | 23 | 51 | 80 | 30 |
| *Fulham* | 42 | 7 | 11 | 24 | 40 | 81 | 25 |

## DIVISION THREE 1968-69

| | | | | | | | |
|---|---|---|---|---|---|---|---|
| **Watford** | 46 | 27 | 10 | 9 | 74 | 34 | 64 |
| **Swindon Town** | 46 | 27 | 10 | 9 | 71 | 35 | 64 |
| Luton Town | 46 | 25 | 11 | 10 | 74 | 38 | 61 |
| Bournemouth & Boscombe Ath. | 46 | 21 | 9 | 16 | 60 | 45 | 51 |
| Plymouth Argyle | 46 | 17 | 15 | 14 | 53 | 49 | 49 |
| Torquay United | 46 | 18 | 12 | 16 | 54 | 46 | 48 |
| Tranmere Rovers | 46 | 19 | 10 | 17 | 70 | 68 | 48 |
| Southport | 46 | 17 | 13 | 16 | 71 | 64 | 47 |
| Stockport County | 46 | 16 | 14 | 16 | 67 | 68 | 46 |
| Barnsley | 46 | 16 | 14 | 16 | 58 | 63 | 46 |
| Rotherham United | 46 | 16 | 13 | 17 | 56 | 50 | 45 |
| Brighton & Hove Albion | 46 | 16 | 13 | 17 | 72 | 65 | 45 |
| Walsall | 46 | 14 | 16 | 16 | 50 | 49 | 44 |
| Reading | 46 | 15 | 13 | 18 | 67 | 66 | 43 |
| Mansfield Town | 46 | 16 | 11 | 19 | 58 | 62 | 43 |
| Bristol Rovers | 46 | 16 | 11 | 19 | 63 | 71 | 43 |
| Shrewsbury Town | 46 | 16 | 11 | 19 | 51 | 67 | 43 |
| Orient | 46 | 14 | 14 | 18 | 51 | 58 | 42 |
| Barrow | 46 | 17 | 8 | 21 | 56 | 75 | 42 |
| Gillingham | 46 | 13 | 15 | 18 | 54 | 63 | 41 |
| *Northampton Town* | 46 | 14 | 12 | 20 | 54 | 61 | 40 |
| *Hartlepool* | 46 | 10 | 19 | 17 | 40 | 70 | 39 |
| *Crewe Alexandra* | 46 | 13 | 9 | 24 | 52 | 76 | 35 |
| *Oldham Athletic* | 46 | 13 | 9 | 24 | 50 | 83 | 35 |

## DIVISION FOUR 1968-69

| | | | | | | | |
|---|---|---|---|---|---|---|---|
| **Doncaster Rovers** | 46 | 21 | 17 | 8 | 65 | 38 | 59 |
| **Halifax Town** | 46 | 20 | 17 | 9 | 53 | 37 | 57 |
| **Rochdale** | 46 | 18 | 20 | 8 | 68 | 35 | 56 |
| **Bradford City** | 46 | 18 | 20 | 8 | 65 | 46 | 56 |
| Darlington | 46 | 17 | 18 | 11 | 62 | 45 | 52 |
| Colchester United | 46 | 20 | 12 | 14 | 57 | 53 | 52 |
| Southend United | 46 | 19 | 13 | 14 | 78 | 61 | 51 |
| Lincoln City | 46 | 17 | 17 | 12 | 54 | 52 | 51 |
| Wrexham | 46 | 18 | 14 | 14 | 61 | 52 | 50 |
| Swansea Town | 46 | 19 | 11 | 16 | 58 | 54 | 49 |
| Brentford | 46 | 18 | 12 | 16 | 64 | 65 | 48 |
| Workington | 46 | 15 | 17 | 14 | 40 | 43 | 47 |
| Port Vale | 46 | 16 | 14 | 16 | 46 | 46 | 46 |
| Chester | 46 | 16 | 13 | 17 | 76 | 66 | 45 |
| Aldershot | 46 | 19 | 7 | 20 | 66 | 66 | 45 |
| Scunthorpe United | 46 | 18 | 8 | 20 | 61 | 60 | 44 |
| Exeter City | 46 | 16 | 11 | 19 | 66 | 65 | 43 |
| Peterborough United | 46 | 13 | 16 | 17 | 60 | 57 | 42 |
| Notts County | 46 | 12 | 18 | 16 | 48 | 57 | 42 |
| Chesterfield | 46 | 13 | 15 | 18 | 43 | 50 | 41 |
| York City | 46 | 14 | 11 | 21 | 53 | 75 | 39 |
| Newport County | 46 | 11 | 14 | 21 | 49 | 74 | 36 |
| Grimsby Town | 46 | 9 | 15 | 22 | 47 | 69 | 33 |
| Bradford Park Avenue | 46 | 5 | 10 | 31 | 32 | 106 | 20 |

## 1969 F.A. Cup

### Semi-finals

| | |
|---|---|
| Manchester City vs Everton | 1-0 |
| West Bromwich Albion vs Leicester City | 0-1 |

### Final

Wembley, 26th April 1969

**Manchester City 1** (Young)

**Leicester City 0**

*Attendance 100,000*

## 1969 Football League Cup

### Semi-finals

| | |
|---|---|
| Arsenal vs Tottenham Hotspur  (1-0, 1-1) | 2-1 |
| Burnley vs Swindon Town  (1-2, 2-1) | 3-3 |

### Play-off

| | |
|---|---|
| Burnley vs Swindon Town | 2-3 |

### Final

Wembley, 15th March 1969

**Swindon Town 3**   (Smart, Rogers 2)

**Arsenal 1**   (Gould)

*Attendance 98,189*

## DIVISION ONE 1969-70

| | | | | | | | |
|---|---|---|---|---|---|---|---|
| **EVERTON** | 42 | 29 | 8 | 5 | 72 | 34 | 66 |
| Leeds United | 42 | 21 | 15 | 6 | 84 | 49 | 57 |
| Chelsea | 42 | 21 | 13 | 8 | 70 | 50 | 55 |
| Derby County | 42 | 22 | 9 | 11 | 64 | 37 | 53 |
| Liverpool | 42 | 20 | 11 | 11 | 65 | 42 | 51 |
| Coventry City | 42 | 19 | 11 | 12 | 58 | 48 | 49 |
| Newcastle United | 42 | 17 | 13 | 12 | 57 | 35 | 47 |
| Manchester United | 42 | 14 | 17 | 11 | 66 | 61 | 45 |
| Stoke City | 42 | 15 | 15 | 12 | 56 | 52 | 45 |
| Manchester City | 42 | 16 | 11 | 15 | 55 | 48 | 43 |
| Tottenham Hotspur | 42 | 17 | 9 | 16 | 54 | 55 | 43 |
| Arsenal | 42 | 12 | 18 | 12 | 51 | 49 | 42 |
| Wolverhampton Wanderers | 42 | 12 | 16 | 14 | 55 | 57 | 40 |
| Burnley | 42 | 12 | 15 | 15 | 56 | 61 | 39 |
| Nottingham Forest | 42 | 10 | 18 | 14 | 50 | 71 | 38 |
| West Bromwich Albion | 42 | 14 | 9 | 19 | 58 | 66 | 37 |
| West Ham United | 42 | 12 | 12 | 18 | 51 | 60 | 36 |
| Ipswich Town | 42 | 10 | 11 | 21 | 40 | 63 | 31 |
| Southampton | 42 | 6 | 17 | 19 | 46 | 67 | 29 |
| Crystal Palace | 42 | 6 | 15 | 21 | 34 | 68 | 27 |
| *Sunderland* | 42 | 6 | 14 | 22 | 30 | 68 | 26 |
| *Sheffield Wednesday* | 42 | 8 | 9 | 25 | 40 | 71 | 25 |

## DIVISION TWO 1969-70

| | | | | | | | |
|---|---|---|---|---|---|---|---|
| **Huddersfield Town** | 42 | 24 | 12 | 6 | 68 | 37 | 60 |
| **Blackpool** | 42 | 20 | 13 | 9 | 56 | 45 | 53 |
| Leicester City | 42 | 19 | 13 | 10 | 64 | 50 | 51 |
| Middlesbrough | 42 | 20 | 10 | 12 | 55 | 45 | 50 |
| Swindon Town | 42 | 17 | 16 | 9 | 57 | 47 | 50 |
| Sheffield United | 42 | 22 | 5 | 15 | 73 | 38 | 49 |
| Cardiff City | 42 | 18 | 13 | 11 | 61 | 41 | 49 |
| Blackburn Rovers | 42 | 20 | 7 | 15 | 54 | 50 | 47 |
| Queen's Park Rangers | 42 | 17 | 11 | 14 | 66 | 57 | 45 |
| Millwall | 42 | 15 | 14 | 13 | 56 | 56 | 44 |
| Norwich City | 42 | 16 | 11 | 15 | 49 | 46 | 43 |
| Carlisle United | 42 | 14 | 13 | 15 | 58 | 56 | 41 |
| Hull City | 42 | 15 | 11 | 16 | 72 | 70 | 41 |
| Bristol City | 42 | 13 | 13 | 16 | 54 | 50 | 39 |
| Oxford United | 42 | 12 | 15 | 15 | 35 | 42 | 39 |
| Bolton Wanderers | 42 | 12 | 12 | 18 | 54 | 61 | 36 |
| Portsmouth | 42 | 13 | 9 | 20 | 66 | 80 | 35 |
| Birmingham City | 42 | 11 | 11 | 20 | 51 | 78 | 33 |
| Watford | 42 | 9 | 13 | 20 | 44 | 57 | 31 |
| Charlton Athletic | 42 | 7 | 17 | 18 | 35 | 76 | 31 |
| *Aston Villa* | 42 | 8 | 13 | 21 | 36 | 62 | 29 |
| *Preston North End* | 42 | 8 | 12 | 22 | 43 | 63 | 28 |

## DIVISION THREE 1969-70

| | | | | | | | |
|---|---|---|---|---|---|---|---|
| **Orient** | 46 | 25 | 12 | 9 | 67 | 36 | 62 |
| **Luton Town** | 46 | 23 | 14 | 9 | 77 | 43 | 60 |
| Bristol Rovers | 46 | 20 | 16 | 10 | 80 | 59 | 56 |
| Fulham | 46 | 20 | 15 | 11 | 81 | 55 | 55 |
| Brighton & Hove Albion | 46 | 23 | 9 | 14 | 57 | 43 | 55 |
| Mansfield Town | 46 | 21 | 11 | 14 | 70 | 49 | 53 |
| Barnsley | 46 | 19 | 15 | 12 | 68 | 59 | 53 |
| Reading | 46 | 21 | 11 | 14 | 87 | 77 | 53 |
| Rochdale | 46 | 18 | 10 | 18 | 69 | 60 | 46 |
| Bradford City | 46 | 17 | 12 | 17 | 57 | 50 | 46 |
| Doncaster Rovers | 46 | 17 | 12 | 17 | 52 | 54 | 46 |
| Walsall | 46 | 17 | 12 | 17 | 54 | 67 | 46 |
| Torquay United | 46 | 14 | 17 | 15 | 62 | 59 | 45 |
| Rotherham United | 46 | 15 | 14 | 17 | 62 | 54 | 44 |
| Shrewsbury Town | 46 | 13 | 18 | 15 | 62 | 63 | 44 |
| Tranmere Rovers | 46 | 14 | 16 | 16 | 56 | 72 | 44 |
| Plymouth Argyle | 46 | 16 | 11 | 19 | 56 | 64 | 43 |
| Halifax Town | 46 | 14 | 15 | 17 | 47 | 63 | 43 |
| Bury | 46 | 15 | 11 | 20 | 75 | 80 | 41 |
| Gillingham | 46 | 13 | 13 | 20 | 52 | 64 | 39 |
| *Bournemouth & Boscombe Ath.* | 46 | 12 | 15 | 19 | 48 | 71 | 39 |
| *Southport* | 46 | 14 | 10 | 22 | 48 | 66 | 38 |
| *Barrow* | 46 | 8 | 14 | 24 | 46 | 81 | 30 |
| *Stockport County* | 46 | 6 | 11 | 29 | 27 | 71 | 23 |

## DIVISION FOUR 1969-70

| | | | | | | | |
|---|---|---|---|---|---|---|---|
| **Chesterfield** | 46 | 27 | 10 | 9 | 77 | 32 | 64 |
| **Wrexham** | 46 | 26 | 9 | 11 | 84 | 49 | 61 |
| **Swansea City** | 46 | 21 | 18 | 7 | 66 | 45 | 60 |
| **Port Vale** | 46 | 20 | 19 | 7 | 61 | 33 | 59 |
| Brentford | 46 | 20 | 16 | 10 | 58 | 39 | 56 |
| Aldershot | 46 | 20 | 13 | 13 | 78 | 65 | 53 |
| Notts County | 46 | 22 | 8 | 16 | 73 | 62 | 52 |
| Lincoln City | 46 | 17 | 16 | 13 | 66 | 52 | 50 |
| Peterborough United | 46 | 17 | 14 | 15 | 77 | 69 | 48 |
| Colchester United | 46 | 17 | 14 | 15 | 64 | 63 | 48 |
| Chester | 46 | 21 | 6 | 19 | 58 | 66 | 48 |
| Scunthorpe United | 46 | 18 | 10 | 18 | 67 | 65 | 46 |
| York City | 46 | 16 | 14 | 16 | 55 | 62 | 46 |
| Northampton Town | 46 | 16 | 12 | 18 | 64 | 55 | 44 |
| Crewe Alexandra | 46 | 16 | 12 | 18 | 51 | 51 | 44 |
| Grimsby Town | 46 | 14 | 15 | 17 | 54 | 58 | 43 |
| Southend United | 46 | 15 | 10 | 21 | 59 | 85 | 40 |
| Exeter City | 46 | 14 | 11 | 21 | 57 | 59 | 39 |
| Oldham Athletic | 46 | 13 | 13 | 20 | 60 | 65 | 39 |
| Workington | 46 | 12 | 14 | 20 | 46 | 64 | 38 |
| Newport County | 46 | 13 | 11 | 22 | 53 | 74 | 37 |
| Darlington | 46 | 13 | 10 | 23 | 53 | 73 | 36 |
| Hartlepool | 46 | 10 | 10 | 26 | 42 | 82 | 30 |
| *Bradford Park Avenue* | 46 | 6 | 11 | 29 | 41 | 96 | 23 |

## 1970 F.A. Cup

### Semi-finals

| | |
|---|---|
| Chelsea vs Watford | 5-1 |
| Manchester United vs Leeds United | 0-0, 0-0, 0-1 |

### Final

Wembley, 11th April 1970

**Chelsea 2**   (Houseman, Hutchinson)
**Leeds United 2 (aet.)**   (Charlton, Jones)

*Attendance 100,000*

### Replay

Old Trafford, 29th April 1970

**Chelsea 2**   (Osgood, Webb)
**Leeds United 1 (aet.)**   (Jones)

*Attendance 62,000*

## 1970 Football League Cup

### Semi-finals

| | | |
|---|---|---|
| Manchester City vs Manchester United (2-1, 2-2) | 4-3 |
| Carlisle United vs West Bromwich Albion (1-0, 1-4) | 2-4 |

### Final

Wembley, 7th March 1970

**Manchester City 2**   (Doyle, Pardoe)
**West Bromwich Albion 1**   (Astle)

*Attendance 97,963*

## DIVISION ONE 1970-71

| | | | | | | | |
|---|---|---|---|---|---|---|---|
| **ARSENAL** | 42 | 29 | 7 | 6 | 71 | 29 | 65 |
| Leeds United | 42 | 27 | 10 | 5 | 72 | 30 | 64 |
| Tottenham Hotspur | 42 | 19 | 14 | 9 | 54 | 33 | 52 |
| Wolverhampton Wanderers | 42 | 22 | 8 | 12 | 64 | 54 | 52 |
| Liverpool | 42 | 17 | 17 | 8 | 42 | 24 | 51 |
| Chelsea | 42 | 18 | 15 | 9 | 52 | 42 | 51 |
| Southampton | 42 | 17 | 12 | 13 | 56 | 44 | 46 |
| Manchester United | 42 | 16 | 11 | 15 | 65 | 66 | 43 |
| Derby County | 42 | 16 | 10 | 16 | 56 | 54 | 42 |
| Coventry City | 42 | 16 | 10 | 16 | 37 | 38 | 42 |
| Manchester City | 42 | 12 | 17 | 13 | 47 | 42 | 41 |
| Newcastle United | 42 | 14 | 13 | 15 | 44 | 46 | 41 |
| Stoke City | 42 | 12 | 13 | 17 | 44 | 48 | 37 |
| Everton | 42 | 12 | 13 | 17 | 54 | 60 | 37 |
| Huddersfield Town | 42 | 11 | 14 | 17 | 40 | 49 | 36 |
| Nottingham Forest | 42 | 14 | 8 | 20 | 42 | 61 | 36 |
| West Bromwich Albion | 42 | 10 | 15 | 17 | 58 | 75 | 35 |
| Crystal Palace | 42 | 12 | 11 | 19 | 39 | 57 | 35 |
| Ipswich Town | 42 | 12 | 10 | 20 | 42 | 48 | 34 |
| West Ham United | 42 | 10 | 14 | 18 | 47 | 60 | 34 |
| *Burnley* | *42* | *7* | *13* | *22* | *29* | *63* | *27* |
| *Blackpool* | *42* | *4* | *15* | *23* | *34* | *66* | *23* |

## DIVISION THREE 1970-71

| | | | | | | | |
|---|---|---|---|---|---|---|---|
| **Preston North End** | 46 | 22 | 17 | 7 | 63 | 39 | 61 |
| **Fulham** | 46 | 24 | 12 | 10 | 68 | 41 | 60 |
| Halifax Town | 46 | 22 | 12 | 12 | 74 | 55 | 56 |
| Aston Villa | 46 | 19 | 15 | 12 | 54 | 46 | 53 |
| Chesterfield | 46 | 17 | 17 | 12 | 66 | 38 | 51 |
| Bristol Rovers | 46 | 19 | 13 | 14 | 69 | 50 | 51 |
| Mansfield Town | 46 | 18 | 15 | 13 | 64 | 62 | 51 |
| Rotherham United | 46 | 17 | 16 | 13 | 64 | 60 | 50 |
| Wrexham | 46 | 18 | 13 | 15 | 72 | 65 | 49 |
| Torquay United | 46 | 19 | 11 | 16 | 54 | 57 | 49 |
| Swansea City | 46 | 15 | 16 | 15 | 59 | 56 | 46 |
| Barnsley | 46 | 17 | 11 | 18 | 49 | 52 | 45 |
| Shrewsbury Town | 46 | 16 | 13 | 17 | 58 | 62 | 45 |
| Brighton & Hove Albion | 46 | 14 | 16 | 16 | 50 | 47 | 44 |
| Plymouth Argyle | 46 | 12 | 19 | 15 | 63 | 63 | 43 |
| Rochdale | 46 | 14 | 15 | 17 | 61 | 68 | 43 |
| Port Vale | 46 | 15 | 12 | 19 | 52 | 59 | 42 |
| Tranmere Rovers | 46 | 10 | 22 | 14 | 45 | 55 | 42 |
| Bradford City | 46 | 13 | 14 | 19 | 49 | 62 | 40 |
| Walsall | 46 | 14 | 11 | 21 | 51 | 57 | 39 |
| *Reading* | *46* | *14* | *11* | *21* | *48* | *85* | *39* |
| *Bury* | *46* | *12* | *13* | *21* | *52* | *60* | *37* |
| *Doncaster Rovers* | *46* | *13* | *9* | *24* | *45* | *66* | *35* |
| *Gillingham* | *46* | *10* | *13* | *23* | *42* | *67* | *33* |

## DIVISION TWO 1970-71

| | | | | | | | |
|---|---|---|---|---|---|---|---|
| **Leicester City** | 42 | 23 | 13 | 6 | 57 | 30 | 59 |
| **Sheffield United** | 42 | 21 | 14 | 7 | 73 | 39 | 56 |
| Cardiff City | 42 | 20 | 13 | 9 | 64 | 41 | 53 |
| Carlisle United | 42 | 20 | 13 | 9 | 65 | 43 | 53 |
| Hull City | 42 | 19 | 13 | 10 | 54 | 41 | 51 |
| Luton Town | 42 | 18 | 13 | 11 | 62 | 43 | 49 |
| Middlesbrough | 42 | 17 | 14 | 11 | 60 | 43 | 48 |
| Millwall | 42 | 19 | 9 | 14 | 59 | 42 | 47 |
| Birmingham City | 42 | 17 | 12 | 13 | 58 | 48 | 46 |
| Norwich City | 42 | 15 | 14 | 13 | 54 | 52 | 44 |
| Queen's Park Rangers | 42 | 16 | 11 | 15 | 58 | 53 | 43 |
| Swindon Town | 42 | 15 | 12 | 15 | 61 | 51 | 42 |
| Sunderland | 42 | 15 | 12 | 15 | 52 | 54 | 42 |
| Oxford United | 42 | 14 | 14 | 14 | 41 | 48 | 42 |
| Sheffield Wednesday | 42 | 12 | 12 | 18 | 51 | 69 | 36 |
| Portsmouth | 42 | 10 | 14 | 18 | 46 | 61 | 34 |
| Orient | 42 | 9 | 16 | 17 | 29 | 51 | 34 |
| Watford | 42 | 10 | 13 | 19 | 38 | 60 | 33 |
| Bristol City | 42 | 10 | 11 | 21 | 46 | 64 | 31 |
| Charlton Athletic | 42 | 8 | 14 | 20 | 41 | 65 | 30 |
| *Blackburn Rovers* | *42* | *6* | *15* | *21* | *37* | *69* | *27* |
| *Bolton Wanderers* | *42* | *7* | *10* | *25* | *35* | *74* | *24* |

## DIVISION FOUR 1970-71

| | | | | | | | |
|---|---|---|---|---|---|---|---|
| **Notts County** | 46 | 30 | 9 | 7 | 89 | 36 | 69 |
| **Bournemouth & Boscombe** | 46 | 24 | 12 | 10 | 81 | 46 | 60 |
| **Oldham Athletic** | 46 | 24 | 11 | 11 | 88 | 63 | 59 |
| **York City** | 46 | 23 | 10 | 13 | 78 | 54 | 56 |
| Chester | 46 | 24 | 7 | 15 | 69 | 55 | 55 |
| Colchester United | 46 | 21 | 12 | 13 | 70 | 54 | 54 |
| Northampton Town | 46 | 19 | 13 | 14 | 63 | 59 | 51 |
| Southport | 46 | 21 | 6 | 19 | 63 | 57 | 48 |
| Exeter City | 46 | 17 | 14 | 15 | 67 | 68 | 48 |
| Workington | 46 | 18 | 12 | 16 | 48 | 49 | 48 |
| Stockport County | 46 | 16 | 14 | 16 | 49 | 65 | 46 |
| Darlington | 46 | 17 | 11 | 18 | 58 | 57 | 45 |
| Aldershot | 46 | 14 | 17 | 15 | 66 | 71 | 45 |
| Brentford | 46 | 18 | 8 | 20 | 66 | 62 | 44 |
| Crewe Alexandra | 46 | 18 | 8 | 20 | 75 | 76 | 44 |
| Peterborough United | 46 | 18 | 7 | 21 | 70 | 71 | 43 |
| Scunthorpe United | 46 | 15 | 13 | 18 | 56 | 61 | 43 |
| Southend United | 46 | 14 | 15 | 17 | 53 | 66 | 43 |
| Grimsby Town | 46 | 18 | 7 | 21 | 57 | 71 | 43 |
| Cambridge United | 46 | 15 | 13 | 18 | 51 | 66 | 43 |
| Lincoln City | 46 | 13 | 13 | 20 | 70 | 71 | 39 |
| Newport County | 46 | 10 | 8 | 28 | 55 | 85 | 28 |
| Hartlepool | 46 | 8 | 12 | 26 | 34 | 74 | 28 |
| Barrow | 46 | 7 | 8 | 31 | 51 | 90 | 22 |

## 1971 F.A. Cup

**Semi-finals**

| | |
|---|---|
| Stoke City vs Arsenal | 2-2, 0-2 |
| Liverpool vs Everton | 2-1 |

**Final**

Wembley, 8th May 1971

**Arsenal 2**  (Kelly, George)
**Liverpool 1 (aet.)**  (Heighway)

*Attendance 100,000*

## 1971 Football League Cup

**Semi-finals**

| | |
|---|---|
| Bristol City vs Tottenham Hotspur (1-1, 0-2) | 1-3 |
| Manchester United vs Aston Villa (1-1, 1-2) | 2-3 |

**Final**

Wembley, 27th February 1971

**Tottenham Hotspur 2**  (Chivers 2)
**Aston Villa 0**

*Attendance 100,000*

## DIVISION ONE 1971-72

| | | | | | | | |
|---|---|---|---|---|---|---|---|
| **DERBY COUNTY** | 42 | 24 | 10 | 8 | 69 | 33 | 58 |
| Leeds United | 42 | 24 | 9 | 9 | 73 | 31 | 57 |
| Liverpool | 42 | 24 | 9 | 9 | 64 | 30 | 57 |
| Manchester City | 42 | 23 | 11 | 8 | 77 | 45 | 57 |
| Arsenal | 42 | 22 | 8 | 12 | 58 | 40 | 52 |
| Tottenham Hotspur | 42 | 19 | 13 | 10 | 63 | 42 | 51 |
| Chelsea | 42 | 18 | 12 | 12 | 58 | 49 | 48 |
| Manchester United | 42 | 19 | 10 | 13 | 69 | 61 | 48 |
| Wolverhampton Wanderers | 42 | 18 | 11 | 13 | 65 | 57 | 47 |
| Sheffield United | 42 | 17 | 12 | 13 | 61 | 60 | 46 |
| Newcastle United | 42 | 15 | 11 | 16 | 49 | 52 | 41 |
| Leicester City | 42 | 13 | 13 | 16 | 41 | 46 | 39 |
| Ipswich Town | 42 | 11 | 16 | 15 | 39 | 53 | 38 |
| West Ham United | 42 | 12 | 12 | 18 | 47 | 51 | 36 |
| Everton | 42 | 9 | 18 | 15 | 37 | 48 | 36 |
| West Bromwich Albion | 42 | 12 | 11 | 19 | 42 | 54 | 35 |
| Stoke City | 42 | 10 | 15 | 17 | 39 | 56 | 35 |
| Coventry City | 42 | 9 | 15 | 18 | 44 | 67 | 33 |
| Southampton | 42 | 12 | 7 | 23 | 52 | 80 | 31 |
| Crystal Palace | 42 | 8 | 13 | 21 | 39 | 65 | 29 |
| *Nottingham Forest* | *42* | *8* | *9* | *25* | *47* | *81* | *25* |
| *Huddersfield Town* | *42* | *6* | *13* | *23* | *27* | *59* | *25* |

## DIVISION TWO 1971-72

| | | | | | | | |
|---|---|---|---|---|---|---|---|
| **Norwich City** | 42 | 21 | 15 | 6 | 60 | 36 | 57 |
| **Birmingham City** | 42 | 19 | 18 | 5 | 60 | 31 | 56 |
| Millwall | 42 | 19 | 17 | 6 | 64 | 46 | 55 |
| Queen's Park Rangers | 42 | 20 | 14 | 8 | 57 | 28 | 54 |
| Sunderland | 42 | 17 | 16 | 9 | 67 | 57 | 50 |
| Blackpool | 42 | 20 | 7 | 15 | 70 | 50 | 47 |
| Burnley | 42 | 20 | 6 | 16 | 70 | 55 | 46 |
| Bristol City | 42 | 18 | 10 | 14 | 61 | 49 | 46 |
| Middlesbrough | 42 | 19 | 8 | 15 | 50 | 48 | 46 |
| Carlisle United | 42 | 17 | 9 | 16 | 61 | 57 | 43 |
| Swindon Town | 42 | 15 | 12 | 15 | 47 | 47 | 42 |
| Hull City | 42 | 14 | 10 | 18 | 49 | 53 | 38 |
| Luton Town | 42 | 10 | 18 | 14 | 43 | 48 | 38 |
| Sheffield Wednesday | 42 | 13 | 12 | 17 | 51 | 58 | 38 |
| Oxford United | 42 | 12 | 14 | 16 | 43 | 55 | 38 |
| Portsmouth | 42 | 12 | 13 | 17 | 59 | 68 | 37 |
| Orient | 42 | 14 | 9 | 19 | 50 | 61 | 37 |
| Preston North End | 42 | 12 | 12 | 18 | 52 | 58 | 36 |
| Cardiff City | 42 | 10 | 14 | 18 | 56 | 69 | 34 |
| Fulham | 42 | 12 | 10 | 20 | 45 | 68 | 34 |
| *Charlton Athletic* | *42* | *12* | *9* | *21* | *55* | *77* | *33* |
| *Watford* | *42* | *5* | *9* | *28* | *24* | *75* | *19* |

## DIVISION THREE 1971-72

| | | | | | | | |
|---|---|---|---|---|---|---|---|
| **Aston Villa** | 46 | 32 | 6 | 8 | 85 | 32 | 70 |
| **Brighton & Hove Albion** | 46 | 27 | 11 | 8 | 82 | 47 | 65 |
| Bournemouth & Boscombe Ath. | 46 | 23 | 16 | 7 | 73 | 37 | 62 |
| Notts County | 46 | 25 | 12 | 9 | 74 | 44 | 62 |
| Rotherham United | 46 | 20 | 15 | 11 | 69 | 52 | 55 |
| Bristol Rovers | 46 | 21 | 12 | 13 | 75 | 56 | 54 |
| Bolton Wanderers | 46 | 17 | 16 | 13 | 51 | 41 | 50 |
| Plymouth Argyle | 46 | 20 | 10 | 16 | 74 | 64 | 50 |
| Walsall | 46 | 15 | 18 | 13 | 62 | 57 | 48 |
| Blackburn Rovers | 46 | 19 | 9 | 18 | 54 | 57 | 47 |
| Oldham Athletic | 46 | 17 | 11 | 18 | 59 | 63 | 45 |
| Shrewsbury Town | 46 | 17 | 10 | 19 | 73 | 65 | 44 |
| Chesterfield | 46 | 18 | 8 | 20 | 57 | 57 | 44 |
| Swansea City | 46 | 17 | 10 | 19 | 46 | 59 | 44 |
| Port Vale | 46 | 13 | 15 | 18 | 43 | 59 | 41 |
| Wrexham | 46 | 16 | 8 | 22 | 59 | 63 | 40 |
| Halifax Town | 46 | 13 | 12 | 21 | 48 | 61 | 38 |
| Rochdale | 46 | 12 | 13 | 21 | 57 | 83 | 37 |
| York City | 46 | 12 | 12 | 22 | 57 | 66 | 36 |
| Tranmere Rovers | 46 | 10 | 16 | 20 | 50 | 71 | 36 |
| *Mansfield Town* | *46* | *8* | *20* | *18* | *41* | *63* | *36* |
| *Barnsley* | *46* | *9* | *18* | *19* | *32* | *64* | *36* |
| *Torquay United* | *46* | *10* | *12* | *24* | *41* | *69* | *32* |
| *Bradford City* | *46* | *11* | *10* | *25* | *45* | *77* | *32* |

## DIVISION FOUR 1971-72

| | | | | | | | |
|---|---|---|---|---|---|---|---|
| **Grimsby Town** | 46 | 28 | 7 | 11 | 88 | 56 | 63 |
| **Southend United** | 46 | 24 | 12 | 10 | 81 | 55 | 60 |
| **Brentford** | 46 | 24 | 11 | 11 | 76 | 44 | 59 |
| **Scunthorpe United** | 46 | 22 | 13 | 11 | 56 | 37 | 57 |
| Lincoln City | 46 | 21 | 14 | 11 | 77 | 59 | 56 |
| Workington | 46 | 16 | 19 | 11 | 50 | 34 | 51 |
| Southport | 46 | 18 | 14 | 14 | 66 | 46 | 50 |
| Peterborough United | 46 | 17 | 16 | 13 | 82 | 64 | 50 |
| Bury | 46 | 19 | 12 | 15 | 73 | 59 | 50 |
| Cambridge United | 46 | 17 | 14 | 15 | 62 | 60 | 48 |
| Colchester United | 46 | 19 | 10 | 17 | 70 | 69 | 48 |
| Doncaster Rovers | 46 | 16 | 14 | 16 | 56 | 63 | 46 |
| Gillingham | 46 | 16 | 13 | 17 | 61 | 67 | 45 |
| Newport County | 46 | 18 | 8 | 20 | 60 | 72 | 44 |
| Exeter City | 46 | 16 | 11 | 19 | 61 | 68 | 43 |
| Reading | 46 | 17 | 8 | 21 | 56 | 76 | 42 |
| Aldershot | 46 | 9 | 22 | 15 | 48 | 54 | 40 |
| Hartlepool | 46 | 17 | 6 | 23 | 58 | 69 | 40 |
| Darlington | 46 | 14 | 11 | 21 | 64 | 82 | 39 |
| Chester | 46 | 10 | 18 | 18 | 47 | 56 | 38 |
| Northampton Town | 46 | 12 | 13 | 21 | 66 | 79 | 37 |
| *Barrow* | *46* | *13* | *11* | *22* | *40* | *71* | *37* |
| Stockport County | 46 | 9 | 14 | 23 | 55 | 87 | 32 |
| Crewe Alexandra | 46 | 10 | 9 | 27 | 43 | 69 | 29 |

## 1972 F.A. Cup

**Semi-finals**

| | |
|---|---|
| Leeds United vs Birmingham City | 3-0 |
| Arsenal vs Stoke City | 1-1, 2-1 |

**Final**

Wembley, 6th May 1972

**Leeds United 1** (Clarke)

**Arsenal 0**

*Attendance 100,000*

## 1972 Football League Cup

**Semi-finals**

| | |
|---|---|
| Stoke City vs West Ham Utd. (1-2, 1-0, 0-0*, 3-2†) | 5-4 |
| Chelsea vs Tottenham Hotspur (3-2, 2-2) | 5-4 |

* 1st play-off at Hillsborough; † 2nd play-off at Old Trafford

**Final**

Wembley, 4th March 1972

**Stoke City 2** (Conroy, Eastham)

**Chelsea 1** (Osgood)

*Attendance 100,000*

## DIVISION ONE 1972-73

| | | | | | | | |
|---|---|---|---|---|---|---|---|
| **LIVERPOOL** | 42 | 25 | 10 | 7 | 72 | 42 | 60 |
| Arsenal | 42 | 23 | 11 | 8 | 57 | 43 | 57 |
| Leeds United | 42 | 21 | 11 | 10 | 71 | 45 | 53 |
| Ipswich Town | 42 | 17 | 14 | 11 | 55 | 45 | 48 |
| Wolverhampton Wanderers | 42 | 18 | 11 | 13 | 66 | 54 | 47 |
| West Ham United | 42 | 17 | 12 | 13 | 67 | 53 | 46 |
| Derby County | 42 | 19 | 8 | 15 | 56 | 54 | 46 |
| Tottenham Hotspur | 42 | 16 | 13 | 13 | 58 | 48 | 45 |
| Newcastle United | 42 | 16 | 13 | 13 | 60 | 51 | 45 |
| Birmingham City | 42 | 15 | 12 | 15 | 53 | 54 | 42 |
| Manchester City | 42 | 15 | 11 | 16 | 57 | 60 | 41 |
| Chelsea | 42 | 13 | 14 | 15 | 49 | 51 | 40 |
| Southampton | 42 | 11 | 18 | 13 | 47 | 52 | 40 |
| Sheffield United | 42 | 15 | 10 | 17 | 51 | 59 | 40 |
| Stoke City | 42 | 14 | 10 | 18 | 61 | 56 | 38 |
| Leicester City | 42 | 10 | 17 | 15 | 40 | 46 | 37 |
| Everton | 42 | 13 | 11 | 18 | 41 | 49 | 37 |
| Manchester United | 42 | 12 | 13 | 17 | 44 | 60 | 37 |
| Coventry City | 42 | 13 | 9 | 20 | 40 | 55 | 35 |
| Norwich City | 42 | 11 | 10 | 21 | 36 | 63 | 32 |
| *Crystal Palace* | *42* | *9* | *12* | *21* | *41* | *58* | *30* |
| *West Bromwich Albion* | *42* | *9* | *10* | *23* | *38* | *62* | *28* |

## DIVISION THREE 1972-73

| | | | | | | | |
|---|---|---|---|---|---|---|---|
| **Bolton Wanderers** | 46 | 25 | 11 | 10 | 73 | 39 | 61 |
| **Notts County** | 46 | 23 | 11 | 12 | 67 | 47 | 57 |
| Blackburn Rovers | 46 | 20 | 15 | 11 | 57 | 47 | 55 |
| Oldham Athletic | 46 | 19 | 16 | 11 | 72 | 54 | 54 |
| Bristol Rovers | 46 | 20 | 13 | 13 | 77 | 56 | 53 |
| Port Vale | 46 | 21 | 11 | 14 | 56 | 69 | 53 |
| Bournemouth | 46 | 17 | 16 | 13 | 66 | 44 | 50 |
| Plymouth Argyle | 46 | 20 | 10 | 16 | 74 | 66 | 50 |
| Grimsby Town | 46 | 20 | 8 | 18 | 67 | 61 | 48 |
| Tranmere Rovers | 46 | 15 | 16 | 15 | 56 | 52 | 46 |
| Charlton Athletic | 46 | 17 | 11 | 18 | 69 | 67 | 45 |
| Wrexham | 46 | 14 | 17 | 15 | 55 | 54 | 45 |
| Rochdale | 46 | 14 | 17 | 15 | 48 | 54 | 45 |
| Southend United | 46 | 17 | 10 | 19 | 61 | 54 | 44 |
| Shrewsbury Town | 46 | 15 | 14 | 17 | 46 | 54 | 44 |
| Chesterfield | 46 | 17 | 9 | 20 | 57 | 61 | 43 |
| Walsall | 46 | 18 | 7 | 21 | 56 | 66 | 43 |
| York City | 46 | 13 | 15 | 18 | 42 | 46 | 41 |
| Watford | 46 | 12 | 17 | 17 | 43 | 48 | 41 |
| Halifax Town | 46 | 13 | 15 | 18 | 43 | 53 | 41 |
| *Rotherham United* | *46* | *17* | *7* | *22* | *51* | *65* | *41* |
| *Brentford* | *46* | *15* | *7* | *24* | *51* | *69* | *37* |
| *Swansea City* | *46* | *14* | *9* | *23* | *51* | *73* | *37* |
| *Scunthorpe United* | *46* | *10* | *10* | *26* | *33* | *72* | *30* |

## DIVISION TWO 1972-73

| | | | | | | | |
|---|---|---|---|---|---|---|---|
| **Burnley** | 42 | 24 | 14 | 4 | 72 | 35 | 62 |
| **Queen's Park Rangers** | 42 | 24 | 13 | 5 | 81 | 37 | 61 |
| Aston Villa | 42 | 18 | 14 | 10 | 51 | 47 | 50 |
| Middlesbrough | 42 | 17 | 13 | 12 | 46 | 43 | 47 |
| Bristol City | 42 | 17 | 12 | 13 | 63 | 51 | 46 |
| Sunderland | 42 | 17 | 12 | 13 | 59 | 49 | 46 |
| Blackpool | 42 | 18 | 10 | 14 | 56 | 51 | 46 |
| Oxford United | 42 | 19 | 7 | 16 | 52 | 43 | 45 |
| Fulham | 42 | 16 | 12 | 14 | 58 | 49 | 44 |
| Sheffield Wednesday | 42 | 17 | 10 | 15 | 59 | 55 | 44 |
| Millwall | 42 | 16 | 10 | 16 | 55 | 47 | 42 |
| Luton Town | 42 | 15 | 11 | 16 | 44 | 53 | 41 |
| Hull City | 42 | 14 | 12 | 16 | 64 | 59 | 40 |
| Nottingham Forest | 42 | 14 | 12 | 16 | 47 | 52 | 40 |
| Orient | 42 | 12 | 12 | 18 | 49 | 53 | 36 |
| Swindon Town | 42 | 10 | 16 | 16 | 46 | 60 | 36 |
| Portsmouth | 42 | 12 | 11 | 19 | 42 | 59 | 35 |
| Carlisle United | 42 | 11 | 12 | 19 | 50 | 52 | 34 |
| Preston North End | 42 | 11 | 12 | 19 | 37 | 64 | 34 |
| Cardiff City | 42 | 11 | 11 | 20 | 43 | 58 | 33 |
| *Huddersfield Town* | *42* | *8* | *17* | *17* | *36* | *56* | *33* |
| *Brighton & Hove Albion* | *42* | *8* | *13* | *21* | *46* | *83* | *29* |

## DIVISION FOUR 1972-73

| | | | | | | | |
|---|---|---|---|---|---|---|---|
| **Southport** | 46 | 26 | 10 | 10 | 71 | 48 | 62 |
| **Hereford United** | 46 | 23 | 12 | 11 | 56 | 38 | 58 |
| **Cambridge United** | 46 | 20 | 17 | 9 | 67 | 57 | 57 |
| **Aldershot** | 46 | 22 | 12 | 12 | 60 | 38 | 56 |
| Newport County | 46 | 22 | 12 | 12 | 64 | 44 | 56 |
| Mansfield Town | 46 | 20 | 14 | 12 | 78 | 51 | 54 |
| Reading | 46 | 17 | 18 | 11 | 51 | 38 | 52 |
| Exeter City | 46 | 18 | 14 | 14 | 57 | 51 | 50 |
| Gillingham | 46 | 19 | 11 | 16 | 63 | 58 | 49 |
| Lincoln City | 46 | 16 | 16 | 14 | 64 | 57 | 48 |
| Stockport County | 46 | 18 | 12 | 16 | 53 | 53 | 48 |
| Bury | 46 | 14 | 18 | 14 | 58 | 51 | 46 |
| Workington | 46 | 17 | 12 | 17 | 59 | 61 | 46 |
| Barnsley | 46 | 14 | 14 | 16 | 58 | 60 | 44 |
| Chester | 46 | 14 | 15 | 17 | 61 | 52 | 43 |
| Bradford City | 46 | 16 | 11 | 19 | 61 | 65 | 43 |
| Doncaster Rovers | 46 | 15 | 12 | 19 | 49 | 58 | 42 |
| Torquay United | 46 | 12 | 17 | 17 | 44 | 47 | 41 |
| Peterborough United | 46 | 14 | 13 | 19 | 71 | 76 | 41 |
| Hartlepool | 46 | 12 | 17 | 17 | 34 | 49 | 41 |
| Crewe Alexandra | 46 | 9 | 18 | 19 | 38 | 61 | 36 |
| Colchester United | 46 | 10 | 11 | 25 | 48 | 76 | 31 |
| Northampton Town | 46 | 10 | 11 | 25 | 40 | 73 | 31 |
| Darlington | 46 | 7 | 15 | 24 | 42 | 85 | 29 |

## 1973 F.A. Cup

**Semi-finals**

| | |
|---|---|
| Arsenal vs Sunderland | 1-2 |
| Leeds United vs Wolverhampton Wanderers | 1-0 |

**Final**

Wembley, 5th May 1973

**Sunderland 1**  (Porterfield)

**Leeds United 0**

*Attendance 100,000*

## 1973 Football League Cup

**Semi-finals**

| | |
|---|---|
| Wolverhampton Wands. vs Tottenham H. (1-2, 2-2) | 3-4 |
| Chelsea vs Norwich City (0-2, 0-1) | 0-3 |

**Final**

Wembley, 3rd March 1973

**Tottenham Hotspur 1**  (Coates)

**Norwich City 0**

*Attendance 100,000*

## DIVISION ONE 1973-74

| | | | | | | | |
|---|---|---|---|---|---|---|---|
| LEEDS UNITED | 42 | 24 | 14 | 4 | 66 | 31 | 62 |
| Liverpool | 42 | 22 | 13 | 7 | 52 | 31 | 57 |
| Derby County | 42 | 17 | 14 | 11 | 52 | 42 | 48 |
| Ipswich Town | 42 | 18 | 11 | 13 | 67 | 58 | 47 |
| Stoke City | 42 | 15 | 16 | 11 | 54 | 42 | 46 |
| Burnley | 42 | 16 | 14 | 12 | 56 | 53 | 46 |
| Everton | 42 | 16 | 12 | 14 | 50 | 48 | 44 |
| Queen's Park Rangers | 42 | 13 | 17 | 12 | 56 | 52 | 43 |
| Leicester City | 42 | 13 | 16 | 13 | 51 | 41 | 42 |
| Arsenal | 42 | 14 | 14 | 14 | 49 | 51 | 42 |
| Tottenham Hotspur | 42 | 14 | 14 | 14 | 45 | 50 | 42 |
| Wolverhampton Wanderers | 42 | 13 | 15 | 14 | 49 | 49 | 41 |
| Sheffield United | 42 | 14 | 12 | 16 | 44 | 49 | 40 |
| Manchester City | 42 | 14 | 12 | 16 | 39 | 46 | 40 |
| Newcastle United | 42 | 13 | 12 | 17 | 49 | 48 | 38 |
| Coventry City | 42 | 14 | 10 | 18 | 43 | 54 | 38 |
| Chelsea | 42 | 12 | 13 | 17 | 56 | 60 | 37 |
| West Ham United | 42 | 11 | 15 | 16 | 55 | 60 | 37 |
| Birmingham City | 42 | 12 | 13 | 17 | 52 | 64 | 37 |
| *Southampton* | 42 | 11 | 14 | 17 | 47 | 68 | 36 |
| *Manchester United* | 42 | 10 | 12 | 20 | 38 | 48 | 32 |
| *Norwich City* | 42 | 7 | 15 | 20 | 37 | 62 | 29 |

## DIVISION THREE 1973-74

| | | | | | | | |
|---|---|---|---|---|---|---|---|
| Oldham Athletic | 46 | 25 | 12 | 9 | 83 | 47 | 62 |
| Bristol Rovers | 46 | 22 | 17 | 7 | 65 | 33 | 61 |
| York City | 46 | 21 | 19 | 6 | 67 | 38 | 61 |
| Wrexham | 46 | 22 | 12 | 12 | 63 | 43 | 56 |
| Chesterfield | 46 | 21 | 14 | 11 | 55 | 42 | 56 |
| Grimsby Town | 46 | 18 | 15 | 13 | 67 | 50 | 51 |
| Watford | 46 | 19 | 12 | 15 | 64 | 56 | 50 |
| Aldershot | 46 | 19 | 11 | 16 | 65 | 52 | 49 |
| Halifax Town | 46 | 14 | 21 | 11 | 48 | 51 | 49 |
| Huddersfield Town | 46 | 17 | 13 | 16 | 56 | 55 | 47 |
| Bournemouth | 46 | 16 | 15 | 15 | 54 | 58 | 47 |
| Southend United | 46 | 16 | 14 | 16 | 62 | 62 | 46 |
| Blackburn Rovers | 46 | 18 | 10 | 18 | 62 | 64 | 46 |
| Charlton Athletic | 46 | 19 | 8 | 19 | 66 | 73 | 46 |
| Walsall | 46 | 16 | 13 | 17 | 57 | 48 | 45 |
| Tranmere Rovers | 46 | 15 | 15 | 16 | 50 | 44 | 45 |
| Plymouth Argyle | 46 | 17 | 10 | 19 | 59 | 54 | 44 |
| Hereford United | 46 | 14 | 15 | 17 | 53 | 57 | 43 |
| Brighton & Hove Albion | 46 | 16 | 11 | 19 | 52 | 58 | 43 |
| Port Vale | 46 | 14 | 14 | 18 | 52 | 58 | 42 |
| *Cambridge United* | 46 | 13 | 9 | 24 | 48 | 81 | 35 |
| *Shrewsbury Town* | 46 | 10 | 11 | 25 | 41 | 62 | 31 |
| *Southport* | 46 | 6 | 16 | 24 | 35 | 82 | 28 |
| *Rochdale* | 46 | 2 | 17 | 27 | 38 | 94 | 21 |

## DIVISION TWO 1973-74

| | | | | | | | |
|---|---|---|---|---|---|---|---|
| Middlesbrough | 42 | 27 | 11 | 4 | 77 | 30 | 65 |
| Luton Town | 42 | 19 | 12 | 11 | 64 | 51 | 50 |
| Carlisle United | 42 | 20 | 9 | 13 | 61 | 48 | 49 |
| Orient | 42 | 15 | 18 | 9 | 55 | 42 | 48 |
| Blackpool | 42 | 17 | 13 | 12 | 57 | 40 | 47 |
| Sunderland | 42 | 19 | 9 | 14 | 58 | 44 | 47 |
| Nottingham Forest | 42 | 15 | 15 | 12 | 57 | 43 | 45 |
| West Bromwich Albion | 42 | 14 | 16 | 12 | 48 | 45 | 44 |
| Hull City | 42 | 13 | 17 | 12 | 46 | 47 | 43 |
| Notts County | 42 | 15 | 13 | 14 | 55 | 60 | 43 |
| Bolton Wanderers | 42 | 15 | 12 | 15 | 44 | 40 | 42 |
| Millwall | 42 | 14 | 14 | 14 | 51 | 51 | 42 |
| Fulham | 42 | 16 | 10 | 16 | 39 | 43 | 42 |
| Aston Villa | 42 | 13 | 15 | 14 | 48 | 45 | 41 |
| Portsmouth | 42 | 14 | 12 | 16 | 45 | 62 | 40 |
| Bristol City | 42 | 14 | 10 | 18 | 47 | 54 | 38 |
| Cardiff City | 42 | 10 | 16 | 16 | 49 | 62 | 36 |
| Oxford United | 42 | 10 | 16 | 16 | 35 | 46 | 36 |
| Sheffield Wednesday | 42 | 12 | 11 | 19 | 51 | 63 | 35 |
| *Crystal Palace* | 42 | 11 | 12 | 19 | 43 | 56 | 34 |
| *Preston North End* | 42 | 9 | 14 | 19 | 40 | 62 | 31 |
| *Swindon Town* | 42 | 7 | 11 | 24 | 36 | 72 | 25 |

Preston North End had one point deducted

## DIVISION FOUR 1973-74

| | | | | | | | |
|---|---|---|---|---|---|---|---|
| Peterborough United | 46 | 27 | 11 | 8 | 75 | 38 | 65 |
| Gillingham | 46 | 25 | 12 | 9 | 90 | 49 | 62 |
| Colchester United | 46 | 24 | 12 | 10 | 73 | 36 | 60 |
| Bury | 46 | 24 | 11 | 11 | 81 | 49 | 59 |
| Northampton Town | 46 | 20 | 13 | 13 | 63 | 48 | 53 |
| Reading | 46 | 16 | 19 | 11 | 58 | 37 | 51 |
| Chester | 46 | 17 | 15 | 14 | 54 | 55 | 49 |
| Bradford City | 46 | 17 | 14 | 15 | 58 | 52 | 48 |
| Newport County | 46 | 16 | 14 | 16 | 56 | 65 | 45 |
| Exeter City | 45 | 18 | 8 | 19 | 58 | 55 | 44 |
| Hartlepool | 46 | 16 | 12 | 18 | 48 | 47 | 44 |
| Lincoln City | 46 | 16 | 12 | 18 | 63 | 67 | 44 |
| Barnsley | 46 | 17 | 10 | 19 | 58 | 64 | 44 |
| Swansea City | 46 | 16 | 11 | 19 | 45 | 46 | 43 |
| Rotherham United | 46 | 15 | 13 | 18 | 56 | 58 | 43 |
| Torquay United | 46 | 13 | 17 | 16 | 52 | 57 | 43 |
| Mansfield Town | 46 | 13 | 17 | 16 | 62 | 69 | 43 |
| Scunthorpe United | 45 | 14 | 12 | 19 | 47 | 64 | 42 |
| Brentford | 46 | 12 | 16 | 18 | 48 | 50 | 40 |
| Darlington | 46 | 13 | 13 | 20 | 40 | 62 | 39 |
| Crewe Alexandra | 46 | 14 | 10 | 22 | 43 | 71 | 38 |
| Doncaster Rovers | 46 | 12 | 11 | 23 | 47 | 80 | 35 |
| Workington | 46 | 11 | 13 | 22 | 43 | 74 | 35 |
| Stockport County | 46 | 7 | 20 | 19 | 44 | 69 | 34 |

Newport County had one point deducted
Scunthorpe United vs Exeter City match not played
Scunthorpe United awarded two points

## 1974 F.A. Cup

**Semi-finals**

| | |
|---|---|
| Burnley vs Newcastle United | 0-2 |
| Leicester City vs Liverpool | 0-0, 1-3 |

**Final**

Wembley, 4th May 1974

**Liverpool 3** (Keegan 2, Heighway)
**Newcastle United 0**

*Attendance 100,000*

## 1974 Football League Cup

**Semi-finals**

| | |
|---|---|
| Norwich City vs Wolverhampton Wanderers (1-1, 0-1) | 1-2 |
| Plymouth Argyle vs Manchester City (1-1, 0-2) | 1-3 |

**Final**

Wembley, 2nd March 1974

**Wolverhampton Wanderers 2** (Hibbitt, Richards)
**Manchester City 1** (Bell)

*Attendance 100,000*

## DIVISION ONE 1974-75

| | | | | | | | |
|---|---|---|---|---|---|---|---|
| **DERBY COUNTY** | 42 | 21 | 11 | 10 | 67 | 49 | 53 |
| Liverpool | 42 | 20 | 11 | 11 | 60 | 39 | 51 |
| Ipswich Town | 42 | 23 | 5 | 14 | 66 | 44 | 51 |
| Everton | 42 | 16 | 18 | 8 | 56 | 42 | 50 |
| Stoke City | 42 | 17 | 15 | 10 | 64 | 48 | 49 |
| Sheffield United | 42 | 18 | 13 | 11 | 58 | 51 | 49 |
| Middlesbrough | 42 | 18 | 12 | 12 | 54 | 40 | 48 |
| Manchester City | 42 | 18 | 10 | 14 | 54 | 54 | 46 |
| Leeds United | 42 | 16 | 13 | 13 | 57 | 49 | 45 |
| Burnley | 42 | 17 | 11 | 14 | 68 | 67 | 45 |
| Queen's Park Rangers | 42 | 16 | 10 | 16 | 54 | 54 | 42 |
| Wolverhampton Wanderers | 42 | 14 | 11 | 17 | 57 | 54 | 39 |
| West Ham United | 42 | 13 | 13 | 16 | 58 | 59 | 39 |
| Coventry City | 42 | 12 | 15 | 15 | 51 | 62 | 39 |
| Newcastle United | 42 | 15 | 9 | 18 | 59 | 72 | 39 |
| Arsenal | 42 | 13 | 11 | 18 | 47 | 49 | 37 |
| Birmingham City | 42 | 14 | 9 | 19 | 53 | 61 | 37 |
| Leicester City | 42 | 12 | 12 | 18 | 46 | 60 | 36 |
| Tottenham Hotspur | 42 | 13 | 8 | 21 | 52 | 63 | 34 |
| *Luton Town* | *42* | *11* | *11* | *20* | *47* | *65* | *33* |
| *Chelsea* | *42* | *9* | *15* | *18* | *42* | *72* | *33* |
| *Carlisle United* | *42* | *12* | *5* | *25* | *43* | *59* | *29* |

## DIVISION TWO 1974-75

| | | | | | | | |
|---|---|---|---|---|---|---|---|
| **Manchester United** | 42 | 26 | 9 | 7 | 66 | 30 | 61 |
| Aston Villa | 42 | 25 | 8 | 9 | 79 | 32 | 58 |
| Norwich City | 42 | 20 | 13 | 9 | 58 | 37 | 53 |
| Sunderland | 42 | 19 | 13 | 10 | 65 | 35 | 51 |
| Bristol City | 42 | 21 | 8 | 13 | 47 | 33 | 50 |
| West Bromwich Albion | 42 | 18 | 9 | 15 | 54 | 42 | 45 |
| Blackpool | 42 | 14 | 17 | 11 | 38 | 33 | 45 |
| Hull City | 42 | 15 | 14 | 13 | 40 | 53 | 44 |
| Fulham | 42 | 13 | 16 | 13 | 44 | 39 | 42 |
| Bolton Wanderers | 42 | 15 | 12 | 15 | 45 | 41 | 42 |
| Oxford United | 42 | 15 | 12 | 15 | 41 | 51 | 42 |
| Orient | 42 | 11 | 20 | 11 | 28 | 39 | 42 |
| Southampton | 42 | 15 | 11 | 16 | 53 | 54 | 41 |
| Notts County | 42 | 12 | 16 | 14 | 49 | 59 | 40 |
| York City | 42 | 14 | 10 | 18 | 51 | 55 | 38 |
| Nottingham Forest | 42 | 12 | 14 | 16 | 43 | 55 | 38 |
| Portsmouth | 42 | 12 | 13 | 17 | 44 | 54 | 37 |
| Oldham Athletic | 42 | 10 | 15 | 17 | 40 | 48 | 35 |
| Bristol Rovers | 42 | 12 | 11 | 19 | 42 | 64 | 35 |
| *Millwall* | *42* | *10* | *12* | *20* | *44* | *56* | *32* |
| *Cardiff City* | *42* | *9* | *14* | *19* | *36* | *62* | *32* |
| *Sheffield Wednesday* | *42* | *5* | *11* | *26* | *29* | *64* | *21* |

## DIVISION THREE 1974-75

| | | | | | | | |
|---|---|---|---|---|---|---|---|
| **Blackburn Rovers** | 46 | 22 | 16 | 8 | 68 | 45 | 60 |
| **Plymouth Argyle** | 46 | 24 | 11 | 11 | 79 | 58 | 59 |
| **Charlton Athletic** | 46 | 22 | 11 | 13 | 76 | 61 | 55 |
| Swindon Town | 46 | 21 | 11 | 14 | 64 | 58 | 53 |
| Crystal Palace | 46 | 18 | 15 | 13 | 66 | 57 | 51 |
| Port Vale | 46 | 18 | 15 | 13 | 61 | 54 | 51 |
| Peterborough United | 46 | 19 | 12 | 15 | 47 | 53 | 50 |
| Walsall | 46 | 18 | 13 | 15 | 67 | 52 | 49 |
| Preston North End | 46 | 19 | 11 | 16 | 63 | 56 | 49 |
| Gillingham | 46 | 17 | 14 | 15 | 65 | 60 | 48 |
| Colchester United | 46 | 17 | 13 | 16 | 70 | 63 | 47 |
| Hereford United | 46 | 16 | 14 | 16 | 64 | 66 | 46 |
| Wrexham | 46 | 15 | 15 | 16 | 65 | 55 | 45 |
| Bury | 46 | 16 | 12 | 18 | 53 | 50 | 44 |
| Chesterfield | 46 | 16 | 12 | 18 | 62 | 66 | 44 |
| Grimsby Town | 46 | 15 | 13 | 18 | 55 | 64 | 43 |
| Halifax Town | 46 | 13 | 17 | 16 | 49 | 65 | 43 |
| Southend United | 46 | 13 | 16 | 17 | 46 | 51 | 42 |
| Brighton & Hove Albion | 46 | 16 | 10 | 20 | 56 | 64 | 42 |
| Aldershot | 46 | 14 | 11 | 21 | 53 | 63 | 38 |
| *Bournemouth* | *46* | *13* | *12* | *21* | *44* | *58* | *38* |
| *Tranmere Rovers* | *46* | *14* | *9* | *23* | *55* | *57* | *37* |
| *Watford* | *46* | *10* | *17* | *19* | *52* | *75* | *37* |
| *Huddersfield Town* | *46* | *11* | *10* | *25* | *47* | *76* | *32* |

Aldershot had one point deducted

## DIVISION FOUR 1974-75

| | | | | | | | |
|---|---|---|---|---|---|---|---|
| **Mansfield Town** | 46 | 28 | 12 | 6 | 90 | 40 | 68 |
| **Shrewsbury Town** | 46 | 26 | 10 | 10 | 80 | 43 | 62 |
| **Rotherham United** | 46 | 22 | 15 | 9 | 71 | 41 | 59 |
| **Chester** | 46 | 23 | 11 | 12 | 64 | 38 | 57 |
| Lincoln City | 46 | 21 | 15 | 10 | 79 | 48 | 57 |
| Cambridge United | 46 | 20 | 14 | 12 | 62 | 44 | 54 |
| Reading | 46 | 21 | 10 | 15 | 63 | 47 | 52 |
| Brentford | 46 | 18 | 13 | 15 | 53 | 45 | 49 |
| Exeter City | 46 | 19 | 11 | 16 | 60 | 63 | 49 |
| Bradford City | 46 | 17 | 13 | 16 | 56 | 51 | 47 |
| Southport | 46 | 15 | 17 | 14 | 56 | 56 | 47 |
| Newport County | 46 | 19 | 9 | 18 | 68 | 75 | 47 |
| Hartlepool | 46 | 16 | 11 | 19 | 52 | 62 | 43 |
| Torquay United | 46 | 14 | 14 | 18 | 46 | 61 | 42 |
| Barnsley | 46 | 15 | 11 | 20 | 62 | 65 | 41 |
| Northampton Town | 46 | 15 | 11 | 20 | 67 | 73 | 41 |
| Doncaster Rovers | 46 | 14 | 12 | 20 | 65 | 79 | 40 |
| Crewe Alexandra | 46 | 11 | 18 | 17 | 34 | 47 | 40 |
| Rochdale | 46 | 13 | 13 | 20 | 59 | 75 | 39 |
| Stockport County | 46 | 12 | 14 | 20 | 43 | 70 | 38 |
| Darlington | 46 | 13 | 10 | 23 | 54 | 67 | 36 |
| Swansea City | 46 | 15 | 6 | 25 | 46 | 73 | 36 |
| Workington | 46 | 10 | 11 | 25 | 36 | 66 | 31 |
| Scunthorpe United | 46 | 7 | 15 | 24 | 41 | 78 | 29 |

## 1975 F.A. Cup

**Semi-finals**

| | |
|---|---|
| West Ham United vs Ipswich Town | 0-0, 2-1 |
| Fulham vs Birmingham City | 1-1, 1-0 |

**Final**

Wembley, 2nd May 1975

**West Ham United 2**  (A. Taylor 2)
**Fulham 0**

*Attendance 100,000*

## 1975 Football League Cup

**Semi-finals**

| | |
|---|---|
| Chester vs Aston Villa (2-2, 2-3) | 4-5 |
| Manchester United vs Norwich City (2-2, 0-1) | 2-3 |

**Final**

Wembley, 1st March 1975

**Aston Villa 1**  (Graydon)
**Norwich City 0**

*Attendance 100,000*

## DIVISION ONE 1975-76

| | | | | | | | |
|---|---|---|---|---|---|---|---|
| **LIVERPOOL** | 42 | 23 | 14 | 5 | 66 | 31 | 60 |
| Queen's Park Rangers | 42 | 24 | 11 | 7 | 67 | 33 | 59 |
| Manchester United | 42 | 23 | 10 | 9 | 68 | 42 | 56 |
| Derby County | 42 | 21 | 11 | 10 | 75 | 58 | 53 |
| Leeds United | 42 | 21 | 9 | 12 | 65 | 46 | 51 |
| Ipswich Town | 42 | 16 | 14 | 12 | 54 | 48 | 46 |
| Leicester City | 42 | 13 | 19 | 10 | 48 | 51 | 45 |
| Manchester City | 42 | 16 | 11 | 15 | 64 | 46 | 43 |
| Tottenham Hotspur | 42 | 14 | 15 | 13 | 63 | 63 | 43 |
| Norwich City | 42 | 16 | 10 | 16 | 58 | 58 | 42 |
| Everton | 42 | 15 | 12 | 15 | 60 | 66 | 42 |
| Stoke City | 42 | 15 | 11 | 16 | 48 | 50 | 41 |
| Middlesbrough | 42 | 15 | 10 | 17 | 46 | 45 | 40 |
| Coventry City | 42 | 13 | 14 | 15 | 47 | 57 | 40 |
| Newcastle United | 42 | 15 | 9 | 18 | 71 | 62 | 39 |
| Aston Villa | 42 | 11 | 17 | 14 | 51 | 59 | 39 |
| Arsenal | 42 | 13 | 10 | 19 | 47 | 53 | 36 |
| West Ham United | 42 | 13 | 10 | 19 | 48 | 71 | 36 |
| Birmingham City | 42 | 13 | 7 | 22 | 57 | 75 | 33 |
| *Wolverhampton Wanderers* | *42* | *10* | *10* | *22* | *51* | *68* | *30* |
| *Burnley* | *42* | *9* | *10* | *23* | *43* | *66* | *28* |
| *Sheffield United* | *42* | *6* | *10* | *26* | *33* | *82* | *22* |

## DIVISION THREE 1975-76

| | | | | | | | |
|---|---|---|---|---|---|---|---|
| **Hereford United** | 46 | 26 | 11 | 9 | 86 | 55 | 63 |
| **Cardiff City** | 46 | 22 | 13 | 11 | 69 | 48 | 57 |
| **Millwall** | 46 | 20 | 16 | 10 | 54 | 43 | 56 |
| Brighton & Hove Albion | 46 | 22 | 9 | 15 | 78 | 53 | 53 |
| Crystal Palace | 46 | 18 | 17 | 11 | 61 | 46 | 53 |
| Wrexham | 46 | 20 | 12 | 14 | 66 | 55 | 52 |
| Walsall | 46 | 18 | 14 | 14 | 74 | 61 | 50 |
| Preston North End | 46 | 19 | 10 | 17 | 62 | 57 | 48 |
| Shrewsbury Town | 46 | 19 | 10 | 17 | 61 | 59 | 48 |
| Peterborough United | 46 | 15 | 18 | 13 | 63 | 63 | 48 |
| Mansfield Town | 46 | 16 | 15 | 15 | 58 | 52 | 47 |
| Port Vale | 46 | 15 | 16 | 15 | 55 | 54 | 46 |
| Bury | 46 | 14 | 16 | 16 | 51 | 46 | 44 |
| Chesterfield | 46 | 17 | 9 | 20 | 69 | 69 | 43 |
| Gillingham | 46 | 12 | 19 | 15 | 58 | 68 | 43 |
| Rotherham United | 46 | 15 | 12 | 19 | 54 | 65 | 42 |
| Chester | 46 | 15 | 12 | 19 | 43 | 62 | 42 |
| Grimsby Town | 46 | 15 | 10 | 21 | 62 | 74 | 40 |
| Swindon Town | 46 | 16 | 8 | 22 | 62 | 75 | 40 |
| Sheffield Wednesday | 46 | 12 | 16 | 18 | 48 | 59 | 40 |
| *Aldershot* | *46* | *13* | *13* | *20* | *59* | *75* | *39* |
| *Colchester United* | *46* | *12* | *14* | *20* | *41* | *65* | *38* |
| *Southend United* | *46* | *12* | *13* | *21* | *65* | *75* | *37* |
| *Halifax Town* | *46* | *11* | *13* | *22* | *41* | *61* | *35* |

## DIVISION TWO 1975-76

| | | | | | | | |
|---|---|---|---|---|---|---|---|
| **Sunderland** | 42 | 24 | 8 | 10 | 67 | 36 | 56 |
| **Bristol City** | 42 | 19 | 15 | 8 | 59 | 35 | 53 |
| **West Bromwich Albion** | 42 | 20 | 13 | 9 | 50 | 33 | 53 |
| Bolton Wanderers | 42 | 20 | 12 | 10 | 64 | 38 | 52 |
| Notts County | 42 | 19 | 11 | 12 | 60 | 41 | 49 |
| Southampton | 42 | 21 | 7 | 14 | 66 | 50 | 49 |
| Luton Town | 42 | 19 | 10 | 13 | 61 | 51 | 48 |
| Nottingham Forest | 42 | 17 | 12 | 13 | 55 | 40 | 46 |
| Charlton Athletic | 42 | 15 | 12 | 15 | 61 | 72 | 42 |
| Blackpool | 42 | 14 | 14 | 14 | 40 | 49 | 42 |
| Chelsea | 42 | 12 | 16 | 14 | 53 | 54 | 40 |
| Fulham | 42 | 13 | 14 | 15 | 45 | 47 | 40 |
| Orient | 42 | 13 | 14 | 15 | 37 | 39 | 40 |
| Hull City | 42 | 14 | 11 | 17 | 45 | 49 | 39 |
| Blackburn Rovers | 42 | 12 | 14 | 16 | 45 | 50 | 38 |
| Plymouth Argyle | 42 | 13 | 12 | 17 | 48 | 54 | 38 |
| Oldham Athletic | 42 | 13 | 12 | 17 | 57 | 68 | 38 |
| Bristol Rovers | 42 | 11 | 16 | 15 | 38 | 50 | 38 |
| Carlisle United | 42 | 12 | 13 | 17 | 45 | 59 | 37 |
| *Oxford United* | *42* | *11* | *11* | *20* | *39* | *59* | *33* |
| *York City* | *42* | *10* | *8* | *24* | *39* | *71* | *28* |
| *Portsmouth* | *42* | *9* | *7* | *26* | *32* | *61* | *25* |

## DIVISION FOUR 1975-76

| | | | | | | | |
|---|---|---|---|---|---|---|---|
| **Lincoln City** | 46 | 32 | 10 | 4 | 111 | 39 | 74 |
| **Northampton Town** | 46 | 29 | 10 | 7 | 87 | 40 | 68 |
| **Reading** | 46 | 24 | 12 | 10 | 70 | 51 | 60 |
| **Tranmere Rovers** | 46 | 24 | 10 | 12 | 89 | 55 | 58 |
| Huddersfield Town | 46 | 21 | 14 | 11 | 56 | 41 | 56 |
| Bournemouth | 46 | 20 | 12 | 14 | 57 | 48 | 52 |
| Exeter City | 46 | 18 | 14 | 14 | 56 | 47 | 50 |
| Watford | 46 | 22 | 6 | 18 | 62 | 62 | 50 |
| Torquay United | 46 | 18 | 14 | 14 | 55 | 63 | 50 |
| Doncaster Rovers | 46 | 19 | 11 | 16 | 75 | 69 | 49 |
| Swansea City | 46 | 16 | 15 | 15 | 66 | 57 | 47 |
| Barnsley | 46 | 14 | 16 | 16 | 52 | 48 | 44 |
| Cambridge United | 46 | 14 | 15 | 17 | 58 | 62 | 43 |
| Hartlepool | 46 | 16 | 10 | 20 | 62 | 78 | 42 |
| Rochdale | 46 | 12 | 18 | 16 | 40 | 54 | 42 |
| Crewe Alexandra | 46 | 13 | 15 | 18 | 58 | 57 | 41 |
| Bradford City | 46 | 12 | 17 | 17 | 63 | 65 | 41 |
| Brentford | 46 | 14 | 13 | 19 | 56 | 60 | 41 |
| Scunthorpe United | 46 | 14 | 10 | 22 | 50 | 59 | 38 |
| Darlington | 46 | 14 | 10 | 22 | 48 | 57 | 38 |
| Stockport County | 46 | 13 | 12 | 21 | 43 | 76 | 38 |
| Newport County | 46 | 13 | 9 | 24 | 57 | 90 | 35 |
| Southport | 46 | 8 | 10 | 28 | 41 | 77 | 26 |
| Workington | 46 | 7 | 7 | 32 | 30 | 87 | 21 |

## 1976 F.A. Cup

### Semi-finals

| | |
|---|---|
| Southampton vs Crystal Palace | 2-0 |
| Manchester United vs Derby County | 2-0 |

### Final

Wembley, 1st May 1976

**Southampton 1** (Stokes)

**Manchester United 0**

*Attendance 100,000*

## 1976 Football League Cup

### Semi-finals

| | |
|---|---|
| Middlesbrough vs Manchester City (1-0, 0-4) | 1-4 |
| Tottenham Hotspur vs Newcastle United (1-0, 1-3) | 2-3 |

### Final

Wembley, 28th February 1976

**Manchester City 2** (Barnes, Tueart)

**Newcastle United 1** (Gowling)

*Attendance 100,000*

## DIVISION ONE 1976-77

| | | | | | | | |
|---|---|---|---|---|---|---|---|
| **LIVERPOOL** | 42 | 23 | 11 | 8 | 62 | 33 | 57 |
| Manchester City | 42 | 21 | 14 | 7 | 60 | 34 | 56 |
| Ipswich Town | 42 | 22 | 8 | 12 | 66 | 39 | 52 |
| Aston Villa | 42 | 22 | 7 | 13 | 76 | 50 | 51 |
| Newcastle United | 42 | 18 | 13 | 11 | 64 | 49 | 49 |
| Manchester United | 42 | 18 | 11 | 13 | 71 | 62 | 47 |
| West Bromwich Albion | 42 | 16 | 13 | 13 | 62 | 56 | 45 |
| Arsenal | 42 | 16 | 11 | 15 | 64 | 59 | 43 |
| Everton | 42 | 14 | 14 | 14 | 62 | 64 | 42 |
| Leeds United | 42 | 15 | 12 | 15 | 48 | 51 | 42 |
| Leicester City | 42 | 12 | 18 | 12 | 47 | 60 | 42 |
| Middlesbrough | 42 | 14 | 13 | 15 | 40 | 45 | 41 |
| Birmingham City | 42 | 13 | 12 | 17 | 63 | 61 | 38 |
| Queen's Park Rangers | 42 | 13 | 12 | 17 | 47 | 52 | 38 |
| Derby County | 42 | 9 | 19 | 14 | 50 | 55 | 37 |
| Norwich City | 42 | 14 | 9 | 19 | 47 | 64 | 37 |
| West Ham United | 42 | 11 | 14 | 17 | 46 | 65 | 36 |
| Bristol City | 42 | 11 | 13 | 18 | 38 | 48 | 35 |
| Coventry City | 42 | 10 | 15 | 17 | 48 | 59 | 35 |
| *Sunderland* | *42* | *11* | *12* | *19* | *46* | *54* | *34* |
| *Stoke City* | *42* | *10* | *14* | *18* | *28* | *51* | *34* |
| *Tottenham Hotspur* | *42* | *12* | *9* | *21* | *48* | *72* | *33* |

## DIVISION TWO 1976-77

| | | | | | | | |
|---|---|---|---|---|---|---|---|
| **Wolverhampton Wanderers** | 42 | 22 | 13 | 7 | 84 | 45 | 57 |
| **Chelsea** | 42 | 21 | 13 | 8 | 73 | 53 | 55 |
| **Nottingham Forest** | 42 | 21 | 10 | 11 | 77 | 43 | 52 |
| Bolton Wanderers | 42 | 20 | 11 | 11 | 75 | 54 | 51 |
| Blackpool | 42 | 17 | 17 | 8 | 58 | 42 | 51 |
| Luton Town | 42 | 21 | 6 | 15 | 67 | 48 | 48 |
| Charlton Athletic | 42 | 16 | 16 | 10 | 71 | 58 | 48 |
| Notts County | 42 | 19 | 10 | 13 | 65 | 60 | 48 |
| Southampton | 42 | 17 | 10 | 15 | 72 | 67 | 44 |
| Millwall | 42 | 15 | 13 | 14 | 57 | 53 | 43 |
| Sheffield United | 42 | 14 | 12 | 16 | 54 | 63 | 40 |
| Blackburn Rovers | 42 | 15 | 9 | 18 | 42 | 54 | 39 |
| Oldham Athletic | 42 | 14 | 10 | 18 | 52 | 64 | 38 |
| Hull City | 42 | 10 | 17 | 15 | 45 | 53 | 37 |
| Bristol Rovers | 42 | 12 | 13 | 17 | 53 | 68 | 37 |
| Burnley | 42 | 11 | 14 | 17 | 46 | 64 | 36 |
| Fulham | 42 | 11 | 13 | 18 | 54 | 61 | 35 |
| Cardiff City | 42 | 12 | 10 | 20 | 56 | 67 | 34 |
| Orient | 42 | 9 | 16 | 17 | 37 | 55 | 34 |
| *Carlisle United* | *42* | *11* | *12* | *19* | *49* | *75* | *34* |
| *Plymouth Argyle* | *42* | *8* | *16* | *18* | *46* | *65* | *32* |
| *Hereford United* | *42* | *8* | *15* | *19* | *57* | *78* | *31* |

## DIVISION THREE 1976-77

| | | | | | | | |
|---|---|---|---|---|---|---|---|
| **Mansfield Town** | 46 | 28 | 8 | 10 | 78 | 33 | 64 |
| **Brighton & Hove Albion** | 46 | 25 | 11 | 10 | 83 | 39 | 61 |
| **Crystal Palace** | 46 | 23 | 13 | 10 | 68 | 40 | 59 |
| Rotherham United | 46 | 22 | 15 | 9 | 69 | 44 | 59 |
| Wrexham | 46 | 24 | 10 | 12 | 80 | 54 | 58 |
| Preston North End | 46 | 21 | 12 | 13 | 64 | 43 | 54 |
| Bury | 46 | 23 | 8 | 15 | 64 | 59 | 54 |
| Sheffield Wednesday | 46 | 22 | 9 | 15 | 65 | 55 | 53 |
| Lincoln City | 46 | 19 | 14 | 13 | 77 | 70 | 52 |
| Shrewsbury Town | 46 | 18 | 11 | 17 | 65 | 59 | 47 |
| Swindon Town | 46 | 15 | 15 | 16 | 68 | 75 | 45 |
| Gillingham | 46 | 16 | 12 | 18 | 55 | 64 | 44 |
| Chester | 46 | 18 | 8 | 20 | 48 | 58 | 44 |
| Tranmere Rovers | 46 | 13 | 17 | 16 | 51 | 53 | 43 |
| Walsall | 46 | 13 | 15 | 18 | 57 | 65 | 41 |
| Peterborough United | 46 | 13 | 15 | 18 | 55 | 65 | 41 |
| Oxford United | 46 | 12 | 15 | 19 | 55 | 65 | 39 |
| Chesterfield | 46 | 14 | 10 | 22 | 56 | 64 | 38 |
| Port Vale | 46 | 11 | 16 | 19 | 47 | 71 | 38 |
| Portsmouth | 46 | 11 | 14 | 21 | 43 | 70 | 36 |
| *Reading* | *46* | *13* | *9* | *24* | *49* | *73* | *35* |
| *Northampton Town* | *46* | *13* | *8* | *25* | *60* | *75* | *34* |
| *Grimsby Town* | *46* | *12* | *9* | *25* | *45* | *69* | *33* |
| *York City* | *46* | *10* | *12* | *24* | *50* | *89* | *32* |

## DIVISION FOUR 1976-77

| | | | | | | | |
|---|---|---|---|---|---|---|---|
| **Cambridge United** | 46 | 26 | 13 | 7 | 87 | 40 | 65 |
| **Exeter City** | 46 | 25 | 12 | 9 | 70 | 46 | 62 |
| **Colchester United** | 46 | 25 | 9 | 12 | 77 | 43 | 59 |
| **Bradford City** | 46 | 23 | 13 | 10 | 78 | 51 | 59 |
| Swansea City | 46 | 25 | 8 | 13 | 92 | 68 | 58 |
| Barnsley | 46 | 23 | 9 | 14 | 62 | 39 | 55 |
| Watford | 46 | 18 | 15 | 13 | 67 | 50 | 51 |
| Doncaster Rovers | 46 | 21 | 9 | 16 | 71 | 65 | 51 |
| Huddersfield Town | 46 | 19 | 12 | 15 | 60 | 49 | 50 |
| Southend United | 46 | 15 | 19 | 12 | 52 | 45 | 49 |
| Darlington | 46 | 18 | 13 | 15 | 59 | 64 | 49 |
| Crewe Alexandra | 46 | 19 | 11 | 16 | 47 | 60 | 49 |
| Bournemouth | 46 | 15 | 18 | 13 | 54 | 44 | 48 |
| Stockport County | 46 | 13 | 19 | 14 | 53 | 57 | 45 |
| Brentford | 46 | 18 | 7 | 21 | 77 | 76 | 43 |
| Torquay United | 46 | 17 | 9 | 20 | 59 | 67 | 43 |
| Aldershot | 46 | 16 | 11 | 19 | 49 | 59 | 43 |
| Rochdale | 46 | 13 | 12 | 21 | 50 | 59 | 38 |
| Newport County | 46 | 14 | 10 | 22 | 42 | 58 | 38 |
| Scunthorpe United | 46 | 13 | 11 | 22 | 49 | 73 | 37 |
| Halifax Town | 46 | 11 | 14 | 21 | 47 | 58 | 36 |
| Hartlepool | 46 | 10 | 12 | 24 | 47 | 73 | 32 |
| Southport | 46 | 3 | 19 | 24 | 33 | 77 | 25 |
| *Workington* | *46* | *4* | *11* | *31* | *41* | *102* | *19* |

## 1977 Football League Cup

### Semi-finals

| | |
|---|---|
| Queen's Park Rangers vs Aston Villa (0-0, 2-2, 0-3*) | 2-5 |
| Everton vs Bolton Wanderers (1-1, 1-0) | 2-1 |

\* Play-off at Highbury

### Final

Wembley, 12th March 1977

**Aston Villa 0**
**Everton 0**

*Attendance 100,000*

### Replay

Hillsborough, 16th March 1977

**Aston Villa 1** (Kenyon (og))
**Everton 1 (aet.)** (Latchford)

*Attendance 55,000*

### 2nd Replay

\* Old Trafford, 13th April 1977

**Aston Villa 3** (Little 2, Nicholl)
**Everton 2 (aet.)** (Latchford, Lyons)

*Attendance 54,749*

## 1977 F.A. Cup

### Semi-finals

| | |
|---|---|
| Leeds United vs Manchester United | 1-2 |
| Everton vs Liverpool | 2-2, 0-3 |

### Final

Wembley, 21st May 1977

**Manchester United 2** (Pearson, J. Greenhoff)
**Liverpool 1** (Case)

*Attendance 100,000*

## DIVISION ONE 1977-78

| | | | | | | | |
|---|---|---|---|---|---|---|---|
| **NOTTINGHAM FOREST** | 42 | 25 | 14 | 3 | 69 | 24 | 64 |
| Liverpool | 42 | 24 | 9 | 9 | 65 | 34 | 57 |
| Everton | 42 | 22 | 11 | 9 | 76 | 45 | 55 |
| Manchester City | 42 | 20 | 12 | 10 | 74 | 51 | 52 |
| Arsenal | 42 | 21 | 10 | 11 | 60 | 37 | 52 |
| West Bromwich Albion | 42 | 18 | 14 | 10 | 62 | 53 | 50 |
| Coventry City | 42 | 18 | 12 | 12 | 75 | 62 | 48 |
| Aston Villa | 42 | 18 | 10 | 14 | 57 | 42 | 46 |
| Leeds United | 42 | 18 | 10 | 14 | 63 | 53 | 46 |
| Manchester United | 42 | 16 | 10 | 16 | 67 | 63 | 42 |
| Birmingham City | 42 | 16 | 9 | 17 | 55 | 60 | 41 |
| Derby County | 42 | 14 | 13 | 15 | 54 | 59 | 41 |
| Norwich City | 42 | 11 | 18 | 13 | 52 | 66 | 40 |
| Middlesbrough | 42 | 12 | 15 | 15 | 42 | 54 | 39 |
| Wolverhampton Wanderers | 42 | 12 | 12 | 18 | 51 | 64 | 36 |
| Chelsea | 42 | 11 | 14 | 17 | 46 | 69 | 36 |
| Bristol City | 42 | 11 | 13 | 18 | 49 | 53 | 35 |
| Ipswich Town | 42 | 11 | 13 | 18 | 47 | 61 | 35 |
| Queen's Park Rangers | 42 | 9 | 15 | 18 | 47 | 64 | 33 |
| *West Ham United* | *42* | *12* | *8* | *22* | *52* | *69* | *32* |
| *Newcastle United* | *42* | *6* | *10* | *26* | *42* | *78* | *22* |
| *Leicester City* | *42* | *5* | *12* | *25* | *26* | *70* | *22* |

## DIVISION THREE 1977-78

| | | | | | | | |
|---|---|---|---|---|---|---|---|
| Wrexham | 46 | 23 | 15 | 8 | 78 | 45 | 61 |
| **Cambridge United** | 46 | 23 | 12 | 11 | 72 | 51 | 58 |
| **Preston North End** | 46 | 20 | 16 | 10 | 63 | 38 | 56 |
| Peterborough United | 46 | 20 | 16 | 10 | 47 | 33 | 56 |
| Chester | 46 | 16 | 22 | 8 | 59 | 56 | 54 |
| Walsall | 46 | 18 | 17 | 11 | 61 | 50 | 53 |
| Gillingham | 46 | 15 | 20 | 11 | 67 | 60 | 50 |
| Colchester United | 46 | 15 | 18 | 13 | 55 | 44 | 48 |
| Chesterfield | 46 | 17 | 14 | 15 | 58 | 49 | 48 |
| Swindon Town | 46 | 16 | 16 | 14 | 67 | 60 | 48 |
| Shrewsbury Town | 46 | 16 | 15 | 15 | 63 | 57 | 47 |
| Tranmere Rovers | 46 | 16 | 15 | 15 | 57 | 52 | 47 |
| Carlisle United | 46 | 14 | 19 | 13 | 59 | 59 | 47 |
| Sheffield Wednesday | 46 | 15 | 16 | 15 | 50 | 52 | 46 |
| Bury | 46 | 13 | 19 | 14 | 62 | 56 | 45 |
| Lincoln City | 46 | 15 | 15 | 16 | 53 | 61 | 45 |
| Exeter City | 46 | 15 | 14 | 17 | 49 | 59 | 44 |
| Oxford United | 46 | 13 | 14 | 19 | 64 | 67 | 40 |
| Plymouth Argyle | 46 | 11 | 17 | 18 | 61 | 68 | 39 |
| Rotherham United | 46 | 13 | 13 | 20 | 51 | 68 | 39 |
| *Port Vale* | *46* | *8* | *20* | *18* | *46* | *67* | *36* |
| *Bradford City* | *46* | *12* | *10* | *24* | *56* | *86* | *34* |
| *Hereford United* | *46* | *9* | *14* | *23* | *34* | *60* | *32* |
| *Portsmouth* | *46* | *7* | *17* | *22* | *41* | *75* | *31* |

## DIVISION TWO 1977-78

| | | | | | | | |
|---|---|---|---|---|---|---|---|
| **Bolton Wanderers** | 42 | 24 | 10 | 8 | 63 | 33 | 58 |
| **Southampton** | 42 | 22 | 13 | 7 | 70 | 39 | 57 |
| **Tottenham Hotspur** | 42 | 20 | 16 | 6 | 83 | 49 | 56 |
| Brighton & Hove Albion | 42 | 22 | 12 | 8 | 63 | 38 | 56 |
| Blackburn Rovers | 42 | 16 | 13 | 13 | 56 | 60 | 45 |
| Sunderland | 42 | 14 | 16 | 12 | 67 | 59 | 44 |
| Stoke City | 42 | 16 | 10 | 16 | 53 | 49 | 42 |
| Oldham Athletic | 42 | 13 | 16 | 13 | 54 | 58 | 42 |
| Crystal Palace | 42 | 13 | 15 | 14 | 50 | 47 | 41 |
| Fulham | 42 | 14 | 13 | 15 | 49 | 49 | 41 |
| Burnley | 42 | 15 | 10 | 17 | 56 | 64 | 40 |
| Sheffield United | 42 | 16 | 8 | 18 | 62 | 73 | 40 |
| Luton Town | 42 | 14 | 10 | 18 | 54 | 52 | 38 |
| Orient | 42 | 10 | 18 | 14 | 43 | 49 | 38 |
| Notts County | 42 | 11 | 16 | 15 | 54 | 62 | 38 |
| Millwall | 42 | 12 | 14 | 16 | 49 | 57 | 38 |
| Charlton Athletic | 42 | 13 | 12 | 17 | 55 | 68 | 38 |
| Bristol Rovers | 42 | 13 | 12 | 17 | 61 | 77 | 38 |
| Cardiff City | 42 | 13 | 12 | 17 | 51 | 71 | 38 |
| *Blackpool* | *42* | *12* | *13* | *17* | *59* | *60* | *37* |
| *Mansfield Town* | *42* | *10* | *11* | *21* | *49* | *69* | *31* |
| *Hull City* | *42* | *8* | *12* | *22* | *34* | *52* | *28* |

## DIVISION FOUR 1977-78

| | | | | | | | |
|---|---|---|---|---|---|---|---|
| **Watford** | 46 | 30 | 11 | 5 | 85 | 38 | 71 |
| **Southend United** | 46 | 25 | 10 | 11 | 66 | 39 | 60 |
| **Swansea City** | 46 | 23 | 10 | 13 | 87 | 47 | 56 |
| **Brentford** | 46 | 21 | 14 | 11 | 86 | 54 | 56 |
| Aldershot | 46 | 19 | 16 | 11 | 67 | 47 | 54 |
| Grimsby Town | 46 | 21 | 11 | 14 | 57 | 51 | 53 |
| Barnsley | 46 | 18 | 14 | 14 | 61 | 49 | 50 |
| Reading | 46 | 18 | 14 | 14 | 55 | 52 | 50 |
| Torquay United | 46 | 16 | 15 | 15 | 57 | 56 | 47 |
| Northampton Town | 46 | 17 | 13 | 16 | 63 | 68 | 47 |
| Huddersfield Town | 46 | 15 | 15 | 16 | 63 | 55 | 45 |
| Doncaster Rovers | 46 | 14 | 17 | 15 | 52 | 65 | 45 |
| Wimbledon | 46 | 14 | 16 | 16 | 66 | 67 | 44 |
| Scunthorpe United | 46 | 14 | 16 | 16 | 50 | 55 | 44 |
| Crewe Alexandra | 46 | 15 | 14 | 17 | 50 | 69 | 44 |
| Newport County | 46 | 16 | 11 | 19 | 65 | 73 | 43 |
| Bournemouth | 46 | 14 | 15 | 17 | 41 | 51 | 43 |
| Stockport County | 46 | 16 | 10 | 20 | 56 | 56 | 42 |
| Darlington | 46 | 14 | 13 | 19 | 52 | 59 | 41 |
| Halifax Town | 46 | 10 | 21 | 15 | 52 | 62 | 41 |
| Hartlepool United | 46 | 15 | 7 | 24 | 51 | 84 | 37 |
| York City | 46 | 12 | 12 | 22 | 50 | 69 | 36 |
| *Southport* | *46* | *6* | *19* | *21* | *52* | *76* | *31* |
| Rochdale | 46 | 8 | 8 | 30 | 43 | 85 | 24 |

## 1978 F.A. Cup

### Semi-finals

| | |
|---|---|
| Ipswich Town vs West Bromwich Albion | 3-1 |
| Arsenal vs Orient | 3-0 |

### Final

Wembley, 6th May 1978

**Ipswich Town 1**   (Osborne)

**Arsenal 0**

*Attendance 100,000*

## 1978 Football League Cup

### Semi-finals

| | |
|---|---|
| Leeds United vs Nottingham Forest (1-3, 2-4) | 3-7 |
| Liverpool vs Arsenal (2-1, 0-0) | 2-1 |

### Final

Wembley, 18th March 1978

**Nottingham Forest 0**

**Liverpool 0 (aet.)**

*Attendance 100,000*

### Replay

Old Trafford, 22nd March 1978

**Nottingham Forest 1**   (Robertson (penalty))

**Liverpool 0**

*Attendance 54,375*

## DIVISION ONE 1978-79

| | | | | | | | |
|---|---|---|---|---|---|---|---|
| LIVERPOOL | 42 | 30 | 8 | 4 | 85 | 16 | 68 |
| Nottingham Forest | 42 | 21 | 18 | 3 | 61 | 26 | 60 |
| West Bromwich Albion | 42 | 24 | 11 | 7 | 72 | 35 | 59 |
| Everton | 42 | 17 | 17 | 8 | 52 | 40 | 51 |
| Leeds United | 42 | 18 | 14 | 10 | 70 | 52 | 50 |
| Ipswich Town | 42 | 20 | 9 | 13 | 63 | 49 | 49 |
| Arsenal | 42 | 17 | 14 | 11 | 61 | 48 | 48 |
| Aston Villa | 42 | 15 | 16 | 11 | 59 | 49 | 46 |
| Manchester United | 42 | 15 | 15 | 12 | 60 | 63 | 45 |
| Coventry City | 42 | 14 | 16 | 12 | 58 | 68 | 44 |
| Tottenham Hotspur | 42 | 13 | 15 | 14 | 48 | 61 | 41 |
| Middlesbrough | 42 | 15 | 10 | 17 | 57 | 50 | 40 |
| Bristol City | 42 | 15 | 10 | 17 | 47 | 51 | 40 |
| Southampton | 42 | 12 | 16 | 14 | 47 | 53 | 40 |
| Manchester City | 42 | 13 | 13 | 16 | 58 | 56 | 39 |
| Norwich City | 42 | 7 | 23 | 12 | 51 | 57 | 37 |
| Bolton Wanderers | 42 | 12 | 11 | 19 | 54 | 75 | 35 |
| Wolverhampton Wanderers | 42 | 13 | 8 | 21 | 44 | 68 | 34 |
| Derby County | 42 | 10 | 11 | 21 | 44 | 71 | 31 |
| *Queen's Park Rangers* | *42* | *6* | *13* | *23* | *45* | *73* | *25* |
| *Birmingham City* | *42* | *6* | *10* | *26* | *37* | *64* | *22* |
| *Chelsea* | *42* | *5* | *10* | *27* | *44* | *92* | *20* |

## DIVISION TWO 1978-79

| | | | | | | | |
|---|---|---|---|---|---|---|---|
| Crystal Palace | 42 | 19 | 19 | 4 | 51 | 24 | 57 |
| Brighton & Hove Albion | 42 | 23 | 10 | 9 | 72 | 39 | 56 |
| Stoke City | 42 | 20 | 16 | 6 | 58 | 31 | 56 |
| Sunderland | 42 | 22 | 11 | 9 | 70 | 44 | 55 |
| West Ham United | 42 | 18 | 14 | 10 | 70 | 39 | 50 |
| Notts County | 42 | 14 | 16 | 12 | 48 | 60 | 44 |
| Preston North End | 42 | 12 | 18 | 12 | 59 | 57 | 42 |
| Newcastle United | 42 | 17 | 8 | 17 | 51 | 55 | 42 |
| Cardiff City | 42 | 16 | 10 | 16 | 56 | 70 | 42 |
| Fulham | 42 | 13 | 15 | 14 | 50 | 47 | 41 |
| Orient | 42 | 15 | 10 | 17 | 51 | 51 | 40 |
| Cambridge United | 42 | 12 | 16 | 14 | 44 | 52 | 40 |
| Burnley | 42 | 14 | 12 | 16 | 51 | 62 | 40 |
| Oldham Athletic | 42 | 13 | 13 | 16 | 52 | 61 | 39 |
| Wrexham | 42 | 12 | 14 | 16 | 45 | 42 | 38 |
| Bristol Rovers | 42 | 14 | 10 | 18 | 48 | 60 | 38 |
| Leicester City | 42 | 10 | 17 | 15 | 43 | 52 | 37 |
| Luton Town | 42 | 13 | 10 | 19 | 60 | 57 | 36 |
| Charlton Athletic | 42 | 11 | 13 | 18 | 60 | 69 | 35 |
| *Sheffield United* | *42* | *11* | *12* | *19* | *52* | *69* | *34* |
| *Millwall* | *42* | *11* | *10* | *21* | *42* | *61* | *32* |
| *Blackburn Rovers* | *42* | *10* | *10* | *22* | *41* | *72* | *30* |

## DIVISION THREE 1978-79

| | | | | | | | |
|---|---|---|---|---|---|---|---|
| Shrewsbury Town | 46 | 21 | 19 | 6 | 61 | 41 | 61 |
| Watford | 46 | 24 | 12 | 10 | 83 | 52 | 60 |
| Swansea City | 46 | 24 | 12 | 10 | 83 | 61 | 60 |
| Gillingham | 46 | 21 | 17 | 8 | 65 | 42 | 59 |
| Swindon Town | 46 | 25 | 7 | 14 | 74 | 52 | 57 |
| Carlisle United | 46 | 15 | 22 | 9 | 53 | 42 | 52 |
| Colchester United | 46 | 17 | 17 | 12 | 60 | 55 | 51 |
| Hull City | 46 | 19 | 11 | 16 | 66 | 61 | 49 |
| Exeter City | 46 | 17 | 15 | 14 | 61 | 56 | 49 |
| Brentford | 46 | 19 | 9 | 18 | 53 | 49 | 47 |
| Oxford United | 46 | 14 | 18 | 14 | 44 | 50 | 46 |
| Blackpool | 46 | 18 | 9 | 19 | 61 | 59 | 45 |
| Southend United | 46 | 15 | 15 | 16 | 51 | 49 | 45 |
| Sheffield Wednesday | 46 | 13 | 19 | 14 | 53 | 53 | 45 |
| Plymouth Argyle | 46 | 15 | 14 | 17 | 67 | 68 | 44 |
| Chester | 46 | 14 | 16 | 16 | 57 | 61 | 44 |
| Rotherham United | 46 | 17 | 10 | 19 | 49 | 55 | 44 |
| Mansfield Town | 46 | 12 | 19 | 15 | 51 | 52 | 43 |
| Bury | 46 | 11 | 20 | 15 | 59 | 65 | 42 |
| Chesterfield | 46 | 13 | 14 | 19 | 51 | 65 | 40 |
| *Peterborough United* | *46* | *11* | *14* | *21* | *44* | *63* | *36* |
| *Walsall* | *46* | *10* | *12* | *24* | *56* | *71* | *32* |
| *Tranmere Rovers* | *46* | *6* | *16* | *24* | *45* | *78* | *28* |
| *Lincoln City* | *46* | *7* | *11* | *28* | *41* | *88* | *25* |

## DIVISION FOUR 1978-79

| | | | | | | | |
|---|---|---|---|---|---|---|---|
| Reading | 46 | 26 | 13 | 7 | 76 | 35 | 65 |
| Grimsby Town | 46 | 26 | 9 | 11 | 82 | 49 | 61 |
| Wimbledon | 46 | 25 | 11 | 10 | 78 | 46 | 61 |
| Barnsley | 46 | 24 | 13 | 9 | 73 | 42 | 61 |
| Aldershot | 46 | 20 | 17 | 9 | 63 | 47 | 57 |
| Wigan Athletic | 46 | 21 | 13 | 12 | 63 | 48 | 55 |
| Portsmouth | 46 | 20 | 12 | 14 | 62 | 48 | 52 |
| Newport County | 46 | 21 | 10 | 15 | 66 | 55 | 52 |
| Huddersfield Town | 46 | 18 | 11 | 17 | 57 | 53 | 47 |
| York City | 46 | 18 | 11 | 17 | 51 | 55 | 47 |
| Torquay United | 46 | 19 | 8 | 19 | 58 | 65 | 46 |
| Scunthorpe United | 46 | 17 | 11 | 18 | 54 | 60 | 45 |
| Hartlepool United | 46 | 13 | 18 | 15 | 57 | 66 | 44 |
| Hereford United | 46 | 15 | 13 | 18 | 53 | 53 | 43 |
| Bradford City | 46 | 17 | 9 | 20 | 62 | 68 | 43 |
| Port Vale | 46 | 14 | 14 | 18 | 57 | 70 | 42 |
| Stockport County | 46 | 14 | 12 | 20 | 58 | 60 | 40 |
| Bournemouth | 46 | 14 | 11 | 21 | 47 | 48 | 39 |
| Northampton Town | 46 | 15 | 9 | 22 | 64 | 76 | 39 |
| Rochdale | 46 | 15 | 9 | 22 | 47 | 64 | 39 |
| Darlington | 46 | 11 | 15 | 20 | 49 | 66 | 37 |
| Doncaster Rovers | 46 | 13 | 11 | 22 | 50 | 73 | 37 |
| Halifax Town | 46 | 9 | 8 | 29 | 39 | 72 | 26 |
| Crewe Alexandra | 46 | 6 | 14 | 26 | 43 | 90 | 26 |

## 1979 F.A. Cup

**Semi-finals**

| | |
|---|---|
| Arsenal vs Wolverhampton Wanderers | 2-0 |
| Manchester United vs Liverpool | 2-2, 1-0 |

**Final**

Wembley, 12th May 1979

**Arsenal 3**   (Talbot, Stapleton, Sunderland)
**Manchester United 2**   (McQueen, McIlroy)

*Attendance 100,000*

## 1979 Football League Cup

**Semi-finals**

| | |
|---|---|
| Nottingham Forest vs Watford (3-1, 0-0) | 3-1 |
| Leeds United vs Southampton (2-2, 0-1) | 2-3 |

**Final**

Wembley, 17th March 1979

**Nottingham Forest 3**   (Birtles 2, Woodcock)
**Southampton 2**   (Peach, Holmes)

*Attendance 100,000*

## DIVISION ONE 1979-80

| | | | | | | | |
|---|---|---|---|---|---|---|---|
| **LIVERPOOL** | 42 | 25 | 10 | 7 | 81 | 30 | 60 |
| Manchester United | 42 | 24 | 10 | 8 | 65 | 35 | 58 |
| Ipswich Town | 42 | 22 | 9 | 11 | 68 | 39 | 53 |
| Arsenal | 42 | 18 | 16 | 8 | 52 | 36 | 52 |
| Nottingham Forest | 42 | 20 | 8 | 14 | 63 | 43 | 48 |
| Wolverhampton Wanderers | 42 | 19 | 9 | 14 | 58 | 47 | 47 |
| Aston Villa | 42 | 16 | 14 | 12 | 51 | 50 | 46 |
| Southampton | 42 | 18 | 9 | 15 | 65 | 53 | 45 |
| Middlesbrough | 42 | 16 | 12 | 14 | 50 | 44 | 44 |
| West Bromwich Albion | 42 | 11 | 19 | 12 | 54 | 50 | 41 |
| Leeds United | 42 | 13 | 14 | 15 | 46 | 50 | 40 |
| Norwich City | 42 | 13 | 14 | 15 | 58 | 66 | 40 |
| Crystal Palace | 42 | 12 | 16 | 14 | 41 | 50 | 40 |
| Tottenham Hotspur | 42 | 15 | 10 | 17 | 52 | 62 | 40 |
| Coventry City | 42 | 16 | 7 | 19 | 56 | 66 | 39 |
| Brighton & Hove Albion | 42 | 11 | 15 | 16 | 47 | 57 | 37 |
| Manchester City | 42 | 12 | 13 | 17 | 43 | 66 | 37 |
| Stoke City | 42 | 13 | 10 | 19 | 44 | 58 | 36 |
| Everton | 42 | 9 | 17 | 16 | 43 | 51 | 35 |
| *Bristol City* | *42* | *9* | *13* | *20* | *37* | *66* | *31* |
| *Derby County* | *42* | *11* | *8* | *23* | *47* | *67* | *30* |
| *Bolton Wanderers* | *42* | *5* | *15* | *22* | *38* | *73* | *25* |

## DIVISION TWO 1979-80

| | | | | | | | |
|---|---|---|---|---|---|---|---|
| **Leicester City** | 42 | 21 | 13 | 8 | 58 | 38 | 55 |
| **Sunderland** | 42 | 21 | 12 | 9 | 69 | 42 | 54 |
| **Birmingham City** | 42 | 21 | 11 | 10 | 58 | 38 | 53 |
| Chelsea | 42 | 23 | 7 | 12 | 66 | 52 | 53 |
| Queen's Park Rangers | 42 | 18 | 13 | 11 | 75 | 53 | 49 |
| Luton Town | 42 | 16 | 17 | 9 | 66 | 45 | 49 |
| West Ham United | 42 | 20 | 7 | 15 | 54 | 43 | 47 |
| Cambridge United | 42 | 14 | 16 | 12 | 61 | 53 | 44 |
| Newcastle United | 42 | 15 | 14 | 13 | 53 | 49 | 44 |
| Preston North End | 42 | 12 | 19 | 11 | 56 | 52 | 43 |
| Oldham Athletic | 42 | 16 | 11 | 15 | 49 | 53 | 43 |
| Swansea City | 42 | 17 | 9 | 16 | 48 | 53 | 43 |
| Shrewsbury Town | 42 | 18 | 5 | 19 | 60 | 53 | 41 |
| Orient | 42 | 12 | 17 | 13 | 48 | 54 | 41 |
| Cardiff City | 42 | 16 | 8 | 18 | 41 | 48 | 40 |
| Wrexham | 42 | 16 | 6 | 20 | 40 | 49 | 38 |
| Notts County | 42 | 11 | 15 | 16 | 51 | 52 | 37 |
| Watford | 42 | 12 | 13 | 17 | 39 | 46 | 37 |
| Bristol Rovers | 42 | 11 | 13 | 18 | 50 | 64 | 35 |
| *Fulham* | *42* | *11* | *7* | *24* | *42* | *74* | *29* |
| *Burnley* | *42* | *6* | *15* | *21* | *39* | *73* | *27* |
| *Charlton Athletic* | *42* | *6* | *10* | *26* | *39* | *78* | *22* |

## DIVISION THREE 1979-80

| | | | | | | | |
|---|---|---|---|---|---|---|---|
| **Grimsby Town** | 46 | 26 | 10 | 10 | 73 | 42 | 62 |
| **Blackburn Rovers** | 46 | 25 | 9 | 12 | 58 | 36 | 59 |
| **Sheffield Wednesday** | 46 | 21 | 16 | 9 | 81 | 47 | 58 |
| Chesterfield | 46 | 23 | 11 | 12 | 71 | 46 | 57 |
| Colchester United | 46 | 20 | 12 | 14 | 64 | 56 | 52 |
| Carlisle United | 46 | 18 | 12 | 16 | 66 | 56 | 48 |
| Reading | 46 | 16 | 16 | 14 | 66 | 65 | 48 |
| Exeter City | 46 | 19 | 10 | 17 | 60 | 68 | 48 |
| Chester | 46 | 17 | 13 | 16 | 49 | 57 | 47 |
| Swindon Town | 46 | 19 | 8 | 19 | 71 | 63 | 46 |
| Barnsley | 46 | 16 | 14 | 16 | 53 | 56 | 46 |
| Sheffield United | 46 | 18 | 10 | 18 | 60 | 66 | 46 |
| Rotherham United | 46 | 18 | 10 | 18 | 58 | 66 | 46 |
| Millwall | 46 | 16 | 13 | 17 | 65 | 59 | 45 |
| Plymouth Argyle | 46 | 16 | 12 | 18 | 59 | 55 | 44 |
| Gillingham | 46 | 14 | 14 | 18 | 49 | 51 | 42 |
| Oxford United | 46 | 14 | 13 | 19 | 57 | 62 | 41 |
| Blackpool | 46 | 15 | 11 | 20 | 62 | 74 | 41 |
| Brentford | 46 | 15 | 11 | 20 | 59 | 73 | 41 |
| Hull City | 46 | 12 | 16 | 18 | 51 | 69 | 40 |
| *Bury* | *46* | *16* | *7* | *23* | *45* | *59* | *39* |
| *Southend United* | *46* | *14* | *10* | *22* | *47* | *58* | *38* |
| *Mansfield Town* | *46* | *10* | *16* | *20* | *47* | *58* | *36* |
| *Wimbledon* | *46* | *10* | *14* | *22* | *52* | *81* | *34* |

## DIVISION FOUR 1979-80

| | | | | | | | |
|---|---|---|---|---|---|---|---|
| **Huddersfield Town** | 46 | 27 | 12 | 7 | 101 | 48 | 66 |
| **Walsall** | 46 | 23 | 18 | 5 | 75 | 47 | 64 |
| **Newport County** | 46 | 27 | 7 | 12 | 83 | 50 | 61 |
| **Portsmouth** | 46 | 24 | 12 | 10 | 91 | 49 | 60 |
| Bradford City | 46 | 24 | 12 | 10 | 77 | 50 | 60 |
| Wigan Athletic | 46 | 21 | 13 | 12 | 76 | 61 | 55 |
| Lincoln City | 46 | 18 | 17 | 11 | 64 | 42 | 53 |
| Peterborough United | 46 | 21 | 10 | 15 | 58 | 47 | 52 |
| Torquay United | 46 | 15 | 17 | 14 | 70 | 69 | 47 |
| Aldershot | 46 | 16 | 13 | 17 | 62 | 53 | 45 |
| Bournemouth | 46 | 13 | 18 | 15 | 52 | 51 | 44 |
| Doncaster Rovers | 46 | 15 | 14 | 17 | 62 | 63 | 44 |
| Northampton Town | 46 | 16 | 12 | 18 | 51 | 66 | 44 |
| Scunthorpe United | 46 | 14 | 15 | 17 | 58 | 75 | 43 |
| Tranmere Rovers | 46 | 14 | 13 | 19 | 50 | 56 | 41 |
| Stockport County | 46 | 14 | 12 | 20 | 48 | 72 | 40 |
| York City | 46 | 14 | 11 | 21 | 65 | 82 | 39 |
| Halifax Town | 46 | 13 | 13 | 20 | 46 | 72 | 39 |
| Hartlepool United | 46 | 14 | 10 | 22 | 59 | 64 | 38 |
| Port Vale | 46 | 12 | 12 | 22 | 56 | 70 | 36 |
| Hereford United | 46 | 11 | 14 | 21 | 38 | 52 | 36 |
| Darlington | 46 | 9 | 17 | 20 | 50 | 74 | 35 |
| Crewe Alexandra | 46 | 11 | 13 | 22 | 35 | 68 | 35 |
| Rochdale | 46 | 7 | 13 | 26 | 33 | 79 | 27 |

## 1980 F.A. Cup

**Semi-finals**

| | |
|---|---|
| West Ham United vs Everton | 1-1, 2-1 |
| Arsenal vs Liverpool | 0-0, 1-1, 1-1, 1-0 |

**Final**

Wembley, 10th May 1980

**West Ham United 1** (Brooking)
**Arsenal 0**

*Attendance 100,000*

## 1980 Football League Cup

**Semi-finals**

| | | |
|---|---|---|
| Swindon Town vs Wolverhampton Wands. (2-1, 1-3) | | 3-4 |
| Nottingham Forest vs Liverpool (1-0, 1-1) | | 2-1 |

**Final**

Wembley, 15th March 1980

**Wolverhampton Wanderers 1** (Gray)
**Nottingham Forest 0**

*Attendance 100,000*

## DIVISION ONE 1980-81

| | | | | | | | |
|---|---|---|---|---|---|---|---|
| **ASTON VILLA** | 42 | 26 | 8 | 8 | 72 | 40 | 60 |
| Ipswich Town | 42 | 23 | 10 | 9 | 77 | 43 | 56 |
| Arsenal | 42 | 19 | 15 | 8 | 61 | 45 | 53 |
| West Bromwich Albion | 42 | 20 | 12 | 10 | 60 | 42 | 52 |
| Liverpool | 42 | 17 | 17 | 8 | 62 | 42 | 51 |
| Southampton | 42 | 20 | 10 | 12 | 76 | 56 | 50 |
| Nottingham Forest | 42 | 19 | 12 | 11 | 62 | 44 | 50 |
| Manchester United | 42 | 15 | 18 | 9 | 51 | 36 | 48 |
| Leeds United | 42 | 17 | 10 | 15 | 39 | 47 | 44 |
| Tottenham Hotspur | 42 | 14 | 15 | 13 | 70 | 68 | 43 |
| Stoke City | 42 | 12 | 18 | 12 | 51 | 60 | 42 |
| Manchester City | 42 | 14 | 11 | 17 | 56 | 59 | 39 |
| Birmingham City | 42 | 13 | 12 | 17 | 50 | 61 | 38 |
| Middlesbrough | 42 | 16 | 5 | 21 | 53 | 61 | 37 |
| Everton | 42 | 13 | 10 | 19 | 55 | 58 | 36 |
| Coventry City | 42 | 13 | 10 | 19 | 48 | 68 | 36 |
| Sunderland | 42 | 14 | 7 | 21 | 52 | 53 | 35 |
| Wolverhampton Wanderers | 42 | 13 | 9 | 20 | 43 | 55 | 35 |
| Brighton & Hove Albion | 42 | 14 | 7 | 21 | 54 | 67 | 35 |
| *Norwich City* | *42* | *13* | *7* | *22* | *49* | *73* | *33* |
| *Leicester City* | *42* | *13* | *6* | *23* | *40* | *67* | *32* |
| *Crystal Palace* | *42* | *6* | *7* | *29* | *47* | *83* | *19* |

## DIVISION THREE 1980-81

| | | | | | | | |
|---|---|---|---|---|---|---|---|
| **Rotherham United** | 46 | 24 | 13 | 9 | 62 | 32 | 61 |
| **Barnsley** | 46 | 21 | 17 | 8 | 72 | 45 | 59 |
| **Charlton Athletic** | 46 | 25 | 9 | 12 | 63 | 44 | 59 |
| Huddersfield Town | 46 | 21 | 14 | 11 | 71 | 40 | 56 |
| Chesterfield | 46 | 23 | 10 | 13 | 72 | 48 | 56 |
| Portsmouth | 46 | 22 | 9 | 15 | 55 | 47 | 53 |
| Plymouth Argyle | 46 | 19 | 14 | 13 | 56 | 44 | 52 |
| Burnley | 46 | 18 | 14 | 14 | 60 | 48 | 50 |
| Brentford | 46 | 14 | 19 | 13 | 52 | 49 | 47 |
| Reading | 46 | 18 | 10 | 18 | 62 | 62 | 46 |
| Exeter City | 46 | 16 | 13 | 17 | 62 | 66 | 45 |
| Newport County | 46 | 15 | 13 | 18 | 64 | 61 | 43 |
| Fulham | 46 | 15 | 13 | 18 | 57 | 64 | 43 |
| Oxford United | 46 | 13 | 17 | 16 | 39 | 47 | 43 |
| Gillingham | 46 | 12 | 18 | 16 | 48 | 58 | 42 |
| Millwall | 46 | 14 | 14 | 18 | 43 | 60 | 42 |
| Swindon Town | 46 | 13 | 15 | 18 | 51 | 56 | 41 |
| Chester | 46 | 15 | 11 | 20 | 38 | 48 | 41 |
| Carlisle United | 46 | 14 | 13 | 19 | 56 | 70 | 41 |
| Walsall | 46 | 13 | 15 | 18 | 59 | 74 | 41 |
| *Sheffield United* | *46* | *14* | *12* | *20* | *65* | *63* | *40* |
| *Colchester United* | *46* | *14* | *11* | *21* | *45* | *65* | *39* |
| *Blackpool* | *46* | *9* | *14* | *23* | *45* | *75* | *32* |
| *Hull City* | *46* | *8* | *16* | *22* | *40* | *71* | *32* |

## DIVISION TWO 1980-81

| | | | | | | | |
|---|---|---|---|---|---|---|---|
| **West Ham United** | 42 | 28 | 10 | 4 | 79 | 29 | 66 |
| **Notts County** | 42 | 18 | 17 | 7 | 49 | 38 | 53 |
| **Swansea City** | 42 | 18 | 14 | 10 | 64 | 44 | 50 |
| Blackburn Rovers | 42 | 16 | 18 | 8 | 42 | 29 | 50 |
| Luton Town | 42 | 18 | 12 | 12 | 61 | 46 | 48 |
| Derby County | 42 | 15 | 15 | 12 | 57 | 52 | 45 |
| Grimsby Town | 42 | 15 | 15 | 12 | 44 | 42 | 45 |
| Queen's Park Rangers | 42 | 15 | 13 | 14 | 56 | 46 | 43 |
| Watford | 42 | 16 | 11 | 15 | 50 | 45 | 43 |
| Sheffield Wednesday | 42 | 17 | 8 | 17 | 53 | 51 | 42 |
| Newcastle United | 42 | 14 | 14 | 14 | 30 | 45 | 42 |
| Chelsea | 42 | 14 | 12 | 16 | 46 | 41 | 40 |
| Cambridge United | 42 | 17 | 6 | 19 | 53 | 65 | 40 |
| Shrewsbury Town | 42 | 11 | 17 | 14 | 46 | 47 | 39 |
| Oldham Athletic | 42 | 12 | 15 | 15 | 39 | 48 | 39 |
| Wrexham | 42 | 12 | 14 | 16 | 43 | 45 | 38 |
| Orient | 42 | 13 | 12 | 17 | 52 | 56 | 38 |
| Bolton Wanderers | 42 | 14 | 10 | 18 | 61 | 66 | 38 |
| Cardiff City | 42 | 12 | 12 | 18 | 44 | 60 | 36 |
| *Preston North End* | *42* | *11* | *14* | *17* | *41* | *62* | *36* |
| *Bristol City* | *42* | *7* | *16* | *19* | *29* | *51* | *30* |
| *Bristol Rovers* | *42* | *5* | *13* | *24* | *34* | *65* | *23* |

## DIVISION FOUR 1980-81

| | | | | | | | |
|---|---|---|---|---|---|---|---|
| **Southend United** | 46 | 30 | 7 | 9 | 79 | 31 | 67 |
| **Lincoln City** | 46 | 25 | 15 | 6 | 66 | 25 | 65 |
| **Doncaster Rovers** | 46 | 22 | 12 | 12 | 59 | 49 | 56 |
| **Wimbledon** | 46 | 23 | 9 | 14 | 64 | 46 | 55 |
| Peterborough United | 46 | 17 | 18 | 11 | 68 | 54 | 52 |
| Aldershot | 46 | 18 | 14 | 14 | 43 | 41 | 50 |
| Mansfield Town | 46 | 20 | 9 | 17 | 58 | 44 | 49 |
| Darlington | 46 | 19 | 11 | 16 | 65 | 59 | 49 |
| Hartlepool United | 46 | 20 | 9 | 17 | 64 | 61 | 49 |
| Northampton Town | 46 | 18 | 13 | 15 | 65 | 67 | 49 |
| Wigan Athletic | 46 | 18 | 11 | 17 | 51 | 55 | 47 |
| Bury | 46 | 17 | 11 | 18 | 70 | 62 | 45 |
| Bournemouth | 46 | 16 | 13 | 17 | 47 | 48 | 45 |
| Bradford City | 46 | 14 | 16 | 16 | 53 | 60 | 44 |
| Rochdale | 46 | 14 | 15 | 17 | 60 | 70 | 43 |
| Scunthorpe United | 46 | 11 | 20 | 15 | 60 | 69 | 42 |
| Torquay United | 46 | 18 | 5 | 23 | 55 | 63 | 41 |
| Crewe Alexandra | 46 | 13 | 14 | 19 | 48 | 61 | 40 |
| Port Vale | 46 | 12 | 15 | 19 | 57 | 70 | 39 |
| Stockport County | 46 | 16 | 7 | 23 | 44 | 57 | 39 |
| Tranmere Rovers | 46 | 13 | 10 | 23 | 59 | 73 | 36 |
| Hereford United | 46 | 11 | 13 | 22 | 38 | 62 | 35 |
| Halifax Town | 46 | 11 | 12 | 23 | 44 | 71 | 34 |
| York City | 46 | 12 | 9 | 25 | 47 | 66 | 33 |

## 1981 F.A. Cup

**Semi-finals**

Tottenham Hotspur vs Wolverhampton Wanderers   2-2, 3-0
Ipswich Town vs Manchester City                                0-1

**Final**

Wembley, 9th May 1981

**Tottenham Hotspur 1**   (Hutchinson (og))
**Manchester City 1**   (Hutchinson)

*Attendance 100,000*

**Replay**

Wembley, 14th May 1981

**Tottenham Hotspur 3**   (Villa 2, Crooks)
**Manchester City 2**   (MacKenzie, Reeves (pen))

*Attendance 92,000*

## 1981 Football League Cup

**Semi-finals**

| | |
|---|---|
| Manchester City vs Liverpool (0-1, 1-1) | 1-2 |
| Coventry City vs West Ham United (3-2, 0-2) | 3-4 |

**Final**

Wembley, 14th March 1981

**Liverpool 1**   (A. Kennedy)
**West Ham United 1 (aet.)**   (Stewart)

*Attendance 100,000*

**Replay**

Villa Park, 1st April 1981

**Liverpool 2**   (Dalglish, R. Kennedy)
**West Ham United 1**   (Goddard)

*Attendance 36,693*

## DIVISION ONE 1981-82

| | | | | | | | |
|---|---|---|---|---|---|---|---|
| **LIVERPOOL** | 42 | 26 | 9 | 7 | 80 | 32 | 87 |
| Ipswich Town | 42 | 26 | 5 | 11 | 75 | 53 | 83 |
| Manchester United | 42 | 22 | 12 | 8 | 59 | 29 | 78 |
| Tottenham Hotspur | 42 | 20 | 11 | 11 | 67 | 48 | 71 |
| Arsenal | 42 | 20 | 11 | 11 | 48 | 37 | 71 |
| Swansea City | 42 | 21 | 6 | 15 | 58 | 51 | 69 |
| Southampton | 42 | 19 | 9 | 14 | 72 | 67 | 66 |
| Everton | 42 | 17 | 13 | 12 | 56 | 50 | 64 |
| West Ham United | 42 | 14 | 16 | 12 | 66 | 57 | 58 |
| Manchester City | 42 | 15 | 13 | 14 | 49 | 50 | 58 |
| Aston Villa | 42 | 15 | 12 | 15 | 55 | 53 | 57 |
| Nottingham Forest | 42 | 15 | 12 | 15 | 42 | 48 | 57 |
| Brighton & Hove Albion | 42 | 13 | 13 | 16 | 43 | 52 | 52 |
| Coventry City | 42 | 13 | 11 | 18 | 56 | 62 | 50 |
| Notts County | 42 | 13 | 8 | 21 | 61 | 69 | 47 |
| Birmingham City | 42 | 10 | 14 | 18 | 53 | 61 | 44 |
| West Bromwich Albion | 42 | 11 | 11 | 20 | 46 | 57 | 44 |
| Stoke City | 42 | 12 | 8 | 22 | 44 | 63 | 44 |
| Sunderland | 42 | 11 | 11 | 20 | 38 | 58 | 44 |
| *Leeds United* | *42* | *10* | *12* | *20* | *39* | *61* | *42* |
| *Wolverhampton Wanderers* | *42* | *10* | *10* | *22* | *32* | *63* | *40* |
| *Middlesbrough* | *42* | *8* | *15* | *19* | *34* | *52* | *39* |

## DIVISION TWO 1981-82

| | | | | | | | |
|---|---|---|---|---|---|---|---|
| **Luton Town** | 42 | 25 | 13 | 4 | 86 | 46 | 88 |
| **Watford** | 42 | 23 | 11 | 8 | 76 | 42 | 80 |
| **Norwich City** | 42 | 22 | 5 | 15 | 64 | 50 | 71 |
| Sheffield Wednesday | 42 | 20 | 10 | 12 | 55 | 51 | 70 |
| Queen's Park Rangers | 42 | 21 | 6 | 15 | 65 | 43 | 69 |
| Barnsley | 42 | 19 | 10 | 13 | 59 | 41 | 67 |
| Rotherham United | 42 | 20 | 7 | 15 | 66 | 54 | 67 |
| Leicester City | 42 | 18 | 12 | 12 | 56 | 48 | 66 |
| Newcastle United | 42 | 18 | 8 | 16 | 52 | 50 | 62 |
| Blackburn Rovers | 42 | 16 | 11 | 15 | 47 | 43 | 59 |
| Oldham Athletic | 42 | 15 | 14 | 13 | 50 | 51 | 59 |
| Chelsea | 42 | 15 | 12 | 15 | 60 | 60 | 57 |
| Charlton Athletic | 42 | 13 | 12 | 17 | 50 | 65 | 51 |
| Cambridge United | 42 | 13 | 9 | 20 | 48 | 53 | 48 |
| Crystal Palace | 42 | 13 | 9 | 20 | 34 | 45 | 48 |
| Derby County | 42 | 12 | 12 | 18 | 53 | 68 | 48 |
| Grimsby Town | 42 | 11 | 13 | 18 | 53 | 65 | 46 |
| Shrewsbury Town | 42 | 11 | 13 | 18 | 37 | 57 | 46 |
| Bolton Wanderers | 42 | 13 | 7 | 22 | 39 | 61 | 46 |
| *Cardiff City* | *42* | *12* | *8* | *22* | *45* | *61* | *44* |
| *Wrexham* | *42* | *11* | *11* | *20* | *40* | *56* | *44* |
| *Orient* | *42* | *10* | *9* | *23* | *36* | *61* | *39* |

## DIVISION THREE 1981-82

| | | | | | | | |
|---|---|---|---|---|---|---|---|
| **Burnley** | 46 | 21 | 17 | 8 | 66 | 45 | 80 |
| **Carlisle United** | 46 | 23 | 11 | 12 | 65 | 50 | 80 |
| **Fulham** | 46 | 21 | 15 | 10 | 77 | 51 | 78 |
| Lincoln City | 46 | 21 | 14 | 11 | 66 | 40 | 77 |
| Oxford United | 46 | 19 | 14 | 13 | 63 | 49 | 71 |
| Gillingham | 46 | 20 | 11 | 15 | 64 | 56 | 71 |
| Southend United | 46 | 18 | 15 | 13 | 63 | 51 | 69 |
| Brentford | 46 | 19 | 11 | 16 | 56 | 47 | 68 |
| Millwall | 46 | 18 | 13 | 15 | 62 | 62 | 67 |
| Plymouth Argyle | 46 | 18 | 11 | 17 | 64 | 56 | 65 |
| Chesterfield | 46 | 18 | 10 | 18 | 57 | 58 | 64 |
| Reading | 46 | 17 | 11 | 18 | 67 | 75 | 62 |
| Portsmouth | 46 | 14 | 19 | 13 | 56 | 51 | 61 |
| Preston North End | 46 | 16 | 13 | 17 | 50 | 56 | 61 |
| Bristol Rovers | 46 | 18 | 9 | 19 | 58 | 65 | 61 |
| Newport County | 46 | 14 | 16 | 16 | 54 | 54 | 58 |
| Huddersfield Town | 46 | 15 | 12 | 19 | 64 | 59 | 57 |
| Exeter City | 46 | 16 | 9 | 21 | 71 | 84 | 57 |
| Doncaster Rovers | 46 | 13 | 17 | 16 | 55 | 68 | 56 |
| Walsall | 46 | 13 | 14 | 19 | 51 | 55 | 53 |
| *Wimbledon* | *46* | *14* | *11* | *21* | *61* | *75* | *53* |
| *Swindon Town* | *46* | *13* | *13* | *20* | *55* | *71* | *52* |
| *Bristol City* | *46* | *11* | *13* | *22* | *40* | *65* | *46* |
| *Chester* | *46* | *7* | *11* | *28* | *36* | *78* | *32* |

Bristol Rovers had two points deducted

## DIVISION FOUR 1981-82

| | | | | | | | |
|---|---|---|---|---|---|---|---|
| **Sheffield United** | 46 | 27 | 15 | 4 | 94 | 41 | 96 |
| **Bradford City** | 46 | 26 | 13 | 7 | 88 | 45 | 91 |
| **Wigan Athletic** | 46 | 26 | 13 | 7 | 80 | 46 | 91 |
| **Bournemouth** | 46 | 23 | 19 | 4 | 62 | 30 | 88 |
| Peterborough United | 46 | 24 | 10 | 12 | 71 | 57 | 82 |
| Colchester United | 46 | 20 | 12 | 14 | 82 | 57 | 72 |
| Port Vale | 46 | 18 | 16 | 12 | 56 | 49 | 70 |
| Hull City | 46 | 19 | 12 | 15 | 70 | 61 | 69 |
| Bury | 46 | 17 | 17 | 12 | 80 | 59 | 68 |
| Hereford United | 46 | 16 | 19 | 11 | 64 | 58 | 67 |
| Tranmere Rovers | 46 | 14 | 18 | 14 | 51 | 56 | 60 |
| Blackpool | 46 | 15 | 13 | 18 | 66 | 60 | 58 |
| Darlington | 46 | 15 | 13 | 18 | 61 | 62 | 58 |
| Hartlepool United | 46 | 13 | 16 | 17 | 73 | 84 | 55 |
| Torquay United | 46 | 14 | 13 | 19 | 47 | 59 | 55 |
| Aldershot | 46 | 13 | 15 | 18 | 57 | 68 | 54 |
| York City | 46 | 14 | 8 | 24 | 69 | 91 | 50 |
| Stockport County | 46 | 12 | 13 | 21 | 48 | 67 | 49 |
| Halifax Town | 46 | 9 | 22 | 15 | 51 | 72 | 49 |
| Mansfield Town | 46 | 13 | 10 | 23 | 63 | 81 | 47 |
| Rochdale | 46 | 10 | 16 | 20 | 50 | 62 | 46 |
| Northampton Town | 46 | 11 | 9 | 26 | 57 | 84 | 42 |
| Scunthorpe United | 46 | 9 | 15 | 22 | 43 | 79 | 42 |
| Crewe Alexandra | 46 | 6 | 9 | 31 | 29 | 84 | 27 |

Mansfield Town had two points deducted

## 1982 F.A. Cup

### Semi-finals

| | |
|---|---|
| Tottenham Hotspur vs Leicester City | 2-0 |
| West Bromwich Albion vs Queen's Park Rangers | 0-1 |

### Final

Wembley, 22nd May 1982

**Tottenham Hotspur 1**   (Hoddle)

**Queen's Park Rangers 1 (aet.)**

*Attendance 100,000*

### Replay

Wembley, 27th May 1982

**Tottenham Hotspur 1**   (Hoddle (pen))

**Queen's Park Rangers 0**

*Attendance 90,000*

## 1982 Football League Cup

### Semi-finals

| | |
|---|---|
| Ipswich Town vs Liverpool (0-2, 2-2) | 2-4 |
| West Brom. Albion vs Tottenham Hotspur (0-0, 0-1) | 0-1 |

### Final

Wembley, 13th March 1982

**Liverpool 3**   (Whelan 2, Rush)

**Tottenham Hotspur 1 (aet.)**   (Archibald)

*Attendance 100,000*

## DIVISION ONE 1982-83

| | | | | | | | |
|---|---|---|---|---|---|---|---|
| LIVERPOOL | 42 | 24 | 10 | 8 | 87 | 37 | 82 |
| Watford | 42 | 22 | 5 | 15 | 74 | 57 | 71 |
| Manchester United | 42 | 19 | 13 | 10 | 56 | 38 | 70 |
| Tottenham Hotspur | 42 | 20 | 9 | 13 | 65 | 50 | 69 |
| Nottingham Forest | 42 | 20 | 9 | 13 | 62 | 50 | 69 |
| Aston Villa | 42 | 21 | 5 | 16 | 62 | 50 | 68 |
| Everton | 42 | 18 | 10 | 14 | 66 | 48 | 64 |
| West Ham United | 42 | 20 | 4 | 18 | 68 | 62 | 64 |
| Ipswich Town | 42 | 15 | 13 | 14 | 64 | 50 | 58 |
| Arsenal | 42 | 16 | 10 | 16 | 58 | 56 | 58 |
| West Bromwich Albion | 42 | 15 | 12 | 15 | 51 | 49 | 57 |
| Southampton | 42 | 15 | 12 | 15 | 54 | 58 | 57 |
| Stoke City | 42 | 16 | 9 | 17 | 53 | 64 | 57 |
| Norwich City | 42 | 14 | 12 | 16 | 52 | 58 | 54 |
| Notts County | 42 | 15 | 7 | 20 | 55 | 71 | 52 |
| Sunderland | 42 | 12 | 14 | 16 | 48 | 61 | 50 |
| Birmingham City | 42 | 12 | 14 | 16 | 40 | 55 | 50 |
| Luton Town | 42 | 12 | 13 | 17 | 65 | 84 | 49 |
| Coventry City | 42 | 13 | 9 | 20 | 48 | 59 | 48 |
| *Manchester City* | 42 | 13 | 8 | 21 | 47 | 70 | 47 |
| *Swansea City* | 42 | 10 | 11 | 21 | 51 | 69 | 41 |
| *Brighton & Hove Albion* | 42 | 9 | 13 | 20 | 38 | 68 | 40 |

## DIVISION THREE 1982-83

| | | | | | | | |
|---|---|---|---|---|---|---|---|
| Portsmouth | 46 | 27 | 10 | 9 | 74 | 41 | 91 |
| Cardiff City | 46 | 25 | 11 | 10 | 76 | 50 | 86 |
| Huddersfield Town | 46 | 23 | 13 | 10 | 84 | 49 | 82 |
| Newport County | 46 | 23 | 9 | 14 | 76 | 54 | 78 |
| Oxford United | 46 | 22 | 12 | 12 | 71 | 53 | 78 |
| Lincoln City | 46 | 23 | 7 | 16 | 77 | 51 | 76 |
| Bristol Rovers | 46 | 22 | 9 | 15 | 84 | 58 | 75 |
| Plymouth Argyle | 46 | 19 | 8 | 19 | 61 | 66 | 65 |
| Brentford | 46 | 18 | 10 | 18 | 88 | 77 | 64 |
| Walsall | 46 | 17 | 13 | 16 | 64 | 63 | 64 |
| Sheffield United | 46 | 19 | 7 | 20 | 62 | 64 | 64 |
| Bradford City | 46 | 16 | 13 | 17 | 68 | 69 | 61 |
| Gillingham | 46 | 16 | 13 | 17 | 58 | 59 | 61 |
| Bournemouth | 46 | 16 | 13 | 17 | 59 | 68 | 61 |
| Southend United | 46 | 15 | 14 | 17 | 66 | 65 | 59 |
| Preston North End | 46 | 15 | 13 | 18 | 60 | 69 | 58 |
| Millwall | 46 | 14 | 13 | 19 | 64 | 77 | 55 |
| Wigan Athletic | 46 | 15 | 9 | 22 | 60 | 72 | 54 |
| Exeter City | 46 | 14 | 12 | 20 | 81 | 104 | 54 |
| Orient | 46 | 15 | 9 | 22 | 64 | 88 | 54 |
| *Reading* | 46 | 12 | 17 | 17 | 64 | 79 | 53 |
| *Wrexham* | 46 | 12 | 15 | 19 | 56 | 76 | 51 |
| *Doncaster Rovers* | 46 | 9 | 11 | 26 | 57 | 97 | 38 |
| *Chesterfield* | 46 | 8 | 13 | 25 | 43 | 68 | 37 |

## DIVISION TWO 1982-83

| | | | | | | | |
|---|---|---|---|---|---|---|---|
| Queen's Park Rangers | 42 | 26 | 7 | 9 | 77 | 36 | 85 |
| Wolverhampton Wanderers | 42 | 20 | 15 | 7 | 68 | 44 | 75 |
| Leicester City | 42 | 20 | 10 | 12 | 72 | 44 | 70 |
| Fulham | 42 | 20 | 9 | 13 | 64 | 47 | 69 |
| Newcastle United | 42 | 18 | 13 | 11 | 75 | 53 | 67 |
| Sheffield Wednesday | 42 | 16 | 15 | 11 | 60 | 47 | 63 |
| Oldham Athletic | 42 | 14 | 19 | 9 | 64 | 47 | 61 |
| Leeds United | 42 | 13 | 21 | 8 | 51 | 46 | 60 |
| Shrewsbury Town | 42 | 15 | 14 | 13 | 48 | 48 | 59 |
| Barnsley | 42 | 14 | 15 | 13 | 57 | 55 | 57 |
| Blackburn Rovers | 42 | 15 | 12 | 15 | 58 | 58 | 57 |
| Cambridge United | 42 | 13 | 12 | 17 | 42 | 60 | 51 |
| Derby County | 42 | 10 | 19 | 13 | 49 | 58 | 49 |
| Carlisle United | 42 | 12 | 12 | 18 | 68 | 70 | 48 |
| Crystal Palace | 42 | 12 | 12 | 18 | 43 | 52 | 48 |
| Middlesbrough | 42 | 11 | 15 | 16 | 46 | 67 | 48 |
| Charlton Athletic | 42 | 13 | 9 | 20 | 63 | 86 | 48 |
| Chelsea | 42 | 11 | 14 | 17 | 51 | 61 | 47 |
| Grimsby Town | 42 | 12 | 11 | 19 | 45 | 70 | 47 |
| *Rotherham United* | 42 | 10 | 15 | 17 | 45 | 68 | 45 |
| *Burnley* | 42 | 12 | 8 | 22 | 56 | 66 | 44 |
| *Bolton Wanderers* | 42 | 11 | 11 | 20 | 42 | 61 | 44 |

## DIVISION FOUR 1982-83

| | | | | | | | |
|---|---|---|---|---|---|---|---|
| Wimbledon | 46 | 29 | 11 | 6 | 96 | 45 | 98 |
| Hull City | 46 | 25 | 15 | 6 | 75 | 34 | 90 |
| Port Vale | 46 | 26 | 10 | 10 | 67 | 34 | 88 |
| Scunthorpe United | 46 | 23 | 14 | 9 | 71 | 42 | 83 |
| Bury | 46 | 23 | 12 | 11 | 74 | 46 | 81 |
| Colchester United | 46 | 24 | 9 | 13 | 75 | 55 | 81 |
| York City | 46 | 22 | 13 | 11 | 88 | 58 | 79 |
| Swindon Town | 46 | 19 | 11 | 16 | 61 | 54 | 68 |
| Peterborough United | 46 | 17 | 13 | 16 | 58 | 52 | 64 |
| Mansfield Town | 46 | 16 | 13 | 17 | 61 | 70 | 61 |
| Halifax Town | 46 | 16 | 12 | 18 | 59 | 66 | 60 |
| Torquay United | 46 | 17 | 7 | 22 | 56 | 65 | 58 |
| Chester | 46 | 15 | 11 | 20 | 55 | 60 | 56 |
| Bristol City | 46 | 13 | 17 | 16 | 59 | 70 | 56 |
| Northampton Town | 46 | 14 | 12 | 20 | 65 | 75 | 54 |
| Stockport County | 46 | 14 | 12 | 20 | 60 | 79 | 54 |
| Darlington | 46 | 13 | 13 | 20 | 61 | 71 | 52 |
| Aldershot | 46 | 12 | 15 | 19 | 61 | 82 | 51 |
| Tranmere Rovers | 46 | 13 | 11 | 22 | 49 | 71 | 50 |
| Rochdale | 46 | 11 | 16 | 19 | 55 | 73 | 49 |
| Blackpool | 46 | 13 | 12 | 21 | 55 | 74 | 49 |
| Hartlepool United | 46 | 13 | 9 | 24 | 46 | 76 | 48 |
| Crewe Alexandra | 46 | 11 | 8 | 27 | 53 | 71 | 41 |
| Hereford United | 46 | 11 | 8 | 27 | 42 | 79 | 41 |

Blackpool had two points deducted

## 1983 F.A. Cup

**Semi-finals**

| | |
|---|---|
| Manchester United vs Arsenal | 2-1 |
| Brighton & Hove Albion vs Sheffield Wednesday | 2-1 |

**Final**

Wembley, 21st May 1983

**Manchester United 2**  (Stapleton, Wilkins)

**Brighton & Hove Albion 2**  (Smith, Stevens)

*Attendance 100,000*

**Replay**

Wembley, 26th May 1983

**Manchester United 4**  (Robson 2, Whiteside, Muhren (pen))

**Brighton & Hove Albion 0**

*Attendance 100,000*

## 1983 Football League Cup

**Semi-finals**

| | |
|---|---|
| Liverpool vs Burnley (3-0, 0-1) | 3-1 |
| Arsenal vs Manchester United (2-4, 1-2) | 3-6 |

**Final**

Wembley, 26th March 1983

**Liverpool 2**  (Kennedy, Whelan)

**Manchester United 1 (aet.)**  (Whiteside)

*Attendance 100,000*

## DIVISION ONE 1983-84

| | | | | | | | |
|---|---|---|---|---|---|---|---|
| LIVERPOOL | 42 | 22 | 14 | 6 | 73 | 32 | 80 |
| Southampton | 42 | 22 | 11 | 9 | 66 | 38 | 77 |
| Nottingham Forest | 42 | 22 | 8 | 12 | 76 | 45 | 74 |
| Manchester United | 42 | 20 | 14 | 8 | 71 | 41 | 74 |
| Queen's Park Rangers | 42 | 22 | 7 | 13 | 67 | 37 | 73 |
| Arsenal | 42 | 18 | 9 | 15 | 74 | 60 | 63 |
| Everton | 42 | 16 | 14 | 12 | 44 | 42 | 62 |
| Tottenham Hotspur | 42 | 17 | 10 | 15 | 64 | 65 | 61 |
| West Ham United | 42 | 17 | 9 | 16 | 60 | 55 | 60 |
| Aston Villa | 42 | 17 | 9 | 16 | 59 | 61 | 60 |
| Watford | 42 | 16 | 9 | 17 | 68 | 77 | 57 |
| Ipswich Town | 42 | 15 | 8 | 19 | 55 | 57 | 53 |
| Sunderland | 42 | 13 | 13 | 16 | 42 | 53 | 52 |
| Norwich City | 42 | 12 | 15 | 15 | 48 | 49 | 51 |
| Leicester City | 42 | 13 | 12 | 17 | 65 | 68 | 51 |
| Luton Town | 42 | 14 | 9 | 19 | 53 | 66 | 51 |
| West Bromwich Albion | 42 | 14 | 9 | 19 | 48 | 62 | 51 |
| Stoke City | 42 | 13 | 11 | 18 | 44 | 63 | 50 |
| Coventry City | 42 | 13 | 11 | 18 | 57 | 77 | 50 |
| *Birmingham City* | *42* | *12* | *12* | *18* | *39* | *50* | *48* |
| *Notts County* | *42* | *10* | *11* | *21* | *50* | *72* | *41* |
| *Wolverhampton Wanderers* | *42* | *6* | *11* | *25* | *27* | *80* | *29* |

## DIVISION THREE 1983-84

| | | | | | | | |
|---|---|---|---|---|---|---|---|
| Oxford United | 46 | 28 | 11 | 7 | 91 | 50 | 95 |
| Wimbledon | 46 | 26 | 9 | 11 | 97 | 76 | 87 |
| Sheffield United | 46 | 24 | 11 | 11 | 86 | 53 | 83 |
| Hull City | 46 | 23 | 14 | 9 | 71 | 38 | 83 |
| Bristol Rovers | 46 | 22 | 13 | 11 | 68 | 54 | 79 |
| Walsall | 46 | 22 | 9 | 15 | 68 | 61 | 75 |
| Bradford City | 46 | 20 | 11 | 15 | 73 | 65 | 71 |
| Gillingham | 46 | 20 | 10 | 16 | 74 | 69 | 70 |
| Millwall | 46 | 18 | 13 | 15 | 71 | 65 | 67 |
| Bolton Wanderers | 46 | 18 | 10 | 18 | 56 | 60 | 64 |
| Orient | 46 | 18 | 9 | 19 | 71 | 81 | 63 |
| Burnley | 46 | 16 | 14 | 16 | 76 | 61 | 62 |
| Newport County | 46 | 16 | 14 | 16 | 58 | 75 | 62 |
| Lincoln City | 46 | 17 | 10 | 19 | 59 | 62 | 61 |
| Wigan Athletic | 46 | 16 | 13 | 17 | 46 | 56 | 61 |
| Preston North End | 46 | 15 | 11 | 20 | 66 | 66 | 56 |
| Bournemouth | 46 | 16 | 7 | 23 | 63 | 73 | 55 |
| Rotherham United | 46 | 15 | 9 | 22 | 57 | 64 | 54 |
| Plymouth Argyle | 46 | 13 | 12 | 21 | 56 | 62 | 51 |
| Brentford | 46 | 11 | 16 | 19 | 69 | 79 | 49 |
| *Scunthorpe United* | *46* | *9* | *19* | *18* | *54* | *73* | *46* |
| *Southend United* | *46* | *10* | *14* | *22* | *55* | *76* | *44* |
| *Port Vale* | *46* | *11* | *10* | *25* | *51* | *83* | *43* |
| *Exeter City* | *46* | *6* | *15* | *25* | *50* | *84* | *33* |

## DIVISION TWO 1983-84

| | | | | | | | |
|---|---|---|---|---|---|---|---|
| Chelsea | 42 | 25 | 13 | 4 | 90 | 40 | 88 |
| Sheffield Wednesday | 42 | 26 | 10 | 6 | 72 | 34 | 88 |
| Newcastle United | 42 | 24 | 8 | 10 | 85 | 53 | 80 |
| Manchester City | 42 | 20 | 10 | 12 | 66 | 48 | 70 |
| Grimsby Town | 42 | 19 | 13 | 10 | 60 | 47 | 70 |
| Blackburn Rovers | 42 | 17 | 16 | 9 | 57 | 46 | 67 |
| Carlisle United | 42 | 16 | 16 | 10 | 48 | 41 | 64 |
| Shrewsbury Town | 42 | 17 | 10 | 15 | 49 | 53 | 61 |
| Brighton & Hove Albion | 42 | 17 | 9 | 16 | 69 | 60 | 60 |
| Leeds United | 42 | 16 | 12 | 14 | 55 | 56 | 60 |
| Fulham | 42 | 15 | 12 | 15 | 60 | 53 | 57 |
| Huddersfield Town | 42 | 14 | 15 | 13 | 56 | 49 | 57 |
| Charlton Athletic | 42 | 16 | 9 | 17 | 53 | 64 | 57 |
| Barnsley | 42 | 15 | 7 | 20 | 57 | 53 | 52 |
| Cardiff City | 42 | 15 | 6 | 21 | 53 | 66 | 51 |
| Portsmouth | 42 | 14 | 7 | 21 | 73 | 64 | 49 |
| Middlesbrough | 42 | 12 | 13 | 17 | 41 | 47 | 49 |
| Crystal Palace | 42 | 12 | 11 | 19 | 42 | 52 | 47 |
| Oldham Athletic | 42 | 13 | 8 | 21 | 47 | 73 | 47 |
| *Derby County* | *42* | *11* | *9* | *22* | *36* | *72* | *42* |
| *Swansea City* | *42* | *7* | *8* | *27* | *36* | *85* | *29* |
| *Cambridge United* | *42* | *4* | *12* | *26* | *28* | *77* | *24* |

## DIVISION FOUR 1983-84

| | | | | | | | |
|---|---|---|---|---|---|---|---|
| York City | 46 | 31 | 8 | 7 | 96 | 39 | 101 |
| Doncaster Rovers | 46 | 24 | 13 | 9 | 82 | 54 | 85 |
| Reading | 46 | 22 | 16 | 8 | 84 | 56 | 82 |
| Bristol City | 46 | 24 | 10 | 12 | 70 | 44 | 82 |
| Aldershot | 46 | 22 | 9 | 15 | 76 | 69 | 75 |
| Blackpool | 46 | 21 | 9 | 16 | 70 | 52 | 72 |
| Peterborough United | 46 | 18 | 14 | 14 | 72 | 48 | 68 |
| Colchester United | 46 | 17 | 16 | 13 | 69 | 53 | 67 |
| Torquay United | 46 | 18 | 13 | 15 | 59 | 64 | 67 |
| Tranmere Rovers | 46 | 17 | 15 | 14 | 53 | 53 | 66 |
| Hereford United | 46 | 16 | 15 | 15 | 54 | 53 | 63 |
| Stockport County | 46 | 17 | 11 | 18 | 60 | 64 | 62 |
| Chesterfield | 46 | 15 | 15 | 16 | 59 | 61 | 60 |
| Darlington | 46 | 17 | 8 | 21 | 49 | 50 | 59 |
| Bury | 46 | 15 | 14 | 17 | 61 | 64 | 59 |
| Crewe Alexandra | 46 | 16 | 11 | 19 | 56 | 67 | 59 |
| Swindon Town | 46 | 15 | 13 | 18 | 58 | 56 | 58 |
| Northampton Town | 46 | 13 | 14 | 19 | 53 | 78 | 53 |
| Mansfield Town | 46 | 13 | 13 | 20 | 66 | 70 | 52 |
| Wrexham | 46 | 11 | 15 | 20 | 59 | 74 | 48 |
| Halifax Town | 46 | 12 | 12 | 22 | 55 | 89 | 48 |
| Rochdale | 46 | 11 | 13 | 22 | 52 | 80 | 46 |
| Hartlepool United | 46 | 10 | 10 | 26 | 47 | 85 | 40 |
| Chester City | 46 | 7 | 13 | 26 | 45 | 82 | 34 |

## 1984 F.A. Cup

**Semi-finals**

| | |
|---|---|
| Everton vs Southampton | 1-0 |
| Watford vs Plymouth Argyle | 1-0 |

**Final**

Wembley, 19th May 1984

**Everton 2**   (Sharp, Gray)

**Watford 0**

*Attendance 100,000*

## 1984 Football League Cup

**Semi-finals**

| | |
|---|---|
| Liverpool vs Walsall (2-2, 2-0) | 4-2 |
| Everton vs Aston Villa (2-0, 0-1) | 2-1 |

**Final**

Wembley, 25th March 1984

**Liverpool 0**

**Everton 0 (aet.)**

*Attendance 100,000*

**Replay**

Maine Road, 28th March 1984

**Liverpool 1**   (Souness)

**Everton 0**

*Attendance 52,089*

## DIVISION ONE 1984-85

| | | | | | | | |
|---|---|---|---|---|---|---|---|
| EVERTON | 42 | 28 | 6 | 8 | 88 | 43 | 90 |
| Liverpool | 42 | 22 | 11 | 9 | 68 | 35 | 77 |
| Tottenham Hotspur | 42 | 23 | 8 | 11 | 78 | 51 | 77 |
| Manchester United | 42 | 22 | 10 | 10 | 77 | 47 | 76 |
| Southampton | 42 | 19 | 11 | 12 | 56 | 47 | 68 |
| Chelsea | 42 | 18 | 12 | 12 | 63 | 48 | 66 |
| Arsenal | 42 | 19 | 9 | 14 | 61 | 49 | 66 |
| Sheffield Wednesday | 42 | 17 | 14 | 11 | 58 | 45 | 65 |
| Nottingham Forest | 42 | 19 | 7 | 16 | 56 | 48 | 64 |
| Aston Villa | 42 | 15 | 11 | 16 | 60 | 60 | 56 |
| Watford | 42 | 14 | 13 | 15 | 81 | 71 | 55 |
| West Bromwich Albion | 42 | 16 | 7 | 19 | 58 | 62 | 55 |
| Luton Town | 42 | 15 | 9 | 18 | 57 | 61 | 54 |
| Newcastle United | 42 | 13 | 13 | 16 | 55 | 70 | 52 |
| Leicester City | 42 | 15 | 6 | 21 | 65 | 73 | 51 |
| West Ham United | 42 | 13 | 12 | 17 | 51 | 68 | 51 |
| Ipswich Town | 42 | 13 | 11 | 18 | 46 | 57 | 50 |
| Coventry City | 42 | 15 | 5 | 22 | 47 | 64 | 50 |
| Queen's Park Rangers | 42 | 13 | 11 | 18 | 53 | 72 | 50 |
| *Norwich City* | *42* | *13* | *10* | *19* | *46* | *64* | *49* |
| *Sunderland* | *42* | *10* | *10* | *22* | *40* | *62* | *40* |
| *Stoke City* | *42* | *3* | *8* | *31* | *24* | *91* | *17* |

## DIVISION THREE 1984-85

| | | | | | | | |
|---|---|---|---|---|---|---|---|
| Bradford City | 46 | 28 | 10 | 8 | 77 | 45 | 94 |
| Millwall | 46 | 26 | 12 | 8 | 73 | 42 | 90 |
| Hull City | 46 | 25 | 12 | 9 | 78 | 49 | 87 |
| Gillingham | 46 | 25 | 8 | 13 | 80 | 62 | 83 |
| Bristol City | 46 | 24 | 9 | 13 | 74 | 47 | 81 |
| Bristol Rovers | 46 | 21 | 12 | 13 | 66 | 48 | 75 |
| Derby County | 46 | 19 | 13 | 14 | 65 | 54 | 70 |
| York City | 46 | 20 | 9 | 17 | 70 | 57 | 69 |
| Reading | 46 | 19 | 12 | 15 | 68 | 62 | 69 |
| Bournemouth | 46 | 19 | 11 | 16 | 57 | 46 | 68 |
| Walsall | 46 | 18 | 13 | 15 | 58 | 52 | 67 |
| Rotherham United | 46 | 18 | 11 | 17 | 55 | 55 | 65 |
| Brentford | 46 | 16 | 14 | 16 | 62 | 64 | 62 |
| Doncaster Rovers | 46 | 17 | 8 | 21 | 72 | 74 | 59 |
| Plymouth Argyle | 46 | 15 | 14 | 17 | 62 | 65 | 59 |
| Wigan Athletic | 46 | 15 | 14 | 17 | 60 | 64 | 59 |
| Bolton Wanderers | 46 | 16 | 6 | 24 | 69 | 75 | 54 |
| Newport County | 46 | 13 | 13 | 20 | 55 | 69 | 52 |
| Lincoln City | 46 | 11 | 18 | 17 | 50 | 51 | 51 |
| Swansea City | 46 | 12 | 11 | 23 | 53 | 80 | 47 |
| *Burnley* | *46* | *11* | *13* | *22* | *60* | *73* | *46* |
| *Orient* | *46* | *11* | *13* | *22* | *51* | *76* | *46* |
| *Preston North End* | *46* | *13* | *7* | *26* | *51* | *100* | *46* |
| *Cambridge United* | *46* | *4* | *9* | *33* | *37* | *95* | *21* |

## DIVISION TWO 1984-85

| | | | | | | | |
|---|---|---|---|---|---|---|---|
| Oxford United | 42 | 25 | 9 | 8 | 84 | 36 | 84 |
| Birmingham City | 42 | 25 | 7 | 10 | 59 | 33 | 82 |
| Manchester City | 42 | 21 | 11 | 10 | 66 | 40 | 74 |
| Portsmouth | 42 | 20 | 14 | 8 | 69 | 50 | 74 |
| Blackburn Rovers | 42 | 21 | 10 | 11 | 66 | 41 | 73 |
| Brighton & Hove Albion | 42 | 20 | 12 | 10 | 54 | 34 | 72 |
| Leeds United | 42 | 19 | 12 | 11 | 66 | 43 | 69 |
| Shrewsbury Town | 42 | 18 | 11 | 13 | 66 | 53 | 65 |
| Fulham | 42 | 19 | 8 | 15 | 68 | 64 | 65 |
| Grimsby Town | 42 | 18 | 8 | 16 | 72 | 64 | 62 |
| Barnsley | 42 | 14 | 16 | 12 | 42 | 42 | 58 |
| Wimbledon | 42 | 16 | 10 | 16 | 71 | 75 | 58 |
| Huddersfield Town | 42 | 15 | 10 | 17 | 52 | 64 | 55 |
| Oldham Athletic | 42 | 15 | 8 | 19 | 49 | 67 | 53 |
| Crystal Palace | 42 | 12 | 12 | 18 | 46 | 65 | 48 |
| Carlisle United | 42 | 13 | 8 | 21 | 50 | 67 | 47 |
| Charlton Athletic | 42 | 11 | 12 | 19 | 51 | 63 | 45 |
| Sheffield United | 42 | 10 | 14 | 18 | 54 | 66 | 44 |
| Middlesbrough | 42 | 10 | 10 | 22 | 41 | 57 | 40 |
| *Notts County* | *42* | *10* | *7* | *25* | *45* | *73* | *37* |
| *Cardiff City* | *42* | *9* | *8* | *25* | *47* | *79* | *35* |
| *Wolverhampton Wanderers* | *42* | *8* | *9* | *25* | *37* | *79* | *33* |

## DIVISION FOUR 1984-85

| | | | | | | | |
|---|---|---|---|---|---|---|---|
| Chesterfield | 46 | 26 | 13 | 7 | 64 | 35 | 91 |
| Blackpool | 46 | 24 | 14 | 8 | 73 | 39 | 86 |
| Darlington | 46 | 24 | 13 | 9 | 66 | 49 | 85 |
| Bury | 46 | 24 | 12 | 10 | 76 | 50 | 84 |
| Hereford United | 46 | 22 | 11 | 13 | 65 | 47 | 77 |
| Tranmere Rovers | 46 | 24 | 3 | 19 | 83 | 66 | 75 |
| Colchester United | 46 | 20 | 14 | 12 | 87 | 65 | 74 |
| Swindon Town | 46 | 21 | 9 | 16 | 62 | 58 | 72 |
| Scunthorpe United | 46 | 19 | 14 | 13 | 83 | 62 | 71 |
| Crewe Alexandra | 46 | 18 | 12 | 16 | 65 | 69 | 66 |
| Peterborough United | 46 | 16 | 14 | 16 | 54 | 53 | 62 |
| Port Vale | 46 | 14 | 18 | 14 | 61 | 59 | 60 |
| Aldershot | 46 | 17 | 8 | 21 | 56 | 63 | 59 |
| Mansfield Town | 46 | 13 | 18 | 15 | 41 | 38 | 57 |
| Wrexham | 46 | 15 | 9 | 22 | 67 | 70 | 54 |
| Chester City | 46 | 15 | 9 | 22 | 60 | 72 | 54 |
| Rochdale | 46 | 13 | 14 | 19 | 55 | 69 | 53 |
| Exeter City | 46 | 13 | 14 | 19 | 57 | 79 | 53 |
| Hartlepool United | 46 | 14 | 10 | 22 | 54 | 67 | 52 |
| Southend United | 46 | 13 | 11 | 22 | 58 | 83 | 50 |
| Halifax Town | 46 | 15 | 5 | 26 | 42 | 69 | 50 |
| Stockport County | 46 | 13 | 8 | 25 | 58 | 79 | 47 |
| Northampton Town | 46 | 14 | 5 | 27 | 53 | 74 | 47 |
| Torquay United | 46 | 9 | 14 | 23 | 38 | 63 | 41 |

## 1985 F.A.Cup

**Semi-finals**

| | |
|---|---|
| Luton Town vs Everton | 1-2 |
| Manchester United vs Liverpool | 2-2, 2-1 |

**Final**

Wembley, 18 May 1985

**Everton 0**

**Manchester United 1**   (Whiteside)

*Attendance 100,000*

## 1985 Football League Cup

**Semi-finals**

| | |
|---|---|
| Sunderland vs Chelsea (1-0, 3-2) | 4-2 |
| Ipswich Town vs Norwich City (1-0, 0-2) | 1-2 |

**Final**

Wembley, 24th March 1985

**Norwich City 1**   (Chisholm (og))

**Sunderland 0**

*Attendance 100,000*

## DIVISION ONE 1985-86

| | | | | | | | |
|---|---|---|---|---|---|---|---|
| **LIVERPOOL** | 42 | 26 | 10 | 6 | 89 | 37 | 88 |
| Everton | 42 | 26 | 8 | 8 | 87 | 41 | 86 |
| West Ham United | 42 | 26 | 6 | 10 | 74 | 40 | 84 |
| Manchester United | 42 | 22 | 10 | 10 | 70 | 36 | 76 |
| Sheffield Wednesday | 42 | 21 | 10 | 11 | 63 | 54 | 73 |
| Chelsea | 42 | 20 | 11 | 11 | 57 | 56 | 71 |
| Arsenal | 42 | 20 | 9 | 13 | 49 | 47 | 69 |
| Nottingham Forest | 42 | 19 | 11 | 12 | 69 | 53 | 68 |
| Luton Town | 42 | 18 | 12 | 12 | 61 | 44 | 66 |
| Tottenham Hotspur | 42 | 19 | 8 | 15 | 74 | 52 | 65 |
| Newcastle United | 42 | 17 | 12 | 13 | 67 | 72 | 63 |
| Watford | 42 | 16 | 11 | 15 | 69 | 62 | 59 |
| Queen's Park Rangers | 42 | 15 | 7 | 20 | 53 | 64 | 52 |
| Southampton | 42 | 12 | 10 | 20 | 51 | 62 | 46 |
| Manchester City | 42 | 11 | 12 | 19 | 43 | 57 | 45 |
| Aston Villa | 42 | 10 | 14 | 18 | 51 | 67 | 44 |
| Coventry City | 42 | 11 | 10 | 21 | 48 | 71 | 43 |
| Oxford United | 42 | 10 | 12 | 20 | 62 | 80 | 42 |
| Leicester City | 42 | 10 | 12 | 20 | 54 | 76 | 42 |
| *Ipswich Town* | *42* | *11* | *8* | *23* | *32* | *55* | *41* |
| *Birmingham City* | *42* | *8* | *5* | *29* | *30* | *73* | *29* |
| *West Bromwich Albion* | *42* | *4* | *12* | *26* | *35* | *89* | *24* |

## DIVISION THREE 1985-86

| | | | | | | | |
|---|---|---|---|---|---|---|---|
| **Reading** | 46 | 29 | 7 | 10 | 67 | 51 | 94 |
| **Plymouth Argyle** | 46 | 26 | 9 | 11 | 88 | 53 | 87 |
| **Derby County** | 46 | 23 | 15 | 8 | 80 | 41 | 84 |
| Wigan Athletic | 46 | 23 | 14 | 9 | 82 | 48 | 83 |
| Gillingham | 46 | 22 | 13 | 11 | 81 | 54 | 79 |
| Walsall | 46 | 22 | 9 | 15 | 90 | 64 | 75 |
| York City | 46 | 20 | 11 | 15 | 77 | 58 | 71 |
| Notts County | 46 | 19 | 14 | 13 | 71 | 60 | 71 |
| Bristol City | 46 | 18 | 14 | 14 | 69 | 60 | 68 |
| Brentford | 46 | 18 | 12 | 16 | 58 | 61 | 66 |
| Doncaster Rovers | 46 | 16 | 16 | 14 | 45 | 52 | 64 |
| Blackpool | 46 | 17 | 12 | 17 | 66 | 55 | 63 |
| Darlington | 46 | 15 | 13 | 18 | 61 | 78 | 58 |
| Rotherham United | 46 | 15 | 12 | 19 | 61 | 59 | 57 |
| Bournemouth | 46 | 15 | 9 | 22 | 65 | 72 | 54 |
| Bristol Rovers | 46 | 14 | 12 | 20 | 51 | 75 | 54 |
| Chesterfield | 46 | 13 | 14 | 19 | 61 | 64 | 53 |
| Bolton Wanderers | 46 | 15 | 8 | 23 | 54 | 68 | 53 |
| Newport County | 46 | 11 | 18 | 17 | 52 | 65 | 51 |
| Bury | 46 | 12 | 13 | 21 | 63 | 67 | 49 |
| *Lincoln City* | *46* | *10* | *16* | *20* | *55* | *77* | *46* |
| *Cardiff City* | *46* | *12* | *9* | *25* | *53* | *83* | *45* |
| *Wolverhampton Wanderers* | *46* | *11* | *10* | *25* | *57* | *98* | *43* |
| *Swansea City* | *46* | *11* | *10* | *25* | *43* | *87* | *43* |

## DIVISION TWO 1985-86

| | | | | | | | |
|---|---|---|---|---|---|---|---|
| **Norwich City** | 42 | 25 | 9 | 8 | 84 | 37 | 84 |
| **Charlton Athletic** | 42 | 22 | 11 | 9 | 78 | 45 | 77 |
| **Wimbledon** | 42 | 21 | 13 | 8 | 58 | 37 | 76 |
| Portsmouth | 42 | 22 | 7 | 13 | 69 | 41 | 73 |
| Crystal Palace | 42 | 19 | 9 | 14 | 57 | 52 | 66 |
| Hull City | 42 | 17 | 13 | 12 | 65 | 55 | 64 |
| Sheffield United | 42 | 17 | 11 | 14 | 64 | 63 | 62 |
| Oldham Athletic | 42 | 17 | 9 | 16 | 62 | 61 | 60 |
| Millwall | 42 | 17 | 8 | 17 | 64 | 65 | 59 |
| Stoke City | 42 | 14 | 15 | 13 | 48 | 50 | 57 |
| Brighton & Hove Albion | 42 | 16 | 8 | 18 | 64 | 64 | 56 |
| Barnsley | 42 | 14 | 14 | 14 | 47 | 50 | 56 |
| Bradford City | 42 | 16 | 6 | 20 | 51 | 63 | 54 |
| Leeds United | 42 | 15 | 8 | 19 | 56 | 72 | 53 |
| Grimsby Town | 42 | 14 | 10 | 18 | 58 | 62 | 52 |
| Huddersfield Town | 42 | 14 | 10 | 18 | 51 | 67 | 52 |
| Shrewsbury Town | 42 | 14 | 9 | 19 | 52 | 64 | 51 |
| Sunderland | 42 | 13 | 11 | 18 | 47 | 61 | 50 |
| Blackburn Rovers | 42 | 12 | 13 | 17 | 53 | 62 | 49 |
| *Carlisle United* | *42* | *13* | *7* | *22* | *47* | *71* | *46* |
| *Middlesbrough* | *42* | *12* | *9* | *21* | *44* | *53* | *45* |
| *Fulham* | *42* | *10* | *6* | *26* | *45* | *69* | *36* |

## DIVISION FOUR 1985-86

| | | | | | | | |
|---|---|---|---|---|---|---|---|
| **Swindon Town** | 46 | 32 | 6 | 8 | 82 | 43 | 102 |
| **Chester City** | 46 | 23 | 15 | 8 | 83 | 50 | 84 |
| **Mansfield Town** | 46 | 23 | 12 | 11 | 74 | 47 | 81 |
| **Port Vale** | 46 | 21 | 16 | 9 | 67 | 37 | 79 |
| Orient | 46 | 20 | 12 | 14 | 79 | 64 | 72 |
| Colchester United | 46 | 19 | 13 | 14 | 88 | 63 | 70 |
| Hartlepool United | 46 | 20 | 10 | 16 | 68 | 67 | 70 |
| Northampton Town | 46 | 18 | 10 | 18 | 79 | 58 | 64 |
| Southend United | 46 | 18 | 10 | 18 | 69 | 67 | 64 |
| Hereford United | 46 | 18 | 10 | 18 | 74 | 73 | 64 |
| Stockport County | 46 | 17 | 13 | 16 | 63 | 71 | 64 |
| Crewe Alexandra | 46 | 18 | 9 | 19 | 54 | 61 | 63 |
| Wrexham | 46 | 17 | 9 | 20 | 68 | 80 | 60 |
| Burnley | 46 | 16 | 11 | 19 | 60 | 65 | 59 |
| Scunthorpe United | 46 | 15 | 14 | 17 | 50 | 55 | 59 |
| Aldershot | 46 | 17 | 7 | 22 | 66 | 74 | 58 |
| Peterborough United | 46 | 13 | 17 | 16 | 52 | 64 | 56 |
| Rochdale | 46 | 14 | 13 | 19 | 57 | 77 | 55 |
| Tranmere Rovers | 46 | 15 | 9 | 22 | 74 | 73 | 54 |
| Halifax Town | 46 | 14 | 12 | 20 | 60 | 71 | 54 |
| Exeter City | 46 | 13 | 15 | 18 | 47 | 59 | 54 |
| Cambridge United | 46 | 15 | 9 | 22 | 65 | 80 | 54 |
| Preston North End | 46 | 11 | 10 | 25 | 54 | 89 | 43 |
| Torquay United | 46 | 9 | 10 | 27 | 43 | 88 | 37 |

## 1986 F.A. Cup

**Semi-finals**

| | |
|---|---|
| Everton vs Sheffield Wednesday | 2-1 |
| Liverpool vs Southampton | 2-0 |

**Final**

Wembley, 10th May 1986

**Everton 1**   (Lineker)

**Liverpool 3**   (Rush 2, Johnston)

*Attendance 98,000*

## 1986 Football League Cup

**Semi-finals**

| | |
|---|---|
| Queen's Park Rangers vs Liverpool (1-0, 2-2) | 3-2 |
| Aston Villa vs Oxford United (2-2, 1-2) | 3-4 |

**Final**

Wembley, 20 April 1985

**Oxford United 3**   ( Hebberd, Houghton, Charles)

**Queen's Park Rangers 0**

*Attendance 90,396*

## DIVISION ONE 1986-87

| | | | | | | | |
|---|---|---|---|---|---|---|---|
| **EVERTON** | 42 | 26 | 8 | 8 | 76 | 31 | 86 |
| Liverpool | 42 | 23 | 8 | 11 | 72 | 42 | 77 |
| Tottenham Hotspur | 42 | 21 | 8 | 13 | 68 | 43 | 71 |
| Arsenal | 42 | 20 | 10 | 12 | 58 | 35 | 70 |
| Norwich City | 42 | 17 | 17 | 8 | 53 | 51 | 68 |
| Wimbledon | 42 | 19 | 9 | 14 | 57 | 50 | 66 |
| Luton Town | 42 | 18 | 12 | 12 | 47 | 45 | 66 |
| Nottingham Forest | 42 | 18 | 11 | 13 | 64 | 51 | 65 |
| Watford | 42 | 18 | 9 | 15 | 67 | 54 | 63 |
| Coventry City | 42 | 17 | 12 | 13 | 50 | 45 | 63 |
| Manchester United | 42 | 14 | 14 | 14 | 52 | 45 | 56 |
| Southampton | 42 | 14 | 10 | 18 | 69 | 68 | 52 |
| Sheffield Wednesday | 42 | 13 | 13 | 16 | 58 | 59 | 52 |
| Chelsea | 42 | 13 | 13 | 16 | 53 | 64 | 52 |
| West Ham United | 42 | 14 | 10 | 18 | 52 | 67 | 52 |
| Queen's Park Rangers | 42 | 13 | 11 | 18 | 48 | 64 | 50 |
| Newcastle United | 42 | 12 | 11 | 19 | 47 | 65 | 47 |
| Oxford United | 42 | 11 | 13 | 18 | 44 | 69 | 46 |
| Charlton Athletic | 42 | 11 | 11 | 20 | 45 | 55 | 44 |
| *Leicester City* | *42* | *11* | *9* | *22* | *54* | *76* | *42* |
| *Manchester City* | *42* | *8* | *15* | *19* | *36* | *57* | *39* |
| *Aston Villa* | *42* | *8* | *12* | *22* | *45* | *79* | *36* |

### Division One/Division Two Play-offs

| | |
|---|---|
| Ipswich Town vs Charlton Athletic | 0-0, 1-2 |
| Leeds United vs Oldham Athletic | 1-0, 1-2 |
| *(Leeds United won on away goals)* | |
| Charlton Athletic vs Leeds United | 1-0, 0-1, 2-1 |
| *(Third game was played at Leeds)* | |

## DIVISION TWO 1986-87

| | | | | | | | |
|---|---|---|---|---|---|---|---|
| **Derby County** | 42 | 25 | 9 | 8 | 64 | 38 | 84 |
| **Portsmouth** | 42 | 23 | 9 | 10 | 53 | 28 | 78 |
| Oldham Athletic | 42 | 22 | 9 | 11 | 65 | 44 | 75 |
| Leeds United | 42 | 19 | 11 | 12 | 58 | 44 | 68 |
| Ipswich Town | 42 | 17 | 13 | 12 | 59 | 43 | 64 |
| Crystal Palace | 42 | 19 | 5 | 18 | 51 | 53 | 62 |
| Plymouth Argyle | 42 | 16 | 13 | 13 | 62 | 57 | 61 |
| Stoke City | 42 | 16 | 10 | 16 | 63 | 53 | 58 |
| Sheffield United | 42 | 15 | 13 | 14 | 50 | 49 | 58 |
| Bradford City | 42 | 15 | 10 | 17 | 62 | 62 | 55 |
| Barnsley | 42 | 14 | 13 | 15 | 49 | 52 | 55 |
| Blackburn Rovers | 42 | 15 | 10 | 17 | 45 | 55 | 55 |
| Reading | 42 | 14 | 11 | 17 | 52 | 59 | 53 |
| Hull City | 42 | 13 | 14 | 15 | 41 | 55 | 53 |
| West Bromwich Albion | 42 | 13 | 12 | 17 | 51 | 49 | 51 |
| Millwall | 42 | 14 | 9 | 19 | 39 | 45 | 51 |
| Huddersfield Town | 42 | 13 | 12 | 17 | 54 | 61 | 51 |
| Shrewsbury Town | 42 | 15 | 6 | 21 | 41 | 53 | 51 |
| Birmingham City | 42 | 11 | 17 | 14 | 47 | 59 | 50 |
| *Sunderland* | *42* | *12* | *12* | *18* | *49* | *59* | *48* |
| *Grimsby Town* | *42* | *10* | *14* | *18* | *39* | *59* | *44* |
| *Brighton & Hove Albion* | *42* | *9* | *12* | *21* | *37* | *54* | *39* |

### Division Two/Division Three Play-offs

| | |
|---|---|
| Gillingham vs Sunderland | 3-2, 3-4 |
| *(Gillingham won on away goals)* | |
| Wigan Athletic vs Swindon Town | 2-3, 0-0 |
| Gillingham vs Swindon Town | 1-0, 1-2, 0-2 |
| *(Third game was played at Swindon)* | |

## DIVISION THREE 1986-87

| | | | | | | | |
|---|---|---|---|---|---|---|---|
| **Bournemouth** | 46 | 29 | 10 | 7 | 76 | 40 | 97 |
| **Middlesbrough** | 46 | 28 | 10 | 8 | 67 | 30 | 94 |
| **Swindon Town** | 46 | 25 | 12 | 9 | 77 | 47 | 87 |
| Wigan Athletic | 46 | 25 | 10 | 11 | 83 | 60 | 85 |
| Gillingham | 46 | 23 | 9 | 14 | 65 | 48 | 78 |
| Bristol City | 46 | 21 | 14 | 11 | 63 | 36 | 77 |
| Notts County | 46 | 21 | 13 | 12 | 77 | 56 | 76 |
| Walsall | 46 | 22 | 9 | 15 | 80 | 67 | 75 |
| Blackpool | 46 | 16 | 16 | 14 | 74 | 59 | 64 |
| Mansfield Town | 46 | 15 | 16 | 15 | 52 | 55 | 61 |
| Brentford | 46 | 15 | 15 | 16 | 64 | 66 | 60 |
| Port Vale | 46 | 15 | 12 | 19 | 76 | 70 | 57 |
| Doncaster Rovers | 46 | 14 | 15 | 17 | 56 | 62 | 57 |
| Rotherham United | 46 | 15 | 12 | 19 | 48 | 57 | 57 |
| Chester City | 46 | 13 | 17 | 16 | 61 | 59 | 56 |
| Bury | 46 | 14 | 13 | 19 | 54 | 60 | 55 |
| Chesterfield | 46 | 13 | 15 | 18 | 56 | 69 | 54 |
| Fulham | 46 | 12 | 17 | 17 | 59 | 77 | 53 |
| Bristol Rovers | 46 | 13 | 12 | 21 | 49 | 75 | 51 |
| York City | 46 | 12 | 13 | 21 | 55 | 79 | 49 |
| *Bolton Wanderers* | *46* | *10* | *15* | *21* | *46* | *58* | *45* |
| *Carlisle United* | *46* | *10* | *8* | *28* | *39* | *78* | *38* |
| *Darlington* | *46* | *7* | *16* | *23* | *45* | *77* | *37* |
| *Newport County* | *46* | *8* | *13* | *25* | *49* | *86* | *37* |

### Division Three/Division Four Play-offs

| | |
|---|---|
| Aldershot vs Bolton Wanderers | 1-0, 2-2 |
| Colchester United vs Wolverhampton Wanderers | 0-2, 0-0 |
| Aldershot vs Wolverhampton Wanderers | 2-0, 1-0 |

## DIVISION FOUR 1986-87

| | | | | | | | |
|---|---|---|---|---|---|---|---|
| **Northampton Town** | 46 | 30 | 9 | 7 | 103 | 53 | 99 |
| **Preston North End** | 46 | 26 | 12 | 8 | 72 | 47 | 90 |
| **Southend United** | 46 | 25 | 5 | 16 | 68 | 55 | 80 |
| Wolverhampton Wanderers | 46 | 24 | 7 | 15 | 69 | 50 | 79 |
| Colchester United | 46 | 21 | 7 | 18 | 64 | 56 | 70 |
| **Aldershot** | 46 | 20 | 10 | 16 | 64 | 57 | 70 |
| Orient | 46 | 20 | 9 | 17 | 64 | 61 | 69 |
| Scunthorpe United | 46 | 18 | 12 | 16 | 73 | 57 | 66 |
| Wrexham | 46 | 15 | 20 | 11 | 70 | 51 | 65 |
| Peterborough United | 46 | 17 | 14 | 15 | 57 | 50 | 65 |
| Cambridge United | 46 | 17 | 11 | 18 | 60 | 62 | 62 |
| Swansea City | 46 | 17 | 11 | 18 | 56 | 61 | 62 |
| Cardiff City | 46 | 15 | 16 | 15 | 48 | 50 | 61 |
| Exeter City | 46 | 11 | 23 | 12 | 53 | 49 | 56 |
| Halifax Town | 46 | 15 | 10 | 21 | 59 | 74 | 55 |
| Hereford United | 46 | 14 | 11 | 21 | 60 | 61 | 53 |
| Crewe Alexandra | 46 | 13 | 14 | 19 | 70 | 72 | 53 |
| Hartlepool United | 46 | 11 | 18 | 17 | 44 | 65 | 51 |
| Stockport County | 46 | 13 | 12 | 21 | 40 | 69 | 51 |
| Tranmere Rovers | 46 | 11 | 17 | 18 | 54 | 72 | 50 |
| Rochdale | 46 | 11 | 17 | 18 | 54 | 73 | 50 |
| Burnley | 46 | 12 | 13 | 21 | 53 | 74 | 49 |
| Torquay United | 46 | 10 | 18 | 18 | 56 | 72 | 48 |
| *Lincoln City* | *46* | *12* | *12* | *22* | *45* | *65* | *48* |

## 1987 F.A. Cup

### Semi-finals

| | |
|---|---|
| Tottenham Hotspur vs Watford | 4-1 |
| Coventry City vs Leeds United | 3-2 |

### Final

Wembley, 16th May 1987

**Coventry City 3**   (Bennett, Houchen, Mabbutt (og))
**Tottenham Hotspur 2**   (C. Allen, Mabbutt)

*Attendance 98,000*

## 1987 Football League Cup

### Semi-finals

| | | |
|---|---|---|
| Arsenal vs Tottenham Hotspur | (0-1, 2-1, 2-1*) | 4-3 |
| Southampton vs Liverpool | (0-0, 0-3) | 0-3 |
| * Play-off | | |

### Final

Wembley, 5th April 1987

**Arsenal 2**   (Nicholas 2)
**Liverpool 1**   (Rush)

*Attendance 96,000*

## DIVISION ONE 1987-88

| | | | | | | | |
|---|---|---|---|---|---|---|---|
| **LIVERPOOL** | 40 | 26 | 12 | 2 | 87 | 24 | 90 |
| Manchester United | 40 | 23 | 12 | 5 | 71 | 38 | 81 |
| Nottingham Forest | 40 | 20 | 13 | 7 | 67 | 39 | 73 |
| Everton | 40 | 19 | 13 | 8 | 53 | 27 | 70 |
| Queen's Park Rangers | 40 | 19 | 10 | 11 | 48 | 38 | 67 |
| Arsenal | 40 | 18 | 12 | 10 | 58 | 39 | 66 |
| Wimbledon | 40 | 14 | 15 | 11 | 58 | 47 | 57 |
| Newcastle United | 40 | 14 | 14 | 12 | 55 | 53 | 56 |
| Luton Town | 40 | 14 | 11 | 15 | 57 | 58 | 53 |
| Coventry City | 40 | 13 | 14 | 13 | 46 | 53 | 53 |
| Sheffield Wednesday | 40 | 15 | 8 | 17 | 52 | 66 | 53 |
| Southampton | 40 | 12 | 14 | 14 | 49 | 53 | 50 |
| Tottenham Hotspur | 40 | 12 | 11 | 17 | 38 | 48 | 47 |
| Norwich City | 40 | 12 | 9 | 19 | 40 | 52 | 45 |
| Derby County | 40 | 10 | 13 | 17 | 35 | 45 | 43 |
| West Ham United | 40 | 9 | 15 | 16 | 40 | 52 | 42 |
| Charlton Athletic | 40 | 9 | 15 | 16 | 38 | 52 | 42 |
| *Chelsea* | *40* | *9* | *15* | *16* | *50* | *68* | *42* |
| *Portsmouth* | *40* | *7* | *14* | *19* | *36* | *66* | *35* |
| *Watford* | *40* | *7* | *11* | *22* | *27* | *51* | *32* |
| *Oxford United* | *40* | *6* | *13* | *21* | *44* | *80* | *31* |

### Division One/Division Two Play-offs

| | |
|---|---|
| Blackburn Rovers vs Chelsea | 0-2, 1-4 |
| Bradford City vs Middlesbrough | 2-1, 0-2 |
| Middlesbrough vs Chelsea | 2-0, 0-1 |

## DIVISION TWO 1987-88

| | | | | | | | |
|---|---|---|---|---|---|---|---|
| **Millwall** | 44 | 25 | 7 | 12 | 72 | 52 | 82 |
| **Aston Villa** | 44 | 22 | 12 | 10 | 68 | 41 | 78 |
| **Middlesbrough** | 44 | 22 | 12 | 10 | 63 | 36 | 78 |
| Bradford City | 44 | 22 | 11 | 11 | 74 | 54 | 77 |
| Blackburn Rovers | 44 | 21 | 14 | 9 | 68 | 52 | 77 |
| Crystal Palace | 44 | 22 | 9 | 13 | 86 | 59 | 75 |
| Leeds United | 44 | 19 | 12 | 13 | 61 | 51 | 69 |
| Ipswich Town | 44 | 19 | 9 | 16 | 61 | 52 | 66 |
| Manchester City | 44 | 19 | 8 | 17 | 80 | 60 | 65 |
| Oldham Athletic | 44 | 18 | 11 | 15 | 72 | 64 | 65 |
| Stoke City | 44 | 17 | 11 | 16 | 50 | 57 | 62 |
| Swindon Town | 44 | 16 | 11 | 17 | 73 | 60 | 59 |
| Leicester City | 44 | 16 | 11 | 17 | 62 | 61 | 59 |
| Barnsley | 44 | 15 | 12 | 17 | 61 | 62 | 57 |
| Hull City | 44 | 14 | 15 | 15 | 54 | 60 | 57 |
| Plymouth Argyle | 44 | 16 | 8 | 20 | 65 | 67 | 56 |
| Bournemouth | 44 | 13 | 10 | 21 | 56 | 68 | 49 |
| Shrewsbury Town | 44 | 11 | 16 | 17 | 42 | 54 | 49 |
| Birmingham City | 44 | 11 | 15 | 18 | 41 | 66 | 48 |
| West Bromwich Albion | 44 | 12 | 11 | 21 | 50 | 69 | 47 |
| *Sheffield United* | *44* | *13* | *7* | *24* | *45* | *74* | *46* |
| *Reading* | *44* | *10* | *12* | *22* | *44* | *70* | *42* |
| *Huddersfield Town* | *44* | *6* | *10* | *28* | *41* | *100* | *28* |

### Division Two/Division Three Play-offs

| | |
|---|---|
| Bristol City vs Sheffield United | 1-0, 1-1 |
| Notts County vs Walsall | 1-3, 1-1 |
| Bristol City vs Walsall | 1-3, 2-0, 0-4 |
| *(Third game played at Walsall)* | |

## 1988 F.A. Cup

**Semi-finals**

| | |
|---|---|
| Liverpool vs Nottingham Forest | 2-1 |
| Luton Town vs Wimbledon | 1-2 |

**Final**

Wembley, 14th May 1988

**Wimbledon 1**  (Sanchez)

**Liverpool 0**

*Attendance 98,203*

## DIVISION THREE 1987-88

| | | | | | | | |
|---|---|---|---|---|---|---|---|
| **Sunderland** | 46 | 27 | 12 | 7 | 92 | 48 | 93 |
| **Brighton & Hove Albion** | 46 | 23 | 15 | 8 | 69 | 47 | 84 |
| **Walsall** | 46 | 23 | 13 | 10 | 68 | 50 | 82 |
| Notts County | 46 | 23 | 12 | 11 | 82 | 49 | 81 |
| Bristol City | 46 | 21 | 12 | 13 | 77 | 62 | 75 |
| Northampton Town | 46 | 18 | 19 | 9 | 70 | 51 | 73 |
| Wigan Athletic | 46 | 20 | 12 | 14 | 70 | 61 | 72 |
| Bristol Rovers | 46 | 18 | 12 | 16 | 68 | 56 | 66 |
| Fulham | 46 | 19 | 9 | 18 | 69 | 60 | 66 |
| Blackpool | 46 | 17 | 14 | 15 | 71 | 62 | 65 |
| Port Vale | 46 | 18 | 11 | 17 | 58 | 56 | 65 |
| Brentford | 46 | 16 | 14 | 16 | 53 | 59 | 62 |
| Gillingham | 46 | 14 | 17 | 15 | 77 | 61 | 59 |
| Bury | 46 | 15 | 14 | 17 | 58 | 57 | 59 |
| Chester City | 46 | 14 | 16 | 16 | 51 | 62 | 58 |
| Preston North End | 46 | 15 | 13 | 18 | 48 | 59 | 58 |
| Southend United | 46 | 14 | 13 | 19 | 65 | 83 | 55 |
| Chesterfield | 46 | 15 | 10 | 21 | 41 | 70 | 55 |
| Mansfield Town | 46 | 14 | 12 | 20 | 48 | 59 | 54 |
| Aldershot | 46 | 15 | 8 | 23 | 64 | 74 | 53 |
| *Rotherham United* | *46* | *12* | *16* | *18* | *50* | *66* | *52* |
| *Grimsby Town* | *46* | *12* | *14* | *20* | *48* | *58* | *50* |
| *York City* | *46* | *8* | *9* | *29* | *48* | *91* | *33* |
| *Doncaster Rovers* | *46* | *8* | *9* | *29* | *40* | *84* | *33* |

### Division Three/Division Four Play-offs

| | |
|---|---|
| Swansea City vs Rotherham United | 1-0, 1-1 |
| Torquay United vs Scunthorpe United | 2-1, 1-1 |
| Swansea City vs Torquay United | 2-1, 3-3 |

## DIVISION FOUR 1987-88

| | | | | | | | |
|---|---|---|---|---|---|---|---|
| **Wolverhampton Wanderers** | 46 | 27 | 9 | 10 | 82 | 43 | 90 |
| **Cardiff City** | 46 | 24 | 13 | 9 | 66 | 41 | 85 |
| **Bolton Wanderers** | 46 | 22 | 12 | 12 | 66 | 42 | 78 |
| Scunthorpe United | 46 | 20 | 17 | 9 | 76 | 51 | 77 |
| Torquay United | 46 | 21 | 14 | 11 | 66 | 41 | 77 |
| **Swansea City** | 46 | 20 | 10 | 16 | 62 | 56 | 70 |
| Peterborough United | 46 | 20 | 10 | 16 | 52 | 53 | 70 |
| Leyton Orient | 46 | 19 | 12 | 15 | 85 | 63 | 69 |
| Colchester United | 46 | 19 | 10 | 17 | 47 | 51 | 67 |
| Burnley | 46 | 20 | 7 | 19 | 57 | 62 | 67 |
| Wrexham | 46 | 20 | 6 | 20 | 69 | 58 | 66 |
| Scarborough | 46 | 17 | 14 | 15 | 56 | 48 | 65 |
| Darlington | 46 | 18 | 11 | 17 | 71 | 69 | 65 |
| Tranmere Rovers | 46 | 19 | 9 | 18 | 61 | 53 | 64 |
| Cambridge United | 46 | 16 | 13 | 17 | 50 | 52 | 61 |
| Hartlepool United | 46 | 15 | 14 | 17 | 50 | 57 | 59 |
| Crewe Alexandra | 46 | 13 | 19 | 14 | 57 | 53 | 58 |
| Halifax Town | 46 | 14 | 14 | 18 | 54 | 59 | 55 |
| Hereford United | 46 | 14 | 12 | 20 | 41 | 59 | 54 |
| Stockport County | 46 | 12 | 15 | 19 | 44 | 58 | 51 |
| Rochdale | 46 | 11 | 15 | 20 | 47 | 76 | 48 |
| Exeter City | 46 | 11 | 13 | 22 | 53 | 68 | 46 |
| Carlisle United | 46 | 12 | 8 | 26 | 57 | 86 | 44 |
| *Newport County* | *46* | *6* | *7* | *33* | *35* | *105* | *25* |

Tranmere Rovers had 2 points deducted
Halifax Town had 1 point deducted

## 1988 Football League Cup

**Semi-finals**

| | |
|---|---|
| Oxford United vs Luton Town  (1-1, 0-2) | 1-3 |
| Everton vs Arsenal  (0-1, 1-3) | 1-4 |

**Final**

Wembley, 24th April 1988

**Luton Town 3**  (B. Stein 2, Wilson)

**Arsenal 2**  (Hayes, Smith)

*Attendance 95,732*

## DIVISION ONE 1988-89

| | | | | | | | |
|---|---|---|---|---|---|---|---|
| **ARSENAL** | 38 | 22 | 10 | 6 | 73 | 36 | 76 |
| Liverpool | 38 | 22 | 10 | 6 | 65 | 28 | 76 |
| Nottingham Forest | 38 | 17 | 13 | 8 | 64 | 43 | 64 |
| Norwich City | 38 | 17 | 11 | 10 | 48 | 45 | 62 |
| Derby County | 38 | 17 | 7 | 14 | 40 | 38 | 58 |
| Tottenham Hotspur | 38 | 15 | 12 | 11 | 60 | 46 | 57 |
| Coventry City | 38 | 14 | 13 | 11 | 47 | 42 | 55 |
| Everton | 38 | 14 | 12 | 12 | 50 | 45 | 54 |
| Queen's Park Rangers | 38 | 14 | 11 | 13 | 43 | 37 | 53 |
| Millwall | 38 | 14 | 11 | 13 | 47 | 52 | 53 |
| Manchester United | 38 | 13 | 12 | 13 | 45 | 35 | 51 |
| Wimbledon | 38 | 14 | 9 | 15 | 50 | 46 | 51 |
| Southampton | 38 | 10 | 15 | 13 | 52 | 66 | 45 |
| Charlton Athletic | 38 | 10 | 12 | 16 | 44 | 58 | 42 |
| Sheffield Wednesday | 38 | 10 | 12 | 16 | 34 | 51 | 42 |
| Luton Town | 38 | 10 | 11 | 17 | 42 | 52 | 41 |
| Aston Villa | 38 | 9 | 13 | 16 | 45 | 56 | 40 |
| *Middlesbrough* | *38* | *9* | *12* | *17* | *44* | *61* | *39* |
| *West Ham United* | *38* | *10* | *8* | *20* | *37* | *62* | *38* |
| *Newcastle United* | *38* | *7* | *10* | *21* | *32* | *63* | *31* |

## DIVISION TWO 1988-89

| | | | | | | | |
|---|---|---|---|---|---|---|---|
| **Chelsea** | 46 | 29 | 12 | 5 | 96 | 50 | 99 |
| **Manchester City** | 46 | 23 | 13 | 10 | 77 | 53 | 82 |
| **Crystal Palace** | 46 | 23 | 12 | 11 | 71 | 49 | 81 |
| Watford | 46 | 22 | 12 | 12 | 74 | 48 | 78 |
| Blackburn Rovers | 46 | 22 | 11 | 13 | 74 | 59 | 77 |
| Swindon Town | 46 | 20 | 16 | 10 | 68 | 53 | 76 |
| Barnsley | 46 | 20 | 14 | 12 | 66 | 58 | 74 |
| Ipswich Town | 46 | 22 | 7 | 17 | 71 | 61 | 73 |
| West Bromwich Albion | 46 | 18 | 18 | 10 | 65 | 41 | 72 |
| Leeds United | 46 | 17 | 16 | 13 | 59 | 50 | 67 |
| Sunderland | 46 | 16 | 15 | 15 | 60 | 60 | 63 |
| Bournemouth | 46 | 18 | 8 | 20 | 53 | 62 | 62 |
| Stoke City | 46 | 15 | 14 | 17 | 57 | 72 | 59 |
| Bradford City | 46 | 13 | 17 | 16 | 52 | 59 | 56 |
| Leicester City | 46 | 13 | 16 | 17 | 56 | 63 | 55 |
| Oldham Athletic | 46 | 11 | 21 | 14 | 75 | 72 | 54 |
| Oxford United | 46 | 14 | 12 | 20 | 62 | 70 | 54 |
| Plymouth Argyle | 46 | 14 | 12 | 20 | 55 | 66 | 54 |
| Brighton & Hove Albion | 46 | 14 | 9 | 23 | 57 | 66 | 51 |
| Portsmouth | 46 | 13 | 12 | 21 | 53 | 62 | 51 |
| Hull City | 46 | 11 | 14 | 21 | 52 | 68 | 47 |
| *Shrewsbury Town* | *46* | *8* | *18* | *20* | *40* | *67* | *42* |
| *Birmingham City* | *46* | *8* | *11* | *27* | *31* | *76* | *35* |
| *Walsall* | *46* | *5* | *16* | *25* | *41* | *80* | *31* |

### Division Two Play-offs

| | |
|---|---|
| Blackburn Rovers vs Watford | 0-0, 1-1 |
| *(Blackburn Rovers won on away goals)* | |
| Swindon Town vs Crystal Palace | 1-0, 0-2 |
| Blackburn Rovers vs Crystal Palace | 3-1, 0-3 |

## 1989 F.A. Cup

### Semi-finals

| | |
|---|---|
| Liverpool vs Nottingham Forest | |
| (abandoned after 6 minutes) | 0-0 |
| Everton vs Norwich City | 1-0 |

### Replay

| | |
|---|---|
| Liverpool vs Nottingham Forest | 3-1 |

### Final

Wembley, 20 May 1989

**Liverpool 3 (aet.)**   (Aldridge, Rush 2)
**Everton 2**   (McCall 2)

*Attendance 82,800*

## DIVISION THREE 1988-89

| | | | | | | | |
|---|---|---|---|---|---|---|---|
| **Wolverhampton Wanderers** | 46 | 26 | 14 | 6 | 96 | 49 | 92 |
| **Sheffield United** | 46 | 25 | 9 | 12 | 93 | 54 | 84 |
| **Port Vale** | 46 | 24 | 12 | 10 | 78 | 48 | 84 |
| Fulham | 46 | 22 | 9 | 15 | 69 | 67 | 75 |
| Bristol Rovers | 46 | 19 | 17 | 10 | 67 | 51 | 74 |
| Preston North End | 46 | 19 | 15 | 12 | 79 | 60 | 72 |
| Brentford | 46 | 18 | 14 | 14 | 66 | 61 | 68 |
| Chester City | 46 | 19 | 11 | 16 | 64 | 61 | 68 |
| Notts County | 46 | 18 | 13 | 15 | 64 | 54 | 67 |
| Bolton Wanderers | 46 | 16 | 16 | 14 | 58 | 54 | 64 |
| Bristol City | 46 | 18 | 9 | 19 | 53 | 55 | 63 |
| Swansea City | 46 | 15 | 16 | 15 | 51 | 53 | 61 |
| Bury | 46 | 16 | 13 | 17 | 55 | 67 | 61 |
| Huddersfield Town | 46 | 17 | 9 | 20 | 63 | 73 | 60 |
| Mansfield Town | 46 | 14 | 17 | 15 | 48 | 52 | 59 |
| Cardiff City | 46 | 14 | 15 | 17 | 44 | 56 | 57 |
| Wigan Athletic | 46 | 14 | 14 | 18 | 55 | 53 | 56 |
| Reading | 46 | 15 | 11 | 20 | 68 | 72 | 56 |
| Blackpool | 46 | 14 | 14 | 13 | 19 | 56 | 59 | 55 |
| Northampton Town | 46 | 16 | 6 | 24 | 66 | 76 | 54 |
| *Southend United* | *46* | *13* | *15* | *18* | *56* | *75* | *54* |
| *Chesterfield* | *46* | *14* | *7* | *25* | *51* | *86* | *49* |
| *Gillingham* | *46* | *12* | *4* | *30* | *47* | *81* | *40* |
| *Aldershot* | *46* | *8* | *13* | *25* | *48* | *78* | *37* |

### Division Three Play-offs

| | |
|---|---|
| Bristol Rovers vs Fulham | 1-0, 4-0 |
| Preston North End vs Port Vale | 1-1, 1-3 |
| Bristol Rovers vs Port Vale | 1-1, 0-1 |

## DIVISION FOUR 1988-89

| | | | | | | | |
|---|---|---|---|---|---|---|---|
| **Rotherham United** | 46 | 22 | 16 | 8 | 76 | 35 | 82 |
| **Tranmere Rovers** | 46 | 21 | 17 | 8 | 62 | 43 | 80 |
| **Crewe Alexandra** | 46 | 21 | 15 | 10 | 67 | 48 | 78 |
| Scunthorpe United | 46 | 21 | 14 | 11 | 77 | 57 | 77 |
| Scarborough | 46 | 21 | 14 | 11 | 67 | 52 | 77 |
| **Leyton Orient** | 46 | 21 | 12 | 13 | 86 | 50 | 75 |
| Wrexham | 46 | 19 | 14 | 13 | 77 | 63 | 71 |
| Cambridge United | 46 | 18 | 14 | 14 | 71 | 62 | 68 |
| Grimsby Town | 46 | 17 | 15 | 14 | 65 | 59 | 66 |
| Lincoln City | 46 | 18 | 10 | 18 | 64 | 60 | 64 |
| York City | 46 | 17 | 13 | 16 | 62 | 63 | 64 |
| Carlisle United | 46 | 15 | 15 | 16 | 53 | 52 | 60 |
| Exeter City | 46 | 18 | 6 | 22 | 65 | 68 | 60 |
| Torquay United | 46 | 17 | 8 | 21 | 45 | 60 | 59 |
| Hereford United | 46 | 14 | 16 | 16 | 66 | 72 | 58 |
| Burnley | 46 | 14 | 13 | 19 | 52 | 61 | 55 |
| Peterborough United | 46 | 14 | 12 | 20 | 52 | 74 | 54 |
| Rochdale | 46 | 13 | 14 | 19 | 56 | 82 | 53 |
| Hartlepool United | 46 | 14 | 10 | 22 | 50 | 78 | 52 |
| Stockport County | 46 | 10 | 21 | 15 | 54 | 52 | 51 |
| Halifax Town | 46 | 13 | 11 | 22 | 69 | 75 | 50 |
| Colchester United | 46 | 12 | 14 | 20 | 60 | 78 | 50 |
| Doncaster Rovers | 46 | 13 | 10 | 23 | 49 | 78 | 49 |
| *Darlington* | *46* | *8* | *18* | *20* | *53* | *76* | *42* |

### Division Four Play-offs

| | |
|---|---|
| Leyton Orient vs Scarborough | 2-0, 0-1 |
| Wrexham vs Scunthorpe United | 3-1, 2-0 |
| Wrexham vs Leyton Orient | 0-0, 1-2 |

## 1989 Football League Cup

### Semi-finals

| | |
|---|---|
| West Ham United vs Luton Town (0-3, 0-2) | 0-5 |
| Nottingham Forest vs Bristol City (1-1, 1-0) | 2-1 |

### Final

Wembley, 9th April 1989

**Nottingham Forest 3**   (Clough 2 (1 pen), Webb)
**Luton Town 1**   (Harford)

*Attendance 76,130*

## DIVISION ONE 1989-90

| LIVERPOOL | 38 | 23 | 10 | 5 | 78 | 37 | 79 |
|---|---|---|---|---|---|---|---|
| Aston Villa | 38 | 21 | 7 | 10 | 57 | 38 | 70 |
| Tottenham Hotspur | 38 | 19 | 6 | 13 | 59 | 47 | 63 |
| Arsenal | 38 | 18 | 8 | 12 | 54 | 38 | 62 |
| Chelsea | 38 | 16 | 12 | 10 | 58 | 50 | 60 |
| Everton | 38 | 17 | 8 | 13 | 57 | 46 | 59 |
| Southampton | 38 | 15 | 10 | 13 | 71 | 63 | 55 |
| Wimbledon | 38 | 13 | 16 | 9 | 47 | 40 | 55 |
| Nottingham Forest | 38 | 15 | 9 | 14 | 55 | 47 | 54 |
| Norwich City | 38 | 13 | 14 | 11 | 44 | 42 | 53 |
| Queen's Park Rangers | 38 | 13 | 11 | 14 | 45 | 44 | 50 |
| Coventry City | 38 | 14 | 7 | 17 | 39 | 59 | 49 |
| Manchester United | 38 | 13 | 9 | 16 | 46 | 47 | 48 |
| Manchester City | 38 | 12 | 12 | 14 | 43 | 52 | 48 |
| Crystal Palace | 38 | 13 | 9 | 16 | 42 | 66 | 48 |
| Derby County | 38 | 13 | 7 | 18 | 43 | 40 | 46 |
| Luton Town | 38 | 10 | 13 | 15 | 43 | 57 | 43 |
| *Sheffield Wednesday* | *38* | *11* | *10* | *17* | *35* | *51* | *43* |
| *Charlton Athletic* | *38* | *7* | *9* | *22* | *31* | *57* | *30* |
| *Millwall* | *38* | *5* | *11* | *22* | *39* | *65* | *26* |

## DIVISION TWO 1989-90

| Leeds United | 46 | 24 | 13 | 9 | 79 | 52 | 85 |
|---|---|---|---|---|---|---|---|
| Sheffield United | 46 | 24 | 13 | 9 | 78 | 58 | 85 |
| Newcastle United | 46 | 22 | 14 | 10 | 80 | 55 | 80 |
| Swindon Town | 46 | 20 | 14 | 12 | 79 | 59 | 74 |
| Blackburn Rovers | 46 | 19 | 17 | 10 | 74 | 59 | 74 |
| Sunderland | 46 | 20 | 14 | 12 | 70 | 64 | 74 |
| West Ham United | 46 | 20 | 12 | 14 | 80 | 57 | 72 |
| Oldham Athletic | 46 | 19 | 14 | 13 | 70 | 57 | 71 |
| Ipswich Town | 46 | 19 | 12 | 15 | 67 | 66 | 69 |
| Wolverhampton Wanderers | 46 | 18 | 13 | 15 | 67 | 60 | 67 |
| Port Vale | 46 | 15 | 16 | 15 | 62 | 57 | 61 |
| Portsmouth | 46 | 15 | 16 | 15 | 62 | 65 | 61 |
| Leicester City | 46 | 15 | 14 | 17 | 67 | 79 | 59 |
| Hull City | 46 | 14 | 16 | 16 | 58 | 65 | 58 |
| Watford | 46 | 14 | 15 | 17 | 58 | 60 | 57 |
| Plymouth Argyle | 46 | 14 | 13 | 19 | 58 | 63 | 55 |
| Oxford United | 46 | 15 | 9 | 22 | 57 | 66 | 54 |
| Brighton & Hove Albion | 46 | 15 | 9 | 22 | 56 | 72 | 54 |
| Barnsley | 46 | 13 | 15 | 18 | 49 | 71 | 54 |
| West Bromwich Albion | 46 | 12 | 15 | 19 | 67 | 71 | 51 |
| Middlesbrough | 46 | 13 | 11 | 22 | 52 | 63 | 50 |
| *Bournemouth* | *46* | *12* | *12* | *22* | *57* | *76* | *48* |
| *Bradford City* | *46* | *9* | *14* | *23* | *44* | *68* | *41* |
| *Stoke City* | *46* | *6* | *19* | *21* | *35* | *63* | *37* |

Swindon Town were promoted through the play-offs. However, they were then immediately relegated for financial irregularities and their promotion place was taken by Sunderland.

### Division Two Play-offs

| Blackburn Rovers vs Swindon Town | 1-2, 1-2 |
|---|---|
| Sunderland vs Newcastle United | 0-0, 2-0 |
| Swindon Town vs Sunderland | 1-0 |

## 1990 F.A. Cup

### Semi-finals

| Crystal Palace vs Liverpool | 4-3 |
|---|---|
| Manchester United vs Oldham Athletic | 3-3, 2-1 |

### Final

Wembley, 12th May 1990

**Manchester United 3**  (Robson, Hughes 2)
**Crystal Palace 3 (aet.)**  (O'Reilly, Wright 2)

*Attendance 80,000*

### Replay

Wembley, 17th May 1990

**Manchester United 1**  (Martin)
**Crystal Palace 0**

*Attendance 80,000*

## DIVISION THREE 1989-90

| **Bristol Rovers** | 46 | 26 | 15 | 5 | 71 | 35 | 93 |
|---|---|---|---|---|---|---|---|
| **Bristol City** | 46 | 27 | 10 | 9 | 76 | 40 | 91 |
| **Notts County** | 46 | 25 | 12 | 9 | 73 | 53 | 87 |
| Tranmere Rovers | 46 | 23 | 11 | 12 | 86 | 49 | 80 |
| Bury | 46 | 21 | 11 | 14 | 70 | 49 | 74 |
| Bolton Wanderers | 46 | 18 | 15 | 13 | 59 | 48 | 69 |
| Birmingham City | 46 | 18 | 12 | 16 | 60 | 59 | 66 |
| Huddersfield Town | 46 | 17 | 14 | 15 | 61 | 62 | 65 |
| Rotherham United | 46 | 17 | 13 | 16 | 71 | 62 | 64 |
| Reading | 46 | 15 | 19 | 12 | 57 | 53 | 64 |
| Shrewsbury Town | 46 | 16 | 15 | 15 | 59 | 54 | 63 |
| Crewe Alexandra | 46 | 15 | 17 | 14 | 56 | 53 | 62 |
| Brentford | 46 | 18 | 7 | 21 | 66 | 66 | 61 |
| Leyton Orient | 46 | 16 | 10 | 20 | 52 | 56 | 58 |
| Mansfield Town | 46 | 16 | 7 | 23 | 50 | 65 | 55 |
| Chester City | 46 | 13 | 15 | 18 | 43 | 55 | 54 |
| Swansea City | 46 | 14 | 12 | 20 | 45 | 63 | 54 |
| Wigan Athletic | 46 | 13 | 14 | 19 | 48 | 64 | 53 |
| Preston North End | 46 | 14 | 10 | 22 | 65 | 79 | 52 |
| Fulham | 46 | 12 | 15 | 19 | 55 | 66 | 51 |
| *Cardiff City* | *46* | *12* | *14* | *20* | *51* | *70* | *50* |
| *Northampton Town* | *46* | *11* | *14* | *21* | *51* | *68* | *47* |
| *Blackpool* | *46* | *10* | *16* | *20* | *49* | *73* | *46* |
| *Walsall* | *46* | *9* | *14* | *23* | *40* | *72* | *41* |

### Division Three Play-offs

| Bolton Wanderers vs Notts County | 1-1, 0-2 |
|---|---|
| Bury vs Tranmere Rovers | 0-0, 0-2 |
| Notts County vs Tranmere Rovers | 2-0 |

## DIVISION FOUR 1989-90

| **Exeter City** | 46 | 28 | 5 | 13 | 83 | 48 | 89 |
|---|---|---|---|---|---|---|---|
| **Grimsby Town** | 46 | 22 | 13 | 11 | 70 | 47 | 79 |
| **Southend United** | 46 | 22 | 9 | 15 | 61 | 48 | 75 |
| Stockport County | 46 | 21 | 11 | 14 | 68 | 62 | 74 |
| Maidstone United | 46 | 22 | 7 | 17 | 77 | 61 | 73 |
| **Cambridge United** | 46 | 21 | 10 | 15 | 76 | 66 | 73 |
| Chesterfield | 46 | 19 | 14 | 13 | 63 | 50 | 71 |
| Carlisle United | 46 | 21 | 8 | 17 | 61 | 60 | 71 |
| Peterborough United | 46 | 17 | 17 | 12 | 59 | 46 | 68 |
| Lincoln City | 46 | 18 | 14 | 14 | 48 | 48 | 68 |
| Scunthorpe United | 46 | 17 | 15 | 14 | 69 | 54 | 66 |
| Rochdale | 46 | 20 | 6 | 20 | 52 | 55 | 66 |
| York City | 46 | 16 | 16 | 14 | 55 | 53 | 64 |
| Gillingham | 46 | 17 | 11 | 18 | 46 | 48 | 62 |
| Torquay United | 46 | 15 | 12 | 19 | 53 | 66 | 57 |
| Burnley | 46 | 14 | 14 | 18 | 45 | 55 | 56 |
| Hereford United | 46 | 15 | 10 | 21 | 56 | 62 | 55 |
| Scarborough | 46 | 15 | 10 | 21 | 60 | 73 | 55 |
| Hartlepool United | 46 | 15 | 10 | 21 | 66 | 88 | 55 |
| Doncaster Rovers | 46 | 14 | 9 | 23 | 53 | 60 | 51 |
| Wrexham | 46 | 13 | 12 | 21 | 51 | 67 | 51 |
| Aldershot | 46 | 12 | 14 | 20 | 49 | 69 | 50 |
| Halifax Town | 46 | 12 | 13 | 21 | 57 | 65 | 49 |
| *Colchester United* | *46* | *11* | *10* | *25* | *48* | *75* | *43* |

### Division Four Play-offs

| Cambridge United vs Maidstone United | 1-1, 2-0 |
|---|---|
| Chesterfield vs Stockport County | 4-0, 2-0 |
| Cambridge United vs Chesterfield | 1-0 |

## 1990 Football League Cup

### Semi-finals

| Nottingham Forest vs Coventry City (2-1, 0-0) | 2-1 |
|---|---|
| Oldham Athletic vs West Ham United (6-0, 0-3) | 6-3 |

### Final

Wembley, 29th April 1990

**Nottingham Forest 1**  (Jemson)
**Oldham Athletic 0**

*Attendance 74,343*

## DIVISION ONE 1990-91

| | | | | | | | |
|---|---|---|---|---|---|---|---|
| ARSENAL | 38 | 24 | 13 | 1 | 74 | 18 | 83 |
| Liverpool | 38 | 23 | 7 | 8 | 77 | 40 | 76 |
| Crystal Palace | 38 | 20 | 9 | 9 | 50 | 41 | 69 |
| Leeds United | 38 | 19 | 7 | 12 | 65 | 47 | 64 |
| Manchester City | 38 | 17 | 11 | 10 | 64 | 53 | 62 |
| Manchester United | 38 | 16 | 12 | 10 | 58 | 45 | 60 |
| Wimbledon | 38 | 14 | 14 | 10 | 53 | 46 | 56 |
| Nottingham Forest | 38 | 14 | 12 | 12 | 65 | 50 | 54 |
| Everton | 38 | 13 | 12 | 13 | 50 | 46 | 51 |
| Tottenham Hotspur | 38 | 11 | 16 | 11 | 51 | 50 | 49 |
| Chelsea | 38 | 13 | 10 | 15 | 58 | 69 | 49 |
| Queen's Park Rangers | 38 | 12 | 10 | 16 | 44 | 53 | 46 |
| Sheffield United | 38 | 13 | 7 | 18 | 36 | 55 | 46 |
| Southampton | 38 | 12 | 9 | 17 | 58 | 69 | 45 |
| Norwich City | 38 | 13 | 6 | 19 | 41 | 64 | 45 |
| Coventry City | 38 | 11 | 11 | 16 | 42 | 49 | 44 |
| Aston Villa | 38 | 9 | 14 | 15 | 46 | 58 | 41 |
| *Luton Town* | *38* | *10* | *7* | *21* | *42* | *61* | *37* |
| *Sunderland* | *38* | *8* | *10* | *20* | *38* | *60* | *34* |
| *Derby County* | *38* | *5* | *9* | *24* | *37* | *75* | *24* |

Arsenal had 2 points deducted
Manchester United had 1 point deducted

## DIVISION TWO 1990-91

| | | | | | | | |
|---|---|---|---|---|---|---|---|
| Oldham Athletic | 46 | 25 | 13 | 8 | 83 | 53 | 88 |
| West Ham United | 46 | 24 | 15 | 7 | 60 | 34 | 87 |
| Sheffield Wednesday | 46 | 22 | 16 | 8 | 80 | 51 | 82 |
| Notts County | 46 | 23 | 11 | 12 | 76 | 55 | 80 |
| Millwall | 46 | 20 | 13 | 13 | 70 | 51 | 73 |
| Brighton & Hove Albion | 46 | 21 | 7 | 18 | 63 | 69 | 70 |
| Middlesbrough | 46 | 20 | 9 | 17 | 66 | 47 | 69 |
| Barnsley | 46 | 19 | 12 | 15 | 63 | 48 | 69 |
| Bristol City | 46 | 20 | 7 | 19 | 68 | 71 | 67 |
| Oxford United | 46 | 14 | 19 | 13 | 69 | 66 | 61 |
| Newcastle United | 46 | 14 | 17 | 15 | 49 | 56 | 59 |
| Wolverhampton Wanderers | 46 | 13 | 19 | 14 | 63 | 63 | 58 |
| Bristol Rovers | 46 | 15 | 13 | 18 | 56 | 59 | 58 |
| Ipswich Town | 46 | 13 | 18 | 15 | 60 | 68 | 57 |
| Port Vale | 46 | 15 | 12 | 19 | 56 | 64 | 57 |
| Charlton Athletic | 46 | 13 | 17 | 16 | 57 | 61 | 56 |
| Portsmouth | 46 | 14 | 11 | 21 | 58 | 70 | 53 |
| Plymouth Argyle | 46 | 12 | 17 | 17 | 54 | 68 | 53 |
| Blackburn Rovers | 46 | 14 | 10 | 22 | 51 | 66 | 52 |
| Watford | 46 | 12 | 15 | 19 | 45 | 59 | 51 |
| Swindon Town | 46 | 12 | 14 | 20 | 65 | 73 | 50 |
| Leicester City | 46 | 14 | 8 | 24 | 60 | 83 | 50 |
| *West Bromwich Albion* | *46* | *10* | *18* | *18* | *52* | *61* | *48* |
| *Hull City* | *46* | *10* | *15* | *21* | *57* | *85* | *45* |

### Division Two Play-offs

| | |
|---|---|
| Brighton & Hove Albion vs Millwall | 4-1, 2-1 |
| Middlesbrough vs Notts County | 1-1, 0-1 |
| Notts County vs Brighton & Hove Albion | 3-1 |

## 1991 F.A. Cup

### Semi-finals

| | |
|---|---|
| Arsenal vs Tottenham Hotspur | 1-3 |
| Nottingham Forest vs West Ham United | 4-0 |

### Final

Wembley, 18th May 1991

**Tottenham Hotspur 2**   (Stewart, Walker (og))
**Nottingham Forest 1**   (Pearce)

*Attendance 80,000*

## DIVISION THREE 1990-91

| | | | | | | | |
|---|---|---|---|---|---|---|---|
| Cambridge United | 46 | 25 | 11 | 10 | 75 | 45 | 86 |
| Southend United | 46 | 26 | 7 | 13 | 67 | 51 | 85 |
| Grimsby Town | 46 | 24 | 11 | 11 | 66 | 34 | 83 |
| Bolton Wanderers | 46 | 24 | 11 | 11 | 64 | 50 | 83 |
| Tranmere Rovers | 46 | 23 | 9 | 14 | 64 | 46 | 78 |
| Brentford | 46 | 21 | 13 | 12 | 59 | 47 | 76 |
| Bury | 46 | 20 | 13 | 13 | 67 | 56 | 73 |
| Bradford City | 46 | 20 | 10 | 16 | 62 | 54 | 70 |
| Bournemouth | 46 | 19 | 13 | 14 | 58 | 58 | 70 |
| Wigan Athletic | 46 | 20 | 9 | 17 | 71 | 54 | 69 |
| Huddersfield Town | 46 | 18 | 13 | 15 | 57 | 51 | 67 |
| Birmingham City | 46 | 16 | 17 | 13 | 45 | 49 | 65 |
| Leyton Orient | 46 | 18 | 10 | 18 | 55 | 58 | 64 |
| Stoke City | 46 | 16 | 12 | 18 | 55 | 59 | 60 |
| Reading | 46 | 17 | 8 | 21 | 53 | 66 | 59 |
| Exeter City | 46 | 16 | 9 | 21 | 58 | 52 | 57 |
| Preston North End | 46 | 15 | 11 | 20 | 54 | 67 | 56 |
| Shrewsbury Town | 46 | 14 | 10 | 22 | 61 | 68 | 52 |
| Chester City | 46 | 14 | 9 | 23 | 46 | 58 | 51 |
| Swansea City | 46 | 13 | 9 | 24 | 49 | 72 | 48 |
| Fulham | 46 | 10 | 16 | 20 | 41 | 56 | 46 |
| *Crewe Alexandra* | *46* | *11* | *11* | *24* | *62* | *80* | *44* |
| *Rotherham United* | *46* | *10* | *12* | *24* | *50* | *87* | *42* |
| *Mansfield Town* | *46* | *8* | *14* | *24* | *42* | *63* | *38* |

### Division Three Play-offs

| | |
|---|---|
| Brentford vs Tranmere Rovers | 2-2, 0-1 |
| Bury vs Bolton Wanderers | 1-1, 0-1 |
| Tranmere Rovers vs Bolton Wanderers | 1-0 |

## DIVISION FOUR 1990-91

| | | | | | | | |
|---|---|---|---|---|---|---|---|
| Darlington | 46 | 22 | 17 | 7 | 68 | 38 | 83 |
| Stockport County | 46 | 23 | 13 | 10 | 84 | 47 | 82 |
| Hartlepool United | 46 | 24 | 10 | 12 | 67 | 48 | 82 |
| Peterborough United | 46 | 21 | 17 | 8 | 67 | 45 | 80 |
| Blackpool | 46 | 23 | 10 | 13 | 78 | 47 | 79 |
| Burnley | 46 | 23 | 10 | 13 | 70 | 51 | 79 |
| Torquay United | 46 | 18 | 18 | 10 | 64 | 47 | 72 |
| Scunthorpe United | 46 | 20 | 11 | 15 | 71 | 62 | 71 |
| Scarborough | 46 | 19 | 12 | 15 | 59 | 56 | 69 |
| Northampton Town | 46 | 18 | 13 | 15 | 57 | 58 | 67 |
| Doncaster Rovers | 46 | 17 | 14 | 15 | 56 | 46 | 65 |
| Rochdale | 46 | 15 | 17 | 14 | 50 | 53 | 62 |
| Cardiff City | 46 | 15 | 15 | 16 | 43 | 54 | 60 |
| Lincoln City | 46 | 14 | 17 | 15 | 50 | 61 | 59 |
| Gillingham | 46 | 12 | 18 | 16 | 57 | 60 | 54 |
| Walsall | 46 | 12 | 17 | 17 | 48 | 51 | 53 |
| Hereford United | 46 | 13 | 14 | 19 | 53 | 58 | 53 |
| Chesterfield | 46 | 13 | 14 | 19 | 47 | 62 | 53 |
| Maidstone United | 46 | 13 | 12 | 21 | 66 | 71 | 51 |
| Carlisle United | 46 | 13 | 9 | 24 | 47 | 89 | 48 |
| York City | 46 | 11 | 13 | 22 | 45 | 57 | 46 |
| Halifax Town | 46 | 12 | 10 | 24 | 59 | 79 | 46 |
| Aldershot | 46 | 10 | 11 | 25 | 61 | 101 | 41 |
| Wrexham | 46 | 10 | 10 | 26 | 48 | 74 | 40 |

### Division Four Play-offs

| | |
|---|---|
| Scunthorpe United vs Blackpool | 1-1, 1-2 |
| Torquay United vs Burnley | 2-0, 0-1 |
| Torquay United vs Blackpool | 2-2 |

*Torquay United won 5-4 on penalties*

## 1991 Football League Cup

### Semi-finals

| | |
|---|---|
| Manchester United vs Leeds United   (2-1, 1-0) | 3-1 |
| Chelsea vs Sheffield Wednesday   (0-2, 1-3) | 1-5 |

### Final

Wembley, 21st April 1991

**Sheffield Wednesday 1**   (Sheridan)
**Manchester United 0**

*Attendance 80,000*

## DIVISION ONE 1991-92

| LEEDS UNITED | 42 | 22 | 16 | 4 | 74 | 37 | 82 |
|---|---|---|---|---|---|---|---|
| Manchester United | 42 | 21 | 15 | 6 | 63 | 33 | 78 |
| Sheffield Wednesday | 42 | 21 | 12 | 9 | 62 | 49 | 75 |
| Arsenal | 42 | 19 | 15 | 8 | 81 | 46 | 72 |
| Manchester City | 42 | 20 | 10 | 12 | 61 | 48 | 70 |
| Liverpool | 42 | 16 | 16 | 10 | 47 | 40 | 64 |
| Aston Villa | 42 | 17 | 9 | 16 | 48 | 44 | 60 |
| Nottingham Forest | 42 | 16 | 11 | 15 | 60 | 58 | 59 |
| Sheffield United | 42 | 16 | 9 | 17 | 65 | 63 | 57 |
| Crystal Palace | 42 | 14 | 15 | 13 | 53 | 61 | 57 |
| Queen's Park Rangers | 42 | 12 | 18 | 12 | 48 | 47 | 54 |
| Everton | 42 | 13 | 14 | 15 | 52 | 51 | 53 |
| Wimbledon | 42 | 13 | 14 | 15 | 53 | 53 | 53 |
| Chelsea | 42 | 13 | 14 | 15 | 50 | 60 | 53 |
| Tottenham Hotspur | 42 | 15 | 7 | 20 | 58 | 63 | 52 |
| Southampton | 42 | 14 | 10 | 18 | 39 | 55 | 52 |
| Oldham Athletic | 42 | 14 | 9 | 19 | 63 | 67 | 51 |
| Norwich City | 42 | 11 | 12 | 19 | 47 | 63 | 45 |
| Coventry City | 42 | 11 | 11 | 20 | 35 | 44 | 44 |
| *Luton Town* | *42* | *10* | *12* | *20* | *38* | *71* | *42* |
| *Notts County* | *42* | *10* | *10* | *22* | *40* | *62* | *40* |
| *West Ham United* | *42* | *9* | *11* | *22* | *37* | *59* | *38* |

## DIVISION TWO 1991-92

| **Ipswich Town** | 46 | 24 | 12 | 10 | 70 | 50 | 84 |
|---|---|---|---|---|---|---|---|
| **Middlesbrough** | 46 | 23 | 11 | 12 | 58 | 41 | 80 |
| Derby County | 46 | 23 | 9 | 14 | 69 | 51 | 78 |
| Leicester City | 46 | 23 | 8 | 15 | 62 | 55 | 77 |
| Cambridge United | 46 | 19 | 17 | 10 | 65 | 47 | 74 |
| **Blackburn Rovers** | 46 | 21 | 11 | 14 | 70 | 53 | 74 |
| Charlton Athletic | 46 | 20 | 11 | 15 | 54 | 48 | 71 |
| Swindon Town | 46 | 18 | 15 | 13 | 69 | 55 | 69 |
| Portsmouth | 46 | 19 | 12 | 15 | 65 | 51 | 69 |
| Watford | 46 | 18 | 11 | 17 | 51 | 48 | 65 |
| Wolverhampton Wanderers | 46 | 18 | 10 | 18 | 61 | 54 | 64 |
| Southend United | 46 | 17 | 11 | 18 | 63 | 63 | 62 |
| Bristol Rovers | 46 | 16 | 14 | 16 | 60 | 63 | 62 |
| Tranmere Rovers | 46 | 14 | 19 | 13 | 56 | 56 | 61 |
| Millwall | 46 | 17 | 10 | 19 | 64 | 71 | 61 |
| Barnsley | 46 | 16 | 11 | 19 | 46 | 57 | 59 |
| Bristol City | 46 | 13 | 15 | 18 | 55 | 71 | 54 |
| Sunderland | 46 | 14 | 11 | 21 | 61 | 65 | 53 |
| Grimsby Town | 46 | 14 | 11 | 21 | 47 | 62 | 53 |
| Newcastle United | 46 | 13 | 13 | 20 | 66 | 84 | 52 |
| Oxford United | 46 | 13 | 11 | 22 | 66 | 73 | 50 |
| *Plymouth Argyle* | *46* | *13* | *9* | *24* | *42* | *64* | *48* |
| *Brighton & Hove Albion* | *46* | *12* | *11* | *23* | *56* | *77* | *47* |
| *Port Vale* | *46* | *10* | *15* | *21* | *42* | *59* | *45* |

### Division Two Play-offs

| Blackburn Rovers vs Derby County | 4-2, 1-2 |
|---|---|
| Cambridge United vs Leicester City | 1-1, 0-5 |
| Blackburn Rovers vs Leicester City | 1-0 |

## 1992 F.A. Cup

### Semi-finals

| Liverpool vs Portsmouth | 1-1, 0-0 |
|---|---|
| Liverpool won 3-1 on penalties | |
| Sunderland vs Norwich | 1-0 |

### Final

Wembley, 9th May 1992

**Liverpool 2**   (Thomas, I. Rush)
**Sunderland 0**

*Attendance 79,544*

## DIVISION THREE 1991-92

| **Brentford** | 46 | 25 | 7 | 14 | 81 | 55 | 82 |
|---|---|---|---|---|---|---|---|
| **Birmingham City** | 46 | 23 | 12 | 11 | 69 | 52 | 81 |
| Huddersfield Town | 46 | 22 | 12 | 12 | 59 | 38 | 78 |
| Stoke City | 46 | 21 | 14 | 11 | 69 | 49 | 77 |
| Stockport County | 46 | 22 | 10 | 14 | 75 | 51 | 76 |
| **Peterborough United** | 46 | 20 | 14 | 12 | 65 | 58 | 74 |
| West Bromwich Albion | 46 | 19 | 14 | 13 | 64 | 49 | 71 |
| Bournemouth | 46 | 20 | 11 | 15 | 52 | 48 | 71 |
| Fulham | 46 | 19 | 13 | 14 | 57 | 53 | 70 |
| Leyton Orient | 46 | 18 | 11 | 17 | 62 | 52 | 65 |
| Hartlepool United | 46 | 18 | 11 | 17 | 57 | 57 | 65 |
| Reading | 46 | 16 | 13 | 17 | 59 | 62 | 61 |
| Bolton Wanderers | 46 | 14 | 17 | 15 | 57 | 56 | 59 |
| Hull City | 46 | 16 | 11 | 19 | 54 | 54 | 59 |
| Wigan Athletic | 46 | 15 | 14 | 17 | 58 | 64 | 59 |
| Bradford City | 46 | 13 | 19 | 14 | 62 | 61 | 58 |
| Preston North End | 46 | 15 | 12 | 19 | 61 | 72 | 57 |
| Chester City | 46 | 14 | 14 | 18 | 56 | 59 | 56 |
| Swansea City | 46 | 14 | 14 | 18 | 55 | 65 | 56 |
| Exeter City | 46 | 14 | 11 | 21 | 57 | 80 | 53 |
| *Bury* | *46* | *13* | *12* | *21* | *55* | *74* | *51* |
| *Shrewsbury Town* | *46* | *12* | *11* | *23* | *53* | *68* | *47* |
| *Torquay United* | *46* | *13* | *8* | *25* | *42* | *68* | *47* |
| *Darlington* | *46* | *10* | *7* | *29* | *56* | *90* | *37* |

### Division Three Play-offs

| Stockport County vs Stoke City | 1-0, 1-1 |
|---|---|
| Peterborough United vs Huddersfield Town | 2-2, 2-1 |
| Peterborough United vs Stockport County | 2-1 |

## DIVISION FOUR 1991-92

| **Burnley** | 42 | 25 | 8 | 9 | 79 | 43 | 83 |
|---|---|---|---|---|---|---|---|
| **Rotherham United** | 42 | 22 | 11 | 9 | 70 | 37 | 77 |
| **Mansfield Town** | 42 | 23 | 8 | 11 | 75 | 53 | 77 |
| **Blackpool** | 42 | 22 | 10 | 10 | 71 | 45 | 76 |
| Scunthorpe United | 42 | 21 | 9 | 12 | 64 | 59 | 72 |
| Crewe Alexandra | 42 | 20 | 10 | 12 | 66 | 51 | 70 |
| Barnet | 42 | 21 | 6 | 15 | 81 | 61 | 69 |
| Rochdale | 42 | 18 | 13 | 11 | 57 | 53 | 67 |
| Cardiff City | 42 | 17 | 15 | 10 | 66 | 53 | 66 |
| Lincoln City | 42 | 17 | 11 | 14 | 50 | 44 | 62 |
| Gillingham | 42 | 15 | 12 | 15 | 63 | 53 | 57 |
| Scarborough | 42 | 15 | 12 | 15 | 64 | 68 | 57 |
| Chesterfield | 42 | 14 | 11 | 17 | 49 | 61 | 53 |
| Wrexham | 42 | 14 | 9 | 19 | 52 | 73 | 51 |
| Walsall | 42 | 12 | 13 | 17 | 48 | 58 | 49 |
| Northampton Town | 42 | 11 | 13 | 18 | 46 | 57 | 46 |
| Hereford United | 42 | 12 | 8 | 22 | 44 | 57 | 44 |
| Maidstone United | 42 | 8 | 18 | 16 | 45 | 56 | 42 |
| York City | 42 | 8 | 16 | 18 | 42 | 58 | 40 |
| Halifax Town | 42 | 10 | 8 | 24 | 34 | 75 | 38 |
| Doncaster Rovers | 42 | 9 | 8 | 25 | 40 | 65 | 35 |
| Carlisle United | 42 | 7 | 13 | 22 | 41 | 67 | 34 |

Aldershot were declared bankrupt and obliged to resign from the League after playing 36 matches, the results of which were declared void.

### Division Four Play-offs

| Barnet vs Blackpool | 1-0, 0-2 |
|---|---|
| Crewe Alexandra vs Scunthorpe United | 2-2, 0-2 |
| Blackpool vs Scunthorpe United | 1-1 |
| *Blackpool won 4-3 on penalties* | |

## 1992 Football League Cup

### Semi-finals

| Nottingham Forest vs Tottenham Hotspur (1-1, 2-1) | 3-2 |
|---|---|
| Middlesbrough vs Manchester United (0-0, 1-2) | 1-2 |

### Final

Wembley, 12th April 1992

**Manchester United 1**   (McClair)
**Nottingham Forest 0**

*Attendance 76,810*

## F.A. PREMIER LEAGUE 1992-93

| | | | | | | | |
|---|---|---|---|---|---|---|---|
| **MANCHESTER UNITED** | 42 | 24 | 12 | 6 | 67 | 31 | 84 |
| Aston Villa | 42 | 21 | 11 | 10 | 57 | 40 | 74 |
| Norwich City | 42 | 21 | 9 | 12 | 61 | 65 | 72 |
| Blackburn Rovers | 42 | 20 | 11 | 11 | 68 | 46 | 71 |
| Queen's Park Rangers | 42 | 17 | 12 | 13 | 63 | 55 | 63 |
| Liverpool | 42 | 16 | 11 | 15 | 62 | 55 | 59 |
| Sheffield Wednesday | 42 | 15 | 14 | 13 | 55 | 51 | 59 |
| Tottenham Hotspur | 42 | 16 | 11 | 15 | 60 | 66 | 59 |
| Manchester City | 42 | 15 | 12 | 15 | 56 | 51 | 57 |
| Arsenal | 42 | 15 | 11 | 16 | 40 | 38 | 56 |
| Chelsea | 42 | 14 | 14 | 14 | 51 | 54 | 56 |
| Wimbledon | 42 | 14 | 12 | 16 | 56 | 55 | 54 |
| Everton | 42 | 15 | 8 | 19 | 53 | 55 | 53 |
| Sheffield United | 42 | 14 | 10 | 18 | 54 | 53 | 52 |
| Coventry City | 42 | 13 | 13 | 16 | 52 | 57 | 52 |
| Ipswich Town | 42 | 12 | 16 | 14 | 50 | 55 | 52 |
| Leeds United | 42 | 12 | 15 | 15 | 57 | 62 | 51 |
| Southampton | 42 | 13 | 11 | 18 | 54 | 61 | 50 |
| Oldham Athletic | 42 | 13 | 10 | 19 | 63 | 74 | 49 |
| *Crystal Palace* | *42* | *11* | *16* | *15* | *48* | *61* | *49* |
| *Middlesbrough* | *42* | *11* | *11* | *20* | *54* | *75* | *44* |
| *Nottingham Forest* | *42* | *10* | *10* | *22* | *41* | *62* | *40* |

## DIVISION ONE 1992-93

| | | | | | | | |
|---|---|---|---|---|---|---|---|
| **Newcastle United** | 46 | 29 | 9 | 8 | 92 | 38 | 96 |
| **West Ham United** | 46 | 26 | 10 | 10 | 81 | 41 | 88 |
| Portsmouth | 46 | 26 | 10 | 10 | 80 | 46 | 88 |
| Tranmere Rovers | 46 | 23 | 10 | 13 | 72 | 56 | 79 |
| **Swindon Town** | 46 | 21 | 13 | 12 | 74 | 59 | 76 |
| Leicester City | 46 | 22 | 10 | 14 | 71 | 64 | 76 |
| Millwall | 46 | 18 | 16 | 12 | 65 | 53 | 70 |
| Derby County | 46 | 19 | 9 | 18 | 68 | 57 | 66 |
| Grimsby Town | 46 | 19 | 7 | 20 | 58 | 57 | 64 |
| Peterborough United | 46 | 16 | 14 | 16 | 55 | 63 | 62 |
| Wolverhampton Wanderers | 46 | 16 | 13 | 17 | 57 | 56 | 61 |
| Charlton Athletic | 46 | 16 | 13 | 17 | 49 | 46 | 61 |
| Barnsley | 46 | 17 | 9 | 20 | 56 | 60 | 60 |
| Oxford United | 46 | 14 | 14 | 18 | 53 | 56 | 56 |
| Bristol City | 46 | 14 | 14 | 18 | 49 | 67 | 56 |
| Watford | 46 | 14 | 13 | 19 | 57 | 71 | 55 |
| Notts County | 46 | 12 | 16 | 18 | 55 | 70 | 52 |
| Southend United | 46 | 13 | 13 | 20 | 54 | 64 | 52 |
| Birmingham City | 46 | 13 | 12 | 21 | 50 | 72 | 51 |
| Luton Town | 46 | 10 | 21 | 15 | 48 | 62 | 51 |
| Sunderland | 46 | 13 | 11 | 22 | 50 | 64 | 50 |
| *Brentford* | *46* | *13* | *10* | *23* | *52* | *71* | *49* |
| *Cambridge United* | *46* | *11* | *16* | *19* | *48* | *69* | *49* |
| *Bristol Rovers* | *46* | *10* | *11* | *25* | *55* | *87* | *41* |

### Division One Play-offs

| | |
|---|---|
| Leicester City vs Portsmouth | 1-0, 2-2 |
| Swindon Town vs Tranmere Rovers | 3-1, 2-3 |
| | |
| Swindon Town vs Leicester City | 4-3 |

## 1993 F.A. Cup

### Semi-finals

| | |
|---|---|
| Sheffield United vs Sheffield Wednesday | 1-2 |
| Arsenal vs Tottenham Hotspur | 1-0 |

### Final

Wembley, 15th May 1993

**Arsenal 1**  (Wright)
**Sheffield Wednesday 1 (aet.)**  (Hirst)

*Attendance 79,347*

### Replay

Wembley, 20th May 1993

**Arsenal 2**  (Wright, Linighan)
**Sheffield Wednesday 1 (aet.)**  (Waddle)

*Attendance 62,267*

## DIVISION TWO 1992-93

| | | | | | | | |
|---|---|---|---|---|---|---|---|
| **Stoke City** | 46 | 27 | 12 | 7 | 73 | 34 | 93 |
| **Bolton Wanderers** | 46 | 27 | 9 | 10 | 80 | 41 | 90 |
| Port Vale | 46 | 26 | 11 | 9 | 79 | 44 | 89 |
| **West Bromwich Albion** | 46 | 25 | 10 | 11 | 88 | 54 | 85 |
| Swansea City | 46 | 20 | 13 | 13 | 65 | 47 | 73 |
| Stockport County | 46 | 19 | 15 | 12 | 81 | 57 | 72 |
| Leyton Orient | 46 | 21 | 9 | 16 | 69 | 53 | 72 |
| Reading | 46 | 18 | 15 | 13 | 66 | 51 | 69 |
| Brighton & Hove Albion | 46 | 20 | 9 | 17 | 63 | 59 | 69 |
| Bradford City | 46 | 18 | 14 | 14 | 69 | 67 | 68 |
| Rotherham United | 46 | 17 | 14 | 15 | 60 | 60 | 65 |
| Fulham | 46 | 16 | 17 | 13 | 57 | 55 | 65 |
| Burnley | 46 | 15 | 16 | 15 | 57 | 59 | 61 |
| Plymouth Argyle | 46 | 16 | 12 | 18 | 59 | 64 | 60 |
| Huddersfield Town | 46 | 17 | 9 | 20 | 54 | 61 | 60 |
| Hartlepool United | 46 | 14 | 12 | 20 | 42 | 60 | 54 |
| Bournemouth | 46 | 12 | 17 | 17 | 45 | 52 | 53 |
| Blackpool | 46 | 12 | 15 | 19 | 63 | 75 | 51 |
| Exeter City | 46 | 11 | 17 | 18 | 54 | 69 | 50 |
| Hull City | 46 | 13 | 11 | 22 | 46 | 69 | 50 |
| *Preston North End* | *46* | *13* | *8* | *25* | *65* | *94* | *47* |
| *Mansfield Town* | *46* | *11* | *11* | *24* | *52* | *80* | *44* |
| *Wigan Athletic* | *46* | *10* | *11* | *25* | *43* | *72* | *41* |
| *Chester City* | *46* | *8* | *5* | *33* | *49* | *102* | *29* |

### Division Two Play-offs

| | |
|---|---|
| Stockport County vs Port Vale | 1-1, 0-1 |
| Swansea City vs West Bromwich Albion | 2-1, 0-2 |
| | |
| West Bromwich Albion vs Port Vale | 3-0 |

## DIVISION THREE 1992-93

| | | | | | | | |
|---|---|---|---|---|---|---|---|
| **Cardiff City** | 42 | 25 | 8 | 9 | 77 | 47 | 83 |
| **Wrexham** | 42 | 23 | 11 | 8 | 75 | 52 | 80 |
| **Barnet** | 42 | 23 | 10 | 9 | 66 | 48 | 79 |
| **York City** | 42 | 21 | 12 | 9 | 72 | 45 | 75 |
| Walsall | 42 | 22 | 7 | 13 | 76 | 61 | 73 |
| Crewe Alexandra | 42 | 21 | 7 | 14 | 75 | 56 | 70 |
| Bury | 42 | 18 | 9 | 15 | 63 | 55 | 63 |
| Lincoln City | 42 | 18 | 9 | 15 | 57 | 53 | 63 |
| Shrewsbury Town | 42 | 17 | 11 | 14 | 57 | 52 | 62 |
| Colchester United | 42 | 18 | 5 | 19 | 67 | 76 | 59 |
| Rochdale | 42 | 16 | 10 | 16 | 70 | 70 | 58 |
| Chesterfield | 42 | 15 | 11 | 16 | 59 | 63 | 56 |
| Scarborough | 42 | 15 | 9 | 18 | 66 | 71 | 54 |
| Scunthorpe United | 42 | 14 | 12 | 16 | 57 | 54 | 54 |
| Darlington | 42 | 12 | 14 | 16 | 48 | 53 | 50 |
| Doncaster Rovers | 42 | 11 | 14 | 17 | 42 | 57 | 47 |
| Hereford United | 42 | 10 | 15 | 17 | 47 | 60 | 45 |
| Carlisle United | 42 | 11 | 11 | 20 | 51 | 65 | 44 |
| Torquay United | 42 | 12 | 7 | 23 | 45 | 67 | 43 |
| Northampton Town | 42 | 11 | 8 | 23 | 48 | 74 | 41 |
| Gillingham | 42 | 9 | 13 | 20 | 48 | 64 | 40 |
| *Halifax Town* | *42* | *9* | *9* | *24* | *45* | *68* | *36* |

Maidstone United were declared bankrupt

### Division Three Play-offs

| | |
|---|---|
| Bury vs York City | 0-0, 0-1 |
| Crewe Alexandra vs Walsall | 5-1, 4-2 |
| | |
| York City vs Crewe Alexandra | 1-1 |
| *York City won 5-3 on penalties* | |

## 1993 Football League Cup

### Semi-finals

| | |
|---|---|
| Crystal Palace vs Arsenal  (1-3, 0-2) | 1-5 |
| Blackburn Rovers vs Sheffield Wednesday (2-4, 1-2) | 3-6 |

### Final

Wembley, 18th April 1993

**Arsenal 2**  (Merson, Morrow)
**Sheffield Wednesday 1**  (Harkes)

*Attendance 74,007*

## F.A. PREMIER LEAGUE 1993-94

| MANCHESTER UNITED | 42 | 27 | 11 | 4 | 80 | 38 | 92 |
|---|---|---|---|---|---|---|---|
| Blackburn Rovers | 42 | 25 | 9 | 8 | 63 | 36 | 84 |
| Newcastle United | 42 | 23 | 8 | 11 | 82 | 41 | 77 |
| Arsenal | 42 | 18 | 17 | 7 | 53 | 28 | 71 |
| Leeds United | 42 | 18 | 16 | 8 | 65 | 39 | 70 |
| Wimbledon | 42 | 18 | 11 | 13 | 56 | 53 | 65 |
| Sheffield Wednesday | 42 | 16 | 16 | 10 | 76 | 54 | 64 |
| Liverpool | 42 | 17 | 9 | 16 | 59 | 55 | 60 |
| Queen's Park Rangers | 42 | 16 | 12 | 14 | 62 | 61 | 60 |
| Aston Villa | 42 | 15 | 12 | 15 | 46 | 50 | 57 |
| Coventry City | 42 | 14 | 14 | 14 | 43 | 45 | 56 |
| Norwich City | 42 | 12 | 17 | 13 | 65 | 61 | 53 |
| West Ham United | 42 | 13 | 13 | 16 | 47 | 58 | 52 |
| Chelsea | 42 | 13 | 12 | 17 | 49 | 53 | 51 |
| Tottenham Hotspur | 42 | 11 | 12 | 19 | 54 | 59 | 45 |
| Manchester City | 42 | 9 | 18 | 15 | 38 | 49 | 45 |
| Everton | 42 | 12 | 8 | 22 | 42 | 63 | 44 |
| Southampton | 42 | 12 | 7 | 23 | 49 | 66 | 43 |
| Ipswich Town | 42 | 9 | 16 | 17 | 35 | 58 | 43 |
| *Sheffield United* | *42* | *8* | *18* | *16* | *42* | *60* | *42* |
| *Oldham Athletic* | *42* | *9* | *13* | *20* | *42* | *68* | *40* |
| *Swindon Town* | *42* | *5* | *15* | *22* | *47* | *100* | *30* |

## DIVISION ONE 1993-94

| **Crystal Palace** | 46 | 27 | 9 | 10 | 73 | 46 | 90 |
|---|---|---|---|---|---|---|---|
| **Nottingham Forest** | 46 | 23 | 14 | 9 | 74 | 49 | 83 |
| Millwall | 46 | 19 | 17 | 10 | 58 | 49 | 74 |
| **Leicester City** | 46 | 19 | 16 | 11 | 72 | 59 | 73 |
| Tranmere Rovers | 46 | 21 | 9 | 16 | 69 | 53 | 72 |
| Derby County | 46 | 20 | 11 | 15 | 73 | 68 | 71 |
| Notts County | 46 | 20 | 8 | 18 | 65 | 69 | 68 |
| Wolverhampton Wanderers | 46 | 17 | 17 | 12 | 60 | 47 | 68 |
| Middlesbrough | 46 | 18 | 13 | 15 | 66 | 54 | 67 |
| Stoke City | 46 | 18 | 13 | 15 | 57 | 59 | 67 |
| Charlton Athletic | 46 | 19 | 8 | 19 | 61 | 58 | 65 |
| Sunderland | 46 | 19 | 8 | 19 | 54 | 57 | 65 |
| Bristol City | 46 | 16 | 16 | 14 | 47 | 50 | 64 |
| Bolton Wanderers | 46 | 15 | 14 | 17 | 63 | 64 | 59 |
| Southend United | 46 | 17 | 8 | 21 | 63 | 67 | 59 |
| Grimsby Town | 46 | 13 | 20 | 13 | 52 | 47 | 59 |
| Portsmouth | 46 | 15 | 13 | 18 | 52 | 58 | 58 |
| Barnsley | 46 | 16 | 7 | 23 | 55 | 67 | 55 |
| Watford | 46 | 15 | 9 | 22 | 66 | 80 | 54 |
| Luton Town | 46 | 14 | 11 | 21 | 56 | 60 | 53 |
| West Bromwich Albion | 46 | 13 | 12 | 21 | 60 | 69 | 51 |
| *Birmingham City* | *46* | *13* | *12* | *21* | *52* | *69* | *51* |
| *Oxford United* | *46* | *13* | *10* | *23* | *54* | *75* | *49* |
| *Peterborough United* | *46* | *8* | *13* | *25* | *48* | *76* | *37* |

### Division One Play-offs

| Derby County vs Millwall | 2-0, 3-1 |
|---|---|
| Tranmere Rovers vs Leicester City | 0-0, 1-2 |
| Leicester City vs Derby County | 2-1 |

## 1994 F.A. Cup

### Semi-finals

| Chelsea vs Luton Town | 2-0 |
|---|---|
| Manchester United vs Oldham Athletic | 1-1, 4-1 |

### Final

Wembley, 14th May 1994

**Manchester United 4** (Cantona 2 (2 pens), Hughes, McClair)

**Chelsea 0**

*Attendance 79,634*

## DIVISION TWO 1993-94

| **Reading** | 46 | 26 | 11 | 9 | 81 | 44 | 89 |
|---|---|---|---|---|---|---|---|
| **Port Vale** | 46 | 26 | 10 | 10 | 79 | 46 | 88 |
| Plymouth Argyle | 46 | 25 | 10 | 11 | 88 | 56 | 85 |
| Stockport County | 46 | 24 | 13 | 9 | 74 | 44 | 85 |
| York City | 46 | 21 | 12 | 13 | 64 | 40 | 75 |
| **Burnley** | 46 | 21 | 10 | 15 | 79 | 58 | 73 |
| Bradford City | 46 | 19 | 13 | 14 | 61 | 53 | 70 |
| Bristol Rovers | 46 | 20 | 10 | 16 | 60 | 59 | 70 |
| Hull City | 46 | 18 | 14 | 14 | 62 | 54 | 68 |
| Cambridge United | 46 | 19 | 9 | 18 | 79 | 73 | 66 |
| Huddersfield Town | 46 | 17 | 14 | 15 | 58 | 61 | 65 |
| Wrexham | 46 | 17 | 11 | 18 | 66 | 77 | 62 |
| Swansea City | 46 | 16 | 12 | 18 | 56 | 58 | 60 |
| Brighton & Hove Albion | 46 | 15 | 14 | 17 | 60 | 67 | 59 |
| Rotherham United | 46 | 15 | 13 | 18 | 63 | 60 | 58 |
| Brentford | 46 | 13 | 19 | 14 | 57 | 55 | 58 |
| Bournemouth | 46 | 14 | 15 | 17 | 51 | 59 | 57 |
| Leyton Orient | 46 | 14 | 14 | 18 | 57 | 71 | 56 |
| Cardiff City | 46 | 13 | 15 | 18 | 66 | 79 | 54 |
| Blackpool | 46 | 16 | 5 | 25 | 63 | 75 | 53 |
| *Fulham* | *46* | *14* | *10* | *22* | *50* | *63* | *52* |
| *Exeter City* | *46* | *11* | *12* | *23* | *52* | *83* | *45* |
| *Hartlepool United* | *46* | *9* | *9* | *28* | *41* | *87* | *36* |
| *Barnet* | *46* | *5* | *13* | *28* | *41* | *86* | *28* |

### Division Two Play-offs

| Burnley vs Plymouth Argyle | 0-0, 3-1 |
|---|---|
| York City vs Stockport County | 0-0, 0-1 |
| Burnley vs Stockport County | 2-1 |

## DIVISION THREE 1993-94

| **Shrewsbury Town** | 42 | 22 | 13 | 7 | 63 | 39 | 79 |
|---|---|---|---|---|---|---|---|
| **Chester City** | 42 | 21 | 11 | 10 | 69 | 46 | 74 |
| **Crewe Alexandra** | 42 | 21 | 10 | 11 | 80 | 61 | 73 |
| **Wycombe Wanderers** | 42 | 19 | 13 | 10 | 67 | 53 | 70 |
| Preston North End | 42 | 18 | 13 | 11 | 79 | 60 | 67 |
| Torquay United | 42 | 17 | 16 | 9 | 64 | 56 | 67 |
| Carlisle United | 42 | 18 | 10 | 14 | 57 | 42 | 64 |
| Chesterfield | 42 | 16 | 14 | 12 | 55 | 48 | 62 |
| Rochdale | 42 | 16 | 12 | 14 | 63 | 51 | 60 |
| Walsall | 42 | 17 | 9 | 16 | 48 | 53 | 60 |
| Scunthorpe United | 42 | 15 | 14 | 13 | 64 | 56 | 59 |
| Mansfield Town | 42 | 15 | 10 | 17 | 53 | 62 | 55 |
| Bury | 42 | 14 | 11 | 17 | 55 | 56 | 53 |
| Scarborough | 42 | 15 | 8 | 19 | 55 | 61 | 53 |
| Doncaster Rovers | 42 | 14 | 10 | 18 | 44 | 57 | 52 |
| Gillingham | 42 | 12 | 15 | 15 | 44 | 51 | 51 |
| Colchester United | 42 | 13 | 10 | 19 | 56 | 71 | 49 |
| Lincoln City | 42 | 12 | 11 | 19 | 52 | 63 | 47 |
| Wigan Athletic | 42 | 11 | 12 | 19 | 51 | 70 | 45 |
| Hereford United | 42 | 12 | 6 | 24 | 60 | 79 | 42 |
| Darlington | 42 | 10 | 11 | 21 | 42 | 64 | 41 |
| Northampton Town | 42 | 9 | 11 | 22 | 44 | 66 | 38 |

### Division Three Play-offs

| Carlisle United vs Wycombe Wanderers | 0-2, 1-2 |
|---|---|
| Torquay United vs Preston North End | 2-0, 1-4 |
| Wycombe Wanderers vs Preston North End | 4-2 |

## 1994 Football League Cup

### Semi-finals

| Manchester Utd. vs Sheffield Wednesday (1-0, 4-1) | 5-1 |
|---|---|
| Tranmere Rovers vs Aston Villa (3-1, 1-3) | 4-4 |

Aston Villa won 5-4 on penalties

### Final

Wembley, 27th March 1994

**Aston Villa 3** (Atkinson, Saunders 2 (1 pen))

**Manchester United 1** (Hughes)

*Attendance 77,231*

## F.A. PREMIER LEAGUE 1994-95

| | | | | | | | |
|---|---|---|---|---|---|---|---|
| **BLACKBURN ROVERS** | 42 | 27 | 8 | 7 | 80 | 39 | 89 |
| Manchester United | 42 | 26 | 10 | 6 | 77 | 28 | 88 |
| Nottingham Forest | 42 | 22 | 11 | 9 | 72 | 43 | 77 |
| Liverpool | 42 | 21 | 11 | 10 | 65 | 37 | 74 |
| Leeds United | 42 | 20 | 13 | 9 | 59 | 38 | 73 |
| Newcastle United | 42 | 20 | 12 | 10 | 67 | 47 | 72 |
| Tottenham Hotspur | 42 | 16 | 14 | 12 | 66 | 58 | 62 |
| Queen's Park Rangers | 42 | 17 | 9 | 16 | 61 | 59 | 60 |
| Wimbledon | 42 | 15 | 11 | 16 | 48 | 65 | 56 |
| Southampton | 42 | 12 | 18 | 12 | 61 | 63 | 54 |
| Chelsea | 42 | 13 | 15 | 14 | 50 | 55 | 54 |
| Arsenal | 42 | 13 | 12 | 17 | 52 | 49 | 51 |
| Sheffield Wednesday | 42 | 13 | 12 | 17 | 49 | 57 | 51 |
| West Ham United | 42 | 13 | 11 | 18 | 44 | 48 | 50 |
| Everton | 42 | 11 | 17 | 14 | 44 | 51 | 50 |
| Coventry City | 42 | 12 | 14 | 16 | 44 | 62 | 50 |
| Manchester City | 42 | 12 | 13 | 17 | 53 | 64 | 49 |
| Aston Villa | 42 | 11 | 15 | 16 | 51 | 56 | 48 |
| *Crystal Palace* | *42* | *11* | *12* | *19* | *34* | *49* | *45* |
| *Norwich City* | *42* | *10* | *13* | *19* | *37* | *54* | *43* |
| *Leicester City* | *42* | *6* | *11* | *25* | *45* | *80* | *29* |
| *Ipswich Town* | *42* | *7* | *6* | *29* | *36* | *93* | *27* |

## DIVISION ONE 1994-95

| | | | | | | | |
|---|---|---|---|---|---|---|---|
| Middlesbrough | 46 | 23 | 13 | 10 | 67 | 40 | 82 |
| Reading | 46 | 23 | 10 | 13 | 58 | 44 | 79 |
| **Bolton Wanderers** | 46 | 21 | 14 | 11 | 67 | 45 | 77 |
| Wolverhampton Wanderers | 46 | 21 | 13 | 12 | 77 | 61 | 76 |
| Tranmere Rovers | 46 | 22 | 10 | 14 | 67 | 58 | 76 |
| Barnsley | 46 | 20 | 12 | 14 | 63 | 52 | 72 |
| Watford | 46 | 19 | 13 | 14 | 52 | 46 | 70 |
| Sheffield United | 46 | 17 | 17 | 12 | 74 | 55 | 68 |
| Derby County | 46 | 18 | 12 | 16 | 66 | 51 | 66 |
| Grimsby Town | 46 | 17 | 14 | 15 | 62 | 56 | 65 |
| Stoke City | 46 | 16 | 15 | 15 | 50 | 53 | 63 |
| Millwall | 46 | 16 | 14 | 16 | 60 | 60 | 62 |
| Southend United | 46 | 18 | 8 | 20 | 54 | 73 | 62 |
| Oldham Athletic | 46 | 16 | 13 | 17 | 60 | 60 | 61 |
| Charlton Athletic | 46 | 16 | 11 | 19 | 58 | 66 | 59 |
| Luton Town | 46 | 15 | 13 | 18 | 61 | 64 | 58 |
| Port Vale | 46 | 15 | 13 | 18 | 58 | 64 | 58 |
| Portsmouth | 46 | 15 | 13 | 18 | 53 | 63 | 58 |
| West Bromwich Albion | 46 | 16 | 10 | 20 | 51 | 57 | 58 |
| Sunderland | 46 | 12 | 18 | 16 | 41 | 45 | 54 |
| *Swindon Town* | *46* | *12* | *12* | *22* | *54* | *73* | *48* |
| *Burnley* | *46* | *11* | *13* | *22* | *49* | *74* | *46* |
| *Bristol City* | *46* | *11* | *12* | *23* | *42* | *63* | *45* |
| *Notts County* | *46* | *9* | *13* | *24* | *45* | *66* | *40* |

### Division One Play-offs

| | |
|---|---|
| Tranmere Rovers vs Reading | 1-3, 0-0 |
| Wolverhampton Wanderers vs Bolton Wanderers | 2-1, 0-2 |
| Bolton Wanderers vs Reading | 4-3 |

## 1995 F.A. Cup

**Semi-finals**

| | |
|---|---|
| Crystal Palace vs Manchester United | 2-2, 0-2 |
| Everton vs Tottenham Hotspur | 4-1 |

**Final**

Wembley, 20th May 1995

**Everton 1**  (Rideout)
**Manchester United 0**

*Attendance 79,592*

## DIVISION TWO 1994-95

| | | | | | | | |
|---|---|---|---|---|---|---|---|
| **Birmingham City** | 46 | 25 | 14 | 7 | 84 | 37 | 89 |
| Brentford | 46 | 25 | 10 | 11 | 81 | 39 | 85 |
| Crewe Alexandra | 46 | 25 | 8 | 13 | 80 | 68 | 84 |
| Bristol Rovers | 46 | 22 | 16 | 8 | 70 | 40 | 82 |
| **Huddersfield Town** | 46 | 22 | 15 | 9 | 79 | 49 | 81 |
| Wycombe Wanderers | 46 | 21 | 15 | 10 | 60 | 46 | 78 |
| Oxford United | 46 | 21 | 12 | 13 | 66 | 52 | 75 |
| Hull City | 46 | 21 | 11 | 14 | 70 | 57 | 74 |
| York City | 46 | 21 | 9 | 16 | 67 | 51 | 72 |
| Swansea City | 46 | 19 | 14 | 13 | 57 | 45 | 71 |
| Stockport County | 46 | 19 | 8 | 19 | 63 | 60 | 65 |
| Blackpool | 46 | 18 | 10 | 18 | 64 | 70 | 64 |
| Wrexham | 46 | 16 | 15 | 15 | 65 | 64 | 63 |
| Bradford City | 46 | 16 | 12 | 18 | 57 | 64 | 60 |
| Peterborough United | 46 | 14 | 18 | 14 | 54 | 69 | 60 |
| Brighton & Hove Albion | 46 | 14 | 17 | 15 | 54 | 53 | 59 |
| Rotherham United | 46 | 14 | 14 | 18 | 57 | 61 | 56 |
| Shrewsbury Town | 46 | 13 | 14 | 19 | 54 | 62 | 53 |
| Bournemouth | 46 | 13 | 11 | 22 | 49 | 69 | 50 |
| *Cambridge United* | *46* | *11* | *15* | *20* | *52* | *69* | *48* |
| *Plymouth Argyle* | *46* | *12* | *10* | *24* | *45* | *83* | *46* |
| *Cardiff City* | *46* | *9* | *11* | *26* | *46* | *74* | *38* |
| *Chester City* | *46* | *6* | *11* | *29* | *37* | *84* | *29* |
| *Leyton Orient* | *46* | *6* | *8* | *32* | *30* | *75* | *26* |

### Division Two Play-offs

| | |
|---|---|
| Bristol Rovers vs Crewe Alexandra | 0-0, 1-1 |
| *Bristol Rovers won on away goals* | |
| Huddersfield Town vs Brentford | 1-1, 1-1 |
| *Huddersfield Town won 4-3 on penalties* | |
| Huddersfield Town vs Bristol Rovers | 2-1 |

## DIVISION THREE 1994-95

| | | | | | | | |
|---|---|---|---|---|---|---|---|
| **Carlisle United** | 42 | 27 | 10 | 5 | 67 | 31 | 91 |
| **Walsall** | 42 | 24 | 11 | 7 | 75 | 40 | 83 |
| **Chesterfield** | 42 | 23 | 12 | 7 | 62 | 37 | 81 |
| Bury | 42 | 23 | 11 | 8 | 73 | 36 | 80 |
| Preston North End | 42 | 19 | 10 | 13 | 58 | 41 | 67 |
| Mansfield Town | 42 | 18 | 11 | 13 | 84 | 59 | 65 |
| Scunthorpe United | 42 | 18 | 8 | 16 | 68 | 63 | 62 |
| Fulham | 42 | 16 | 14 | 12 | 60 | 54 | 62 |
| Doncaster Rovers | 42 | 17 | 10 | 15 | 58 | 43 | 61 |
| Colchester United | 42 | 16 | 10 | 16 | 56 | 64 | 58 |
| Barnet | 42 | 15 | 11 | 16 | 56 | 63 | 56 |
| Lincoln City | 42 | 15 | 11 | 16 | 54 | 55 | 56 |
| Torquay United | 42 | 14 | 13 | 15 | 54 | 57 | 55 |
| Wigan Athletic | 42 | 14 | 10 | 18 | 53 | 60 | 52 |
| Rochdale | 42 | 12 | 14 | 16 | 44 | 67 | 50 |
| Hereford United | 42 | 12 | 13 | 17 | 45 | 62 | 49 |
| Northampton Town | 42 | 10 | 14 | 18 | 45 | 67 | 44 |
| Hartlepool United | 42 | 11 | 10 | 21 | 43 | 69 | 43 |
| Gillingham | 42 | 10 | 11 | 21 | 46 | 64 | 41 |
| Darlington | 42 | 11 | 8 | 23 | 43 | 57 | 41 |
| Scarborough | 42 | 8 | 10 | 24 | 49 | 70 | 34 |
| Exeter City | 42 | 8 | 10 | 24 | 36 | 70 | 34 |

### Division Three Play-offs

| | |
|---|---|
| Mansfield Town vs Chesterfield | 1-1, 2-5 |
| Preston North End vs Bury | 0-1, 0-1 |
| Chesterfield vs Bury | 2-0 |

## 1995 Football League Cup

**Semi-finals**

| | |
|---|---|
| Liverpool vs Crystal Palace  (1-0, 1-0) | 2-0 |
| Swindon Town vs Bolton Wanderers  (2-1, 1-3) | 3-4 |

**Final**

Wembley, 2nd April 1995

**Liverpool 2**  (McManaman 2)
**Bolton Wanderers 1**  (Thompson)

*Attendance 75,595*

## F.A. PREMIER LEAGUE 1995-96

| | | | | | | | |
|---|---|---|---|---|---|---|---|
| **MANCHESTER UNITED** | 38 | 25 | 7 | 6 | 73 | 35 | 82 |
| Newcastle United | 38 | 24 | 6 | 8 | 66 | 37 | 78 |
| Liverpool | 38 | 20 | 11 | 7 | 70 | 34 | 71 |
| Aston Villa | 38 | 18 | 9 | 11 | 52 | 35 | 63 |
| Arsenal | 38 | 17 | 12 | 9 | 49 | 32 | 63 |
| Everton | 38 | 17 | 10 | 11 | 64 | 44 | 61 |
| Blackburn Rovers | 38 | 18 | 7 | 13 | 61 | 47 | 61 |
| Tottenham Hotspur | 38 | 16 | 13 | 9 | 50 | 38 | 61 |
| Nottingham Forest | 38 | 15 | 13 | 10 | 50 | 54 | 58 |
| West Ham United | 38 | 14 | 9 | 15 | 43 | 52 | 51 |
| Chelsea | 38 | 12 | 14 | 12 | 46 | 44 | 50 |
| Middlesbrough | 38 | 11 | 10 | 17 | 35 | 50 | 43 |
| Leeds United | 38 | 12 | 7 | 19 | 40 | 57 | 43 |
| Wimbledon | 38 | 10 | 11 | 17 | 55 | 70 | 41 |
| Sheffield Wednesday | 38 | 10 | 10 | 18 | 48 | 61 | 40 |
| Coventry City | 38 | 8 | 14 | 16 | 42 | 60 | 38 |
| Southampton | 38 | 9 | 11 | 18 | 34 | 52 | 38 |
| *Manchester City* | 38 | 9 | 11 | 18 | 33 | 58 | 38 |
| *Queen's Park Rangers* | 38 | 9 | 6 | 23 | 38 | 57 | 33 |
| *Bolton Wanderers* | 38 | 8 | 5 | 25 | 39 | 71 | 29 |

## DIVISION ONE 1995-96

| | | | | | | | |
|---|---|---|---|---|---|---|---|
| **Sunderland** | 46 | 22 | 17 | 7 | 59 | 33 | 83 |
| **Derby County** | 46 | 21 | 16 | 9 | 71 | 51 | 79 |
| Crystal Palace | 46 | 20 | 15 | 11 | 67 | 48 | 75 |
| Stoke City | 46 | 20 | 13 | 13 | 60 | 49 | 73 |
| **Leicester City** | 46 | 19 | 14 | 13 | 66 | 60 | 71 |
| Charlton Athletic | 46 | 17 | 20 | 9 | 57 | 45 | 71 |
| Ipswich Town | 46 | 19 | 12 | 15 | 79 | 69 | 69 |
| Huddersfield Town | 46 | 17 | 12 | 17 | 61 | 58 | 63 |
| Sheffield United | 46 | 16 | 14 | 16 | 57 | 54 | 62 |
| Barnsley | 46 | 14 | 18 | 14 | 60 | 66 | 60 |
| West Bromwich Albion | 46 | 16 | 12 | 18 | 60 | 68 | 60 |
| Port Vale | 46 | 15 | 15 | 16 | 59 | 66 | 60 |
| Tranmere Rovers | 46 | 14 | 17 | 15 | 64 | 60 | 59 |
| Southend United | 46 | 15 | 14 | 17 | 52 | 61 | 59 |
| Birmingham City | 46 | 15 | 13 | 18 | 61 | 64 | 58 |
| Norwich City | 46 | 14 | 15 | 17 | 59 | 55 | 57 |
| Grimsby Town | 46 | 14 | 14 | 18 | 55 | 69 | 56 |
| Oldham Athletic | 46 | 14 | 14 | 18 | 54 | 50 | 56 |
| Reading | 46 | 13 | 17 | 16 | 54 | 63 | 56 |
| Wolverhampton Wanderers | 46 | 13 | 16 | 17 | 56 | 62 | 55 |
| Portsmouth | 46 | 13 | 13 | 20 | 61 | 69 | 52 |
| *Millwall* | 46 | 13 | 13 | 20 | 43 | 63 | 52 |
| *Watford* | 46 | 10 | 18 | 18 | 62 | 70 | 48 |
| *Luton Town* | 46 | 11 | 12 | 23 | 40 | 64 | 45 |

### Division One Play-offs

| | |
|---|---|
| Charlton Athletic vs Crystal Palace | 1-2, 0-1 |
| Leicester City vs Stoke City | 0-0, 1-0 |
| Leicester City vs Crystal Palace | 2-1 |

## DIVISION TWO 1995-96

| | | | | | | | |
|---|---|---|---|---|---|---|---|
| **Swindon Town** | 46 | 25 | 17 | 4 | 71 | 34 | 92 |
| **Oxford United** | 46 | 24 | 11 | 11 | 76 | 39 | 83 |
| Blackpool | 46 | 23 | 13 | 10 | 67 | 40 | 82 |
| Notts County | 46 | 21 | 15 | 10 | 63 | 39 | 78 |
| Crewe Alexandra | 46 | 22 | 7 | 17 | 77 | 60 | 73 |
| **Bradford City** | 46 | 22 | 7 | 17 | 71 | 69 | 73 |
| Chesterfield | 46 | 20 | 12 | 14 | 56 | 51 | 72 |
| Wrexham | 46 | 18 | 16 | 12 | 76 | 55 | 70 |
| Stockport County | 46 | 19 | 13 | 14 | 61 | 47 | 70 |
| Bristol Rovers | 46 | 20 | 10 | 16 | 57 | 60 | 70 |
| Walsall | 46 | 19 | 12 | 15 | 60 | 45 | 69 |
| Wycombe Wanderers | 46 | 15 | 15 | 16 | 63 | 59 | 60 |
| Bristol City | 46 | 15 | 15 | 16 | 55 | 60 | 60 |
| Bournemouth | 46 | 16 | 10 | 20 | 51 | 70 | 58 |
| Brentford | 46 | 15 | 13 | 18 | 43 | 49 | 58 |
| Rotherham United | 46 | 14 | 14 | 18 | 54 | 62 | 56 |
| Burnley | 46 | 14 | 13 | 19 | 56 | 68 | 55 |
| Shrewsbury Town | 46 | 13 | 14 | 19 | 58 | 70 | 53 |
| Peterborough United | 46 | 13 | 13 | 20 | 59 | 66 | 52 |
| York City | 46 | 13 | 13 | 20 | 58 | 73 | 52 |
| *Carlisle United* | 46 | 12 | 13 | 21 | 57 | 72 | 49 |
| *Swansea City* | 46 | 11 | 14 | 21 | 43 | 79 | 47 |
| *Brighton & Hove Albion* | 46 | 10 | 10 | 26 | 46 | 69 | 40 |
| *Hull City* | 46 | 5 | 16 | 25 | 36 | 78 | 31 |

### Division Two Play-offs

| | |
|---|---|
| Bradford City vs Blackpool | 0-2, 3-0 |
| Crewe Alexandra vs Notts County | 2-2, 0-1 |
| Bradford City vs Notts County | 2-0 |

## DIVISION THREE 1995-96

| | | | | | | | |
|---|---|---|---|---|---|---|---|
| **Preston North End** | 46 | 23 | 17 | 6 | 78 | 38 | 86 |
| **Gillingham** | 46 | 22 | 17 | 7 | 49 | 20 | 83 |
| **Bury** | 46 | 22 | 13 | 11 | 66 | 48 | 79 |
| **Plymouth Argyle** | 46 | 22 | 12 | 12 | 68 | 49 | 78 |
| Darlington | 46 | 20 | 18 | 8 | 60 | 42 | 78 |
| Hereford United | 46 | 20 | 14 | 12 | 65 | 47 | 74 |
| Colchester United | 46 | 18 | 18 | 10 | 61 | 51 | 72 |
| Chester City | 46 | 18 | 16 | 12 | 72 | 53 | 70 |
| Barnet | 46 | 18 | 16 | 12 | 65 | 45 | 70 |
| Wigan Athletic | 46 | 20 | 10 | 16 | 62 | 56 | 70 |
| Northampton Town | 46 | 18 | 13 | 15 | 51 | 44 | 67 |
| Scunthorpe United | 46 | 15 | 15 | 16 | 67 | 61 | 60 |
| Doncaster Rovers | 46 | 16 | 11 | 19 | 49 | 60 | 59 |
| Exeter City | 46 | 13 | 18 | 15 | 46 | 53 | 57 |
| Rochdale | 46 | 14 | 13 | 19 | 57 | 61 | 55 |
| Cambridge United | 46 | 14 | 12 | 20 | 61 | 71 | 54 |
| Fulham | 46 | 12 | 17 | 17 | 57 | 63 | 53 |
| Lincoln City | 46 | 13 | 14 | 19 | 57 | 73 | 53 |
| Mansfield Town | 46 | 11 | 20 | 15 | 54 | 64 | 53 |
| Hartlepool United | 46 | 12 | 13 | 21 | 47 | 67 | 49 |
| Leyton Orient | 46 | 12 | 11 | 23 | 44 | 63 | 47 |
| Cardiff City | 46 | 11 | 12 | 23 | 41 | 64 | 45 |
| Scarborough | 46 | 8 | 16 | 22 | 39 | 69 | 40 |
| Torquay United | 46 | 5 | 14 | 27 | 30 | 84 | 29 |

### Division Three Play-offs

| | |
|---|---|
| Colchester United vs Plymouth Argyle | 1-0, 1-3 |
| Hereford United vs Darlington | 1-2, 1-2 |
| Plymouth Argyle vs Darlington | 1-0 |

## 1996 F.A. Cup

### Semi-finals

| | |
|---|---|
| Chelsea vs Manchester United | 1-2 |
| Aston Villa vs Liverpool | 0-3 |

### Final

Wembley, 11th May 1996

**Manchester United 1** (Cantona)
**Liverpool 0**

*Attendance 79,007*

## 1996 Football League Cup

### Semi-finals

| | |
|---|---|
| Birmingham City vs Leeds United (1-2, 0-3) | 1-5 |
| Arsenal vs Aston Villa (2-2, 0-0) | 2-2 |
| Aston Villa won on the away goals rule | |

### Final

Wembley, 24th March 1996

**Aston Villa 3** (Milosevic, Taylor, Yorke)
**Leeds United 0**

*Attendance 77,056*

## F.A. PREMIER LEAGUE 1996-97

| | | | | | | | |
|---|---|---|---|---|---|---|---|
| **MANCHESTER UNITED** | 38 | 21 | 12 | 5 | 76 | 44 | 75 |
| Newcastle United | 38 | 19 | 11 | 8 | 73 | 40 | 68 |
| Arsenal | 38 | 19 | 11 | 8 | 62 | 32 | 68 |
| Liverpool | 38 | 19 | 11 | 8 | 62 | 37 | 68 |
| Aston Villa | 38 | 17 | 10 | 11 | 47 | 34 | 61 |
| Chelsea | 38 | 16 | 11 | 11 | 58 | 55 | 59 |
| Sheffield Wednesday | 38 | 14 | 15 | 9 | 50 | 51 | 57 |
| Wimbledon | 38 | 15 | 11 | 12 | 49 | 46 | 56 |
| Leicester City | 38 | 12 | 11 | 15 | 46 | 54 | 47 |
| Tottenham Hotspur | 38 | 13 | 7 | 18 | 44 | 51 | 46 |
| Leeds United | 38 | 11 | 13 | 14 | 28 | 38 | 46 |
| Derby County | 38 | 11 | 13 | 14 | 45 | 58 | 46 |
| Blackburn Rovers | 38 | 9 | 15 | 14 | 42 | 43 | 42 |
| West Ham United | 38 | 10 | 12 | 16 | 39 | 48 | 42 |
| Everton | 38 | 10 | 12 | 16 | 44 | 57 | 42 |
| Southampton | 38 | 10 | 11 | 17 | 50 | 56 | 41 |
| Coventry City | 38 | 9 | 14 | 15 | 38 | 54 | 41 |
| *Sunderland* | 38 | 10 | 10 | 18 | 35 | 53 | 40 |
| *Middlesbrough* | 38 | 10 | 12 | 16 | 51 | 60 | 39 |
| *Nottingham Forest* | 38 | 6 | 16 | 16 | 31 | 59 | 34 |

Middlesbrough had 3 points deducted

## DIVISION ONE 1996-97

| | | | | | | | |
|---|---|---|---|---|---|---|---|
| **Bolton Wanderers** | 46 | 28 | 14 | 4 | 100 | 53 | 98 |
| **Barnsley** | 46 | 22 | 14 | 10 | 76 | 55 | 80 |
| Wolverhampton Wanderers | 46 | 22 | 10 | 14 | 68 | 51 | 76 |
| Ipswich Town | 46 | 20 | 14 | 12 | 68 | 50 | 74 |
| Sheffield United | 46 | 20 | 13 | 13 | 75 | 52 | 73 |
| **Crystal Palace** | 46 | 19 | 14 | 13 | 78 | 48 | 71 |
| Portsmouth | 46 | 20 | 8 | 18 | 59 | 53 | 68 |
| Port Vale | 46 | 17 | 16 | 13 | 58 | 55 | 67 |
| Queen's Park Rangers | 46 | 18 | 12 | 16 | 64 | 60 | 66 |
| Birmingham City | 46 | 17 | 15 | 14 | 52 | 48 | 66 |
| Tranmere Rovers | 46 | 17 | 14 | 15 | 63 | 56 | 65 |
| Stoke City | 46 | 18 | 10 | 18 | 51 | 57 | 64 |
| Norwich City | 46 | 17 | 12 | 17 | 63 | 68 | 63 |
| Manchester City | 46 | 17 | 10 | 19 | 59 | 60 | 61 |
| Charlton Athletic | 46 | 16 | 11 | 19 | 52 | 66 | 59 |
| West Bromwich Albion | 46 | 14 | 15 | 17 | 68 | 72 | 57 |
| Oxford United | 46 | 16 | 9 | 21 | 64 | 68 | 57 |
| Reading | 46 | 15 | 12 | 19 | 58 | 67 | 57 |
| Swindon Town | 46 | 15 | 9 | 22 | 52 | 71 | 54 |
| Huddersfield Town | 46 | 13 | 15 | 18 | 48 | 61 | 54 |
| Bradford City | 46 | 12 | 12 | 22 | 47 | 72 | 48 |
| *Grimsby Town* | 46 | 11 | 13 | 22 | 60 | 81 | 46 |
| *Oldham Athletic* | 46 | 10 | 13 | 23 | 51 | 66 | 43 |
| *Southend United* | 46 | 8 | 15 | 23 | 42 | 86 | 39 |

### Division One Play-offs

| | |
|---|---|
| Crystal Palace vs Wolverhampton Wanderers | 3-1, 1-2 |
| Sheffield United vs Ipswich Town | 1-1, 2-2 |
| *Sheffield United won on away goals* | |
| Crystal Palace vs Sheffield United | 1-0 |

## 1997 F.A. Cup

### Semi-finals

| | |
|---|---|
| Middlesbrough vs Chesterfield | 3-3, 3-0 |
| Wimbledon vs Chelsea | 0-3 |

### Final

Wembley, 17th May 1997

**Chelsea 2** (Di Matteo, Newton)

**Middlesbrough 0**

*Attendance 79,160*

## 1997 Football League Cup

### Semi-finals

| | |
|---|---|
| Leicester City vs Wimbledon (0-0, 1-1) | 1-1 |
| *Leicester City won on the away goals rule* | |
| Stockport County vs Middlesbrough (0-2, 1-0) | 1-2 |

## DIVISION TWO 1996-97

| | | | | | | | |
|---|---|---|---|---|---|---|---|
| **Bury** | 46 | 24 | 12 | 10 | 62 | 38 | 84 |
| **Stockport County** | 46 | 23 | 13 | 10 | 59 | 41 | 82 |
| Luton Town | 46 | 21 | 15 | 10 | 71 | 45 | 78 |
| Brentford | 46 | 20 | 14 | 12 | 56 | 43 | 74 |
| Bristol City | 46 | 21 | 10 | 15 | 69 | 51 | 73 |
| **Crewe Alexandra** | 46 | 22 | 7 | 17 | 56 | 47 | 73 |
| Blackpool | 46 | 18 | 15 | 13 | 60 | 47 | 69 |
| Wrexham | 46 | 17 | 18 | 11 | 54 | 50 | 69 |
| Burnley | 46 | 19 | 11 | 16 | 71 | 55 | 68 |
| Chesterfield | 46 | 18 | 14 | 14 | 42 | 39 | 68 |
| Gillingham | 46 | 19 | 10 | 17 | 60 | 59 | 67 |
| Walsall | 46 | 19 | 10 | 17 | 54 | 53 | 67 |
| Watford | 46 | 16 | 19 | 11 | 45 | 38 | 67 |
| Millwall | 46 | 16 | 13 | 17 | 50 | 55 | 61 |
| Preston North End | 46 | 18 | 7 | 21 | 49 | 55 | 61 |
| Bournemouth | 46 | 15 | 15 | 16 | 43 | 45 | 60 |
| Bristol Rovers | 46 | 15 | 11 | 20 | 47 | 50 | 56 |
| Wycombe Wanderers | 46 | 15 | 15 | 16 | 51 | 56 | 55 |
| Plymouth Argyle | 46 | 12 | 18 | 16 | 47 | 58 | 54 |
| York City | 46 | 13 | 13 | 20 | 47 | 68 | 52 |
| *Peterborough United* | 46 | 11 | 14 | 21 | 55 | 73 | 47 |
| *Shrewsbury Town* | 46 | 11 | 13 | 22 | 49 | 74 | 46 |
| *Rotherham United* | 46 | 7 | 14 | 25 | 39 | 70 | 35 |
| *Notts County* | 46 | 7 | 14 | 25 | 33 | 59 | 35 |

### Division Two Play-offs

| | |
|---|---|
| Bristol City vs Brentford | 1-2, 1-2 |
| Crewe Alexandra vs Luton Town | 2-1, 2-2 |
| Crewe Alexandra vs Brentford | 1-0 |

## DIVISION THREE 1996-97

| | | | | | | | |
|---|---|---|---|---|---|---|---|
| **Wigan Athletic** | 46 | 26 | 9 | 11 | 84 | 51 | 87 |
| **Fulham** | 46 | 25 | 12 | 9 | 72 | 38 | 87 |
| **Carlisle United** | 46 | 24 | 12 | 10 | 67 | 44 | 84 |
| **Northampton Town** | 46 | 20 | 12 | 14 | 67 | 44 | 72 |
| Swansea City | 46 | 21 | 8 | 17 | 62 | 58 | 71 |
| Chester City | 46 | 18 | 16 | 12 | 55 | 43 | 70 |
| Cardiff City | 46 | 20 | 9 | 17 | 56 | 54 | 69 |
| Colchester United | 46 | 17 | 17 | 12 | 62 | 51 | 68 |
| Lincoln City | 46 | 18 | 12 | 16 | 70 | 69 | 66 |
| Cambridge United | 46 | 18 | 11 | 17 | 53 | 59 | 65 |
| Mansfield Town | 46 | 16 | 16 | 14 | 47 | 45 | 64 |
| Scarborough | 46 | 16 | 15 | 15 | 65 | 68 | 63 |
| Scunthorpe United | 46 | 18 | 9 | 19 | 59 | 62 | 63 |
| Rochdale | 46 | 14 | 16 | 16 | 58 | 58 | 58 |
| Barnet | 46 | 14 | 16 | 16 | 46 | 51 | 58 |
| Leyton Orient | 46 | 15 | 12 | 19 | 50 | 58 | 57 |
| Hull City | 46 | 13 | 18 | 15 | 44 | 50 | 57 |
| Darlington | 46 | 14 | 10 | 22 | 64 | 78 | 52 |
| Doncaster Rovers | 46 | 14 | 10 | 22 | 52 | 66 | 52 |
| Hartlepool United | 46 | 14 | 9 | 23 | 53 | 66 | 51 |
| Torquay United | 46 | 13 | 11 | 22 | 46 | 62 | 50 |
| Exeter City | 46 | 12 | 12 | 22 | 48 | 73 | 48 |
| Brighton & Hove Albion | 46 | 13 | 10 | 23 | 53 | 70 | 47 |
| *Hereford United* | 46 | 11 | 14 | 21 | 50 | 65 | 47 |

Brighton & Hove Albion had two points deducted

### Division Three Play-offs

| | |
|---|---|
| Cardiff City vs Northampton Town | 0-1, 2-3 |
| Chester City vs Swansea City | 0-0, 0-3 |
| Northampton Town vs Swansea City | 1-0 |

### Final

Wembley, 6th April 1997

**Leicester City 1** (Heskey)

**Middlesbrough 1 (aet.)** (Ravanelli)

*Attendance 76,757*

### Replay

Hillsborough, 16th April 1997

**Leicester City 1** (Claridge)

**Middlesbrough 0**

*Attendance 39,428*

## F.A. PREMIER LEAGUE 1997-98

| | | | | | | | |
|---|---|---|---|---|---|---|---|
| **ARSENAL** | 38 | 23 | 9 | 6 | 68 | 33 | 78 |
| Manchester United | 38 | 23 | 8 | 7 | 73 | 26 | 77 |
| Liverpool | 38 | 18 | 11 | 9 | 68 | 42 | 65 |
| Chelsea | 38 | 20 | 3 | 15 | 71 | 43 | 63 |
| Leeds United | 38 | 17 | 8 | 13 | 57 | 46 | 59 |
| Blackburn Rovers | 38 | 16 | 10 | 12 | 57 | 52 | 58 |
| Aston Villa | 38 | 17 | 6 | 15 | 49 | 48 | 57 |
| West Ham United | 38 | 16 | 8 | 14 | 56 | 57 | 56 |
| Derby County | 38 | 16 | 7 | 15 | 52 | 49 | 55 |
| Leicester City | 38 | 13 | 14 | 11 | 51 | 41 | 53 |
| Coventry City | 38 | 12 | 16 | 10 | 46 | 44 | 52 |
| Southampton | 38 | 14 | 6 | 18 | 50 | 55 | 48 |
| Newcastle United | 38 | 11 | 11 | 16 | 35 | 44 | 44 |
| Tottenham Hotspur | 38 | 11 | 11 | 16 | 44 | 56 | 44 |
| Wimbledon | 38 | 10 | 14 | 14 | 34 | 46 | 44 |
| Sheffield Wednesday | 38 | 12 | 8 | 18 | 52 | 67 | 44 |
| Everton | 38 | 9 | 13 | 16 | 41 | 56 | 40 |
| *Bolton Wanderers* | *38* | *9* | *13* | *16* | *41* | *61* | *40* |
| *Barnsley* | *38* | *10* | *5* | *23* | *37* | *82* | *35* |
| *Crystal Palace* | *38* | *8* | *9* | *21* | *37* | *71* | *33* |

## DIVISION ONE 1997-98

| | | | | | | | |
|---|---|---|---|---|---|---|---|
| **Nottingham Forest** | 46 | 28 | 10 | 8 | 82 | 42 | 94 |
| **Middlesbrough** | 46 | 27 | 10 | 9 | 77 | 41 | 91 |
| Sunderland | 46 | 26 | 12 | 8 | 86 | 50 | 90 |
| **Charlton Athletic** | 46 | 26 | 10 | 10 | 80 | 49 | 88 |
| Ipswich Town | 46 | 23 | 14 | 9 | 77 | 43 | 83 |
| Sheffield United | 46 | 19 | 17 | 10 | 69 | 54 | 74 |
| Birmingham City | 46 | 19 | 17 | 10 | 60 | 35 | 74 |
| Stockport County | 46 | 19 | 8 | 19 | 71 | 69 | 65 |
| Wolverhampton Wanderers | 46 | 18 | 11 | 17 | 57 | 53 | 65 |
| West Bromwich Albion | 46 | 16 | 13 | 17 | 50 | 56 | 61 |
| Crewe Alexandra | 46 | 18 | 5 | 23 | 58 | 65 | 59 |
| Oxford United | 46 | 16 | 10 | 20 | 60 | 64 | 58 |
| Bradford City | 46 | 14 | 15 | 17 | 46 | 59 | 57 |
| Tranmere Rovers | 46 | 14 | 14 | 18 | 54 | 57 | 56 |
| Norwich City | 46 | 14 | 13 | 19 | 52 | 69 | 55 |
| Huddersfield Town | 46 | 14 | 11 | 21 | 50 | 72 | 53 |
| Bury | 46 | 11 | 19 | 16 | 42 | 58 | 52 |
| Swindon Town | 46 | 14 | 10 | 22 | 42 | 73 | 52 |
| Port Vale | 46 | 13 | 10 | 23 | 56 | 66 | 49 |
| Portsmouth | 46 | 13 | 10 | 23 | 51 | 63 | 49 |
| Queen's Park Rangers | 46 | 10 | 19 | 17 | 51 | 63 | 49 |
| *Manchester City* | *46* | *12* | *12* | *22* | *56* | *57* | *48* |
| *Stoke City* | *46* | *11* | *13* | *22* | *44* | *74* | *46* |
| *Reading* | *46* | *11* | *9* | *26* | *39* | *78* | *42* |

### Division One Play-offs

| | |
|---|---|
| Ipswich Town vs Charlton Athletic | 0-1, 0-1 |
| Sheffield United vs Sunderland | 2-1, 0-2 |
| Charlton Athletic vs Sunderland | 4-4 |
| *Charlton Athletic won 7-6 on penalties* | |

## 1998 F.A. Cup

### Semi-finals

| | |
|---|---|
| Sheffield United vs Newcastle United | 0-1 |
| Wolverhampton Wanderers vs Arsenal | 0-1 |

### Final

Wembley, 16th May 1998

**Arsenal 2** (Overmars, Anelka)
**Newcastle United 0**

*Attendance 79,183*

## DIVISION TWO 1997-98

| | | | | | | | |
|---|---|---|---|---|---|---|---|
| **Watford** | 46 | 24 | 16 | 6 | 67 | 41 | 88 |
| **Bristol City** | 46 | 25 | 10 | 11 | 69 | 39 | 85 |
| **Grimsby Town** | 46 | 19 | 15 | 12 | 55 | 37 | 72 |
| Northampton Town | 46 | 18 | 17 | 11 | 52 | 37 | 71 |
| Bristol Rovers | 46 | 20 | 10 | 16 | 70 | 64 | 70 |
| Fulham | 46 | 20 | 10 | 16 | 60 | 43 | 70 |
| Wrexham | 46 | 18 | 16 | 12 | 55 | 51 | 70 |
| Gillingham | 46 | 19 | 13 | 14 | 52 | 47 | 70 |
| Bournemouth | 46 | 18 | 12 | 16 | 57 | 52 | 66 |
| Chesterfield | 46 | 16 | 17 | 13 | 46 | 44 | 65 |
| Wigan Athletic | 46 | 17 | 11 | 18 | 64 | 66 | 62 |
| Blackpool | 46 | 17 | 11 | 18 | 59 | 67 | 62 |
| Oldham Athletic | 46 | 15 | 16 | 15 | 62 | 54 | 61 |
| Wycombe Wanderers | 46 | 14 | 18 | 14 | 51 | 53 | 60 |
| Preston North End | 46 | 15 | 14 | 17 | 56 | 56 | 59 |
| York City | 46 | 14 | 17 | 15 | 52 | 58 | 59 |
| Luton Town | 46 | 14 | 15 | 17 | 60 | 64 | 57 |
| Millwall | 46 | 14 | 13 | 19 | 43 | 54 | 55 |
| Walsall | 46 | 14 | 12 | 20 | 43 | 52 | 54 |
| Burnley | 46 | 13 | 13 | 20 | 55 | 65 | 52 |
| *Brentford* | *46* | *11* | *17* | *18* | *50* | *71* | *50* |
| *Plymouth Argyle* | *46* | *12* | *13* | *21* | *55* | *70* | *49* |
| *Carlisle United* | *46* | *12* | *8* | *26* | *57* | *73* | *44* |
| *Southend United* | *46* | *11* | *10* | *25* | *47* | *79* | *43* |

### Division Two Play-offs

| | |
|---|---|
| Fulham vs Grimsby Town | 1-1, 0-1 |
| Bristol Rovers vs Northampton Town | 3-1, 0-3 |
| Grimsby Town vs Northampton Town | 1-0 |

## DIVISION THREE 1997-98

| | | | | | | | |
|---|---|---|---|---|---|---|---|
| **Notts County** | 46 | 29 | 12 | 5 | 82 | 43 | 99 |
| **Macclesfield Town** | 46 | 23 | 13 | 10 | 63 | 44 | 82 |
| **Lincoln City** | 46 | 20 | 15 | 11 | 60 | 51 | 75 |
| **Colchester United** | 46 | 21 | 11 | 14 | 72 | 60 | 74 |
| Torquay United | 46 | 21 | 11 | 14 | 68 | 59 | 74 |
| Scarborough | 46 | 19 | 15 | 12 | 67 | 58 | 72 |
| Barnet | 46 | 19 | 13 | 14 | 61 | 51 | 70 |
| Scunthorpe United | 46 | 19 | 12 | 15 | 56 | 52 | 69 |
| Rotherham United | 46 | 16 | 19 | 11 | 67 | 61 | 67 |
| Peterborough United | 46 | 18 | 13 | 15 | 63 | 51 | 67 |
| Leyton Orient | 46 | 19 | 12 | 15 | 62 | 47 | 66 |
| Mansfield Town | 46 | 16 | 17 | 13 | 64 | 55 | 65 |
| Shrewsbury Town | 46 | 16 | 13 | 17 | 61 | 62 | 61 |
| Chester City | 46 | 17 | 10 | 19 | 60 | 61 | 61 |
| Exeter City | 46 | 15 | 15 | 16 | 68 | 63 | 60 |
| Cambridge United | 46 | 14 | 18 | 14 | 63 | 57 | 60 |
| Hartlepool United | 46 | 12 | 23 | 11 | 61 | 53 | 59 |
| Rochdale | 46 | 17 | 7 | 22 | 56 | 55 | 58 |
| Darlington | 46 | 14 | 12 | 20 | 56 | 72 | 54 |
| Swansea City | 46 | 13 | 11 | 22 | 49 | 62 | 50 |
| Cardiff City | 46 | 9 | 23 | 14 | 48 | 52 | 50 |
| Hull City | 46 | 11 | 8 | 27 | 56 | 83 | 41 |
| Brighton & Hove Albion | 46 | 6 | 17 | 23 | 38 | 66 | 35 |
| *Doncaster Rovers* | *46* | *4* | *8* | *34* | *30* | *113* | *20* |

Leyton Orient had 3 points deducted

### Division Three Play-offs

| | |
|---|---|
| Barnet vs Colchester United | 1-0, 1-3 |
| Scarborough vs Torquay United | 1-3, 1-4 |
| Colchester United vs Torquay United | 1-0 |

## 1998 Football League Cup

### Semi-finals

| | |
|---|---|
| Liverpool vs Middlesbrough (2-1, 0-2) | 2-3 |
| Arsenal vs Chelsea (2-1, 1-3) | 3-4 |

### Final

Wembley, 29th March 1998

**Chelsea 2** (Sinclair, Di Matteo)
**Middlesbrough 0 (aet.)**

*Attendance 77,698*

## F.A. PREMIER LEAGUE 1998-99

| | | | | | | | |
|---|---|---|---|---|---|---|---|
| **MANCHESTER UNITED** | 38 | 22 | 13 | 3 | 80 | 37 | 79 |
| Arsenal | 38 | 22 | 12 | 4 | 59 | 17 | 78 |
| Chelsea | 38 | 20 | 15 | 3 | 57 | 30 | 75 |
| Leeds United | 38 | 18 | 13 | 7 | 62 | 34 | 67 |
| West Ham United | 38 | 16 | 9 | 13 | 46 | 53 | 57 |
| Aston Villa | 38 | 15 | 10 | 13 | 51 | 46 | 55 |
| Liverpool | 38 | 15 | 9 | 14 | 68 | 49 | 54 |
| Derby County | 38 | 13 | 13 | 12 | 40 | 45 | 52 |
| Middlesbrough | 38 | 12 | 15 | 11 | 48 | 54 | 51 |
| Leicester City | 38 | 12 | 13 | 13 | 40 | 46 | 49 |
| Tottenham Hotspur | 38 | 11 | 14 | 13 | 47 | 50 | 47 |
| Sheffield Wednesday | 38 | 13 | 7 | 18 | 41 | 42 | 46 |
| Newcastle United | 38 | 11 | 13 | 14 | 48 | 54 | 46 |
| Everton | 38 | 11 | 10 | 17 | 42 | 47 | 43 |
| Coventry City | 38 | 11 | 9 | 18 | 39 | 51 | 42 |
| Wimbledon | 38 | 10 | 12 | 16 | 40 | 63 | 42 |
| Southampton | 38 | 11 | 8 | 19 | 37 | 64 | 41 |
| *Charlton Athletic* | 38 | 8 | 12 | 18 | 41 | 56 | 36 |
| *Blackburn Rovers* | 38 | 7 | 14 | 17 | 38 | 52 | 35 |
| *Nottingham Forest* | 38 | 7 | 9 | 22 | 35 | 69 | 30 |

## DIVISION ONE 1998-99

| | | | | | | | |
|---|---|---|---|---|---|---|---|
| **Sunderland** | 46 | 31 | 12 | 3 | 91 | 28 | 105 |
| **Bradford City** | 46 | 26 | 9 | 11 | 82 | 47 | 87 |
| Ipswich Town | 46 | 26 | 8 | 12 | 69 | 32 | 86 |
| Birmingham City | 46 | 23 | 12 | 11 | 66 | 37 | 81 |
| Watford | 46 | 21 | 14 | 11 | 65 | 56 | 77 |
| Bolton Wanderers | 46 | 20 | 16 | 10 | 78 | 59 | 76 |
| Wolverhampton Wanderers | 46 | 19 | 16 | 11 | 64 | 43 | 73 |
| Sheffield United | 46 | 18 | 13 | 15 | 71 | 66 | 67 |
| Norwich City | 46 | 15 | 17 | 14 | 62 | 61 | 62 |
| Huddersfield Town | 46 | 15 | 16 | 15 | 62 | 71 | 61 |
| Grimsby Town | 46 | 17 | 10 | 19 | 40 | 52 | 61 |
| West Bromwich Albion | 46 | 16 | 11 | 19 | 69 | 76 | 59 |
| Barnsley | 46 | 14 | 17 | 15 | 59 | 56 | 59 |
| Crystal Palace | 46 | 14 | 16 | 16 | 58 | 71 | 58 |
| Tranmere Rovers | 46 | 12 | 20 | 14 | 63 | 61 | 56 |
| Stockport County | 46 | 12 | 17 | 17 | 49 | 60 | 53 |
| Swindon Town | 46 | 13 | 11 | 22 | 59 | 81 | 50 |
| Crewe Alexandra | 46 | 12 | 12 | 22 | 54 | 78 | 48 |
| Portsmouth | 46 | 11 | 14 | 21 | 57 | 73 | 47 |
| Queen's Park Rangers | 46 | 12 | 11 | 23 | 52 | 61 | 47 |
| Port Vale | 46 | 13 | 8 | 25 | 45 | 75 | 47 |
| *Bury* | 46 | 10 | 17 | 19 | 35 | 60 | 47 |
| *Oxford United* | 46 | 10 | 14 | 22 | 48 | 71 | 44 |
| *Bristol City* | 46 | 9 | 15 | 22 | 57 | 80 | 42 |

### Division One Play-offs

| | |
|---|---|
| Bolton Wanderers vs Ipswich Town | 1-0, 3-4 |
| *Bolton Wanderers won on away goals* | |
| Watford vs Birmingham City | 1-0, 0-1 |
| *Watford won 7-6 on penalties* | |
| Watford vs Bolton Wanderers | 2-0 |

## DIVISION TWO 1998-99

| | | | | | | | |
|---|---|---|---|---|---|---|---|
| **Fulham** | 46 | 31 | 8 | 7 | 79 | 32 | 101 |
| **Walsall** | 46 | 26 | 9 | 11 | 63 | 47 | 87 |
| **Manchester City** | 46 | 22 | 16 | 8 | 69 | 33 | 82 |
| Gillingham | 46 | 22 | 14 | 10 | 75 | 44 | 80 |
| Preston North End | 46 | 22 | 13 | 11 | 78 | 50 | 79 |
| Wigan Athletic | 46 | 22 | 10 | 14 | 75 | 48 | 76 |
| Bournemouth | 46 | 21 | 13 | 12 | 63 | 41 | 76 |
| Stoke City | 46 | 21 | 6 | 19 | 59 | 63 | 69 |
| Chesterfield | 46 | 17 | 13 | 16 | 46 | 44 | 64 |
| Millwall | 46 | 17 | 11 | 18 | 52 | 59 | 62 |
| Reading | 46 | 16 | 13 | 17 | 54 | 63 | 61 |
| Luton Town | 46 | 16 | 10 | 20 | 51 | 60 | 58 |
| Bristol Rovers | 46 | 13 | 17 | 16 | 65 | 56 | 56 |
| Blackpool | 46 | 14 | 14 | 18 | 44 | 54 | 56 |
| Burnley | 46 | 13 | 16 | 17 | 54 | 73 | 55 |
| Notts County | 46 | 14 | 12 | 20 | 52 | 61 | 54 |
| Wrexham | 46 | 13 | 14 | 19 | 43 | 62 | 53 |
| Colchester United | 46 | 12 | 16 | 18 | 52 | 70 | 52 |
| Wycombe Wanderers | 46 | 13 | 12 | 21 | 52 | 58 | 51 |
| Oldham Athletic | 46 | 14 | 9 | 23 | 48 | 66 | 51 |
| *York City* | 46 | 13 | 11 | 22 | 56 | 80 | 50 |
| *Northampton Town* | 46 | 10 | 18 | 18 | 43 | 57 | 48 |
| *Lincoln City* | 46 | 13 | 7 | 26 | 42 | 74 | 46 |
| *Macclesfield Town* | 46 | 11 | 10 | 25 | 43 | 63 | 43 |

### Division Two Play-offs

| | |
|---|---|
| Wigan Athletic vs Manchester City | 1-1, 0-1 |
| Preston North End vs Gillingham | 1-1, 0-1 |
| Manchester City vs Gillingham | 2-2 |
| *Manchester City won 3-1 on penalties* | |

## DIVISION THREE 1998-99

| | | | | | | | |
|---|---|---|---|---|---|---|---|
| **Brentford** | 46 | 26 | 7 | 13 | 79 | 56 | 85 |
| **Cambridge United** | 46 | 23 | 12 | 11 | 78 | 48 | 81 |
| **Cardiff City** | 46 | 22 | 14 | 10 | 60 | 39 | 80 |
| **Scunthorpe United** | 46 | 22 | 8 | 16 | 69 | 58 | 74 |
| Rotherham United | 46 | 20 | 13 | 13 | 79 | 61 | 73 |
| Leyton Orient | 46 | 15 | 12 | 19 | 68 | 59 | 72 |
| Swansea City | 46 | 19 | 14 | 13 | 56 | 48 | 71 |
| Mansfield Town | 46 | 19 | 10 | 17 | 60 | 58 | 67 |
| Peterborough United | 46 | 18 | 12 | 16 | 72 | 56 | 66 |
| Halifax Town | 46 | 17 | 15 | 14 | 58 | 56 | 66 |
| Darlington | 46 | 18 | 11 | 17 | 69 | 58 | 65 |
| Exeter City | 46 | 17 | 12 | 17 | 47 | 50 | 63 |
| Plymouth Argyle | 46 | 17 | 10 | 19 | 58 | 54 | 61 |
| Chester City | 46 | 13 | 18 | 15 | 57 | 66 | 57 |
| Shrewsbury Town | 46 | 14 | 14 | 18 | 52 | 63 | 56 |
| Barnet | 46 | 14 | 13 | 19 | 54 | 71 | 55 |
| Brighton & Hove Albion | 46 | 16 | 7 | 23 | 49 | 66 | 55 |
| Southend United | 46 | 14 | 12 | 20 | 52 | 58 | 54 |
| Rochdale | 46 | 13 | 15 | 18 | 42 | 55 | 54 |
| Torquay United | 46 | 12 | 17 | 17 | 47 | 58 | 53 |
| Hull City | 46 | 14 | 11 | 21 | 44 | 62 | 53 |
| Hartlepool United | 46 | 13 | 12 | 21 | 52 | 65 | 51 |
| Carlisle United | 46 | 11 | 16 | 19 | 43 | 53 | 49 |
| *Scarborough* | 46 | 14 | 6 | 26 | 50 | 77 | 48 |

### Division Three Play-offs

| | |
|---|---|
| Leyton Orient vs Rotherham United | 0-0, 0-0 |
| *Leyton Orient won 4-2 on penalties* | |
| Swansea City vs Scunthorpe United | 1-0, 1-3 |
| Scunthorpe United vs Leyton Orient | 1-0 |

## 1999 F.A. Cup

### Semi-finals

| | |
|---|---|
| Newcastle United vs Tottenham Hotspur | 2-0 (aet) |
| Manchester United vs Arsenal | 0-0, 2-1 (aet) |

### Final

Wembley, 22nd May 1999

**Manchester United 2**    (Sheringham, Scholes)
**Newcastle United 0**

*Attendance 79,101*

## 1999 Football League Cup

### Semi-finals

| | |
|---|---|
| Sunderland vs Leicester City (1-2, 1-1) | 2-3 |
| Tottenham Hotspur vs Wimbledon (0-0, 1-0) | 1-0 |

### Final

Wembley, 21st March 1999

**Tottenham Hotspur 1**    (Nielsen)
**Leicester City 0**

*Attendance 77,892*

## F.A. PREMIER LEAGUE 1999-2000

| MANCHESTER UNITED | 38 | 28 | 7 | 3 | 97 | 45 | 91 |
|---|---|---|---|---|---|---|---|
| Arsenal | 38 | 22 | 7 | 9 | 73 | 43 | 73 |
| Leeds United | 38 | 21 | 6 | 11 | 58 | 43 | 69 |
| Liverpool | 38 | 19 | 10 | 9 | 51 | 30 | 67 |
| Chelsea | 38 | 18 | 11 | 9 | 53 | 34 | 65 |
| Aston Villa | 38 | 15 | 13 | 10 | 46 | 35 | 58 |
| Sunderland | 38 | 16 | 10 | 12 | 57 | 56 | 58 |
| Leicester City | 38 | 16 | 7 | 15 | 55 | 55 | 55 |
| West Ham United | 38 | 15 | 10 | 13 | 52 | 53 | 55 |
| Tottenham Hotspur | 38 | 15 | 8 | 15 | 57 | 49 | 53 |
| Newcastle United | 38 | 14 | 10 | 14 | 63 | 54 | 52 |
| Middlesbrough | 38 | 14 | 10 | 14 | 46 | 52 | 52 |
| Everton | 38 | 12 | 14 | 12 | 59 | 49 | 50 |
| Coventry City | 38 | 12 | 8 | 18 | 47 | 54 | 44 |
| Southampton | 38 | 12 | 8 | 18 | 45 | 62 | 44 |
| Derby County | 38 | 9 | 11 | 18 | 44 | 57 | 38 |
| Bradford City | 38 | 9 | 9 | 20 | 38 | 68 | 36 |
| *Wimbledon* | *38* | *7* | *12* | *19* | *46* | *74* | *33* |
| *Sheffield Wednesday* | *38* | *8* | *7* | *23* | *38* | *70* | *31* |
| *Watford* | *38* | *6* | *6* | *26* | *35* | *77* | *24* |

## DIVISION ONE 1999-2000

| Charlton Athletic | 46 | 27 | 10 | 9 | 79 | 45 | 91 |
|---|---|---|---|---|---|---|---|
| Manchester City | 46 | 26 | 11 | 9 | 78 | 40 | 89 |
| Ipswich Town | 46 | 25 | 12 | 9 | 71 | 42 | 87 |
| Barnsley | 46 | 24 | 10 | 12 | 88 | 67 | 82 |
| Birmingham City | 46 | 22 | 11 | 13 | 65 | 44 | 77 |
| Bolton Wanderers | 46 | 21 | 13 | 12 | 69 | 50 | 76 |
| Wolverhampton Wanderers | 46 | 21 | 11 | 14 | 64 | 48 | 74 |
| Huddersfield Town | 46 | 21 | 11 | 14 | 62 | 49 | 74 |
| Fulham | 46 | 17 | 16 | 13 | 49 | 41 | 67 |
| Queen's Park Rangers | 46 | 16 | 18 | 12 | 62 | 53 | 66 |
| Blackburn Rovers | 46 | 15 | 17 | 14 | 55 | 51 | 62 |
| Norwich City | 46 | 14 | 15 | 17 | 45 | 50 | 57 |
| Tranmere Rovers | 46 | 15 | 12 | 19 | 57 | 68 | 57 |
| Nottingham Forest | 46 | 14 | 14 | 18 | 53 | 55 | 56 |
| Crystal Palace | 46 | 13 | 15 | 18 | 57 | 67 | 54 |
| Sheffield United | 46 | 13 | 15 | 18 | 59 | 71 | 54 |
| Stockport County | 46 | 13 | 15 | 18 | 55 | 67 | 54 |
| Portsmouth | 46 | 13 | 12 | 21 | 55 | 66 | 51 |
| Crewe Alexandra | 46 | 14 | 9 | 23 | 46 | 67 | 51 |
| Grimsby Town | 46 | 13 | 12 | 21 | 41 | 67 | 51 |
| West Bromwich Albion | 46 | 10 | 19 | 17 | 43 | 60 | 49 |
| *Walsall* | *46* | *11* | *13* | *22* | *52* | *77* | *46* |
| *Port Vale* | *46* | *7* | *15* | *24* | *48* | *69* | *36* |
| *Swindon Town* | *46* | *8* | *12* | *26* | *38* | *77* | *36* |

### Division One Play-offs

| Birmingham City vs Barnsley | 0-4, 2-1 |
|---|---|
| Bolton Wanderers vs Ipswich Town | 2-2, 3-5 |
| Ipswich Town vs Barnsley | 4-2 |

## DIVISION TWO 1999-2000

| Preston North End | 46 | 28 | 11 | 7 | 74 | 37 | 95 |
|---|---|---|---|---|---|---|---|
| Burnley | 46 | 25 | 13 | 8 | 69 | 47 | 88 |
| Gillingham | 46 | 25 | 10 | 11 | 79 | 48 | 85 |
| Wigan Athletic | 46 | 22 | 17 | 7 | 72 | 38 | 83 |
| Millwall | 46 | 23 | 13 | 10 | 76 | 50 | 82 |
| Stoke City | 46 | 23 | 13 | 10 | 68 | 42 | 82 |
| Bristol Rovers | 46 | 23 | 11 | 12 | 69 | 45 | 80 |
| Notts County | 46 | 18 | 11 | 17 | 61 | 55 | 65 |
| Bristol City | 46 | 15 | 19 | 12 | 59 | 57 | 64 |
| Reading | 46 | 16 | 14 | 16 | 57 | 63 | 62 |
| Wrexham | 46 | 17 | 11 | 18 | 52 | 61 | 62 |
| Wycombe Wanderers | 46 | 16 | 13 | 17 | 56 | 53 | 61 |
| Luton Town | 46 | 17 | 10 | 19 | 61 | 65 | 61 |
| Oldham Athletic | 46 | 16 | 12 | 18 | 50 | 55 | 60 |
| Bury | 46 | 13 | 18 | 15 | 61 | 64 | 57 |
| Bournemouth | 46 | 16 | 9 | 21 | 59 | 62 | 57 |
| Brentford | 46 | 13 | 13 | 20 | 47 | 61 | 52 |
| Colchester United | 46 | 14 | 10 | 22 | 59 | 82 | 52 |
| Cambridge United | 46 | 12 | 12 | 22 | 64 | 65 | 48 |
| Oxford United | 46 | 12 | 9 | 25 | 43 | 73 | 45 |
| *Cardiff City* | *46* | *9* | *17* | *20* | *45* | *67* | *44* |
| *Blackpool* | *46* | *8* | *17* | *21* | *49* | *77* | *41* |
| *Scunthorpe United* | *46* | *9* | *12* | *25* | *40* | *74* | *39* |
| *Chesterfield* | *46* | *7* | *15* | *24* | *34* | *63* | *36* |

### Division Two Play-offs

| Millwall vs Wigan Athletic | 0-0, 0-1 |
|---|---|
| Stoke City vs Gillingham | 3-2, 0-3 |
| Gillingham vs Wigan Athletic | 3-2 |

## DIVISION THREE 1999-2000

| Swansea City | 46 | 24 | 13 | 9 | 51 | 30 | 85 |
|---|---|---|---|---|---|---|---|
| Rotherham United | 46 | 24 | 12 | 10 | 72 | 36 | 84 |
| Northampton Town | 46 | 25 | 7 | 14 | 63 | 45 | 82 |
| Darlington | 46 | 21 | 16 | 9 | 66 | 36 | 79 |
| Peterborough United | 46 | 22 | 12 | 12 | 63 | 54 | 78 |
| Barnet | 46 | 21 | 12 | 13 | 59 | 53 | 75 |
| Hartlepool United | 46 | 21 | 9 | 16 | 60 | 49 | 72 |
| Cheltenham Town | 46 | 20 | 10 | 16 | 50 | 42 | 70 |
| Torquay United | 46 | 19 | 12 | 15 | 62 | 52 | 69 |
| Rochdale | 46 | 18 | 14 | 14 | 57 | 54 | 68 |
| Brighton & Hove Albion | 46 | 17 | 16 | 13 | 64 | 46 | 67 |
| Plymouth Argyle | 46 | 16 | 18 | 12 | 55 | 51 | 66 |
| Macclesfield Town | 46 | 18 | 11 | 17 | 66 | 61 | 65 |
| Hull City | 46 | 15 | 14 | 17 | 43 | 43 | 59 |
| Lincoln City | 46 | 15 | 14 | 17 | 67 | 69 | 59 |
| Southend United | 46 | 15 | 11 | 20 | 53 | 61 | 56 |
| Mansfield Town | 46 | 16 | 8 | 22 | 50 | 65 | 56 |
| Halifax Town | 46 | 15 | 9 | 22 | 44 | 58 | 54 |
| Leyton Orient | 46 | 13 | 13 | 20 | 47 | 52 | 52 |
| York City | 46 | 12 | 16 | 18 | 39 | 53 | 52 |
| Exeter City | 46 | 11 | 11 | 24 | 46 | 72 | 44 |
| Shrewsbury Town | 46 | 9 | 13 | 24 | 40 | 67 | 40 |
| Carlisle United | 46 | 9 | 12 | 25 | 42 | 75 | 39 |
| *Chester City* | *46* | *10* | *9* | *27* | *44* | *79* | *39* |

### Division Three Play-offs

| Barnet vs Peterborough United | 1-2, 0-3 |
|---|---|
| Hartlepool United vs Darlington | 0-2, 0-1 |
| Peterborough United vs Darlington | 1-0 |

## 2000 F.A. Cup

### Semi-finals

| Bolton Wanderers vs Aston Villa | 0-0 |
|---|---|

Aston Villa won 4-1 on penalties

| Newcastle United vs Chelsea | 1-2 |
|---|---|

### Final

Wembley, 20th May 2000

**Chelsea 1**   (Di Matteo)
**Aston Villa 0**

*Attendance 78,217*

## 2000 Football League Cup

### Semi-finals

| Bolton Wanderers vs Tranmere Rovers (0-1, 0-3) | 0-4 |
|---|---|
| Aston Villa vs Leicester City (0-0, 0-1) | 0-1 |

### Final

Wembley, 27th February 2000

**Leicester City 2**   (Elliott 2)
**Tranmere Rovers 1**   (Kelly)

*Attendance 74,313*

## F.A. PREMIER LEAGUE 2000-2001

| | | | | | | | |
|---|---|---|---|---|---|---|---|
| MANCHESTER UNITED | 38 | 24 | 8 | 6 | 79 | 31 | 80 |
| Arsenal | 38 | 20 | 10 | 8 | 63 | 38 | 70 |
| Liverpool | 38 | 20 | 9 | 9 | 71 | 39 | 69 |
| Leeds United | 38 | 20 | 8 | 10 | 64 | 43 | 68 |
| Ipswich Town | 38 | 20 | 6 | 12 | 57 | 42 | 66 |
| Chelsea | 38 | 17 | 10 | 11 | 68 | 45 | 61 |
| Sunderland | 38 | 15 | 12 | 11 | 46 | 41 | 57 |
| Aston Villa | 38 | 13 | 15 | 10 | 46 | 43 | 54 |
| Charlton Athletic | 38 | 14 | 10 | 14 | 50 | 57 | 52 |
| Southampton | 38 | 14 | 10 | 14 | 40 | 48 | 52 |
| Newcastle United | 38 | 14 | 9 | 15 | 44 | 50 | 51 |
| Tottenham Hotspur | 38 | 13 | 10 | 15 | 47 | 54 | 49 |
| Leicester City | 38 | 14 | 6 | 18 | 39 | 51 | 48 |
| Middlesbrough | 38 | 9 | 15 | 14 | 44 | 44 | 42 |
| West Ham United | 38 | 10 | 12 | 16 | 45 | 50 | 42 |
| Everton | 38 | 11 | 9 | 18 | 45 | 59 | 42 |
| Derby County | 38 | 10 | 12 | 16 | 37 | 59 | 42 |
| *Manchester City* | 38 | 8 | 10 | 20 | 41 | 65 | 34 |
| *Coventry City* | 38 | 8 | 10 | 20 | 36 | 63 | 34 |
| *Bradford City* | 38 | 5 | 11 | 22 | 30 | 70 | 26 |

## DIVISION ONE 2000-2001

| | | | | | | | |
|---|---|---|---|---|---|---|---|
| **Fulham** | 46 | 30 | 11 | 5 | 90 | 32 | 101 |
| **Blackburn Rovers** | 46 | 26 | 13 | 7 | 76 | 39 | 91 |
| **Bolton Wanderers** | 46 | 24 | 15 | 7 | 76 | 45 | 87 |
| Preston North End | 46 | 23 | 9 | 14 | 64 | 52 | 78 |
| Birmingham City | 46 | 23 | 9 | 14 | 59 | 48 | 78 |
| West Bromwich Albion | 46 | 21 | 11 | 14 | 60 | 52 | 74 |
| Burnley | 46 | 21 | 9 | 16 | 50 | 54 | 72 |
| Wimbledon | 46 | 17 | 18 | 11 | 71 | 50 | 69 |
| Watford | 46 | 20 | 9 | 17 | 76 | 67 | 69 |
| Sheffield United | 46 | 19 | 11 | 16 | 52 | 49 | 68 |
| Nottingham Forest | 46 | 20 | 8 | 18 | 55 | 53 | 68 |
| Wolverhampton Wanderers | 46 | 14 | 13 | 19 | 45 | 48 | 55 |
| Gillingham | 46 | 13 | 16 | 17 | 61 | 66 | 55 |
| Crewe Alexandra | 46 | 15 | 10 | 21 | 47 | 62 | 55 |
| Norwich City | 46 | 14 | 12 | 20 | 46 | 58 | 54 |
| Barnsley | 46 | 15 | 9 | 22 | 49 | 62 | 54 |
| Sheffield Wednesday | 46 | 15 | 8 | 23 | 52 | 71 | 53 |
| Grimsby Town | 46 | 14 | 10 | 22 | 43 | 62 | 52 |
| Stockport County | 46 | 11 | 18 | 17 | 58 | 65 | 51 |
| Portsmouth | 46 | 10 | 19 | 17 | 47 | 59 | 49 |
| Crystal Palace | 46 | 12 | 13 | 21 | 57 | 70 | 49 |
| *Huddersfield Town* | 46 | 11 | 15 | 20 | 48 | 57 | 48 |
| *Queen's Park Rangers* | 46 | 7 | 19 | 20 | 45 | 75 | 40 |
| *Tranmere Rovers* | 46 | 9 | 11 | 26 | 46 | 77 | 38 |

### Division One Play-offs

| | |
|---|---|
| Birmingham City vs Preston North End | 1-0, 1-2 |
| *Preston North End won 4-2 on penalties* | |
| West Bromwich Albion vs Bolton Wands. | 2-2, 0-3 |
| Bolton Wanderers vs Preston North End | 3-0 |

## 2001 F.A. Cup

### Semi-finals

| | |
|---|---|
| Arsenal vs Tottenham Hotspur | 2-1 |
| Wycombe Wanderers vs Liverpool | 1-2 |

### Final

The Millennium Stadium, Cardiff, 12th May 2001

**Arsenal 1** (Ljungberg)
**Liverpool 2** (Owen 2)

*Attendance 72,500*

## DIVISION TWO 2000-2001

| | | | | | | | |
|---|---|---|---|---|---|---|---|
| **Millwall** | 46 | 28 | 9 | 9 | 89 | 38 | 93 |
| **Rotherham United** | 46 | 27 | 10 | 9 | 79 | 55 | 91 |
| Reading | 46 | 25 | 11 | 10 | 86 | 52 | 86 |
| **Walsall** | 46 | 23 | 12 | 11 | 79 | 50 | 81 |
| Stoke City | 46 | 21 | 14 | 11 | 74 | 49 | 77 |
| Wigan Athletic | 46 | 19 | 18 | 9 | 53 | 42 | 75 |
| Bournemouth | 46 | 20 | 13 | 13 | 79 | 55 | 73 |
| Notts County | 46 | 19 | 12 | 15 | 62 | 66 | 69 |
| Bristol City | 46 | 18 | 14 | 14 | 70 | 56 | 68 |
| Wrexham | 46 | 17 | 12 | 17 | 65 | 71 | 63 |
| Port Vale | 46 | 16 | 14 | 16 | 55 | 49 | 62 |
| Peterborough United | 46 | 15 | 14 | 17 | 61 | 66 | 59 |
| Wycombe Wanderers | 46 | 15 | 14 | 17 | 46 | 53 | 59 |
| Brentford | 46 | 14 | 17 | 15 | 56 | 70 | 59 |
| Oldham Athletic | 46 | 15 | 13 | 18 | 53 | 65 | 58 |
| Bury | 46 | 16 | 10 | 20 | 45 | 59 | 58 |
| Colchester United | 46 | 15 | 12 | 19 | 55 | 59 | 57 |
| Northampton Town | 46 | 15 | 12 | 19 | 46 | 59 | 57 |
| Cambridge United | 46 | 14 | 11 | 21 | 61 | 77 | 53 |
| Swindon Town | 46 | 13 | 13 | 20 | 47 | 65 | 52 |
| *Bristol Rovers* | 46 | 12 | 15 | 19 | 53 | 57 | 51 |
| *Luton Town* | 46 | 9 | 13 | 24 | 52 | 80 | 40 |
| *Swansea City* | 46 | 8 | 13 | 25 | 47 | 73 | 37 |
| *Oxford United* | 46 | 7 | 6 | 33 | 53 | 100 | 27 |

### Division Two Play-offs

| | |
|---|---|
| Stoke City vs Walsall | 0-0, 2-4 |
| Wigan Athletic vs Reading | 0-0, 1-2 |
| Walsall vs Reading | 3-2 |

## DIVISION THREE 2000-2001

| | | | | | | | |
|---|---|---|---|---|---|---|---|
| **Brighton & Hove Albion** | 46 | 28 | 8 | 10 | 73 | 35 | 92 |
| **Cardiff City** | 46 | 23 | 13 | 10 | 95 | 58 | 82 |
| **Chesterfield** | 46 | 25 | 14 | 7 | 79 | 42 | 80 |
| Hartlepool United | 46 | 21 | 14 | 11 | 71 | 54 | 77 |
| Leyton Orient | 46 | 20 | 15 | 11 | 59 | 51 | 75 |
| Hull City | 46 | 19 | 17 | 10 | 47 | 39 | 74 |
| **Blackpool** | 46 | 22 | 6 | 18 | 74 | 58 | 72 |
| Rochdale | 46 | 18 | 17 | 11 | 59 | 48 | 71 |
| Cheltenham Town | 46 | 18 | 14 | 14 | 59 | 52 | 68 |
| Scunthorpe United | 46 | 18 | 11 | 17 | 62 | 52 | 65 |
| Southend United | 46 | 15 | 18 | 13 | 55 | 53 | 63 |
| Mansfield Town | 46 | 15 | 13 | 18 | 64 | 72 | 58 |
| Plymouth Argyle | 46 | 15 | 13 | 18 | 54 | 61 | 58 |
| Macclesfield Town | 46 | 14 | 14 | 18 | 51 | 62 | 56 |
| Shrewsbury Town | 46 | 15 | 10 | 21 | 49 | 65 | 55 |
| Kidderminster Harriers | 46 | 13 | 14 | 19 | 47 | 61 | 53 |
| York City | 46 | 13 | 13 | 20 | 42 | 63 | 52 |
| Lincoln City | 46 | 12 | 15 | 19 | 58 | 66 | 51 |
| Exeter City | 46 | 12 | 14 | 20 | 40 | 58 | 50 |
| Darlington | 46 | 12 | 13 | 21 | 44 | 56 | 49 |
| Torquay United | 46 | 12 | 13 | 21 | 52 | 77 | 49 |
| Carlisle United | 46 | 11 | 15 | 20 | 42 | 65 | 48 |
| Halifax Town | 46 | 12 | 11 | 23 | 54 | 68 | 47 |
| *Barnet* | 46 | 12 | 9 | 25 | 67 | 81 | 45 |

Chesterfield had 9 points deducted

### Division Three Play-offs

| | |
|---|---|
| Blackpool vs Hartlepool United | 2-0, 3-1 |
| Hull City vs Leyton Orient | 1-0, 0-2 |
| Blackpool vs Leyton Orient | 4-2 |

## 2001 Football League Cup

### Semi-finals

| | | |
|---|---|---|
| Ipswich Town vs Birmingham City (1-0, 1-4) | | 2-4 |
| Crystal Palace vs Liverpool (2-1, 0-5) | | 2-6 |

### Final

The Millennium Stadium, Cardiff, 25th February 2001

**Birmingham City 1** (Purse (pen))
**Liverpool 1 (aet.)** (Fowler)

*Attendance 73,500*

*Liverpool won 5-4 on penalties.*

## F.A. PREMIER LEAGUE 2001-2002

| | | | | | | | |
|---|---|---|---|---|---|---|---|
| **ARSENAL** | 38 | 26 | 9 | 3 | 79 | 36 | 87 |
| Liverpool | 38 | 24 | 8 | 6 | 67 | 30 | 80 |
| Manchester United | 38 | 24 | 5 | 9 | 87 | 45 | 77 |
| Newcastle United | 38 | 21 | 8 | 9 | 74 | 52 | 71 |
| Leeds United | 38 | 18 | 12 | 8 | 53 | 37 | 66 |
| Chelsea | 38 | 17 | 13 | 8 | 66 | 38 | 64 |
| West Ham United | 38 | 15 | 8 | 15 | 48 | 57 | 53 |
| Aston Villa | 38 | 12 | 14 | 12 | 46 | 47 | 50 |
| Tottenham Hotspur | 38 | 14 | 8 | 16 | 49 | 53 | 50 |
| Blackburn Rovers | 38 | 12 | 10 | 16 | 55 | 51 | 46 |
| Southampton | 38 | 12 | 9 | 17 | 46 | 54 | 45 |
| Middlesbrough | 38 | 12 | 9 | 17 | 35 | 47 | 45 |
| Fulham | 38 | 10 | 14 | 14 | 36 | 44 | 44 |
| Charlton Athletic | 38 | 10 | 14 | 14 | 38 | 49 | 44 |
| Everton | 38 | 11 | 10 | 17 | 45 | 57 | 43 |
| Bolton Wanderers | 38 | 9 | 13 | 16 | 44 | 62 | 40 |
| Sunderland | 38 | 10 | 10 | 18 | 29 | 51 | 40 |
| *Ipswich Town* | *38* | *9* | *9* | *20* | *41* | *64* | *36* |
| *Derby County* | *38* | *8* | *6* | *24* | *33* | *63* | *30* |
| *Leicester City* | *38* | *5* | *13* | *20* | *30* | *64* | *28* |

## DIVISION ONE 2001-2002

| | | | | | | | |
|---|---|---|---|---|---|---|---|
| **Manchester City** | 46 | 31 | 6 | 9 | 108 | 52 | 99 |
| **West Bromwich Albion** | 46 | 27 | 8 | 11 | 61 | 29 | 89 |
| Wolverhampton Wanderers | 46 | 25 | 11 | 10 | 76 | 43 | 86 |
| Millwall | 46 | 22 | 11 | 13 | 69 | 48 | 77 |
| **Birmingham City** | 46 | 21 | 13 | 12 | 70 | 49 | 76 |
| Norwich City | 46 | 22 | 9 | 15 | 60 | 51 | 75 |
| Burnley | 46 | 21 | 12 | 13 | 70 | 62 | 75 |
| Preston North End | 46 | 20 | 12 | 14 | 71 | 59 | 72 |
| Wimbledon | 46 | 18 | 13 | 15 | 63 | 57 | 67 |
| Crystal Palace | 46 | 20 | 6 | 20 | 70 | 62 | 66 |
| Coventry City | 46 | 20 | 6 | 20 | 59 | 53 | 66 |
| Gillingham | 46 | 18 | 10 | 18 | 64 | 67 | 64 |
| Sheffield United | 46 | 15 | 15 | 16 | 53 | 54 | 60 |
| Watford | 46 | 16 | 11 | 19 | 62 | 56 | 59 |
| Bradford City | 46 | 15 | 10 | 21 | 69 | 76 | 55 |
| Nottingham Forest | 46 | 12 | 18 | 16 | 50 | 51 | 54 |
| Portsmouth | 46 | 13 | 14 | 19 | 60 | 72 | 53 |
| Walsall | 46 | 13 | 12 | 21 | 51 | 71 | 51 |
| Grimsby Town | 46 | 12 | 14 | 20 | 50 | 72 | 50 |
| Sheffield Wednesday | 46 | 12 | 14 | 20 | 49 | 71 | 50 |
| Rotherham United | 46 | 10 | 19 | 17 | 52 | 66 | 49 |
| *Crewe Alexandra* | *46* | *12* | *13* | *21* | *47* | *76* | *49* |
| *Barnsley* | *46* | *11* | *15* | *20* | *59* | *86* | *48* |
| *Stockport County* | *46* | *6* | *8* | *32* | *42* | *102* | *26* |

### Division One Play-offs

| | |
|---|---|
| Birmingham City vs Millwall | 1-1, 1-0 |
| Norwich City vs Wolverhampton Wanderers | 3-1, 0-1 |
| Birmingham City vs Norwich City | 1-1 |
| *Birmingham won 4-2 on penalties* | |

## 2002 F.A. Cup

### Semi-finals

| | |
|---|---|
| Fulham vs Chelsea | 0-1 |
| Middlesbrough vs Arsenal | 0-1 |

### Final

The Millennium Stadium, Cardiff, 4th May 2002

**Arsenal 2**   (Parlour, Ljungberg)

**Chelsea 0**

*Attendance 73,963*

## DIVISION TWO 2001-2002

| | | | | | | | |
|---|---|---|---|---|---|---|---|
| **Brighton & Hove Albion** | 46 | 25 | 15 | 6 | 66 | 42 | 90 |
| **Reading** | 46 | 23 | 15 | 8 | 70 | 43 | 84 |
| Brentford | 46 | 24 | 11 | 11 | 77 | 43 | 83 |
| Cardiff City | 46 | 23 | 14 | 9 | 75 | 50 | 83 |
| **Stoke City** | 46 | 23 | 11 | 12 | 67 | 40 | 80 |
| Huddersfield Town | 46 | 21 | 15 | 10 | 65 | 47 | 78 |
| Bristol City | 46 | 21 | 10 | 15 | 68 | 53 | 73 |
| Queen's Park Rangers | 46 | 19 | 14 | 13 | 60 | 49 | 71 |
| Oldham Athletic | 46 | 18 | 16 | 12 | 77 | 65 | 70 |
| Wigan Athletic | 46 | 16 | 16 | 14 | 66 | 51 | 64 |
| Wycombe Wanderers | 46 | 17 | 13 | 16 | 58 | 64 | 64 |
| Tranmere Rovers | 46 | 16 | 15 | 15 | 63 | 60 | 63 |
| Swindon Town | 46 | 15 | 14 | 17 | 46 | 56 | 59 |
| Port Vale | 46 | 16 | 10 | 20 | 51 | 62 | 58 |
| Colchester United | 46 | 15 | 12 | 19 | 65 | 76 | 57 |
| Blackpool | 46 | 14 | 14 | 18 | 66 | 69 | 56 |
| Peterborough United | 46 | 15 | 10 | 21 | 64 | 59 | 55 |
| Chesterfield | 46 | 13 | 13 | 20 | 53 | 65 | 52 |
| Notts County | 46 | 13 | 11 | 22 | 59 | 71 | 50 |
| Northampton Town | 46 | 14 | 7 | 25 | 54 | 79 | 49 |
| *Bournemouth* | *46* | *10* | *14* | *22* | *56* | *71* | *44* |
| *Bury* | *46* | *11* | *11* | *24* | *43* | *75* | *44* |
| *Wrexham* | *46* | *11* | *10* | *25* | *56* | *89* | *43* |
| *Cambridge United* | *46* | *7* | *13* | *26* | *47* | *93* | *34* |

### Division Two Play-offs

| | |
|---|---|
| Huddersfield Town vs Brentford | 0-0, 1-2 |
| Stoke City vs Cardiff City | 1-2, 2-0 |
| Stoke City vs Brentford | 2-0 |

## DIVISION THREE 2001-2002

| | | | | | | | |
|---|---|---|---|---|---|---|---|
| **Plymouth Argyle** | 46 | 31 | 9 | 6 | 71 | 28 | 102 |
| **Luton Town** | 46 | 30 | 7 | 9 | 96 | 48 | 97 |
| **Mansfield Town** | 46 | 24 | 7 | 15 | 72 | 60 | 79 |
| **Cheltenham Town** | 46 | 21 | 15 | 10 | 66 | 49 | 78 |
| Rochdale | 46 | 21 | 15 | 10 | 65 | 52 | 78 |
| Rushden & Diamonds | 46 | 20 | 13 | 13 | 69 | 53 | 73 |
| Hartlepool United | 46 | 20 | 11 | 15 | 74 | 48 | 71 |
| Scunthorpe United | 46 | 19 | 14 | 13 | 74 | 56 | 71 |
| Shrewsbury Town | 46 | 20 | 10 | 16 | 64 | 53 | 70 |
| Kidderminster Harriers | 46 | 19 | 9 | 18 | 56 | 47 | 66 |
| Hull City | 46 | 16 | 13 | 17 | 57 | 51 | 61 |
| Southend United | 46 | 15 | 13 | 18 | 51 | 54 | 58 |
| Macclesfield Town | 46 | 15 | 13 | 18 | 41 | 52 | 58 |
| York City | 46 | 16 | 9 | 21 | 54 | 67 | 57 |
| Darlington | 46 | 15 | 11 | 20 | 60 | 71 | 56 |
| Exeter City | 46 | 14 | 13 | 19 | 48 | 73 | 55 |
| Carlisle United | 46 | 12 | 16 | 18 | 49 | 56 | 52 |
| Leyton Orient | 46 | 13 | 13 | 20 | 55 | 71 | 52 |
| Torquay United | 46 | 12 | 15 | 19 | 46 | 63 | 51 |
| Swansea City | 46 | 13 | 12 | 21 | 53 | 77 | 51 |
| Oxford United | 46 | 11 | 14 | 21 | 53 | 62 | 47 |
| Lincoln City | 46 | 10 | 16 | 20 | 44 | 62 | 46 |
| Bristol Rovers | 46 | 11 | 12 | 23 | 40 | 60 | 45 |
| *Halifax Town* | *46* | *8* | *12* | *26* | *39* | *84* | *36* |

### Division Three Play-offs

| | |
|---|---|
| Hartlepool United vs Cheltenham Town | 1-1, 1-1 |
| *Cheltenham Town won 5-4 on penalties* | |
| Rushden & Diamonds vs Rochdale | 2-2, 2-1 |
| Cheltenham Town vs Rushden & Diamonds | 3-1 |

## 2002 Football League Cup

### Semi-finals

| | |
|---|---|
| Chelsea vs Tottenham Hotspur  (2-1, 1-5) | 3-6 |
| Sheffield Wednesday vs Blackburn Rovers (1-2, 2-4) | 3-6 |

### Final

The Millennium Stadium, Cardiff, 24th February 2002

**Blackburn Rovers 2**   (Jansen, Cole)

**Tottenham Hotspur 1**   (Ziege)

*Attendance 72,500*

## F.A. PREMIER LEAGUE 2002-2003

| | | | | | | | |
|---|---|---|---|---|---|---|---|
| **MANCHESTER UNITED** | 38 | 25 | 8 | 5 | 74 | 34 | 83 |
| Arsenal | 38 | 23 | 9 | 6 | 85 | 42 | 78 |
| Newcastle United | 38 | 21 | 6 | 11 | 63 | 48 | 69 |
| Chelsea | 38 | 19 | 10 | 9 | 68 | 38 | 67 |
| Liverpool | 38 | 18 | 10 | 10 | 61 | 41 | 64 |
| Blackburn Rovers | 38 | 16 | 12 | 10 | 52 | 43 | 60 |
| Everton | 38 | 17 | 8 | 13 | 48 | 49 | 59 |
| Southampton | 38 | 13 | 13 | 12 | 43 | 46 | 52 |
| Manchester City | 38 | 15 | 6 | 17 | 47 | 54 | 51 |
| Tottenham Hotspur | 38 | 14 | 8 | 16 | 51 | 62 | 50 |
| Middlesbrough | 38 | 13 | 10 | 15 | 48 | 44 | 49 |
| Charlton Athletic | 38 | 14 | 7 | 17 | 45 | 56 | 49 |
| Birmingham City | 38 | 13 | 9 | 16 | 41 | 49 | 48 |
| Fulham | 38 | 13 | 9 | 16 | 41 | 50 | 48 |
| Leeds United | 38 | 14 | 5 | 19 | 58 | 57 | 47 |
| Aston Villa | 38 | 12 | 9 | 17 | 42 | 47 | 45 |
| Bolton Wanderers | 38 | 10 | 14 | 14 | 41 | 51 | 44 |
| *West Ham United* | *38* | *10* | *12* | *16* | *42* | *59* | *42* |
| *West Bromwich Albion* | *38* | *6* | *8* | *24* | *29* | *65* | *26* |
| *Sunderland* | *38* | *4* | *7* | *27* | *21* | *65* | *19* |

## DIVISION ONE 2002-2003

| | | | | | | | |
|---|---|---|---|---|---|---|---|
| **Portsmouth** | 46 | 29 | 11 | 6 | 97 | 45 | 98 |
| **Leicester City** | 46 | 26 | 14 | 6 | 73 | 40 | 92 |
| Sheffield United | 46 | 23 | 11 | 12 | 72 | 52 | 80 |
| Reading | 46 | 25 | 4 | 17 | 61 | 46 | 79 |
| **Wolverhampton Wanderers** | 46 | 20 | 16 | 10 | 81 | 44 | 76 |
| Nottingham Forest | 46 | 20 | 14 | 12 | 82 | 50 | 74 |
| Ipswich Town | 46 | 19 | 13 | 14 | 80 | 64 | 70 |
| Norwich City | 46 | 19 | 12 | 15 | 60 | 49 | 69 |
| Millwall | 46 | 19 | 9 | 18 | 59 | 69 | 66 |
| Wimbledon | 46 | 18 | 11 | 17 | 76 | 73 | 65 |
| Gillingham | 46 | 16 | 14 | 16 | 56 | 65 | 62 |
| Preston North End | 46 | 16 | 13 | 17 | 68 | 70 | 61 |
| Watford | 46 | 17 | 9 | 20 | 54 | 70 | 60 |
| Crystal Palace | 46 | 14 | 17 | 15 | 59 | 52 | 59 |
| Rotherham United | 46 | 15 | 14 | 17 | 62 | 62 | 59 |
| Burnley | 46 | 15 | 10 | 21 | 65 | 89 | 55 |
| Walsall | 46 | 15 | 9 | 22 | 57 | 69 | 54 |
| Derby County | 46 | 15 | 7 | 24 | 55 | 74 | 52 |
| Bradford City | 46 | 14 | 10 | 22 | 51 | 73 | 52 |
| Coventry City | 46 | 12 | 14 | 20 | 46 | 62 | 50 |
| Stoke City | 46 | 12 | 14 | 20 | 45 | 69 | 50 |
| *Sheffield Wednesday* | *46* | *10* | *16* | *20* | *56* | *73* | *46* |
| *Brighton & Hove Albion* | *46* | *11* | *12* | *23* | *49* | *67* | *45* |
| *Grimsby Town* | *46* | *9* | *12* | *25* | *48* | *85* | *39* |

### Division One Play-offs

| | |
|---|---|
| Nottingham Forest vs Sheffield United | 1-1, 3-4 |
| Wolverhampton Wanderers vs Reading | 2-1, 1-0 |
| Wolverhampton Wanderers vs Sheffield United | 3-0 |

## 2003 F.A. Cup

### Semi-finals

| | |
|---|---|
| Arsenal vs Sheffield United | 1-0 |
| Southampton vs Watford | 2-1 |

### Final

The Millennium Stadium, Cardiff, 17th May 2003

**Arsenal 1** (Pires)
**Southampton 0**

*Attendance 73,726*

## DIVISION TWO 2002-2003

| | | | | | | | |
|---|---|---|---|---|---|---|---|
| **Wigan Athletic** | 46 | 29 | 13 | 4 | 68 | 25 | 100 |
| **Crewe Alexandra** | 46 | 25 | 11 | 10 | 76 | 40 | 86 |
| Bristol City | 46 | 24 | 11 | 11 | 79 | 48 | 83 |
| Queen's Park Rangers | 46 | 24 | 11 | 11 | 69 | 45 | 83 |
| Oldham Athletic | 46 | 22 | 16 | 8 | 68 | 38 | 82 |
| **Cardiff City** | 46 | 23 | 12 | 11 | 68 | 43 | 81 |
| Tranmere Rovers | 46 | 23 | 11 | 12 | 66 | 57 | 80 |
| Plymouth Argyle | 46 | 17 | 14 | 15 | 63 | 52 | 65 |
| Luton Town | 46 | 17 | 14 | 15 | 67 | 62 | 65 |
| Swindon Town | 46 | 16 | 12 | 18 | 59 | 63 | 60 |
| Peterborough United | 46 | 14 | 16 | 16 | 51 | 54 | 58 |
| Colchester United | 46 | 14 | 16 | 16 | 52 | 56 | 58 |
| Blackpool | 46 | 15 | 13 | 18 | 56 | 64 | 58 |
| Stockport County | 46 | 15 | 10 | 21 | 65 | 70 | 55 |
| Notts County | 46 | 13 | 16 | 17 | 62 | 70 | 55 |
| Brentford | 46 | 14 | 12 | 20 | 47 | 56 | 54 |
| Port Vale | 46 | 14 | 11 | 21 | 54 | 70 | 53 |
| Wycombe Wanderers | 46 | 13 | 13 | 20 | 59 | 66 | 52 |
| Barnsley | 46 | 13 | 13 | 20 | 51 | 64 | 52 |
| Chesterfield | 46 | 14 | 8 | 24 | 43 | 73 | 50 |
| *Cheltenham Town* | *46* | *10* | *18* | *18* | *53* | *68* | *48* |
| *Huddersfield Town* | *46* | *11* | *12* | *23* | *39* | *61* | *45* |
| *Mansfield Town* | *46* | *12* | *8* | *26* | *66* | *97* | *44* |
| *Northampton Town* | *46* | *10* | *9* | *27* | *40* | *79* | *39* |

### Division Two Play-offs

| | |
|---|---|
| Cardiff City vs Bristol City | 1-0, 0-0 |
| Oldham Athletic vs Queen's Park Rangers | 1-1, 0-1 |
| Cardiff City vs Queen's Park Rangers | 1-0 |

## DIVISION THREE 2002-2003

| | | | | | | | |
|---|---|---|---|---|---|---|---|
| **Rushden & Diamonds** | 46 | 24 | 15 | 7 | 73 | 47 | 87 |
| **Hartlepool United** | 46 | 24 | 13 | 9 | 71 | 51 | 85 |
| **Wrexham** | 46 | 23 | 15 | 8 | 84 | 50 | 84 |
| **Bournemouth** | 46 | 20 | 14 | 12 | 60 | 48 | 74 |
| Scunthorpe United | 46 | 19 | 15 | 12 | 68 | 49 | 72 |
| Lincoln City | 46 | 18 | 16 | 12 | 46 | 37 | 70 |
| Bury | 46 | 18 | 16 | 12 | 57 | 56 | 70 |
| Oxford United | 46 | 19 | 12 | 15 | 57 | 47 | 69 |
| Torquay United | 46 | 16 | 18 | 12 | 71 | 71 | 66 |
| York City | 46 | 17 | 15 | 14 | 52 | 53 | 66 |
| Kidderminster Harriers | 46 | 16 | 15 | 15 | 62 | 63 | 63 |
| Cambridge United | 46 | 16 | 13 | 17 | 67 | 70 | 61 |
| Hull City | 46 | 14 | 17 | 15 | 58 | 53 | 59 |
| Darlington | 46 | 12 | 18 | 16 | 58 | 59 | 54 |
| Boston United | 46 | 15 | 13 | 18 | 55 | 56 | 54 |
| Macclesfield Town | 46 | 14 | 12 | 20 | 57 | 63 | 54 |
| Southend United | 46 | 17 | 3 | 26 | 47 | 59 | 54 |
| Leyton Orient | 46 | 14 | 11 | 21 | 51 | 61 | 53 |
| Rochdale | 46 | 12 | 16 | 18 | 63 | 70 | 52 |
| Bristol Rovers | 46 | 12 | 15 | 19 | 50 | 57 | 51 |
| Swansea City | 46 | 12 | 13 | 21 | 48 | 65 | 49 |
| Carlisle United | 46 | 13 | 10 | 23 | 52 | 78 | 49 |
| *Exeter City* | *46* | *11* | *15* | *20* | *50* | *64* | *48* |
| *Shrewsbury Town* | *46* | *9* | *14* | *23* | *62* | *92* | *41* |

Boston United had 4 points deducted

### Division Three Play-offs

| | |
|---|---|
| Bury vs Bournemouth | 0-0, 1-3 |
| Lincoln City vs Scunthorpe United | 5-3, 1-0 |
| Bournemouth vs Lincoln City | 5-2 |

## 2003 Football League Cup

### Semi-finals

| | |
|---|---|
| Manchester United vs Blackburn Rovers (1-1, 3-1) | 4-2 |
| Sheffield United vs Liverpool (2-1, 0-2 aet) | 2-3 |

### Final

The Millennium Stadium, Cardiff, 2nd March 2003

**Liverpool 2** (Gerrard, Owen)
**Manchester United 0**

*Attendance 74,500*

## F.A. PREMIER LEAGUE 2003-2004

| ARSENAL | 38 | 26 | 12 | 0 | 73 | 26 | 90 |
|---|---|---|---|---|---|---|---|
| Chelsea | 38 | 24 | 7 | 7 | 67 | 30 | 79 |
| Manchester United | 38 | 23 | 6 | 9 | 64 | 35 | 75 |
| Liverpool | 38 | 16 | 12 | 10 | 55 | 37 | 60 |
| Newcastle United | 38 | 13 | 17 | 8 | 52 | 40 | 56 |
| Aston Villa | 38 | 15 | 11 | 12 | 48 | 44 | 56 |
| Charlton Athletic | 38 | 14 | 11 | 13 | 51 | 51 | 53 |
| Bolton Wanderers | 38 | 14 | 11 | 13 | 48 | 56 | 53 |
| Fulham | 38 | 14 | 10 | 14 | 52 | 46 | 52 |
| Birmingham City | 38 | 12 | 14 | 12 | 43 | 48 | 50 |
| Middlesbrough | 38 | 13 | 9 | 16 | 44 | 52 | 48 |
| Southampton | 38 | 12 | 11 | 15 | 44 | 45 | 47 |
| Portsmouth | 38 | 12 | 9 | 17 | 47 | 54 | 45 |
| Tottenham Hotspur | 38 | 13 | 6 | 19 | 47 | 57 | 45 |
| Blackburn Rovers | 38 | 12 | 8 | 18 | 51 | 59 | 44 |
| Manchester City | 38 | 9 | 14 | 15 | 55 | 54 | 41 |
| Everton | 38 | 9 | 12 | 17 | 45 | 57 | 39 |
| *Leicester City* | *38* | *6* | *15* | *17* | *48* | *65* | *33* |
| *Leeds United* | *38* | *8* | *9* | *21* | *40* | *79* | *33* |
| *Wolverhampton Wanderers* | *38* | *7* | *12* | *19* | *38* | *77* | *33* |

## DIVISION ONE 2003-2004

| Norwich City | 46 | 28 | 10 | 8 | 79 | 39 | 94 |
|---|---|---|---|---|---|---|---|
| West Bromwich Albion | 46 | 25 | 11 | 10 | 64 | 42 | 86 |
| Sunderland | 46 | 22 | 13 | 11 | 62 | 45 | 79 |
| West Ham United | 46 | 19 | 17 | 10 | 67 | 45 | 74 |
| Ipswich Town | 46 | 21 | 10 | 15 | 84 | 72 | 73 |
| **Crystal Palace** | **46** | **21** | **10** | **15** | **72** | **61** | **73** |
| Wigan Athletic | 46 | 18 | 17 | 11 | 60 | 45 | 71 |
| Sheffield United | 46 | 20 | 11 | 15 | 65 | 56 | 71 |
| Reading | 46 | 20 | 10 | 16 | 55 | 57 | 70 |
| Millwall | 46 | 18 | 15 | 13 | 55 | 48 | 69 |
| Stoke City | 46 | 18 | 12 | 16 | 58 | 55 | 66 |
| Coventry City | 46 | 17 | 14 | 15 | 67 | 54 | 65 |
| Cardiff City | 46 | 17 | 14 | 15 | 68 | 58 | 65 |
| Nottingham Forest | 46 | 15 | 15 | 16 | 61 | 58 | 60 |
| Preston North End | 46 | 15 | 14 | 17 | 69 | 71 | 59 |
| Watford | 46 | 15 | 12 | 19 | 54 | 68 | 57 |
| Rotherham United | 46 | 13 | 15 | 18 | 53 | 61 | 54 |
| Crewe Alexandra | 46 | 14 | 11 | 21 | 57 | 66 | 53 |
| Burnley | 46 | 13 | 14 | 19 | 60 | 77 | 53 |
| Derby County | 46 | 13 | 13 | 20 | 53 | 67 | 52 |
| Gillingham | 46 | 14 | 9 | 23 | 48 | 67 | 51 |
| *Walsall* | *46* | *13* | *12* | *21* | *45* | *65* | *51* |
| *Bradford City* | *46* | *10* | *6* | *30* | *38* | *69* | *36* |
| *Wimbledon* | *46* | *8* | *5* | *33* | *41* | *89* | *29* |

### Division One Play-offs

| Crystal Palace vs Sunderland | 3-2, 1-2 |
|---|---|
| *Crystal Palace won 5-4 on penalties* | |
| Ipswich Town vs West Ham United | 1-0, 0-2 |
| | |
| Crystal Palace vs West Ham United | 1-0 |

## 2004 F.A. Cup

### Semi-finals

| Arsenal vs Manchester United | 0-1 |
|---|---|
| Sunderland vs Millwall | 0-1 |

### Final

The Millennium Stadium, Cardiff, 22nd May 2004

**Manchester United 3** (Ronaldo, Van Nistelrooy 2)
**Millwall 0**

*Attendance 71,350*

## DIVISION TWO 2003-2004

| Plymouth Argyle | 46 | 26 | 12 | 8 | 85 | 41 | 90 |
|---|---|---|---|---|---|---|---|
| **Queen's Park Rangers** | **46** | **22** | **17** | **7** | **80** | **45** | **83** |
| Bristol City | 46 | 23 | 13 | 10 | 58 | 37 | 82 |
| **Brighton & Hove Albion** | **46** | **22** | **11** | **13** | **64** | **43** | **77** |
| Swindon Town | 46 | 20 | 13 | 13 | 76 | 58 | 73 |
| Hartlepool United | 46 | 20 | 13 | 13 | 76 | 61 | 73 |
| Port Vale | 46 | 21 | 10 | 15 | 73 | 63 | 73 |
| Tranmere Rovers | 46 | 17 | 16 | 13 | 59 | 56 | 67 |
| AFC Bournemouth | 46 | 17 | 15 | 14 | 56 | 51 | 66 |
| Luton Town | 46 | 17 | 15 | 14 | 69 | 66 | 66 |
| Colchester United | 46 | 17 | 13 | 16 | 52 | 56 | 64 |
| Barnsley | 46 | 15 | 17 | 14 | 54 | 58 | 62 |
| Wrexham | 46 | 17 | 9 | 20 | 50 | 60 | 60 |
| Blackpool | 46 | 16 | 11 | 19 | 58 | 65 | 59 |
| Oldham Athletic | 46 | 12 | 21 | 13 | 66 | 60 | 57 |
| Sheffield Wednesday | 46 | 13 | 14 | 19 | 48 | 64 | 53 |
| Brentford | 46 | 14 | 11 | 21 | 52 | 69 | 53 |
| Peterborough United | 46 | 12 | 16 | 18 | 58 | 58 | 52 |
| Stockport County | 46 | 11 | 19 | 16 | 62 | 70 | 52 |
| Chesterfield | 46 | 12 | 15 | 19 | 49 | 71 | 51 |
| *Grimsby Town* | *46* | *13* | *11* | *22* | *55* | *81* | *50* |
| *Rushden & Diamonds* | *46* | *13* | *9* | *24* | *60* | *74* | *48* |
| *Notts County* | *46* | *10* | *12* | *24* | *50* | *78* | *42* |
| *Wycombe Wanderers* | *46* | *6* | *19* | *21* | *50* | *75* | *37* |

### Division Two Play-offs

| Hartlepool United vs Bristol City | 1-1, 1-2 |
|---|---|
| Swindon Town vs Brighton & Hove Albion | 0-1, 2-1 |
| *Brighton & Hove Albion won 4-3 on penalties* | |
| | |
| Brighton & Hove Albion vs Bristol City | 1-0 |

## DIVISION THREE 2003-2004

| Doncaster Rovers | 46 | 27 | 11 | 8 | 79 | 37 | 92 |
|---|---|---|---|---|---|---|---|
| Hull City | 46 | 25 | 13 | 8 | 82 | 44 | 88 |
| Torquay United | 46 | 23 | 12 | 11 | 68 | 44 | 81 |
| Huddersfield Town | 46 | 23 | 12 | 11 | 68 | 52 | 81 |
| Mansfield Town | 46 | 22 | 9 | 15 | 76 | 62 | 75 |
| Northampton Town | 46 | 22 | 9 | 15 | 58 | 51 | 75 |
| Lincoln City | 46 | 19 | 17 | 10 | 68 | 47 | 74 |
| Yeovil Town | 46 | 23 | 5 | 18 | 70 | 57 | 74 |
| Oxford United | 46 | 18 | 17 | 11 | 55 | 44 | 71 |
| Swansea City | 46 | 15 | 14 | 17 | 58 | 61 | 59 |
| Boston United | 46 | 16 | 11 | 19 | 50 | 54 | 59 |
| Bury | 46 | 15 | 11 | 20 | 54 | 64 | 56 |
| Cambridge United | 46 | 14 | 14 | 18 | 55 | 67 | 56 |
| Cheltenham Town | 46 | 14 | 14 | 18 | 57 | 71 | 56 |
| Bristol Rovers | 46 | 14 | 13 | 19 | 50 | 61 | 55 |
| Kidderminster Harriers | 46 | 14 | 13 | 19 | 45 | 59 | 55 |
| Southend United | 46 | 14 | 12 | 20 | 51 | 63 | 54 |
| Darlington | 46 | 14 | 11 | 21 | 53 | 61 | 53 |
| Leyton Orient | 46 | 13 | 14 | 19 | 48 | 65 | 53 |
| Macclesfield Town | 46 | 13 | 13 | 20 | 54 | 69 | 52 |
| Rochdale | 46 | 12 | 14 | 20 | 49 | 58 | 50 |
| Scunthorpe United | 46 | 11 | 16 | 19 | 69 | 72 | 49 |
| *Carlisle United* | *46* | *12* | *9* | *25* | *46* | *69* | *45* |
| *York City* | *46* | *10* | *14* | *22* | *35* | *66* | *44* |

### Division Three Play-offs

| Lincoln City vs Huddersfield Town | 1-2, 2-2 |
|---|---|
| Northampton Town vs Mansfield Town | 0-2, 3-1 |
| *Mansfield Town won 5-4 on penalties* | |
| | |
| Huddersfield Town vs Mansfield Town | 0-0 |
| *Huddersfield won 4-1 on penalties* | |

## 2004 Football League Cup

### Semi-finals

| Arsenal vs Middlesbrough (0-1, 1-2) | 1-3 |
|---|---|
| Bolton vs Aston Villa (5-2, 0-2) | 5-4 |

### Final

The Millennium Stadium, Cardiff, 29th February 2004

**Bolton Wanderers 1** (Davies)
**Middlesbrough 2** (Job, Zenden)

*Attendance 72,634*

## F.A. PREMIER LEAGUE 2004-2005

| | | | | | | | |
|---|---|---|---|---|---|---|---|
| **CHELSEA** | 38 | 29 | 8 | 1 | 72 | 15 | 95 |
| Arsenal | 38 | 25 | 8 | 5 | 87 | 36 | 83 |
| Manchester United | 38 | 22 | 11 | 5 | 58 | 26 | 77 |
| Everton | 38 | 18 | 7 | 13 | 45 | 46 | 61 |
| Liverpool | 38 | 17 | 7 | 14 | 52 | 41 | 58 |
| Bolton Wanderers | 38 | 16 | 10 | 12 | 49 | 44 | 58 |
| Middlesbrough | 38 | 14 | 13 | 11 | 53 | 46 | 55 |
| Manchester City | 38 | 13 | 13 | 12 | 47 | 39 | 52 |
| Tottenham Hotspur | 38 | 14 | 10 | 14 | 47 | 41 | 52 |
| Aston Villa | 38 | 12 | 11 | 15 | 45 | 52 | 47 |
| Charlton Athletic | 38 | 12 | 10 | 16 | 42 | 58 | 46 |
| Birmingham City | 38 | 11 | 12 | 15 | 40 | 46 | 45 |
| Fulham | 38 | 12 | 8 | 18 | 52 | 60 | 44 |
| Newcastle United | 38 | 10 | 14 | 14 | 47 | 57 | 44 |
| Blackburn Rovers | 38 | 9 | 15 | 14 | 32 | 43 | 42 |
| Portsmouth | 38 | 10 | 9 | 19 | 43 | 59 | 39 |
| West Bromwich Albion | 38 | 6 | 16 | 16 | 36 | 61 | 34 |
| *Crystal Palace* | *38* | *7* | *12* | *19* | *41* | *62* | *33* |
| *Norwich City* | *38* | *7* | *12* | *19* | *42* | *77* | *33* |
| *Southampton* | *38* | *6* | *14* | *18* | *45* | *66* | *32* |

## THE CHAMPIONSHIP 2004-2005

| | | | | | | | |
|---|---|---|---|---|---|---|---|
| **Sunderland** | 46 | 29 | 7 | 10 | 76 | 41 | 94 |
| **Wigan Athletic** | 46 | 25 | 12 | 9 | 79 | 35 | 87 |
| Ipswich Town | 46 | 24 | 13 | 9 | 85 | 56 | 85 |
| Derby County | 46 | 22 | 10 | 14 | 71 | 60 | 76 |
| Preston North End | 46 | 21 | 12 | 13 | 67 | 58 | 75 |
| **West Ham United** | 46 | 21 | 10 | 15 | 66 | 56 | 73 |
| Reading | 46 | 19 | 13 | 14 | 51 | 44 | 70 |
| Sheffield United | 46 | 18 | 13 | 15 | 57 | 56 | 67 |
| Wolverhampton Wanderers | 46 | 15 | 21 | 10 | 72 | 59 | 66 |
| Millwall | 46 | 18 | 12 | 16 | 51 | 45 | 66 |
| Queens Park Rangers | 46 | 17 | 11 | 18 | 54 | 58 | 62 |
| Stoke City | 46 | 17 | 10 | 19 | 36 | 38 | 61 |
| Burnley | 46 | 15 | 15 | 16 | 38 | 39 | 60 |
| Leeds United | 46 | 14 | 18 | 14 | 49 | 52 | 60 |
| Leicester City | 46 | 12 | 21 | 13 | 49 | 46 | 57 |
| Cardiff City | 46 | 13 | 15 | 18 | 48 | 51 | 54 |
| Plymouth Argyle | 46 | 14 | 11 | 21 | 52 | 64 | 53 |
| Watford | 46 | 12 | 16 | 18 | 52 | 59 | 52 |
| Coventry City | 46 | 13 | 13 | 20 | 61 | 73 | 52 |
| Brighton & Hove Albion | 46 | 13 | 12 | 21 | 40 | 65 | 51 |
| Crewe Alexandra | 46 | 12 | 14 | 20 | 66 | 86 | 50 |
| *Gillingham* | *46* | *12* | *14* | *20* | *45* | *66* | *50* |
| *Nottingham Forest* | *46* | *9* | *17* | *20* | *42* | *66* | *44* |
| *Rotherham United* | *46* | *5* | *14* | *27* | *35* | *69* | *29* |

### The Championship Play-offs

| | |
|---|---|
| West Ham United vs Ipswich Town | 2-2, 2-0 |
| Preston North End vs Derby County | 2-0, 0-0 |
| West Ham United vs Preston North End | 1-0 |

## 2005 F.A. Cup

### Semi-finals

| | |
|---|---|
| Arsenal vs Blackburn Rovers | 3-0 |
| Manchester United vs Newcastle United | 4-1 |

### Final

The Millennium Stadium, Cardiff, 21st May 2005

**Arsenal 0**

**Manchester United 0** **(aet.)**

*Attendance 71,876*

*Arsenal won 5-4 on penalties*

## LEAGUE ONE 2004-2005

| | | | | | | | |
|---|---|---|---|---|---|---|---|
| **Luton Town** | 46 | 29 | 11 | 6 | 87 | 48 | 98 |
| **Hull City** | 46 | 26 | 8 | 12 | 80 | 53 | 86 |
| Tranmere Rovers | 46 | 22 | 13 | 11 | 73 | 55 | 79 |
| Brentford | 46 | 22 | 9 | 15 | 57 | 60 | 75 |
| **Sheffield Wednesday** | 46 | 19 | 15 | 12 | 77 | 59 | 72 |
| Hartlepool United | 46 | 21 | 8 | 17 | 76 | 66 | 71 |
| Bristol City | 46 | 18 | 16 | 12 | 74 | 57 | 70 |
| AFC Bournemouth | 46 | 20 | 10 | 16 | 77 | 64 | 70 |
| Huddersfield Town | 46 | 20 | 10 | 16 | 74 | 65 | 70 |
| Doncaster Rovers | 46 | 16 | 18 | 12 | 65 | 60 | 66 |
| Bradford City | 46 | 17 | 14 | 15 | 64 | 62 | 65 |
| Swindon Town | 46 | 17 | 12 | 17 | 66 | 68 | 63 |
| Barnsley | 46 | 14 | 19 | 13 | 69 | 64 | 61 |
| Walsall | 46 | 16 | 12 | 18 | 65 | 69 | 60 |
| Colchester United | 46 | 14 | 17 | 15 | 60 | 50 | 59 |
| Blackpool | 46 | 15 | 12 | 19 | 54 | 59 | 57 |
| Chesterfield | 46 | 14 | 15 | 17 | 55 | 62 | 57 |
| Port Vale | 46 | 17 | 5 | 24 | 49 | 59 | 56 |
| Oldham Athletic | 46 | 14 | 10 | 22 | 60 | 73 | 52 |
| Milton Keynes Dons | 46 | 12 | 15 | 19 | 54 | 68 | 51 |
| *Torquay United* | *46* | *12* | *15* | *19* | *55* | *79* | *51* |
| *Wrexham* | *46* | *13* | *14* | *19* | *62* | *80* | *43* |
| *Peterborough United* | *46* | *9* | *12* | *25* | *49* | *73* | *39* |
| *Stockport County* | *46* | *6* | *8* | *32* | *49* | *98* | *26* |

Wrexham had 10 points deducted

### League One Play-offs

| | |
|---|---|
| Sheffield Wednesday vs Brentford | 1-0, 2-1 |
| Hartlepool United vs Tranmere Rovers | 2-0, 0-2 |
| *Hartlepool United won 6-5 on penalties* | |
| Sheffield Wednesday vs Hartlepool United | 4-2 |

## LEAGUE TWO 2004-2005

| | | | | | | | |
|---|---|---|---|---|---|---|---|
| **Yeovil Town** | 46 | 25 | 8 | 13 | 90 | 65 | 83 |
| **Scunthorpe United** | 46 | 22 | 14 | 10 | 69 | 42 | 80 |
| **Swansea City** | 46 | 24 | 8 | 14 | 62 | 43 | 80 |
| **Southend United** | 46 | 22 | 12 | 12 | 65 | 46 | 78 |
| Macclesfield Town | 46 | 22 | 9 | 15 | 60 | 49 | 75 |
| Lincoln City | 46 | 21 | 8 | 17 | 76 | 66 | 71 |
| Northampton Town | 46 | 20 | 12 | 14 | 62 | 51 | 72 |
| Darlington | 46 | 20 | 12 | 14 | 57 | 49 | 72 |
| Rochdale | 46 | 16 | 18 | 12 | 54 | 48 | 66 |
| Wycombe Wanderers | 46 | 17 | 14 | 15 | 58 | 52 | 65 |
| Leyton Orient | 46 | 16 | 15 | 15 | 65 | 67 | 63 |
| Bristol Rovers | 46 | 13 | 21 | 12 | 60 | 57 | 60 |
| Mansfield Town | 46 | 15 | 15 | 16 | 56 | 56 | 60 |
| Cheltenham Town | 46 | 16 | 12 | 18 | 51 | 54 | 60 |
| Oxford United | 46 | 16 | 11 | 19 | 50 | 63 | 59 |
| Boston United | 46 | 14 | 16 | 16 | 62 | 58 | 58 |
| Bury | 46 | 14 | 16 | 16 | 54 | 54 | 58 |
| Grimsby Town | 46 | 13 | 17 | 16 | 47 | 51 | 56 |
| Notts County | 46 | 13 | 13 | 20 | 46 | 62 | 52 |
| Chester City | 46 | 12 | 16 | 18 | 43 | 69 | 52 |
| Shrewsbury Town | 46 | 11 | 16 | 19 | 48 | 53 | 49 |
| Rushden & Diamonds | 46 | 10 | 14 | 22 | 42 | 63 | 44 |
| *Kidderminster Harriers* | *46* | *10* | *9* | *27* | *38* | *81* | *39* |
| *Cambridge United* | *46* | *8* | *16* | *22* | *39* | *62* | *30* |

Cambridge United had 10 points deducted

### League Two Play-offs

| | |
|---|---|
| Lincoln City vs Macclesfield Town | 1-0, 1-1 |
| Northampton Town vs Southend United | 0-0, 0-1 |
| Southend United vs Lincoln City | 2-0 |

## 2005 Football League Cup

### Semi-finals

| | |
|---|---|
| Chelsea vs Manchester United (0-0, 2-1) | 2-1 |
| Liverpool vs Watford (1-0, 1-0) | 2-0 |

### Final

The Millennium Stadium, Cardiff, 27th February 2005

**Chelsea 3** (Gerrard (og), Drogba, Kezman)

**Liverpool 2** **(aet.)** (Riise, Nunez)

*Attendance 78,000*

## F.A. PREMIER LEAGUE 2005-2006

| | | | | | | | |
|---|---|---|---|---|---|---|---|
| **CHELSEA** | 38 | 29 | 4 | 5 | 72 | 22 | 91 |
| Manchester United | 38 | 25 | 8 | 5 | 72 | 34 | 83 |
| Liverpool | 38 | 25 | 7 | 6 | 57 | 25 | 82 |
| Arsenal | 38 | 20 | 7 | 11 | 68 | 31 | 67 |
| Tottenham Hotspur | 38 | 18 | 11 | 9 | 53 | 38 | 65 |
| Blackburn Rovers | 38 | 19 | 6 | 13 | 51 | 42 | 63 |
| Newcastle United | 38 | 17 | 7 | 14 | 47 | 42 | 58 |
| Bolton Wanderers | 38 | 15 | 11 | 12 | 49 | 41 | 56 |
| West Ham United | 38 | 16 | 7 | 15 | 52 | 55 | 55 |
| Wigan Athletic | 38 | 15 | 6 | 17 | 45 | 52 | 51 |
| Everton | 38 | 14 | 8 | 16 | 34 | 49 | 50 |
| Fulham | 38 | 14 | 6 | 18 | 48 | 58 | 48 |
| Charlton Athletic | 38 | 13 | 8 | 17 | 41 | 55 | 47 |
| Middlesbrough | 38 | 12 | 9 | 17 | 48 | 58 | 45 |
| Manchester City | 38 | 13 | 4 | 21 | 43 | 48 | 43 |
| Aston Villa | 38 | 10 | 12 | 16 | 42 | 55 | 42 |
| Portsmouth | 38 | 10 | 8 | 20 | 37 | 62 | 38 |
| *Birmingham City* | *38* | *8* | *10* | *20* | *28* | *50* | *34* |
| *West Bromwich Albion* | *38* | *7* | *9* | *22* | *31* | *58* | *30* |
| *Sunderland* | *38* | *3* | *6* | *29* | *26* | *69* | *15* |

## THE CHAMPIONSHIP 2005-2006

| | | | | | | | |
|---|---|---|---|---|---|---|---|
| **Reading** | 46 | 31 | 13 | 2 | 99 | 32 | 106 |
| **Sheffield United** | 46 | 26 | 12 | 8 | 76 | 46 | 90 |
| **Watford** | 46 | 22 | 15 | 9 | 77 | 53 | 81 |
| Preston North End | 46 | 20 | 20 | 6 | 59 | 30 | 80 |
| Leeds United | 46 | 21 | 15 | 10 | 57 | 38 | 78 |
| Crystal Palace | 46 | 21 | 12 | 13 | 67 | 48 | 75 |
| Wolverhampton Wanderers | 46 | 16 | 19 | 11 | 50 | 42 | 67 |
| Coventry City | 46 | 16 | 15 | 15 | 62 | 65 | 63 |
| Norwich City | 46 | 18 | 8 | 20 | 56 | 65 | 62 |
| Luton Town | 46 | 17 | 10 | 19 | 66 | 67 | 61 |
| Cardiff City | 46 | 16 | 12 | 18 | 58 | 59 | 60 |
| Southampton | 46 | 13 | 19 | 14 | 49 | 50 | 58 |
| Stoke City | 46 | 17 | 7 | 22 | 54 | 63 | 58 |
| Plymouth Argyle | 46 | 13 | 17 | 16 | 39 | 46 | 56 |
| Ipswich Town | 46 | 14 | 14 | 18 | 53 | 66 | 56 |
| Leicester City | 46 | 13 | 15 | 18 | 51 | 59 | 54 |
| Burnley | 46 | 14 | 12 | 20 | 46 | 54 | 54 |
| Hull City | 46 | 12 | 16 | 18 | 49 | 55 | 52 |
| Sheffield Wednesday | 46 | 13 | 13 | 20 | 39 | 52 | 52 |
| Derby County | 46 | 10 | 20 | 16 | 53 | 67 | 50 |
| Queens Park Rangers | 46 | 12 | 14 | 20 | 50 | 65 | 50 |
| *Crewe Alexandra* | *46* | *9* | *15* | *22* | *57* | *86* | *42* |
| *Millwall* | *46* | *8* | *16* | *22* | *35* | *62* | *40* |
| *Brighton & Hove Albion* | *46* | *7* | *17* | *22* | *39* | *71* | *38* |

### The Championship Play-offs

| | |
|---|---|
| Leeds United vs Preston North End | 1-1, 2-0 |
| Crystal Palace vs Watford | 0-3, 0-0 |
| Watford vs Leeds United | 3-0 |

## 2006 F.A. Cup

### Semi-finals

| | |
|---|---|
| Chelsea vs Liverpool | 1-2 |
| Middlesbrough vs West Ham United | 0-1 |

### Final

The Millennium Stadium, Cardiff, 13th May 2006

**Liverpool 3**   (Cisse, Gerrard 2)

**West Ham United 3   (aet.)**   (Carragher (og), Ashton, Konchesky)

*Attendance 74,000*

*Liverpool won 3-1 on penalties*

## LEAGUE ONE 2005-2006

| | | | | | | | |
|---|---|---|---|---|---|---|---|
| **Southend United** | 46 | 23 | 13 | 10 | 72 | 43 | 82 |
| **Colchester United** | 46 | 22 | 13 | 11 | 58 | 40 | 79 |
| Brentford | 46 | 20 | 16 | 10 | 72 | 52 | 76 |
| Huddersfield Town | 46 | 19 | 16 | 11 | 72 | 59 | 73 |
| **Barnsley** | 46 | 18 | 18 | 10 | 62 | 44 | 72 |
| Swansea City | 46 | 18 | 17 | 11 | 78 | 55 | 71 |
| Nottingham Forest | 46 | 19 | 12 | 15 | 67 | 52 | 69 |
| Doncaster Rovers | 46 | 20 | 9 | 17 | 55 | 51 | 69 |
| Bristol City | 46 | 18 | 11 | 17 | 66 | 62 | 65 |
| Oldham Athletic | 46 | 18 | 11 | 17 | 58 | 60 | 65 |
| Bradford City | 46 | 14 | 19 | 13 | 51 | 49 | 61 |
| Scunthorpe United | 46 | 15 | 15 | 16 | 68 | 73 | 60 |
| Port Vale | 46 | 16 | 12 | 18 | 49 | 54 | 60 |
| Gillingham | 46 | 16 | 12 | 18 | 50 | 64 | 60 |
| Yeovil Town | 46 | 15 | 11 | 20 | 54 | 62 | 56 |
| Chesterfield | 46 | 14 | 14 | 18 | 63 | 73 | 56 |
| AFC Bournemouth | 46 | 12 | 19 | 15 | 49 | 53 | 55 |
| Tranmere Rovers | 46 | 13 | 15 | 18 | 50 | 52 | 54 |
| Blackpool | 46 | 12 | 17 | 17 | 56 | 64 | 53 |
| Rotherham United | 46 | 12 | 16 | 18 | 52 | 62 | 52 |
| *Hartlepool United* | *46* | *11* | *17* | *18* | *44* | *59* | *50* |
| *Milton Keynes Dons* | *46* | *12* | *14* | *20* | *45* | *66* | *50* |
| *Swindon Town* | *46* | *11* | *15* | *20* | *46* | *65* | *48* |
| *Walsall* | *46* | *11* | *14* | *21* | *47* | *70* | *47* |

### League One Play-offs

| | |
|---|---|
| Barnsley vs Huddersfield Town | 0-1, 3-1 |
| Swansea City vs Brentford | 1-1, 2-0 |
| Swansea City vs Barnsley | 2-2 |
| *Barnsley won 4-3 on penalties* | |

## LEAGUE TWO 2005-2006

| | | | | | | | |
|---|---|---|---|---|---|---|---|
| **Carlisle United** | 46 | 25 | 11 | 10 | 84 | 42 | 86 |
| **Northampton Town** | 46 | 22 | 17 | 7 | 63 | 37 | 83 |
| **Leyton Orient** | 46 | 22 | 15 | 9 | 67 | 51 | 81 |
| Grimsby Town | 46 | 22 | 12 | 12 | 64 | 44 | 78 |
| **Cheltenham Town** | 46 | 19 | 15 | 12 | 65 | 53 | 72 |
| Wycombe Wanderers | 46 | 18 | 17 | 11 | 72 | 56 | 71 |
| Lincoln City | 46 | 15 | 21 | 10 | 65 | 53 | 66 |
| Darlington | 46 | 16 | 15 | 15 | 58 | 52 | 63 |
| Peterborough United | 46 | 17 | 11 | 18 | 57 | 49 | 62 |
| Shrewsbury Town | 46 | 16 | 13 | 17 | 55 | 55 | 61 |
| Boston United | 46 | 15 | 16 | 15 | 50 | 60 | 61 |
| Bristol Rovers | 46 | 17 | 9 | 20 | 59 | 67 | 60 |
| Wrexham | 46 | 15 | 14 | 17 | 61 | 54 | 59 |
| Rochdale | 46 | 14 | 14 | 18 | 66 | 69 | 56 |
| Chester City | 46 | 14 | 12 | 20 | 53 | 59 | 54 |
| Mansfield Town | 46 | 13 | 15 | 18 | 59 | 66 | 54 |
| Macclesfield Town | 46 | 12 | 18 | 16 | 60 | 71 | 54 |
| Barnet | 46 | 12 | 18 | 16 | 44 | 57 | 54 |
| Bury (-1) | 46 | 12 | 17 | 17 | 45 | 57 | 52 |
| Torquay United | 46 | 13 | 13 | 20 | 53 | 66 | 52 |
| Notts County | 46 | 12 | 16 | 18 | 48 | 63 | 52 |
| Stockport County | 46 | 11 | 19 | 16 | 57 | 78 | 52 |
| *Oxford United* | *46* | *11* | *16* | *19* | *43* | *57* | *49* |
| *Rushden & Diamonds* | *46* | *11* | *12* | *23* | *44* | *76* | *45* |

Bury had one point deducted

### League Two Play-offs

| | |
|---|---|
| Lincoln City vs Grimsby Town | 0-1, 1-2 |
| Wycombe Wanderers vs Cheltenham Town | 1-2, 0-0 |
| Cheltenham Town vs Grimsby Town | 1-0 |

## 2006 Football League Cup

### Semi-finals

| | |
|---|---|
| Blackburn Rovers vs Manchester United (1-1, 1-2) | 2-3 |
| Wigan Athletic vs Arsenal (1-0, 1-2 aet) | 2-2 |

Wigan Athletic won on the away goals rule

### Final

The Millennium Stadium, Cardiff, 26th February 2006

**Manchester United 4**   (Rooney 2, Saha, Ronaldo)

**Wigan Athletic 0**

*Attendance 66,866*

## F.A. PREMIER LEAGUE 2006-2007

| | | | | | | | |
|---|---|---|---|---|---|---|---|
| **MANCHESTER UNITED** | 38 | 28 | 5 | 5 | 83 | 27 | 89 |
| Chelsea | 38 | 24 | 11 | 3 | 64 | 24 | 83 |
| Liverpool | 38 | 20 | 8 | 10 | 57 | 27 | 68 |
| Arsenal | 38 | 19 | 11 | 8 | 63 | 35 | 68 |
| Tottenham Hotspur | 38 | 17 | 9 | 12 | 57 | 54 | 60 |
| Everton | 38 | 15 | 13 | 10 | 52 | 36 | 58 |
| Bolton Wanderers | 38 | 16 | 8 | 14 | 47 | 52 | 56 |
| Reading | 38 | 16 | 7 | 15 | 52 | 47 | 55 |
| Portsmouth | 38 | 14 | 12 | 12 | 45 | 42 | 54 |
| Blackburn Rovers | 38 | 15 | 7 | 16 | 52 | 54 | 52 |
| Aston Villa | 38 | 11 | 17 | 10 | 43 | 41 | 50 |
| Middlesbrough | 38 | 12 | 10 | 16 | 44 | 49 | 46 |
| Newcastle United | 38 | 11 | 10 | 17 | 38 | 47 | 43 |
| Manchester City | 38 | 11 | 9 | 18 | 29 | 44 | 42 |
| West Ham United | 38 | 12 | 5 | 21 | 35 | 59 | 41 |
| Fulham | 38 | 8 | 15 | 15 | 38 | 60 | 39 |
| Wigan Athletic | 38 | 10 | 8 | 20 | 37 | 59 | 38 |
| **Sheffield United** | 38 | 10 | 8 | 20 | 32 | 55 | 38 |
| **Charlton Athletic** | 38 | 8 | 10 | 20 | 34 | 60 | 34 |
| **Watford** | 38 | 5 | 13 | 20 | 29 | 59 | 28 |

## THE CHAMPIONSHIP 2006-2007

| | | | | | | | |
|---|---|---|---|---|---|---|---|
| **Sunderland** | 46 | 27 | 7 | 12 | 76 | 47 | 88 |
| **Birmingham City** | 46 | 26 | 8 | 12 | 67 | 42 | 86 |
| **Derby County** | 46 | 25 | 9 | 12 | 62 | 46 | 84 |
| West Bromwich Albion | 46 | 22 | 10 | 14 | 81 | 55 | 76 |
| Wolverhampton Wndrs | 46 | 22 | 10 | 14 | 59 | 56 | 76 |
| Southampton | 46 | 21 | 12 | 13 | 77 | 53 | 75 |
| Preston North End | 46 | 22 | 8 | 16 | 64 | 53 | 74 |
| Stoke City | 46 | 19 | 16 | 11 | 62 | 41 | 73 |
| Sheffield Wednesday | 46 | 20 | 11 | 15 | 70 | 66 | 71 |
| Colchester United | 46 | 20 | 9 | 17 | 70 | 56 | 69 |
| Plymouth Argyle | 46 | 17 | 16 | 13 | 63 | 62 | 67 |
| Crystal Palace | 46 | 18 | 11 | 17 | 59 | 51 | 65 |
| Cardiff City | 46 | 17 | 13 | 16 | 57 | 53 | 64 |
| Ipswich Town | 46 | 18 | 8 | 20 | 64 | 59 | 62 |
| Burnley | 46 | 15 | 12 | 19 | 52 | 49 | 57 |
| Norwich City | 46 | 16 | 9 | 21 | 56 | 71 | 57 |
| Coventry City | 46 | 16 | 8 | 22 | 47 | 62 | 56 |
| Queens Park Rangers | 46 | 14 | 11 | 21 | 54 | 68 | 53 |
| Leicester City | 46 | 13 | 14 | 19 | 49 | 64 | 53 |
| Barnsley | 46 | 15 | 5 | 26 | 53 | 85 | 50 |
| Hull City | 46 | 13 | 10 | 23 | 51 | 67 | 49 |
| *Southend United* | 46 | 10 | 12 | 24 | 47 | 80 | 42 |
| *Luton Town* | 46 | 10 | 10 | 26 | 53 | 81 | 40 |
| *Leeds United* | 46 | 13 | 7 | 26 | 46 | 72 | 36 |

Leeds United had 10 points deducted

### The Championship Play-offs

| | |
|---|---|
| Southampton vs Derby County | 1-2, 3-2 |

*Derby County won 4-3 on penalties*

| | |
|---|---|
| Wolverhampton Wands. vs West Bromwich Albion | 2-3, 0-1 |
| Derby County vs West Bromwich Albion | 1-0 |

## LEAGUE ONE 2006-2007

| | | | | | | | |
|---|---|---|---|---|---|---|---|
| **Scunthorpe United** | 46 | 26 | 13 | 7 | 73 | 35 | 91 |
| **Bristol City** | 46 | 25 | 10 | 11 | 63 | 39 | 85 |
| **Blackpool** | 46 | 24 | 11 | 11 | 76 | 49 | 83 |
| Nottingham Forest | 46 | 23 | 13 | 10 | 65 | 41 | 82 |
| Yeovil Town | 46 | 23 | 10 | 13 | 55 | 39 | 79 |
| Oldham Athletic | 46 | 21 | 12 | 13 | 69 | 47 | 75 |
| Swansea City | 46 | 20 | 12 | 14 | 69 | 53 | 72 |
| Carlisle United | 46 | 19 | 11 | 16 | 54 | 55 | 68 |
| Tranmere Rovers | 46 | 18 | 13 | 15 | 58 | 53 | 67 |
| Millwall | 46 | 19 | 9 | 18 | 59 | 62 | 66 |
| Doncaster Rovers | 46 | 16 | 15 | 15 | 52 | 47 | 63 |
| Port Vale | 46 | 18 | 6 | 22 | 64 | 65 | 60 |
| Crewe Alexandra | 46 | 17 | 9 | 20 | 66 | 72 | 60 |
| Northampton Town | 46 | 15 | 14 | 17 | 48 | 51 | 59 |
| Huddersfield Town | 46 | 14 | 17 | 15 | 60 | 69 | 59 |
| Gillingham | 46 | 17 | 8 | 21 | 56 | 77 | 59 |
| Cheltenham Town | 46 | 15 | 9 | 22 | 49 | 61 | 54 |
| Brighton & Hove Albion | 46 | 14 | 11 | 21 | 49 | 58 | 53 |
| AFC Bournemouth | 46 | 13 | 13 | 20 | 50 | 64 | 52 |
| Leyton Orient | 46 | 12 | 15 | 19 | 61 | 77 | 51 |
| *Chesterfield* | 46 | 12 | 11 | 23 | 45 | 53 | 47 |
| *Bradford City* | 46 | 11 | 14 | 21 | 47 | 65 | 47 |
| *Rotherham United* | 46 | 13 | 9 | 24 | 58 | 75 | 38 |
| *Brentford* | 46 | 8 | 13 | 25 | 40 | 79 | 37 |

Rotherham United had 10 points deducted

### League One Play-offs

| | |
|---|---|
| Yeovil Town vs Nottingham Forest | 0-2, 5-2 |
| Oldham Athletic vs Blackpool | 1-2, 1-3 |
| Blackpool vs Yeovil Town | 2-0 |

## LEAGUE TWO 2006-2007

| | | | | | | | |
|---|---|---|---|---|---|---|---|
| **Walsall** | 46 | 25 | 14 | 7 | 66 | 34 | 89 |
| **Hartlepool United** | 46 | 26 | 10 | 10 | 65 | 40 | 88 |
| **Swindon Town** | 46 | 25 | 10 | 11 | 58 | 38 | 85 |
| Milton Keynes Dons | 46 | 25 | 9 | 12 | 76 | 58 | 84 |
| Lincoln City | 46 | 21 | 11 | 14 | 70 | 59 | 74 |
| **Bristol Rovers** | 46 | 20 | 12 | 14 | 49 | 42 | 72 |
| Shrewsbury Town | 46 | 18 | 17 | 11 | 68 | 46 | 71 |
| Stockport County | 46 | 21 | 8 | 17 | 65 | 54 | 71 |
| Rochdale | 46 | 18 | 12 | 16 | 70 | 50 | 66 |
| Peterborough United | 46 | 18 | 11 | 17 | 70 | 61 | 65 |
| Darlington | 46 | 17 | 14 | 15 | 52 | 56 | 65 |
| Wycombe Wanderers | 46 | 16 | 14 | 16 | 52 | 47 | 62 |
| Notts County | 46 | 16 | 14 | 16 | 55 | 53 | 62 |
| Barnet | 46 | 16 | 11 | 19 | 55 | 70 | 59 |
| Grimsby Town | 46 | 17 | 8 | 21 | 57 | 73 | 59 |
| Hereford United | 46 | 14 | 13 | 19 | 45 | 53 | 55 |
| Mansfield Town | 46 | 14 | 12 | 20 | 58 | 63 | 54 |
| Chester City | 46 | 13 | 14 | 19 | 40 | 48 | 53 |
| Wrexham | 46 | 13 | 12 | 21 | 43 | 65 | 51 |
| Accrington Stanley | 46 | 13 | 11 | 22 | 70 | 81 | 50 |
| Bury | 46 | 13 | 11 | 22 | 46 | 61 | 50 |
| Macclesfield Town | 46 | 12 | 12 | 22 | 55 | 77 | 48 |
| *Boston United* | 46 | 12 | 10 | 24 | 51 | 80 | 46 |
| *Torquay United* | 46 | 7 | 14 | 25 | 36 | 63 | 35 |

### League Two Play-offs

| | |
|---|---|
| Bristol Rovers vs Lincoln City | 2-1, 5-3 |
| Shrewsbury Town vs Milton Keynes Dons | 0-0, 2-1 |
| Bristol Rovers vs Shrewsbury Town | 3-1 |

## 2007 F.A. Cup

### Semi-finals

| | |
|---|---|
| Blackburn Rovers vs Chelsea | 1-2 |
| Watford vs Manchester United | 1-4 |

### Final

Wembley, 19th May 2007

**Chelsea 1**  (Drogba)
**Manchester United 0**  (aet.)

*Attendance 89,826*

## 2007 Football League Cup

### Semi-finals

| | |
|---|---|
| Tottenham Hotspur vs Arsenal (2-2, 1-3 aet) | 3-5 |
| Wycombe Wanderers vs Chelsea (1-1, 0-4) | 1-5 |

### Final

The Millennium Stadium, Cardiff, 25th February 2007

**Chelsea 2**  (Drogba 2)
**Arsenal 1**  (Walcott)

*Attendance 70,073*

## F.A. PREMIER LEAGUE 2007-2008

| | | | | | | | |
|---|---|---|---|---|---|---|---|
| **MANCHESTER UNITED** | 38 | 27 | 6 | 5 | 80 | 22 | 87 |
| Chelsea | 38 | 25 | 10 | 3 | 65 | 26 | 85 |
| Arsenal | 38 | 24 | 11 | 3 | 74 | 31 | 83 |
| Liverpool | 38 | 21 | 13 | 4 | 67 | 28 | 76 |
| Everton | 38 | 19 | 8 | 11 | 55 | 33 | 65 |
| Aston Villa | 38 | 16 | 12 | 10 | 71 | 51 | 60 |
| Blackburn Rovers | 38 | 15 | 13 | 10 | 50 | 48 | 58 |
| Portsmouth | 38 | 16 | 9 | 13 | 48 | 40 | 57 |
| Manchester City | 38 | 15 | 10 | 13 | 45 | 53 | 55 |
| West Ham United | 38 | 13 | 10 | 15 | 42 | 50 | 49 |
| Tottenham Hotspur | 38 | 11 | 13 | 14 | 66 | 61 | 46 |
| Newcastle United | 38 | 11 | 10 | 17 | 45 | 65 | 43 |
| Middlesbrough | 38 | 10 | 12 | 16 | 43 | 53 | 42 |
| Wigan Athletic | 38 | 10 | 10 | 18 | 34 | 51 | 40 |
| Sunderland | 38 | 11 | 6 | 21 | 36 | 59 | 39 |
| Bolton Wanderers | 38 | 9 | 10 | 19 | 36 | 54 | 37 |
| Fulham | 38 | 8 | 12 | 18 | 38 | 60 | 36 |
| *Reading* | *38* | *10* | *6* | *22* | *41* | *66* | *36* |
| *Birmingham City* | *38* | *8* | *11* | *19* | *46* | *62* | *35* |
| *Derby County* | *38* | *1* | *8* | *29* | *20* | *89* | *11* |

## THE CHAMPIONSHIP 2007-2008

| | | | | | | | |
|---|---|---|---|---|---|---|---|
| **West Bromwich Albion** | 46 | 23 | 12 | 11 | 88 | 55 | 81 |
| **Stoke City** | 46 | 21 | 16 | 9 | 69 | 55 | 79 |
| **Hull City** | 46 | 21 | 12 | 13 | 65 | 47 | 75 |
| Bristol City | 46 | 20 | 14 | 12 | 54 | 53 | 74 |
| Crystal Palace | 46 | 18 | 17 | 11 | 58 | 42 | 71 |
| Watford | 46 | 18 | 16 | 12 | 62 | 56 | 70 |
| Wolverhampton Wanderers | 46 | 18 | 16 | 12 | 53 | 48 | 70 |
| Ipswich Town | 46 | 18 | 15 | 13 | 65 | 56 | 69 |
| Sheffield United | 46 | 17 | 15 | 14 | 56 | 51 | 66 |
| Plymouth Argyle | 46 | 17 | 13 | 16 | 60 | 50 | 64 |
| Charlton Athletic | 46 | 17 | 13 | 16 | 63 | 58 | 64 |
| Cardiff City | 46 | 16 | 16 | 14 | 59 | 55 | 64 |
| Burnley | 46 | 16 | 14 | 16 | 60 | 67 | 62 |
| Queens Park Rangers | 46 | 14 | 16 | 16 | 60 | 66 | 58 |
| Preston North End | 46 | 15 | 11 | 20 | 50 | 56 | 56 |
| Sheffield Wednesday | 46 | 14 | 13 | 19 | 54 | 55 | 55 |
| Norwich City | 46 | 15 | 10 | 21 | 49 | 59 | 55 |
| Barnsley | 46 | 14 | 13 | 19 | 52 | 65 | 55 |
| Blackpool | 46 | 12 | 18 | 16 | 59 | 64 | 54 |
| Southampton | 46 | 13 | 15 | 18 | 56 | 72 | 54 |
| Coventry City | 46 | 14 | 11 | 21 | 52 | 64 | 53 |
| *Leicester City* | *46* | *12* | *16* | *18* | *42* | *45* | *52* |
| *Scunthorpe United* | *46* | *11* | *13* | *22* | *46* | *69* | *46* |
| *Colchester United* | *46* | *7* | *17* | *22* | *62* | *86* | *38* |

### The Championship Play-offs

| | |
|---|---|
| Watford vs Hull City | 0-2, 1-4 |
| Crystal Palace vs Bristol City | 1-2, 1-2 |
| Hull City vs Bristol City | 1-0 |

## 2008 F.A. Cup

### Semi-finals

| | |
|---|---|
| Barnsley vs Cardiff City | 0-1 |
| West Bromwich Albion vs Portsmouth | 0-1 |

### Final

Wembley, 17th May 2008

**Portsmouth 1**   (Kanu)
**Cardiff City 0**

*Attendance 89,874*

## LEAGUE ONE 2007-2008

| | | | | | | | |
|---|---|---|---|---|---|---|---|
| **Swansea City** | 46 | 27 | 11 | 8 | 82 | 42 | 92 |
| **Nottingham Forest** | 46 | 22 | 16 | 8 | 64 | 32 | 82 |
| **Doncaster Rovers** | 46 | 23 | 11 | 12 | 65 | 41 | 80 |
| Carlisle United | 46 | 23 | 11 | 12 | 64 | 46 | 80 |
| Leeds United | 46 | 27 | 10 | 9 | 72 | 38 | 76 |
| Southend United | 46 | 22 | 10 | 14 | 70 | 55 | 76 |
| Brighton & Hove Albion | 46 | 19 | 12 | 15 | 58 | 50 | 69 |
| Oldham Athletic | 46 | 18 | 13 | 15 | 58 | 46 | 67 |
| Northampton Town | 46 | 17 | 15 | 14 | 60 | 55 | 66 |
| Huddersfield Town | 46 | 20 | 6 | 20 | 50 | 62 | 66 |
| Tranmere Rovers | 46 | 18 | 11 | 17 | 52 | 47 | 65 |
| Walsall | 46 | 16 | 16 | 14 | 52 | 46 | 64 |
| Swindon Town | 46 | 16 | 13 | 17 | 63 | 56 | 61 |
| Leyton Orient | 46 | 16 | 12 | 18 | 49 | 63 | 60 |
| Hartlepool United | 46 | 15 | 9 | 22 | 63 | 66 | 54 |
| Bristol Rovers | 46 | 12 | 17 | 17 | 45 | 53 | 53 |
| Millwall | 46 | 14 | 10 | 22 | 45 | 60 | 52 |
| Yeovil Town | 46 | 14 | 10 | 22 | 38 | 59 | 52 |
| Cheltenham Town | 46 | 13 | 12 | 21 | 42 | 64 | 51 |
| Crewe Alexandra | 46 | 12 | 14 | 20 | 47 | 65 | 50 |
| *AFC Bournemouth* | *46* | *17* | *7* | *22* | *62* | *72* | *48* |
| *Gillingham* | *46* | *11* | *13* | *22* | *44* | *73* | *46* |
| *Port Vale* | *46* | *9* | *11* | *26* | *47* | *81* | *38* |
| *Luton Town* | *46* | *11* | *10* | *25* | *43* | *63* | *33* |

Leeds United had 15 points deducted
AFC Bournemouth and Luton Town had 10 points deducted

### League One Play-offs

| | |
|---|---|
| Southend United vs Doncaster Rovers | 0-0, 1-5 |
| Leeds United vs Carlisle United | 1-2, 2-0 |
| Doncaster Rovers vs Leeds United | 1-0 |

## LEAGUE TWO 2007-2008

| | | | | | | | |
|---|---|---|---|---|---|---|---|
| **Milton Keynes Dons** | 46 | 29 | 10 | 7 | 82 | 37 | 97 |
| **Peterborough United** | 46 | 28 | 8 | 10 | 84 | 43 | 92 |
| **Hereford United** | 46 | 26 | 10 | 10 | 72 | 41 | 88 |
| **Stockport County** | 46 | 24 | 10 | 12 | 72 | 54 | 82 |
| Rochdale | 46 | 23 | 11 | 12 | 77 | 54 | 80 |
| Darlington | 46 | 22 | 12 | 12 | 67 | 40 | 78 |
| Wycombe Wanderers | 46 | 22 | 12 | 12 | 56 | 42 | 78 |
| Chesterfield | 46 | 19 | 12 | 15 | 76 | 56 | 69 |
| Rotherham United | 46 | 21 | 11 | 14 | 62 | 58 | 64 |
| Bradford City | 46 | 17 | 11 | 18 | 63 | 61 | 62 |
| Morecambe | 46 | 16 | 12 | 18 | 59 | 63 | 60 |
| Barnet | 46 | 16 | 12 | 18 | 56 | 63 | 60 |
| Bury | 46 | 16 | 11 | 19 | 58 | 61 | 59 |
| Brentford | 46 | 17 | 8 | 21 | 52 | 70 | 59 |
| Lincoln City | 46 | 18 | 4 | 24 | 61 | 77 | 58 |
| Grimsby Town | 46 | 15 | 10 | 21 | 55 | 66 | 55 |
| Accrington Stanley | 46 | 16 | 3 | 27 | 49 | 83 | 51 |
| Shrewsbury Town | 46 | 12 | 14 | 20 | 56 | 65 | 50 |
| Macclesfield Town | 46 | 11 | 17 | 18 | 47 | 64 | 50 |
| Dagenham & Redbridge | 46 | 13 | 10 | 23 | 49 | 70 | 49 |
| Notts County | 46 | 10 | 18 | 18 | 37 | 53 | 48 |
| Chester City | 46 | 12 | 11 | 23 | 51 | 68 | 47 |
| *Mansfield Town* | *46* | *11* | *9* | *26* | *48* | *68* | *42* |
| *Wrexham* | *46* | *10* | *10* | *26* | *38* | *70* | *40* |

Rotherham United had 10 points deducted

### League Two Play-offs

| | |
|---|---|
| Wycombe Wanderers vs Stockport County | 1-1, 0-1 |
| Darlington vs Rochdale | 2-1, 1-2 |
| *Rochdale won 5-4 on penalties* | |
| Rochdale vs Stockport County | 2-3 |

## 2008 Football League Cup

### Semi-finals

| | |
|---|---|
| Chelsea vs Everton (2-1, 1-0) | 3-1 |
| Arsenal vs Tottenham Hotspur (1-1, 1-5) | 2-6 |

### Final

Wembley, 24th February 2008

**Chelsea 1**   (Drogba)
**Tottenham Hotspur 2 (aet.)**   (Berbatov (pen), Woodgate)

*Attendance 87,660*

## F.A. PREMIER LEAGUE 2008-2009

| | | | | | | | |
|---|---|---|---|---|---|---|---|
| **MANCHESTER UNITED** | 38 | 28 | 6 | 4 | 68 | 24 | 90 |
| Liverpool | 38 | 25 | 11 | 2 | 77 | 27 | 86 |
| Chelsea | 38 | 25 | 8 | 5 | 68 | 24 | 83 |
| Arsenal | 38 | 20 | 12 | 6 | 68 | 37 | 72 |
| Everton | 38 | 17 | 12 | 9 | 55 | 37 | 63 |
| Aston Villa | 38 | 17 | 11 | 10 | 54 | 48 | 62 |
| Fulham | 38 | 14 | 11 | 13 | 39 | 34 | 53 |
| Tottenham Hotspur | 38 | 14 | 9 | 15 | 45 | 45 | 51 |
| West Ham United | 38 | 14 | 9 | 15 | 42 | 45 | 51 |
| Manchester City | 38 | 15 | 5 | 18 | 58 | 50 | 50 |
| Wigan Athletic | 38 | 12 | 9 | 17 | 34 | 45 | 45 |
| Stoke City | 38 | 12 | 9 | 17 | 38 | 55 | 45 |
| Bolton Wanderers | 38 | 11 | 8 | 19 | 41 | 53 | 41 |
| Portsmouth | 38 | 10 | 11 | 17 | 38 | 57 | 41 |
| Blackburn Rovers | 38 | 10 | 11 | 17 | 40 | 60 | 41 |
| Sunderland | 38 | 9 | 9 | 20 | 34 | 54 | 36 |
| Hull City | 38 | 8 | 11 | 19 | 39 | 64 | 35 |
| *Newcastle United* | *38* | *7* | *13* | *18* | *40* | *59* | *34* |
| *Middlesbrough* | *38* | *7* | *11* | *20* | *28* | *57* | *32* |
| *West Bromwich Albion* | *38* | *8* | *8* | *22* | *36* | *67* | *32* |

### The Championship Play-offs

| | |
|---|---|
| Preston North End vs Sheffield United | 1-1, 0-1 |
| Burnley vs Reading | 1-0, 2-0 |
| Sheffield United vs Burnley | 0-1 |

## THE CHAMPIONSHIP 2008-2009

| | | | | | | | |
|---|---|---|---|---|---|---|---|
| **Wolverhampton Wanderers** | 46 | 27 | 9 | 10 | 80 | 52 | 90 |
| **Birmingham City** | 46 | 23 | 14 | 9 | 54 | 37 | 83 |
| Sheffield United | 46 | 22 | 14 | 10 | 64 | 39 | 80 |
| Reading | 46 | 21 | 14 | 11 | 72 | 40 | 77 |
| **Burnley** | 46 | 21 | 13 | 12 | 72 | 60 | 76 |
| Preston North End | 46 | 21 | 11 | 14 | 66 | 54 | 74 |
| Cardiff City | 46 | 19 | 17 | 10 | 65 | 53 | 74 |
| Swansea City | 46 | 16 | 20 | 10 | 63 | 50 | 68 |
| Ipswich Town | 46 | 17 | 15 | 14 | 62 | 53 | 66 |
| Bristol City | 46 | 15 | 16 | 15 | 54 | 54 | 61 |
| Queen's Park Rangers | 46 | 15 | 16 | 15 | 42 | 44 | 61 |
| Sheffield Wednesday | 46 | 16 | 13 | 17 | 51 | 58 | 61 |
| Watford | 46 | 16 | 10 | 20 | 68 | 72 | 58 |
| Doncaster Rovers | 46 | 17 | 7 | 22 | 42 | 53 | 58 |
| Crystal Palace | 46 | 15 | 12 | 19 | 52 | 55 | 57 |
| Blackpool | 46 | 13 | 17 | 16 | 47 | 58 | 56 |
| Coventry City | 46 | 13 | 15 | 18 | 47 | 58 | 54 |
| Derby County | 46 | 14 | 12 | 20 | 55 | 67 | 54 |
| Nottingham Forest | 46 | 13 | 14 | 19 | 50 | 65 | 53 |
| Barnsley | 46 | 13 | 13 | 20 | 45 | 58 | 52 |
| Plymouth Argyle | 46 | 13 | 12 | 21 | 44 | 57 | 51 |
| *Norwich City* | *46* | *12* | *10* | *24* | *57* | *70* | *46* |
| *Southampton* | *46* | *10* | *15* | *21* | *46* | *69* | *45* |
| *Charlton Athletic* | *46* | *8* | *15* | *23* | *52* | *74* | *39* |

### League One Play-offs

| | |
|---|---|
| Scunthorpe United vs Milton Keynes Dons | 1-1, 0-0 |
| *Scunthorpe United won 7-6 on penalties* | |
| Millwall vs Leeds United | 1-0, 1-1 |
| Scunthorpe United vs Millwall | 3-2 |

## 2009 F.A. Cup

### Semi-finals

| | |
|---|---|
| Arsenal vs Chelsea | 1-2 |
| Manchester United vs Everton | 0-1 (aet) |
| Everton won 4-2 on penalties | |

### Final

Wembley, 30th May 2009

**Chelsea 2**  (Drogba, Lampard)
**Everton 1**  (Saha)

*Attendance 89,391*

## LEAGUE ONE 2008-2009

| | | | | | | | |
|---|---|---|---|---|---|---|---|
| **Leicester City** | 46 | 27 | 15 | 4 | 84 | 39 | 96 |
| **Peterborough United** | 46 | 26 | 11 | 9 | 78 | 54 | 89 |
| Milton Keynes Dons | 46 | 26 | 9 | 11 | 83 | 47 | 87 |
| Leeds United | 46 | 26 | 6 | 14 | 77 | 49 | 84 |
| Millwall | 46 | 25 | 7 | 14 | 63 | 53 | 82 |
| **Scunthorpe United** | 46 | 22 | 10 | 14 | 82 | 63 | 76 |
| Tranmere Rovers | 46 | 21 | 11 | 14 | 62 | 49 | 74 |
| Southend United | 46 | 21 | 8 | 17 | 58 | 61 | 71 |
| Huddersfield Town | 46 | 18 | 14 | 14 | 62 | 65 | 68 |
| Oldham Athletic | 46 | 16 | 17 | 13 | 66 | 65 | 65 |
| Bristol Rovers | 46 | 17 | 12 | 17 | 79 | 61 | 63 |
| Colchester United | 46 | 18 | 9 | 19 | 58 | 58 | 63 |
| Walsall | 46 | 17 | 10 | 19 | 61 | 66 | 61 |
| Leyton Orient | 46 | 15 | 11 | 20 | 45 | 57 | 56 |
| Swindon Town | 46 | 12 | 17 | 17 | 68 | 71 | 53 |
| Brighton & Hove Albion | 46 | 13 | 13 | 20 | 55 | 70 | 52 |
| Yeovil Town | 46 | 12 | 15 | 19 | 41 | 66 | 51 |
| Stockport County | 46 | 16 | 12 | 18 | 59 | 57 | 50 |
| Hartlepool United | 46 | 13 | 11 | 22 | 66 | 79 | 50 |
| Carlisle United | 46 | 12 | 14 | 20 | 56 | 69 | 50 |
| *Northampton Town* | *46* | *12* | *13* | *21* | *61* | *65* | *49* |
| *Crewe Alexandra* | *46* | *12* | *10* | *24* | *59* | *82* | *46* |
| *Cheltenham Town* | *46* | *9* | *12* | *25* | *51* | *91* | *39* |
| *Hereford United* | *46* | *9* | *7* | *30* | *42* | *79* | *34* |

Stockport County had 10 points deducted

## LEAGUE TWO 2008-2009

| | | | | | | | |
|---|---|---|---|---|---|---|---|
| **Brentford** | 46 | 23 | 16 | 7 | 65 | 36 | 85 |
| **Exeter City** | 46 | 22 | 13 | 11 | 65 | 50 | 79 |
| **Wycombe Wanderers** | 46 | 20 | 18 | 8 | 54 | 33 | 78 |
| Bury | 46 | 21 | 15 | 10 | 63 | 43 | 78 |
| **Gillingham** | 46 | 21 | 12 | 13 | 58 | 55 | 75 |
| Rochdale | 46 | 19 | 13 | 14 | 70 | 59 | 70 |
| Shrewsbury Town | 46 | 17 | 18 | 11 | 61 | 44 | 69 |
| Dagenham & Redbridge | 46 | 19 | 11 | 16 | 77 | 53 | 68 |
| Bradford City | 46 | 18 | 13 | 15 | 66 | 55 | 67 |
| Chesterfield | 46 | 16 | 15 | 15 | 62 | 57 | 63 |
| Morecambe | 46 | 15 | 18 | 13 | 53 | 56 | 63 |
| Darlington | 46 | 20 | 12 | 14 | 61 | 44 | 62 |
| Lincoln City | 46 | 14 | 17 | 15 | 53 | 52 | 59 |
| Rotherham United | 46 | 21 | 12 | 13 | 60 | 46 | 58 |
| Aldershot Town | 46 | 14 | 12 | 20 | 59 | 80 | 54 |
| Accrington Stanley | 46 | 13 | 11 | 22 | 42 | 59 | 50 |
| Barnet | 46 | 11 | 15 | 20 | 56 | 74 | 48 |
| Port Vale | 46 | 13 | 9 | 24 | 44 | 66 | 48 |
| Notts County | 46 | 11 | 14 | 21 | 49 | 69 | 47 |
| Macclesfield Town | 46 | 13 | 8 | 25 | 45 | 77 | 47 |
| AFC Bournemouth | 46 | 17 | 12 | 17 | 59 | 51 | 46 |
| Grimsby Town | 46 | 9 | 14 | 23 | 51 | 69 | 41 |
| *Chester City* | *46* | *8* | *13* | *25* | *43* | *81* | *37* |
| *Luton Town* | *46* | *13* | *17* | *16* | *58* | *65* | *26* |

Darlington had 10 points deducted
Rotherham United had 17 points deducted
AFC Bournemouth had 17 points deducted
Luton Town had 30 points deducted

### League Two Play-offs

| | |
|---|---|
| Shrewsbury Town vs Bury | 0-1, 1-0 |
| *Shrewsbury Town won 4-3 on penalties* | |
| Rochdale vs Gillingham | 0-0, 1-2 |
| Gillingham vs Shrewsbury Town | 1-0 |

## 2009 Football League Cup

### Semi-finals

| | | |
|---|---|---|
| Derby County vs Manchester United | (1-0, 2-4) | 3-4 |
| Tottenham Hotspur vs Burnley | (4-1, 2-3) | 6-4 |

### Final

Wembley, 1st March 2009

**Manchester United 0**
**Tottenham Hotspur 0 (aet.)**

*Attendance 88,217*

*Manchester United won 4-1 on penalties*

## F.A. PREMIER LEAGUE 2009-2010

| | | | | | | | |
|---|---|---|---|---|---|---|---|
| **CHELSEA** | **38** | **27** | **5** | **6** | **103** | **32** | **86** |
| Manchester United | 38 | 27 | 4 | 7 | 86 | 28 | 85 |
| Arsenal | 38 | 23 | 6 | 9 | 83 | 41 | 75 |
| Tottenham Hotspur | 38 | 21 | 7 | 10 | 67 | 41 | 70 |
| Manchester City | 38 | 18 | 13 | 7 | 73 | 45 | 67 |
| Aston Villa | 38 | 17 | 13 | 8 | 52 | 39 | 64 |
| Liverpool | 38 | 18 | 9 | 11 | 61 | 35 | 63 |
| Everton | 38 | 16 | 13 | 9 | 60 | 49 | 61 |
| Birmingham City | 38 | 13 | 11 | 14 | 38 | 47 | 50 |
| Blackburn Rovers | 38 | 13 | 11 | 14 | 41 | 55 | 50 |
| Stoke City | 38 | 11 | 14 | 13 | 34 | 48 | 47 |
| Fulham | 38 | 12 | 10 | 16 | 39 | 46 | 46 |
| Sunderland | 38 | 11 | 11 | 16 | 48 | 56 | 44 |
| Bolton Wanderers | 38 | 10 | 9 | 19 | 42 | 67 | 39 |
| Wolverhampton Wanderers | 38 | 9 | 11 | 18 | 32 | 56 | 38 |
| Wigan Athletic | 38 | 9 | 9 | 20 | 37 | 79 | 36 |
| West Ham United | 38 | 8 | 11 | 19 | 47 | 66 | 35 |
| *Burnley* | *38* | *8* | *6* | *24* | *42* | *82* | *30* |
| *Hull City* | *38* | *6* | *12* | *20* | *34* | *75* | *30* |
| *Portsmouth* | *38* | *7* | *7* | *24* | *34* | *66* | *19* |

Portsmouth had 9 points deducted

## THE CHAMPIONSHIP 2009-2010

| | | | | | | | |
|---|---|---|---|---|---|---|---|
| **Newcastle United** | **46** | **30** | **12** | **4** | **90** | **35** | **102** |
| **West Bromwich Albion** | **46** | **26** | **13** | **7** | **89** | **48** | **91** |
| Nottingham Forest | 46 | 22 | 13 | 11 | 65 | 40 | 79 |
| Cardiff City | 46 | 22 | 10 | 14 | 73 | 54 | 76 |
| Leicester City | 46 | 21 | 13 | 12 | 61 | 45 | 76 |
| **Blackpool** | **46** | **19** | **13** | **14** | **74** | **58** | **70** |
| Swansea City | 46 | 17 | 18 | 11 | 40 | 37 | 69 |
| Sheffield United | 46 | 17 | 14 | 15 | 62 | 55 | 65 |
| Reading | 46 | 17 | 12 | 17 | 68 | 63 | 63 |
| Bristol City | 46 | 15 | 18 | 13 | 56 | 65 | 63 |
| Middlesbrough | 46 | 16 | 14 | 16 | 58 | 50 | 62 |
| Doncaster Rovers | 46 | 15 | 15 | 16 | 59 | 58 | 60 |
| Queens Park Rangers | 46 | 14 | 15 | 17 | 58 | 65 | 57 |
| Derby County | 46 | 15 | 11 | 20 | 53 | 63 | 56 |
| Ipswich Town | 46 | 12 | 20 | 14 | 50 | 61 | 56 |
| Watford | 46 | 14 | 12 | 20 | 61 | 68 | 54 |
| Preston North End | 46 | 13 | 15 | 18 | 58 | 73 | 54 |
| Barnsley | 46 | 14 | 12 | 20 | 53 | 69 | 54 |
| Coventry City | 46 | 13 | 15 | 18 | 47 | 64 | 54 |
| Scunthorpe United | 46 | 14 | 10 | 22 | 62 | 84 | 52 |
| Crystal Palace | 46 | 14 | 17 | 15 | 50 | 53 | 49 |
| *Sheffield Wednesday* | *46* | *11* | *14* | *21* | *49* | *69* | *47* |
| *Plymouth Argyle* | *46* | *11* | *8* | *27* | *43* | *68* | *41* |
| *Peterborough United* | *46* | *8* | *10* | *28* | *46* | *80* | *34* |

Crystal Palace had 10 points deducted

### The Championship Play-offs

| | |
|---|---|
| Blackpool vs Nottingham Forest | 2-1, 4-3 |
| Leicester City vs Cardiff City | 0-1, 3-2 |
| *Cardiff City won 4-3 on penalties* | |
| Blackpool vs Cardiff City | 3-2 |

## 2010 F.A. Cup

### Semi-finals

| | |
|---|---|
| Aston Villa vs Chelsea | 0-3 |
| Tottenham Hotspur vs Portsmouth | 0-2 (aet) |

### Final

Wembley, 15th May 2010

**Chelsea 1**　(Drogba)
**Portsmouth  0**

*Attendance  88,335*

## LEAGUE ONE 2009-2010

| | | | | | | | |
|---|---|---|---|---|---|---|---|
| **Norwich City** | **46** | **29** | **8** | **9** | **89** | **47** | **95** |
| **Leeds United** | **46** | **25** | **11** | **10** | **77** | **44** | **86** |
| **Millwall** | **46** | **24** | **13** | **9** | **76** | **44** | **85** |
| Charlton Athletic | 46 | 23 | 15 | 8 | 73 | 57 | 84 |
| Swindon Town | 46 | 22 | 16 | 8 | 71 | 48 | 82 |
| Huddersfield Town | 46 | 23 | 11 | 12 | 82 | 56 | 80 |
| Southampton | 46 | 23 | 14 | 9 | 85 | 47 | 73 |
| Colchester United | 46 | 20 | 12 | 14 | 64 | 52 | 72 |
| Brentford | 46 | 14 | 20 | 12 | 55 | 52 | 62 |
| Walsall | 46 | 16 | 14 | 16 | 60 | 63 | 62 |
| Bristol Rovers | 46 | 19 | 5 | 22 | 59 | 70 | 62 |
| Milton Keynes Dons | 46 | 17 | 9 | 20 | 60 | 68 | 60 |
| Brighton & Hove Albion | 46 | 15 | 14 | 17 | 56 | 60 | 59 |
| Carlisle United | 46 | 15 | 13 | 18 | 63 | 66 | 58 |
| Yeovil Town | 46 | 13 | 14 | 19 | 55 | 59 | 53 |
| Oldham Athletic | 46 | 13 | 13 | 20 | 39 | 57 | 52 |
| Leyton Orient | 46 | 13 | 12 | 21 | 53 | 63 | 51 |
| Exeter City | 46 | 11 | 18 | 17 | 48 | 60 | 51 |
| Tranmere Rovers | 46 | 14 | 9 | 23 | 45 | 72 | 51 |
| Hartlepool United | 46 | 14 | 11 | 21 | 59 | 67 | 50 |
| *Gillingham* | *46* | *12* | *14* | *20* | *48* | *64* | *50* |
| *Wycombe Wanderers* | *46* | *10* | *15* | *21* | *56* | *76* | *45* |
| *Southend United* | *46* | *10* | *13* | *23* | *51* | *72* | *43* |
| *Stockport County* | *46* | *5* | *10* | *31* | *35* | *95* | *25* |

Southampton had 10 points deducted
Hartlepool United had 3 points deducted

### League One Play-offs

| | |
|---|---|
| Swindon Town vs Charlton Athletic | 2-1, 1-2 |
| *Swindon Town won 5-4 on penalties* | |
| Huddersfield Town vs Millwall | 0-0, 0-2 |
| Millwall vs Swindon Town | 1-0 |

## LEAGUE TWO 2009-2010

| | | | | | | | |
|---|---|---|---|---|---|---|---|
| **Notts County** | **46** | **27** | **12** | **7** | **96** | **31** | **93** |
| **Bournemouth** | **46** | **25** | **8** | **13** | **61** | **44** | **83** |
| **Rochdale** | **46** | **25** | **7** | **14** | **82** | **48** | **82** |
| Morecambe | 46 | 20 | 13 | 13 | 73 | 64 | 73 |
| Rotherham United | 46 | 21 | 10 | 15 | 55 | 52 | 73 |
| Aldershot Town | 46 | 20 | 12 | 14 | 69 | 56 | 72 |
| *Dagenham & Redbridge* | *46* | *20* | *12* | *14* | *69* | *58* | *72* |
| Chesterfield | 46 | 21 | 7 | 18 | 61 | 62 | 70 |
| Bury | 46 | 19 | 12 | 15 | 54 | 59 | 69 |
| Port Vale | 46 | 17 | 17 | 12 | 61 | 50 | 68 |
| Northampton Town | 46 | 18 | 13 | 15 | 62 | 53 | 67 |
| Shrewsbury Town | 46 | 17 | 12 | 17 | 55 | 54 | 63 |
| Burton Albion | 46 | 17 | 11 | 18 | 71 | 71 | 62 |
| Bradford City | 46 | 16 | 14 | 16 | 59 | 62 | 62 |
| Accrington Stanley | 46 | 18 | 7 | 21 | 62 | 74 | 61 |
| Hereford United | 46 | 17 | 8 | 21 | 54 | 65 | 59 |
| Torquay United | 46 | 14 | 15 | 17 | 64 | 55 | 57 |
| Crewe Alexandra | 46 | 15 | 10 | 21 | 68 | 73 | 55 |
| Macclesfield Town | 46 | 12 | 18 | 16 | 49 | 58 | 54 |
| Lincoln City | 46 | 13 | 11 | 22 | 42 | 65 | 50 |
| Barnet | 46 | 12 | 12 | 22 | 47 | 63 | 48 |
| Cheltenham Town | 46 | 10 | 18 | 18 | 54 | 71 | 48 |
| *Grimsby Town* | *46* | *9* | *17* | *20* | *45* | *71* | *44* |
| *Darlington* | *46* | *8* | *6* | *32* | *33* | *87* | *30* |

### League Two Play-offs

| | |
|---|---|
| Aldershot Town vs Rotherham United | 0-1, 0-2 |
| Dagenham & Redbridge vs Morecambe | 6-0, 1-2 |
| Dagenham & Redbridge vs Rotherham United | 3-2 |

## 2010 Football League Cup

### Semi-finals

| | |
|---|---|
| Blackburn Rovers vs Aston Villa (0-1, 4-6) | 4-7 |
| Manchester City vs Manchester United (2-1, 1-3) | 3-4 |

### Final

Wembley, 28th February 2010

**Aston Villa  1**　(Milner pen)
**Manchester United  2**　(Owen, Rooney)

*Attendance  88,596*

## F.A. PREMIER LEAGUE 2010-2011

| | | | | | | | |
|---|---|---|---|---|---|---|---|
| **MANCHESTER UNITED** | 38 | 23 | 11 | 4 | 78 | 37 | 80 |
| Chelsea | 38 | 21 | 8 | 9 | 69 | 33 | 71 |
| Manchester City | 38 | 21 | 8 | 9 | 60 | 33 | 71 |
| Arsenal | 38 | 19 | 11 | 8 | 72 | 43 | 68 |
| Tottenham Hotspur | 38 | 16 | 14 | 8 | 55 | 46 | 62 |
| Liverpool | 38 | 17 | 7 | 14 | 59 | 44 | 58 |
| Everton | 38 | 13 | 15 | 10 | 51 | 45 | 54 |
| Fulham | 38 | 11 | 16 | 11 | 49 | 43 | 49 |
| Aston Villa | 38 | 12 | 12 | 14 | 48 | 59 | 48 |
| Sunderland | 38 | 12 | 11 | 15 | 45 | 56 | 47 |
| West Bromwich Albion | 38 | 12 | 11 | 15 | 56 | 71 | 47 |
| Newcastle United | 38 | 11 | 13 | 14 | 56 | 57 | 46 |
| Stoke City | 38 | 13 | 7 | 18 | 46 | 48 | 46 |
| Bolton Wanderers | 38 | 12 | 10 | 16 | 52 | 56 | 46 |
| Blackburn Rovers | 38 | 11 | 10 | 17 | 46 | 59 | 43 |
| Wigan Athletic | 38 | 9 | 15 | 14 | 40 | 61 | 42 |
| Wolverhampton Wanderers | 38 | 11 | 7 | 20 | 46 | 66 | 40 |
| *Birmingham City* | 38 | 8 | 15 | 15 | 37 | 58 | 39 |
| *Blackpool* | 38 | 10 | 9 | 19 | 55 | 78 | 39 |
| *West Ham United* | 38 | 7 | 12 | 19 | 43 | 70 | 33 |

### The Championship Play-offs

| | |
|---|---|
| Nottingham Forest vs Swansea City | 0-0, 1-3 |
| Reading vs Cardiff City | 0-0, 3-0 |
| Swansea City vs Reading | 4-2 |

## THE CHAMPIONSHIP 2010-2011

| | | | | | | | |
|---|---|---|---|---|---|---|---|
| **Queen's Park Rangers** | 46 | 24 | 16 | 6 | 71 | 32 | 88 |
| **Norwich City** | 46 | 23 | 15 | 8 | 83 | 58 | 84 |
| **Swansea City** | 46 | 24 | 8 | 14 | 69 | 42 | 80 |
| Cardiff City | 46 | 23 | 11 | 12 | 76 | 54 | 80 |
| Reading | 46 | 20 | 17 | 9 | 77 | 51 | 77 |
| Nottingham Forest | 46 | 20 | 15 | 11 | 69 | 50 | 75 |
| Leeds United | 46 | 19 | 15 | 12 | 81 | 70 | 72 |
| Burnley | 46 | 18 | 14 | 14 | 65 | 61 | 68 |
| Millwall | 46 | 18 | 13 | 15 | 62 | 48 | 67 |
| Leicester City | 46 | 19 | 10 | 17 | 76 | 71 | 67 |
| Hull City | 46 | 16 | 17 | 13 | 52 | 51 | 65 |
| Middlesbrough | 46 | 17 | 11 | 18 | 68 | 68 | 62 |
| Ipswich Town | 46 | 18 | 8 | 20 | 62 | 68 | 62 |
| Watford | 46 | 16 | 13 | 17 | 77 | 71 | 61 |
| Bristol City | 46 | 17 | 9 | 20 | 62 | 65 | 60 |
| Portsmouth | 46 | 15 | 13 | 18 | 53 | 60 | 58 |
| Barnsley | 46 | 14 | 14 | 18 | 55 | 66 | 56 |
| Coventry City | 46 | 14 | 13 | 19 | 54 | 58 | 55 |
| Derby County | 46 | 13 | 10 | 23 | 58 | 71 | 49 |
| Crystal Palace | 46 | 12 | 12 | 22 | 44 | 69 | 48 |
| Doncaster Rovers | 46 | 11 | 15 | 20 | 55 | 81 | 48 |
| *Preston North End* | 46 | 10 | 12 | 24 | 54 | 79 | 42 |
| *Sheffield United* | 46 | 11 | 9 | 26 | 44 | 79 | 42 |
| *Scunthorpe United* | 46 | 12 | 6 | 28 | 43 | 87 | 42 |

### League One Play-offs

| | |
|---|---|
| AFC Bournemouth vs Huddersfield Town | 1-1, 3-3 |
| *Huddersfield Town won 4-2 on penalties* | |
| Milton Keynes Dons vs Peterborough United | 3-2, 0-2 |
| Peterborough United vs Huddersfield Town | 3-0 |

## 2011 F.A. Cup

### Semi-finals

| | |
|---|---|
| Bolton Wanderers vs Stoke City | 0-5 |
| Manchester City vs Manchester United | 1-0 |

### Final

Wembley, 14th May 2011

**Manchester City 1** (Yaya Touré)
**Stoke City 0**

*Attendance 88,643*

## LEAGUE ONE 2010-2011

| | | | | | | | |
|---|---|---|---|---|---|---|---|
| **Brighton & Hove Albion** | 46 | 28 | 11 | 7 | 85 | 40 | 95 |
| **Southampton** | 46 | 28 | 8 | 10 | 86 | 38 | 92 |
| Huddersfield Town | 46 | 25 | 12 | 9 | 77 | 48 | 87 |
| **Peterborough United** | 46 | 23 | 10 | 13 | 106 | 75 | 79 |
| Milton Keynes Dons | 46 | 23 | 8 | 15 | 67 | 60 | 77 |
| Bournemouth | 46 | 19 | 14 | 13 | 75 | 54 | 71 |
| Leyton Orient | 46 | 19 | 13 | 14 | 71 | 62 | 70 |
| Exeter City | 46 | 20 | 10 | 16 | 66 | 71 | 70 |
| Rochdale | 46 | 18 | 14 | 14 | 63 | 55 | 68 |
| Colchester United | 46 | 16 | 14 | 16 | 57 | 63 | 62 |
| Brentford | 46 | 17 | 10 | 19 | 55 | 62 | 61 |
| Carlisle United | 46 | 16 | 11 | 19 | 60 | 62 | 59 |
| Charlton Athletic | 46 | 15 | 14 | 17 | 62 | 66 | 59 |
| Yeovil Town | 46 | 16 | 11 | 19 | 56 | 66 | 59 |
| Sheffield Wednesday | 46 | 16 | 10 | 20 | 67 | 67 | 58 |
| Hartlepool United | 46 | 15 | 12 | 19 | 47 | 65 | 57 |
| Tranmere Rovers | 46 | 15 | 11 | 20 | 53 | 60 | 56 |
| Oldham Athletic | 46 | 13 | 17 | 16 | 53 | 62 | 56 |
| Notts County | 46 | 14 | 8 | 24 | 46 | 60 | 50 |
| Walsall | 46 | 12 | 12 | 22 | 56 | 75 | 48 |
| *Dagenham & Redbridge* | 46 | 12 | 11 | 23 | 52 | 70 | 47 |
| *Bristol Rovers* | 46 | 11 | 12 | 23 | 48 | 82 | 45 |
| *Plymouth Argyle* | 46 | 15 | 7 | 24 | 51 | 74 | 42 |
| *Swindon Town* | 46 | 9 | 14 | 23 | 50 | 72 | 41 |

Plymouth Argyle had 10 points deducted

## LEAGUE TWO 2010-2011

| | | | | | | | |
|---|---|---|---|---|---|---|---|
| **Chesterfield** | 46 | 24 | 14 | 8 | 85 | 51 | 86 |
| **Bury** | 46 | 23 | 12 | 11 | 82 | 50 | 81 |
| **Wycombe Wanderers** | 46 | 22 | 14 | 10 | 69 | 50 | 80 |
| Shrewsbury Town | 46 | 22 | 13 | 11 | 72 | 49 | 79 |
| Accrington Stanley | 46 | 18 | 19 | 9 | 73 | 55 | 73 |
| **Stevenage** | 46 | 18 | 15 | 13 | 62 | 45 | 69 |
| Torquay United | 46 | 17 | 18 | 11 | 74 | 53 | 68 |
| Gillingham | 46 | 17 | 17 | 12 | 67 | 57 | 68 |
| Rotherham United | 46 | 17 | 15 | 14 | 75 | 60 | 66 |
| Crewe Alexandra | 46 | 18 | 11 | 17 | 87 | 65 | 65 |
| Port Vale | 46 | 17 | 14 | 15 | 54 | 49 | 65 |
| Oxford United | 46 | 17 | 12 | 17 | 58 | 60 | 63 |
| Southend United | 46 | 16 | 13 | 17 | 62 | 56 | 61 |
| Aldershot Town | 46 | 14 | 19 | 13 | 54 | 54 | 61 |
| Macclesfield Town | 46 | 14 | 13 | 19 | 59 | 73 | 55 |
| Northampton Town | 46 | 11 | 19 | 16 | 63 | 71 | 52 |
| Cheltenham Town | 46 | 13 | 13 | 20 | 56 | 77 | 52 |
| Bradford City | 46 | 15 | 7 | 24 | 43 | 68 | 52 |
| Burton Albion | 46 | 12 | 15 | 19 | 56 | 70 | 51 |
| Morecambe | 46 | 13 | 12 | 21 | 54 | 73 | 51 |
| Hereford United | 46 | 12 | 17 | 17 | 50 | 66 | 50 |
| Barnet | 46 | 12 | 12 | 22 | 58 | 77 | 48 |
| *Lincoln City* | 46 | 13 | 8 | 25 | 45 | 81 | 47 |
| *Stockport County* | 46 | 9 | 14 | 23 | 48 | 96 | 41 |

Torquay United had 1 point deducted
Hereford United had 3 points deducted

### League Two Play-offs

| | |
|---|---|
| Torquay United vs Shrewsbury Town | 2-0, 0-0 |
| Stevenage Borough vs Accrington Stanley | 2-0, 1-0 |
| Stevenage Borough vs Torquay United | 1-0 |

## 2011 Football League Cup

### Semi-finals

| | |
|---|---|
| Ipswich Town vs Arsenal (1-0, 0-3) | 1-3 |
| West Ham United vs Birmingham City (2-1, 1-3 aet) | 3-4 |

### Final

Wembley, 27th February 2011

**Arsenal 1** (Van Persie)
**Birmingham City 2** (Zigic, Martins)

*Attendance 88,851*

## F.A. PREMIER LEAGUE 2011-2012

| | | | | | | | |
|---|---|---|---|---|---|---|---|
| **MANCHESTER CITY** | 38 | 28 | 5 | 5 | 93 | 29 | 89 |
| Manchester United | 38 | 28 | 5 | 5 | 89 | 33 | 89 |
| Arsenal | 38 | 21 | 7 | 10 | 74 | 49 | 70 |
| Tottenham Hotspur | 38 | 20 | 9 | 9 | 66 | 41 | 69 |
| Newcastle United | 38 | 19 | 8 | 11 | 56 | 51 | 65 |
| Chelsea | 38 | 18 | 10 | 10 | 65 | 46 | 64 |
| Everton | 38 | 15 | 11 | 12 | 50 | 40 | 56 |
| Liverpool | 38 | 14 | 10 | 14 | 47 | 40 | 52 |
| Fulham | 38 | 14 | 10 | 14 | 48 | 51 | 52 |
| West Bromwich Albion | 38 | 13 | 8 | 17 | 45 | 52 | 47 |
| Swansea City | 38 | 12 | 11 | 15 | 44 | 51 | 47 |
| Norwich City | 38 | 12 | 11 | 15 | 52 | 66 | 47 |
| Sunderland | 38 | 11 | 12 | 15 | 45 | 46 | 45 |
| Stoke City | 38 | 11 | 12 | 15 | 36 | 53 | 45 |
| Wigan Athletic | 38 | 11 | 10 | 17 | 42 | 62 | 43 |
| Aston Villa | 38 | 7 | 17 | 14 | 37 | 53 | 38 |
| Queens Park Rangers | 38 | 10 | 7 | 21 | 43 | 66 | 37 |
| *Bolton Wanderers* | *38* | *10* | *6* | *22* | *46* | *77* | *36* |
| *Blackburn Rovers* | *38* | *8* | *7* | *23* | *48* | *78* | *31* |
| *Wolverhampton Wanderers* | *38* | *5* | *10* | *23* | *40* | *82* | *25* |

### The Championship Play-offs

| | |
|---|---|
| West Ham United vs Cardiff City | 2-0, 3-0 |
| Birmingham City vs Blackpool | 0-1, 2-2 |
| West Ham United vs Blackpool | 2-1 |

## THE CHAMPIONSHIP 2011-2012

| | | | | | | | |
|---|---|---|---|---|---|---|---|
| **Reading** | 46 | 27 | 8 | 11 | 69 | 41 | 89 |
| **Southampton** | 46 | 26 | 10 | 10 | 85 | 46 | 88 |
| **West Ham United** | 46 | 24 | 14 | 8 | 81 | 48 | 86 |
| Birmingham City | 46 | 20 | 16 | 10 | 78 | 51 | 76 |
| Blackpool | 46 | 20 | 15 | 11 | 79 | 59 | 75 |
| Cardiff City | 46 | 19 | 18 | 9 | 66 | 53 | 75 |
| Middlesbrough | 46 | 18 | 16 | 12 | 52 | 51 | 70 |
| Hull City | 46 | 19 | 11 | 16 | 47 | 44 | 68 |
| Leicester City | 46 | 18 | 12 | 16 | 66 | 55 | 66 |
| Brighton & Hove Albion | 46 | 17 | 15 | 14 | 52 | 52 | 66 |
| Watford | 46 | 16 | 16 | 14 | 56 | 64 | 64 |
| Derby County | 46 | 18 | 10 | 18 | 50 | 58 | 64 |
| Burnley | 46 | 17 | 11 | 18 | 61 | 58 | 62 |
| Leeds United | 46 | 17 | 10 | 19 | 65 | 68 | 61 |
| Ipswich Town | 46 | 17 | 10 | 19 | 69 | 77 | 61 |
| Millwall | 46 | 15 | 12 | 19 | 55 | 57 | 57 |
| Crystal Palace | 46 | 13 | 17 | 16 | 46 | 51 | 56 |
| Peterborough United | 46 | 13 | 11 | 22 | 67 | 77 | 50 |
| Nottingham Forest | 46 | 14 | 8 | 24 | 48 | 63 | 50 |
| Bristol City | 46 | 12 | 13 | 21 | 44 | 68 | 49 |
| Barnsley | 46 | 13 | 9 | 24 | 49 | 74 | 48 |
| *Portsmouth* | *46* | *13* | *11* | *22* | *50* | *59* | *40* |
| *Coventry City* | *46* | *9* | *13* | *24* | *41* | *65* | *40* |
| *Doncaster Rovers* | *46* | *8* | *12* | *26* | *43* | *80* | *36* |

Portsmouth had 10 points deducted

### League One Play-offs

| | |
|---|---|
| Sheffield United vs Stevenage | 0-0, 1-0 |
| Huddersfield Town vs Milton Keynes Dons | 2-0, 1-2 |
| Sheffield United vs Huddersfield Town | 0-0 |

*Huddersfield Town won 8-7 on penalties*

## 2012 F.A. Cup

**Semi-finals**

| | |
|---|---|
| Liverpool vs Everton | 2-1 |
| Tottenham Hotspur vs Chelsea | 1-5 |

**Final**

Wembley, 5th May 2012

**Chelsea 2**   (Ramires, Drogba)

**Liverpool 1**   (Carroll)

*Attendance 89,102*

## LEAGUE ONE 2011-2012

| | | | | | | | |
|---|---|---|---|---|---|---|---|
| **Charlton Athletic** | 46 | 30 | 11 | 5 | 82 | 36 | 101 |
| **Sheffield Wednesday** | 46 | 28 | 9 | 9 | 81 | 48 | 93 |
| Sheffield United | 46 | 27 | 9 | 10 | 92 | 51 | 90 |
| **Huddersfield Town** | 46 | 21 | 18 | 7 | 79 | 47 | 81 |
| Milton Keynes Dons | 46 | 22 | 14 | 10 | 84 | 47 | 80 |
| Stevenage | 46 | 21 | 10 | 15 | 69 | 44 | 73 |
| Notts County | 46 | 18 | 19 | 9 | 75 | 63 | 73 |
| Carlisle United | 46 | 18 | 15 | 13 | 65 | 66 | 69 |
| Brentford | 46 | 18 | 13 | 15 | 63 | 52 | 67 |
| Colchester United | 46 | 13 | 20 | 13 | 61 | 66 | 59 |
| Bournemouth | 46 | 15 | 13 | 18 | 48 | 52 | 58 |
| Tranmere Rovers | 46 | 14 | 14 | 18 | 49 | 53 | 56 |
| Hartlepool United | 46 | 14 | 14 | 18 | 50 | 55 | 56 |
| Bury | 46 | 15 | 11 | 20 | 60 | 79 | 56 |
| Preston North End | 46 | 13 | 15 | 18 | 54 | 68 | 54 |
| Oldham Athletic | 46 | 14 | 12 | 20 | 50 | 66 | 54 |
| Yeovil Town | 46 | 14 | 12 | 20 | 59 | 80 | 54 |
| Scunthorpe United | 46 | 10 | 22 | 14 | 55 | 59 | 52 |
| Walsall | 46 | 10 | 20 | 16 | 51 | 57 | 50 |
| Leyton Orient | 46 | 13 | 11 | 22 | 48 | 75 | 50 |
| *Wycombe Wanderers* | *46* | *11* | *10* | *25* | *65* | *88* | *43* |
| *Chesterfield* | *46* | *10* | *12* | *24* | *55* | *81* | *42* |
| *Exeter City* | *46* | *10* | *12* | *24* | *46* | *75* | *42* |
| *Rochdale* | *46* | *8* | *14* | *24* | *47* | *81* | *38* |

## LEAGUE TWO 2011-2012

| | | | | | | | |
|---|---|---|---|---|---|---|---|
| **Swindon Town** | 46 | 29 | 6 | 11 | 75 | 32 | 93 |
| **Shrewsbury Town** | 46 | 26 | 10 | 10 | 66 | 41 | 88 |
| **Crawley Town** | 46 | 23 | 15 | 8 | 76 | 54 | 84 |
| Southend United | 46 | 25 | 8 | 13 | 77 | 48 | 83 |
| Torquay United | 46 | 23 | 12 | 11 | 63 | 50 | 81 |
| Cheltenham Town | 46 | 23 | 8 | 15 | 66 | 50 | 77 |
| **Crewe Alexandra** | 46 | 20 | 12 | 14 | 67 | 59 | 72 |
| Gillingham | 46 | 20 | 10 | 16 | 79 | 62 | 70 |
| Oxford United | 46 | 17 | 17 | 12 | 59 | 48 | 68 |
| Rotherham United | 46 | 18 | 13 | 15 | 67 | 63 | 67 |
| Aldershot Town | 46 | 19 | 9 | 18 | 54 | 52 | 66 |
| Port Vale | 46 | 20 | 9 | 17 | 68 | 60 | 59 |
| Bristol Rovers | 46 | 15 | 12 | 19 | 60 | 70 | 57 |
| Accrington Stanley | 46 | 14 | 15 | 17 | 54 | 66 | 57 |
| Morecambe | 46 | 14 | 14 | 18 | 63 | 57 | 56 |
| AFC Wimbledon | 46 | 15 | 9 | 22 | 62 | 78 | 54 |
| Burton Albion | 46 | 14 | 12 | 20 | 54 | 81 | 54 |
| Bradford City | 46 | 12 | 14 | 20 | 54 | 59 | 50 |
| Dagenham & Redbridge | 46 | 14 | 8 | 24 | 50 | 72 | 50 |
| Northampton Town | 46 | 12 | 11 | 23 | 56 | 79 | 47 |
| Plymouth Argyle | 46 | 10 | 16 | 20 | 47 | 64 | 46 |
| Barnet | 46 | 12 | 10 | 24 | 52 | 79 | 46 |
| *Hereford United* | *46* | *10* | *14* | *22* | *50* | *70* | *44* |
| *Macclesfield Town* | *46* | *8* | *13* | *25* | *39* | *64* | *37* |

Port Vale had 10 points deducted

### League Two Play-offs

| | |
|---|---|
| Southend United vs Crewe Alexandra | 0-1, 2-2 |
| Torquay United vs Cheltenham Town | 0-2, 1-2 |
| Cheltenham Town vs Crewe Alexandra | 0-2 |

## 2012 Football League Cup

**Semi-finals**

| | |
|---|---|
| Crystal Palace vs Cardiff City  (1-0, 0-1 aet) | 1-1 |
| Cardiff City won 3-1 on penalties | |
| Manchester City vs Liverpool  (0-1, 2-2) | 2-3 |

**Final**

Wembley, 26th February 2012

**Cardiff City 2**   (Mason, Turner)

**Liverpool 2 (aet.)**   (Skrtel, Kuyt)

*Attendance 88,851*

*Liverpool won 3-2 on penalties*

## F.A. PREMIER LEAGUE 2012-2013

| Team | P | W | D | L | F | A | Pts |
|---|---|---|---|---|---|---|---|
| **MANCHESTER UNITED** | 38 | 28 | 5 | 5 | 86 | 43 | 89 |
| Manchester City | 38 | 23 | 9 | 6 | 66 | 34 | 78 |
| Chelsea | 38 | 22 | 9 | 7 | 75 | 39 | 75 |
| Arsenal | 38 | 21 | 10 | 7 | 72 | 37 | 73 |
| Tottenham Hotspur | 38 | 21 | 9 | 8 | 66 | 46 | 72 |
| Everton | 38 | 16 | 15 | 7 | 55 | 40 | 63 |
| Liverpool | 38 | 16 | 13 | 9 | 71 | 43 | 61 |
| West Bromwich Albion | 38 | 14 | 7 | 17 | 53 | 57 | 49 |
| Swansea City | 38 | 11 | 13 | 14 | 47 | 51 | 46 |
| West Ham United | 38 | 12 | 10 | 16 | 45 | 53 | 46 |
| Norwich City | 38 | 10 | 14 | 14 | 41 | 58 | 44 |
| Fulham | 38 | 11 | 10 | 17 | 50 | 60 | 43 |
| Stoke City | 38 | 9 | 15 | 14 | 34 | 45 | 42 |
| Southampton | 38 | 9 | 14 | 15 | 49 | 60 | 41 |
| Aston Villa | 38 | 10 | 11 | 17 | 47 | 69 | 41 |
| Newcastle United | 38 | 11 | 8 | 19 | 45 | 68 | 41 |
| Sunderland | 38 | 9 | 12 | 17 | 41 | 54 | 39 |
| *Wigan Athletic* | 38 | 9 | 9 | 20 | 47 | 73 | 36 |
| *Reading* | 38 | 6 | 10 | 22 | 43 | 73 | 28 |
| *Queen's Park Rangers* | 38 | 4 | 13 | 21 | 30 | 60 | 25 |

### The Championship Play-offs

| | |
|---|---|
| Watford vs Leicester City | 0-1, 3-1 |
| Brighton & Hove Albion vs Crystal Palace | 0-0, 0-2 |
| Crystal Palace vs Watford | 1-0 (aet) |

## THE CHAMPIONSHIP 2012-2013

| Team | P | W | D | L | F | A | Pts |
|---|---|---|---|---|---|---|---|
| **Cardiff City** | 46 | 25 | 12 | 9 | 72 | 45 | 87 |
| **Hull City** | 46 | 24 | 7 | 15 | 61 | 52 | 79 |
| Watford | 46 | 23 | 8 | 15 | 85 | 58 | 77 |
| Brighton & Hove Albion | 46 | 19 | 18 | 9 | 69 | 43 | 75 |
| Crystal Palace | 46 | 19 | 15 | 12 | 73 | 62 | 72 |
| Leicester City | 46 | 19 | 11 | 16 | 71 | 48 | 68 |
| Bolton Wanderers | 46 | 18 | 14 | 14 | 69 | 61 | 68 |
| Nottingham Forest | 46 | 17 | 16 | 13 | 63 | 59 | 67 |
| Charlton Athletic | 46 | 17 | 14 | 15 | 65 | 59 | 65 |
| Derby County | 46 | 16 | 13 | 17 | 65 | 62 | 61 |
| Burnley | 46 | 16 | 13 | 17 | 62 | 60 | 61 |
| Birmingham City | 46 | 15 | 16 | 15 | 63 | 69 | 61 |
| Leeds United | 46 | 17 | 10 | 19 | 57 | 66 | 61 |
| Ipswich Town | 46 | 16 | 12 | 18 | 48 | 61 | 60 |
| Blackpool | 46 | 14 | 17 | 15 | 62 | 63 | 59 |
| Middlesbrough | 46 | 18 | 5 | 23 | 61 | 70 | 59 |
| Blackburn Rovers | 46 | 14 | 16 | 16 | 55 | 62 | 58 |
| Sheffield Wednesday | 46 | 16 | 10 | 20 | 53 | 61 | 58 |
| Huddersfield Town | 46 | 15 | 13 | 18 | 53 | 73 | 58 |
| Millwall | 46 | 15 | 11 | 20 | 51 | 62 | 56 |
| Barnsley | 46 | 14 | 13 | 19 | 56 | 70 | 55 |
| *Peterborough United* | 46 | 15 | 9 | 22 | 66 | 75 | 54 |
| *Wolverhampton Wanderers* | 46 | 14 | 9 | 23 | 55 | 69 | 51 |
| *Bristol City* | 46 | 11 | 8 | 27 | 59 | 84 | 41 |

### League One Play-offs

| | |
|---|---|
| Brentford vs Swindon Town | 1-1, 3-3 (aet) |
| *Brentford won 5-4 on penalties* | |
| Yeovil Town vs Sheffield United | 0-1, 2-0 |
| Yeovil Town vs Brentford | 2-1 |

## LEAGUE ONE 2012-2013

| Team | P | W | D | L | F | A | Pts |
|---|---|---|---|---|---|---|---|
| **Doncaster Rovers** | 46 | 25 | 9 | 12 | 62 | 44 | 84 |
| **Bournemouth** | 46 | 24 | 11 | 11 | 76 | 53 | 83 |
| Brentford | 46 | 21 | 16 | 9 | 62 | 47 | 79 |
| **Yeovil Town** | 46 | 23 | 8 | 15 | 71 | 56 | 77 |
| Sheffield United | 46 | 19 | 18 | 9 | 56 | 42 | 75 |
| Swindon Town | 46 | 20 | 14 | 12 | 72 | 39 | 74 |
| Leyton Orient | 46 | 21 | 8 | 17 | 55 | 48 | 71 |
| Milton Keynes Dons | 46 | 19 | 13 | 14 | 62 | 45 | 70 |
| Walsall | 46 | 17 | 17 | 12 | 65 | 58 | 68 |
| Crawley Town | 46 | 18 | 14 | 14 | 59 | 58 | 68 |
| Tranmere Rovers | 46 | 19 | 10 | 17 | 58 | 48 | 67 |
| Notts County | 46 | 16 | 17 | 13 | 61 | 49 | 65 |
| Crewe Alexandra | 46 | 18 | 10 | 18 | 54 | 62 | 64 |
| Preston North End | 46 | 14 | 17 | 15 | 54 | 49 | 59 |
| Coventry City | 46 | 18 | 11 | 17 | 66 | 59 | 55 |
| Shrewsbury Town | 46 | 13 | 16 | 17 | 54 | 60 | 55 |
| Carlisle United | 46 | 14 | 13 | 19 | 56 | 77 | 55 |
| Stevenage | 46 | 15 | 9 | 22 | 47 | 64 | 54 |
| Oldham Athletic | 46 | 14 | 9 | 23 | 46 | 59 | 51 |
| Colchester United | 46 | 14 | 9 | 23 | 47 | 68 | 51 |
| *Scunthorpe United* | 46 | 13 | 9 | 24 | 49 | 73 | 48 |
| *Bury* | 46 | 9 | 14 | 23 | 45 | 73 | 41 |
| *Hartlepool United* | 46 | 9 | 14 | 23 | 39 | 67 | 41 |
| *Portsmouth* | 46 | 10 | 12 | 24 | 51 | 69 | 32 |

Coventry City had 10 points deducted
Portsmouth had 10 points deducted

## LEAGUE TWO 2012-2013

| Team | P | W | D | L | F | A | Pts |
|---|---|---|---|---|---|---|---|
| **Gillingham** | 46 | 23 | 14 | 9 | 66 | 39 | 83 |
| **Rotherham United** | 46 | 24 | 7 | 15 | 74 | 59 | 79 |
| **Port Vale** | 46 | 21 | 15 | 10 | 87 | 52 | 78 |
| Burton Albion | 46 | 22 | 10 | 14 | 71 | 65 | 76 |
| Cheltenham Town | 46 | 20 | 15 | 11 | 58 | 51 | 75 |
| Northampton Town | 46 | 21 | 10 | 15 | 64 | 55 | 73 |
| **Bradford City** | 46 | 18 | 15 | 13 | 63 | 52 | 69 |
| Chesterfield | 46 | 18 | 13 | 15 | 60 | 45 | 67 |
| Oxford United | 46 | 19 | 8 | 19 | 59 | 60 | 65 |
| Exeter City | 46 | 18 | 10 | 18 | 63 | 62 | 64 |
| Southend United | 46 | 16 | 13 | 17 | 61 | 55 | 61 |
| Rochdale | 46 | 16 | 13 | 17 | 68 | 70 | 61 |
| Fleetwood Town | 46 | 15 | 15 | 16 | 55 | 57 | 60 |
| Bristol Rovers | 46 | 16 | 12 | 18 | 60 | 69 | 60 |
| Wycombe Wanderers | 46 | 17 | 9 | 20 | 50 | 60 | 60 |
| Morecambe | 46 | 15 | 13 | 18 | 55 | 61 | 58 |
| York City | 46 | 12 | 19 | 15 | 50 | 60 | 55 |
| Accrington Stanley | 46 | 14 | 12 | 20 | 51 | 67 | 54 |
| Torquay United | 46 | 13 | 14 | 19 | 55 | 62 | 53 |
| AFC Wimbledon | 46 | 14 | 11 | 21 | 54 | 76 | 53 |
| Plymouth Argyle | 46 | 13 | 13 | 20 | 46 | 55 | 52 |
| Dagenham & Redbridge | 46 | 13 | 12 | 21 | 55 | 62 | 51 |
| *Barnet* | 46 | 13 | 12 | 21 | 47 | 59 | 51 |
| *Aldershot Town* | 46 | 11 | 15 | 20 | 42 | 60 | 48 |

### League Two Play-offs

| | |
|---|---|
| Burton Albion vs Bradford City | 3-2, 1-3 |
| Cheltenham Town vs Northampton Town | 0-1, 0-1 |
| Bradford City vs Northampton Town | 3-0 |

## 2013 F.A. Cup

### Semi-finals

| | |
|---|---|
| Millwall vs Wigan Athletic | 0-2 |
| Chelsea vs Manchester City | 1-2 |

### Final

Wembley, 11th May 2013

**Manchester City 0**
**Wigan Athletic 1**   (Watson)

*Attendance 86,254*

## 2013 Football League Cup

### Semi-finals

| | |
|---|---|
| Bradford City vs Aston Villa (3-1, 1-2) | 4-3 |
| Chelsea vs Swansea City (0-2, 0-0) | 0-2 |

### Final

Wembley, 24th February 2013

**Swansea City 5**   (Dyer 2, Michu, De Guzmán 2)
**Bradford City 0**

*Attendance 82,597*